THE BARBOUR
COLLECTION
OF CONNECTICUT TOWN
VITAL RECORDS

THE BARBOUR COLLECTION
OF CONNECTICUT TOWN
VITAL RECORDS

ANDOVER 1848–1879

ASHFORD 1710–1851

AVON 1830–1851

Compiled by
Lorraine Cook White

Genealogical Publishing Co., Inc.

INTRODUCTION

As early as 1640 the Connecticut Court of Election ordered all magistrates to keep a record of the marriages they performed. In 1644 the registration of births and marriages became the official responsibility of town clerks and registrars, with deaths added to their duties in 1650. From 1660 until the close of the Revolutionary War these vital records of birth, marriage, and death were generally well kept, but then for a period of about two generations until the mid-nineteenth century, the faithful recording of vital records declined in some towns.

General Lucius Barnes Barbour was the Connecticut Examiner of Public Records from 1911 to 1934 and in that capacity directed a project in which the vital records kept by the towns up to about 1850 were copied and abstracted. Barbour previously had directed the publication of the Bolton and Vernon vital records for the Connecticut Historical Society. For this new project he hired several individuals who were experienced in copying old records and familiar with the old script.

Barbour presented the completed transcriptions of town vital records to the Connecticut State Library where the information was typed onto printed forms. The form sheets were then cut, producing twelve small slips from each sheet. The slips for most towns were then alphabetized and the information was then typed a second time on large sheets of rag paper, which were subsequently bound into separate volumes for each town. The slips for all towns were then interfiled, forming a statewide alphabetized slip index for most surviving town vital records.

The dates of coverage vary from town to town, and of course the records of some towns are more complete than others. Altogether the entire Barbour Collection--one of the great genealogical manuscript collections and one of the last to be published--covers 137 towns and comprises 14,333 typed pages. This present volume is a transcription of the vital records of the first three towns covered in the Collection. Many more such volumes are contemplated.

TABLE OF CONTENTS

ABBREVIATIONS

ae.----age
b.-----born
d.-----died or day or daughter
J.P.---Justice of Peace
m.-----married or month
N. S.--- New Style
O. S.----Old Style
res.---resident
s.-----son
w.-----wife
wid.---widow
y.-----year

THE BARBOUR
COLLECTION
OF CONNECTICUT TOWN
VITAL RECORDS

ANDOVER VITAL RECORDS
1848 - 1879

BISHOP, (cont.) Page

BURNAP, (cont.)   Page

Mary J., single, d. Aug. 11, 1870, ae 33   58

Mary K., wid. of D., & d. of Joseph & Ruth **KINGSBURY,** d. Nov. 21.
1873, ae 86   60

Nathan, farmer, ae 51, & w. Phebe N., ae 43, had d., b. Oct. 6, 1848   13

Phebe, b. Willington, married, d. Mar. 25, 1879, ae 72   62

____, d. N., d. Oct. 6, 1848, ae [ ]   42

BURNETT, Rosa A., had d., d. Oct. 10, 1880, ae 7 h.   63

BUTLER, Mary L., houseworker, b. Lebanon, res. Lebanon, d. [ ], 1850 ae 39   43

BUTTON, Cha[rle]s G., soldier, single, d. Apr. 5, 1865, at Point of Rock, Va.
ae 25   56

Frances, housekeeper, b. Plainfield, married, d. May 24, 1854, ae 46   45

CAMWELL, Dan, laborer, ae 35, had s., b. Sept. [ ], 1848   14

CAPEN, Betsey, b. Hartford, wid., d. Mar. 4, 1871, ae 94 y. 7 m.   59

CARBURG, ____, female, d. Sept. [ ], 1869, ae [ ]   57

CARY, William, s. Patrick, laborer, ae 26, & Bridget, ae 24, b. July 22, 1849   13

William, d. July 29, 1849, ae 7 d.   42

CHADWICK, James A., of East Windsor, ;m. Lucy M. **JONES,** of Andover,
April. 27, 1851, by Rev. Roswell G. Lamb, at the house of Amasa
Jones   2

James A., d. Aug. 12, 1863, on the passage home from New Orleans,
La. Was a private in Co. C., 25th Reg. C. V. His children were
Janett A., ae 13, Sarah A., ae 12, Elliott L., ae 9, Mary L., ae 5, and
Anna F., ae 4   65

James A., soldier, married, d. [1863], at Sea, ae 35   54

Sarah Augusta, d. James A.,farmer, ae 25, & Lucy M., ae 20, b. Mar. 28,
1853   16

CHAPMAN, Betsa M., b. Ashford, res. Ashford, d. [ ], 1850 ae 7   43

Howmor S., b. Hartford, o. Ruoh & Adolino (**STORRS**), d. Apr. 17, 1876,
ae 3 y. 11 m.   61

CHAPPELL, CHAPPEL, Harriet M., of Andover, m. William W. **STRONG,**
of Hebron, Oct. 3, 1849, by Rev. Roswell G. Lamb   1

Harriet M., ae 23, b. Hebron, res. Andover, m. W[illia]m W. **STRONG,**
farmer, ae 26, b. Hebron, res. Andover, Oct. 3, 1849, by Roswell G.
Lamb   40

Nancy, housekeeper, b. Hebron, wid. of Z., d. Jan. 30, 1872, ae 79   59

Zenas, farmer, married, d. Jan. 7, 1864, ae 85   55

CHENEY, CHENNEY, Ann, b. Windham, single, d. Oct, 2, 1853, ae 16   45

Henry M., soldier, b. Willimantic, single, d. Apr. 23,[1862], ae 19 at
Morehead City, N. C.   53

Marvin, farmer, b. Hampton, married, d. May 29, 1873, ae 61   60

CLEVELAND, CLEAVLAND, Fanny A., d. W[illia]m N., blacksmith, ae 29,
& Permelia, ae 32, b. Apr. 8, 1848   12

Harriet S., d. William N., blacksmith, ae 32, & Parmelia S., ae 35, b.
June 6, 1850   14

Henry F., merchant, s. W[illia]m H. & Pamelia (**STANDISH**), single,
d. May 4, 1876, ae 32   61

CLYDE, Peter S., of Derry, N. H., m. Mariah H. **PERKINS** of Andover, Feb.
17, 1850, by Rev. Roswell G. Lamb   1

CLYDE, (cont.)   Page
Peter S. R. R. contractor, ae 29, b. Derry N. H., m Mariah H.
    PERKINS, ae 29, of Andover, Feb., 17, 1850, by Rev. Roswell G.
    Lamb   40
Rosa Maria, d. Jan. 11, 1859, ae 4   50
Sarah M., d. Peter, rr. contactor, ae 33, & Maria, ae 30, res. Fair Haven, b.
    Sept. 13, 1850   15
COLVIN, Annie F., see under Annie F. **PORTER**   58
COOK, Bela, farmer, b. Coventry, married, d. Oct. 25, 1866, ae 75 y. 7 m. 28
    d.   56
W[illia]m, hatter, ae 31, m. Martha E. A. **HENDEE,** housekeeper, ae
    22, b. of Andover, Dec. 26, 1852, by Rev. Alpha Miller   3
W[illia]m, farmer, & hatter, ae 31, b. Andover, res. Andover, m. Martha
    E. A. **HENDEE,** ae 22, b. Andover, res. Andover, Dec. 26, 1852, by
    Rev. Alpha Miller   41
W[illia]m, farmer, married, d. June 16, 1867 ae 46   57
CROSS, Rhoda, housekeeper, colored, b. Griswold, married, d. Jan. 24, 1868,
    ae 61   57
CURLEY, Francis, s. Patrick, laborer, ae 35, b. Feb. 4, 1849   14
CURTIS, CURTISS, Betsey, see under Betsey **DRAKE**   63
Lucy, houseworker, ae 22, b. Coventry, res. Andover, m. Charles H.
    LOOMIS, farmer, ae 30, of Andover, [ ], 1850, by Smith A. Miller   40
DAGGETT, Bets[e]y, housekeeper, b. Coventry, single, d. Aug. 19, 1861, ae
    67   52
Isaiah, teacher, b. Andover, married, d. Apr. 21. 1854, ae 68 y. 8 m. 45
Lucy H. A., ae 20, of Andover, m. Henry **ENSIGN,** tailor, ae 22, of East
    Hartford, Oct. 20, 1847, by Rev. James Ely, of Bolton   39
Sally, housekeeper, b. Columbia, wid., d. Jan. 22, 1854, ae 83 y. 3 m. 45
DEAN, ___, male, d. July 8, 1864, ae 46   55
DORRANCE, Emily, A., ae 32, b. Canterbury, res. Andover, m. Mahlon
    WATROUS, mechanic, b. Waltow, N. Y., res. Coventry, Nov. 23,
    1854, by Sam[ue]ll Griswold   3
George A., joiner, ;b. Lebanon, married, d. May 16, 1860, ae 29   51
George Henry, s. of William, taverner, ae 37, & Hepsy, ae 38, b. Dec. 10.
    1849   14
Gershom, farmer, b. Westerly, R. I., d. July 19, 1852, ae 84   43
Harriet S., w. of Appleton **DORRANCE** & d. of Caleb & Mary
    STEWART, b. in Lebanon, d. Dec. 28, 1874, ae 65   60
Hepsey P., housekeeper, b. Rocky Hill , married, d. May 12, 1871, ae 61 59
Loisa, b. Griswold, single, d. Gershom & Sarah, d. Feb. 10, 1880, ae 64 63
Mary, housekeeper, b. Griswold, single, d. Gershom & Sarah, d. Mar. 29,
    1877   61
Roselle Stewart, d. Appleton, mason, ae 47, & Harriet, ae 39, b. Sept. 13,
    1848   13
Sarah, b. Saybrook, res. Andover, d. May 11, 1848, ae 70   42
William, Capt., d. Dec. 6, 1879   61
William, Capt., b. Griswold, wid., s. Gershom & Sarah, d. Dec. 6, 1879,
    ae 67   62
W[illia]m G., book-keeper, single, s. W[illia]m & Hepsey (**GOODRICH**),

DORRANCE,(cont.)
    d. Feb. 20, 1877, ae 29 y. 10 m. 18 d. 61
DRAKE, Betsey, housework, b. Coventry, wid., d. of Abijah & Hulda
    CURTISS, d. Sept. 23, 1880, ae 83 63
DRINKWATTER, Nabby, housekeeper, b. Groton, married, d. Jan. 9, 1856,
    ae 68 46
DUFF, Stephen, b. Bolton, d. Oct., 29, 1861, ae 15 52
EATON, Nannie F., housekeeper, b. Tolland, res. New York, married, d. Oct.
    28, 1868, ae 36 57
EDGERTON, EDGARTON, Asa B., of Mansfield, m. Olive R. **HYDE,** of
    Andover, July 15, 1849, by Rev. Alpha Miller 1
    Asa B., farmer, ae 48, b. Mansfield, res. Mansfield, m. 3rd w. Olive R.
    HYDE, ae 33, b. Lebanon, July 15, 1849, by Rev. Alpha Miller 39
    Parthena D., housekeeper, b. Coventry, wid., d. Feb. 1, 1871, ae 81 y. 10
    m. 59
EDWARDS, Marina, b. Coventry, single, d. Dec. 14, 1854, ae 55 y 46
    Mary Ann, ae 34, b. Coventry, res. Andover, m. Francis **THAYER,** ae
    33, b. Vernon, res. Coventry, Oct. 5, 1856, by Rev. Urijah
    Underwood 3
ENSIGN, Henry, tailor, ae 22, of East Hartford, m. Lucy H. A. **DAGGETT,** ae
    20, of Andover, Oct. 20, 1847, by Rev. James Ely of Bolton 39
ENSWORTH, Sophia K., housekeeper, b. East Hartford, married, d. May 18,
    [1864], ae 69 55
EVANS, Ellen, servant, colored, b. Hebron, res. Hebron, d. Oct. [ ], 1849, ae
    18 43
FITCH, A. Parker, s. Alfred H., shoemaker, ae 29, & Martha P., ae 31, b. Jan.
    6, 1848 12
    Alfred H., shoemaker, married, d. Dec. 25, 1855, ae 36 46
    Alfred H., d. Mar. 31, 1867, ae 2 1/2 m. 57
    Cynthia M, housekeeper, b. Columbia, married, d. Dec. 5, [1862], ae 25 53
    Eunice, housekeeper, b. Windham, wid., d. Mar, 31, 1858, ae 74 49
FOOTE, Jerusha, dressmaker, b. Colchester, single, d. Joel & Abigail, d. Mar.
    2, 1876, ae 87 y. 1 m. 28 d. 61
    Julius, farm laborer, b. Columbia, single, d. Oct. 15, 1873, ae 91 60
FOSS, Walter, s. Aaron, carpenter, ae 30, & Elvira T., ae 26, res. Bolton, b.
    Oct. 26, 1849 14
FREEMAN, A stillborn male, colored, Feb. 29, 1856 47
FULLER, Andrus & w. Mary A., had stillborn son July 6, 1855 46
    David O., of Columbia, m. Jane C. **HUTCHINS,** of Bolton, Aug. 21,
    1849, by Rev. Alpha Miller 1
    George F., s. Josiah A., farmer, ae 23, & Mary, ae 19, b. Sept. 28, 1850 15
    Mary Ann, d. Andrew, farmer, ae 21, & Mary B., ae 14, b. Aug. 9, 1848 13
    Mary Ann, d. Aug. 31, 1848, ae 22 d. 42
    Mary Ann, housekeeper, married, d. July 12, 1855, ae 21 46
    Mary E., d. Andrew, farmer, ae 21, & Mary, ae 14, b. July 29, 1848 12
GOODRICH, Eli, farmer, b. Bolton, single, d. Sept. 3, [1863], ae 15 54
GRISWOULD, Geo[rge] H., shoemaker, ae 28, & w. Lucinda W., ae 26, had
    dau. b. Feb. 2, 1853 16
GROVER, Anson R., of Coventry, m. Charlotte N. **PERKINS,** of Andover,

GROVER, (cont.)   Page
   [Dec.] 25, [1850], by Rev. Charles Hyde, of Coventry   1
   Anson R. hatter, ae 26, b. Coventry, res. Coventry, m. Charlotte
     N. PERKINS, ae 24, b. Hebron, Dec. 25, 1850, by Rev. Charles
     Hyde   40
   William J., m. Josephine A. **SPELLMAN,** b. of Rockville, Nov. 12,
     1848, by Rev. Alpha Miller   1
HALL, Josiah D., s. Adrastus, farmer, ae 36, & Lucretia, ae 40, b. July 9, 1848   12
HANLEY, Mary, d. John, laborer, ae 33, b. Nov. [ ], 1848   14
HENDEE, Amelia B., housekeeper, b. Stonington, wid., d. Nov. 27, 1870, ae
   81   58
   Eliphalet, farmer, married, d. Oct. 29, [1863], ae 80   54
   Leonard, married, d. Sept. 2, 1859, ae 71   50
   Martha E. A., housekeeper, ae 22, m. W[illia]m Cook, hatter, ae 31, b. of
     Andover, Dec. 26, 1852, by Rev. Alpha Miller   3
   Martha E. A., ae 22, b. Andover, res. Andover, m. W[illia]m Cook, farmer
     & hatter, ae 31, b. Andover, res. Andover, Dec. 26, 1852, by Rev.
     Alpha Miller   41
   Mary, housekeeper, b. Coventry, single, d. Sept. 18, 1868, ae 87   57
   Sarah B., housekeeper, b. Canterbury, wid. of Leonard & dau. of Jacob
     BACON & Martha (**CLARK**), d. Aug. 10, 1876, ae 80   61
HENDICA, Thomas, s. Michael, laborer, ae 32, b. Jan. 17, 1849   14
HIGGINS, Michael, s. Thomas, laborer, ae 35, & Mary, ae 34, b. July 8, 1849   13
HOLDRIDGE, Robert, laborer, b. Hebron, single, d. Aug. [ ], 1857, ae 96   48
HOLSTED, Geo[rge], & w. Mary (colored) had dau. d. Apr. 30, 1856, ae 2
   wk.   47
HOPKINS. _____, housekeeper, res. Middletown, wid., d. Feb. [ ], 1874, ae
   8[ ].   60
HORTON, Bryon W., d. July 17, 1871, ae 1 y. 1 m.   59
   Sarah, housekeeper, b. Lebanon, married, d. Jan. 18, 1856, ae 71   47
HOUSE, Franklin Pierce, s. Joel L., farmer, & Celia, b. Nov. 16, 1852   16
   Jane, housekeeper, w. of Samuel, d. May 4, 1876, ae 45   61
   Jane M., d. Dec. 10, 1864, ae 5 m.   55
   Joel L., farmer, married, d. Dec. 19, 1869, ae 58   57
   Lydia Ann, d. Joel L., farmer, ae 45 & Celia, ae 43, b. Feb. [ ], 1850   14
HUBBARD, Betsey, b. Ellington, wid., d. Apr. 16, 1866, ae 82 y. 6 m. 1 d.   56
HURLBURT, George Edgar, s. George R., hatter & farmer, ae 26, & Cina O.,
   ae 23, b. Oct. 11, 1848   13
HURLEY, John, operator R. R., b. Ireland, married, d. Mar. 23, 1875, ae 40   60
HUTCHINS, Jane C., of Bolton, m. David O. **FULLER,** of Columbia, Aug.
   21, 1849, by Rev. Alpha Miller   1
HUTCHINSON, HUTCHENSON, Alice Celestia, d. Bezaleel, grocer, butcher,
   farmer, ae 50, & Lydia Ann, ae 38, b. Sept. 20, 1848   13
   Bezaleel, farmer, s. Bezaleel & Betsey, d. Nov. 14, 1880, ae 82 y. 7 m.   63
   Geo[rge] H. & w. Emily had dau. d. Sept. 5, 1855, ae 1 hr.   46
   Lewis, ae 44 & w. Caroline S., ae 41, had son b. Nov. 20, 1850   15
   Mary, A., d. Lewis, farmer, ae 41, & Caroline S., ae 38, b. Feb. 1, 1848   12
   Orrin O., d. Sept, [ ], 1848, ae 3   42
HYDE, Abbey B., housekeeper, b. Stockbridge, Mass., wid. of Rev. A. S.,

HYDE, (cont.) Page
d. Apr. 7, 1872, ae 72 y. 6 m. 59
Olive R., of Andover, m. Asa B. **EDGARTON** of Mansfield, July 15,
1849, by Rev. Alpha Miller 1
Olive R., ae 33, b. Lebanon, m. Asa B. **EDGARTON,** farmer, ae 48, b.
Mansfield, res. Mansfield, July 15, 1849, by Rev. Alpha Miller 39
ISHAM, Electa, b. Hebron, single, d. May 15, 1861, ae 35 52
JOHNSON, Benjamin Franklin, farmer, single, s. Charles F. & Harriet C.,
d. Mar. 27, 1881, ae 18 y. 6 m. 2 d. 64
JONES, Amasa, farmer, b. Coventry, married, d. Oct. 10, 1859, ae 60 50
Amos, farmer, widower, d. Feb. 21. 1856, ae 93 47
Caroline M., housekeeper, b. Glastenbury, married, d. Oct. 12, 1855, ae 20 46
Charles H., farmer, b. Coventry, res. Andover, d. Oct. 19, [1847], ae 26 42
Dwight C., b. Hartford, d. Aug. 27, 1855, ae 1 y. 1 m. 46
Elizabeth, ae 16, m. Alfred **BISHOP,** farmer, ae 20, b. Bolton, res.
Andover, Nov. 12, 1848, by Horace J. Jones 39
Hannah Elisabeth, of Andover, m. Alfred **BISHOP,** of Bolton, Nov. 12,
1848, by Horace I. Jones, J. P. 1
Julia A., housekeeper, b. Salem, w. of Randall, dau. of W[illia]m
LATHAM, d. Dec. 18, 1876, ae 33 y. 4 m. 12 d. 61
Lavina, housekeeper, b. Coventry, wid., d. Aug. 18, 1868, ae 68 57
Leonard, Jr., farmer, ae 19, b. Glastenbury, res. Coventry, m. Mary
LOCKWOOD, ae 17, b. Marlborough, Sept. 19, 1847, by Rev.
Alpha Miller 39
Lucy M., of Andover, m. James A. **CHADWICK,** of East Windsor, Apr.
27, 1851, by Rev. Roswell G. Lamb, at the house of Amasa Jones 2
Lucy M., houseworker, ae 18, b. Coventry, res. Andover, m. James A.
SHADWICK, farmer, ae 22, b. Coventry, res. Windsor, Apr. 27,
1851, by Rev. Roswell G. Lamb 40
Phebe S., housekeeper, b. Lyme, married, d. Mar. 31, 1855, ae 49 46
Sarah Jane, m. David W. **POST,** b. of Andover, Oct. 20, 1851, by Rev.
Roswell G. Lamb 2
Thomas K., farmer, b. Coventry, married, s. Noah & Dolly, d. Mar. 25,
[1878], ae 80 y. 4 m. 19 d. 62
William C., m. Harriet N. **PERKINS,** b. of Andover, Apr. 5, 1852, by
Rev. Alpha Miller 2
W[illia]m C., depot agent, wid., d. June 10, 1858, ae 33 49
_____, male, d. Aug. 20, 1869, ae 8 d. 57
KELLY, Hannah, see under Hannah **MURPHY** 62
KING, Thomas J., laborer, b. Coventry, wid., d. Jan. 20, 1863, ae 45 54
KINGSBURY, Amelia, Mrs., b. East Hartford,.d. July 9, 1848, ae 52 42
Emily M., teacher & seamstress, single, d. Sept. 21, 1867, ae 39 y. 11 m. 57
Henry N., s. Henry M., farmer, ae 29, & Emely, ae 21, b. Aug. 7, 1849 14
Henry M., farmer, ae 30, & w. Emily, ae 22, had dau, b. Feb. 1, 1851 15
Joseph, farmer, ae 62, b. Andover, res. Andover, m. 2d w. Sarah **VORRA,**
ae 52, b. East Hartford, res. Manchester, Apr. 10, 1853, by Rev.
Alpha Miller 41
Joseph, farmer, married, d. Mar. 17, [1864], ae 72 55
Mary K., see Mary K. **BURNAP** 60

LOOMIS, (cont.)   Page
Mary, L., d. Charles H., farmer, ae 30, & Lucy M., ae 23, b.
    June 8, 1851   15
Minerva, d. Mar. 25, 1857, ae 11   47
Monroe, s. Willard N., farmer, ae 40, & Susan A., ae 37, b. Oct. 20, 1848   13
Susan A., housekeeper, b. Columbia, married, d. Jan. 30, [1859], ae 46   50
Timothy, farmer, married, d. May 17, 1860, ae 74   51
Willard B., farmer, ae 44 & w. Susan A., ae 43, had son b. Oct. 28, 1853   16
LORD, Chloe, housekeeper, b. Columbia, d. of Manly, wid, of Elisha, d. Nov.
    6, 1874, ae 73   60
Hannah, housekeeper, b. South Windsor, married, d. Feb. 7, 1866, ae 29 y.
    9 m. 6 d   56
LOVELAND, Clarysa, housekeeper, b. Coventry, married, d. Feb. 12, [1862],
    ae 30   53
Selden, & w. Clarissa had dau., who d. Mar. 10, 1856   47
_____, dau. st. b. Oct. 22, 1854   45
LYMAN, Amoret M., houseworker, d. Jan.[ ], 1850, ae 15   43
Austin L., s. Harvey, farmer, ae 35, & Harriet, b. Aug. 16, 1850   14
Clarissa H., housekeeper, wid. of N., d. Aug. 27, 1872, ae 83   59
Delia, housekeeper, single, d. Nov. 18, 1870, ae 83   58
Eglah Medora, d. Elavel, farmer, ae 43, & Harriet, ae 37, b. Jan. 24, 1851   15
Harvey L., d. Aug. 21, 1858, ae 12 y. 11 m. 21 d.   49
Josiah, d. Sept. 12, 1848, ae 64   42
Juliaett A., b. Andover, res. Andover, d. Apr. 1, 1848, ae 4   42
Lucy H., housekeeper, married, d. June 6, 1872, ae 70   59
Nathan, farmer, b. Coventry, d. Oct. 8, 1850, ae 65   43
MACK, Henry, or Pomp, colored, b. Columbia, res. Windham, d. Apr. 19,
    [1862], ae 6 y.   53
Timothy, laborer, colored, res. Columbia, s. Geo[rge], d. Apr. 14, 1876,
    ae 21   61
MANLY, Chloe, see under Chloe **LORD**   60
MAPLES, Lydia, see under Lydia Maples **PARK**   63
McDUFF, Stephen C., s. John, paper maker, ae 40, & Philenda, ae 34, b. Feb.
    17, 1847   12
McGILLYCUDDY, Daniel, s. Daniel, laborer, ae 40, b. Dec. 6, 1848   14
MERDOCK, Ezekiel, farmer, b. Bristol, R. I., single, d. July 9, 1861, ae 42   52
MILLER, Alpha, clergyman, b. Winchester, married, d. Mar. 29, 1867, ae 75 y.
    2 m. 11 d.   57
Esther H., housekeeper, b. North Coventry, wid., d. Apr. 10, 1870, ae 75   58
Fanny S., of Andover, m. Edward **REED**, of Lanesville, O., Sept. 26,
    1849, by Rev. Alpha Miller   1
Fanny S., school-teacher, ae 25, of Lanesville, O., m. Edward **REED**,
    book merchant, ae 27, b. Andover, res. Lanesville, O., Sept. 26,
    1849, by Rev. Alpha Miller   40
Hannah, Mrs., b. North Coventry, d. Jan. 28, 1848, ae 49   42
MONEHUE, John, job worker, b. Ireland, married, d. Aug. 11,[1862], ae 36 y.
    2 m.   53
MOULTON, Lyman, ae 24, m. Cornelia **LOCKWOOD**, ae 18, b. in Hebron,

MOULTON, (cont.)   Page
    Apr. 1, 1855, by Leonard Hendee   3
MURPHY, Hannah, housewife, b. Ireland, w. of John, & dau. of John &
    Abbey, KELLY, d. Jan. 20, 1878, ae 30   62
    John & w. Hannah (KELLY) had child st. b. Jan. 20, 1878 62
NEWCOMB, Orestus, s. Ralph, cabinet maker, ae 30, & Jane E., ae 22, res.
    Bolton, b. July 1, 1849   14
NORTON, W[illia]m, silver plater, b. Hebron, widower, d. June 26, [1862],
    ae 75   53
O'HAYER, Patrick, s. Owen, laborer, ae 30, b. Sept. 4, 1848   14
PAGE, Lydia, b. Hebron, res. Hebron, wid., d. Nov. 1, 1860, ae 70   51
PALMER, Andrew, laborer, b. Windsor, colored, married, d. Jan. 6, 1857   47
    Dian, housekeeper, colored, b. Windsor, married, d. Jan. 6, 1857 ae 75 47
PARK, Lydia MAPLES, housekeeper, wid., of Abijah, dau. of [ ] MAPLES,
    d. July 16, 1880, ae 83.   63
PARKER, Adelbert E., s. Edwin B., farmer, ae 28, & Adelade, ae 20, b. May
    14, 1851   15
    Hannah, pauper, b. Coventry, res. Andover, d. Apr. [ ], [1848], ae 84 42
PAYSON, Samuel, mechanic, b. Sharon, Mass., married, d. aug. 22, 1858, ae
    70   49
PENHALLER, _____, male d. Oct, 24, 1856, ae 2 wk.   47
PERKINS, Adeline, housekeeper, b. Columbia, married, d. Jan. 25, 1857, ae 23 47
    Betsey M., single, d. June 23, 1858, ae 48   49
    Charlotte N., of Andover, m. Anson R. GROVER, of Coventry, [Dec.]
    25, [1850], by Rev. Charles Hyde, of Coventry   1
    Charlotte N., ae 24, b. Hebron, m. Anson R. GROVER, hatter, ae 26, b.
    Coventry, res. Coventry, Dec. 25, 1850, by Rev. Charles Hyde 40
    Chester, farmer, b. Hebron, d. Mar. 28, 1851, ae 65   43
    Effie Leona, d. Mar. 20, [1864], ae 1   55
    Elisha, farmer, widower, s. Elisha & Submit (PAYNE), d. Sept. 14, 1878,
    ae 89, y. 3 m. 24 d.   62
    Ella L., d. May 4, 1857, ae 6 1/2 m.   48
    Fanny, housekeeper, b. Hebron, wid., d. Dec. 24, 1863, at Willimantic, ae
    76   54
    George, millwright, married, d. Aug. 30, 1858, ae 75 y. 1 m. 13 d. 49
    Harriet N., m. William C. JONES, b. of Andover, Apr. 5, 1852, by Rev.
    Alpha Miller   2
    John, farmer, s. Asa, widower, d. Oct. [ ], 1873, ae 84 60
    Lucy, housekeeper, b. Hebron, married, d. May 27, 1866, ae 72 y. 11 m.
    9 d.   56
    Luther M., & w. Adaline had dau., who d. Sept. 27, 1856 47
    Mariah H., of Andover, m. Peter S. CLYDE, of Derry, N. H., Feb. 17,
    1850, by Rev. Roswell G. Lamb   1
    Mariah H., ae 29, of Andover, m. Peter S. CLYDE, rr. contractor, ae 29,
    b. Derry, N. H., Feb. 17, 1850, by Rev. Roswell G. Lamb 40
    Sarah M., d. Aug. 26, 1865, ae 3 m.   56
    Sophia, w. of Elisha, d. July 13, 1875, ae 84   60
PHELPS, Alfred, s. Gurley, farmer, ae 45, & Anna E., ae 31, b. Apr. 30, 1848 12
    Alfred, d. Apr. 30, 1848 ae 15 h.   42

PHELPS, (cont.)   Page
    Gurley, farmer, ae 49, & w. Ann E., ae 34, had dau. b. July 21, 1851   15
    Henry G., s. Gurley, farmer, ae 46, & Ann Eliza, ae 32, b. Aug. 25, 1849   14
POLK, Philurd, housewife, wid., b. in Columbia, dau. of Harvey & Sarah
    LINCOLN, d. Mar. 10, 1880, ae 60   63
PORTER, Abner, s. Francis A., farmer, ae 31, & Julia Ann A., ae 28, b. Sept.
    24, 1847   12
    Abner H., d. July 2, 1853, ae 5 y. 9 m.   44
    Annie F., w. of Francis E., & dau. of Davis & Mahala COLVIN, b. in
       Warwick, R. I., d. Sept. 2, 1870, ae 20   58
    Annie F., d. Leonard & Lucy (MAINE), d. June 24, 1876, ae 6 y. 1 m.
       19 d.   61
    Ellen J., d. Dec. 20, 1860, ae 4 m. 28 d.   51
    Emily, b. Coventry, wid., d. July 27, 1880, ae 85   63
    Francis, farmer, b. Hebron, married, d. June 12, 1872, ae 56 y. 9 m.   59
    Kingsley H., d. July 6, 1851, ae 19 m.   43
    Sarah A., housekeeper, b. Torrington, married, d. Dec. 19, 1861, ae 30   52
    _____, d. Mar. 6, 1865, ae 1 d. (st. b.)   56
POST, David W., m. Sarah Jane JONES, b. of Andover, Oct. 20, 1851, by
    Rev. Roswell G. Lamb   2
    Dolly, housekeeper, New York, married, d. Jan. 7, 1870, ae 65 (?)   58
    Erastus, farmer, b. Columbia, married, d. Aug. 9, [1863], ae 72   54
    Geo[rge] C., d. Mar. 10, 1869, ae 10 m. 18 d.   57
    Thaddeus W., soldier, b. Hebron, single, d. Nov. 28, 1864, at Annapolis,
       Md., Hospital, ae 21   55
PRENTICE, Anna, housekeeper, b. N. Stonington, married, dau. of William T.
    & Catherine BROWNING, d. Sept. 16, 1878, ae 84   62
REED, Edward, of Lanesville, O., m. Fanny S. MILLER, of Andover, Sept.
    26, 1849, by Rev. Alpha Miller   1
    Edward, book merchant, ae 27, b. Andover, res. Lanesville, O., m. Fanny
       S. MILLER, school teacher, ae 25, of Lanesville, O., Sept. 26, 1849,
       by Rev. Alpha Miller   40
RIDER, Watson & w. Zada had dau. d. Jan. 21, 1854, ae 2 d.   45
ROGERS Asenath, of Andover, m. George WEATHERBY, of Nunday
    Valley, N. Y. May 27, 1849, by Rev. Alpha Miller   1
    Asenath, ae 47, b. Mansfield, m. George WEATHERBY, farmer, ae 57,
       b. Nunday, N. Y., res. Andover, May 27, 1849, by Rev. Alpha Miller   39
    Harmony, w. of Sam[ue]l, d. May 6, 1875, ae 82   60
    Josiah, farmer, b. (unknown), d. May 2, 1848, ae 79   42
    Mary O., ae 21, b. Andover, res. Columbia, m. Edwin C. BOLLES,
       farmer, ae 25, b. Columbia, res. Columbia, June 3, 1851, by Rev.
       Alpha Miller   40
    Mary O., of Andover, m. Edwin C. BOLLES, of Columbia, June 3, 1851,
       by Rev. Alpha Miller   2
ROOD, Julius J., farmer, ae 29, & w. Julia A., ae 28, had son b. May 30, 1851 15
    Julius J., soldier, married, d. Feb. 2, 1864, ae 46, at Martinsburg, Va.   55
    Julius J., d. Feb. 3, 1864, at Martinsburg, Va. Was private in Co. G., 18th
       Reg. C. V.His children were Charles, ae 9, Caroline, ae 8, Rosa E. ae
       6   65

Page

SPRAGUE, (cont.)   Page

Sarah M., d. Norman & Laura P., d. Sept. 30, 1873, ae 28   60

Timothy Dwight, editor, d. Oct. 8, 1849, ae 30   43

W[illia]m, m. farmer, single, d. Jan. 27, 1870, ae 32   58

William Buel, s. Benjamin, farmer, ae 58, & Sarah, ae 39, b. May 6, 1849   13

STANDISH, Fanny, housekeeper, b. Groton, wid., d. July 9, 1870, ae 83   58

Fanny L., housework, b. Preston, single, d. Amasa & Fanny (GEER), d. Mar. 8, 1881, ae 72 y. 4 m.   64

STEWART, Harriet, see under Harriet S. DORRANCE   60

STRICKLAND, Andrew, farmer, b. East Glastenbury, married, d. Apr. 10, 1870, ae 65   58

STRONG, Lucy H., housekeeper, b. Belchertown, Mass., married, d. Aug. 13, 1856, ae 61   47

W[illia]m, Cyrus, s. W[illia]m W., farmer, ae 29, & Harriett M., ae 29, b. July 12, 1853   16

William W., of Hebron, m. Harriet M. CHAPPEL, of Andover, Oct. 3, 1849, by Rev. Roswell G. Lamb   1

W[illia]m W., farmer, ae 26, b. Hebron, res. Andover, m. Harriet M. CHAPPELL, ae 23, b. Hebron, res. Andover, Oct. 3, 1849, by Roswell G. Lamb   40

W[illia]m W., farmer, married, s. Geo[rge] & Anna B., b. Hebron, d. Nov. 5, 1874, ae 51   60

SWAN, Annah L., of Andover, m. Daniel E. SKINNER, of Hartford, Nov. 12, 1848, by Rev. Alpha Miller   1

John, laborer, married, d. July 17, 1866, ae 66 y. 6 m. 13 d.   56

TABOR, Margaret C., see Margaret C. BOWEN   61

THAYER, Francis, ae 33, b. Vernon, res. Coventry, m. Mary Ann EDWARDS, ae 34, b. Coventry, res. Andover, Oct. 5, 1856, by Rev. Urijah Underwood   3

THOMPSON, Dwight C., s. Eugene W. & Hattie, d. Feb. 24, 1875, ae 6 d.   60

Eugenee, d. Eugene & Harriet, d. Jan. 9. 1874, ae 5 d.   60

Mariah S., housekeeper, b. New London, married, d. Sept. 13, 1869, ae 30 y.   57

TICKNOR, Ansel, joiner, ae 38, & Emily, ae 41, had son, b. May 13, 1849   14

Ellen M., ae 17, of Andover, m. Edward H. WELLS, ae 23, b. Middletown, Feb. 7, 1855, by Urijah Underwood   3

TOPLIFF, Fanny, d. Dec. 21, 1863, ae 10   54

TRACY, Chester, shoemaker, b. Franklin, res. Coventry, d. Jan. [ ], 1850, ae 62   43

TRAPP, Samuel, blacksmith, b. Coventry, wid., d. Sept. 27, 1854, ae 70   45

VORRA, Elizabeth A., ae 30, b. Manchester, Ct., res. Andover, m. Mahlon WATROUS, ae 35, b. Walton, N. Y., res. Coventry, Nov. 26, 1857, by Rev. John R. Freeman   3

Sarah, ae 52, b. East Hartford, res. Manchester, m. 2d h. Joseph KINGSBURY, farmer, ae 62, b. Andover, res. Andover, Apr. 10., 1853, by Rev. Alpha Miller   41

WAKEFIELD, Lovinea, housekeeper, b. Bolton, married, d. Aug. 14, 1861, ae 22   52

WALKER, Phebe BILLINGS, housewife, wid. of Rev. Levi, d. Peleg &

14 BARBOUR COLLECTION

WALKER, (cont.)   Page
    Kiza **BARROWS**, d. Feb. 11, 1880, ae 92   63
WALLACE, Edward, b. Bolton, d. Aug. 7, 1849, ae 5 m.   42
WALLEN, Julia, ae 17, m. Lewis **BLISH**, mechanic, ae 23, res. Columbia,
    [ ], by Rev. Roswell[1], P. Lamb   40
    Julia A., of Andover, m. Lewis **BLISH** , of Columbia, Mar. 23, 1851, by
    Rev. Roswell G. Lamb, at her father's house   1
WARTIS, Marvin, laborer, colored, b. Lisbon, married, d. Mar. 2, 1872, ae 66   59
WATROUS, Ichabod, mechanic, b. Hebron, married, d. Aug. 21, [1862], ae 69   53
    Mahlon, mechanic, ae 32, b. Walton, N. Y., res. Coventry, m. Emily A.
    DORRANCE, ae 32, b. Canterbury, res. Andover, Nov. 23, 1854,
    by Sam[ue]l Griswold   3
    Mahlon, ae 35, b. Walton, N. Y., res. Coventry, m. 2d w. Elizabeth A.
    VORR, ae 30, b. in Manchester, Ct., res. Andover, Nov. 26, 1857,
    by Rev. John R. Freeman   3
WATSON, Fidelia C., housekeeper, res. Columbia, married, d. Aug. 31. 1866,
    ae 33   56
WEATHERBY, George, of Nunday Valley, N. Y., m. Asenath **ROGERS**, of
    Andover, May 27, 1849, by Rev. Alpha Miller   1
    George, farmer, ae 57, b. Nunday, N. Y. res. Andover, m. 3rd w. Asenath
    ROGERS, ae 47, b. Mansfield, May 27, 1849, by Rev. Alpha
    Miller   39
WEBSTER. Abigail, housekeeper, b. Lebanon, wid., d. Aug. 10, 1864, ae 58   55
    George W., hotel keeper, b. Exeter, married, d. May 25, 1873, ae 47   60
    Joel C., farmer, b. Hebron, widower, d. Aug. 6, 1861, ae 33   52
    Lucy A., b. Hebron, married, d. Oct. 6, 1860, ae 30   51
    Orpha E., d. John L., farmer, ae 42, & Mary, ae 37, b. Dec. 27, 1848   14
    Willie A., s. Cha[rle]s N., farmer, ae 29, & Sarah E., ae 29, b. Sept. 23,
    1850   15
WELLES, WELLS, Charles, s. William & Samantha, colored, d. July 18,
    1880, ae 8 m. 16 d.   63
    Edward H., ae 23, b. Middletown, m. Ellen M. **TICKNER***, ae 17, Feb.
    7, 1855, by Urijah Underwood (* Of Andover)   3
    Harriet, b. Eastbury, wid., dau. of Stewart, colored, d. Jan. 3, 1880, ae 81   63
WEST, Sherman, of Hartford, m. Amanda W. **ABBEY**, of Andover, Apr. 10,
    1850, by Rev. Alpha Miller   1
    Sherman, chandler, ae 30, b. Vernon, res. Hartford, m. Amanda **ABBEY**,
    houseworker, ae 34, b. Coventry, res. Hartford, [ ] 1850, by Smith
    A. Miller   40
WHITCOMB, Amelia, d. Nov. 21. 1864, ae 7 y. 7 m.   55
    Emma M., d. Mar. 20, 1865, ae 2 y.   56
WHITE, Adonijah, physician, b. Hebron, married, d. June 6, 1853, ae 58   44
    Edgar S., s. George H., farmer, ae 35, & Lucia, ae 35, b. Feb. 20, 1848   13
    Edith H., d. Apr. 9, 1872, ae 1 y.   59
    Eleazer S., farmer, & w. Frances had son b. Feb. 19, 1853   16
    Harriet, housekeeper, b. Hebron, single, d. Mar. 24, 1872, ae 71 y. 5 m.   59
    Jane C., housewife, d. John F. & H. W. **BINGHAM**, d. Nov. 19, 1873,
    ae 35   60
    John P., farmer, b. Andover, married, d. Sept. 24, 1854, ae 71   54

WHITE, (cont.) Page

Nancy, single, d. Mar. 6, 1865, ae 85   56

Patrick, his wife, b. in Ireland, d. Sept. [ ], 1848, ae about 30   42

Patrick, his son, d. Sept. [ ], 1848, ae about 4 m.   42

Roxelany, housekeeper, b. Hebron, wid., d. May 26, [1862], ae 79   53

Sarah R., d. Eleazer S., farmer, ae 39, & Frances, ae 28, b. Nov. 12, 1848   14

WILBER, Louisa J., d. Aug. 11, 1858, ae 1 y. 11m.   49

Nathan, b. Marlborough, single, d. Nov. [ ], 1856, ae 87   47

WILLIAMS, George Henry, b. South Coventry, d. Sept. 18, 1867, ae 2 y. 20 d.   57

Naomi, housekeeper, b. Windsor, wid., d. Apr. 6, 1854, ae 72   45

Orlando J., of Columbia, m. Louiza M. LATHROP, of Andover, Apr. 28,

1852, by Rev. Fred[eric]k D. Avery   2

Samuel, farmer, b. Douglass, Mass., wid., d. Apr. 9, 1854, ae 84 y.   45

WOODWORTH, Charles, farm laborer, b. South Coventry, married, s. Asa &

Sarah, d. Jan. 22, 1879, ae 59   62

WRIGHT, Jennie L., housekeeper, b. Andover, res. Huntington, married, d.

Mar. 11, [1862], ae 25   53

YEOMANS, Henry C., d. Dec. 21, 1870, ae 1 y. 1 m   58

NO SURNAME

A negro d. Mar. 20, 1861, ae 1 d.   52

A male st. b. Aug. 15, 1870   58

ASHFORD VITAL RECORDS
1710 - 1851

ABBOTT, ABBOT, ABBITT, ABBIT, ABIT (cont),

	Vol.	Page
David, s. John & Mary, b. Apr. 19, 1758	1	17
Esther, d. Nathan & Elisabeth, b. Mar. 14, 1798	4	73
Girdan, s. Joseph & Anna, b. Apr. 24, 1801	4	275
Hannah, [d. Nath[anie]ll, Jr. & Esther], b. Sept. 16, 1740	1	29
Hannah, d. John & Mary, b. Aug. 1, 1776	3	43
Henry, s. Benj[ami]n & Maryan, b. Nov. 11, 1746; d. Jan. 29, 1747/8	2	61
Henry, s. Benjamin & Maryan, b. June 3, 1749	2	61
John, [s Nath[anie]ll, Jr. & Esther], b. Sept. 22, 1742	1	29
John, m. Mary WRIGHT, Nov. 21, 1750, by James Bicknell, Esq.	1	17
John, s. John & Mary, b. Oct. 18, 1751	1	17
John, 3rd, d. Nov. 22, 1782	3	43
John, s. Abial & Jean, b. July 3, 1787; d. Oct. 18, 1790	4	248
Joseph, s. Nathaniel & Mary, b. Oct. 22, 1716	A	1
Joseph, s. Nath[anie]ll & Mary, b. Feb. 22, 1716	A	1
Joseph, s. John & Mary, b. Feb. 13, 1771	3	43
Joseph, s. Samuel & Elisabeth, b. Dec. 19, 1773	4	102
Joseph, s. Joshua & Lydia, b. Feb. 12, 178/9 (sic)	1	50
Joseph, m Anna SKINNER, Mar. 6, 1794	4	275
Joseph, Capt., m. Lucinda H. BAKER, b. of Ashford, [May] 7, [1846], by Jonathan King. Intention published May 3, 1846	5	97
Joshua, s. Nathaniel & Mary, b. Feb. 22, 1711	A	1
Joshua, s. Joshua & Lidea, b. Mar. 10, 1739/40	1	50
Judah, d. John & Mary, b. Nov., 29, 1760	3	43
Leda, d. Joshua & Ledea, [b.] Feb. 27, 1737/8	1	50
Lois, d. Nathan & Elisabeth, b. June 18, 1800	4	73
Lucy, d. Nathan & Elisabeth, b. Oct. 1, 1793	4	73
Lydia, see under Leda		
Marcy, d. Joshua & Lidea, b. June 2, 1744	1	50
Mary, d. Nathanael, Jr. & Esther, b. Apr. 22, 1734	1	29
Mol[l]ey, m. Ebenezer WRIGHT, Nov. 21, 1784	4	238
Molly, d. Nathan & Elisabeth, b. May 31, 1791	4	73
Nathan, s. Nathan & [E]unis, b. May 17, 1744	2	37
Nathan, [s. Nath[anie]ll, Jr. & Esther], b. Dec. 6, 1744	1	29
Nathan, s. John & Mary, b. July 30, 1763	3	43
Nathan, m. Elizabeth BORN, Aug. 31, 1785	4	73
Nathan, m. Huldah SKINNER, Oct. 16, 1808	4	240
Nathaniel, s. Nathaniel & Mary, b. May 22, 1714	A	1
Nathanael, Jr., m. Esther LYON, Apr. 16, 1734, by Philip Eastman, J. P.	1	29
Nathan[i]el, s. Nath[anie]ll, Jr. & Esther, b. July 18, 1737	1	29
Phebe, d. Nathan & Elizabeth, b. July 11, 1789	4	73
Phillip, s. Stephen & Freelove, b. Oct. 21, 1753	1	94
Rebeckah, d. Joshua & Lidyea, b. May 4, 1746	1	50
R[e]uben, s. Stephen, b. Apr. 15, 1774	3	106

ABBOTT, ABBOT, ABBITT, ABBIT, ABIT, (cont.)

Roxey, d. Joseph & Anna, b. Sept. 5, 1794;d. Mar. 30, 1795   4   275

Samuel, s. Joshua & Lidea, b. Feb. 6, 1741/2   1   50

Stephen, s. Nathanael, Jr. & [Esther], b. Nov. 10, 1735   1   29

Stephen, Capt., d. Sept. 29, 1801   3   106

Susannah, m. Stephen **BURGES**, Jr., Sept. 15, 1773   4   81

Thomas, s. Joshua & Lidda, b. Mar. 16, 1735/6   1   50

Warner, s. Amos & Sarah, b. May 18, 1801   4   39

Warner, of Otison, N. Y. , m. Sophia **EASTMAN**, of Ashford,
Oct. 10, 1827, by Rev. Philo Judson   5   29

William, s. Samuel & Elisabeth, b. Apr. 24, 1778   4   102

ADAMS, Abnur, s. Thomas & Abiga[i]ll, b. Aug. 10, 1733   1   27

Asa, s. Thomas & Abigail, b. Jan. 13, 1726/7   A   10

Asa, s. Thomas & Abiga[i]ll, b. Apr. 4, 1729   1   27

Dwight R., instructor, ae 27, of Canterbury, m. Sarah J.
HOUGH, ae 27, of Eastford, Oct.[ ], 1849, by Cha[rle]s
Peabody   5   142-3

George, m. Laura **PRESTON**, b. of Ashford, May 7, 1835, by
W[illia]m Livesey, Minister   5   56

Isaiah, s. Tho[ma]s & Abigaill, b. Nov. 7, 1723   1   27

James Augustus, s. James A. & Olive, b. Feb. 15, 1820   6   27

Jane, m. David **KENDALL**, Feb. 8, 1738/9, by Rev. Mr. Avery   1   28

John, m. Adeline **PRESTON**, b. of Ashford, Apr. 29, 1824, by
Rev. W[illia]m Storrs   5   14

John Quincy, s. John B. & Adaline, b. Mar. 22, 1826   6   61

Julia A., of Stafford, m. Henry L. **FULLER**, of Ashford, Aug.
10, 1851, by Rev. Cha[rle]s Hyde   5   107

Nathan, s. Tho[ma]s & Abigaill, b. July 1, 1731   1   27

Nathan, S. Thomas & Abigail, b. May 16, 1736   1   27

Nathan Preston, s. John B. & Adeline, b. Dec. 30, 1828   6   61

Nehemiah T., of Hampton, m. Louisa W. **PALMER**, of
Ashford, Oct. 19, 1836, by Rev. J. Hall   5   62

Olive, d. William & Olive, b. Aug. 7, 1798   4   243

Olive, d. James A. & Olive, b. Jan., 20, 1818   6   27

Susan, of Pomfret, m. Roswell **EASTMAN**, of Hartford, Nov.
11, [1841], by Francis Williams   5   79

_____. s. Thomas & Abigail, b. Nov. 7, 1723   A   8

AGARD, Amos, s. James & Abigail, b. June 23, 1735   1   47

ALBRO, William, m. Abigail **SCARBOROUGH**, b. of Ashford,
[Mar.] 8, 1829, by Rev. Reuben Torrey, Eastford   5   33

ALDRICH, Harty, of Thompson, m. Ephraim **CARPENTER**, of
Ashford, Dec. 7, 1829, by Edward S. Keyes, J. P.   5   37

ALLEN, Almira, m. Jarvis **CHAPMAN**, Mar. 13, 1825, by Amos
Babcock, Elder. Intention published.   5   18

Angenette, of Ashford, m. Merrick **CLEMENCE** of
Southbridge, Nov. 26, 1845, by Rev. Renssalear O.Putney   5   96

ALLEN, (cont.)	Vol.	Page
Azubah, w. Daniel, d. Apr. 25, 1776	4	85
Benjamin, m. Rebeckah **BISHOP**, Dec. 31, 1717	A	4
Cryus, s. Dan[ie]ll, Jr. & Mary, b. oct. 14, 1771	4	33
Daniel, Jr. , m. Mary **SUMNER**, Feb. 19, 1764	4	33
Daniel, s. Dan[ie]ll, Jr. & Mary, b. Jan. 9, 1777	4	33
David, Jr., m. Lydia **ABBE**, May 6, 1776	4	85
David, s. David, Jr. & Silva, b. Feb. 4, 1784	4	85
Ephraim, m. Hannah **SUMNER**, Mar. 6, 180[ ]	4	84
Experience, d. Ephraim & Hannah, b. Oct. 12, 1800; d, May 12, 1806	4	84
Experience, d. Ephraim & Hannah, d. May 12, 1806	4	84
Geals(?), s. John & Mary, b. June 11, 1740	1	76
Hannah, d. John & Mary, b. Oct. 21, 1742	1	76
Hannah, d. Dan[ie]ll, Jr. & Mary, b. Sept. 2, 1774	4	33
Hannah, d. David, Jr. & Silva, b. Aug. 21, 1792	4	85
Ira, s. John & Sarah, b. Mar. 25, 1784; d. Jan. 23, 1788	4	240
Ira, of Thompson, m. Calista **BASS**, of Ashford, Nov. 23, 1834, by Rev. Stephen Hitchcock	5	55
James, m. Lucy **WHIPPLE**, b. of Ashford, June 6, 1830, by Rev. Philo Judson	5	39
John, s. John & Mary, b. July 27, 1745	1	76
John, m. Sarah **KENDAL**, Jan. 1, 1784	4	240
John, s. John & Sarah, b. Dec. 24, 1789	4	240
Lucy, m. Jonathan **CHAFFE**, May 1, 1776	4	107
Mary, d. John & Mary, b. Feb. 5, 1737/8	1	63
Mary, d. John & Mary, b. Feb. 9, 1737/8	1	76
Mary, m. Cyril **BROWN**, Sept. 15, 1768	4	89
Mary, d. Ephraim & Hannah, b. July 2, 1805	4	84
Mary, of Ashford, m. Oliver **CARPENTER**, Jr., of Killingly, Mar. 16, 1843, by Rev. John Howson	5	84
Molly, m. Olcutt **FISHER**, Jan. 28, 1773	4	72
Philip, s. David, Jr. & Silva, b. Oct. 11, 1781	4	85
Polley, m. John Newman **SUMNER**, June 8, 1797	4	24
Rachel, m. John **CHEDLE**, May 11, 1768	3	58
Rosammund, d. Daniel, Jr. & Mary, b. June 5, 1768	4	33
Samuell, m. Elisabeth **PARRY**, May 30, 1754, by Mr. Stephen Williams, of Woodstock	1	83
Solomon, s. David, Jr. & Silva, b. Nov. 17, 1789	4	85
Thomas, s. John & Sarah, b. Oct. 17, 1786; d. Jan. 14, 1788	4	240
Timothy, Rev., of Ashford, m. Mrs. Dorothy **REED** of Norwich, Jan. 6, 1761, by Rev. Peter Powers, Newent, Norwich	3	20
Woodward B., m. Mary Ann **WHIPPLE**, Nov. 19, 1840, by John N. Whipple	5	76
Yeals (?), see under Geals		
Zachariah, s. David, Jr. & Silva, b. Mar. 21, 1786	4	85

	Vol.	Page
ALMY, William T., of Norwich, m. Percy S. **PALMER**, of Ashford, Jan. 8, 1845, by Rev. Cha[rle]s Hyde	5	93
[ALTON], ALLTON, Betsey, m. Zephaniah **SHERMAN**, Nov. 15, 1804	4	272
AMES, [see also **EMES**], Sarah, m. Aaron **BOSWORTH**, Mar. 28, 1771	4	79
Thomas, of East Lyme, m. Lucinda **COLE**, of Verona, May 9, 1844, by Rev. Geo[rge] Mixter	5	89
AMIDOWN, AMMIDOW, AMIDON, Abel, s. Joseph & Patience, b. Mar. 14, 1767	4	17
Abner, s. Joseph & Patience, b. Feb. 9, 1774	4	17
Asahel, s. Joseph & Patience, b. Jan. 17, 1776	4	17
Caleb, s. Joseph & Patience, b. July 12, 1781	4	17
Cheney, s. Joseph & Patience, b. Sept. 3, 1783	4	17
Chloe, d. Joseph & Patience, b. Apr. 10, 1764	4	17
Dan, s. Experience J. & Elizabeth, b. Feb. 12, 1823	4	60
Ebenezer, s. Jedidiah, d. May 29, 1803	4	270
Eunice, d. Joseph & Patience, b. Sept. 13, 1762	4	17
Experiance J., m. Elisabeth **WALKER**, Jan. 5, 1807	4	60
Experience J., farmer, b. Willington, res. Ashford, d. Aug, 22, 1850, ae 72	5	150-1
Experiance Johnson, s. Ex[periance] Johnson & Elisabeth, b. May 13, 1813	4	60
Hannah, d. Joseph & Patience, b. Oct. 5, 177[ ]	4	17
Hannah, m. Amasa **CHAPMAN** Oct. 13, 1796	4	289
Hannah, w. Jedidiah, d. May 16, 1813	4	270
Hannah, d. Jedidiah & Hannah, d. Mar. 14, 1826	4	270
Harris, s. Jedidiah, d. Apr. 28, 1806	4	270
Henry, d. Mar. 5, 1778	4	17
Horatio, m. Marion **STRONG**, Oct. 14, 1819	6	56
Horatio Lyman, s. Horatio & Marion, b. Dec. 23, 1825	6	56
Jedadiah, s. Henery & Sarah, b. Aug. 3, 1753	1	82
Jedidiah, s. Jedidiah & Hannah, b. Mar. 2, 1800	4	270
Jedidiah Sanford, [s. Horatio & Marion], b. Sept. 19, 1834	6	56
Jonathan, s. Henery, Jr. & Sarah, b. Feb.7, 1759	1	106
Louisa, d. Experiance J. & Elisabeth, b. Oct. 3, 1809	4	60
Louisa M., teacher, d. Aug, 12, 1850, ae 20	5	150-1
Maria Louisa, [d. Horatio & Marion], b. Sept. 26, 1829	6	56
Mehatiah, d. Joseph & Patience, b. Mar. 22, 1787	4	17
Melatiah, d. May 17, 1780	4	17
Molly, d. Henery, Jr. & Sarah, b. Aug. 26, 1761	3	129
Moses, s. Henery, Jr. & Sarah, b. Apr. 17, 1756	1	106
Polley, [twin with Salla], d. Jedidiah & Hannah, b. June 22, 1797	4	270
Rhoda, d. Joseph & Patience, b. Apr. 7, 177[ ]	4	17
Salla, [twin with Polley], d Jedidiah & Hannah, b. June 22,1797	4	270

	Vol.	Page
AMIDOWN, AMMIDOW, AMIDON, (cont.)		
Salla, m. David WRIGHT Nov. 8, 1821	4	277
Sally, m. Daniel WRIGHT, b. of Ashford, Nov. 8, 1821, by		
Rev. W[illia]m Storrs	5	5
Wealthy, d. Jedidiah, d. Aug. 14, 1798	4	270
Wealthy Matilda, of Ashford, m. Hosea VINTON, of		
Woodstock, Jan. 28, 1841, by Rev. Alvin Bennett	5	77
ANDREWS, Asahel, s. John & Hannah, b. June 28, 1732	1	5
Benjamin B., m. Lucy B. SNOW, b. of Ashford, Mar. 8, 1830,		
by Rev. Philo Judson	5	38
Benjamin Norriss, s. Benjamin B. & Lucy B., b. Mar. 27, 1832	6	70
Cordelia F., m. Bradford LYON, b. of Ashford, Jan. 31, 1830,		
by Rev. Philo Judson	5	38
Lucy Ann Griggs, d. Benjamin B. & Lucy B., b. Aug. 10, 1830	6	70
Mary Ann, d. John & Hannah, b. July 25, 1727	1	5
Maryan, m. Benj[ami]n ABBOTT, Jan. 16, 1745/6	2	61
Stephen, s. John & Hannah, b. Nov. 30, 1724	1	5
ANTHONY, Eliza, m. Samuel G. REYNOLDS, [Feb.] 16, [1824],		
by Rueben Torrey, Eastford	5	12
ANTRAM, Jeremiah, s. Francis, & Eunice, b. Sept. 13, 1790	4	237
ARMOUR, Danford, of Lenox, N. Y., m. Julia A. BROOKS of		
Ashford, Conn., Nov. 27, 1825, by Amos Babcock, Elder.		
Intention published.	5	20
ARMSTRONG, Mary, M. Jeremiah ABBE, June 18, 1760	3	39
ARNOLD, Charles M., of Ashford, m. Mary A. TOWN, of Union,		
Mar. 1, 1846, by Rev. Renssalear O. Putney	5	96
Daniel S., m. Lovisa MIXTER, b. of Ashford, Apr. 15, 1845,		
by Rev. Geo[rge] Mixter	5	93
Dedama, of Ashford, m. Jabez STARKWEATHER, Jr. of		
Mansfield, Jan. 26, 1830, by Rev. Ezekiel Skinner	5	38
Diadama, m. Palmer SOUTHWORTH, b. of Ashford, Apr. 15,		
1845, by Rev. Geo[rge] Mixter	5	93
Ezra P., m. Esther LYON, b. of Eastford, Oct. 19, 1846, by		
Francis Williams	5	97
George, of Woodstock, m. Sally WHITNEY, of Ashford, July		
11, 1822, by Rev. Isaac Hall	5	6
Henry H., m. Mary MORSE, b. of Ashford, [June] 4, [1837],		
by Rev. Reuben Torrey, Eastford	5	64
James B., m. Adaline A. BILL, b. of Ashford, Jan. 1, 1843, by		
Elder R. V. Lyon, Mansfield	5	83
Mary A., d. James B., farmer, ae 29, & Adaline A., ae 25, b.		
Oct. 11, 1847	5	126/7
Moses L., m. Mary W. BOLLES, b. of Ashford, May 30,		
1842, by Rev. C. C. Barnes	5	81
Zuriel P., m. Susan FRANKLIN, b. of Ashford, Aug. 4, 1833,		

	Vol.	Page
ARNOLD, (cont.)		
by Rev. W[illia]m Livesey	5	51
ASHCRAFT, Mary, m. Asa **RICHARDS**, Jr., Aug. 19, 1804	4	102
ASHLEY, Henry, of Chaplin, m. Elizabeth **CLARK**, of Ashford,		
Sept. 17, 1838, by Rev. Cha[rle]s Hyde	5	68
ASPINWALL, Lucretia, d. Claras[s] **SNOW**, b. Mar. 30, 1807	4	71
ATWOOD, Cindarilla, of Ashford, m. Sidney **WORK**, of Stafford,		
[Nov.] 2, [1834], by Rev. Dexter Munger	5	55
Ellen Lucinda, d. Milvern H. & Lucinda, b. Sept. 23, 1845	6	99
Jerusha C., b. Nov. 11, 1810; m. John P. **SHUMWAY**, Nov.		
11, 1830; d. Apr. 4, 1849	6	91
John, of Mansfield, m. Sophronia **WRIGHT**, of Ashford, Mar.		
6, 1844, by Rev. Ezekiel Skinner	5	88
Lorrin S., of Mansfield, m. Elvira **COOLEY**, of Ashford, Sept.		
24, 1844, by Rev. Cha[rle]s Hyde	5	91
Melvin H., of Mansfield, m. Lucinda **COOLEY** of Ashford,		
Oct. 23, 1843, by Cha[rle]s Hyde	5	86
Orrel S., of Willington, m. Austin S. **SOUTHWARTS**, of		
Mansfield, Feb. 2, 1836, by Amos Babcock	5	58
AUSTIN, Aaron,Capt., of Suffield, Conn., m. Content Ann		
WENTWORTH, of Dear Island, Me., Nov. 28, 1822, by		
Edward Keyes, J. P.	5	7
Delilah, d. Jacob & Joanna, b. Aug. 3, 1805	4	88
Henry W., of Woodstock, m. Cynthia M. **FULLER**, of Ashford		
(Westford Society), Jan. 8, 1844, by [Rev.] R.V. Lyon,		
Westford	5	87
Henry Wotherill, s Jacob & Joanna, b. May 6, 1807	4	88
Lydia J., d. Thomas M., hatter, ae 27, & Mary T., ae 22, b.		
Nov. 27, 1849	5	140-1
Parmelia, d. Jacob. & Joanna, b. May 10, 1804	4	88
Thomas McDonough, m. Mary Tabor **GREEN**, b. of		
Ashford, May 28, 1843, by Rev. Ezekiel Skinner	5	85
AVERILL, AVEREL, AVERIL, AVERELL, Aaron, s. James &		
Mary, b. Oct. 6, 1768	3	25
Aaron, s. James [& Mary], d. Sept. 28, 1775	3	25
Abigail, d. James & Mary, b. May 28, 1762	3	25
Benjamin, . James & Mary, b. Aug. 15, 1765	3	25
Elizabeth, of Preston, m. David **PELER**, of Ashford, Dec. 7,		
1722, by Rev. Salmon Treat, at Preston	A	6
Ephraim, s. James & Mary, b. Sept. 24, 1757; d. Nov. 23, 1757	1	103
Ephraim, s. James & Mary, b. Sept. 21, 1758	1	103
George, s. Jonathan & Anna, b. May 25, 178[ ]	4	283
Hearta, [child] of Jonathan & Anna, b. Dec. 11, 179[ ]	4	283
Jabez, s. James & Mary, b. Aug. 29, 1770	3	25
James, m. Mary **WALKER**, Mar. 3, 1757	1	103
James, s. James & Mary, b. Dec. 14, 1763	3	25

	Vol.	Page
AVERILL, AVEREL, AVERIL, AVERELL, (cont.)		
Jonathan, m. Anna WATKINS(?), Dec. 4, 1784	4	283
Mary, d. James & Mary, b. July 28, 1760	3	25
Mary, w. James, d. Nov. 21, 1774	3	25
Rex, s. Jonathan & Anna, b. Apr. 29, 1784	4	283
Stata, [child] of Jonathan & Anna, b. Aug. 26, [ ]	4	283
Stephen, s. James & Mary, b. Aug. 11, 1773	3	25
Stephen, s. James [& Mary] d. Sept. 10, 1775	3	25
William Pitt, s. Jonathan & Anna, b. Nov. 7, 178[ ] ; d. Jan. 10, 1789	4	283
AVERY, Almira, seamstress, d. [1848 or 9], ae 52	5	138-9
Betsy, d. Abel [ ]	4	3
Celia, m. Henry CURTIS, Jr., Nov. 28, 1816	6	18
David, s. John & Sarah, b. Aug. 4, 1760 ; d. Jan. 1, 1764	3	38
Elisha, s. Jonathan & Chloe, b. Nov. 5, 1774	4	70
Hannah, d. John & Sarah, b. Aug. 3, 1754	1	87
Hannah, d. John & Sarah, b. Aug. 3, 1754 ; d. Aug. 9, 1757	3	38
Han[n]ah, d. Jonathan & Chloe, b. Feb. 22, 1777	4	70
John, m. Sarah BICKNELL, Dec. 11, 1751	3	38
John, s. John & Sarah, b. Mar. 5, 1756	1	92
John, s. John & Sarah, b. Mar. 5, 1756	3	38
John, d. June 5, 1772	3	38
Jonathan, Jr., m. Hannah HUMPHREY, Dec. 6, 1749, by Rev. John Bass	2	19
Jonathan, Jr., d. Jan. 15, 1749/50	2	19
Jonathan, s. Jonathan & Hannah, b. July 2, 1750	2	19
Jonathan, [twin with Lyd[i]a, s. John & Sarah, b. Mar. 20, 1757; d. one day after birth	3	38
Jonathan, Dr., d. June 12, 1761	3	38
Jonathan, s. John & Sarah, b. June 26, 1762	3	38
Jonathan, m. Chloe WALES, Nov. 29, 1773	4	70
Lydia, w. Dr. Jonathan, d. Feb. 10, 1753	1	80
Lyd[i]a, [twin with Jonathan, d. John & Sarah, b. Mar. 20, 1757	3	38
Matilda, d. John & Sarah, b. Apr. 13, 1767	3	38
Melinda, d. John, d. Feb. 7, 1769	3	38
Polley, d. Jonath[an] & Chloe, b. Feb. 21, 1779	4	70
Robert, s. John & Sarah, b. Aug. 6, 1758 ; d. Aug. 31, 1760	3	38
Sally, d. John & Sarah, b. Sept. 6, 1765	3	38
Salla, m. Solomon FARNAM, Nov. 23, 1786	4	269
Samuel W., of Stafford, m. Almira BUTLER, of Ashford, Dec. 27, 1831, by Rev. David Bennett	5	46
Sarah, d. John & Sarah, b. July 23, 1753 ; d. Aug. 27, 1753	2	23
Sarah, d. John & Sarah, b. July 23, 1753 ; d. Aug. 21, 1753	3	38
Sarah, w. John, d. Dec.[ ], 1771	3	38

Vol. Page

BABBITT, BABAT, Celia A., of Brookfield, m. Ephraim BURR, of
Millbury, Mass., Jan. 26, 1834, by Rev. Ezekiel Skinner   5   52
Persis, ae 59, b. N. Brookfield, Mass., m. Hiram JOHNSON,
ae 49, b. Vermont, res. Sturbridge, Sept. 24, 1848, by
Rev. Cha[rle]s B. Adams   5   136-7
Sally, m. Danford CHAPMAN, July 24, 1825, by Henry
Curtis, Elder   5   19
Tryphenia, of Brookfield, Mass., m. Henry GRAVES, Sept. 18,
1836, by Alvan Underwood   5   61
BABCOCK, BADCOCK, BABCOK, Achsah, see under Ashsah
Amos, m. Anna WADKINS, Oct. 25, 1737   1   73
Amos, s. Amos & Anna, b. Jan. 11, 1748/9   2   80
Annah, d. Amos & Annah, b. Nov. 16, 1751   2   80
Annah, [d. Elijah & Elisabeth], b. Dec. 28, 1767   4   54
Annah, m. Ebenezer WALES, Dec. 26, 1773   4   84
Archibald, s. Timothy & Esther, b. Mar. 8, 1780   4   78
Ashsah, d. Timothy & Esther, b. July 30, 1788   4   78
Dwight, s. Thomas P. & Emelia, b. Jan. 1, 1816   6   23
Edwin C., s. Amos & Esther, b. Feb. 1, 1825   6   86
Elyah, s. Amos & Anna, b. Feb. 8, 1742   (Elijah)   1   73
Elijah, m. Elisabeth BASSETT, May 1, 1762   3   78
Elijah, m. Elisabeth BASSET[T], May 2, 1762   4   54
Elisabeth, [d. Elijah & Elisabeth], b. Apr. 4, 1772   4   54
Elisabeth, w. Elijah, d. June 2, 1776   4   54
Horace, s. Amos & Annah, b. Nov. 12, 1762   2   80
Lydia, d. Timothy & Esther, b. May 14, 1791 ; d. Dec. 19,1794   4   78
Mariham, d. Amos & Annah, b. Apr. 6, 1757   2   80
Mehitable, s. [Elijah & Elisabeth], b. May 30, 1766   4   54
Palmer, s. Timothy & Esther, b. Nov. 26, 1793   4   78
Palmer, s. Tho[ma]s P. & Emelia, b. Aug. 25, 1819   6   23
Percy, of Liberty, N. Y., m. Sampson KEYES, of Ashford, Jan.
6, 1824, by Rev. Philo Judson   5   12
Prudance, d. Elijah & Elisabeth, b. May 25, 1776   4   54
Ralph, s. Elijah & Elisabeth, b. Feb. 20, 1774   4   54
Rocksalena, d. Elijah & Elisabeth, b. Apr. 19, 1763   3   78
Roxalena, [d. Elijah & Elisabeth], b. Apr. 19, 1763   4   54
Rozell, s. Amos & Annah, b. Nov. 1, 1764   2   80
Sanford, s. Tho[ma]s P. & Emelia, b. Oct. 3, 1817   6   23
Sarah, d. Amos & Anna, b. Aug. 1, 1746   1   73
Selenda, d. Elijah & Elizabeth, b. Mar. [ ], 1754   3   78
S[e]lenda, [d. Elijah & Elisabeth], b. Mar. 24, 1764   4   54
Stephen, s. Amos & Anna, b. Mar. 20, 1740   1   73
Thomas P., m. Emeline RAZE, Dec. 23, 1814   6   23
Timothy, s. Timothy & Est[h]er, b. Apr. 16, 1777   4   78
Timothy, d. Mar. 27, 1814, ae 66   4   78

	Vol.	Page.
BABCOCK, BADCOCK, BABCOK, (cont.)		
We[a]lthy, d. Timothy & Esther, b. May 27, 1785	4	78
William, s. Amos & Anna, b. Aug. 30, 1744	1	73
William, s. Amos, d. Oct. 11, 1748	2	80
William, [s. Elijah & Elisabeth], b. Dec. 24, 1769	4	54
William S., of Toledo, O., m. Caroline S. WHALEY, of		
Ashford, Oct. 24, 1842, by Rev. Cha[rle]s Hyde	5	82
BACKUS, BECKUS, Aaron, s. Adonijah & Anna, b. Dec. 13, 1756	1	98
Adonijah, m. Anna FULLER, Apr. 5, 1755	1	98
Anna, d. Adonijah, Jr., b. Oct. 9, 1795	4	260
Anne, d. Adonijah & Anne, b. Apr. 25, 1759	1	110
Anne, w. Adonijah, d. Apr. 11, 1794	3	123
Eli Nathaniel, s. Timothy J. & Sally, b. Jan. 11, 1845	6	97
Herbert Roland, s. Joseph, pedler, & Mary J., b. Apr. 5, 1849	5	132-3
Joseph, pedler, ae 27, b. Chaplin, res. Ashford, m. Mary J.		
CLARKE, ae 19, Aug. 8, 1848, by Rev. Erastus		
Dickinson	5	136-7
Josiah, s. Adonijah & Anne, b. Dec. 17, 1762	3	123
Libea, d. Adonijah & Anna, b. Mar. 4, [ ]	4	7
Mary, d. Adonijah & Anne, b. Dec. 16, 1760	3	49
Percy, d. Jeremiah & Percy, b. Feb. 25, 1791	4	263
Polly, d. Adonijah, Jr., b. Oct. 23, 1799	4	260
Roxey, d. Jeremiah & Percy, b. May 25, 1799	4	263
Stephen Gennins, s. Esther Chapman, b. June 17, 1811	4	101
Susan, d. Timothy J. & Sally, b. Aug. 19, 1839	6	97
Zilpha, d. Timothy J. & Sally, b. June 21, 1842	6	97
----hen, s. Jeremiah & Parcy, b. Jan. 19, 1794	4	96
----, d. Zalmon, farmer, & C[ ], b. June[ ], 1850	5	140-1
BADGER, BAGER, Olice, d. John & Bridget, b. Nov. 5, 1870		
(Alice?)	4	118
Dorathy, d. John & Bridget, b. Feb. 10, 1787	4	118
Edmund, [s. Ezekiel & Doratha], b. [ ] 23, 1773	4	88
Elisabeth, d. Ezek[i]el & Dorithy, b. Dec. 18, 1756	1	96
Ezekiel, m. Dorothy SCARBOROUGH, Apr. 3, 1755, by Mr.		
Stephen Williams, of Woodstock	1	88
James, s. Nath[anie]ll & Rebeckah, b. July 29, 1744	1	95
James, s. Ezekiel & Doratha, b. Feb.9, 1777	4	88
James, s. John & Bridget, b. Mar. 12, 1789	4	118
Jesse, s,. John & Bridget, b. Dec. 5, 1778 (sic)	4	118
John, m. Olice TUFTS, May 12, 1778 (sic)	4	118
John, s. John & Bridget, b. Feb. 1, 1785	4	118
Lucetta P., m. Frank WEEKS, b. of Ashford, Dec. 11, 1842,		
by Rev. F. Williams	5	83
Lucretia, m. Amos WEEKS, Jr., Oct. 29, 1837, by Amasa		
Lyon, J. P.	5	66

	Vol.	Page
BADGER, BAGER,(cont.)		
Mary, d. John & Bridget, b. Dec. 2,1782	4	118
Mary, of Ashford, m. Benjamin **FRANKLIN**, of Brookfield,		
Mass., June 14, 1846, by Rev. Edward A. Lyon	5	98
Olice, see under Alice		
Patience, d. Ezekiel & Doratha, b. May 10, 1776	4	88
Patience, m. Nathan **LYON**, Apr. 10, 1788	4	258
Rebecca, m. John **PARRY**, Jr., May 2, 1755, by Stephen		
Williams	1	95
Rebeckah, [d. Ezekiel & Doratha], b. Jan. 1, 1768	4	88
Rebeckah, m. John **PECK**, Jr. Nov. 12, 1788	4	230
Rhode, m. John **EWING**, Dec. 4, 1761	4	19
Sarah, [d. Ezekiel & Doratha], b. Apr. 26, 1771	4	88
Sarah had d. Myre Ingrehan, b. Feb. 2, 1798	4	88
Sarah, m. Elisha **PECK**, Sept. 23, 1802	4	34
BAILEY, BALEY, Ann, d. John & Clarina, b. Jan. 10, 1798	4	75
Ann, m. Israel D. **CHAFFEE**, 2d, May 27, 1818	6	20
Asa, s. John & Clarina, b. Feb. 2, 1793	4	75
Claris[s]a, d. John & Clarina, b. Mar, 25, 1794	4	75
John, m. Clarina **SNOW**, Aug. 30, 1792	4	75
Leushe, d. John & Clarina, b. Apr. 10, 1796	4	75
Louisa, m. David **BAKER**, Dec. 2, 1819	6	25
Sally, m. Erastus **LATHROP**, Sept. 21, 1807	6	66
BAITAN, James, of New Bedford, m. Levina **DENNIS**, of Ashford,		
Sept. 20, 1831 by [ ], Eastford	5	44
BAKER, Anne, d. Jonathan & Easter, b. May 28, 1755	2	33
Benjamin L. , of Woodstock, m. Susan **WHITMAN**, of		
Ashford, Sept. 30, 1838, by Elias C. Scott	5	69
Caroline Jain, d. David & Louisa, b. Mar. 22, 1831	6	25
David, m. Louisa **BALEY**, Dec., 2, 1819	6	25
David Ruggles, s. David & Louisa, b. Nov. 17, 1820	6	25
Eleazer, s. [Eleazer] & Hannah, b. June 1, 1795	4	284
Emily, m. Leander **WALBRIDGE**, b. of Ashford, Nov. 20,		
1853, by Rev. P. Mathewson	5	110
Easther, d. Jonathan & Easther, b. Aug. 1, 1743 ; d. Oct. 13,		
1748	2	33
Easter, d. Jonathan & Easter, b. Apr. 15, 1751	2	33
Eunis, d. Robert & Deborah, b. Mar. 27, 1768	3	55
George, m. Eliza D. **CHAFFEE**, b. of Ashford, May 6, 1832,		
by Rev. David Bennett	5	47
George H., s. Mary, farmer, ae 49, & Enoch E., ae 48, b. Nov.		
18, 1850	5	148-9
Hannah, d. Eleazer & Hannah, b. Oct. 4, 1797	4	284
Henry Watter, s. David & Louisa, b. Nov. 15, 1825	6	25
James Dwight, s. David & Louisa, b. May 25, 1828	6	25
John, [s. Robert & Deborah], b. May 4, 1755	3	55

	Vol.	Page
BAKER, (cont.)		
John, Jr., m. Betsey J. **WHEATON,** b. of Ashford,		
Dec. 16. 1838, by Rev. Alvan Underwood	5	70
John W., m. Sarah **WHITE,** b. of Ashford, Sept. 15, 1850, by		
Rev. John M. Hunt	5	105
John W., farmer, ae 22, of Ashford, m. Sarah H. **WHITE,** ae		
19, b. Canterbury, Sept. 15, 1850, by Rev. John M. Hunt	5	148-9
Jonathan, m. Easther **WOODCOCK,** June 17, 1740	2	33
Jonathan, s. Jonathan & Easter, b. Feb. 12, 1745/6	2	33
Jonathan, [s. Robert & Deborah], b. May 4, 1755	3	55
Joseph, s. Eleazer & Hannah, b. June 21, 1800	4	284
Joshua, s. Jonathan & Easter, b. Apr. 3, 1759	2	33
Lucinda H., of Ashford, m. Capt. Joseph **ABBOTT,** b. of		
Ashford, [May] 7,[1846], by Jonathan King. Intention		
published May 3, 1846	5	97
Lucy Elvina, d. David & Louisa, b. Aug. 6, 1823	6	25
Marcy, [d. Robert & Deborah], b. Apr. 4, 1761* (*Entry		
scratched out)	3	55
Molly, [d. Robert & Deborah], b. Feb. 16, 1759	3	55
Olive, [d. Robert & Deborah], b. Feb. 23, 1751	3	55
Patty, [d. Robert & Deborah], b. July 14, 1757	3	55
Phebee, d. Jonathan & Easter, b. Oct. 16, 1761	2	33
Reuben W., of Plainsfield, m. Sarah **FARNHAM,** of Ashford,		
July 12, 1847, by Charles Peabody	5	101
Reuben W., laborer, b. Pomfret, res. Ashford, m. Keziah		
UTLEY, his 5th w., b. Ashford, May [ ], 1850, by		
Cha[rle]s Peabody	5	142-3
Robert, [s. Robert & Deborah], b. Apr. 7, 1763	3	55
Samuel, s. Jonathan & Easther, b. Jan. 12, 1748/9	2	33
Samuel, [s.Robert & Deborah], b. Aug. 28, 1752	3	55
Sarah, dark housekeeper, b. Hampton, res. Ashford, d. Sept. 25,		
1848, ae 78	5	136-7
BALDWEN, Patien[c]e, m. Joseph **RUSS,** Jr., Jan, 22, 1734/5	1	49
BANCROFT, Lucy, m. Jesse **FOSTER,** Aug. 30, 1803	4	103
BARBER, William, of Pomfret, m. Azuba **SPAULDING,** of		
Ashford, Eastford Society, Mar. 4, 1823, by Rev. Philo		
Judson	5	8
BARK, Aphia, m. Nathan **EASTMAN,** Apr. 29, 1795	4	63
BARLOW, Darius R., s. Reuben M., farmer, & Sophia S., b. July 3,		
1848	5	126-7
Reuben M., of Woodstock, m. Eunice S. **SNOW,** of Ashford,		
Apr. 17, 1844, by R. V. Lyon	5	89
BARNES, Lydia, m. Charles **SAMSON,** Mar. 4, 1813	6	2
BARNET, ----, w. John, d. Nov. 11, 1723	A	8
BARNEY, BANEY, Bettey, d. Joseph, Jr.& Sybil, b. Jan. 28, 1777	4	24
Jacob, s. Joseph, Jr. & Sybil, b. Aug. 29, 1770	4	24

	Vol.	Page
BARNEY, BANEY, (cont.)		
Jonathan, s. Joseph, Jr. & Sybil, b. Apr. 23, 1768	4	24
Joseph, Jr., m. Sybel **CHAPMAN**, Dec. 5, 1764	4	24
Phebe, m. Hovey **PRESTON**, Nov. 23, 1773	4	68
Sarah, m. W[illia]m **SNELL** Dec. 26, 1758	3	7
Susan[n]ah, m. Trupe **CHAPMAN**, Mar. 29, 1759	3	11
Susanna, d. Joseph, Jr. & Sybil, b. June 11, 1774	4	24
BARROWS, Bradley, of Mansfield, m. Betsey **KENT**, of Ashford, Nov. 12, 1840, by Rev. Ezekiel Skinner	5	75
Charles, m. Susan **GORTON**, [Feb.] 1, 1837, by Rev. Reuben Torrey, Eastford	5	63
Cordelia E., ae 17, b. Mansfield, m. Orrin E. **SQUIER**, laborer, ae 22, b. Ashford, res. Willington. Aug. 5, 1849, by Washington Munger	5	142-3
Harlow E., of Mansfield, m. Mary **TANDO**, of Weathersfield, Sept, 13, 1834, by Amos Babcock	5	54
Lydia, m. David Torrey, Dec. 28, 1790	4	95
Lydia, m. Edward **FRINK**, Feb. 4, 1802	4	37
Minerva, d. Harlow E., steelyard maker, ae 37, & Mary Ann, ae 30, b. Jan. 18, 1848	5	126-7
Roger, of Ashford, m. Rebeckah **PARKER**, of Mansfield, Sept, 24, 1826, by Rev. Philo Judson	5	24
BARRY, Sarah, m. Jonathan **PIDGE**, Apr. 13, 1749	2	29
BARTHBY, Ichabod, m. Harriet **SIMMONS**, b. of Ashford, Oct. 24, 1827, by Rev. Philo Judson	5	29
BARTLETT, BARTLET, Abner, s. Ira & Betty, b. July 6, 1802	4	42
Anny, of Ashford, m. Ira **LAWSON**, of Union, [Jan.,] 15, [1837], by Rev. Reuben Torrey, Eastford	5	63
Daniel, of Woodstock, m. Lucy P. **HOWARD**, of Ashford, June 27, 1836, by Rev. Leonard Gage	5	60
Eliza, d. Ira & Betty, b. July 14, 1805	4	42
Elezebeth, m. Jonathan **CARPENTER**, May 22, 1794	3	112
Elizabeth, m. Jonathan **CARPENTER**, May 22, 1794	4	248
Elizabeth, of Ashford, m. Parley **HOWLET**, of Woodstock, Mar. 4, 1827, by Edward S. Keyes, J. P. Intention published	5	26
Jean, m. Abial **ABBOTT**, June 8, 1786	4	248
John, s. John S. & Louisa, b. June 13, 1839	6	90
Louisa, d. John S. & Louisa, b. June 29, 1837	6	90
Nathan C., of Ashford, m. Sarah **RATHBURN**, of Thompson, Sept. 13, 1840, by Henry Work, J. P.	5	75
Roxana, m. Hiram **BOSWORTH**, b. of Ashford, Jan. 3, 1830, by Edward S. Keyes, J. P.	5	37
Sabrina, of Ashford, m. Isaac **COON**, of Hopkinton, R. I., Jan. 4, 1829, by Edward S. Keyes. J. P.	5	33

BARTLETT, BARTLET, (cont.)	Vol.	Page
Smith S. C., of Sutton, Mass., m. Mary M. **DOW** of Ashford, Sept. 13, 1837, by Rev. Hall	5	65
BASS, [see also **BOSS**], Adeline M. m. Pascal H. **MATTHEWS,** b. of Eastford, June 30, 1844, by Francis Williams, Eastford	5	90
Calista, d. Luther & Esther, b. May 22, 1811	6	1
Calista, of Ashford, m. Ira **ALLEN,** of Thompson, Nov. 23, 1834, by Rev. Stephen Hitchcock	5	55
David, [twin with Jonathan], s. Samuel & Hannah, b. Oct. 31, 1785	4	61
Enoch, s. Sam[ue]ll & Hannah, b. Jan. 27, 1783	4	61
Eunis, d. Samuel & Hannah, b. Feb. 27, 1775	4	61
Hannah Woodward, d. Luther & Charlotte, b. June 12, 1809	6	1
Jemima, d. Sam[ue]ll, d. June 11, 1800, ae 31	4	61
John, Rev., Mr., m. Mrs. Mary **DENESON,** Nov. 24, 1743, by Rev. Martin Cabot	2	36
John, s. Rev. John & Mary, b. June 5, 1746	2	36
John, s. [Rev.] Mr. John & Mary, b. Oct. 24, 1751	2	36
Jonathan, [twin with David], s. Samuel & Hannah, b. Oct. 31, 1785	4	61
Lauraette, m. Halstein **BROWN,** of Union, Sept. 18, 1842, by Washington Munger	5	82
Lavel, s. Samuel & Hannah, b. Apr. 9, 1779	4	61
Lavel, s. Sam[ue]ll, d. Mar. 25, 1800, ae 21	4	61
Loensa E., m. Erskine C. **ELY.,** b. of Eastford, May 3, 1847, by Francis Williams	5	100
Luther, s. Samuel & Hannah, b. Feb. 15, 1773	4	61
Luther, m. Charlotte **BRANSON,** Feb. 25, 1808	6	1
Mary, d. Rev. John & Mary, b. Dec. 24, 1747	2	36
Mary, d. Sam[ue]ll & Hannah, b. Mar. 29, 1781	4	61
Milicent, d. Sam[ue]ll & Hannah, b. Mar. 29, 1777	4	61
Otis Branson, s. Luther & Esther, b. June 28, 1814	6	1
Sam[ue]ll, s. Sam[ue]ll & Hannah , b. Nov. 2, 1787	4	61
Trifene, d. Samuel & Hannah, b. Oct. 6, 1771	4	61
BASSETT, BASSET,Elisabeth, m. Elijah **BABCOCK,** May 1,1762	3	78
Elisabeth, m. Elijah **BABCOCK,** May 2, 1762	4	54
------, of Killingly, m. [ ]**COPELAND,** Oct. 29, 1832, by Rev. Philo Judson	5	49
BATES, Eunice, m. Ephraim **BLISS,** farmer, black, July 25, 1849, b Reuben Macey, Esq.	5	136-7
Mary, of West Greenwich, R. I. , m. Jonathan **WEEKS,** of Ashford, [June] 27, [1836], by Rev. Reuben Torrey, of Eastford	5	60
Sally, m. Ephraim **BLISS,** Aug. 5, 1849, by Reuben Marcy, J. P.	5	104

	Vol.	Page
BATES, (cont.)		
William, of Ashford, m. Mariet R. **CROWEL**, of Woodstock, (colored), Nov. 27, 1842, by Rev. F. Williams	5	83
BAXTER, Samuel H., of Mansfield, m. Sarah **SPRAGUE**, of Ashford, Nov. 8, 1841, by Rev. Charles C. Barnes	5	79
BECKUS, [see under **BACKUS**]		
BEDLOW, Hannah, d. Sylvanus & Hannah, b. Oct. 17, 1798	4	247
Hannah, w. Sylvanus, d. Sept. 30, 1849	4	247
Joseph, s. Sylvanus & Hannah, b. Aug. 24, 1796	4	247
Joseph, m. Ann **GRIGGS**, b. of Ashford, Apr. 21, 1824, by Rev. Philo Judson	5	14
Sylvanus, d. July 6, 1835	4	247
BEEBE, BEEBEE, Adin, s. Joshua, Jr. & Mary, b. June 30, 1761	3	98
Prudance, m. Jacob **KENDAL**, Jan. 12, 1761	3	4
-----, 2nd s. Joshua & Mary, b. Nov. 25, 1764	3	98
BELDEN, BELDING, Elizabeth, of Ashford, m. Samuel **VINTON**, of Hartford, Nov. 10, 1850, by Rev. F. P. Coe	5	105
--------, d. A[a]ron, mechanic, ae 40, of Mass., & Thankful, ae 38, b. Feb. 16, 1849	5	132-3
BELLAMAY, Esther, m. John **SIBLEY**, Apr. 4, 1793	4	276
BEMIS, BEMISS, BEEMIS, BEMES, BIMES, Abner, s. John & Prissilah, b. Sept. 10, 1779	4	114
Alexander, s. Ephraim, & Lyd[i]a, b. Apr. 9, 1756	4	114
David, s. Ephraim & Lidy, b. Mar. 25, 1754	1	84
David, s. John & Prissilah, [b.] Feb. 6, 1781	4	114
Diadama, d. Jno. & Pressilah, b. June 3, 1784	4	114
Elijah, s. Epherem & Lidy, b. Aug. 29, 1746	1	73
Ephrem, s. Epherem & Lidia, b. Oct. 16, 1741	1	73
Epherem, [s. Epharem & Lydia], d. Aug. 15, 1742	1	73
Epherem, [s. Epharem & Lydia], b. Feb. 25, 1744/5	1	73
Ephraim Simeon, s. Simeon & Salla, b. Feb,. 8, 1794	4	277
Eunice, d. Jno, & Prissilah, [b.] Sept. 18, 1782	4	114
Joanna, d. Epherem, b. May 6, 1748	1	73
Johannah, m. Berry **BOWEN**, Oct. 6, 1785	4	48
John, s. Ephraim & Lyd[i]a, b. Mar. 18, 1752	1	93
John, m. Prissilah **GOODAIL**, Nov. 25, 1778	4	114
Jonathan, s. Ephraim & Lidia, b. May 20, 1750	1	73
Jonathan, m. Mary **GRIGGS**, Jan. 20, 1774	4	74
Jonathan, s. Jonathan & Mary, b. Mar. 6, 1780	4	74
Lucrecia, d. Jonathan & Mary, b. Apr. 8, 1778	4	74
Mary, [d. Epharem & Lydia], d. Aug. 21, 1742	1	73
Mary, d. Jonathan & Mary, b. July 29, 1776	4	74
Phebe, d. Jonathan & Mary, b. Sept. 10, 1786	4	74
Sarah, [d. Epharem & Lydia], b. May 28, 1743	1	73
Sarah, d. Jonathan & Mary, b. June 28, 1774	4	74
Silas, s. Jonathan & Mary, b. Jan. 20, 1782	4	74

	Vol.	Page
BEMIS, BEMISS, BEEMIS, BEMES, BIMES, (cont.)		
Simeon, m. Salla **RUSS**, July 26, 1793	4	277
Stephen, s. Ephraim & Mary, b. Nov. 29, 1773	1	73
Thomas, s. Jon[a]th[an], & Mary, b. May 31, 1789	4	74
Zaruiah, m. Elias **WILLSON**, Oct. 1, 1789	4	108
---------. [child] of Ephraim & Mary, b. Aug. 18, 1766	4	6
---------, [child] of Ephraim] & Mary, b. Nov. 24, 1769	4	6
BENJAMIN, Marcy, m. Azariah **RUSS**, May 21, 1761	4	70
BENNETT, BENNET, Abner R., m Chloe Ann **FULLER**, May 26, 1844, by Rev. Washington Munger	5	90
Alvin W., of Wilbraham, Mass., m. Mary **HOLMAN**, of Ashford, Apr. 20, 1842, by Rev. Alvin Bennett	5	81
Chloe, d. John & Sarah, b. June 3, 1760	2	60
Corlis, of Tolland, m. Lavina **IDE**, of Ashford, [Apr.] 9, [1838], by Rev. Cha[rle]s Hyde	5	67
David, Elder, m. Clariss **FARNHAM**, b. of Ashford, Feb. 26, 1832, by Rev. Ezekiel Skinner	5	46
Est[h]er, m. Ephraim **LYON**, July 5, 1762	3	67
Eunice, d. John & Sarah, b. Mar. 19, 1758	2	60
Luchrese, d. John & Sarah, b. Dec. 20. 1762	2	60
Smith, of Monroe, m. Elista M. **SNOW**, of Ashford, Oct. 2, 1831, by Rev. David Bennett	5	45
Syria E., of Scituate, R. I., m.Sally **COOPER**, of Plainfield, Aug. 15, 1822, by Rev. Philo Judson	5	7
BENTON, James, [s. Simon & Mary], b. Oct. 3, 1735	1	A
Mary, [d. Simon & Mary], b. May 12, 1728	1	A
Richard, [s. Simon & Mary], b. May 27, 1731	1	A
BERRY, Mary, m. Nath[anie]ll **FULLER**, Jr., Sept. 30, 1736, by Philip Eastman, J. P	1	49
BETTIS, Anna, of Ashford, m. Parker **HARRIS**, of Mansfield, Oct. 8, [1826], by Ezekiel Skinner	5	24
BEULEY, Samuel D., m. Martha S. **GREEN**, Apr. 6, 1845, by Rev. Renssalear O. Putney	5	93
BIBBINS, Anne, m. William **CHAFFE**, July 21, 1762	3	104
Aurther, d. June 6, 1759	1	105
BICKNELL, BICKNEL, BICKNAL, BECKNAL, BEKNAL,		
Aavis, d. Eben[eze]r & Mary, b. Aug. 27, 1771	3	30
Abigail, d. Zachariah & Katham, b. May 6, 1741	1	31
Abigail, d. W[illia]m & Ama, b. Aug. 5, 1762	2	57
Ama, d. William & Ama, b. Jan. 2, 1775 ; d. Oct. 7, 1781	4	80
Ama, w. William, d. June 22, 1807	4	80
Anna, d. Sam[uel] & Deborah, b. Apr. 16, 1768	4	107
Anna, w. William, d. June 22, 1807	2	56
An[n]e, [d. Zachariah & Kathran], b. Oct. 1, 1726	1	31
Anne, m. Ebenezer **BYLES**, Nov. 28, 1745, by Mr. John Bass	2	49

	Vol.	Page
BICKNELL, BICKNEL, BICKNAL BECKNAL, BEKNAL,(cont)		
Anne, d. William, b. [ ]* (*Entry scratched out)	3	30
Anne, d. Sam[ue]ll & Deborah, b. [ ]	4	17
Asa, s. Peter & Rachel, b. Apr. 13, 1747	1	55
Avis, see under **AAVIS**		
Benjamin *, s. Eben[eze]r & Mary, b. Sept. 14, 1773 (*First		
written Asa	3	30
Betsey, d. William & Ama, b. Sept. 17, 1779	4	80
Bets[e]y, d. Zach[ariah], Jr. & Phebe, b. July 7, 1788	4	253
Betsey, d. Zach[ariah], Jr. d. Nov. 1, 1790	4	253
Betsey, d. Zach[ariah], Jr. & Phebe, b. Sept. 25, 1791	4	253
Betsey, m. Moses **RICHARDS**, Dec. 12, 1811	6	37
Briana, d. John, Jr. & Anna, b. Dec. 6, 1781	4	232
Carthrine, d. Eben[eze]r & Mary, b. Feb. 23, 1767	3	30
Charlot[t]a, d. Sam[ue]ll & Deborah, b. June 27, 1763	4	17
Charlot[t]a, d. Sam[ue]l & Deborah, b. June 27, 1763	4	107
Cynthya, d. Nathan & B[e]ulah, b. Aug. 21, 1763	3	108
David, s. Sam[uel] & Deborah, b. Nov. 13, 1775 : d. Apr. 2,		
1776	4	107
David Watson, s. Sam[ue]ll, Jr. & Salla, b. May 4, 1800	4	252
Deborah, d. Sam[ue]ll, Jr. & Salla, b. Dec. 4, 1802	4	252
Deborah, m. George **PALMER**, Oct. 9, 1826, by Rev. Philo		
Judson	5	24
Ebenezer, [s. Zachariah & Kathran], b. Aug. 15, 1732	1	31
Ebenezer, m.Mary **PARRY**,Dec. 1, 1755, by James Bicknell,JP	1	90
Ebenezer, s. Ebenezer & Mary b. Oct. 19, 1756	1	95
Edward, s. Sam[ue]l & Salla, b. Sept. 18, 1816	4	252
Elijah, s. Nathan & B[e]ulah, b. Apr. 4, 1765	3	108
Elezebeth, m. James **HALE**, Jr., May 17, 1739, by Rev. James		
Hale	1	77
Elizabeth, w. Zacheriah, & d. of Edward **SUMNER**, d. Aug.		
30, 1752	1	80
Elisabeth, [d. Sam[ue]ll & Deborah], b. Oct. 24, 1758	1	105
Elizabeth, d. Sam[ue]ll & Deborah, b. Oct. 24, 1758	4	17
Elisabeth, d. Sam[uel] & Deborah, b. Oct. 24, 1758	4	107
Elisabeth, d. Eben[eze]r & Mary, b. Nov. 18, 1762	3	30
Elisabeth, m. Lemuel **CLARKE**, Nov. 25, 1779	4	70
Emaline, d. Sam[ue]l, Jr. & Salla, b. Nov. 3, 1807	4	252
Emeline, of Ashford, m. Ashbel **WOODWARD**, of Franklin,		
May 31, 1832, by Rev. Philo Judson	5	48
Emily L., m. Peter **PLATT**, b. of Ashford, Nov. 13, 1853, by		
Rev. P. Mathewson	5	110
Ephraim Parry, s. Eben[eze]r & Mary, b. Feb. 15, 1769	3	30
Erastus, s. Sam[ue]ll, Jr. & Salla, b. Dec. 1, 1804	4	252
Erastas, m. Catherine **WORK**, b. of Ashford, June 3, 1835, by		
Rev. R. Torrey, Eastford	5	56

	Vol.	Page
BICKNELL, BICKNEL, BICKNAL, BECKNAL, BEKNAL(cont)		
Esther, d. W[illia]m & Ama, b. Nov. 28, 1765	2	57
Eunis, d. Sam[ue]ll & Deborah, b. Dec. 21, 1756	1	105
Eunice, m. David TORREY, Feb. 12, 1778	4	95
Hannah, d. Joshua & Hannah, b. Nov. 10, 1721	A	6
Hannah, d. Zachariah & Kathren, b. Oct. 18, 1738	1	31
Hannah, d. James, Jr. & Comfort, Mar. 20, 1756	1	93
Hannah, d. Sam[ue]ll & Deborah, b. Nov. 14, 1760	4	17
Hannah, d. Sam[uel] & Deborah, ;b. Nov. 14, 1760	4	107
Hannah, w. Timothy, d. Aug. 8, 1768	4	23
Hannah, m. John WOODWARD, Apr. 24, 1783	4	17
Hannah, d. Jno. Jr. & Anna, b. Nov. 26, 1783	4	232
Harriet Eliza, d. Zachariah, Jr., farmer, ae 50, & Eliza, ae 39, b. Apr. 12, 1849	5	132-3
Idah, d. W[illia]m & Ama, b. Feb. 25, 1773	2	57
Irany, d. John & Irany, b. May 18, 1852, O. S.	1	82
Irana, d. John, Jr. & Anna, b. July 16, 1789	4	232
Isaac, s. Nathan & B[e]ulah, b. June 23, 1770	3	108
Jereshua, d. Zachariah & Katharn, b. Dec. 1, 1739	1	31
Joanna, d. Will[ia]m & Anna, b. Dec. 5, 1768	2	57
John, [s. Zacharia & Kathran], b. Apr. 22, 1725	1	31
John, m. Irane POWEL, Dec. 24, 1751, O. S.	1	82
John, s. John & Iorany, b. Nov. 27, 1755	1	90
John, s. John, Jr. & Anna, b. Feb. 8, 1786	4	232
Joseph, s. Joshua & Hannah, b. Nov. 21, 1732 ; d. the 20th day of Dec. next following	1	38
Joshua, s. Joshua & Hannah, b. Mar. 8, 1722/3	A	7
Josiah, s. Eben[eze]r & Mary, b. Dec. 4, 1760	3	30
Julia M., m. William D. CARPENTER, Oct. 28, 1846, by Charles Peabody	5	98
Laura, d. Sam[ue]ll, Jr. & Salla, b. Oct. 25, 1810	4	252
Laura, of Ashford, m. Edward B. EDWARDS, of Berlin, Conn., May 6, 1829, by Rev. Philo Judson	5	35
Lucius,[twin with Rufus] s. Zachariah & Phebe, b. Jan 11,1808	4	253
Mary, [d. Zachariah & Kathran], b. Feb. 15, 1728	1	31
Molley, d. Eben[eze]r & Mary, b. Mar. 1, 1765	3	30
Nancey, d. John, Jr. & Anna, b. May 8, 1791	4	232
Nathan, s. Zachariah & Kathren, b. Feb. 8, 1736/7	1	31
Nathan, m. B[e]ulah MEDCALF, Nov. 18, 1762	3	108
Nathan, s. Nathan & B[e]ulah, b. Dec. 22, 1774	3	108
Nathan[i]ell, s. Eben[eze]r & Mary, b. July 9, 1758	1	102
Nathaniel, s. Nathan & B[e]ulah, b. Oct. 2, 1768	3	108
Olive, d. Joshua & Hannah, b. Feb. 6, 1733/4	1	38
Parry, s. Eben[eze]r & Mary, b. Feb. 15, 1769* (*Entry crossed out)	3	30
Peter, s. Peter & Rachel, b. Jan. 11, 1736	1	55

	Vol.	Page
BICKNELL, BICHNEL, BICKNAL, BECKNAL BEKNAL,(cont)		
Peter, s. Peter & Rachel, b. July 24, 1745	1	55
Phebe, d. Zach[ariah] & Phebe, b. Mar. 24, 1803	4	253
Phebe, of Ashford, m. George COLLINS, of Wilbraham,		
Mass., Nov. 30, 1820, by Rev. Philo Judson	5	1
Rachel, d. Peter & Rachel, b. Dec. 9, 1737	1	55
Roxee, d. Sam[uel] & Deborah, b. Feb. 24, 1771	4	107
Roxcey, m. John FRINK, Feb. 7, 1793	4	76
Rufus, [twin with Lucius], s. Zachariah & Phebe, b. Jan. 11,		
1808	4	253
Sal, d. Sam[uel] & Deborah, b. Jan. 19, 1766	4	107
Salley, d. Sam[ue]ll & Deborah, b. Jan. 19, 1766	4	17
Sally, d. William & Anna, B. Jan. 3, 1771	2	57
Salla, d. Zach[ariah], Jr. & Phebe, b. May 4, 1794	4	253
Sally, m. Samuel COLLINS, Dec. 1, 1814	6	41
Samuel, [s. Zachariah & Kathran], b. July 10, 1729	1	31
Samuel, m. Deborah RICE, Nov. 13, 1755	4	107
Sam[ue]ll. m. Deborah RICE, Nov. 14, 1755	1	105
Samuel, s. Sam[eul] & Deborah, b. June 20, 1773	4	107
Sam[ue]ll, Jr., m. Salla MARCY, Nov. 14, 1799	4	252
Samuel, s. Sam[ue]l & Salla, b. June 5, 1814	4	252
Sapphira, d. W[illia]m, Jr. & Nancy, b. July 25, 1808	4	54
Sarah, [d. Zachariah & Kathran], b. Apr. 29, 1731	1	31
Sarah, m. John AVERY, Dec. 11, 1751	3	38
Sarah E., d. Samuel, Jr., farmer, ae 36, & Esther, ae 24, b. Feb.		
12, 1850	5	140-1
Sibbel, d. Nathan & B[e]ulah, b. Nov. 7, 1766	3	108
Sophia, m. Judathan HAMMOND, b. of Ashford, Oct. 29,		
1827, by Rev. Philo Judson	5	29
Timothy, s. Zachariah & Cathrain, b. Dec. 8, 1733	1	31
Timothy, s. W[illia]m & Ama, b. Jan. 30, 1767	2	57
Willliam, s. Zach[a]riah & Kathuran, [b.] May 29, 1735	1	31
William, m. Ama EATON, Nov. 15, 1759	2	57
W[illia]m. s. William & Ama, b. June 17, 1777	4	80
William, Jr., m. Nancy BYLES, May 5, 1803	4	54
William, d. Jan. 15, 1813, in the 78th y. of his age	2	56
William, d. Jan. 15, 1813, in the 78th y. of his age	4	80
William Dwight, s. W[illia]m, Jr. & Nancy, b. Apr. 13, 1814	4	54
Zachariah, [s. Zachariah & Kathran], b. May 5, 1723	1	31
Zachariah, Capt., d. Jan. 30, 1750/51	1	31
Zechariah, m. Elisabeth STEB[B]ENS, Apr. 22, 1756	2	57
Zachariah, s. W[illia]m & Ama, b. Aug. 21, 1760	2	57
Zachariah, Jr., m. Phebe KENDALL, Dec. 13, 1787	4	253
Zachariah, d. Apr. 6, 1798	2	58
Zachariah, s. Zach[ariah] & Phebe, b. Sept. 17, 1798	4	253
Zachariah, Jr., m. Sally GAYLORD, b. of Ashford, Jan. 21,		

BICKNELL, BICHNEL, BICHNAL, BECHNAL, BEKNAL(cont)	Vol.	Page
1823,by Rev. Philo Judson	5	8
Zachariah, Jr., m. Eliza WORK, b. of Ashford, Jan. 7, 1841, by Rev. Charles Hyde	5	76
Zachariah, Jr. d. Dec. 28, 1850, ae 52	5	150-1
----------, d. Nathan & B[e]ulah, b. Jan. 18, 1773	3	108
BIDWELL, Horace, of Manchester, m. Eliza BOWEN, of Ashford, Nov. 24, 1831, by Rev. Benjamin Paine	5	46
BIGGS, Charles Henry, s. Abram & Mary, b. Dec. 18, 1824	6	93
Edwin Alonzo, s. Abram & Mary, b. Nov. 21, 1829	6	93
Harriet Sophronia, d. Abram & Mary, b. Aug. 17, 1837	6	93
BILL, Adaline A., m. James B. ARNOLD, b. of Ashford, Jan. 1, 1843, by Elder R. V. Lyon, Mansfield	5	83
Alvin Herbert, s. Roswell & Olive, b. Mar. 31, 1841	6	97
Roswell Clark, s. Roswell & Olive, b. Sept. 1, 1838	6	97
---------, of Chaplin, m. [ ] EASTMAN, of Ashford, Oct. 9, 1831, by Rev. Philo Judson	5	45
BILLINGS, Bethyah, m. Theophelas CLERK, Dec. 5, 1745, by Rev. Mr. Mosely	2	58
BINGHAM, Clarissa, Mrs., of Ashford, m. James FRANKLIN, of Brooklyn, Sept. 17, 1823, by Rev. Hubble Loomis	5	10
BIRCHARD, BURCHARD, Betsey, m. Daniel KNOWLTON, Jr., Apr. 4, 1793	4	60
Betty, d. Phinias & Lydia, b. Oct. 11, 1768	4	57
Gurdin, s. Phinias & Lydia, b. Oct. 5, 1773	4	57
Gordin, m. Anna WALKER, Sept. 16, 1798	4	59
Harvey, s. Gordin & Anna, b. Apr. 17, 1799	4	59
Lois, d. Phinias & Lydia, b. May 2, 1776	4	57
Mima, d. Phinehas & Lydia, b. Oct. 26, 1787	4	57
Phebe, d. Phin[e]has & Lydia, b. Apr. 16, 1783	4	57
Phinias, s. Phinias & Lydia, b. Nov. 22, 1771	4	57
Polley, d. Phineas & Lydia, b. Aug. 11, 1777	4	57
BIRGE, [see under BURGE]		
BISBEE, Joseph A., m. Eliza BRAMIN, May, 12, 1844, by Rev. Washington Munger	5	89
BISHOP, Frederick H., s. George R., mechanic, ae 38, & Adeline, ae 37, b. Mar. 30, 1849	5	134-5
George R., of Grafton, Mass., m. Addeline COE, of Ashford, (Westford Society), Oct. 10, 1836, by Rev. Lent S. Hough, of Chaplin	5	62
Hiram, of Woodstock, m. Sabrina CHAPMAN, of Ashford, [ ], by Rev. Luke Wood	5	41
Mary, d. David & Rebeckah, b. Dec. 28, 1715	A	1
Mary, m. Zephaniah PRESTON, May 25, 178[ ]	4	65
Rebeckah, m. Benjamin ALLEN, Dec. 31, 1717	A	4
Theodore, of Middletown, m. Esther CHAFFEE, of Ashford,		

	Vol.	Page
BISHOP, (cont.)		
Dec. 27, 1835, by Amos Babcock	5	58
BLAKE, Rhoda, d. Calvin & Rhoda, b. Oct. 31, 1803	4	65
Sarah, d. Calvin & Rhoda, b. Nov. 25, 1801	4	65
BLANCHER, Chester, s. Jedediah & Martha, b. June 7, 1773	3	68
Daniel, d. Dec. 10, 1753	1	92
Daniel, d. Dec. 10, 1753	1	93
Daniel, s. Jedediah, d. Oct. 6, 1759	1	108
Ebenezer, s. Jedediah & Martha, b. Sept. 17, 1767 ; d. June 24, 1769	3	68
Hannah, d. Jedediah & Martha, b. June. 16, 1766	3	68
Jedediah, m. Martha **CHAPMAN**, Nov. 13, 1754	1	92
Jedediah, m. Martha **CHAPMAN**, Nov. 13, 1754	1	93
Jedediah, s. Jedediah & Martha, b. Sept. 29, 1762	3	68
Mehitable, m. James **WHITON**, Mar. 15, 1758	1	99
Samuel, Jr., d. Mar. 19, 1753	1	92
Samuel, Jr., d. Mar. 19, 1753	1	93
Samuel, s. Jedediah & Martha, b. Mar. 10, 1756	1	92
Samuel, s. Jedediah & Martha, b. Mar. 10, 1756	1	93
Samuel, d. Oct. 13, 1759	1	108
Simion, s. Jedediah & Martha, b. Aug. 7, 1764	3	68
Thomas, s. Jed[ed]iah & Martha, b. June 18, 1769	3	68
Willard, s. Jedediah & Martha, b. Nov. 27, 1771	3	68
BLISS, Ephraim, farmer, black, m. Eunice **BATES**, July 25, 1849, by Reuben Macey, Esq.	5	136-7
Ephraim, m. Sally **BATES**, Aug. 5, 1849, by Reuben Marcy, J. P.	5	104
BLODGETT. Alden W., of Stafford, m. Caroline C. **CHAPMAN**, of Ashford, Oct. 2, 1839, by Rev. Samuel J. Curtis, of Woodstock	5	71
BODWELL, Mary, m. William B. **FRANKLIN**, Aug. 18, 1816	6	33
BOLLES, BOLLS, Aliphaz, s. Matthew & [Anna], d. Dec. 30, 1800	4	280
[Al]iphaz Hibbard, s. Matthew & Anna, b. June 10, 1796 ; d. Dec. 30, 1800	4	280
Anna Hibbard, d. Matthew & Anna, b. Feb. 28, 1798	4	280
Armenius, s. David, Jr. & Elizabeth, b. May 16, 1795	4	246
Augustus, s. David & Susannah, b. Dec. 28, 1776	4	56
Augustus, m. Fanny **TROWBRIDGE**, Nov. 27, 1798	4	29
Augustus Leverett, s. Augustus & Fanny, b. Nov. 23, 1803	4	29
Caroline, ae 22, m. Eli **CLARK**, shoemaker, ae 25, of Ashford, June [ ], 1850, by Lyman Leffingwell	5	142-3
Caroline M., m. Eli **CLARK**, Jr., b. of Ashford, May 1, 1850, by Rev. Lyman Leffingwell	5	105
Caroline Matilda, d. Matthew & Anna, b. Feb. 19, 1804	4	280
Caroline Matilda, d. Lorenzo & Mary W., b. June 19, 1827	6	103
Charles, s. David & Susannah, b. Feb. 19, 1775	4	56
Charles, s. David, d. Feb. 27, 1790	4	56

	Vol.	Page
BOLLES, BOLLS, (cont.)		
David, s. David & Susannah, b. Sept. 26, 1765	4	56
David, Jr., m.Elizabeth **DOW**, Nov. 12, 1786	4	246
David, Capt., had born to Rose, negro servant, Phillis, b. Nov. 19, 1786, Flora, b. Jan. 30, 1788, Phebe, b. Mar. 12, 1791	4	56
David, Elder, d. Feb. 14, 1807, ae 64 y. 1 m.	4	56
David, s. Mathew & Anna, b. Mar. [ ], 1811	4	280
David, s. Lorenzo & Mary W., b. May 4, 1830 ; d. May 4, 1832	6	103
David, s. Lorenzo & Mary W. b. Aug. 10, 1832 ; d. May 27, 1836	6	103
David Charles, s. David, Jr. & Elizabeth, b. Feb. 2, 1793	4	246
Ebenezer, s. David & Susannah, b. Mar. 28, 1772 ; d. Feb. 27, 1777	4	56
Elisha Trowbridge, s. Lorenzo & Mary W., b. Apr. 20, 1825	6	103
Eliza, of Ashford, m. Asa B. **CLARK**, of Ithaca, N. Y., Oct. 17, 1837, by Rev. Reuben Torrey, Eastford	5	66
Enoch, s. Lorenzo & Mary W., b. Sept. 28, 1838	6	103
Esther, m. David **CLARK**, Jan. 4, 1807	4	82
James Grant, s. Matthew & Anna, b. Jan. 17, 1802	4	280
Jerusha Pride, d. Matthew & Anna, b. Mar. 12, 1800	4	280
John, s. Lorenzo & Mary W., b. Dec. 1, 1835	6	103
John Augustus, s. Matthew & Anna, b. Apr. 16, 1809	4	280
Lorenzo, m. Mary Work **TROWBRIDGE**, Oct. 13, 1819	6	103
Lorenzo, s. Lorenzo & Mary W., b. Oct. 13, 1822	6	103
Lucius, s. David & Susannah, b. Sept. 25, 1779	4	56
Maria, m. Henry **WORK**, Jr., Apr. 23, 1817	6	34
Mary Ann Frances, d. Augustus & Fanny, b. Aug. 30, 1799	4	29
Mary W., m. Moses L. **ARNOLD**, b. of Ashford, May 30, 1842, by Rev. C. C. Barnes	5	81
Mary Work, d. Lorenzo & Mary W., b. July 4, 1820	6	103
Matilda, d. David & Susannah, b. Sept. 22, 1783	4	56
Mat[t]hew, s. David & Susannah, b. Apr. 21, 1769	4	56
Mat[t]hew, m. Anna **HIBBARD**, Sept. 15, 1793	4	280
Matthew, s. Matthew & Anna, b. June 11, 1807	4	280
Rowland J., of Pomfret, m. Betsey **LAWTON**, of Chaplin, Jan. 2, 1853, by Rev. P. Mathewson	5	109
Susan, d. Augustus & Fanny, b. Jan. 27, 1805	4	29
Susanna, d. David, Jr. & Elizabeth, b. July 30, 1787	4	246
Susanna, w. Elder David, d. Nov. 2, 1807, ae 63 y. 7 m.	4	56
[S]usanna Elisabeth, d. Matthew & Anna, b. Aug. 31, 1794	4	280
---------, infant s. Lorenzo & Mary W., b. Nov. 5, 1834 ; d. Nov. 8, 1834	6	103
BOONE, Richard, of Berlin, N. Y. m. Martha A. **SKINNER**, of Ashford, Feb. 26, 1844, by Rev. Ezekiel Skinner	5	88
BOOTH, Hannah W., m. Bartlett **SEAMMANS**, b. of Ashford, Sept. 30, 1821, by Rev. Isaac Hall	5	4

BORN, [see under **BOWEN**]

BOSS, [see also **BASS**], Hannah W., of Ashford, m. James
    MERCER, of Union, Sept. 15, 1831, by Rev. Stephen
    Hitchcock   5   44

BOSTON, James, m. Mary **HALL**, Sept. 14, 1843, by Nathan B.
    Lyon, J. P.   5   85

------, male, black, d. Jan. [ ], 1850   5   144-5

BOSWORTH, Aaron, m. Sarah **AMES**, Mar. 28, 1771   4   79

Abigail, [twin with Alen], d. John & Mary, b. Nov. 7, 1758   3   113

Abigail, m. Ezra **KNOWLTON**, Oct. 10, 1786   4   270

Abigail, d. Allen & Mary, b. July 18, 1793   4   233

Abigail, w. Allen, d. Apr. 2, 1802   4   233

Abigail, of Ashford, m. Amaziah **SAWTELLE**, of Hartford,
    May 6, 1829, by Rev. Philo Judson   5   35

Allen, s. Benj[ami]n & Jemima, b. July 29, 1735   1   45

Al[l]en, [twin with Abigail], s. John & Mary, b. Nov. 7, 1758   3   113

Allen, s. Eben[eze]r & Elisabeth, b. Mar. 27, 1768   3   114

Allen, m. Mary **PEABODY**, Apr. 4, 1782   4   233

Allen, m. Sarah **HARWOOD**, Nov. 18, 1802   4   233

Alva Southworth, s. Leonard & Polly, b. June 12, 1815   6   10

Asenath, d. Aaron & Sarah, b. Apr. 3, 1789   4   79

Benjamin, s. Ebe[neze]r & Elisabeth, b. Jan. 16, 1762   3   114

Bette, d. Aaron & Sarah, b. Apr. 23, 1787   4   79

Bridget, d. Benjamin & Jemima, b. Sept. 18, 1733   1   45

Bridget, m. Thomas **KNOWLTON**, Dec. 8, 1756   1   95

Charles Smith, s. Allen & Sarah, b. June 3, 1811   4   233

Clarissa, m. Joseph **DORSET**, Jr., b. of Ashford, [Nov.] 28,
    [1833], by Rev. Reuben Torrey, Eastford   5   52

Clarissa M., m. Harvey **DEAN**, b. of Ashford, Nov. 4, 1832, by
    Tho[ma]s Dow, J. P.   5   49

Danforth H., s. Hiram, b. Oct. 3, 1835   6   81

David, of Avon, m. Sarah **BOSWORTH**, of Ashford, May 31,
    1840, by Rev. James W. Woodward, Eastford   5   75

Delosha, d. Abram* & Sarah, b. Sept. 5, 1815 (*Allen?)   4   233

Ebenezer, s. Benj[ami]n & Jemima, b. Aug. 23, 1736   1   45

Ebenezer, m. Elesabeth **FLETCHER**, May 17, 1759   3   114

Eben[eze]r, s. Eben[eze]r & Elisabeth, b. May 5, 1770   3   114

Elisabeth, m. Jeremiah **CONIALL**, June 26, 1769   4   40

Esther, d. John & Mary, b. May 30, 1761   3   113

Ethan, s. Aaron & Sarah, b. July 30, 1785   4   79

Eunice, m. John **DOUGLASS**, b. of Ashford, Apr. 12, 1821,
    by Rev. William Storrs   5   3

Ezra, m. Lucretia **CARPENTER**, Jan. 1, 1833, by Rev.
    Leonard Gage   5   50

Ezra Harwood, s. Allen & Sarah, b. Jan. 23, 1804   4   233

Hannah, m. John **BROWN**, Nov. 23, 1769   4   102

Hervey, d. Aaron & Sarah, b. Oct. 22, 1783   4   79

BOSWORTH,(cont.)	Vol.	Page
Hiram, s. Allen & Sarah, b. Sept. 6, 1805	4	233
Hiram, m.Roxana **BARTLET[T]**, b. of Ashford, Jan. 3, 1830,		
by Edward S. Keyes, J. P.	5	37
Hopestill, d. Benjamin & Jemima, b. Sept. 7, 1729, at Bristoll	1	45
Jacob, m. Ruth **SQUIRE**, Oct. 6, 1743	2	49
Jemima, d. Benjamin [& Jemima], b. Dec. 25, 1730	1	45
Jemima, d. Eben[eze]r & Elisabeth, b. Feb. 6, 1766	3	114
John, m. Mehitibal **CHENEY**, Nov. 19, 1781	3	113
Judath, m. Ezra **SMITH**, May 23, 1745	1	68
Julia, d. Leonard & Polly, b. Aug. 10, 1811	6	10
Julia, of Ashford, m. Jeduthan **PAULLE**, of Tolland, Feb. 7,		
1831, by Daniel Knowlton, J. P.	5	41
Leonard, m Polly **SOUTHWORTH** Mar. 12, 1809	6	10
Lois, m. Ephraim **LYON**, June 18, 1832, by Amasa Lyon, J. P.	5	48
Marcus Leonard, s. Leonard & Polly, b. Jan. 25, 1810	6	10
Mary, d. Benjamin & Jemima, b. Mar. 3, 1731/2	1	45
Mary, d. Ebe[neze]r, & Elesabeth, b. June 1, 1760	3	114
Mary, m. John **CHEEDLE**, Nov. 5, 1761	3	58
Mary, d. Aaron & Sarah, b. Apr. 22, 1777	4	79
Mary, d. Allen & Mary, b. Oct. 27. 1786	4	233
Mary, of Ashford, m. Hopkins **STONE**, of Cranston, R. I., Jan.		
2, 1825, by Levi Work, J. P.	5	17
Mary G., m. Horatio **CARPENTER**, b. of Ashford, [Mar.] 25,		
1832, by Rev. Reuben Torrey, Eastford	5	47
Nathan, s. Allen & Sarah, b. June 30, 1807	4	233
Nathan Allen, s. Hiram, b. Mar. 24, 1833	6	81
Nathan Ames, s. Aaron & Sarah, b. Feb. 27, 1772 ; d. Sept. 5,		
1775	4	79
Olive, d. Aaron & Sarah, b. Dec. 17, 1773 ; d. Apr. 13, 1777	4	79
Parney, d. Aaron & Sarah, b. Dec. 28, 1791	4	79
Rachel, d. Eben[eze]r & Elisabeth, b. Feb. 15, 1764	3	114
Rosette, of Ashford, m. Lucius **CHAMBERLAIN**, of		
Mansfield, Nov. 19, 1840, by Rev. David Bennett	5	76
Roxse, d. Allen & Mary, b. Mar. 13, 1783	4	233
Ruth, d. Jacob & Ruth, b. Apr. 29, 1744	2	49
Sanford, s. Abram* & Sarah, b. Feb. 25, 1813 (*Allen?)	4	233
Sarah, d. Aaron & Sarah, b. Sept. 8, 1781	4	79
Sarah, d. Allen & Sarah, b. Apr. 30, 1818	4	233
Saray, m. David **DEAN**, Dec. 14, 1828, by Levi Works, J. P.	5	34
Sarah, of Ashford, m. David **BOSWORTH**, [of] Avon, May		
31, 1840, By Rev. James W. Woodward, Eastford	5	75
Seth Fletcher, s. Eben[eze]r & Elisabeth, b. May 5, 1773 ; d.		
Aug. 10, 1776	3	114
Stil[l]man Whitman, s. Allen & Sarah, b. May 2, 1809	4	233
William Henry, s. Hiram, b. Feb. 26, 1831	6	81
BOTHAM, Frances C., of Eastford, m. Edward T. **ELLIS** of		
Ashford, Nov. 27, 1851, by Rev. P. Mathewson	5	108

	Vol.	Page
BOUTELL, BOUTWEL, BOUTWELL, BOUTELLE,		
BOUTWILL, BOUTLE, BOUTEVEL, Abner, s. Jacob & Jerusha,		
b. Oct. 24, 1773	3	79
Abner m. Lucinda HINDFIELD, b. of Ashford, Apr. 24, 1821,		
by Rev. Isaac Hall	5	3
Anna, d. Jacob, Jr. & Eunis, b. Sept. 29, 1762	3	79
Anna, d. Ezra & Cynthia, b. Oct. 29, 1790	4	265
Cynthia, d. Ezra & Cynthia, b. July 15, 1792	4	265
Cynthia A., d. Ezra W. & Patty, b. Feb. 4. 1841	6	66
Dan, s. James & Chloe, b. June 29, 1782	4	119
Eliza, d. Jacob & Sybel, b. Aug. 3, 1828	6	69
Emily, d. Thomas E., b. Aug. 17, 1827	6	81
Eunis, w. Jacob, Jr., d. Jan. 18, 1772	3	79
Eunice, d. Jacob, Jr. & Jerusha, b. Aug. 29, 1779	3	79
Ezra, s. Jacob, Jr. & Eunis, b. Feb. 27, 1770	3	79
Ezra, m. Cynthia WILLIAMS, Mar. 25, 1790	4	265
Ezra W., farmer, of Ashford, d. Apr. 9, 1848, ae 49	5	130-1
Ezra W[illia]m, s. Ezra & Cynthia, b. Feb. 3, 1799	4	265
Henry, s. Thomas E., b. Sept. 9, 1833	6	81
Ira, s. James & Chloe, b. Jan. 20, 1785	4	119
Jacob, m. Rebeckah SNOW, Oct. 11, 1739	1	60
Jacob, s. Jacob & Rebeckah, b. Aug. 23, 1740	1	60
Jacob, Jr., m. Eunis DREW, June 20, 1759	3	79
Jacob, Jr. m. Jerusha FOLLET, Oct. 1, 1772	3	79
Jacob, s. Jacob & Jerusha, b. Nov. 3, 1775	3	79
Jacob, s. Jacob, Jr. [& Jerusha], d. Sept. 12, 1777	3	79
Jacob, Jr., d. Jan. 23, 1789	3	79
Jacob, s. James & Chloe, b. Oct. 17, 1791	4	119
Jacob, d. May 6, 1794	1	60
Jacob, m. Sybel SNOW, Oct. 24, 1827, by Israel P. Fuller,		
Stafford, Conn.	5	28
James, s. Jacob & Eunis, b. July 30, 1760	1	111
James, s. Jacob & Eunice, b. July 30, 1760	3	79
James, m. Chloey PRESTON, , Nov. 15, 1781	4	119
James, s. James & Chloe, b. Feb. 25, 1800	4	119
James, m. Julia Ann PRESTON, b. of Ashford, Mar. 22, 1824,		
by Rev. Philo Judson	5	13
John, s. Jacob, Jr. & Eunis, b. Sept. 23, 1767	3	79
John, s. James & Chloe, b. Sept. 1, 1789	4	119
Laura Fitts, d. Thomas E. & Sally, b. Mar. 29, 1842	6	81
Lucius, s. James & Chloe, b. May 14, 1805 ; d. Apr. 27, 1817	4	119
Lusha, [twin with Marsha], d. James & Chloe, b. Sept. 12,		
1797 ; d. Sept. 7. 1800	4	119
Lydia, d. Ezra & Cynthia, b. Aug. 13, 1894	4	265
Lydia, m. Hosea SMITH, Jan. 12, 1814	6	21
Marcia, m. Amasa ROBINSON, b. of Ashford, "last evening"		
[June 1, 1835], by Rev. Job Hall	5	56
Marsha, [twin with Lusha], d. James & Chloe, b. Sept. 12,1797	4	119

	Vol.	Page
BOUTELL, BOUTWEL, BOUTWELL, BOUTELLE,		
BOUTWILL, BOUTLE, BOUTEVEL, (cont.)		
Mary, d. Ezra & Cynthia, b. Mar. 23, 1797	4	265
Nancy K., d. Ezra William & Patty, b. Sept. 3, 1826	6	66
Patty, housekeeper, d. May 11, 1848, ae 47	5	130-1
Rebeckah, d. Jacob & Rebeckah, b. Mar. 4, 1742/3	1	60
Rebeckah, d. Jacob, d. Sept. 3, 1748	1	60
Rebeckah, w. Jacob, d. Dec. 9, [1]772	1	60
Salla, d. James & Chloe, b. Apr. 16, 1807	4	119
Samuel, s. Jacob & Eunis, b. Nov. 22, 1765	3	79
Sophia C., m. Ebenezer **KINGSBURY**, b. of Ashford, Apr. 7,		
1829, by Rev. Philo Judson	5	35
Sophia Caroline, d. Ezra & Cynth[i]a, b. Oct. 12, 1804	4	265
Thomas E., m. Sally **BUTTER**, b. of Ashford, Apr. 4, 1826, by		
Rev. Philo Judson	5	22
Thomas Ewing, s. Ezra & Cynthia, b. Sept. 14, 1802	4	265
Willard, s. James & Chloe, b. Aug. 20, 1794	4	119
William, m. Patty **SMITH**, of Ashford, Apr. 21, 1825, by Rev.		
Philo Judson	5	18
William D., s. Ezra W. & Patty, b. Oct. 11, 1834	6	66
BOWEN, BOWING, BOWIN, BOWN, BORN, Aaron, s. John &		
Elizabeth, b. May 6, 1749	1	5
Abia, d. Benj[amin], & Abia, b. Mar. 19, 1764	3	64
Abia, m. Elijah **BURNAM**, Jan. 2, 1782	4	244
Abigail, m. Amasa **CHAPMAN**, b. of Ashford, Feb. 28,		
[1836], by Dexter Munger	5	59
Achsah, d. John & Abigail, b. May 15, 1794	4	234
Almirey, d. John & Abigail, b. June 4, 1802	4	234
Ann, m. Stephen F. **BURNHAM**, b. of Ashford, Jan. 4, 1830,		
by Rev. Philo Judson	5	37
Benj[amin], s. John & Elizabeth, b. Jan. 3, 1735/6	1	5
Benj[amin], s. Benj[amin] & Abian, b. Mar. 11, 1761 ; d. Apr.		
19, 1763	3	64
Benj[amin], s. Benj[amin] & Abia, b. Dec . 27, 1765	3	64
Benjamin, s. John & Abigail, b. May 5, 1782	4	234
Berry, m. Johannah **BEMISS**, Oct. 6. 1785	4	48
Berry, d. July 22, 1794	4	48
Betsey, d. John & Abigail, b. Dec. 14, 1798	4	234
Charles, of Pomfret, m. Laura **WHITMORE**, of Ashford, July		
11, 1841, by Rev. Charles C. Barnes	5	78
Eben[eze]r, s. John & Abigail, b. June 2, 1786 ; d. Sept. 28,		
1788	4	234
Elisha, s. John & Abigail, b. June 26, 1792	4	234
Eliza, of Ashford, m. Horace **BIDWELL**, of Manchester, Nov.		
24, 1831, by Rev. Benjamin Paine	5	46
Eliza B., of Ashford, m. Oliver **BRAMAN**, of Willington,		
[Mar.] 29, [1835], by Rev. Dexter Bullard	5	56
[Eliza]beth, d. Joseph & Thankfull, b. Feb. 13, 176[ ]	4	98

	Vol.	Page
BOWEN, BOWING, BOWIN, BOWN, BORN, (cont.)		
Elizabeth, m. Nathan **ABBOTT**, Aug. 31. 1785	4	73
Ephraim,. s. Berry & Johannah, b. Apr. 29, 1788	4	48
Erastus, see under Rastus		
Filis, d. John & Elizabeth, b. May 4, 1745	1	5
Jabez, m. Mary Ann **MOSELEY**, b. of Ashford, [Mar.] 17,		
[1834], by Rev. Reuben Torrey, Eastford	5	53
Jane M., m. George W. **GREEN**, b. of Ashford, Mar. 26, 1846,		
by Francis Williams	5	96
John, s. John & Elezebeth, b. Sept. 24, 1732	1	5
John, s. John & Elisabeth, b. Oct. 5, 1755	1	5
John, m. Abigail **CHUBB**, July 12, 1781	4	234
John, s. John & Abigail, b. Aug. 4, 1790	4	234
Joseph, s. John & Elizabeth b. May 17, 1741	1	5
[Joseph], m. Thankfull **CHANDLER**, Oct. 28, 1764	4	98
Moses, s. John & Elisabeth, b. Mar. 31, 1755* (*Probably		
1750 or 51)	1	5
Oliver, m. Betsey **HORTON**, Mar. 7, 1837, Eastford, by Rev.		
Reuben Torrey	5	64
Peter, s. John & Elezebeth, b. July 5, 1734	1	5
Phyllis, see under Filis		
Rastus, s. John & Abigail, b. June 4, 1796	4	234
Roxey, d. John & Abigail, b. June 15, 1784	4	234
Salley, d. Christopher & Elisabeth, b. Feb. 1, 1779	4	104
Stoddard, s. John & Elisabeth, b. Aug. 23, 1752	1	5
William. s. Christopher & Elisabeth, b. May 29, 1781	4	104
--------, s. Joseph & Thankfull, b. Dec. 24, 1766	4	98
--------, s. Joseph & Thankfull, b. July 11, 1767	4	98
-----ng, d. Joseph & Thankfull, b. Apr. 12, 1769 ; [d.] June 3,		
1769	4	98
--------, s. Joseph & Thankfull, b. Aug. 4, 1772	4	98
--------, s. Joseph & Thankfull, b. Apr. 30, 1773	4	98
--------, d. Joseph & Thankfull b. Apr. 27, 1776	4	98
--------, s. Joseph & Thankfull, b. Mar. 16, 1777	4	98
BOYDEN, Calvin, d. May 26, 1831, ae 35	6	72
BOYNTON, Benjamin C., of East Windsor, m. Hannah		
CHAPMAN, of Ashford, Apr. 8, 1848, by Rev. D.		
Bancroft	5	102
BRADLEY, Roxey, m. David **SEARS**, Jr., Feb. 4, 1808	4	123
BRAGG, BRAG, Abigail, d. Tho[ma]s & Abigail, b. Feb. 6, 1772	4	47
Abigail, w. Tho[ma]s, d. Jan. 17, 1785	4	47
Abigail, w. Tho[ma]s. d. Oct. 17, 1815	4	47
Benjamin, s. Tho[ma]s & Abigail, b. May 20, 1776	4	47
Celinda, [see under Sallinday]		
Clarase, d. Tho[ma]s & Abigail, b. Jan. 13, 1785	4	47
Daniel Royce, s. Tho[ma]s & Abigail, b. Feb. 17, 1795	4	47
Ebenezer, s. Tho[ma]s & Abigail, b. Mar. 8, 1774	4	47

	Vol.	Page
BRAGG, BRAG, (cont.)		
Ire, s. Tho[ma]s & Abigail, b. Mar. 31,1797	4	47
Jemima, d. Tho[ma]s & Abigail, b. July 30, 1780	4	47
Lydia Powers, d. Thomas & Abigail, b. Apr. 16, 1788	4	47
Mary Hayward, d. Tho[ma]s & Abigail, b. Jan. 8, 1791	4	47
Persis, d. Tho[ma]s, d. Nov. 22, 1790	4	47
Persis, d. Thomas & Abigail, b. Dec. 16, 17[ ]	4	47
Ruth Rice, d. Tho[ma]s & Abigail, b. Jan. 1, 1793	4	47
Sallinday, d. Tho[ma]s & Abigail, b. Jan. 23, 1770	4	47
Thomas, m. Abigail **LEE**, b. of Ashford, Dec. 6, 1768, by Elijah Whiton, J. P.	4	47
Thomas, m. Abigail **BRANDON**, Aug. 8, 1785	4	47
Thomas, s. Thomas & Abigail, b. Apr. 22, 1786	4	47
BRAMAN, BRAMIN, Eliza, m. Joseph A. **BISBEE**, May 12, 1844, by Rev. Washington Munger	5	89
Elizabeth, b. Thompson, res. Ashford, d. June 16, 1851, ae 58	5	150-1
Oliver, of Willington, m. Eliza B. **BOWEN**, of Ashford, [Mar.] 29, [1835], by Rev. Dexter Bullard	5	56
Thomas A., m. Mary **GREENE**, b. of Pomfret, [Dec.] 10, [1834], by Rev. R. Torrey, Eastford	5	55
BRANDON, BRANDAN, Abigail, m. Thomas **BRAGG**, Aug. 8, 1785	4	47
Charles, m. Abigail **ROYCE**, m. Apr. 1, 1773	4	90
Charles, s. Charles & Abigail, b. Apr. 1, 1774	4	90
Charles, s. Charles W. & Martha, b. Oct. [ ], 1798	4	19
Charles Willis, m. Martha **KNOWLTON**, June 12, 1796	4	19
Elisabeth, d. Charles & Abigail, b. Feb. 24, 1776	4	90
Rebecca, d. Charles W. & Martha, b. Sept. 24, 1796	4	19
BRANSON, Charlotte, m. Luther **BASS**, Feb. 25, 1808	6	1
BRAYFORD, Elisabeth Mrs., m. Joseph **SKINNER**, b. of Ashford, Dec. 15, 1762, at Woodstock, by Stephen Williams	3	64
BRIERLY, John, m. Eliza **MILLER**, b. of Southbridge, Mass., Mar. 27, 1844, by Rev. Stephen Cushing	5	88
BRIGGS, Abram, of Cambin, m. Mary **SIMMONS**, of Ashford, Apr. 1, 1824, by Edward Keyes, J. P.	5	13
Elisphal, m. Uriah **CARPENTER**, Apr. 14, 1785	4	66
BROCKER, Gennet, of New Haven, m. George **GILMER**, of Ashford, May 13, 1832, by Rev. David Bennett	5	47
BRONSON, [see under **BRANSON**]		
BROOKS, Abigail, m. Samson **KYES**, Sept. 22, 1742, by Rev. Mr. Hale	1	69
Abihail, d. John & Abigail, b. Sept. 23, 1763	3	98
Abijah, [s. Abijah & Lucy], b. Nov. 22, 1761	3	50
Abijah, s. Abijah & Lucy, d. Aug. 3, 1777	3	50
Abijah, s. Nathaniel & Lucy, b. Apr. 1, 1787	4	251
Abijah, Dea., d. Nov. 13, 1791	3	50
Abijah, m. Sally **STEVENS**, Dec. 19, 1811	6	15
Abijah, d. Nov. 19, 1843	6	15

BROWN, (cont.)	Vol.	Page
15, 1843, by Francis Williams, Eastford	5	85
Alva, [d. Magoldus & Margaret], b. Oct. 25, 1822	6	83
Anna, d. Obadiah & Anna, b. Sept. 14, 1750	2	46
Betsey, d. Cyril & Mary, b. Apr. 27, 1774	4	89
Bets[e]y, d. Roswell & Bets[e]y, b. Nov. 11, 1802	4	256
Betsey, m.Jessemiah Post RIDER, b. of Ashford, Nov. 30, 1820, by Rev. Isaac Hall	5	1
Betsey, m. Jeremiah Post RIDER, b. of Ashford, Nov. 30, 1820, by Rev. Isaac Hall	6	26
Cassander, m. Lovia M. TUFTS, b. of Ashford, [Jan.] 5, [1840], by Rev. Reuben Torrey, Eastford	5	73
Charles, s. Roswell & Bets[e]y, b. July 7, 1797	4	256
Cyril m. Mary ALLEN Sept. 15, 1768	4	89
Cyril, s. David & Molley, b. May 26, 1792	4	117
Cyrus, s. Roswell & Betsey, b. Aug. 18, 1795	4	256
Cyrus, m. Olive SPAULDING, Apr. 4, 1820, by Edward Keyes, J. P.	6	32
David, m. Molley WATSON, Nov. 23, 1777	4	117
David, [twin with Susannah], s. John & Hannah, b. Apr. 19, 1783	4	102
David, s. David & Molley, b. July 12, 1788	4	117
Edward Holstein, s. Holstein, farmer, & Mary, b. Dec. 25, 1847	5	126-7
Elias, s. John & Hannah, b. Feb. 11, 1778	4	102
Eliphalet, of Windham, m. Ermina PRESTON of Ashford, Mar. 27, 1829, by Rev. Luke Wood	5	34
Ephraim, of New Milford, m. Tryphenia CHAPMAN, of Ashford, Aug. 10, 1823, by Reuben Torrey, Eastford	5	10
Esther, d. John & Hannah, b. July 14, 1788	4	102
Halstein, of Union, m. Lauraette BASS, Sept. 18, 1842, by Rev. Washington Munger	5	82
Hannah, d. John & Hannah, b. Dec. 11, 1785	4	102
Harriet, of Ashford, m. David MARGAIN, of Old Brimfield, Mass., Nov. 16, 1826, by Rev. Amos Babcock, Jr. Intention published	5	25
Herrette, d. Roswell & Bets[e]y, b. July 7, 1807	4	256
Huldah, [d. Magoldus & Margaret], b. Oct. 16, 1825	6	83
Huldah, m. Andrew CHAPMAN, b. of Ashford, Jan. 1, 1843, by Rev. Amos Snell	5	83
Isaiah, s. John & Hannah, b. Aug. 25, 1790	4	102
James, s. Obadiah & Anna, b. Apr. 11, 1761	2	46
James, s. Cyril & Mary, b. Nov. 5, 1783	4	89
James, s. David & Molley, b. July 30, 1790	4	117
John, m. Hannah BOZWORTH, Nov. 23, 1769	4	102
John, s. John & Hannah, b. Feb. 1, 1776 ; d. Mar. 11, 1779	4	102
Lewis A., of Mansfieldd, m. Mrs. Mary Ann BUTLER, of Ashford, Nov. 12, 1854, by Rev. Charles Chamberlain	5	111
Lucinda, Mrs., m. John KEITH, b. of Eastford, Mar. 16, 1840, by Rev. R. W. Allen, Eastford	5	74

	Vol.	Page
BROWN, (cont.)		
Lucinda, of Ashford, m. Elijah F. **OWEN,** of		
Chaplin, Dec. 17, 1843, by Rev. L. W. Blood	5	86
Luther, s. John & Hannah, b. Feb. 4, 1781	4	102
Magaldus, m. Margaret **SCARBOROUGH,** Mar. [ ], 1817	6	83
Margaret, [w. Magoldus], d. Aug. 17, 1834	6	83
Mary, d. Obadiah & An[n], b. Aug. 1748	2	46
Mary, d. Cyril & Mary, b. June 21, 1769	4	89
Mary, of Ashford, d. of Anna, m. Manuel **PORTER,** of Palmer		
Mass., Sept. 10, 1821, by John Warren, J. P.	5	4
Mary Ann, of Ashford, m. Dan **RUSS,** of Chaplin, Nov. 30,		
1837, by Amos Babaock	5	66
Micah, s. Cyril & Mary, b. Apr. 27, 1776	4	89
Molley, d. David & Molley, b. Apr. 25, 1784	4	117
Nabba, d. David & Molley, b. June 3, 1782	4	117
Nelson, [s. Magoldus & Margaret], b. Dec. 23, 1830	6	83
Newman, s. Roswell & Bets[e]y, b. Aug. 3, 1799	4	256
Obadiah, m. Ann **WADKINS,** May 9, 1744, by Rev. Mr. John		
Bass	2	46
Percy, d. Cyril & Mary, b. Mar. 25, 1778	4	89
Rachel, d. Obadiah & Anne, b. Feb. 6, 1744/5	2	46
Rebec[[c]a, d. David & Molley, b. July 11, 1786	4	117
Rhoda, of Ashford, Conn., m. Calvin S. **SWAN,** of Northfield,		
Mass., Feb. 12, 1824, by Rev. Ella Dunham	5	12
Richard A., of R. I., m. Julia R. **TRACY,** of Seconk, Mass.,		
May 16, 1823, by Philip Hayward, J. P.	5	9
Roswel[l], m. Betsey **MARCH,** Nov. 24, 1788	4	256
Roswell, s. Roswell & Betsey, b. Mar. 19, 1789 ; d. Sept. 19,		
1793	4	256
Sabrina, d. William & Wealthey, b. Dec. 29, 1820	6	42
Sally, d. Cyril & Mary, b. Mar. 19, 1771	4	89
Salla, m. John **BUTLER,** Dec. 7, 1790	4	288
Samuel, s. Obadiah & Anna, b. Sept. 15, 1758	2	46
Samuel Watson, s. David & Molly, b. Nov. 28, 1779	4	117
Sa[p]phira, [d.] Roswell & Betsey, b. Oct. 19, 1793	4	256
Susannah, [twin with David], d. John & Hannah, b. Apr. 19,		
1783	4	102
Susanna, of Ashford, m. Rufus Stafford **SPINK,** of Pomfret,		
Sept. 24, 1826, by Nathan Hayward, J. P	5	23
Susey, d. Roswell& Betsey, b. Dec. 8, 1790	4	256
Tabithy, d. John & Hannah, b. Nov. 23, 1771 ; d.Feb. 18, 1776	4	102
Thaddas, s. Obadiah & Ann, b. Apr. 23, 1747	2	46
Thaddas, s. Obadiah & Anna, b. Sept. 4, 1755	2	46
Wealthy Sophronia, d. William & Wealthy, b. Nov. 21, 1818	6	42
Willaim, s. Cyril & Mary, b. Aug. 27, 1780	4	89
William, m. Phebe **LEONARD,** b. of Ashford, Nov. 10,		
[1824], by Ezekiel Skinner	5	16
William Dexter, s. William & Wealthy, b. Oct. 23, 1816	6	42
-----, infant of [David & Molley], b. Nov. 9, 1778 ; d. Nov.		

	Vol.	Page
BROWN, (cont.)		
10, 1778	4	117
BUCK, Augustus, of Killingly, m. Lucy **BROOKS**, of Ashford, May 4, 1830, by Rev. Ezekiel Skinner	5	39
George, of Killingly, m. Phila Ann **WILLIAMS**, of Ashford, June 5, 1831, by Rev. Reuben Torrey, of Eastford	5	43
BUCKLAND, Salley, m. Thomas **MOSELEY**, Sept. 22, 1803	4	29
BUFFINGTON, Anna, d. William & Candice, b. Apr. 19, 1781 ; d. Nov. 19, 1786	4	262
Candace, d. W[illia]m, & Candace, b. April 11, 1785 ; d. Oct. 21, 1786	4	262
Candace Cornelia, d. James & Julia, b. Nov. 12, 1836 ; d. May 6, 1837	6	52
Daniel, s. W[illia]m, & Candace, b. Aug. 4, 1793	4	262
Daniel, s. James & Julia, b. Apr. 22, 1838	6	52
David, s. W[illia]m & Candace, b. July 3, 1798	4	262
Dyiany, d. W[illia]m & Candace, b. Mar. 16, 1788 ; d. May 31, 1788	4	262
Flavia Julina, d. James & Julia, b. Mar. 9, 1834 ; d. May 11, 1837	6	52
James, s. W[illia]m & Candace, b. Dec. 30, 1795	4	262
James, s. James & Julia, b. Aug. 11, 1829	6	52
James, farmer, ae 53, of Ashford, m. 2d w. Lucy **FLINT**, ae 47, Feb. 8, 1849, by Rev. Cha[rle]s S. Adams	5	136-7
Mary Jane, d. James & Julia, b. July 29, 1827	6	52
Oliver, s. W[illia]m & Candace, b. Aug. 13, 1813	4	263
Phebe, d. William & Candice, b. Jan. 13, 1779	4	262
Phebe, m. Shubael **CHAPMAN**, Aug. 20, 1800	4	113
Phebe, d. James & Julia, b. July 19, 1825	6	52
Polley, d. William & Candice, b. Feb. 16, 1783 ; d. Nov. 11, 1786	4	262
Polley, d. W[illia]m & Candace, b. Mar. 25, 1800	4	262
Royal, s. W[illia]m & Candace, b. July 17, 1791	4	262
William, s. W[illia]m & Candace, b. June 21, 1789	4	262
William, s. W[illia]m, d. Dec 29, 1813	4	263
William, Jr., m. Marcy **PEARL**, Jan. 1, 181[ ]	4	95
William Ethan, s. James & Julia, b. Dec. 12, 1831	6	52
BUGBEE, BUGBE, Abiel, s. Abiel & Hannah, b. Jan. 2, 1774	4	79
Abigail, m. Joseph **WILLSON** Feb. 28, 1714/15, by Rev. James Hale	1	28
Adem, s. Abial & Hannah, b. Mar. 18, 1778	4	79
Alexander Don Carliss, [s. Amos & Eunice], b. July 6, 1827	6	49
Almira, of Ashford, m. Benjamin **CHAMBERLAIN**, of Woodstock, Aug. 26, 1827, by Rev. George B. Atwell, of Woodstock	5	28
Amasa, s. Sam[ue]ll & Thankful, b. Dec. 13, 1791	4	118
Amate, m. Richard **LEA[C]H**, May 2, 1739	1	74
Amos, [s. Josiah & Polasene], b. Nov. 3, 1749	1	53
Amos, m. Martha **WOODWARD**, Mar. 21, 1782	4	226

	Vol.	Page
BUGBEE, BUGBE, (cont.)		
Amos, s. Amos & Martha, b. Dec. 8, 1782	4	226
Amos, d. Feb. 15, 1804	4	226
Amos, m. Mary DUNHAM, Sept. 10, 1816	6	49
Amos, Capt., m. Eunice RICHMOND, b. of Ashford, Apr. 15,		
1822, by Rev. James Grow, of Pomfret	5	6
Amos, m. Eunice RICHMOND, Apr. 15, 1822	6	49
Anna, d. Josiah & Sarah, b. Mar. 5, 1729/30	1	29
Anna, m. Bartholomy PORTER, Oct. 9, 1751	2	30
Bethyah, m. Nehemiah WATKINS, May 25, 1726	A	10
Billings, s. James & Thirza, b. Mar. 22, 1786	6	39
Billings, m. Mary JONES, May 13, 1815	6	37
Calvin, s. Abial & Hannah, b. Apr. 19, 1780	4	79
Caroline, d. Amos & Martha, b. Dec. 27, 1785	4	226
Caroline, d. Billings & Mary, b. Oct. 9, 1821	6	37
Caroline, d. Billings & Mary, b. Mar. 1, 1829	6	37
Charlotte, d. Billings & Mary, b. Feb. 10, 1831	6	37
C[h]loe, m. Amasa LYON, 2d, b. of Ashford, Mar. 18, 1842,		
by Rev. Ezekiel Skinner	5	80
David, s. Abiel & Hannah, b. Feb. 2, 1776	4	79
Delotia, of Ashford, m. John S. MARCY, of Woodstock, Sept.		
1, [1845], by Rev. Renesalaer P. Putney, North Ashford	5	95
Dorothy, d. Peltiah & Dorothy, b. Sept. 19, 1749	2	23
Ebenezer, s. John & Elezebeth, b. Sept. 2, 1740	1	26
Ebenezer, s. Edward, b. May 9, 1741	1	47
Ebenezer, s. Edward, d. Aug. 21, 1761	1	46
Edward, m. Lida [W]RIGIIT, May 22, 1739	1	47
Edward, [s. Edward], b. Oct. 8, 1748	1	27
Edward Grosvenor, s. Billings & Mary, b. Apr. 14, 1827	6	37
Edwin, [s. Amos] & Eunice, b. June 30, 1825	6	49
Eleazer G., of Union, m. Sarah Ann DAY, of Eastford, Dec.		
28, 1845, by Francis Williams	5	96
Elisha Jones, s. Billings & Mary, b. Oct. 12, 1819	6	37
Elizabeth, d. Amos & Martha, b. Dec. 17, 1787	4	226
Easther, d. Josiah & Sarah, b. June 24, 1726	A	10
Esther, d. Edward & Lid[i]a, b. June 4, 1746	1	47
Esther, m. Ingoldsbe WORK, July 11, 1771	2	20
Eunis, d. Nathaniel & Sarah, b. Dec. 13, 1748	2	23
Frank, s. Amos & Martha, b. Feb. 18, 1794	4	226
Hannah, d. Nathaniel & Sarah, b. Sept. 8, 1751	2	23
Hannah, d. Edward & Lydia, b. June 15, 1754	1	46
Hannah, d. Edward, d. July 4, 1770	1	46
Hannah, d. James & Thirza, b. June 7, 1782	6	39
Hannah, of Ashford, m. John CHAPMAN, of Little Valley, N.		
Y., Apr. 26, 1825, by Amos Babcock, Elder. Intention		
published	5	19
Henriette A., [d. Amos & Eunice], b. June 28, 1839 ; d. Mar.		
18, 1843	6	49

	Vol.	Page
BUGBEE, BUGBE (cont.)		
James, s. Edward & Lydia, b. Mar. 15,1758	1	46
James, s. James & Thirza, b. May 12, 1784	6	39
James, m. Thirza **WELCH**, [ ]	6	39
James Deloss, s. Billings & Mary, b. Apr. 11, 1824	6	37
Jane Antionette, [d. Amos & Eunice], b. Apr. 17, 1832	6	49
John, m. Elezebeth **LEBRET**, Nov. 9, 1732	1	26
John Calhoun, [s. Amos & Eunice], b. Apr. 24, 1837	6	49
Jonathan, [s. Josiah & Polasene], b. June 30, 1741	1	53
Joseph, s. John & Elezebeth, b. July 3, 1738	1	26
Joseph, [s. Josiah & Polasene], b. Aug. 17, 1743	1	53
Josiah, s. Josiah, Jr. & Polasene, b. Sept. 10, 1736	1	53
Josiah, Dr., d. Dec. 23, 1751	1	29
Josiah, Jr., m. Hannah **WELCH**, June 14, 1770	4	44
Josiah, s. Sam[ue]ll & Thankful, b. Apr. 11, 1784	4	118
Josiah, d. Apr. 21, 1787	1	53
Keziah, d. John & Elezebeth, b. Feb. 12, 1735/6	1	26
Lemuel, s. Edward & Lydia, b. Aug. 11, 1751	1	46
Levi, s. Amos & Martha, b. Apr. 4, 1792 ; d. Sept. 15, 1795	4	226
Lois, m. Joseph W. **MARCY**, b. of Ashford, Apr. 22, 1832, by Rev. Leonard Gage	5	47
Louisa Josephine, [d. Amos & Eunice], b. May 2, 1834 ; d. Mar. 21, 1839	6	49
Maria, d. Amos & Martha, b. Apr. 6, 1803	4	226
Maria, of Ashford, m. Aaron **GOULD**, of Ware, Mass., Dec. 6, 1840, by Rev. Alvin Bennett	5	76
Martha, d. Amos & Martha, b. Jan. 30, 1784	4	226
Martha, wid. Amos, d. Jan. 8, 1847	4	226
Mary, d. Billings & Mary, b. Aug. 3, 1817	6	37
Mary, w. Amos, d. Apr. 10, 1819	6	49
Mary Emeline, d. Amos & Eunice, b. Jan. 31. 1823	6	49
Mehetebel, d. John & Elezebeth, b. Sept. 19, 1733	1	26
Minor, s. Amos & Martha, b. Mar. 1, 1799	4	226
Miram, d. Edward & Lidia, b. Sept. 4, 1743	1	47
Nabby, d. Abel & Eunis, b. June 12, 1776	4	92
Nathaniel, s. Josiah & Sarah, b. Apr. 5, 1721	A	6
Nathaniel, m. Sarah **JOHNSON**, Jan. 22, 1746	2	23
Nathaniel, Jr. [s.] Nathaniel, b. Mar. 9, 1747 ; d. Sept. 16, 1749	2	23
Olive, m. Archalus **STOWEL**, Nov. 4, 1791	4	19
Patrick Henry, [s. Amos & Eunice], b. Sept. 17, 1829	6	49
Palatiah, s. Josiah & Sarah, b. May 4, 1723	A	7
Pel[e]tiah, m. Dorothy **RIGBE**, Nov. 4, 1747, by Rev. Mr. John Bass	2	23
Pel[e]tiah, s. Pel[e]tiah & Dorithy, b. June 24, 1748	2	23
Peter, [s.] Nathaniel & Sarah, b. Jan. 20, 1750	2	23
Pheneliphe, m. John **CHAPMAN**, Apr. 15, 1716 (sic), by Rev. Mr. James Hale	1	61
Pollyseana, d. Josiah & Pollyseane, b. Apr. 15, 1756	1	53

	Vol.	Page
BULLARD, (cont.)		
Babcock, Elder. Intention published	5	16
BULLOCK, Elijah, s. Nathan & Hulda, b. Feb. 16, 1772	3	78
Hulda, d. Nathan & Hulda, b. Oct. 30, 1763 ; d. Apr. 11, 1767	3	78
Hulda, d. Nathan & Hulda, b. Aug. 10, 1767	3	78
Israel, s. Nathan & Hulda, b. Sept. 14, 1769	3	78
Nathan, s. Nathan, d. May 4, 1767	3	78
Rebeckah, d. Nathan & Hulda, b. Oct. 13, 1761	3	78
BURBANK, Electe, d. Elias & Meriam, b. July 18, 1775	4	101
Elias, m. Meriam **DIMOCK,** Oct. 15, 1774	4	101
Elias, s. Elias & Meriam, [b.] Feb.9, 1778	4	101
BURCHARD, [see under **BIRCHARD**]		
BURGE, [see also **BURGES**], Freelove, d. Benjamin & Susan[n]ah, b. July 14, 1731	1	5
Martha, m. George **CHEDAL,** Aug. 16, 1721, by James Hale	A	9
Mary, d. Stephen & Mary, b. Jan. 14, 1742/3	1	48
Susannah, [d. Stephen & Mary], b. July 6, 1741	1	48
BURGES [see also **BURGE**], Abigail, d. Stephen & Susanna, b. Apr. 7, 1776	4	81
Anna, d. Benj[ami]n, b. May 26, 1753	4	13
Benjamin, s. Benj[ami]n, b. Mar. 26, 1749	4	13
Benjamin, s. Stephen & Susannah, b. Aug. 30, 1774	4	81
Joseph, s. Benj[ami]n, b. Apr. 18, 1757	4	13
Mary, d. Stephen, b. Feb. 16, 1763	4	13
Philip, s. Stephen & Susanna, b. Mar. 30, 1778	4	81
Stephen, s. Benj[ami]n, b. Jan. 12, 1751	4	13
Stephen, Jr., m. Susannah **ABBOTT,** Sept. 15, 1773	4	81
Stephen, s. Stephen & Susanna, b. May 30, 1780	4	81
BURLEY, BURLEIGH, Joseph, s. Joseph C., retailer of spirits, b. Mar. 18, 1849	5	134-5
Mary, m. Amos **HAYWARD,** Nov. 27, 1817	6	30
BURNAP, Sibel, of Windham, m. John **KNOX,** of Ashford, Nov. 30, 1773	4	91
BURNHAM, BURNAM,Abia, d. Elijah & A[b]ina, b. Sept. 10,1784	4	244
Abigail, m. Sumner **RICHARDS,** Mar. 20, 1827, by Rev. Reuben Torrey, Eastford	5	27
Alba, s. Joseph & Elisabeth, b. May 17, 1786	4	94
Chester, s. Roswell & Esther, b. June 28, 1788	4	245
Clirana, m. John **LUMMISS,** Jan. 18, 1781	4	122
Dolley, d. Freeman & Abigail, b. Oct. 18, 1796	4	262
Elijah, m. Abina **BOWIN,** Jan. 2, 1782	4	244
Elisabeth, m. Benj[ami]n **SABIN,** May 10, 1763	4	34
Elisabeth, d. Freeman & Abigail, b. Jan. 18, 1793	4	262
Esther, d. Nathan & Esther, b. Apr. 6, 1782	4	241
Esther, d. Roswell & Betsey, b. June 10, 1800	4	245
Esther, m. Patrick **CARPENTER,** Mar. 29, 1827, by Rev. Reuben Torrey, Eastford	5	27
[E]unice, d. Joseph & Elisabeth, b. May 25, 177[ ]	5	27

	Vol.	Page
BURNHAM, BURNAM, (cont.)		
Eunice, m. Amos SNOW, June 27, 1797	4	20
Hiram B., m. Hannah H. MARCY, b. of Ashford, [May] 5, [1839], by Rev. Erastus Benton	5	70
Isaac, d. Oct. 14, 1807	4	94
Jacob, s. Elijah & Abina, b. Aug. 13, 1782	4	244
Joseph, m. Elisabeth DURKEE, June 13, 1776	4	94
Joseph, s. Joseph & Elisabeth, b. Feb. 23, 1782	4	94
Joseph C., m. Sarah A. WALKER, b. of Ashford, Nov. 26, 1846, by Rev. Edward A. Lyon, Eastford	5	99
Jotham, s. Roswell & Esther, b. Dec. 19, 1785	4	245
Lucy, d. Roswell & Esther, b. Apr. 13, 1784	4	245
Lucy, of Ashford, m. Horace TROWBRIDGE, of North Providence, R. I. "last evening", [Aug. 31. 1836], by Rev. J. Hall	5	61
Lucy Ann, m. Elisha ROBINS, b. of Ashford, May 1, 1842, by Rev. Charles C. Barnes	5	81
Lyman, s. Nathan & Esther, b. May 8, 1786	4	241
Nathan, m. Esther LYON, Dec. 13, 1781	4	241
Nathan, s. Nathan & Esther, b. Mar. 23, 1784	4	241
Polley, d. Elijah & Abina, b. Nov. 3, 1786	4	244
Roswell, m. Esther CHILD, Oct. 23, 1783	4	245
Royal, m. Sarah SOUTHWORTH, [July] 15, [1832], by Reuben Torrey, Eastford	5	48
Rufus, s. Joseph & Elisabeth, b. Apr. 26, 1784	4	94
Rufus, s. Freeman & Abigail, b. Aug. 6. 1790	4	262
Stephen F., m. Ann BOWEN, b. of Ashford, Jan, 4, 1830, by Rev. Philo Judson	5	37
Stephen Fielder, s. Roswell & Betsey, b. May 17, 1797	4	245
Triphene, d. Joseph & Elisabeth, b. Dec. 22, 1778	4	94
Tryphena, m. Alva SIMMONS, Dec. 4. 1800	4	81
Vilote, m. Daniel CHANDLER, Dec. 24, 1754, by Joseph Pitken, Esc.	1	87
BURR, Ephraim, of Millbury, Mass., m. Celia A. BABBITT, of Brookfield, Jan. 26, 1834, by Rev. Ezekiel Skinner	5	52
BURTON, Mark, s. Simon & Marah, b. Apr. 7, 1718	A	6
Martha, d. Simon & Marah, b. Aug. 11, 1714	A	6
Simon, s. Simon & Mary, b. Oct. 7, 1722	A	6
BUTLER, Abigail, d. Benj[ami]n & Patty, b. Nov. 6, 1796	4	50
Almira, d. Stephen & Mehetable, b. July 31, 1797	4	15
Almira, of Ashford, m. Samuel W. AVERY, of Stafford, Dec. 27, 1831, by Rev. David Bennett	5	46
Altheah, d. Tho[ma]s & Elisabeth, b. Feb. 19, 1763	3	115
Barzaldia, s. Benj[ami]n & Patty, b. Aug. 12, 1798	4	50
Barzaldai, m. Catharine DOW, Apr. 21, 1823, by Philo Judson	5	9
Benjamin, s. Thomas & Elisabeth, b. Feb. 8, 1771	3	115
Benjamin, m. Patty HOWE, Dec. 12, 1793	4	50
Betsey, m. Oliver CLARK, Dec. 19, 1802	6	14

	Vol.	Page
BUTLER, (cont.)		
Betsey W., of Ashford, m. Philo **HILLS**, of		
Marlborough, [May] 9, [1836], by Rev. J. Hall	5	59
Catharine Elizabeth, d. Barzillia & Catharine, b. May 4, 1824	6	50
C[h]loe, [twin with Lyd[i]a], d. Ele[a]zar, b. June 13, 1760	2	78
Craft, s. Tho[ma]s & Elisabeth, b. Feb. 23, 1776	3	115
Elither, m. Nathan **HUNTINGTON**, May 31, 1798	4	104
Hipzibah, m. Josiah **HENDEE**, Feb. 16, 1791	4	89
James H., m. Polly **FITTS** b. of Ashford, Oct. 19, 1825, by		
Rev. Philo Judson	5	20
James Harne, s. Benj[ami]n & Patty, b. Aug. 6, 1801	4	50
Jemima, d. Thomas & Elisabeth, b. Mar. 28, 1761	3	115
Jemima, m. Marverick **JOHNSON**, Oct. 25, 1787	4	259
John, s. Tho[ma]s & Elisabeth, b. Oct. 23, 1764	3	115
John, m. Salla **BROWN**, Dec. 7, 1790	4	288
Joseph, m. Elizabeth **DOW**, b. of Ashford, Sept. 4, 1827, by		
Rev. Philo Judson	5	28
Josiah, s. Tho[ma]s & Elisabeth, b. Nov. 14, 1766	3	115
[J]osiah, s. John & Salla, b. Mar. 7, 1793	4	288
Lyd[i]a, [twin with C[h]loe], d. Ele[a]zar, b. June, 13, 1760	2	78
Martha, of Ashford, m. Royal **KEITH**, of Douglass, Mass.,		
May 2, 1837, by Rev. J. Hall	5	64
Mary Ann, Mrs., of Ashford, m. Lewis A. **BROWN**, of		
Mansfield, Nov. 12, 1854, by Rev. Charles Chamberlain	5	111
Mehetable, d. Stephen & Mehetable, b. June 13, 178[ ]	4	15
Mahitable, w. Stephen, d. Nov. [ ], 1827	4	15
Sally, m. Thomas E. **BOUTELL**, b. of Ashford, Apr. 4, 1826,		
by Rev. Philo Judson	5	22
Sam[ue]ll Warren, s. Benj[ami]n & Patty, b. May 23, 1803	4	50
Stephen, m. Mehetable **ROBINSON**, Mar. 6, 178[ ]	4	15
Thomas, s. Thomas & Elisabeth, b. Nov. 27,1768	3	115
Thomas, d. Nov. 29, 1787	3	115
BUTTS, Lovice, d. James & Elizabeth, b. Mar. 20, 1782	4	123
Luther, s. James & Elisabeth, b. Sept. 4, 1783	4	123
BYLES, BILES, Abigail, [d.] Ebenezer & Anne, b. Mar. 16, 1751	2	49
Abigail, d. Josias & Abigail, b. Jan. 14, 1799	4	112
Abigail, m. Rufus **PEARL**, Oct. 27, 1816	6	12
Abigail, d. Elisha & Sophia, b. Nov. 1, 1816	6	4
Abigail, w. Josias, d. Jan. 5, 1829	4	112
Abigail, of Ashford, m. Stephen **WHITON**, of East Hartford,		
Apr. 14, 1845, by Rev. Cha[rle]s Hyde	5	93
Andrew Huntington, s. Elisha & Sophia, b. Oct. 3, 1820	6	4
Anne, d. Ebenezer & Anne, b. May 17, 1749	2	49
Anne, m. Simeon **SMITH**, Feb. 18, 1766	4	38
Anne, w. Eben[eze]r, d. Apr. 25, 1776	2	49
Cornelius, s. Eben[eze]r & Betsey, b. Mar. 9, 1815	4	281
Ebenezer, b. Mar. 26, 1723 ; came to Ashford Mar. 10, 1743\4		
married Anne **BICKNELL**, Nov. 28, 1745, by Mr. John		
Bass	2	49

BYLES, BILES, (cont.)   Vol.   Page
Ebenezer, s. Josias & Abigail, b. July 4, 1780   4   112
Ebenezer, d. Nov. 12, 1805, in the 83 y. of his age   2   49
Ebenezer, m, Betsa MARCY, Mar. 21, 180[ ]   4   281
Edwin, s. Eben[eze]r & Betsey, b. July 29, 1820   4   281
Elisha, s. Josias & Abigail, b. Jan. 28, 1788   4   112
Elisha, m. Sophis HUNTINGTON, Jan. 28, 1813   6   4
Elizabeth Ann, d. Eben[eze]r & Betsey, b. Nov. 4. 1816 ; d.
    Feb. 15, 1821   4   281
Elizabeth Ann, d. Eben[eze]r & Betsey, b. Jan. 29, 182[ ]   4   281
Josiah, [no information given]   3   112
Josias, s. Ebene[ze]r & Anne, b. Nov. 13, 1756   2   49
Josias, m. Abigail CLARK, Nov. 18, 1779   4   112
Josias, d. June 25, 1834, ae 77 y. 7 m.   4   112
Julia, d. Eben[eze]r & Betsey, b. Jan. 8, 1[ ]   4   281
Junius, s. Elisha & Sophia, b. Mar. 31. 1814   6   4
Lucy, d. Elisha & Sophia, b. Sept. 13, 1819   6   4
Mariet, m. Benjamin C. SIMMONS, b. of Ashford, Apr. 29,
    1824, by Rev. Philo Judson   5   14
Maryetta, d. Ebenezer & Betsa, b. Apr. 2, 1806   4   281
Marv, [d.] Ebenezer & Anne, b. Mar. 26, 1753, O. S.   2   49
Mary, d. Eben[eze]r, d. Nov. 19, 1762   2   49
Matthew Marcy, s. Eben[eze]r & Betsey, b. Apr. 1, 1809   4   281
Nancy, d. Josias & Abigail, b. Dec. 16, 1781   4   112
Nancy, m. William BICKNELL, Jr. May 5, 1803   4   54
Polley, d. Josias & Abigail, b. Mar. 27, 1792   4   112
Polly, m. Michael RICHMOND, Mar. 3, 1814   6   7
Roxalana, d.Josias & Abigail, b. Apr. 5, 1789 ; d. Feb. 15,1791 4 112
Roxalana, d. Josias & Abigail, b. Aug. 25, 1796   4   112
Salla, d. Josias & Abigail, b. Sept. 30, 1785 ; d. Feb. 12, 1791 4 112
Salla, d. Josias & Abigail, b. Nov. 27, 1793   4   112
Sarah, d. Eben[eze]r & Anne, b. Nov. 10, 1758   2   49
Sarah, d. Eben[eze]r & Betsey, b. Sept. 29, 1813   4   281
Sophia, housekeeper, d. Nov. 7, 1849, ae 58   5   144-5
William Dwight, s. Eben[eze]r & Betsey, b. July 29, 1807 4   281
Zuriah, d. Elisha & Sophia, b. Dec. 31, 1831   6   4
CADA, [see also CADY], Hiram, of Hartford, m. Merian
    KNOWLTON, of Ashford, Nov. 24, 1831, by Rev.
    David Bennett   5   45
CADWELL,Jerusha, m. Rev. Elisha HUTCHINSON, July 16, 1778 4 108
CADY, [see also CADA], George, m. Lucinda H. SIMMONS, b. of
    Ashford, Apr. 14, 1841, by Rev. Cha[rle]s Hyde   5   78
Mary A. H., m. Philo CHAFFEE, b. of Ashford, Sept. 1, 1851,
    by Rev. P. Mathewson   5   107
CAMPBELL, Almira, of Union, resident of Westford, m. Josiah R.
    JAMES, Oct. 26, 1836, by Alvan Underwood   5   63
CANADA, Chloe, m. Reuben PARKER, Aug. 5, 1792   4   261
Phila, m. John Westley SQUIR[E], Jan. 26, 1812   4   53
Rensselaer, of Chaplin, m. Catharine Mariah SQUIER, of

	Vol.	Page
CANADA, (cont.)		
Ashford, Aug. 30, 1834 by Amos Babcock, Elder	5	54
CANLY, [see under CONLY		
CARD, Amy A., m. John R. MILLER, b. of Ashford, Nov. 28,		
1850, by Rev. Lyman Leffingwell	5	106
Amey A., ae 19, b. Mass., m. John R. MILLER, farmer, ae 22,		
b. N. Y. State, res. Ashford, Nov. [ ], 1850, by Lyman		
Leffington	5	148-9
CARDER, Chester W., of Killingly, m. Sarah THOMPSON, of		
Ashford, Jan. 11, 1837, by Rev. Reuben Torrey, Eastford	5	63
CAREY, [see under CARY]		
CARLE (?), James, s. Abigail Kindal, b. Nov. 11, 1773	4	123
CARPENTER, CARPINTER, Abiel, s. Amos & Mary, b. Aug. 2,		
1746	2	56
Abial Cheney, s. Dyer & Martha, b. Oct. 21, 1816 ; d. July 19,		
1820	6	21
Abigail, m. John SEAIRLS, b. of Ashford, May, 11, 1753, by		
Rev. Mr. Stephen Williams	1	80
Abigail, of Ashford, m. Alason PECK, of Abington, Pomfret,		
[Apr.] 13, [1829], by Rev. Reuben Torrey, Eastford	5	35
Aeleser(?), d. Jonah & Se[r]viah, b. Sept. 19, 1772	4	71
Alfred, s. Uriah & Elisphal, b. Dec. 27, 1789	4	66
Alfred Patrick, s. Palmer, b. Oct. 29, 1835	6	79
Almira Maria, d. Joseph T. & Almira F., b. Feb. 20, 1831	6	70
Amasa, s. Benjamin & Joanna, b. Dec. 23, 176[ ]sic	3	2
Amasa, of Woodstock, m. Susa P. RICHMOND, of Ashford,		
Oct. 7, 1830, by Rev. Samuel Backus	5	40
Amelia, d. Comfort & Prissilla, b. Feb. 13, 1799	4	251
Amos, m. Mary GOULD, Apr. 3, 1746	2	56
Ann, m. John HAYWARD, Nov. 11,1734, by Philip Eastman,		
J. P.	1	45
Anna, d. Uriah & Sarah, b. Jan. 1, 1745/6	1	44
Benjamin, s. Benj[ami]n & Joannah, b. Oct. 28, 1760	3	2
Caleb, s. Uriah & Sarah, b. Dec. 1, 1755	2	36
Candace, m. George W. TAFT, b. of Montague, Mass., July		
20, 1839, by Rev. Alvan Underwood	5	71
Charles Victor, s. Patrick & Esther, b. Apr. 2, 1850	6	64
Chester, s. Jonah & Serviah, b. July 3, 1780	4	71
Chester Whitman, s. Dyer & Martha, b. Aug. 8, 1812	6	21
Comfort, m. Prissilla HAYWARD, Nov. 15, 1786	4	251
Dan, s. Uriah & Sarah, b. June 13, 1750	2	36
Dan, s. Uriah & Sarah, b. June 19, 1750	1	44
Daniel, s. Joel & Rebeckah, b. Feb. 1, 1769	4	28
David, s. Uriah & Sarah, b. Jan. 28, 1759	2	36
David, s. Uriah & Elisphal, b. Feb. 11, 1809	4	66
David, m. Polly JAMES, b. of Ashford, Feb. 23, 1834, by Rev.		
Ezekiel Skinner	5	53
Dyer, s. Jonah & Serviah, b. Apr. 22, 1786	4	71
Dyer, m. Martha GIBBS, Sept. 19, 1811	6	21

	Vol.	Page

CARPENTER, CARPINTER, (cont.)

Dyer, s. Dyer & Martha, b. Dec. 15, 1819	6	21
Elias, s. Uriah & Elisphal, b. Jan. 29, 1786	4	66
Elisha, [s. Uriah B.], b. Jan. 14, 1824	6	83
Elezebeth, d. Uriah & Sarah, b. June 21, 1749 ; [d.] Aug. 25, 1749	1	44
Elizabeth, m. Stephen SCARBOROUGH, b. of Ashford, Mar. 8, 1821, by Rev. Stephen Haskell	5	2
Ellen I., d. William D., farmer, ae 29, & Julia M., ae 20, b. Aug. 20, 1847	5	126-7
Ephraim, of Ashford, m. Harty ALDRICH, of Thompson, Dec. 7, 1829, by Edward S. Keyes, J. P.	5	37
Ephraim Keyes, s. Levi & Hannah, b. Oct. 1, [ ]	4	7
Ephraim Lorin, s. Uriah & Elisphal, b. Jan. 20, 1799	4	66
Freelove, m. Josiah CHANDLER, Nov. 5. 1747	2	74
Fridus Chapman, [s. Palmer] b.Oct. 5, 1820	6	79
George W., s. Samuel H. & Lois, b. Mar. 24, 1821	6	49
Grace, d. Uriah & Sarah, b. Aug. 21, 1734	1	44
Hezekiah, s. Uriah & Sarah, b. Dec. 8, 1736	1	44
Horatio, s. Uriah & Elisphal, b. Jan. 6, 1806	4	66
Horatio, [s. Uriah B.], b. June 6, 1826	6	83
Horatio, m. Mary G. BOSWORTH, b. of Ashford, [Mar.] 25, 1832, by Rev. Reuben Torrey, Eastford	5	47
Huldah, m. John GRIGGS, Nov. 26, 1807	4	108
Izabel, d. Uriah & Sarah, b. July 8, 1743	1	44
Izabel, d. Uriah [& Sarah], d. Aug. 20, 1749	1	44
Iszabel, d. Uriah & Sarah, b. May 5, 1753	2	36
Jairus Thawlin, [s. Palmer], b. Feb. 14, 1822	6	79
James Milton, [s. Uriah B.], b. Aug. 26, 1834	6	83
Joanna, d. Benj[ami]n & Joannah, b. Oct. 24, 1763	3	2
Joel, m. Rebecca PIT[T]S, July 3, 1755, by Stephen Williams	1	89
Joel, s. Joel & Rebeckah, b. Jan. 21, 1765	4	28
John Briggs, [s. Uriah B.], b. Dec. 2, 1820	6	83
Jonah, s. Jonah & Serviah, b. Oct. 4, 1777	4	71
Jonah, d. Jan. 31, 1805	4	71
Jonah Davison, [twin with Joseph Titus], s. Joseph T. & {Huldah] b. Apr. 12, 1805 ; d. Apr. [ ], 1805	4	96
Jonah Orlando, s. Dyer & Martha, b. Apr. 9, 1818	6	21
Jonathan, s. Uriah & Sarah, b. Nov. 24, 1738	1	44
Jonathan, [s. Uriah & Sarah], d. Feb. 18, 1747/8	1	44
Jonathan, s. Dan & Sarah, b. Apr. 11, 1752	1	52
Jonathan, s. Jonathan & Rebeck, b. Feb. 14, 1772 *(* or 1792)	3	2
Jonathan, m. Elezebeth BARTLETT, May 22, 1794	3	112
Jonathan, m. Elizabeth BARTLET[T], May 22, 1794	4	248
Jonathan, [s. Jonathan & Elezebeth], b. May 4, 1797	3	112
Jonathan, s. Jonathan & Elizabeth, b. May 4, 1797	4	248
Joseph T., m. Huldah DAVISON, Apr. 15, 1800	4	96
Joseph T. , M. Almira FITTS, b. of Ashford, Apr. 12, 1829,		

CARPENTER, CARPINTER, (cont.)	Vol.	Page
by Ezekiel Skinner	4	34
Joseph Titus, s. Jonah & Se[r]viah, b. Jan. 2, 1774	4	71
Joseph Titus, [twin with Jonah Davison], s. Joseph T. & [Huldah], b. Apr. 12, 1805	4	96
[Jose]ph Titus, d. Apr. 11, 1805	4	96
Josiah, s. Jonah & Serviah, b. June 29, 1783	4	71
Judson, [s. Uriah B.], b. Jan. 31, 1833	6	83
Levi, m. Hannah KEYES, Jan.13, 17[ ]	4	7
Leviny, d. Comfort, & Prissilla, b. Aug. 1, 1796	4	251
Lois, m. Benjamin ROBBINS, Oct. 21, 1784	4	237
Loren Niles, s. Palmer, b. Dec. 22, 1838	6	79
Lucian Palmer, [s. Palmer], b. Dec. 2, 1824	6	79
Lucinda Gibbs, d. Dyer & Martha, b. July 4, 1814	6	21
Lucius, [s. Uriah B.], b. Nov. 23, 1814	6	83
Lucius, m. Freelove P. ABBE, of Ashford, Jan. 6, 1841, by Rev. R. W. Allen	5	77
Lucius, m. Sylvia C. DAY, [Mar.] 23, [1843], by F. Williams	5	84
Lucretia, m. Ezra BOSWORTH, Jan. 1, 1833, by Rev. Leonard Gage	5	50
Lurilla, d. Comfort, & Prissilla, b. Aug. 1, 1793	4	251
Luretta*, m. Amos TROWBRIDGE, Feb. 10, 1813 *(Lurilla?)	6	20
Marian, m. Thomas CHAPMAN, Jr., Apr. 11, 1813	6	23
Mary, m. Sam[u]el HUMPHREY, Feb. 9, 1737/8	1	59
Mary, d. Benj[ami]n, & Johannah, b. Apr. 12, 1755	1	88
Mary Cemantha, [d. Palmer], b. May 3, 1830	6	79
Nabby, d. Joseph T. & Huldah, b. Dec. 19. 1802	4	96
Nelson, s. Joseph T. & Huldah, b. Jan. 12, 1801	4	96
Noah, s. Comfort & Prissilla, b. Apr. 10, 1790	4	251
Oliver, Jr., of Killingly, m. Mary ALLEN, of Ashford, Mar. 16, 1843, by Rev. John Howson	5	84
Palmer, s. Uriah & Elisphal, b. Apr. 1, 1795	4	66
Palmer, Jr., m. Lydia SCARBOROUGH, Oct. 7, 1839, by Elder Henry Greenslit. Intention published	5	71
Patrick, s. Uriah & Elisphal, b. May 21, 1801	4	66
Patrick m. Esther BURNHAM, Mar. 29, 1827, by Rev. Reuben Torrey, Eastford	5	27
Patrick Henry, s. Patrick & Esther, b. July 20, 1828	6	64
Patty, of Ashford, m. Hezekiah SIMMONS, of Woodstock, Jan. 11, 1829, by Levi Works, J. P.	5	33
Patty Amanda, [d. Palmer], b. Feb. 23, 1828	6	79
Phebe, d. Joel & Rebeckah, b. June 4, 1760	1	109
Polley, d. Uriah & Elisphal, b. May 3, 1804	4	66
Rebeckah, d. Dan & Sarah, b. Aug. 20, 1738	1	52
Roxana, [d. Uriah B.], b. July 29, 1817	6	83
Roxana, m. Daniel WILBUR, b. of Ashford, Dec. 3, 1843, by Francis Williams	5	87
Roxsey, d. Levi & Hannah, b. Nov. 24, [ ]	4	7
Rufus B., m. Almira H. BROWN, b. of Ashford, Oct. 15,		

	Vol.	Page
CARPENTER, CARPINTER, (cont.)		
1843, by Francis Williams, Eastford	5	85
Rufus Bulkley, [s. Uriah B.] b. Jan. 24, 1819	6	83
Samuel H., farmer, d. Dec. [ ], 1850, ae 63	5	150-1
Samuel Ha[y]ward, s. Comfort & Pressilla, b. Jan. 26, 1788	4	251
Sam[ue]ll Hayward, s. Jonathan & Elizabeth, b. May 19, 1795	4	248
Sam[ue]l Howard, [s. Jonathan & Elezebeth], b. May, 19, 1795	3	112
Sarah, m. Peter **WALKER,** Nov. 13, 1783	4	266
Sarah, m. Ezra **GROSVENOR,** May 4, 1786	4	246
Serviah, see under Zerviah		
Stephen, s. Benj[ami]n & Joannah, b. Dec. 18, 1758	1	104
Sylvester, s. Don & Mehitable, b. Oct. 29, 1799	4	114
Uriah, m. Sarah **HAYWARD,** Nov. 28, 1733, by Philip Eastman, J. P.	1	44
Uriah, s. Uriah & Sarah, b. Jan. 6, 1740/41	1	44
Uriah, m. Elisphal **BRIGGS,** Apr. 14, 1785	4	66
Uriah Briggs, s. Uriah & Elisphal, b. Apr. 30, 1792	4	66
Uriah L., m. Emily A. **CHILDS,** b. of Eastford, Dec. 1, 1846, by Francis Williams	5	99
Uriah Lafayette, s. Palmer, b. Nov. 3, 1818	6	79
William D., s. Samuel H. & Lois, b. Oct 19, 1818	6	49
William D., m. Julia M. **BICKNELL,** Oct. 28, 1846, by Charles Peabody	5	98
Serviah, d. Dan & Sarah, b. Apr. 17, 1736	1	52
Zerviah, m. Barnibus **EDDY,** Nov. 1, 1750, by Rev. Mr. Stephen Williams	1	81
------, d. Joel & Rebeckah, b. Feb. 13, 1[1756] ; d. Mar. 3,1756	1	91
------. s. Wllllam D., farmer, & Julia M., b. June 25, 1849	5	134-5
CARR, Almira, d. W[illia]m & Elithear, Sept. 5, 1807	4	281
Benj[amin], s. W[illia]m & Elithear, b. Sept. 7, 1805	4	281
Betsey, d, W[illia]m & Ellitheah, b. Sept. 25, 179[ ]	4	281
Lucy, d. William & Ellitheah, b. Aug. 5, 1798	4	281
Numan, s. William & Ellitheah, b. Apr. 1, 180[ ]	4	281
Samuel, s. William & Ell[itheah], b. Sept. 20, 1796	4	281
Sophia, d. William & Ellithiar, b. Feb. 3, 1800	4	281
Wightman, s. William & Ellitheah, b. Aug. 18, 1801	4	281
William, s. William & Ellitheah, b. Mar. [ ]	4	281
CARTER,, Mary, m. Stephen **TANNER,** b. of Ashford, Jan. 14, 1827, by Rev. Luke Wood	5	25
CARY, Catherine, [d. Henry], b. Mar. 13, 1743/4 ; d. Nov. 27, 1749	2	48
Chloa, [d. Henry], b. June 6, 1746	2	48
Daniel, m. Jerusha **PARISH,** b. of Ashford, Dec. 5, 1822, by Rev. John Paine, of Hampton	5	7
Elezebeth, [d. Henry], b. Aug. 18, 1739	2	48
Easther, [d. Henry], b. Oct. 8, 1737	2	48
Henry, [s. Henry], b. Aug. 19, 1745	2	48
John Paul, [s. Henry], b. Aug. 6, 1750	2	48
Marcy, [d. Henry], b. Aug. 28, 1735	2	48

	Vol.	Page
CARY, (cont.)		
Mary, [d. Henry], b. Nov. 17, 1741	2	48
CASE, Alice, see under Ellese		
Bettse, d. Elip]h]alet & Experiance, b. Aug, 26, 1784	3	4
Daniel, s. Barnard & Phebe, b. Aug. 7, 1782	4	120
Elip[h]alet, m. Experiance [ ], Nov. 26, 1778	3	4
Ellese, m. Samuel **WALKER**, Jr., Dec. 14, 1775	4	99
Ephraim, [twin with Phebe], s. Barnard & Phebe, b. Dec. 26, 1780	4	120
Experience, of Ashford, m. William **WATROUS**, of Pomfret, County of Windsor, State of Vt., Sept. 21, 1823, by Thomas Dow, J. P.	5	11
Naomi, d. Eliphalet & Experience, b. Nov. 25, 1785	3	4
Phebe, [twin with Ephraim, d. Barnard & Phebe, b. Dec. 26, 1780	4	120
Phebe, w. Barnard, d. Feb. 1, 1785	4	120
Ruth, m. Elisha **HUNTINGTON**, June 12, 1777	4	105
William, s. Barnard & Phebe, b. Feb 24, 1784	4	120
CASEY, Ellen M., d. Michael, farmer, ae 30, & [ ] ae 34, b. July 27, 1850	5	140-1
CAVARY, [see under **CRARY**]		
CHAFFEE, CHAFFE, Abigill, d. Jonathan & Abigaill, b. Dec. 17, 1740	1	20
Abigail, d. Benj[ami]n & Perseala, b. Mar. 26, 1743	1	74
Abigail, w. Artherton, d. Feb. 12, 1755	1	96
Abigail, m. Ephraim **KEYES**, Jr., Dec. 20, 1760	3	12
Abigail, m. Jacob **ORCUTT**, Jan. 1, 1771	4	55
Abigail, d. Josiah & Elizabeth, b. Mar. 4, 1771	3	18
Abigail, w. Johath[a]n, d. Jan. 19, 1773	1	20
Abigail S., d. Reuben & Hannah, b. Apr. 29, 1819	6	87
Abigail S., of Ashford, m. Rufus **PEARL**, of Hartford, May 6, 1840, by Rev. Alvan Underwood	5	74
Abner, s. David, d. Sept. 18, 1755	2	27
Abner, s. David, Jr. & Prissilla, b. Aug. 3, 1762	3	128
Abner, m. Judith **WALKER**, Dec. 9, 1790	4	21
Albigence, s. Josiah, Jr. & Joanna, b. Apr. 14, 1790	4	257
Albigence, m. Lucy **STREETER**, Sept. 15, 1811	6	1
Albigence Lyman, s. Albigence & Lucy, b. Aug. 9, 1813	6	1
Alfred, m. Minerve **PRESTON**, b. of Ashford, May 24, 1837, by Alvan Underwood	5	64
Alfred, farmer, ae 38, m. 2d w. Almira **DEANS**, ae 27, b. Woodstock, res. Ashford, Apr. 4, 1849, by Rev. R. O. Putney	5	136-7
Alse, d. Elihu & Alse, b. Nov. 14, 1806	6	61
Alse, d. Elihu & Alse, d. Mar. 17, 1812	6	51
Alice Ann, see under Else Ann		
Almyra, d. Fred[e]ric & Elisabeth, b. Feb. 28, 1794	4	254

	Vol.	Page
CHAFFEE, CHAFFE,(cont.)		
Almira, m. John KNOWLTON, Nov. 30, 1815	6	19
Alpheus, s. Jonathan & Salla, b. Dec. 31, 1794	4	258
Ama, d. David & Martha, b. Sept. 2, 1759	2	27
Amanda, d. Frederick & Elisabeth, b. Mar. 6, 1801	4	254
Amanda, d. Amos & Eunice, b. July 4, 1801	4	35
Amanda, d. Frederick, d. Mar. 29, 1802	4	254
Amanda, m. Chauncey HORTON, b. of Ashford, Sept. 30, 1824, by Rev. W[illia]m Storrs	5	16
Amos, m. Harmony CRARY, Oct. 1, 1797	4	116
Amos, m. Eunice CUMMINGS, Jan. 1, 1799	4	35
Amos, s. Amos & Harmany, b. Oct. 14, 1806	4	116
Amos, Jr., m. Mary CURTIS, [Sept.] 14, [1834], by Rev. R. Torrey, Eastford	5	54
Amos, Capt., of Ashford, m. Mrs. Elizabeth WEEKS, of Windham, Oct. 27, 1844, by Jared D. Richmond, J. P.	5	91
Amos, farmer, d. Jan. 27, 1850, ae 75	5	144-5
Amos C., m. Loiza CHAPMAN, Oct. 4, 1836, by Alvan Underwood	5	61
Amos Cummings, s. Amos & Eunice, b. Mar. 11, 1812	4	35
Amy, d. Abner & Judith, b. Aug.7, 1791	4	21
Amy, m. Abner WHITON, Oct. [ ], 1814	6	43
Andrew B., s. Reuben & Hannah, b. July 27, 1837	6	87
Anna, d. Abner & Judith, b. Oct. 18, 1794	4	21
Anna, of Ashford, m. Reuben ROBINSON, of Mansfield, Feb. 13, 1822, by Rev. W[illia]m Storrs	5	5
Anna B., m. Elijah FORDHAM, Oct. 3, 1838, by Thomas Dow, J. P.	5	69
Anna Bib[b]ins, d. Amos & Harmany, b. Mar. 24, 1811	4	116
Anna Emily, d. [Amos, Jr. & Mary], b. June 11, 1840	6	84
Anson, s. Frederick & Elisabeth, b. Nov. 17, 1804	4	254
Artherton, m. Rachal FULLER Mar. 25, 1756	1	96
Atherton, s. Atherton & Abigail, b. May, 15, 1752	1	76
Benj[ami]n, m. Hannah CHAPMAN, Nov. 2, 1738	1	38
Benj[ami]n, m. Hannah CHAPMAN, Nov. 2, 1738	1	74
Benjamin, s. Benjamin & Hannah, b. Jan. 18, 1739/40 ; d. Sept. 13, 1740	1	74
[Benj[ami]n], m. Pessalla GREEN, Feb. 26, 1741	1	74
Benj[ami]n, m. Rebec[c]ah WHITON, Nov. 29, 1792	4	273
Bet[t]y, d. Atherton & Abigail, b. May 9, 1749	1	75
Carpenter, s. Jonathan & Abigail, b. Jan. 25, 1749/50	1	20
Carpenter, s. Josiah & Elisabeth, b. Feb. 27, 1774	3	18
Carpenter, s. Jon[a]th[an], d. Apr. 23, 1776	1	19
Catharine, d. Elihu & Al[i]ce, b. Sept. 2, 1808	4	100
Catharine, d. Elihu & Al[i]se, b. Sept. 2 1808	6	61
Charles, d. Nov. 10, 1850, ae 10 m.	5	150-1
Charles T., s. Alfred, farmer, ae 39, & Almira, ae 29, b. Dec. 29, 1849	5	140-1

CHAFFEE, CHAFFE, (cont.)	Vol.	Page
Chloa, d. Atherton & Rachal, b. Sept, 21, 1758 ; d. Apr. 21, 1760	1	76
Clasard(?),* s. Artherton & Rachal, b.Jan. 20, 1757 *(Claford?)	1	96
Cyrus, s. Amos & Harmany, b. Feb. 11, 1803	4	116
Dan, s. Amos & Eunice, b. July 30, 1815	4	35
Daniel Knowlton, s. Frederick & Elisabeth, b. Nov. 21, 1802	4	254
David, m. [Pr]ysilla ROBBINS, Nov. 6, 1761	3	128
David, s. David, Jr. & Pressilla, b. July 25, 1772	3	128
[Da]vid, d. Feb. 19, 1784	3	128
David, s. Josiah Jr. & Joanna, b. Feb. 3, 1798	4	257
David, d. Oct. 3, 18[ ]	3	128
David C., s. Amos, farmer, ae 43, & Mary, ae 36, b. Dec. 1, 1849	5	140-1
David C., d. Feb. 1, 1850, ae 2 m.	5	144-5
Deliveran[c]e, d. Joathan & Abigail, b. Feb. 6, 1742/3	1	20
[Delivera]nce, m. [Jonah ROGERS], Dec. 11, 1766 (See index of original volume for supplied data)	4	8
Delotia, d. Amos & Harmany, b. Dec. 7, 1804	4	116
Doratha, [d. David], d. Oct. 10, 1755	2	27
Doratha, d. David & Martha, b. Jan. 11, 1756	2	27
[Dorcas], Mrs., of Woodstock, m. Francis CHAFFEE, of Ashford, Oct. 6, 1767, in Woodstock, by Rev. Abiel Lenard	4	8
Dwight P., d. Sept. 22 1847, ae 7 m. (sic)	5	128-9
Dwight Preston, s. Alfred, farmer, ae 39, & Minerva, ae 41, b. Sept. 22, 1847	5	126-7
[Ebe]nezer, s. David & Prissilla, b. Oct.2, 1784 ; d. Aug. 18, 1786	3	128
Ebenezer, s. Abner & Judith, b. Nov. 29, 1796	4	21
Ebenezer, m. Hannah SMITH, b. of Ashford, Mar. 21, 1822, by Rev. W[illia]m Storrs	5	5
Ebenezer Justus, s. Fred[eric]k & Betsey, b. Aug. 25, 1815 ; d. Jan.27, 1819	4	254
Eleheu, s. Josiah & Elesebeth, b. May 6, 1777	3	18
Elihu, m. Al[i]ce READ, Aug. 31, 1806	4	100
Elihu, m. Else PROUD, Aug. 31, 1806	6	61
Elihu, s. Elihu & Al[i]ce, b. Aug. 5 1810	4	100
Elihu, s. Elihu & Alse, b. Aug. 5, 1810	6	61
Eliza D., m. George BAKER, b. of Ashford, May 6, 1832, by Rev. David Bennett	5	47
Elisabeth, d. David & Martha, b. Apr. 11, 1753	2	27
Elisabeth, d. Josiah & Elisabeth, b. July 29, 1762	3	18
Elisabeth, d. Fridrick & Elisabeth, b. Sept. 16, 1790	4	254
Elisabeth, d. Jonathan, Jr. & Elisabeth, [b.] Oct. 28, 1803	4	245
Elisabeth, w. Frederick, d. Nov. 19, 1806	4	254
Elizabeth, m. Sylvanus SHI[R]TLEFF, Mar. 4, 1813	6	60
Else Ann, d. Elihu & Alse, b. Sept. 2, 1815	6	61
Else, see also Alse		

CHAFFEE, CHAFFE, (cont.)	Vol.	Page
Emory, s. Elihu & Alse, b. Apr. 30, 1818	6	61
Ephraim, s. Josiah & Elisabeth, b. May 9, 1779 ; d. Sept. 25, 1779	3	18
Ephraim Pendleton, s. Amos & Harmany, b. Mar. 4, 1815	4	116
Erastus, s. Amos & Harmany, b. May 26, 1801 ; d. Aug. 27, 1802	4	116
Erastus, s. Amos & Eunice, b. Aug. 10, 1803	4	35
Est[h]er, d. David, Jr. & Pressilla, b. Nov. 5 1767	3	128
Esther, of Ashford, m. Theodore BISHOP, of Middletown, Dec. 27, 1835, by Amos Babcock	5	58
Eunice, d. W[illia]m & Anne, b. Feb. 28, 1763	3	104
Eunice, of Ashford, m. Albert SIMMONS, of Mansfield, Nov. 28, 1831, by Rev. David Bennett	5	45
Eunice, housekeeper, d. Oct. 9, 1849, ae 77	5	144-5
Experan[c]e, d. Atherton & Abigail, b. Apr. 2, 1745	1	75
Fydelia, d. Josiah & Elisabeth, b. Mar. 16, 1760	3	18
Fidelia, d. Josiah, Jr. & Joanna, b. Feb. 14, 1791	4	257
Francis, of Ashford, m. Mrs. [Dorcas] [CH]AFFEE, of Woodstock, Oct. 6, 1767, in Woodstock, by Rev. Abiel Le[o]nard	4	8
Frances Green, s. Benj[amin], b. Apr. 6, 1745	1	74
[Fra]ncis Green, d. July 3, 1786	4	8
Fred[e]rick, s. Josiah & Elizabeth, b. Mar. 6, 1767	3	18
Fred[e]rick, m. Elisabeth KNOWLTON, Mar. 6, 1788	4	254
Fred[e]rick, s. Fred[e]rick & Elisabeth, b. Jan. 7, 1789	4	254
Frederick, Jr., m. Catherine Spring KNOWLTON, June 12, 1814	6	9
Frederick, m. Betsey SHURTLIFF, Nov. 13, 1814	4	254
Gurdon, s. Amos & Harmany, b. Feb. 14, 1799 ; d. July 1, 1799	4	116
Gurdon Amos, s. Amos, Jr. & Mary, b. May 10, 1837	6	84
Guy, of Onondaga, N.Y., m. Almira CHAPMAN, of Ashford, Sept. 22, 1836, by Alvan Underwood	5	61
Hannah, d. Jonathan & Abiga[i]l, b. Nov. 28, 1733	1	20
Hannah, w. Benj[ami]n, d. Jan. 18, 1739/40	1	74
Hannah, d. Benj[ami]n & Peseala, b. Jan. 16, 1740/41 ; d. the 26th of the same month	1	74
Hannah, d. Abner & Judith, b. Nov. 30, 1792	4	21
Hannah, d. Fred[e]rick & Elisabeth, b. June 19, 1798	4	254
Hannah, 3rd, of Ashford, m. Lucius ELDREDGE, of Willington, Jan. 21, 1824, by Rev. William Storrs	5	12
Hannah, of Ashford, m. Elijah ELDRIDGE, Jr. of Willington, Nov. 22, 1837, by Amos Babcock	5	67
Hannah E., d. Reuben & Hannah, b. Apr. 6, 1828	6	87
Harmony C., of Ashford, m. Zelotes P. HISCOCK, of Woodstock, July 15, 1844, by Rev. Cha[rle]s Hyde	5	90
Harmany Claudine, d. Amos & Harmany, b. Aug. 23, 1817	4	116
Harmony Levina, d. W[illia]m F.& Mary Ann, b. Mar. 26,1841	6	95

	Vol.	Page
CHAFFEE, CHAFFE, (cont.)		
Harriet Maria, d. W[illia]m F. & Mary Ann, b. June 3, 1842	6	95
Hiram, s. Amos & Eunice, b. Dec. 6, 1805	4	35
Ida Issabella, d. Alfred, farmer, ae 40, & Almira, ae 29, b. Feb. 17, 1851	5	146-7
Israel d., 2nd, m. Ann BA[I]LEY, May 27, 1818	6	20
Israel Dimuck, s. Josiah & Elisabeth, b. July 7, 1772	3	18
Israel Dimick, s. Josiah, Jr. & Joanna, b. May 23, 1796	4	257
James, s. Jonathan & Lucy, b. May 21, 1777 ; d. May 14, 1778	4	107
Jemimah, d. Joseph & Hannah, b. Feb. 1, 1757	2	82
Jemima, m. Elijah CHAPMAN, Dec. 8, 1779	4	101
Joannah, d. David & Marthe, b. Jan. 3, 1749/50	2	27
Joanna, m. Joseph WHITON, Jr., Oct. 4, 1770	4	52
Joanna, d. Josiah & Joanna, b. Aug. 29, 1800	4	257
Joel, s. Josiah, Jr. & Joanna, b. Mar. 16, 1794	4	257
John, of Woodstock, m. Elizebath HAYWARD, of Ashford, Nov. 4, 1735, by Philip Eastman, J.P.	1	45
John H., s. Reuben & Hannah, b. Feb. 11, 1818	6	87
Jonathan, m. Abigail LYON, June 1, 1727, by Rev. James Hale	A	11
Jonathan, s. Jonathan & Abigail, b. Apr. 21, 1728 ; d. same day	1	20
Jonathan, s. Jonathan & Abiga[i]l, b. May 11, 1746	1	20
Jonathan, s. Willian & Anne, b. Feb. 11, 1765	3	104
Jonathan, m. Lucy ALLEN, May 1, 1776	4	107
Jonathan, s. Jonathan & Lucy, b. Nov. 26, 1780	4	107
Jonathan, d. Feb. 9, 1785	1	43
Jonathan, m. Salla FARNAM, Nov. 26, 1789	4	258
Jonathan, Jr., m. Elisabeth JAMES, Nov. 4, 1802	4	245
Jose, s. Jonathan & Salla, b. May 30, 1791	4	258
Joseph, s. Joseph & Hannah, b. May 31, 1759	2	82
Josiah, s. Jonathan & Abigail, b. Feb. 10, 1728/9	1	20
[Jos]iah, m. Elesabeth [DIM]MOCK, [Ap]ril 11, 1760	1	108
Josiah, s. Josiah & Elisabeth, b. Apr. 26, 1766	3	18
Josiah, Jr., m. Joanna PARKER, Mar. 26, 1789	4	257
Josiah, d. Apr. 24, 1800, in the 72nd y. of his age	3	18
Josiah, s. Josiah & Joanna, b. Nov. 9, 1805	4	257
Juliaette, d. W[illia]m F. & Mary Ann, b. Sept. 12, 1843	6	95
Laura W., m. Simeon DEAN, b. of Eastford, Nov. 17, 1846, by Francis Williams	5	99
Letetia Ann, d. Israel D., 2d, & Ann, b. Feb. 23, 1821	6	20
Lois, d. David, Jr. & Pressilla, b. Jan. 16, 1765	3	128
Louis, d. Abner & Judith, b. Sept. 24, 1798	4	21
Lois, of Ashford, m. Phillip CORBIN, of Union, Nov. 30, 1820, by W[illia]m Storrs	5	1
Luis, of Ashford, m. Philip CORBIN, of Union, Nov. 30, 1820, by W[illia]m Storrs	6	26
Lucy Emily, d. Albigence & Lucy, b. Jan. 28, 1812	6	1
Marg[a]rat, d. Artherton & Abigail, b. Apr. 18, 175[ ] ; d. Mar. 17, 1755	1	96

CHAFFEE, CHAFFE, (cont.)	Vol.	Page
Mariette, see under Maryette		
Martha, m. Job TYLER, Oct. 6, 1757	3	8
[Mar]tha, d. Sept. 20, 1790	3	128
Martha Susan, d. Amos, Jr. & Mary, b. June 22, 1839	6	84
Mary, d. Atherton & Abiga[i]l, b. Feb. 15, 1739/40	1	75
Mary Jane, d. Amos, Jr. b. July 27, 1835	6	84
Maryette, d. Ebenezer & Hannah, b. Dec. 9, 1822	6	45
Minerva, housewife, d. Nov. 8, 1848, ae 40	5	136-7
Molley, d. Jonathan & Lucy, b. Feb. 25, 1779	4	107
Nancy Carpenter, d. Fred[e]rick & Elisabeth, b. Feb. 25, 1796	4	254
Numan, s. Josiah & Joanna, b. May 3, 1802	4	257
Origin W., s. Reuben & Hannah, b. Jan. 22, 1825	6	87
Orran, s. Benja[min] & Rebec[c]ah, b. Sept. 22, 1793	4	273
Orvil Sidney, s. Frederick, Jr. & Catharine, b. June 13, 1815	6	9
Percey, d. Ebenezer & Presillah, b. Nov. 10, 1778	3	110
Percey, d. Jonathan & Lucy, b. July 29, 1782	4	107
Philo, s. Ebenezer & Hannah, b. Aug. 5, 1826	6	45
Philo, m. Mary A.H. CADY, b. of Ashford, Sept. 10, 1851, by Rev. P. Mathewson	5	107
Prissilla, w. Benjamin, d. Sept. 6, 1768	3	64
Prissilla, w. David, d. May 13, 1814	3	128
Rebeckah, d. Joseph & Hannah, b. Aug. 4, 1749	2	82
R[e]uben, s. Jonathan & Lucy, b. Mar. 5 1784	4	107
Reuben H., s. Reuben & Hannah, b. Aug. 10, 1830	6	87
Rosette Jane, d. Frederick & Betsey, b. Oct. 31, 1818	4	254
Sarah, d. Joseph & Hannah, b. Sept. 10, 175[ ]	2	82
Sarah, d. David & Martha, b. July 10, 1763	2	27
Semantha, d. Amos & Eunice, b. Jan. 31, 1808	4	35
Sophronia, d. Amos & Eunice, b. Sept. 26, 1799 ; d. June 11, 1801	4	35
Squir[e], s. Benj[amin] & Persela, b. July 18, 1747* (*Entry crossed out	1	74
Squire, s. Atherton & Abigail, b. July 18, 1747	1	75
Susan[n]ah, d. Jonathan & Abigaill, b. Sept. 10, 1738	1	20
Susannah, d. Josiah & Elisabeth, b. May 19, 1792	3	18
Susanna, d. Fred[e]rick & Elisabeth, b. June 26, 1792	4	254
Susanna, 2d, of Ashford, m. Ephraim WYLLYS, of Manchester, [Mar.] 12, [1840], by Daniel Knowlton, J.P.	5	73
Tabitha, d Elihu & Alse, b. Apr. 10, 1813	6	61
Thomas, s. Jonathan & Abigaill, b. Apr. 8, 1731	1	20
Thomas, s. Joseph & Hannah, b. July 3, 1754	2	82
Tryphena, d. William & Anne, b. Mar. 16, 1767	3	104
Will[ia]m, s. Jonathan & Hannah, b. July 30, 1736	1	20
William, m. Anne BIBBINS, July 21, 1762	3	104
William, d. June 5, 1771	3	104
William, s. Josiah & Elesabath b. Oct. 27, 1775 ; d. Aug. 21, 1776	3	18
William, s. Abner & Judith, b. Apr. 21, 1801	4	21

	Vol.	Page
CHAFFEE, CHAFFE, (cont.)		
William F., m. Mary Ann **PARKER,** b. of		
Ashford, May 12, 1840, by Rev. Alvan. Underwood	5	74
William Fox, s. Amos & Harmany, b. Apr. 20, 1809	4	116
----cis, s. Francis & Dorcas, b. Aug. 18, 1776	4	8
----in, s. Francis Green & Dorcas, b. Apr. 20, 1786	4	8
-----, d. Francis & Dorcas, b. Nov. 17, 1767	4	8
-----, s. Francies & Dorcas, b. June 28, 1771	4	8
-----, s. Francies & Dorcas, b. June 15, 1773	4	8
-----, s. David, Jr. & Pressilla, b. June 2, 1774	3	128
-----, d. Francies & Dorcas, b. Sept. 29, 1779	4	8
----aces, d. Francis & Dorcas, b. Mar. 18, 1782	4	8
----aniel, s. David & Prissilla, b. Nov. 10, 17[ ] Nov. 15,		
1776	3	128
---rah, d. David & Prissilla, b. May [ ]	3	128
---niel, s. David & Prissilla, b. Oct. 10, [ ]	3	128
------* (Probably the marriagae of a woman, Entry missing)	4	98
CHAMBERLAIN, CHAMBERLIN, Benjamin, of Woodstock, m.		
Almira **BUGBEE,** of Ashford, Aug. 26, 1827, by Rev.		
George B. Atwell, of Woodstock	5	28
Betsey, m. John **PIKE,** June 28, 1804	4	287
Lucius, of Mansfield, m. Rosette **BOSWORTH,** of Ashford,		
Nov. 19, 1840, by Rev. David Bennett	5	76
Sarah, m. John **TOMSEN,** Oct. 4, 1770	4	65
Wells, m. Philena **TAFT,** b. of Ashford, [Feb.] 17, [1840]. by		
Rev. Reuben Torrey, Eastford	5	73
CHANA, [see under **CHENEY**]		
CHANDLER, CHANDLAR, , Alice, see under Ellice and Ellis		
Benj[ami]n, s. Stephen & Mary, b. May 31, 1785	3	3
Daniel, m. Vilote **BURNHAM,** Dec. 24, 1754, by Joseph		
Pitken, Esq.	1	87
Ellis, w. Steven, d. Jan. 17, 1782	3	3
Ellice, d. Stephen & Sarah, b. Nov. 27, 1791	3	3
Hannah, d. Josiah & Freelove, b. July 23, 1751	2	74
James, s. Stephen & Ellis, b. July 25, 1763	3	3
Joel, s. Stephen & Ellis, b. Mar. 10, 1765	3	3
Josiah, m. Freelove **CARPENTER,** Nov. 5, 1747	2	74
Lois, d. Steven & Sarah, b. Oct. 18, 1797	3	12
Mary, m. Joseph **SNOW,** Jr., Nov. 18, 1762	3	74
Mary, w. Stephen, d. Mar. 10, 1787	3	3
Mary, m. Edmund **SPALDING,** Sept. 20, 1809	4	103
Nathan, s. Josiah & Freelove, b. Nov. 16, 1748 ; d. Dec. 17,		
1748	2	74
R[e]uben, s. Joseph, d. May 7, 1751	2	24
Stephen, m. Mary **PRESTON,**, June [ ], 1784	3	3
Stephen, m. Sarah **ROGERS,** July 3, 1790	3	3
Stevens, s. Stevens & Ellis, b. Nov. 12, 1781	3	3
Thankfull, m. [Joseph **BOW]EN,** Oct. 28, 1764	4	98
Thomas, of Pomfret, m. Lucinda **WARREN,** of Ashford, Dec.		

CHAPMAN, (cont.)	Vol.	Page
Ashford, Apr. 8, 1850, in Williamantic, by Rev.		
Henry Branley	5	105
CHAPMAN, Clarasena, d. Jacob & Ellinah, b. May 26, 1777	3	121
Coziah, see under Keziah		
Cynth[i]a, d. Elijah & Esther, b. Mar. 21, 1804	4	101
Cynthia, m. William MATHEWS, Sept. 17, 1827, by Amasa		
Lyon, J. P.	5	28
Danford, m. Sally BABAT, July 24, 1825, by Henry Curtis,		
Elder	5	19
David, s. Jonathan & Dorcas, b. Sept. 13, 1751	2	67
David, m. Sarah CHUBB, Mar. 4, 1772	4	51
David, s. David & Sarah, b. Feb. 21, 1782	4	51
David, m. Sarah PECK(?), Aug. 3, 1793	4	51
Deliverence, d. Benj[ami]n & Lois, b. Dec. 1, 1772	4	64
Diana, d. Thomas, Jr. & Marion, b. July 17, 1818	6	23
Dillee, d. Elijah & Esther, b. Nov. 16, 1798	4	101
Ditta*, m. Stephen WOOD, b. of Ashford, Apr. 11, 1824, by		
Edward Keyes, J. P. (*Dilla?)	5	13
Dorcas, d. Jonathan & Dorcas, b. Mar. 30, 1763 ; d. June 14,		
1766	2	67
Darcus, d. David & Sarah, b. Sept. 9, 1772	4	51
Ebenezer, s. Throop & Susannah, b. Nov. 27, 1763	3	11
Ebenezer, s. David & Sarah, b. Dec. 9, 1786	4	51
Eli, [twin with Levi], s. Elijah & Esther, b. Apr. 26, 1796	4	101
Elias, [s. Thomas & Mary], b. May 26, 1749	1	52
Elias, m. Saras FLINT, Jan. 31, 1771	4	45
Elias, m. Elesabeth SLATE, Feb. 12, 1778	4	62
Elias, s. Elias & Elisabeth, b. Nov. 2, 1788	4	62
Elias, Jr., m. Abibatena OLNEY, Oct. 19, 1814	6	35
Elijah, s. Jonathan, & Dorcas, b. Dec. 2, 1753	2	67
Elijah, m. Jemima CHAFFEE, Dec. 8, 1779	4	101
Elijah, s. Jonathan, Jr. & Mary, b. May 9, 1788	4	46
Elijah, m. Esther GINNINGS, Mar. 25, 1793	4	101
Elijah, d. May 31, 1804	4	101
Elijah, s. Stephen, 2d, & Roxey, b. May 8, 1805	4	69
Elisha, s. Elias & Elisabeth, b. May 17, 1793	4	62
Elisha, s. Elias, Jr. & Abibatena, b. Oct. 8, 1819	6	35
Elizabeth, m. Gould LYON, Apr. 12, 1726	A	10
Elisabeth, d. Elias & Elisabeth, b. Nov. 16, 1778	4	62
Elisabeth, d. Jacob & Ellinah, b. Apr. 25, 1780	3	121
Elisabeth, m. Stephen ELDRIDGE, Jan. 10, 1804	4	62
Elizabeth, d. Elias, Jr. & Abibatena, b. Oct. 3, 1817	6	35
Emeline P., of Ashford, m. John HALL, Jr., of Holland,		
Mass., Aug. 13, 1848, by Rev. Ezekiel Skinner	5	103
Emma F., m. Hiram THOMAS, Jan. 23, 1844, by Francis		
Williams, Eastford	5	87
Esther, d. Throop & Susannah, b. July 13, 1766	3	11
Esther, d. Elijah & Jemima, b. July 11, 1781	4	101

	Vol.	Page
CHAPMAN (cont.)		
Esther had s. Stephen Gennins Backus, b.June 17, 1811	4	101
Esther, d. Nov. 7, 1840	4	101
Eunice, d. Joseph & Keziah, b. June 2, 1780	4	63
Eveline, m. Daniel **SHERMAN**, b. of Ashford, Jan. 13, 1837,		
by Rev. Stephen Cushing	5	65
Ezekiel, s. Elias & Elisabeth, b. Oct. 9, 1785	4	62
Fielder, s. Jonathan, Jr. & Mary, b. Mar. 31, 1790	4	46
George W., s. Danford & Sally, b. Dec. 4, 1825	6	101
Gideon F., s. Thomas & Marion, b. Apr. 18, 1823	6	23
Gideon F., m. Almira C. **CHAPMAN**, b. of Ashford, Oct. 5,		
1845, by Rev. Renssalear O. Putney, North Ashford	5	95
Hannah, m. Benj[ami]n **CHAFFE[E]**, Nov. 2, 1738	1	38
Hannah, m. Benj[ami]n **CHAF[F]E[E]**, Nov. 2, 1738	1	74
Hannah, d. Jonathan & Dorcas, b. Sept. 2, 1768	2	67
Hannah, d. Joseph & Keziah, b. Oct. 20, 1791	4	63
Hannah, d. Luther & Betsey, b. Aug. 1, 1807	4	27
Hannah, of Ashford, m. Benjamin C. **BOYNTON**, of East		
Windsor, Apr. 8, 1848, by Rev. D. Bancroft	5	102
Harriet C., m. Royal **CHAPMAN**, b. of Ashford, Nov. 5, 1848,		
by Rev. Charles Peabody	5	103
Harvey, s. Benj[ami]n, Jr. & El[e]aner, b. Jan. 14, 1809	4	77
Hulde, d. Will[ia]m & Abigail, b. Jan.1, 1724/5	A	8
Huldah, d. Jonathan, Jr. & Mary, b. Apr. 19, 1772	4	46
Huldah, d. Jonathan, Jr. [& Mary], d. Dec. 3, 1786	4	46
Huldah, d. Jonathan & Dorcas, b. Apr. 1, [ ]* (*Entry		
scratched out)	2	68
Irena, [twin with Triphene], d. Elijah & Esther, b. Jan. 11, 1801	4	101
Irene, m. Jared **PARISH**, b. of Ashford, June 2, 1822, by Rev.		
Philo Judson	5	6
Jacob, s. John & Phenelephe, b. Sept. 7, 1739	1	61
Jacob, m. Ellinah **KENDAL**, Mar. 17, 1762	3	121
Jacob, Jr., m. Phebe **SLADE**, Apr. 16, 1805	4	272
James, s. Jonathan & Dorcas, b. Oct. 28, 1756; d Dec. 12, 1760	2	67
James, s. Jonathan, Jr. & Mary, b. Jan. 19, 1774	4	46
James, m. Emily **MOORE**, b. of Ashford, Jan. 1, 1829, by		
Rev. Ezekiel Skinner	5	32
Jarvis, m. Almira **ALLEN**, Mar. 13, 1825, by Amos Babcock,		
Elder Intention published	5	18
Jedido, of Tolland, m. Elijah **GRIGGS** of Abington, Conn.,		
[Sept.] 8, [1831], by Reuben Torrey, Eastford	5	44
Jemima, w. Elijah, d. Dec. 7, 1792	4	101
John, m. Pheneliphe **BUGBE**, Apr. 15, 1716 (sic), by Rev. Mr.		
James Hale	1	61
John, d. Jan. 23, 1731/2	1	9
John, s. John & Phenelephe, b. Oct. 8, 1737	1	61
John, m. Sibbel **DIMMOCK**, May 9, 1759	3	120
John, s. Jonathan & Dorcas, b. Apr. 10, 1766	2	67

CHAPMAN, (cont.)	Vol.	Page
John,, of Littlevalley, N. Y., m. Hannah		
BUGBEE, of Ashford, Apr. 26, 1825, by Amos Babcock,		
Elder, Intention published	5	19
Jonathan, m. Dorcas CHUB[B], Jan. 28, 1747/8	2	67
Jonathan, s. Jonathan & Dorcus, b. Mar. 28, 1749	2	67
Jonathan, Jr., m. Mary HOAR, Sept. 5, 1771	4	46
Jonathan, s. Jonathan, Jr. & Mary, [b.] Sept. 26, 1776	4	46
Jonathan, d. Jan. 7, 1802	2	68
Joseph, [s. Thomas & Mary], b. May 9, 1747	1	52
Joseph, s. Joseph & Keziah, b. May 26, 1771	4	63
Coziah Ford, d. Joseph & Keziah, b. Apr. 23, 1774	4	63
Kyal(?), s. Elias & Elisabeth, b. July 4, 1781 (Thyal?)	4	62
Levi, s. R[e]uben & Rhoda, b. June 18, 1784	4	242
Levi, [twin with Eli], s. Elijah & Esther b. Apr. 26, 1796 ; d. Mar. 15, 1798	4	101
Lois, d. David & Sarah, b. Jan. 3, 1777	4	51
Lois, d. Benjamin & Lois, b. Dec. 12, 1778	4	64
Lois, m. Freeman SNOW, May 18, 1797	4	48
Lois M., of Ashford, m. Jesse T. HALL, of Stafford, Apr. 3, 1850, By Rev. Ezekiel Skinner	5	105
Lois S., of Ashford, m. John L. KEEZER, of Union, Oct. 11, 1835, by Rev. Alvan Underwood, Westford	5	57
Lois Susan, d. Thomas, Jr. & Marion, b. Nov. 4, 1815	6	23
Louiza, d. Elias, Jr. & Abibatena, b. June 23, 1815	6	35
Loiza, m. Amos C. CHAFFEE, Oct. 4, 1836, by Alvan Underwood	5	61
Lovina, d. Benjamin & Lois, b. Oct. 30, 1786	4	64
Lucinde, d. Jon[a]th[an], Jr. & Mary, b. May 12, 1792	4	46
Lucinde, m. Samuel WHITNEY, Jr., Jan. 21, 1816	6	35
Luis, s. Elijah & Esther, b. June 16, 1794	4	101
Luther, s. Elijah & Jemima, b. Feb. 14, 1783	4	101
Luther, m. Betsey LEOPARD, Aug, 8, 1805	4	27
Lydia, d. Thomas, Jr. & Mary, b. Apr. 19, 1773	4	63
Lydia, d. Benj[ami]n & Lois, b. Oct. 28, 1784	4	64
Marriette, miller, d. Apr. 26, 1848, ae 21	5	130-1
Maryette, d. Aug. 30, 1848, ae 6 wk.	5	138-9
Martha, d. Sept. 7, 1716	1	61
Martha, [d. Thomas & Mary], b. July 2, 1735	1	52
Martha, m. Jedediah BLANCHER, Nov. 13, 1754	1	92
Martha, m. Jedediah BLANCHER, Nov. 13, 1754	1	93
Martha, d. Danford & Sally, b. Apr. 16, 1842	6	101
Mary, m. Isaac KENDALL, Jr. Mar. 15, 1731/2, by Mr. James Hale	1	6
Mary, [d. Thomas & Mary], b. Nov. 26, 1732	1	52
Mary, d. John & Pheneliphe, b. Feb. 26, 1749/50	1	61
Mary, d. Jacob & Ellinah, b. June 1, 1774	3	121
Mary, d. Jonathan, Jr. & Mary, b. Dec. 26, 1778	4	46
Mary, d. Benjamin & Lois, b. Dec. 29, 1782	4	64

CHAPMAN, (cont.)	Vol.	Page
Marvette, see under Mariette		
Mercy, d. Trupe & Susan[n]ah, b. Jan. 15, 1762	3	11
Nancy J., d. Thomas & Maria, b. July 2, 1827	6	23
Olive, m. Danforth HAYWARD, Sept. 22, 1811	6	31
Olover, s. Jonathan, Jr. & Mary, b. Nov. 6, 1783	4	46
Otis, s. Jacob, Jr. & Phebe, b. Jan. 8, 1806	4	272
Parcy, d. Jonathan, Jr. & Mary, b. Feb. 28, 1781	4	46
Percy, d. Tho[ma[s, 3rd & Prissilla, b. Sept. 27, 1784	4	252
Phenelephe, d. Sept. 7, 1716	1	61
Penelope, d. John & Penelope, b. Jan. 15, 1742/3	1	61
Philinda, m. Jonathan WEEKES, Jr., Feb. 24, 1828, by Amasa Lyon, J. P.	5	30
Phinehas, s. Elias & Sarah, b. Apr. 14, 1773	4	62
Priscilla L., of Ashford, m. John B. HATCH, of Union, [Sept.] 6, [1835], by Dexter Munger	5	57
Rachel, d. David & Sarah, b. Aug. 2, 1784	4	51
R[e]ubin, s. Jonathan & Dorcas, b. Mar. 20, 1761	2	67
Reuben, m. Rhoda PECK, Nov. 21, 1782	4	242
Reuben, s. Elijah & Jemima, b. Nov. 6, 1792	4	101
Reubin, s. Stephen, 2d, & Roxey, b. Dec. 22, 1806	4	69
R[e]ubin, s. Amos & Syball, b. Oct, 15, 1808	6	11
Rossel, s. Thom[ma]s, 3rd, & Prissilla, b. June 10, 1778	4	252
Royal, m. Harriet C. CHAPMAN, b. of Ashford, Nov, 5, 1848, by Rev. Charles Peabody	5	103
Sebra, d. Jacob & Ellinah, b. June 12, 1763	3	121
Sebra, see also Ceber		
Sabrina, of Ashford, m. Hiram BISHOP, of Woodstock, [ ], by Rev. Luke Wood	5	41
Sally Maria, d. Shubael, Jr. & Sally, b. Aug, 20, 1826	6	57
Salome M., of Ashford, m. Dr. Silas T. LINDSEY, of Union, Nov. 4, 1851, by Rev. Samuel J. Curtis, of Union	5	107
Samuel, s. Tho[ma]s, 3rd, & Prissilla, b. June 28, 1780	4	252
Samuel, farmer, b. Willington, res. Ashford, d. July [ ], 1851, ae 62	5	150-1
Sarah, d. John & Penelepe, b. Feb. 23, 1747/8	1	61
Sarah, d. David & Sarah, b. Nov. 16, 1774	4	51
Sarah, d. Joseph & Keziah, b. May 10, 1776	4	63
Sarah, w. Elias, d. Aug. 26, 1777	4	62
Sarah, w. David, d. May 22, 1793	4	51
Sarah, d. Danford & Sally, b. Dec. 20, 1829	6	101
Sarah, housekeeper, d. Oct. 25, 1847, ae 61	5	130-1
Sarah, ae 18, of Ashford, m. Samuel YOUNG, farmer, ae 27, of Stafford, Dec. 13, 1847, by Ezekiel Skinner	5	128-9
Sarah, of Ashford, m. Samuel YOUNG, of Stafford, Dec. 19, 1847, by Rev. Ezekiel Skinner	5	102
Saslenda, d. Jacob & Ellinah, b. Apr. 24, 1768	3	121
Servial, m. Amos KENDAL, Jan. 29, 1772 ; d. Aug. 11, 1804	4	69
Servial, see also Zerviah		

CHAPMAN, (cont.)	Vol.	Page
Shubael, s. Benj[ami]n & Lois, b. Nov. 1, 1775	4	64
Shubael, m. Phebe BUFFINGTON, Aug. 20, 1800	4	113
Shubael, s. Shubael & Phebe, b. Feb. 2, 1801	4	113
Smith, s. Jonathan, Jr. & Mary, b. Feb. 21, 1786	4	46
Stephen, s. Jacob & Ellinah, b. Oct. 5, 1765	3	121
Stephen, 2d, m. Roxey COGSHELL, Feb. 24, 1805	4	69
Stephen, Jr., m. Mariah SLADE, b. of Ashford, Sept. 16, 1824,		
by John Nichols	5	15
Stephen, farmer, d. Feb. 5, 1848, ae 82	5	130-1
Stephen, farmer, d. Mar. 12, 1850, ae 46	5	144-5
Susan A., m. Edwin P. LEWIS, Nov. 5, 1848, by Rev. Charles		
Peabody	5	103
Sybbel, [d. Thomas & Mary], b. Aug. 4, 1744	1	52
Sybel, m. Joseph BARNEY, Jr. Dec. 5, 1764	4	24
Thiah, d. Elias & Sarah, b. May 8, 1771	4	45
Thyah, d. Elias & Sarah, b. May 8, 1771	4	62
Thomas, m. Mary THROOP, Jan. 26, 1729, by Rev. Mr.		
Solomon Williams	1	52
Tho[ma]s, [s. Thomas & Mary], b. Jan. 3, 1731	1	52
Thomas, s. Elias & Sarah, b. May 7, 1775	4	62
Tho[ma]s, 3rd, m. Prissilla LEACH, Dec. 18, 1777	4	252
Thomas, s. Tho[ma[s, 3rd, & Prissilla, b. Dec. 1, 1791	4	252
Thomas, d. Mar. 2, 1793	1	52
Thomas, s. Amos & Syball, b. Jan. 20, 1813	6	11
Thomas, Jr., m. Marian CARPENTER, Apr. 11, 1813	6	23
Throop, [s. Thomas & Mary], b. Mar. 25, 1739	1	52
Trupe, m. Susan[n]ah BARNEY, Mar. 29, 1759	3	11
Thyah, see under Thiah		
Thyal, see under Kyal		
Triphene, d. Reuben & Rhoda, b. Sept. 3, 1786	4	242
Triphene, [twin with Irena], d. Elijah & Esther, b. Jan. 11,1801	4	101
Tryphenia, of Ashford, m. Ephraim BROWN, of New Milford,		
Aug. 10, 1823, by Reuben Torrey, Eastford	5	10
Wealthy Jane, d. Danford & Sally, b. Dec. 31. 1838	6	101
Will[ia]m, s. John & Phenelephe, b. Mar. 22, 1740/41	1	61
Will[ia]m, [s. Thomas & Mary], b. Nov. 21, 1741	1	52
William, s. Trupe & Susannah, b. Apr. 10, 1760	3	11
William, s John & Sibble, b. Apr. 25, 1763	3	120
Zerviah, d. John & Penelepe, b. May 8, 1745	1	61
Zurviah, d. Tho[ma]s, 3rd, & Prissilla, b. Nov. 23, 1782	4	252
Zerviah, see also Servial		
Ziba, s. Luther & Betsey, b. Jan. 4, 1806	4	27
Zolinda, [d.] Amos & Syball, b. Feb. 25, 1810	6	11
--------, child of Stephen, farmer, ae 43, & Maria, ae 42, b. July		
19, 1848	5	128-9
CHASE, Rebeckah, m. Joseph GRIGGS, Nov. 17, 1774	4	74
CHEDLE, CHEDAIL, CHADLE, CHEDAL, CHEEDLE, Adah,		
d. Increas[e] & Anne, b. Apr. 3, 1775	3	56

	Vol.	Page
CHEDLE, CHEDAIL, CHADLE, CHEDAL, CHEEDLE, (cont.),		
Alvah, s. Increase & Anne, b. Jan. 23, 1763 ; d. Feb. 22, 1763	3	56
Alvah, s. Increas[e] & Anna, b. Apr. 13, 1764	3	56
Alvah, s. Increas[e], d. Mar. 17, 1766	3	56
Ann, d. George & Martha, b. Jan. 18, 1740/41	1	47
Anne, Increase & Anne, b. Aug. 24, 1761 ; d. Sept. 18, 1764	3	56
Asa, s. George & Martha, b. Oct. 6, 1734	1	47
Asa, m. Martha HADDICK, Nov. 5, 1760	3	109
Asa, s. Asa & Martha, b. Aug. 5, 1762	3	109
Avis, d. Increas[e] & Anne, b. Apr. 17, 1770	3	56
Benj[amin], s. George & Martha, b. Aug. 30, 1738	1	47
Cleve, d. Asa & Martha, b. Feb. 29, 1768	3	109
Elizebeth, d. George & Martha, b. Mar. 5, 1725/6	1	47
Elisabeth, d. Increase & Anna b. Dec. 31, 1759	1	109
George, m. Martha BURGE, Aug. 16, 1721, by James Hale	A	9
George, s. Increas[e] & Anna, b. May 17, 1768	3	56
Increas[e], s. George & Martha, b. Oct. 8, 1727	1	47
Increase, m. Anna (Illegible), July 22, 1759	1	109
Izet, d. Increas[e] & Anne, b. Feb. 4, 1766	3	56
Izet, d. Increas[e], d. Jan. 28, 1788	3	56
John, s. George & Martha, b. Aug. 26, 1732	1	47
John, m. Mary BOSWORTH, Nov. 5, 1761	3	58
John, s. John & Mary, b. July 6, 1762 ; d. July 16, 1762	3	58
John, s. John & Mary, b. July 25, 1763	3	58
John, m. Rachel ALLEN, May 11, 1768	3	58
John, s. Asa & Martha, b. May 26, 1771	3	109
Mary, [twin with William], d. George & Martha, b Apr. 5, 1743	1	47
Mary, w. John, d. Jan. 19, 1767	3	58
Mary, d. John & Rachel, b. Feb. 1, 1769	3	58
Polle, d. Increas[e] & Anne, b. May 29, 1777	3	56
Ruth, d. Asa & Martha, b. Apr. 24, 1765	3	109
Samuell Allen, s. Increas[e] & Anne, b. Sept. 18, 1772	3	56
Susannah, d. George & Martha, b. Apr. 8, 1730	1	47
Timothy Bosworth, s. John & Mary, b. June 4, 1765	3	58
William, [twin with Mary], s. George & Martha, b. Apr. 5, 1743	1	47
CHENEY,CHENY, CHANA, Abigail, w. Benj[ami]m, d. Sept. 20, 1790	4	14
Benj[ami]n, s. Will[ia]m & Ruth, b. June 20, 1744	1	76
Benjamin, m. Abigail PARRY, May 30, 1765	4	14
Benjamin, s. Benj[ami]n & Abigail, b. Sept, 12, 1777	4	14
Byall, [child of Benj[ami]n & Abigail], b. Aug. 10, 1773	4	14
Daniel, s. Benj[ami]n & Abigail, b. June 9, 1771	4	14
Danforth, s. Thomas & Mary, b. Oct. 29, 1794	4	72
Ebenezer, s. Will[ia]m & Ruth, b. May 23, 1740	1	76
Ebenezer, m. Prissillah LYON, Mar. 2, 1760	3	110
Ebenezer, s. Eben[eze]r & Presillah, b. Aug. 6, 1769	3	110

	Vol.	Page
CHENEY, CHENY, CHANA, (cont.)		
Elisabeth, [d. Benj[ami]n & Abigail] b. Aug. 27, 1775	4	14
Elizabeth, d. Will[ia]m & Ruth, b. Sept. 6, 1752	1	80
Hannah, d. Benj[ami]n & Abigail, b. Dec. 19,17.'3	4	14
Harray, s. Thomas & Meary, b. Mar. 30, 1793	4	72
Huldah, d. Benj[ami]n & Abigail, b. Sept. 9, 1767	4	14
John, s. William & Ruth, b. Mar. 14, 174[ ]	4	14
John, s. W[illia]m, d. Nov. 10, 1754	3	105
John, s. Ebenezer & Presillah, b. Aug. 11, 1772	3	110
John, s. Benj[ami]n & Abigail, b. Aug. 17, 1781	4	14
John, s. Thomas & Mary, b. Dec. 5, 1804	4	72
Jonathan Stowel, s. Thomas & Mary, b. Dec. 31, 1802	4	72
Joseph, s. Ebeneze r & Presillah, b. Oct. 11, 1774	3	110
Mary, Ebe[neze]r & Pressillah, b. Feb. 16, 1762	3	110
Mary, see also Mary **FELSHAW**	3	105
Mehitable, d. Benj[ami]n & Abigail, b. Sept. 26, 1765	4	14
Mehitibal, m. John **BOSWORTH**, Nov. 19, 1781	3	113
Nabba, d. Benj[ami]n & Abigail, b. May 17, 1779	4	14
Polley, d. Thomas & Mary, b. Apr. 1, 1800	4	72
Ruth, w. W[illia]m, d. Oct. 10, 1756	3	105
Ruth, d. Eben[eze]r & Presillah, b. Apr. 7, 1767	3	110
Ruth, d. Benj[ami]n & Abigail, b. July 31, 1788	4	14
Silence, s. Ebe[neze]r & Pressillah, b. Oct.9, 176 ; d. same day	3	110
Tho[ma]s, s. Will[ia]m & Ruth, b. July 1, 1742	1	76
Thomas, s. Benj[ami]n & Abigail, b. June 24, 1769	4	14
Thomas, m, Meary **STOWIEL**, Oct. 4, 1792	4	72
Thomas, s. Thomas & Mary, b. Sept. 12, 1796	4	72
Will[ia]m, m. Ruth **EASTMAN**, Mar. 14, 1738/9	1	76
William, s. William & Ruth, b. Apr. 17, 1747	3	105
William, m. Mehetable **CHUB[B]**, Feb. 1, 1757	3	105
William, s. Eben[eze]r & Presillah, b. Apr. 12, 1765	3	110
William, s. Ebenezer, b. Apr. 12, 1765 * (*Entry crossed out)	4	13
William, s. Benj[ami]n & Abigail, b. Feb. 17, 1785	4	14
W[illia]m E., of Manchester, m. Clarissa C. **PRESTON**, of		
East Ashford, May 13, 1835, by Rev. R. Torrey,		
Ashford, East	5	56
CHESTER, Harden H., m. Esther H. **WHALEY**, b. of		
Ashford, Mar. 30, 1841, by Rev. Cha[rle]s Hyde	5	78
Mary, of Ashford, m. Edward B. **WATERS**, of Providence, R.		
I. Oct. 6, 1847, by Charles Peabody	5	101
CHILD, CHILDS, Edwin S., of Woodstock, m. Juliaette		
RICHMOND, of Ashford, [Aug. 28, 1843,] by D.		
Bullard	5	85
Emily A., m. Uriah L. **CARPENTER**, b. of Eastford, Dec. 1,		
1846, by Francis Williams	5	99
Esther, m. Roswell **BURNAM**, Oct. 23, 1783	4	245
Isaac N. shoemaker, ae 25, b.Woodstock, res. Eastford, m.Sarah		
JOHNSON, ae 20, Jan. 1, 1848, by Francis Williams	5	128-9

	Vol.	Page
CHISON, David, m. Sally SNELL, b. of Ashford, Oct. 17, 1831, by Rev. Ezekiel Skinner	5	44
CHUBB, CHUB, COHUBB, Abigail, d. Benjamin & Mary, b. Sept. 10, 1756	2	75
Abigail, m. John BOWEN, July 12, 1781	4	234
Ann, d. William & Rachal, b. Dec. 26, 1756	2	53
Ann, had s. Rozzel b. Jan. 3, 1779	4	120
Ann, m. Benjamin FARNAM, Mar. 28, 1781	4	120
Benj[ami]n, s. Joseph & Mehetable, b. Oct, 29, 1721	A	9
Benjamin, [s. Joseph & Meheteball], b. Oct. 29, 1721	1	36
Benjamin, m. Mary WOODCOCK, Nov. 15, 1748, by Mr. John Bass	2	75
Benjamin, s. Benjamin & Mary, b. June 18, 1750	2	75
Benjamin, m. Hannah GENINGS, Jan. 28, 1773	4	65
Caleb, s. Joseph & Mehetable, b. Sept. 6, 1715	A	2
Caleb, s. Joseph & Meheteball, b. Sept. 6, 1715	1	36
Caleb, m. Leah SQUIRE, June 20, 1743, by Sqr, Grosvener	2	62
Caleb, d. Mar. 18, 1749	2	62
David, s. Will[ia]m & Rachel, b. Sept. 26, 1746 ; d. Jan. 20, 1748/9	2	53
David, s. Benjamin & Mary, b. Jan. 17, 1760	1	108
Dorkas, [d. Joseph & Meheteball], b. Aug. 16, 1731	1	36
Dorcas, m. Jonathan CHAPMAN Jan. 28, 1747/8	2	67
Ezekiel, s. Joseph & Mehetable, b. Aug. 10, 1726	A	5
Ezekiel, [s. Joseph & Meheteball], b. Aug. 11, 1726	1	36
Ezek[i]el, d. Jan. 12, 1753	1	80
Feeba, see under Phebe		
Hannah, d. Joseph & Mehetable, b. Sept. 6, 1725	A	9
Hannah, [d. Joseph & Meheteball], b. Sept. 6, 1725	1	36
Hannah, d. William & Rachel, b. May 4, 1749	2	53
Hannah, m. Jonathan SNOW, Mar. 30, 1773	4	58
Harmona, d. William & Rachal, b. Jan. 19, 1765	2	53
Joseph, s. Joseph & Mehetable, b. Dec. 28, 1719	A	9
Joseph, [s. Joseph & Meheteball], b. Dec. 28, 1719	1	36
Joseph, d. Jan. 20, 1731/2, ae 41 y.	1	36
Joseph, m. Mehetebel LYON, Apr. 10, 1749, by Mr. Bass	2	27
Joseph, s. Benj[ami]n & Mary, b. Mar. 9, 1754	2	75
Joseph, d. May 24, 175(?)	1	81
Mehetebel, m. David SMITH, Aug. 28, 1733, by Sqr. Eastman, J. P.	1	36
Mehetable, m. William CHENEY, Feb. 1, 1757	3	105
Feeba, d. William & Mary, b. July 16, 1754	2	75
Presillah, d. Joseph & Mehitable, b. July 4, 1718	A	4
Persillah, [d. Joseph & Meheteball], b. July 4, 1718	1	36
Persecellah, d. Caleb & Leah, b. Apr. 3, 1747	2	62
Prissilla, m. Nathaniel HAYWARD, Nov. 13, 1777	3	14
Rachel, [twin with Sarah], d. William & Rachel, b. Oct. 20, 1751	2	53

CHUBB, CHUB, COHUBB, (cont.)	Vol.	Page
Rozzel, s. Ann, b. Jan. 3, 1779	4	120
Sarah, [d. Joseph & Meheteball], b. July 24, 1729	1	36
Sarah, [twin with Rachel], d. William & Rachel, b. Oct. 20, 1751	2	53
Sarah, m. David **CHAPMAN**, Mar. 4, 1772	4	51
William, s. Joseph & Mehetable, b. Nov. 26, 1723	A	9
William, [s. Joseph & Meheteball], b. Nov. 26, 1723	1	36
Will[ia]m, m. Rachel **SQUIRE**, Nov. 13, 1745, by Rev. Mr. Bass	2	53
William, s. William & Rachal, b. Apr. 23, 1761	2	53
CHURCH, Emily A., d. John, farmer, ae 46, & Lucretia, ae 44, b. [ ], 1851	5	146-7
[E]unis, m. Isa[a]ce **ABBE**, b. of Ashford, Apr. 5, 1753, by Eb[eneze]r Wales, J. P.	1	82
--------, st. b. d. John, farmer, ae 44, & Lucretia, ae 42, b. Mar. 11, 1849	5	132-3
CLARK, CLARKE, CLERK, Abel, s. John & Phebe, b. Sept. 6, 1788	4	109
Abel, s. John, d. May 27, 1812	4	109
Abel, s. Oliver & Betsey, b. Apr. 2, 1819	6	14
Abigail, m. Josias **BYLES**, Nov. 18, 1779	4	112
Abigail, d. John & Phebe, b. Dec. 25, 1790 ; d. May 7, 1809	4	109
Alanson, s. Eli & Mary, b. Aug. 19, 1822	6	48
Alfred, s. Lemuel & Elizabeth, b. Aug. 30, 1780	4	70
Almira, d. Lemuel & Elisabeth, b. May 26, 1800	4	70
Almira, m. Henry **THOMAS** b. of Ashford, Mar. 18, 1844, by L. W. Blood	5	88
Ama L., of Chaplin, m. Ezra W. **SMITH**, of Ashford, Feb. 28, 1843, by F. Williams, Intention published	5	84
Amasa, of Hampton, m. Hannah **CLARK**, of Ashford, Dec. 3, 1834, by Dexter Bullard	5	55
Andrew, s. Eli & Mary, b. Aug. 4, 1834	6	48
Andrew Judson, s. Dyer & Lucinda, b. Apr. 11, 1809	4	89
Anna, d. John & Phebe, b. Jan. 23, 1786 ; d. Aug. 11, 1805	4	109
Asa, B., of Ithica, N. Y., m. Eliza **BOLLES**, of Ashford, Oct. 17, 1837, by Rev. Reuben Torrey, Eastford	5	66
Asa Bolles, s. David, & Esther, b. Feb. 11, 1810	4	82
Benj[ami]n, Capt., had negro Ginnei, b. Aug. 16, 1719 ; Prince, negro child of Silva, b. Feb. 27, 1795	2	25
Benjamin, m. Hannah **TIFFANEY**, Dec. 17, 1747	2	25
Benjamin, s. Theophilus & Bethyah, b. June 15, 1750	2	58
Benjamin, Esq., d. Jan. 28, 1804	2	25
Betsey, d. Eli & Mary, b. July 24, 1820	6	48
Calvin, m. Mary **SNOW**, [June 12, [1825], by Rev. Reuben Torrey, Eastport * (*Eastford?)	5	19
Ceazer, basketmaker, black, d. June [ ], 1849, ae 84	5	138-9
Charles, of Brooklyn, Conn., m. Tabitha **PALMER**, of Ashford, Sept. 30, 1833, by Rev. James Porter	5	52

CLARK, CLARKE, CLERK, (cont.)	Vol.	Page
Charles T., s. George, farmer, ae 32, & Zilpha, ae 33, b. Aug. 3, 1850	5	146-7
Charles T., of Chaplin, m. Lydia E. FRANKLIN, of Ashford, [Jan. 30, 1834], by Rev. Ezekiel Skinner	5	53
Charles W., of East Windsor, m. Sophronia E. FAY, of Pomfret, July 6, 1845, by Rev. Geo[rge] Mixter	5	94
Cornelia, d. Eli & Mary, b. Sept. 29, 1826	6	48
Daniel, of Ellington, m. Lovina WHITE, of [Ashford], Feb. 12, [1833], by S. M. Wheelock, at Westford	5	50
Daniel R., s. Eli & Mary, b. May 13, 1831	6	48
Daniel Russell, s. John & Phebe, b. May 29, 1796	4	109
David, s. Lemuel & Elizabeth, b. Aug. 13, 1783	4	70
David, m. Esther BOLLS, Jan. 4, 1807	4	82
David, s. David & Esther, b. Feb. 14, 1812	4	82
Dyer Andrew, s. Dyer H. & Augusta A., b. Oct. 24, 1841	6	92
Dyer Howe, s. Dyer & Lucinda, b. May 23, 1817	4	89
Earl S., s. Dyer H., farmer, ae 34, & Augusta, ae 31, b. Jan. 26, 1851	5	146-7
Eben, s. Eliphalet & Hepsabeth, b. Mar. 23, 1786	4	268
Edmund, s. Eliphalet & Hepsabeth, b. Nov. 27, 1789	4	268
Eli, s. John & Phebe, b. Aug. 5, 1793	4	109
Eli, s. Eli & Mary, b. Aug. 28, 1824	6	48
Eli, Jr., m. Caroline M. BOLLES, b. of Ashford, May 1, 1850, by Rev. Lyman Leffingwell	5	105
Eli, shoemaker, ae 25, of Ashford, m. Caroline BOLLES ae 22, of Ashford, June [ ], 1850, by Lyman Leffingwell	5	142-3
Eliphalet, s. Lemuel & Elizabeth, b. Jan. 27, 1782	4	70
Eliphalet, m. Hephzibah FAY, June 1, 1785	4	268
Elizabeth, d. Lemuel & Elizabeth, b. July 21, 1785	4	70
Elizabeth, d. Oliver & Betsey, b. Feb. 6, 1815	6	14
Elizabeth, of Ashford, m. Henry ASHLEY, of Chaplin, Sept. 17, 1838, by Rev. Cha[rle]s Hyde	5	68
Elizabeth H., of Ashford, m. W[illia]m R. MAY, of Pomfret, Nov, 27, 1846, by Rev. Renssalear O. Putney	5	99
Erastus, s. Lemuel & Elisabeth, b. Aug. 15, 1787	4	70
Erastus, s. David & Esther, b. Oct. 22, 1807	4	82
Easther, m. Timothy EASTMAN, Apr. 15, 1739, by Mr. Hale	1	72
Esther, m. [Simeon TIFFANY], Dec. 28, 1775	4	99
Eunice, w. John, d. June 24, 1816	4	109
Francis P., of Chaplin, m. Jelina WOODWARD, of Ashford, Mar. 11, 1830, by William Ely	5	38
Frances P., of Chaplin, m. Matilda HUNTINGTON, of Ashford, Mar. 22, 1836, by Rev. Alvin Underwood	5	59
Hannah, of Ashford, m. Amasa CLARK, of Hampton, Dec. 3, 1834, by Dexter Bullard	5	55
Hannah Emily, d. John & Hannah, b. May 31, 1820	4	109
Harriet, d. Oliver & Betsey, b. Nov. 21, 1807	6	14
Harriet M., m. Lyman D. HEWES, b. of Ashford, Feb. 13,1851		

	Vol.	Page
CLARK, CLARKE, CLERK, (cont.)		
Harvey, s. Hosea & Surviah, b. Aug. 7, 1795	4	268
Hosea, s. Hosea & Surviah, b. Sept. 6, 1797	4	268
John, m. Phebe **RUSSEL[L]**, Nov. 25, 1779	4	109
John, s. John & Phebe, b. Aug. 31. 1780	4	109
John, m. Eunice **STAPLES**, Aug. [ ], 1812	4	109
John, m. Hannah **MOSELEY**, Oct. 4, 1816	4	109
John, s. Eli & Mary, b. July 18, 1828	6	48
Joseph Howard, s. Eli & Mary, b. Sept. 22, 1837	6	48
Joseph Howard, s. Eli & Mary, d. Oct. 5, 1839	6	48
Julia Sabrina, d. Dyer H. & Augusta A., b. Nov. 26, 1839	6	92
Laura, d. Oliver & Betsey, b. Aug. 24, 1823	6	14
Lemuel, m. Elisabeth **BICKNAL**, Nov. 25, 1779	4	70
Lemuel Bicknell, s. Lemuel & Elisabeth, b. Feb. 19, 1792	4	70
Lois, m. Amos **KENDAL**, Sept. 25, 1805	4	69
Lucinda, d. Dyer & Lucinda, b. July 30, 1802	4	89
Lucinda H., m. Jeseph B. **SIMMONS**, b. of Ashford, Feb. 19, 1829, by Rev. Philo Judson	5	33
Lydia, m. Thomas **DOW**, Apr. 2, 1799	4	93
Mary, w. Eli, d. Nov. 1, 1837	6	48
Mary J., ae 19, m. Joseph **BACKUS**, pedler, ae 27, b. Chaplin, res. Ashford, Aug. 8, 1848, by Rev. Erastus Dickinson	5	136-7
Mary W, m. Jon[a]than **SKINNER**, b. of Ashford, Mar. 22, 1838, by Rev. Erastus Benton, of Eastford	5	68
Molly, m. William **TIFFANY**, Nov. 16, 1775	4	89
Nancy, d. Oliver & Betsey, b. Feb. 1, 1811	6	14
Nathan Fay, s. Eliphalet & Hepsabeth, b. Dec. 25, 1790	4	268
Nehemiah Howe, s. Dyer & Lucinda, b. June 13, 1805	4	89
Newman, s. Oliver & Betsey, b. Apr. 14, 1803	6	14
Olive, m. Billy **SNOW**, Dec.11, 1787	4	16
Olive, d. Lemuel & Elisabeth, b. Apr. 26, 1798	4	70
Olover, s. John & Phebe, b. Aug. 1, 1782	4	109
Oliver, m. Betsey **BUTLER**, Dec. 19, 1802	6	14
Oliver, farmer, b. Middletown, res. Ashford, d. Aug. [ ], 1850, ae 68	5	150-1
Orrin A., s. Henry T., farmer, & Jerusha, b. Nov. [ ], 1849	5	140-1
Owin, s. Lemuel & Elisabeth, b. Mar. 13, 1796	4	70
Percey, of Ashford, m. Rev. Isreal G. **ROSE**, of Canterbury, [Nov.] 22, [1826], by Rev. Reuben Torrey, Eastford	5	25
Phebe, d. John & Phebe, b. Mar. 12, 1784	4	109
Phebe, w. John, d. Jan. 14, 1811	4	109
Polley, d. Lemuel & Elisabeth, b. Oct. 5, 1789	4	70
Rousewell, s. Oliver & Betsey, b. Mar. 17, 1813	6	14
Rufus, s. Oliver & Betsey, b. Sept. 23, 1809	6	14
Sabrina Howe, d. Dyer & Lucinda, b. Nov. 3, 1799	4	89
Sab[r]ina How[e], m. Clark **GRANT**, June 15, 1819	6	36
Sabrina, see also Sussbrana		
Samuel, s. Theophilus & Bethiah, b. Nov. 9, 1752	1	80

	Vol.	Page
CLARK, CLARKE, CLERK, (cont.)		
Samuel, s. Theophilus & Bethiah, b. Nov. 9, 1752	2	58
Sissbrana, d. Oliver & Betsey, b. Aug. 14, 1816	6	14
Sylvester, s. Hosea & Surviah, b. Oct. 8, 1793	4	268
Tamma, m. Josiah **HENDE**, Nov. 16, 1775	4	89
Theophilus, d. Oct. 7, 1737, ae 67	1	16
Theophelas, m. Bethyah **BILLINGS**, Dec. 5, 1745, by Rev. Mr. Mosely	2	58
Theophilus, s. Theophilus & Bethyah, b. Aug. 12, 1748	2	58
Wade, s. Hosea & Surviah, b. Jan. 23, 1800	4	268
Wheedon, m. Cynthia **SNOW** b. of Ashford, Feb. 3, 1825, by Rev. Philo Judson	5	17
William, s. Theophilas & Bethya, b. Nov. 19, 1746	2	58
CLEMENCE, Merrick, of Southbridge, m. Angenette **ALLEN**, of Ashford, Nov. 26, 1845, by Rev. Renssalear O. Putney	5	96
CLOUGH, George W., of Warwick, R. I., m. Desire N. **SCRANTON**, of Ashford, Oct. 26, 1828, by Amos Babcock, Elder, Intention published	5	32
COBURN, Charrity, [twin with Samuel], d. Samuel & Judaith, b. Feb. 3, 1754	1	88
Noah M., of Union, m. Harriet **POTTER**, of Ashford, Oct. 3, 1824, by Nathan Hayward, J. P.	5	15
Samuel, [twin with Charrity], s. Samuel & Judiath, b. Feb. 3, 1854	1	88
COE, Addeline, of Ashford, (Westford Society), m. George R. **BISHOP**, of Grafton, Mass., Oct. 10, 1836, by Rev. Lent S. Hough, of Chaplin	5	62
Mary Ann, of Ashford, d. of Isaac, m. Charles **COLLAR**, of Grafton, Mass., Mar. 29, 1829, by Elder Dexter Bullard	5	34
Sally E., of Ashford, m. Jotham W. **TAFT**, of Grafton, Mass., Nov. 7, 1836, by Rev. Alfred Burnham	5	63
COGSHELL, Roxey, m. Stephen **CHAPMAN**, 2nd, Feb. 24, 1805	4	69
COLBURN, Tryphena, m. Amariah **CRANE**, June 21, 1782	4	235
COLE, Elizabeth, d. Feb. 16, 1833	4	123
Lucinda, of Verona, m. Thomas **AMES** of East Lyme, May 9, 1844, by Rev. Geo[rge] Mixter	5	89
COLLAR, COLLER, Charles, of Grafton, Mass., m. Mary Ann **COE**, of Ashford, d. of Isaac, Mar. 29, 1829, by Elder Dexter Bullard	5	34
Coziah, m. Stephen **UTLEY**, b. of Ashford, Dec. 6, 1830, by Rev. Philo Judson	5	41
Ezekiel, m. Baziah *JORDAN, June 12, 1823, by Ezekiel Skinner (*Keziah?)	5	10
Keziah, see under Coziah		
COLLINS, George, of Wilbraham, Mass., m. Phebe **BICKNELL**, of Ashford, Conn. , Nov. 30, 1820, by Rev. Philo Judson	5	1
George, of Wilbraham, Mass., m. Phebe **RICHMOND**, of Ashford, Nov. 30, 1820, by Rev. Philo Judson	6	26

COLLINS, (cont.)	Vol.	Page
John, s. George & Phebe, b. Oct. 1, 1826	6	52
Julia, d. George & Phebe, b. Aug. 20, 1824	6	52
Rufus B., s. Samuel & Sally, b. Jan. 17, 1817 ; d. Mar. 23, 1817	4	41
Samuel, m. Sally BICKNELL, Dec. 1, 1814	6	41
Sanford B., s. Samuel & Sally, b. Aug. 30, 1821	6	41
Sarah Ann, d. Samuel & Sally, b. Dec. 18, 1825	6	41
Sophronia H., d. Samuel & Sally, b. Aug. 17, 1818 ; d. Nov. 14, 1820	6	41
COLTON, Esther, m. John PERKINS, Feb. 20, 1804	4	43
COMINS, COMMINS, [see under CUMMINGS]		
CONANT, Joseph, of Mansfield, m. Parmelia GAYLORD, of Ashford, [Sept.] 4, [1833], by Rev. Reuben Torrey, Eastford	5	51
Sally, m. Nathan UTLEY, Dec. 25, 1804	6	29
Sarah, m. Peter SMITH, Sept. 11, 1768	4	16
CONIALL, Daniel, s. Jeremiah & Elisabeth, b. Apr. 5, 1770	4	40
Jeremiah, m. Elisabeth BOSWORTH, June 26, 1769	4	40
CONLY, Sarah, m. David SMITH, Apr. 13, 1809	4	12
CONVERSE, Denison, m. Elizabeth LATHAM, Mar. 24, "last", [1830], by Reuben Torrey, Eastford	5	39
Horace, m. Almira SPRAGUE, [Sept.] 4, 1834, by Reuben Torrey, Eastford	5	54
Horace, m. Hulda SCARBOROUGH, b. of Ashford, Sept. 3, [1837], by Rev. Elias Sharpe, at the home of Alfred Brown, Westford Society	5	65
Joseph, of Stafford, m. Tenta YOUNG, of Ashford, May 18, 1834, by Amasa Lyon, J. P.	5	54
Nancy, m. Samuel LAMB, Dec. 12, 1812	6	3
Palmer, m. Betsey TAYLER, b. of Ashford, June 5, 1821, by Rev. Isaac Hall	5	3
COOK, Justin W., of Ashford, m. William C. WILLIAMS, of Roxbury, Litchfield County, June 9. 1827, by Rev. Philo Judson	5	28
Mary Ann, ae 26, b. Killingly, Ct., m. George MILLER, shoemaker, ae 21, b. Providence, R. I., res. Ashford, July 23, 1848, by Cha[rle]s S. Adams	5	128-9
COOLEY, COOLY, Andrew, s. Rowe & Mira, b. Aug. 14, 1830	6	73
Chester, s. Rowe & Mira, b. Dec. 29, 1813	6	73
Clark, s. Rowe & Mira, b. Mar. 13, 1818	6	73
Elvira, of Ashford, m. Lorrin S. ATWOOD, of Mansfield, Sept. 24, 1844, by Rev. Cha[rle]s Hyde	5	91
Emily, d. Rowe & Mira, b. Apr. 7, 1823	6	73
Emily, m. Edwin JOHNSON, b. of Ashford, [Jan.] 1, [1843], by Rev. Cha[rle]s Hyde	5	83
Francis, s. Rowe & Mira, b. Mar. 14, 1816	6	73
Lucinda, d. Rowe & Mira, b. Sept. 13, 1825	6	73
Lucinda, of Ashford, m. Melvin H. ATWOOD, of		

	Vol.	Page
CORBIN, CORBAN, (cont.)		
1719	A	6
Samuel, [twin with Elezebeth], s. Thomas & Sarah, b. Dec. 26,		
1719	1	24
Sarah, d. Thomas & Sarah, b. May 1, 1738	1	23
Sylvia, m. William **WALKER,** Jr., May 28, 1806	4	78
Thomas, s. Thomas & Sarah, b. Feb. 16, 1724/5	A	9
Thomas, s. Thomas & Sarah, b. Feb. 16, 1724/5	1	24
Timothy, s. Thomas & Sarah, b. May 14, 1735	1	24
COREY, William M., of Hampton, m. Chloe **SOUTHERBY,** of		
Pomfret, Dec. 12, 1842, by Rev. F. Williams	5	83
CORNEL, Sarah, of Willmantown, m. Joseph **SNOW,** of Ashford,		
May 7, 1735, by Rev. Mr. James [Hale]	1	54
CORRARY, [see under **CRARY**]		
CORRY, Daniel B., m. Irena **STORY,** Mar. 31, 1833, by Rev.		
David Bennett	5	51
CORTICE, [See also **CURTIS**], Ebenezer, s. Jonathan & Dorothy,		
b. Apr. 20, 1764	2	41
Jonathan, m. Dorothy **MASON,** Nov. 16, 1752	2	41
COTTON, Charles A., of Hartford, m. Mary R. **GRANT,** of		
Ashford, Nov. 5, 1833, by Rev. James Porter	5	52
COY, COYE, Archibald, s. Luke & Ceber, b. June 4, 1793	4	36
Betty, d. Stephen & Anna, b. [ ]	4	7
Ele[a]nor, d. Luke & Ceber, b. Dec. 11, 1891	4	36
Hannah, m. Joseph **HOLMES,** Dec. 31, 1760	3	48
Hannah, d. Setphen & Anna, b. [ ]	4	7
John, s. Stephen & Anna, b. Aug. 12, 17[ ]	4	7
Luke, m. Ceber **CHAPMAN,** Nov. 2, 1786	4	36
Stephen, s. Stephen & Anna, b. Sept. 21, [ ]	4	7
Sylenda, d. Luke & Ceber, b. Oct. 2, 1787	4	36
Vine, s. Stephen & Anna, b. Feb. 16, 17[ ]	4	7
CRAM*, Phebe, m. Moses **STILES,** Jan, 8, 1735, by Rev. Mr.		
Mosle (***CRANE?**)	1	75
CRANE, CRAIN, [see also **CRAM**], Abigail, d. Roger & Sarah, b.		
Sept. 14, 1786	4	244
Alford, s. Amariah & Tryphena, b. Jan. 13, 1783	4	235
Amariah, m. Tryphena **COLBURN,** June 21, 1782	4	235
Cyrus, s. Roger & Sarah, b. June 23, 1790	4	244
Frances, d. Amariah & Tryphena, b. Sept. 1, 1784	4	235
Orraman, s. Amariah & Tryphena, b. Jan. 13, 1783	4	235
Rebeckah, m. Solomon **SMITH,** Oct. 28, 1773	4	77
Roger, m. Sarah **WHITON,** May 20, 1784	4	244
Samuel, s. Roger & Sarah, b. July 28, 1788	4	244
CRARY, CORRARY, CAVARY, Hannah, m. Ezekiel **SIBLEY,**		
Sept. 24, 1778	4	103
Harmony, m. Amos **CHAFFEE,** Oct. 1, 1797	4	116
Joseph, s. Roger & Mary, b. Mar. 29, 1758	1	105
Mehitable, m. David **CUMMINGS,** Dec. 17, 1761	3	122
Rebakah, m. Salvanus **SNOW,** Nov. 9, 1752, by James		

	Vol.	Page
CRARY, CORRARY, CAVARY, (cont.)		
Bicknell, J. P.	2	47
Roger, s. Roger & Mary, b. July 7, 1754	1	85
Sarah, d. Roger & Mary, b. Aug. 21, 1760	3	62
Sarah, m. Jacob **UTLEY**, Dec. 5, 1781	4	225
Thiah, m. Samuell **WALKER**, Nov. 15, 1769	4	49
CROCKER, Hannah, m. Elijah **WHITON**, Nov. 23, 1758	1	101
Lucy, d. Nathan & Lucy, b. Aug. 18, 1798	4	62
CROSS, David, s. David & Ann, b. Dec. 13, 1754	1	88
Gracey, of Ashford, m. Lewis W. **MOSELEY**, of Hampton, Dec. 12, 1824, by Jared Andrus, Chaplin	5	16
Timothy Squire, s. David & Anne, b. Nov. 5, 1759	1	108
CROUCH, William, of Brimfield, Mass., m. Sarah **WEDGE**, of Ashford, Apr. 2, 1838, by Rev. Reuben Torrey, Eastford	5	67
CROWEL, Mariet R., of Woodstock, m. William **BATES** of Ashford, (people of color), Nov. 27, 1842, by Rev. F. Williams	5	83
CUMMINGS, COMMINS, COMMINGS, COMINS, David, m. Mehitable **CRARY**, Dec. 17, 1761	3	122
David, s. David & Mehitable, b. Feb. 3, 1771	3	122
Ellenah, d. James & Rachel, b. Jan. 22, 1754 (Eleanor)	1	104
El[l]anah, [m.] John **WELCH**, [ ]	4	3
Elisabeth, [d. James & Rachel], b. Mar. 7, 1756	1	104
Eunice, m. Amos **CHAFFEE**, Jan. 1, 1799	4	35
Eunice E., d. Jason G., factory operative, of Oxford, Mass., ae 24, & Lucy A., ae 21, b. June 20, 1850	5	140-1
Eunice E., d. June 20, 1850, ae 6 h.	5	144-5
Hannah, d. David & Mehitable, b. July 20, 1768	3	122
James, of Willington, m. Sarah **WILLSON**, Mar. 18, 1746/7	2	61
James, s. James & Rachel, b. Apr. 19, 1761	3	45
Joseph, s. John & Elisabeth, b. May 20, 1760	3	45
Lissa, David & Mehetable, b. Apr. 4, 1766	3	122
Molley, [d. James & Rachel], b. June 2, 1758	1	104
Patty, d. David & Mehetable, b. July 6, 1762	3	122
Permelia H., of Ashford, m. Ruel **DEAN**, of Wales, Mass., Oct. 2, 1832, by Rev. Philo Judson	5	49
William, s. William & Mary, b. Sept. 30, 1754	1	88
CURRIER, John W., of North Troy, Vt., m. Betsey **JAMES**, of Palmer, Mass., Apr. 15, 1849, by Rev. Ezekiel Skinner	5	103
John W., mechanic, ae 52, b. Ashford, res. North Troy, Vt., m. 2d w. Betsey **JAMES** ae 43, of Palmer, Mass., Apr. 15, 1849, by Rev. Ezekiel Skinner	5	136-7
CURTIS, CURTISS, CURTEES, CURTICE, {see also **CORTICE,** } Alice, see under Ellis		
Amasa, s. Francis & Betty, b. June 24, 1771	4	33
Calvin, s. Francies & Betty, b. July 29, 1778	4	33
Celia, d. Henry, Jr. & Celia, d. Jan. 30, 1826	6	18
Celia, d. Henry, Jr. & Celia, b. Sept. 13, 1820	6	18
Charles Mark, s. Henry, Jr. & Celia, b. Aug. 1, 1834	6	18

	Vol.	Page
CURTIS, CURTISS, CURTEES, CURTICE, (cont.)		
Chloe, d. Henry, b. Dec. 29, 1798	4	270
C[h]loe, m. James **HIMES**, b. of Ashford, Mar. 31, 1822, by Nathan Hayward, J. P.	5	6
Cumfort, d. Francis & Betty, b. Nov. 18, 1773	4	33
Deliverence, d. Francies & Betty, b. Feb. 26, 1776	4	33
Electa, d. Henry, Jr. & Celia, b. Apr. 16, 1823	6	18
Electa, of Ashford, m. W[illia]m H. **STONE**, of Southbridge, Mass., Oct. 26, 1846, by Rev. R. V. Lyon, Westford Society	5	99
Ellis, d. Ransom & Allis, b. Nov. 12, 1782	4	49
Frances, William & Mehetebel, b. July 15, 1743	2	69
Francis, m. Betty **ROBBINS**, Nov, 17, 1768	4	33
Harriet Livermore, d. Henry, Jr. & Celia, b. Sept, 23, 1825	6	17
Henry, s. William & Meheteble, b. Aug. 17, 1750	2	69
Henry, s. Henry, b. Aug. 7, 1792	4	270
Henry, Jr., m. Celia **AVERY**, Nov. 28, 1816	6	18
Henry Francis, s. Henry, Jr. & Celia, b. Dec. 31, 1817	6	18
Henry Francis, s. Henry, Jr. & Celia, b. Mar. 21, 1822	6	18
James, s. Ransom & Allice, b. Mar. 19, 1779	4	49
John Sullivan, s. Samuel & Mary, b. Feb. 23, 1826	6	21
Jonathan, m. Mary **PRESTON**, Jan. 12, 1775	2	41
Joseph, s. Ransom & Allice, b. Dec. 7, 1771	4	49
Lydia, d. Henry, b. July 1, 1796	4	270
Mary, d. Samuel & Mary, b. Apr. 18, 181[ ]	6	21
Mary, m. Amos **CHAFFEE**, Jr., [Sept.]14, [1834], by Rev. R. Torrey, Eastford	5	54
Molley, d. Henry, b. Feb. 15, 1774	4	270
Ranson, s. Will[ia]m & Mehetebel, b. Oct. 23, 1745	2	69
Samuel, s. Henry, b. July 22, 1794	4	270
Samuel Noah, s. Sam[ue]l & Mary, b. Nov. 17, 181[ ]	6	21
Sarah Emila, d. Sam[ue]l & Mary, b. July 28, 1822	6	21
Seldon, m. Martha A. **SKINNER**, June 5, 1853, by Rev. Ezekiel Skinner, Westford	5	110
Stephen Decatur, s. Samuel & Mary, b. Apr. 4, 183[ ]	6	21
Susan[n]a, d. William & Mehetebel, b. Mar. 1, 1747/8	2	69
Susannah, m. Timothy **EASTMAN**, Jr., Feb. [ ]	4	5
William Parrish, s. Samuel & Mary, b. Sept. 30, 1831	6	21
CUSHMAN, Thomas, of Willilngton, m. Lydia **MARCY**, of Ashford, Feb. 13, 1828, by Rev. Philo Jusdson	5	30
CUTLER, Abner, s. Jonathan & Anna, b. June 6, 1738	1	13
Ebenezer, s. Jonathan & Anna, b. Nov. 1, 1736	1	13
Jonathan, m. Annah **GENINGS**, Apr. 16, 1733 by Rev. James Hale	1	13
Jonathan, s. Jonathan & Anna, b. Dec. 10,1733	1	13
Joseph, s. Jonathan & Anna, b. Dec. 7, 1735 ; d. 24th day of the same month	1	14
Mary, d. Jonathan & Anna, b. Mar. 15, 1740	1	13

	Vol.	Page
DADEY, Darbey, m. Hannah **SNOW**, b. of Ashford, Sept. 21, 1851,		
by Rev. P. Mathewson	5	107
DANA, Anderson, m. Susannah **HUNTINGTON**, June 1, 1757	3	5
Anderson, s. Anderson & Susannah, b. Aug. 11, 1765	3	5
Anderson, d. July 3, 1778. "Was killed at Kingstown,		
Susquehannah"	3	5
Anna, d. Jedadiah & Eliz[a]beth, b. Jan. 22, 1747/8 ; d. Nov. 6,		
1754	1	41
Anna, d. Jedidiah, Jr. & Lucy, b. Sept. 16, 1783	4	249
Apia, [child of Jacob, Jr. & Patience], b. Nov. 9, 1754	1	89
Ariel, s. Anderson & Susannah, b. Mar. 17, 1767	3	5
Benjamin, [twin with Joseph], s. Jedidiah & Elezebeth, b. Jan.		
20, 1731/2 ; d. same day	1	41
Clarina, d. Jedidiah, Jr.& Lucy, b. Oct. 14, 1773	4	149
Daniel, s. Anderson & Susannah, b. Sept. 16, 1760	3	5
Daniel, s. Jedediah, Jr. & Lucy b. Deca. 3, 1785	4	249
Eleazer, s. Anderson & Susanna, b. Aug. 12, 1772	3	5
Elener, [twin with Persala], d. Jacob & Abiga[i]l, b. Apr. 4,		
1745	2	55
Elizabeth, d. Jedediah & Elezebeth, b. Oct. 10, 1743	1	41
Elisabeth, m. John **LAISELL**, Apr. 18, 1770	4	76
Elizabeth, d. Jed[idiah], Jr. & Lucy, b. June 8, 1771	4	249
Elizabeth, w. Jedediah, d. Jan. 30, 1786	1	41
Eunis, d. Anderson & Susannah, b. May 10, 1758	3	5
James, s. Jedediah & Elezebeth, b. Oct. 9, 1735	1	41
Jedediah, s. Jedediah & Elezebeth, b. Aug. 9, 1739	1	41
Jedidiah, Jr. , m. Lucy **HOLT**, Nov. 27, 1770	4	249
Jedidiah, s. Jedidia, Jr. & Lucy, b. Nov. 8, 1778	4	249
Jedediah, d. Mar. 28, 1787	1	41
Jonathan, s. Jedidiah & Elezebeth, b. Apr. 9, 1733	1	41
Joseph, [twin with Benjamin], s. Jedidiah & Elezebeth, b. Jan.		
20, 1731/2 ; d. same day	1	41
Levina, [d. Jacob, Jr. & Patience], b. Feb. 6, 1747	1	89
Levina, m. John **SOUTHWORTH**, Feb. 20, 1770	6	19
Lisey, [d. Jacob, Jr. & Patience], b. Aug. 12, 1752	1	89
Lucy, d. Jedidiah, Jr. & Lucy, b. July 8, 1772	4	249
Nelly, [d. Jacob, Jr. & Patience], b. Sept. 24, 1750	1	89
Polley, d. Jedediah, Jr. & Lucy, b. Jan. 15, 1781	4	249
Persala, [twin with Elener, d. Jacob & Abiga[i]l, b. Apr. 4,		
1745	2	55
Presilla, m. Daniel **FENNEY**, Feb. 14, 1771	4	53
Salley, d. Jedidiah, Jr. & Lucy, b. Mar. 23, 1777	4	249
Sarah, d. Jacob & Abigail, b. Apr. 6, 1743	2	55
Silas, s. Jedidiah, Jr. & Lucy, b. Mar. 9, 1775	4	249
Solomon, s. Jedediah & Elezebeth, b. Aug. 22, 1741	1	41
Susannah, d. Anderson & Susannah, b. Jan. 16, 1762	3	5
Sylve[s]ter, s. Anderson & Susannah, b. July, 4, 1769	3	5
Will[ia]m, s. Jedediah & Elezebeth, b. Aug. 9, 1737	1	41

	Vol.	Page
DANES, [see under **DEAN**]		
DANIELSON, James had d. Marriam b. to Dorithy **HUMPHRY,**		
Jan. 7, 1748/9	1	12
DARLIN, George W., of Dorset, Vt., m. Martha C. **MARCY,** of		
Ashford, May, 17, 1847, by Charles Peabody	5	100
DARRY, Dorcose, d. John & Sarah, b. Dec. 31, 1715 [sic]	A	1
Dorathy, d. John & Sarah, b. Apr. 10, 1713	A	1
Hepcebath, d. John & Sarah, b. Sept. 20, 1715	A	1
James, s. John & Sarah, [b.] Dec. 22, 1711	A	1
---------, d. John & Sarah, b. Aug. 9, 1710	A	1
DAVIS, Aaron, of Dudley, Mass., m. Electa **MUMFORD,** of		
Ashford, Oct. 20, 1824, by Reuben Torrey, Eastford	5	16
Dinah, m. David **EATON,** Oct. 19, 1732	1	64
Edward E., of Newburyport, Mass., m. Harriet		
HUNTINGTON, of Eastford, June 30, 1846, by Francis		
Williams	5	97
Eliza Ann, m. Erastus **NEWPORT,** b. of Ashford, May 29,		
1831, by Rev. David Bennett	5	43
Esther, m. Isaac **DEXTER,** Dec. 12, 1745	2	57
Francis, m. Dimmis **WRIGHT,** b. of Ashford, [Dec.] 26,		
[1835], by Rev. R. Torrey, Eastford	5	58
Henry H., m. Melissa **NEWPORT,** b. of Ashford, Apr. 3,		
[1842], by Francis Williams, Eastford	5	80
Polly, d. Willard & Sarah, b. Nov. 2, 1793	4	288
Walter, s. Willard & Sarah, b. Aug. 16, 1788	4	288
DAVISON, Betsey, d. Tho[ma]s & Eunice, b. June 5, 1780	4	108
Hannah, d. Zephaniah & Susannah, b. Feb.7, 1775	4	19
Huldah, m. Joseph T. **CARPENTER,** Apr. 15, 1800	4	96
John, s. Zephaniah & Susannah, b. Nov. 20, 1763	4	19
Norman, s. Paul & Salla, b. Aug. 19, 1786	4	11
Samuel, s. Zephaniah & Susannah, b. Feb.7, 1773	4	19
Sarah, d. Zepheniah & susannah, b. Apr. 4, 178[ ]	4	19
Susanna, d. Zepheniah & Susannah, b. July 24, 17[ ]	4	19
Tho[ma]s, m. Eunice **PAREL,** Aug. 26, 1779	4	108
Zephaniah, s. Zephania & Susannah, b. Oct. 26, 1765	4	19
DAWLEY, Joseph F., manufacturer, b. R. I., res. Willington, m.		
Elvira **ROBBINS,** of Ashford, Mar. 24, 1850, by		
Washington Munger	5	142-3
DAY, Lucia M., m. Elisha D. **HUNTINGTON,** b. of Eastford, Aug.		
11, 1844, by Francis Williams	5	90
Sarah Ann, of Eastford, m. Eleazer G. **BUGBEE** of Union,		
Dec. 28, 1845, by Francis Williams	5	96
Sylvia C., m. Lucius **CARPENTER,** [Mar.] 23, [1843], by F.		
Williams	5	84
DEAN, DEANS, DANES, DEEN, Abigail, of Ashford, m. Isaac		
KEITH, of Easton, Mass., Feb 8, 1829, by Rev. Reuben		
Torrey, Eastford	5	33
Albe, s. Leonard & Hannah, b. Jan. 6, 1802	4	238

	Vol.	Page
DEAN, DEANS, DANES, DEEN, (cont.)		
Almira, ae 27, b. Woodstock, res. Ashford, m. Alfred		
CHAFFEE, farmer, ae 38, Apr. 4, 1849, by Rev. R. O		
Putney	5	136-7
Carolina, [twin with -----], d. Elijah & Irena, b. Sept. 12, 1811	4	10
Charles, s. Ezra & Jemimah, b. Mar. 29, 1783	4	238
Clarissa, m. Virgilius M. GOODELL, b. of Ashford, Apr. 11,		
1842, by Rev. C. C. Barnes	5	81
David, m. Saray BOSWORTH, Dec. 14, 1828, by Levi Works,		
J. P.	5	34
[E]lijah, m. Irena SUMNER, Sept. 27, 1791	4	10
Ephraim, s. Simeon & Tamezine, b. Sept. 21, 1782	4	66
Easter, m. Thomas HIGANS, Nov. 11, 1753	1	81
Eunis, d. Simeon & Tamesine, b. Aug. 24, 1775	4	66
Eunice, d. Leonard & Hannah, b. Nov. 15, 1800	4	238
Eunice, m. Ebenezer JAMES, b. of Ashford, July 14, 1836, by		
Amos Babcock	5	60
Ezra, s. Ezra & Jemimah, b. Dec. 8, 1778	4	238
Hannah P., m. Chauncey PALMER, b. of Ashford, Nov. 3,		
1836, by Rev. Stephen Cushing, Eastford	5	63
Harvey, m. Clarissa M. BOSWORTH, b. of Ashford, Nov. 4,		
1832, by Thom[ma]s Dow, J. P.	5	49
Jemime, d. Simeon & Tamezin, b. Aug. 28, 1770	4	66
John S., m. Hannah M. KNOWLTON, b. of Ashford, May 16,		
1838, by Amos Babcock	5	68
Leonard, s. Simeon & Tamezine, b. Oct. 11, 1779	4	66
Leonard, m. Hannah PHILLIPS, Feb. 13, 1800	4	238
Leonard, farmer, d. Aug. 12, 1848, ae 69	5	138-9
Lydia, d. Ezra & Jemimah, b. May 13, 1785	4	238
Mary, d. Zephaniah & Hannah, b. July 1, 1756	1	94
Mary, d. Simeon & Tamezine, b. June 23, 1773	4	66
Oxenbridge, s. Oxenbridge & Abiga[i]l, b. July 7, 1746	2	43
Parcle, s. Simeon & Tama, b. Jan. 8, 1763	2	37
Philip, s. Ezra & Jemimah, b. Feb. 17, 1781	4	238
Prudence, m. Joseph HAYWARD, Sept. 18, 1751	2	26
Ruel, of Wales, Mass., m. Permelia H. CUMMINGS, of		
Ashford, Oct. 2, 1832, by Rev. Philo Judson	5	49
Samvel, s. Oxenbridge & Abiga[i]l, b. July 21, 1744	2	43
Simeon, m. Tamezine BUGBEE, June 24, 1762	4	66
Simeon, m. Laura W. CHAFFEE, b. of Eastford, Nov. 17,		
1846, by Francis Williams	5	99
Zepheniah, m. Hannah HAYWARD, Oct. 2, 1755, by Mr.		
Stephen Williams	1	94
-----hn Norman, s. Elijah & Irena, b. Oct. 12, 1792	4	10
----muel, s. Elijah & Irena, b. Aug. 27, 1794	4	10
----isa, d. Elijah & Irena, b. Sept. 17, 1796	4	10
----iah, s. Elijah & Irena, b. Sept. 12, 1798	4	10
----isa, d. Elijah & Irena, b. Apr. 17, 1800	4	10
----es, s. Elijah & Irena, b. Mar. 26, 1802	4	10

DIMOCK, DIMICK, DIMMICK, DIMMUCK, DIMMOCK,(cont)

	Vol.	Page
[s. Ebeneze r], b. May 8, 1750	2	34
Abigail, d. Timothy & Merriam, b. Jan. 21, 1728/9	1	16
Abigail, d. Shuba[e]l, d. Dec. 11, 1737	1	16
Abigail, d. Ebenezer & Mary, b. Mar. 12, 1739/40	1	15
Abigail, m. Caleb WALKER, Oct. 23, 1796	4	40
Ann, d. Timothy & Mirriam, b. Dec. 8, 1726	1	16
Asa, s. Shub[a]el, d. Oct. 29, 1740	1	16
Asa, s. Shub[a]el & Persilla, b. Dec. 18, 1740	1	16
Benj[ami]n, s. John & Hannah, [b.] Dec. 1, 1739	1	A
Benjamins, s. Ebenezer & Mary, b. Sept. 30, 1757	4	21
Benjamin, s. John [& Hannah], d. Nov. 10, 1759	1	A
Bettey, d. Daniel & Zilpah, b. Feb. 29, 1776	4	115
Birsha, m. Abel KNOWLTON, Apr. 16, 1795	4	119
Dan[i]el, s. Shub[a]el & Persilla, [b.] Sept. 24, 1736	1	16
Daniel, [s. Ebenezer], b. July 15, 1750 (1753?)	2	34
Daniel, s. Daniel & Zilpah, b. Apr. 19, 1778	4	115
Desire, d. Daniel & Zelpah, b. Mar. 10, 1788	4	115
Ebene zer, m. Mary KYES, Sept. 27, 1739, by Rev. James Hale	1	15
Ebene zer, s. Ebenezer & Mary, b. Dec. 11, 1741	2	34
Ebene zer, [s. Ebenezer], b. Sept. 10, 1747	2	34
Elias, s. Eben[eze]r & Mary, b. July 4, 1750	4	21
Elias, m. Lydia WARREN, Jan. 26, 1785	4	257
Elesabeth, m. [Jos]iah CHAFFE, [Ap]ril 11, 1760	1	108
Hannah, d. John & Hannah, b. Aug. 20, 1729	1	A
Hannah, m. Samvel THATCHER, Dec. 18, 1749	2	18
Hulda, d. Timothy & Hulda, b. Jan. 22, 1771	4	54
Huldah, m. Philip HASTAN, Sept. 21, 1794	4	118
John, m. Mary* KINDALL Oct 10, 1728 (*Overwritten to read "Hannah")	1	A
John, s. John & Hannah, b. Nov. 9, 1731 ; July 10, 1748	1	A
John, s. John & Hannah, b. Oct. 19, 1748	1	A
Joseph, s. John & Hannah, b. Oct. 7, 1733 ; d. July 22, 1748	1	A
Justin, s. Elias & Lydia, b. Aug. 5, 1800	4	257
Mary, d. Ebenezer & Mary, b. Apr. 13, 1743	2	34
Mary, d. Timothy & Hulda, b. July 25, 1772	4	54
Marriam, d. Timothy & Marriam, b. June 5, 1731 (Meriam)	1	16
Meriam, [d. Ebenezer], Apr. 29, 1755 (Birth)	2	34
Meriam, m. Elias BURBANK, Oct. 15, 1774	4	101
(Mores),Moses s. Eben[eze]r & Mary, b. June 25, 1754 (1764)	4	121
( ) were corrections to original manuscript on microfilm		
Otis, s. Elias & Lydia, b. Nov. 26, 1786	4	257
Richard, s. Daniel & Zilpah, b. May 24, 1780	4	115
Salley, d. Daniel & Zilpha, b. June 12, 1774	4	115
Shub[a]el, s. Shub[a]el & Persela, [b.] July 16, 1737 ; d. Nov. 8, 1740	1	16
Solomon, s. Ebenezer, b. Apr. 29, 1745	2	34
Seble, d. John & Han[n]ah, b. Jan. 9, 1736/7	1	A

	Vol.	Page
DIMOCK, DIMICK, DIMMICK, DIMMUCK,DIMMOCK,(cont.)		
Sibbel, m. John **CHAPMAN**. May 9, 1759	3	120
Sybil, s. Elias & Lydia, b. June 1, 1792	4	257
Tarzah, d. Daniel & Zilpah, b. Apr. 21, 1783	4	115
Timothy m. Marian **FULLER**, Mar. 10, 1725/6, by Rev.		
Eben[eze]r Williams	A	10
Timothy, m. Marriam **FULLER**, Mar. 10, 1725/6	1	16
Timothy, s. Timothy & Marriam, b. Dec. 6, 1733	1	16
Timothy, m. Hulda **SNOW**, Dec. 21, 1767	4	54
Timothy, s. Daniel & Zilpah, b. June 2, 1785	4	115
Timothy Dwight, s. Claras[s]a Snow, b. Feb. 27, 1820	4	71
Urrilla, d. Elias & Lydia, b. June 25, 1789	4	257
DIVINE, William H., of Hartford, m. Julia B. **LATHROP**, of		
Ashford, Oct. 29, 1832, by Rev. Philo Judson	5	49
DODGE, Augustus, m. Mary **LYON**, b. of Ashford, [Feb.] 3.		
[1831]. by Rev. Reuben Torrey, of Eastford	5	41
Augustus, m. Mary **TILDEN**, b. of Ashford, Apr. 5, 1835, by		
W[illia]m Livesey, Elder	5	56
James, of Woodstock, m. Nancy **PIERCE**, of Ashford, Jan. 3,		
1836, by Edward S. Keyes, J. P.	5	58
Palmer, of Belchertown, Mass., m. Ruth **THAYER**, of		
Amherst, Mass., [Aug.] 13, [1824], by Ezekiel Skinner	5	14
DOORE, Hannah H., m. Andrew **CHAPMAN**, b. of Ashford, Oct.		
19, 1851, by Rev. Amos Snell	5	108
DORRY, [see under **DARRY**]		
DORSET, DORSETT, [see also **DOWSET**], Benjamin Bosworth, s.		
Joseph, Jr. & Clarissa, b. Aug. 23, 1834	6	88
Daniel Brewster, m. Harriet **PRESTON**, [b. of Eastford], Nov,		
16, [1841], by Francis Williams	5	79
Joseph, of Union, m. Mary **WHITMARSH**, of Ashford, Jan.		
14, 1821, by Elder Isaac Hall	5	1
Joseph, of Union m. Mary **HITCHOCK**, of Ashford, Jan. 14,		
1821, by Rev. Isaac Hall	6	26
Joseph, Jr., m. Clarissa **BOSWORTH**, b. of Ashford, [Nov.]		
28, [1833], by Rev. Reuben Torrey, Eastford	5	52
DOUBLEDE, Joseph, s. Joseph & Elisabeth, b. Feb. 19, 1762	3	15
DOUGLASS, Hannah, m. Chester **WEBSTER**, b. of Ashford,		
Woods, [Nov.] 28, [1839], by Rev. Reuben Torrey,		
Eastford	5	72
John, m. Eunice **BOSWORTH**, b. of Ashford, Apr. 12, 1821,		
by Rev. William Storrs	5	3
DOW, Abal, s. Daniel & Elesabeth, b. July 3, 1757	1	99
Abel, m. Olive **ROGERS**, Sept. 28, 1784	4	267
Abel, d. Jan. 6, 1826	4	267
Catharine, d. Thomas & Lydia, b. July 2, 1801	4	93
Catharine, m. Barzillai **BUTLER**, Apr. 21, 1823, by Philo		
Judson	5	9
Syrus, s. Daniel & Elesabeth, b. June 17, 1764	3	72

DOW, (cont.)	Vol.	Page
Daniel, s. Daniel & Elesabeth, b. Feb. 19, 1772	3	72
Daniel, d. June 8, 1772	3	72
Elesabeth, d. Daniel & Elesabeth, b. July 30, 1766	3	72
Elizabeth, m. David **BOLLES,** Jr. Nov. 12, 1786	4	246
Elisabeth, d. Elisabeth **WORK,** b. Jan. 4, 1792	4	58
Elizabeth, d. Aug. 24, 1805	3	72
Elisabeth, d. Thomas & Lydia, b. Sept. 1, 1809	4	93
Elizabeth, m. Joseph **BUTLER,** b. of Ashford, Sept. 4, 1827, by Rev. Philo Judson	5	28
Hendrick, s. Daniel & Elesabeth, b. Feb. 5, 1761	3	72
Henry Laurens, s. Thomas & Lydia, b. Sept. 20, 1803	4	93
Joseph Clark, s. Thomas & Lydia, b. July 7, 1805	4	93
Laura, d. Abel & Olive, b. June 16, 1796	4	267
Lois, d. Abel & Olive, b. Dec. 1, 1790	4	267
Maritha, d. Tho[ma]s & Lydia, b. Apr. 30, 1816	4	93
Mary A., of Ashford, m. Emery C. **HAWES,** of Springfield, Mass., May 3, 1847, by Charles Peabody	5	100
Mary Ann, d. Henry L. & Mary, b. Sept. 15, 1828	6	69
Mary M., of Ashford, m. Smith S. C. **BARTLETT,** of Sutton, Mass., Sept. 13, 1837, by Rev. J. Hall	5	65
Salla, d. Abel & Olive, b. Nov. 28, 1785	4	267
Thomas, s. Daniel & Elesabeth, b. Sept. 26, 1769	3	72
Thomas, m. Lydia **CLARK,** Apr. 2, 1799	4	93
Thomas, farmer, d. Nov. [ ], 1850, ae 81	5	150-1
Thomas H., s. Thomas & Lydia, b. July 31, 1818	4	93
William, s. Abel & Olive, b. Mar. 6, 1788	4	267
DOWSET, DAWSET, [see also **DORSET**], Amos, s. Lawrance & Lucey, b. Jan. 6, 1754	4	236
Anna, d. Lawrance & Lucey, b. Dec. 31, 1773	4	236
Betsey, d. Lawrence & Lucey, b. Mar. 5, 1766	4	236
Filisity, see under Philis		
Jonathan, s. Lawrance & Lucey, b. June 27, 1758	4	236
Joseph, s. Lawrance & Lucey, b. June 16, 1775	4	236
Lawrance, s. Lawrance & Lucey, b. Jan. 15, 1764	4	236
Lucey, d. Lawrance & Lucey, b. Dec. 13, 1777	4	236
Mary, d. Lawrance & Lucey, b. May 2, 1762	4	236
Olover, s. Lawrance & Lucey, b. July 17, 1771	4	236
Philis, d. Lawrance & Lucey, b. Sept. 20, 1756	4	236
Filisity, m. Isaiah **SPARKS,** Dec. 9, 1779	4	239
Philimon, S. Lawrance & Lucey, b. Apr. 27, 1769	4	236
DRAPER, Joseph, m. Martha **FARNHAM,** Sept. 10, 1821, by Rev. Philo Judson	5	4
Mary Ann, m. Moses **WEDGE,** Apr. 4, 1819	6	38
DRESSER,Lewis A., b. Pomfret, res. Ashford, d. Aug. 6, 1848, ae 8	5	136-7
DREW, Eunis, m. Jacob **BOUTWELL,** Jr., June 20, 1759	3	79
DRICE, Grace, m. Thomas **SQUIER,** Dec. 4, 1716	A	3
Rebeckah, d. William & Mary, b. Mar. 8, 1717/18	A	4
DUDLEY, Edwin P., m. Esther M. **PARKER,** b. of Ashford,		

DUDLEY, (cont.)	Vol.	Page
Dec. 23, 1851, by Rev. P. Mathewson	5	108
John, s. Nicholas & Prissila, b. Mar. 19, 1784	4	231
Nicholas, m. Prisila WHITON, Nov. 12, 1778	4	231
Prisila, d. Nicholas & Prissila, b. Mar. 8, 1782	4	231
DUNHAM, Barnes, s. Jabez, b. Sept. 23, 1821	6	87
Barnes G., shoemaker, ae 28, of Ashford, m. Jane E. GRANT,		
ae 24, b. Willington, res. Ashford, Feb. 27, 1849, by		
Rev. Washington Munger	5	136-7
Cephas, s. Jabez, b. Aug. 3, 1819	6	87
Elizabeth J., d. Barnes G., farmer, ae 29, & Elizabeth J., ae 27,		
b. Nov. 16, 1849	5	140-1
George, of Mansfield, m. Adaline NORTH[R]UP, of Chaplin,		
Nov. 23, 1845, by Rev. Geo[rge] Mixter	5	95
Hannah, d. John & Abial, b. Mar. 10, 1775 ; d. May 19, 1775	4	247
Hannah, d. Royal & Prissilia(?), b. Dec. 21, 1807	4	98
Hannah, d. Jabez, b. Apr. 24, 1809	6	87
Jabez, s. John & Abial, b. Feb. 6, 1779	4	247
John, s. Jabez, b. July 8, 1812	6	87
Martha, d. Jabez, b. June 24, 1816	6	87
Mary, m. Amos BUGBEE, Sept. 10, 1816	6	49
Sally, d. Jabez, b. Dec. 1, 1810	6	87
Salome, Mrs., m. Daniel READ, b. of Ashford, Sept. 13, 1848,		
by Charles Peabody	5	103
Saloma, ae 60, m. Daniel READ, farmer, ae 70, of Ashford,		
Sept. 27, 1848, by Rev. Charles Peabody	5	136-7
Thomas F., s. Jabez, b. Aug. 7, 1831	6	87
--------, s. Barnes G., shoemaker, ae 30, & Elizabeth J., ae 28,		
b. Apr. 3, 1851	5	146-7
DUNN, Sarah, of Ashford, m. Emery SIMMONS, of Woodstock,		
May 19, 1844, by Erastus Dickinson	5	89
DUNTEN, Sarah, m. Josiah HOLMES, Oct. 27, 1757	2	70
DUNWORTH, George, of Hampton, m. Abigail WHITTAM, of		
Ashford, Sept. 27, 1821, by Rev. William Storrs	5	4
DURFEE, Samuel B., of Providence, R. I., m. Miranda		
MUMFORD, of Ashford, Dec. 27, 1831, by Rev.		
Benjamin Paine	5	46
DURGY, Lois, m. Asa HAMMOND, Jan. 12, 1758	1	105
DURHAM*, Abiel, of Hampton, m. Clarissa LUMMIS, of Ashford,		
Nov. 22, 1820, by W[illia]m Storrs (*DURKEE?)	5	1
DURKEE, Abiel, of Hampton, m. Clarissa LUMMIS, of Ashford,		
Nov. 22, 1820, by W[illia]m, Storrs (See Abiel		
DURHAM)	6	26
Charles C., s. Whitman C., hatter, ae 23, & Emily A., ae 21, b.		
Dec.7, 1849	5	140-1
Elisabeth, m. Joseph BURNHAM, June 13, 1776	4	94
Frank, s. Ralph, hatter, ae 22, & Emily, ae 20, b. May 11, 1849	5	132-3
Olive, Mrs., m. Luther WARREN, Sept. 30, 1847, by Charles		
Peabody	5	101

	Vol.	Page
DURKEE, (cont.)		
Olive, ae 51, b. Mansfield, res. Ashford, m. 2d h.		
Luther **WARREN**, farmer, ae 75, of Ashford, Sept. 30,		
1847, by Charles Peabody	5	128-9
Ralph, m. Emily **LINCOLN**, Nov. 22, 1847, by Cha[rle]s		
Peabody	5	102
Ralph, hatter, ae 21, b. Mansfield, res. Ashford, m. Emily A.		
LINCOLN, ae 18, of Ashford, Nov. 22, 1847, by		
Charles Peaody	5	128-9
Whitman C., m. Eveline O. **LINCOLN**, b. of Ashford, Nov.		
23, 1846, by Charles Peabody	5	98
DYER, Patiance, m. Jonathan **GOULD**, [ ]	4	286
Waty, m. [Joshua] **FARNH[AM]**, Mar. 31, 179[ ]	4	285
EASTMAN, Abigail, d. Philip & Mary, b. Aug. 1, 1735 ; d. May		
16, 1737	1	4
Abigail, d. Sam[ue]ll & Thankfull, b. Jan. 20, 1743/4	2	32
Abigaill, d. Philip, b. Mar. 6, 1746	1	6
Abigail, d. Sam[ue]ll & Dorothy, b. Jan. 8, 1764	2	30
Abigail Soper, d, Neal & Hannah, b. July 14, 1768	3	17
Alcy Sophia, d. Rufus, b. Jan. 20, 1839	6	90
Anne, d. Eben[eze]r & Mary, b. July 9, 1759	3	102
Asael, s. Peter & Abigail, b. Mar. 7, 1763	3	17
Beniamin, s. Ebenezer & Mary, b. Nov. 7, 1753	1	82
Benj[ami]n, s. Ebe[neze]r & Mary, b. Nov. 10, 175[ ]	3	102
Benj[ami]n, [s. Eben[eze]r & Mary], b. July 26, 1763	3	102
Benjamin, s. Timothy & Est[h]er, b. Oct. 6, 1765	4	32
Benjamin, m. Marsylva **JONES**, Nov. 8, 1796	4	18
Benjamin F., m. Martha **KNOWLTON**, b. of Ashford, May 22,		
"last", [1826], by Ezekiel Skinner	5	23
Betsey, d. Roswell & Abigail, b. Nov. 17, 1805	4	123
Betsey, m. Jonathan A. **JAMES**, Mar. 23, 1826, by Rev.		
Amos Babcock, Jr. Intention published	5	22
Charles, s. Neeal & Hannah, b. Feb. 10, 1761	3	17
Clark, s. Timothy, b. Sept. 30, 1763	1	72
Cumfort, d. Jonathan & Elisabeth, b. June 9, 1762	2	19
Craft, of Grafton, Mass., m. Mrs. Betsey A. **HILL**, of		
Williamantic, Mar. 2, 1851, by Rev. P. Mathewson	5	106
Craft, shoemaker, of Ashford, m. Bets[e]y W. **HILL**, Mar. 2,		
1851, by P. Mathewson	5	148-9
Dorothy, d. Sam[ue]ll & Dorothy, b. Sept. 1, 1761	2	30
Ebenezer, s. Philip & Mary, b. Feb 16, 1719/20	A	6
Ebenezer, s. Philip & Mary, b. Feb. 16, 1719/20	1	4
Ebenezer, m. Mary **FLETCHER**, July 17, 1751	3	102
Ebenezer, s. [Ebenezer] & Mary, b. Nov. 10, 175[ ] ; d. Nov.		
12, 1754	3	102
Ebenezer, s. Eben[ez]r & Mary, b. Oct. 4, 1757	3	102
Ebenezer, s. Nathan & Aphia, b. May 8, 1797	4	63
Elezebeth, d. Philip, & Mary, b. Mar. 31. 1731	1	4
Elesabeth, d. Eben[eze]r & Mary, b. May 16, 1752	3	102

	Vol.	Page
EASTMAN, (cont.)		
Elisabeth had [d.] Johanna Hil[l]l, b. May 2, 1756	3	105
Erastus Snell, s. Roswell & Abigail, b. Jan.7, 1808	4	123
Esther, d. Timothy & Esther, b. Apr. [ ], 1749	1	72
Esther, d. Phillip & Elisabeth, b. [ ]	4	5
Eunis, d. Eben[eze]r & Mary, b. Feb. 11, 1756	3	102
Eunice, d. Benj[ami]n & Marsylva, b. Sept. 5, 1797	4	18
Fielder, s. Benj[ami]n & Marsylva, b. May 11, 1801	4	18
George Henry, s. Rufus, b. Sept. 3, 1837 ; d. Aug. 2, 1839	6	90
Hannah, d. Philip & Mary, b. Sept. 23, 1733	1	4
Hannah, d. Timothy & Easther, b. Nov. 9, 1752	1	72
Hulday, d. Jonathan & Elizebeth, b. Sept. 12, 1750	2	19
Jemima, d. Timothy, Jr. & Susanna, b. [ ]	4	5
Joanna, d. Samvel & Thankfull, b. July 7, 1746;d. Feb. 2, 1749	2	32
Joannah, d. Samvel & Thankfull, b. June 6, 1749	2	32
Jonathan, s. Philip & Mary, b. June 3, 1724	A	8
Jonathan, s. Philip & Mary, b. June 3, 1724	1	4
Jonathan, m. Elizaabeth PI[E]RCE, Nov. 23, 1749, by Rev. John Bass	2	19
Jonathan, s. Jonathan & Elisabeth, b. Oct. 7, 1760	2	19
Joseph, s. Timothy & Easther, b. Jan. 24, 1739/40	1	72
Joseph, s. Timo[thy] [& Easther], d. Sept. 27, 1759	1	72
Josiah, s. Timothy & Est[h]er, b. July 26, 1760	1	111
Justis, s. Peter & Abigail, b. Nov. 22, 1777	3	17
Levina, d. Timo[thy], Jr. & Susannah, b.[ ]	4	5
Lucinda, d. Nathan & Aphia, b. Sept. 8, 1798	4	63
Lucinda, m. Edmund LYON, Dec. 1, 1819	6	24
Lucy, d. Samuell & Thankfull, b. Sept. 29, 1753	2	32
Lucy Ann, d. Erasmus S., farmer, ae 39, & Lucina, ad 36, b. Oct. 8, 1847	5	128-9
Lucy Ann, d. Sept. 27, 1849, ae 11 m.	5	144-5
Lydia, d. Neal & Hannah, b. Nov. 27, 1771	3	17
Mary, m. John RICE, Oct. 22, 1724	A	9
Mary, d. Philip, b. Jan. 10, 1744	1	6
Mary, d. Samvel & Thankfull, b. June 20, 1751	2	32
Mary, [w. Phillip], d. July 20, 1752	1	4
Mary, d. Neal & Hannah, b. Dec. 25, 1764	3	17
Mary, d. Eben[eze]r & Mary, b. Sept. 15, 1767	3	102
Mary, d. Benj[ami]n & Marsylva, b. June 2, 1799	4	18
Mary, d. Phillip & Elizabeth, b. [ ]	4	5
Mehitable, d. Timo[thy], Jr. & Susannah, b. [ ] ; d. Aug. 27, 1775	4	5
Mol[l]e, d. Timo[thy],Jr. & Susannah, b. [ ]	4	5
Nathan, [s. Eben[eze]r & Mary], b. June 28, 1765	3	102
Nathan, m. Aphia BARK, Apr. 29, 1795	4	63
Nathan, s. Nathan & Aphia, b. Dec. 19, 1795	4	63
Nathan, Jr. , m. Louis HANDALL, b. of Ashford, Nov. 4, 1821, by Levi Work, J. P.	5	5

EASTMAN, (cont.)	Vol.	Page
Neal, m. Hannah JOHNSON, Oct. 13, 1759,		
Rev. Mr. Stephen Williams	1	106
Otis, s. Justin, b.[ ]	4	5
Peter, s. Phillip & Mary, b. May 3, 1726	A	10
Peter, s. Philip & Mary, b. Feb. 22, 1727/8	1	4
Peter, [s. Philip & Mary], d. Apr. 12, 1737, in the 10th y. of his		
age	1	4
Peter, s. Philip, Jr., b. Sept. 18, 1737	1	6
Peter, s. Timothy & Esther, b. July 25, 1746	1	72
Peter, m. Abigail HILL, Oct. 17, 1762	3	17
Phebe, d. Philip & Elesabeth, b. [ ]	4	5
Phillip, Esq., d. Mar. 25, 1741	1	4
Philip, s. Timothy & Easther, b. Jan. 17, 1741/2	1	72
Phillip, s. Peter & Abigail, b. Sept. 19, 1773	3	17
Philip, Jr., m. Elizabeth HODGES, [ ]	4	5
Roswel[l], s. Peter & Abigail, b. Dec. 18, 1780	3	17
Roswell, of Hartford, m. Susan ADAMS, of Pomfret, Nov. 11,		
[1841], by Francis Williams	5	79
Rufus Alexander, s. Rufus, b. Jan. 11, 1832 ; d. July 28, 1839	6	90
Russell Smith, s. Rufus, b. Feb. 6, 1834	6	90
Ruth, d. Philip & Mary, b. Apr. 23, 1722	1	4
Ruth, d. Philip & Mary, b. Apr. 23, 1722	A	6
Ruth, m. Will[ia]m CHEN[E]Y, Mar. 14, 1738/9	1	76
Ruth, d. Samuel & Dorothy, b. Mar. 20, 1766	2	30
Samuel, s. Philip & Mary, b. May 17, 1716	A	3
Samuel, s. Philip & Mary, b. May 17, 1716	1	4
Sam[ue]ll, M. Thankfull REED, Feb 25, 1742/3	2	32
Sam[ue]ll, m. Dorothy GAGGAIL, Mar. 1, 1759	2	32
Sarah, d. Philip, b. May 10, 1741	1	6
Sarah, d. Jonathan & Elizebath, b. May 27, 1752	2	19
Sarah, m. John PRESTON, Jr., Nov. 15, 1759	3	16
Sarah, d. Eben[eze]r & Mary, b. Aug. 7, 1761	3	102
Sarah, m. Samuel UTLEY, Jan. 7, 1790	4	233
Seth, s. Eben[eze]r & Mary, b. Feb 9, 1771	3	102
Sophia, of Ashford, m. Warner ABBOTT, of Otison, N. Y. ,		
Oct. 10, 1827, by Rev. Philo Judson	5	29
Susannah, d. Timo[thy], Jr. & Susanna, b. [ ]	4	5
Sibbell, d. Timothy & Est[h]er, b. Feb. 5, 1755 ; d. Dec. 6,		
1757	1	72
Sibbell, d. Timothy & Est[h]er, b. Aug. 31. 1758	1	72
Thankfull, d. Samuel & Thankfull, b. Feb. 16, 1756	2	32
Timothy, s. Phillip & Mary, b. Mar. 5, 1717/18	A	3
Timothy, s. Philip & Mary, b. Mar. 5, 1717/18	1	4
Timothy, m. Easther CLARK, Apr. 15, 1739, by Mr. Hale	1	72
Timothy, s. Timothy & Easther, b. Apr. 24, 1744	1	72
Timothy, Jr., m. Susannah CURTISS, Feb. [ ]	4	5
Tryphina, d. Peter & Abigail, b. Oct. 2, 1765	3	17
Tryphena, m. Boaz WHITON, Jan. 31. 1788	4	254

EASTMAN, (cont.)	Vol.	Page
-----, of Ashford, m. [ ]BILL, of Chaplin,		
Oct. 9, 1831, by Rev. Philo Judson	5	45
EATON, EATAN, Abel, s. Calvin & Elisabeth, b. Oct. 14, 1775	3	59
Abigaill, d. Nathan[i]el & Easter, d. Nov. 26, 1731	1	10
Abigail, d. Nathan[e]el & Easther, b. May 20, 1738	1	62
Abigaill, d. Nathan[i]el, d. Oct. 23, 1742	1	62
Abigail, d. Ebenezer & Mary, b. Apr. 26, 175[ ]	1	97
Almon, s. Elizabeth, b. May 18, 1788	3	59
Ama, m. William BICKNELL, Nov.15, 1759	2	57
Amy, d. Nathan[i]el & Easther, b. Nov. 26, 1739	1	62
Ann, d. Nathan[i]el, d. Oct. 2, 1738	1	62
Ann, d. Joshua & Ann, b. Oct. 11, 1749 ; d. Nov. 24, 1750	1	70
An[n]a, d. Nathan[i]el & Est[h]er, b. Feb. 19, 1732/3	1	10
Anna, m. Reuben PARKER, Oct. 9, 1788	4	261
Anna, d. Josiah & Anna, b. Mar. 15, 1790	4	14
An[n]e, d. Joshua & An[n]e, b. Nov. 20, 1738 ; d. Dec. 20, 1740	1	70
Anne, d. Calvin & Elesabeth, b. June 19, 1768	3	59
Anne, d. Josiah & Sibbel, b. July 14, 1774	3	37
Anne, d. David & Patience, b. Apr. 14, 1[ ]	1	97
Asa, s. David & Bethyah, b. Mar. 16, 1745/6	1	64
Asa, m. Abigail GOODALE, Nov. 5, 1772	4	87
Asa, s. Asa & Abigail, b. May 27, 1780	4	87
Asa, s. James & Fanny, b. Mar. 6, [ ]	4	97
Avis, d. Nat, Jr. & Sarah, b. Feb. 15, 1775	4	34
Azel, s. Josiah & Sibbel, b. Apr. 21, 1769	3	37
Bethyah, w. David & d. of Tho[ma]s TIFFANY, d. Dec. 11, 1748	1	63
Bethiah, d. Asa & Abigail, b. Jan. 22, 1774	4	87
Beulah, d. Josiah & Sibbel, b. July 13, 1763	3	37
Calvin, s. Nathan[i]el & Easter, b. Jan. 10, 1730 ; d. Mar. 29, 1733	1	10
Calvin, s. Nathan[ie]l & Easter, b. Aug. 11, 1736	1	10
Calvin, m. Elesabeth, WORK, Dec. 8, 1757	1	99
Calvin, s. Calvin & Elisabeth, b. Apr. 7, 1762; d. Jan. 31. 1764	3	59
Calvin, d. Nov. 22, 1787	3	59
Calvin, s. James & Fanny, b. Dec. 21, [ ]	4	97
Catharine, d. Stephen & Fannela, b. Apr. 2, 1782	4	230
Charles, s. Samuel & Chloe, b. July 9, 1769	4	12
Chloe, w. Samuel, d. May 22, 1776	4	12
Chloe, d. Samuel & Martha, b. Mar. 16, 1780	4	12
Chloe, d. Erastus & Polley, b. Jan. 1, 1798	4	228
David, m. Dinah DAVIS, Oct. 19, 1732	1	64
David, s. David & Dinah, b. Aug. 4, 1738	1	64
David, m. Bethyah TIFFANY, Mar. 11, 1741/2, by Rev. James Hale	1	64
David, m. Patiance KENDAL, July 20, 1749, by Sqr.. Bicknel	1	63
David, Jr., m. Mary PRESTON, June 29, 1757	1	107

EATON, EATAN, (cont.)	Vol.	Page
David, s. Asa & Abigail, b. Jan. 6, 1778	4	87
Desire, [twin with Freelove], d. Eben[eze]r & Mary, b. May 29, 1778	3	10
Desire, m. Alva ROGERS, Sept. 8, 1803	4	105
Diadamy, d. Eben[eze]r & Mary, b. Apr. 3, 1763	3	10
Dilley, d. Eben[eze]r & Mary, b. Jan. 13, 1776	3	10
Dinah, d. David, Jr. & Mary, b. Sept. 5, 1757	1	107
Ebenezer, s. Tho[ma]s, d. Dec. 19, 1739	1	62
Ebenezer, s. Nathan[i]el & Easther, b. Jan. 21, 1740/41	1	62
Eben[eze]r, m. Mary HUMPHREY, May, 12, 1753	3	10
Eben[eze]r, s. Eben[eze]r & Mary, b. Dec. 18, 1760	3	10
Edwin, of Chapllin, m. Caroline GAYLORD, of Ashford, Jan. 12, 1831, by Rev. Philo Judson	5	41
Elijah, s. Nathan[i]el & Easther, b. Aug. 24, 1742	1	62
Elisabeth, d. Calvin & Elizabeth, b. Feb. 9, 1765	3	59
Elisabeth, d. Ebenezer & Mary, b. Jan. 6, 1767	3	10
Elizabeth had s. Almon, b. May 18, 1788	3	59
Elisabeth, d. Calvin, d. Jan. 11, 1790	3	59
Elisabeth, d. Sept. 29, 1790	3	59
Elmiria, d. James & Fanny, b. Ju[ ] 23, 1815	4	97
Ephrem, s. David & Dinah, b. Oct. 2, 1736	1	64
Erastus, s. Samuel & Chloe, b. May 6, 1775	4	12
Easter, d. Nathan[i]el & Easter, b. Apr. 5, 1728	1	10
Easther, d. Nathan[i]el, d. Nov. 6, 1748* (*Entry crossed out)	1	62
Easter, d. Calvin & Elisabeth, b. Sept. 7, 1758	1	101
Est[h]er, w. Nath[anie]ll, d. Sept. 14, 1769	1	62
Easter, m. Tiras PRESTON, Nov. 2, 1773	4	68
Ethalmay, d. Josiah & Anna, b. Jan. 8, 1785	4	14
Eunis, d. Eben[eze]r & Mary, b. Mar. 19, 1765	3	10
Ezekiel, s. David & Bethyah, b. Dec. 7, 1747	1	64
Fanny, d. James & Fanny, b. May [ ]	4	97
Freelove, [twin with Desire], d. Eben[eze]r & Mary, b. May 29, 1778	3	10
Hannah, d. Dec. 20, 1748	1	23
Hannah, d. Ebenezer & Mary, b. Feb. 1, 1771	3	10
Horris, s. Erastus & Polley, b. Apr. 13, 1796 (Perhaps Harris)	4	228
Ira, s. Josiah & Sibbel, b. Mar. 2, 1772	3	37
James, s. Calvin & Elisabeth, b. Aug. 3, 1780	3	59
James, s. Asa & Abigail, b. June 10, 1782	4	87
James, s. David & Patience, b. Aug. 9, 1759	1	108
James, m. Fanny RICHARDS, May 1, [ ]	4	97
John, s. Nathan[i]el & Easther, b. Aug. 20, 1745	1	62
Joshua, m. Ann WOODCOCK, Dec. 14, 1737, by Rev. Mr. Hale	1	70
Joshua, d. Mar. 27, 1785	1	70
Joshua, s. Josiah & Anna, [b.] May 23, 1787	4	14
Josiah, s. David & Dinah, b. Oct. 18, 1733	1	64
Josiah, m. Sibbel JOHNSON, Oct. 24, 1754, by James		

EATON, EATAN, (cont.)	Vol.	Page
Bicknell, Esq.	1	87
Josiah, s. Josiah & Sibble, b. Feb. 25, 1757	1	95
Josiah, d. Apr. 13, 1777	3	37
Josiah, m. Anna KNOWLTON, Apr. 23, 1780	4	14
Josiah, s. Josiah & Anna, b. Dec. 22, 1782	4	14
Josiah, of Ashford, m. Mrs. Elizabeth GREEN, of Union, Mar. 6, [1834], by Job Cushman	5	53
Kadniel, s. Stephen & Fannela, b. Jan. 20, 1786 (Thadniel?)	4	230
Lenda, d. Nathan & Phebee, b. July 4, 1780	4	116
Loa, d. Stephen & Fannella, b. June 26, 1784	4	230
Lucinda, d. Josiah & Sibbill, b. Apr. 11, 1767	3	37
Lida, d. Nathan[i]el & Easther, b. Jan. 30, 1743/4	1	62
Lydia, w. Thomas, d. Aug. 29, 1748, in the 69th y. of her age	1	15
Lydia, d. Nath[anie]ll, d. Nov. 6, 1748	1	23
Lydia, d. Nathaneal & Esther, b. June 4, 1749	1	23
Martha, d. Calvin & Elisabeth, b. May 28, 1760	1	110
Mary, d. David & Bethyah, b. Feb. 11, 1742/3 ; d. the 14th day of the same month	1	64
Mary, d. David & Patience, b. May 24, 1752	1	15
Mary, d. Ebenezer & Mary b. Feb. 13, 1759	1	102
Mary, w. David, Jr., d. Jan. 18, 1760	1	107
Metilda, d. Calvin & Elisabeth, b. Sept. 6, 1772	3	59
Mavarick, s. Josiah & Sibbel, b. July 24, 1755	1	91
Mehetebel, d. Joshua & Ann, b. Oct. 17, 1740	1	70
Mehetiable, m. William KNOWLTON, Dec. 15, 1757	1	102
Meriam, d. Ebenezer & Mary, b. Feb. 17, 1769	3	10
Nabby, d. Asa & Abigail, b. Aug. 16, 1784	4	87
Nathan, s. Ebenezer & Mary, b. Aug. 29, 1755	1	89
Nathan, m. Phebee BROOKS, Dec. 16, 1779	4	116
Nathan[i]el, m. Easter PERRY, May 31, 1727, by Rev. James Hale	1	10
Nathan[i]el, s. Nathan[i]el & Easter, b. Mar. 10, 1731/2 ; d. [Mar.] 16, [1731/2]	1	10
Nathaniel, s. Nathaniel & Easter, b. Feb. 2, 1734/5	1	10
Nath[anie]ll, Jr. , m. Sarah JOHNSON, Nov, 13, 1755, by James Bicknell, J. P.	1	90
Nath[anie]ll, d. Mar. 15, 1785	1	62
Origen, s. Josiah & Sibbell, b. May 8, 1765	3	37
Polley, d. Josiah & Sibbel, b. Jan. 3, 1777	3	37
Polley, d. Josiah & Anna, b. Dec. 30, 1780	4	14
Roxeelana, d. Nath[anie]ll, Jr. & Sarah, b. Nov. 5, 1772	4	34
Salla, d. Nath[anie]ll & Sarah, b. Mar. 14, 1770	4	34
Samvel, s. Joshua & Ann, b. Nov. 14, 1742	1	70
[Samu]el, m. Chloe STEDMAN, Sept. 23, 1765, by Elijah Whiton, J. P.	4	12
Samuel, m. Martha TUBBS, Dec. 11, 1777	4	12
Samuel, s. Samuel & Martha, b. July 13, 1778	4	12
Sarah, d. David & Patience, b. Aug. 17, 1754	1	85

	Vol.	Page
EATON, EATAN, (cont.)		
Simeon, s. David & Bethyah, b. July 3,		
1744 ; d. Nov. 20, 1748, in the 5th y. of his age	1	64
Simeon, s. David & Patian[c]e, b. Apr. 16, 1750	1	64
Simeon, s. Asa & Abigail, b. May 21, 1775	4	87
Stephen, s. Josiah & Sibble, b. May 4, 1761	3	37
Stephen, m. Fannela **KNOWLTON,** Nov. 12, 1781	4	230
Sibbel, d, Josiah & Sibbel, b. Apr. 1, 1759	1	108
Thankfull, d. Ebenezer & Mary, b. Feb. 2, 1773	3	10
Thirzey, d. James & Fanny, b. Aug. [ ]	4	97
Thomas, d. Aug. 14, 1748, in the 73rd y. of his age	1	15
William, s. Josiah & Anna, b. June 26, 1792 ; d. Oct. 31, 1797	4	14
Zilpah, d. Calvin & Elisabeth, b. June 3, 1770	3	59
Zilpah, d. Calvin, d. Aug. 29, 1790	3	59
----lemon, s. Samuel & Chloe, b. Jan. 17, 1766	4	12
----rill, s. Samuel & Chloe, b. Dec. 16, 1767	4	12
----oswell, s. Samuel & Chloe, b. Mar, 9, 1773	4	12
----bby, d. Samuel & Chloe, b. Apr. 18, 1771	4	12
EDDY, Barnibus, m. Zerorah **CARPENTER,** Nov. 1, 1750, by Rev.		
Mr. Stephen Williams	1	81
Hannah, d. Barnabas & Zeruiah, b. Apr. 13, 1754	2	20
Levi, s. Joel & Rachel, b. June 19, 1748	2	30
Othniel, s. Joel & Rachel, b. May 30, 1751	2	30
William, s. Benj[ami]n & Joany, b. Sept. 8, 1761	3	index
EDGERTON, EGERTON, Asa B., of Mansfield, m. Mahala		
MOSELEY, of Ashford, Nov, 16, 1829, by Amasa		
Lyon, J. P.	5	36
Huldah, m. Alton **SHERMAN,** b. of Ashford, Nov. 27, 1834,		
by W[illia]m Livescy, Elder, Eastford	5	55
Laura L., m. John **SHERMAN,** b. of Ashford, Feb. 6, 1842, by		
Rev. Charles C. Barnes	5	80
EDWARDS, Edward B., of Berlin, Conn., m. Laura **BICKNELL,** of		
Ashford, May 6, 1829, by Rev. Philo Judson	5	35
ELDRIDGE, ELDRID, ELDREDGE, Abigail, w. Hezekiah, d. July		
20, 17[ ]	3	129
Abigail, d. Elijah & Bethiah, b. Nov. 24, 1800	4	23
Alanson, s. Micah & Anna, b. Nov. 16, 1781, at Salsbury,		
Conn.	4	22
Anna, d. Micah & Anna, b. Mar. 10, 1786, at Cootcootsocky,		
N. Y	4	22
Armina, d. Stephen & Elisabeth, b. Jan. 7, 1807	4	62
David, s. Elisha & Abigail, b. Feb. 13, 1766	4	22
Deidamia, d. Micah & Anna, b. Jan. 16, 1780, at New Winsor,		
Mass.	4	22
Elijah, m. Bethiah **CHAPMAN,** Mar. 17, 1791	4	265
Elijah, s. Elijah & Bethiah, b. Sept. 4, 1794	4	23
Elijah, Jr., of Willington, m. Hannah **CHAFFEE,** of Ashford,		
Nov. 22, 1837, by Amos Baabcock	5	67
Elisabeth, d. Elijah & Bethiah, b. Jan. 13, 1805	4	23

	Vol.	Page
EWING, EWINGS, EWINS, (cont.)		
Alexander, s. Alex[ande]r, Jr. & Lydia, b. May 28, 1768	4	18
Ann, [d. Alexander & Jean], b. May 1, 1741	4	18
Avis, see under Aavis		
Catharine, [d. Alexander & Jean], b. Oct. 23, 1737	4	18
Eunice, d. Alex[ande]r, Jr. & Lydia, b. June 1, 1766	4	18
Jeen, [d. Alexander & Jean], b. Nov. 2, 1735 ; d. Sept. 11, 1754	4	18
John, [s. Alexander & Jean], b. Dec. 20, 1739	4	18
John, m. Rhode **BADGER**, Dec. 4. 1761	4	19
Lydia, d. Alex[ande]r, Jr. & Lydia, b. Dec. 13, 1761	4	18
Marthew, [s. Alexander & Jean], b. Mar. 11, 1749 ; d. Sept. 9, 1754	4	18
Mary, d. Alexander & Mary, b. Feb. 14, , 1733/4	1	13
Mary, m. Samuell **HOLMES**, Aug. 1, 1754	1	84
Mary, d. John & Rhoda, b. May 6, 1763	4	11
Matthew, see under Marthew		
Sall, m. Benjamin **HOW**, Sept. 13, 1766	4	37
Sam[ue]ll, [s. Alexander & Jean], b. Oct. 15, 1745 ; d. Sept. 2, 1754	4	18
Samuel, s. Alex[ande]r, Jr. & Lydia, b. July 14, 1773	4	18
Sarah, [d. Alexander & Jean], b. May 15,1743	4	18
Thomas, [s. Alexander & Jean], b. Dec. 7, 1755	4	18
Will[ia]m, [s. Alexander & Jean], b. Oct. 20, 1747 ; d. Sept. 7, 1754	4	18
William, s. Alex[ande]r, Jr. & Lydia, b. May 15, 1763	4	18
FARNHAM, FARHAM, FARNUM, [see also **VANRUM.** Abigail, d. Manassah, Jr. & Patience, b. Jan. 8, 1763	3	77
Abigail, m. Ephraim **HAYWARD**, Feb. 26, 1789	4	260
Ame, d. Mana[sa]h & Patience, b. Oct. 13, 1776	3	77
Ame, d. Manas[s]ah & Patience, d. Mar. 8, 1813, ae 37	3	77
Amy E., b. Middletown, res. Ashford, d. Aug. [ ], 1850, ae 2	5	150-1
Asa, s. Asa & Lydia, b. July 23, 1760	4	12
Asa, s. Solomon & Salla, b. May 8, 1794	4	269
Asa, s. Jonathan & Eunice, b. June 17, 1802	4	246
Asa, m. Elizabeth **WOODARD**, b. of Ashford, (Westford Society) May 1, 1825, by Levi Smith, at Westford Society	5	18
Asa Antione Dubrilla, s. Asa & Elizabeth, b. May 6, 1830	6	62
[A]ugustus, s. Rufus & Betsey, b. Feb. 5, 1816	4	12
Avery, s. Solomon & Salla, b. July 16, 1796	4	269
Benjamin, m. Ann **CHUBB**, Mar. 28, 1781	4	120
Benj[ami]n, d. May 5, 1807	4	160
Betsey, [twin with Sally], d. Eliasah & Sally, b. Aug. 6, 1805	4	227
Betsey, housekeeper, d. Sept. 19, 1848, ae 37	5	138-9
Caroline, d. Rufus & Betsey, b. June 19, 1807	4	12
Caroline, of Ashford, m. Keith W. **WHITE**, of Uxbridge, Mass., Dec. 7, 1829, by Rev. Luke Wood	5	37

	Vol.	Page
FARNHAM, FARNAM, FARNUM, (cont.)		
Clarissa, d. Elijah & Thankful, b. Nov. 21, 1793	4	273
Clarissa, m. Elder David **BENNETT**, b. of Ashford, Feb. 26, 1832, by Rev. Ezekiel Skinner	5	46
Eleasaph, s. Asa & Lydia, b. July 25, 1769	4	12
Elijah, s. Manassah & Patience, b. Sept. 26, 1768	3	77
Elijah, m. Thankful **ROBINSON**, Aug. 4, 1793	4	273
Elithar, s. Benj[ami]n & Ann, b. Oct. 14, 1788	4	120
Elisabeth, m. Daniel **KNOWLTON**, Nov. 3, 1763	3	20
Elisabeth, d. Manassah & Patience, b. Nov. 17, 1773	3	77
Elisabeth, d. Benj[ami]n & Ann, b. Mar. 20, 1793	4	120
Ephraim, s. Manassah & Patience, b. Oct. 10, 1760	1	111
Ephraim, s. Man[a]ssah, d. Oct. 20, 1776	3	77
Ephraim, s. Benj[ami]n & Ann, b. Apr. 22, 1782	4	120
Erastus, s. Solomon & Salla, b. Sept. 12, 1802	4	269
Eunice, m. Silas **SNOW**, Dec. 16, 1782	4	230
Hannah, d. Asa & Lydia, b. Nov. 2, 1775	4	12
Harrison, d. Aug. 31, 1848, ae 8	5	138-9
Henry Tayler, s. Orris & Susan, b. July 29, 1846	6	102
Horace, m. Susan **WILLIAMS**, b. of Westford, Nov. 24, 1844, by R. V. Lyon, in Westford Society	5	92
Icy, d. Isaac & Mehetable, b. June 21, 1796	4	84
Ira, s. Elijah & Thankful, b. Oct. 24, 1795 ; d. Mar. 17, 1823, ae 28	4	273
Isaac, s. Manassah, Jr. & Patience, b. Oct. 11, 1766	3	77
Isaac, m. Mehetable **SNOW**, Oct. 15, 1792	4	84
Jane Elizabeth, d. Asa & Elizabeth, b. Feb. 25, 1827	6	62
Jemima, d. Joseph & Carthrine, b. July 1, 1773	4	71
Jeremiah, s. Rufus & Betsey, b. Jan. 6, 1809	4	12
John, s. Asa, d. Mar. 17, 1767	4	12
John, s. Manassah & Patience, b. Mar. 31, 1771	3	77
Jonathan, s. Asa & Lydia, b. Mar. 13, 1767	4	12
Jonathan, m. Eunice **SNELL**, Mar. 20, 1794	4	246
Joseph, m. Carthrine **SPRING**, Mar. 15, 1770	4	71
Joseph, s. Benj[ami]n & Ann, b. Mar. 24, 1784	4	120
[Joshua], m. Waty **DYER**, Mar. 31, 179[ ]	4	285
Lucy, d. Rufus & Betsey, b. July 28, 1804	4	70
Lucy, of Ashford, m. Joshua C. **STRANAHAN**, of Plainfield, Apr. 20, 1824, by Rev. Luke Wood, Westford	5	31
Luenda, d. Solomon & Salla, b. Sept. 17, 1791	4	269
Lyd[i]a, d. Asa & Lyd[i]a, b. Feb. 24, 1758	1	102
Lydia, d. Eliasaph & Sally, b. Jan. 22, 1803	4	227
Manasseh, d. May 16, 1808	3	77
Manus Ciesa, s. Rufus & Betsey, b. Jan. 6, 1814	4	12
Maria Elizabeth, d. William, shoemaker, mulatto, ae 24, & Sophronia, ae 28, b. Dec. 11, 1847	5	126-7
Martha, m. Joseph **DRAPER**, Sept. 10, 1821, by Rev. Philo Judson	5	4

	Vol.	Page
FARNHAM, FARNAM, FARNUM, (cont.)		
Mary, d. Ephraim & Hannah, b. Feb. 8, 1806	4	265
Metilda, d. Solomon & Salla, b. Sept. 13, 1787	4	269
Matilda, m. Alvan **KIMBAL** Apr. 1, 1806	4	122
Mehetable, d. Isaac & Mehetable, b. May 23, [ ]	4	84
Nabby, d. Isaac & Mehetable, b. Aug. 26, 1793	4	84
Orphe, d. Elujah & Thankful, b. Mar. 26, 1801	4	273
Orin, s. Elijah & Thankful, b. May 19, 1803 ; d. Apr. 11, 1816	4	273
Orris, s. Elijah & Thankful, b. Jan. 16, 1797	4	273
Parmer, s. Elijah & Thankful, b. Jan. 9, 1800; d. Aug. 15, 1800	4	273
Roxey, d. Benj[ami]n & Ann, b. Sept. 12, 1798	4	120
Ruahamah, ae 22, dark, of Ashford, m. Hezekiah **CORBIN**, shoemaker, ae 21, white, b. Woodstock, res. Ashford, July 19, 1849, by Rev. Charles Peabody	5	136-7
Rufus, m. Betsey **GROVER**, Nov. 26, 1801	4	70
Rufus, s. Rufus & Betsey, b. Nov. 2, 1802	4	70
Sally, d. Joseph & Carthrine, b. Feb. 11, 1771	4	71
Salla, d. Solomon & Salla, b. Sept. 11, 1789	4	269
Salla, m. Jonathan **CHAFFEE**, Nov. 26, 1789	4	258
Sally, [twin with Betsey], d. Eliasah & Sally, b. Aug. 6, 1805	4	227
Sarah, d. Asa & Lydia, b. May 23, 1778	4	12
Sarah, d. Isaac & Mehetable, b. Sept. 4, 1798	4	84
Sarah, of Ashford, m. Reuben W. **BAKER**, of Plainsfield, July 12, 1847, by Charles Peabody	5	101
Selinia, d. Orres & Susan, b. Jan. 25, 1845	6	102
Solomon, m. Salla **AVERY**, Nov. 23, 1786	4	269
Sophia, d. Eph[rai]m & Hannah, b. Oct. 4, 1807	4	265
Stephen, s. Manassah, Jr. & Patience, b. Feb. 3, 1765	3	77
Stephen, s. Rufus & Betsey, b. July 7, 1811	4	12
Susan, Mrs., of Ashford, m. Henry H. **FELCH**, of Willington, Mar. 27, 1854, by Rev. P. Mathewson	5	110
Sylvester G., m. Mary **WHITAN**, b. of Ashford, Mar. 1, 1827, by Rev. Levi Wood	5	26
Sylvester Gilbert, s. Jon[a]th[an] & Eunice, b. Sept. 13, 1796	4	246
Tryphena, d. Benj[ami]n & Ann, b. Feb. 25, 1791	4	120
Tryphena, m. Amaziah **RUSS**, Nov. 10, 1811	4	26
Weltha, d. Elijah & Thankful, b. Sept. 14, 1798	4	273
William, s. William & Ann, b. Aug. 15, 1718	A	4
William, s. Benj[ami]n & Ann, b. Dec. 26, 1786	4	120
William, m. Sophronia **WILSON**, Sept. 5, 1847, by Charles Peabody	5	101
William, shoemaker, mulatto, ae 24, of Ashford, m. Sophronia, **WILLSON**, white, ae 28, Sept. 5, 1847, by Charles Peabody	5	128-9
William, s. William, shoemaker, dark, & Sophronia, white, b. Jan. 1, 1849	5	132-3
W[illia]m H., b. Middletown, res. Ashford, d. Aug. [ ], 1850 ae 1	5	150-1

	Vol.	Page
FARNHAN, FARNAM, FARNUM, (cont.)		
-----, [child of] Joshua, d. Jan. 28, 179[ ]	4	285
----, [s.] Joshua & Waty, b. Sept. 20, 179[ ]	4	285
----, s. Joshua & Waty, b. Oct. 23, 179[ ]	4	285
----, d. Joshua & Waty, b. Oct. 4, [ ]	4	285
---, d. Joshua, d. Aug. [ ]	4	285
----d. Joshua & Waty, b. Sept.[ ]	4	285
FARRER, FFARRER, Anne, d. Isaac & Mary, [b.] Aug, 13, 1707	A	3
Isaac, s. Isaac & Mary, b. Apr. 2, 1702, at Wooburn	A	3
Jacob, s. Isaac & Mary, b. June 11, 1705, at Woobourne	A	3
Janet, d. Isaac & Mary, b. Mar. 1, 1713, at Woobourne, d;		
same day	A	3
Jeduthan, s. Isaac & Mary, b. May 23, 1717	A	3
Joanna, d. Isaac & Mary, b. Mar. 17, 1711, at Wooburn	A	3
John, s. Isaac & Mary, b. Jan. 7, 1704, at Woobourne	A	3
Jonathan, s. Isaac & Mary, b. Apr. 28, 1709, in Woobourne	A	3
Lucy, d. Isaac & Mary, b. Oct. 8, 1714, at Woobourne	A	3
Mary, d. Isaac & Mary, b. Dec. 6, 1699, at Wooburn	A	3
Samuel, s. Isaac & Mary, b. Oct. 10, 1719	A	5
FAY, Dinah, d. Jedediah & Elisabeth, b. Sept. 21, 1754	1	86
Elisabeth, d. Jedediah & Elisabeth, b. Feb. 20, 1753	1	83
Ephraim Brigham, s. Jedediah & Elisabeth, b. June 7, 1764	3	53
Hannah, d. Jedidiah, Jr. & Martha, b. [ ]	4	5
Hepzibeth, d. Jedediah & Elisabeth, b. Apr. 29, 1762	3	53
Hephzibah, m. Eliphalet **CLARK,** June 1, 1785	4	268
Jedediah, s. Jedediah & Elisabeth, b. Apr. 21, 1760	3	53
Jedediah, s. Jedediah & Elisabeth, b. Apr. 22, 1760	1	110
Lucy, of Ashford, m. Miner **PARKER,** of Mansfield, Mar. 11,		
1821, by Rev. Philo Judson	5	2
Nancy, d. Jedidiah, Jr. & Martha, b. Feb. 10, [ ]	4	5
Nathan, s. Jedediah & Elisabeth, b. Mar. 2, 1768	3	53
Nathan, s. Jedidiah, Jr. & Martha, b. Feb. 15, [ ]	4	5
Nathan, s. Jedidiah, Jr. & Martha, b. Sept. 5, [ ]	4	5
Pattey, d. Jedidiah & Martha, b. May 3, [ ]	4	5
Sophronia E., of Pomfret, m. Charles W. **CLARK,** of East		
Windsor, July 6, 1845, by Rev. Geo[rge] Mixter	5	94
----ah, d. Jeded[iah] & Elisabeth, b. Sept. 10, 1756	1	94
FELCH, Henry H., of Willington, m. Mrs. Susan **FARNHAM,** of		
Ashford, Mar. 27, 1854, by Rev. P. Mathewson	5	110
FELSHAW, Mary, mother to W[illia]m **CHENEY,** d. May 15, 1760	3	105
FENNEY, [see under **FINNEY**]		
FENTON, Aurgusta, m. Daniel **READ,** July 5, 1798	4	282
Elisha, of Chaplin, m. Mary Ann **SNOW,** of Ashford, Nov. 30,		
1851, by Rev. P. Mathewson	5	108
Rebec[c]ah, m. Daniel **KNOWLTON,** Apr. 24, 1788	3	20
FERGUSON, Adaline, of Hartford, m. John **WHITMORE,** of		
Ashford, Sept. 18, 1853, by Rev. Ezekiel Skinner	5	110
FIELDS, Lorin, of Somers, m. Mary Ann E. **DEMON,** of Ashford,		

	Vol.	Page
FITTS, (cont.)		
Joseph P., s. Eben[eze]r F. & Nancy, b. Dec. 23, 1818	4	72
Lucy, of Pomfret, m. Parker **PARRISH**, of Woodstock, Sept.		
22, 1830, by Rev. Reuben Torrey, Eastford	5	40
Lyman, of Pomfret, m. Harriet M. **RICHARDS**, of Ashford,		
June 2, 1847, by Charles Peabody	5	100
Maria, m. Selden **MOSELEY**, b. of Ashford, Oct. 11, 1832, by		
Rev. Philo Judson	5	49
Nancy, d. Eben[eze]r F. & Nancy, b. July 20, 1807	4	72
Nancy, of Ashford, m. Jason W. **R[H]OADES**, of Chaplin,		
Nov. 25, 1830, by Rev. Ezekiel Skinner	5	40
Polley, d. Daniel & Elisabeth, b. July 6, 1775 ; d, [ ]	4	85
Polley, m. James H. **BUTLER**, b. of Ashford, Oct. 19, 1825,		
by Rev. Philo Judson	5	20
Polly Green, d. Eben[eze]r F. & Nancey, b. Aug. 17, 1803	4	72
Rhoda, d. Daniel & Elisabeth, b. May 27, 1787	4	85
[Ste]phen, m. Polly **KNOWLTON**, [ ]	4	283
[Ste]phen, s. Stephen & Polley, b. Oct. [ ]	4	283
Susannah, d. Eben[eze]r F. & Nancy, b. July 27, 1816	4	72
Thomas Knowlton, s. Stephen, Jr. & Waty, b. Oct. 23, 1831	6	77
----Knowlton, s. Stephen & Polley, [b.] July 11, 1807	4	283
----ah, d. Stephen & Polley, b. [ ]	4	283
FLETCHER, Elesabeth, m. Ebenezer **BOSWORTH**, May 17, 1759	3	114
Hannah, m. John **WATKINS**, Oct. 26, 1749	1	87
Mary, m. Ebenezer **EASTMAN**, July 17, 1751	3	102
FLINT, Aaron, m. Joanna **WHITON**, Nov. 25, 1830, by Rev. Luke		
Wood	5	41
Aaron, farmer, b. Windham, res. Ashford, d. Feb. 9, 1849, ae		
90	5	138-9
Adaline, Mrs., of Ashford, m. John **SEAVER**, of Sturbridge,		
Mass., Mar. 19, 1834, by Job Cushman	5	53
Ann Maria, of Ashford, m. Alvin **UNDERWOOD**, of Monson,		
Mass., June 29, 1842, by Rev. J. M. Bidwell	5	81
Anna, d. Jonathan & Molley, b. Apr. 20, 1794	4	237
Charles, d. June 29, 1848, ae 52	5	130-1
Ceyrel, s. Jonathan & Molley, b. Jan. 8, 1785	4	237
Elisha, s. Jonathan & Molley, b. Apr. 7, 1787	4	237
Elisabeth, m. Oliver **HINTCHER**, Apr. 20, 1758	3	27
Emeline, of Ashford, m. Lebbeus J. **PECK**, of Canton, Nov.		
24, 1831, by Rev. Joseph P. Tyler	5	46
Joseph, s. Jonathan & Molley, b. Mar. 15, 1789	4	237
Lucy, ae 47, m. James **BUFFINGTON**, farmer, ae 53, of		
Ashford, Feb. 8, 1849, by Rev. Cha[rle]s S. Adams	5	136-7
Mary, m. Thomas **YOUNG**, Mar. 2, 1796	4	50
Mary J., of Hampton, m. Albert **HADSON**, of Ashford, Oct.		
23, 1842, by Rev. Cha[rle]s Hyde	5	82
Salley, d. Jonathan & Molley, b. Apr. 19, 1796	4	237

	Vol.	Page
FLINT, (cont.)		
Sarah, m. Elias **CHAPMAN**, Jan. 31, 1771	4	45
Sarah, m. James **WALKER**, June 14. 1787	4	266
FLOYD, David, of Long Island, m. Abby **LEWIS**, of Brooklyn,		
Conn., [June] 6, [1825], by Reuben Torrey, Eastford	5	19
FOLLET, El[i]sabeth, m. Thomas **TIFFANY**, Apr. 15, 1777	4	110
Irene, m. Joseph **TRISCOT**, Nov. 30, 1773	4	81
Jerusha, m. Jacob **BOUTWEL**, Jr., Oct. 1, 1772	3	79
FOLSON, FULSOM, Ebenezer, s. Isarel & Rachel, b. Dec. 17,		
1727	1	13
Sarah, d. Isarel & Rachel, b. June 16, 1725	1	13
----, s. Israel & Rachel, b. Sept. 11, [ ]	A	8
FORD, Danforth U., factory operative, b. Chaplin, res. Ashford, d.		
Apr. 9, 1851, ae 33	5	150-1
Stephen, of Chaplin, m. Lorana **JOHNSON**, of Ashford, May		
5, 1832, by Rev. Philo Judson	5	47
FORDHAM, Elijah, m. Anna B. **CHAFFEE**, Oct. 3, 1838, by		
Thomas Dow, J. P.	5	69
FOSTER, Abraham, s. Sam[ue]ll, Jr. & Judeth, b. May 2, 1748	2	64
Abraham, m. Methiah **OULDS**, Sept. 21, 1769	4	30
Abraham, s. Abraham & Mehetable, b. Oct. 23, 1775	4	30
Ann, d. Samuel & Ruth, b. June 21, 1737	1	39
Hannah, d. Samvel, Jr. & Judah, b. Nov. 8, 1751	2	64
Jesse, m. Lucy **BANCROFT**, Aug. 30, 1803	4	103
Jonathan, s. Samuel & Ruth, b. May 24, 1742	1	39
Joseph P., s. Jesse & Lucy, b. Aug. 26, 1806	4	103
Judah, d. Samuell, Jr. & Judah,, b. Nov. 13, 1753	2	64
Mary, d. Samuel & Ruth, b. Apr. 11, 1735 ; d. Sept. 4, 174?,		
in the 8th y. of her age	1	39
Mehitable, d. Jesse & Lucy, b. Dec. 6, 1804	4	103
Meletiah, d. Abraham & Melatiah, b. Aug. 9, 1770	4	30
Ruth, d. Samuel & Ruth, b. Sept. 22, 1732 ; d. Sept. 13, 1742,		
in the 10th y. of her age	1	39
Ruth, d. Samvel, Jr. & Judeth, b. Mar. 1, 1749/50	2	64
Ruth, w. Samuell, d. Nov. 17, 1753	2	64
Samuel, m. Ruth **SNOW**, Dec. 3, 1724	A	10
Samuel, m. Ruth **SNOW**, Dec. 3, 1724	1	39
Samuel, s. Sam[ue]ll & Ruth, b. Mar. 1, 1725/6	A	10
Samuel, s. Samuel & Ruth, b. Mar. 1, 1725/6	1	39
Sam[ue]ll, Jr., m. Judath **KNOWLTON**, June 24, 1747, by		
Rev. Mr. John Bass	2	64
Samuel, Jr., d. Nov. 21, 1753	2	64
Samuel, s. Abraham & Melatiah, b. Oct. 23, 1772	4	30
Sarah, d. Sam[ue]ll & Ruth, b. Aug, 12, 1739	1	39
Susannah, d. Samuel & Ruth, b. Mar. 7, 1729/10 (sic) ; d. Aug.		
28, 1742, in the 13th y. of her age	1	39
FRANKLIN, Ann Maria, d. W[illia]m, B. & Mary, b. May 5, 1821	6	33
Ann Maria, m. Gilbert **GREEN**, b. of Ashford, Oct. 10, 1842,		
by Francis Williams, Eastford. Intention published	5	82

	Vol.	Page
FRANKLIN, (cont.)		
Benjamin, d. Oct. 30, 1822	6	38
Benjamin, of Brookfield, Mass., m. Mary **BADGER**, of		
Ashford, June 14, 1846, by Rev. Edward A. Lyon	5	98
Benjamin Addison, s. Benjamin & Susannah, b. Sept. 23, 1814	6	38
Cynthia, housekeeper, d. July [ ], 1850, ae 19	5	144-5
James, of Brooklyn, m. Mrs. Clarissa **BINGHAM**, of Ashford,		
Sept. 17, 1823, by Rev. Hubble Loomis	5	10
John, s. W[illia]m B. & Mary, b. Jan. 13, 1819	6	33
Lydia, d. Benjamin & Susannah, b. June 17, 1818	6	38
Lydia E., of Ashford, m. Charles T. **CLARK**, of Chaplin, [ ],		
by Rev. Ezekiel Skinner	5	53
Lydia Emeline, d. W[illia]m B. & Mary, b. Jan. 3, 1817	6	33
Sarah Ann, of Ashford, m. Jeremiah **CORBIN**, of Woodstock,		
June 21, 1847, by Benj[ami]n C. Simmons, J. P.	5	100
Susan, m. Zuriel P. **ARNOLD**, b. of Ashford, Aug. 4, 1833, by		
Rev. W[illia]m Livesey	5	51
Susannah Sophia, d. Benjamin & Susannah, b. May 14, 1821	6	38
William B., m. Mary **BODWELL**, Aug. 18, 1816	6	33
FREEMAN, Alice W., m. Pierre V. C. **SPOKE**, b. of Ashford, Nov.		
13, 1831, by Rev. Ezekiel Skinner	5	45
Harriet, m. Benajah **GREEN**, b. of Ashford, Apr. 12, 1822, by		
Reuben Torrey, Eastford	5	6
Keziah, m. Benj[ami]n **SNOW**, Oct. 20, 1737, by Rev. Mr.		
Eleazer Williams	1	65
Lovina, m. Thomas **DENNIS**, b. of Ashford, Apr. 12, 1822, by		
Reuben Torrey, Eastford	5	6
FRINK, Cathaine, d. John & Roxalana, b. Feb. 3, 1808	4	76
Edward, s. John & Mary, b. May 19, 1775	4	76
Edward, m. Lydia **BARROWS**, Feb. 4, 1802	4	37
Elias, s. John & Mary, b. Oct. 28, 1769	4	76
John, s. John & Mary, b. Feb. 27, 1772	4	76
John m. Roxcey **BICKNELL**, Feb.7, 1793	4	76
John, s. John & Roxcey, b. Oct. 26, 1795	4	76
Lydia, d. Edward & Lydia, b. Feb. 19, 1804	4	37
Maria, d. John & Roxey, b. Dec. 24, 1804	4	76
Mary, d. John & Mary, b. Feb. 4, 1768	4	76
Roxey, d. John & Roxey, b. Nov. 5, 1799	4	76
FULLER, Aaron, s. Nathaniel & Ann, b. Oct. 31, 1706	A	2
A[a]ron, d. Feb. 23, 1742/3	1	25
Abiga[i]ll, d. James & Abiga[i]ll, b. July 8, 1728	1	9
Abraham, s. Nathaniel & Ann, b. Aug. 29, 1714 ; d. Sept. 18,		
same year, buried in Mansfield	A	2
Abraham, s. Nathaniel & Ann, b. Jan. 7, 1715/6	A	2
Abram, s. Nathaniel & Ann, d. Sept. 28, 1719	A	5
Abram, s. Nathaniel & Ann, b. Oct. 7, 1719	A	5
Ann, [w. of Nathaniel], b. June 3, 1677, in Newport, R. I.	A	2
Ann, d. Nathaniel & Ann, b. Aug. 18, 1699, in Rehobath	A	2
Ann, d. Aaron & Hannah, b. Dec. 11, 1734	1	25

FULLER, (cont.)	Vol.	Page
Ann, w. Nath[anie]ll, d. June 13, 1737, in the 61st		
y. of her age	1	25
Anna, m. Adonijah BECKUS, Apr. 5, 1755	1	98
Anne, d. Nathaniel & Ann, d. Sept. 11, 1715	A	5
Chloe Ann, m. Abner R. BENNETT, May 26, 1844, by Rev.		
Washington Munger	5	90
Cynthia M., of Ashford (Westford Society), m. Henry W.		
AUSTIN, of Woodstock, Jan. 8, 1844, by [Rev.] R. V.		
Lyon, Westford	5	87
Deborah, m. Ebenezer OWEN, June 1, 1772	4	59
Dinah, d. James & Abigail, b. Dec. 29, 1718	A	5
Ebenezer, s. A[a]ron & Hannah, b. Dec. 4, 1741	1	25
Elisha, s. Jacob & Elizabeth, b. Mar. 14, 1719/20	1	11
Elezeb[e]th, m. Philip SQUIRE, Oct. 17, 1715, by Ele[a]zer		
Willi[a]ms, of Mansfield	1	22
Elizabeth, m. Philip SQUIER, Oct. 27, 1715, by Ebenezer		
Williams, of Mansfield	A	5
Elizabeth, d. Matthais & Elizabeth, b. Feb. 14, 1716/17	A	3
Elizabeth, d. James & Abigail, b. June 15, 1721	A	5
Elizabeth, [twin with John], d. Mather & Elizabeth, b. June 8,		
1724	A	8
Elisabeth, m. Daniel FITTS, Jan. 1, 1775	4	85
Elisabeth, d. Jacob & Lydia, b. May 16, 1777	4	26
Emily Miranda, d. Willard, farmer, ae 30, & Almira, ae 31, b.		
Oct. 1, 1847	5	128-9
Esther, d. Nathaniel & Ann, b. Aug. 15, 1712	A	2
Easter, d. Nath[anie]ll & Mary, b. Sept. 13, 175(?)	1	81
Eunice, m. Jonathan HUGHES, Dec. 16, 1790	4	94
Hannah, d. Jacob [& Elezebeth], b. June 1, 1725	1	11
Hannah, m. Peter WALKER, Mar. 17, 1748	2	76
Hannah, m. John WARREN, Jr., Dec. 29, 1797	4	86
Hannah, m. Asahel KIMBALL, Apr. 17, 1803	6	10
Harriet, ae 20, b. Providence, R. I., m. Daniel SHIRTLEFF,		
hat braider, ae 25, of Ashford, Apr. 27, 1849, by Isaac		
Sherman	5	136-7
Henry L., of Ashford, m. Julia A. ADAMS, of Stafford, Aug.		
10, 1851, by Rev. Cha[rle]s Hyde	5	107
Hezekiah, s. James & Abigail, b. Mar. 2, 1724/5	A	9
Hitty, d. Jacob & Lydia, b. Jan. 26, 1767	4	26
Jacob, m. Elisebeth MAGOON, Apr. 1, 1719, by Rev. James		
Hale	1	11
Jacob, s. Jacob & Lydia, b. May 16, 1776	4	26
James, m. Abigail YEWARD*, Dec. 12, 1717 (LENARD?)	A	4
James, s. Nathan[i]el & Mary, b. Mar. 13, 1744	1	50
John, [twin with Elizabeth], s. Mather & Elizabeth, b. June 8,		
1724	A	8
Joseph, s. Jacob & Lydia, b. Mar. 14, 1771	4	26
Joshua, s. Jacob & Lydia, b. Dec. 29, 1768	4	26

	Vol.	Page
FULLER, (cont.)		
Lois, m. Amos **JUSTIN**, May 25, 1810	6	27
Marian, m. Timothy **DIMOCK**, Mar. 10, 1725/6, by Rev.		
Eben[eze]r Williams	A	10
Marriam, m. Timothy **DIMOCK**, Mar. 10, 1725/6	1	16
Mariam, see also Meriam		
Mary, d. Jacob [& Elezebeth], b. Jan. 6, 1722/3	1	11
Mary, d. Nath[anie]ll & Mary, b. Apr. 8, 1750	1	50
Mary, m. Phinehas **WATKINS**, Oct. 24, 1752, by Tho[ma]s		
Tiffany, Esq, Mr. Mil[l]s paid* for him & c. (*Uncertain)	2	40
Mather, s. Mather & Elizabeth, b. July 2, 1719	A	8
Meriam, d. Nathaniel & Ann, b. Mar. 10, 1790, in Windham	A	2
Meriam, see also Mariam		
Moses, s. Nathaniel & Ann, b. July 26, 1698, in Rehobath ; d.		
Oct. 18, in the same year	A	2
Moses, s. Nathaniel & Ann, b. Sept. 14, 1702, in Windham	A	2
Nathaniel, s. Jonathan & Elizabeth, b. Mar. 1, 1675, in		
Rehobath	A	2
Nathaniel, s. Nathaniel & Ann, b. Jan. 24, 1709/10, in		
Mansfield	A	2
Nath[anie]ll, Jr., m. Mary **BERRY**, Sept. 30, 1736, by Philip		
Eastman, J. P.	1	49
Noah, s. Mather & Elizabeth, b. Aug. 30, 1721	A	8
Peter, s. Nath[anie]ll, Jr. & Mary, b. Sept. 13, 1738	1	49
Rachal, m. Artherton **CHAFFE**, Mar. 25, 1756	1	96
Sarah, d. Nathaniel & Ann, b. Oct. 9, 1717	A	4
Sarah, [d. Jacob & Elezebeth], b. Feb. 19, 1727/8	1	11
Sarah, d. Nath[anie]ll, d. May 9, 1729	1	25
Sarah, d. Nathan[i]el & Mary, b. Sept. 10, 1741	1	49
Susannah, d. Nathaniel & Ann, b. Aug. 22, 1704, in Windham	A	2
Thomas, of Hampton, m. Margaret S. **PRESTON**, of Ashford,		
Mar. 4, 1827, by Rev. Philo Judson	5	26
Willard, of Willington, m. Minerva **WALKER**, of Ashford,		
May 19, 1831, by Rev. Luke Wood	5	43
William, s. James & Abigail, b. Mar. 13, 1722/3	A	7
----, s. Nath[anie]ll, Jr. & Mary, b. Aug. 17, [ ] ; d. 21st of		
same month	1	49
FULSOM, [see under **FOLSOM**]		
GAGGILL, GAGGAIL, Dorothy, m. Sam[ue]ll **EASTMAN**, Mar.		
1, 1759	2	32
Hannah, d. John & Dor[o]they, b. Dec. 19, 1753	2	72
GALLUP, Nathan, Jr., of Windham, m. Sarah T. **MURPHY**, of		
Ashford, Feb. 17, 1850, by Rev. P. Mathewson, of the		
Tolland Baptist Church	5	104
Nathan, Jr., pedler, ae 21, b. Windham, res. Ashford, m. Sarah		
T. **MURPHY**, ae 18, b. Ashford, Feb. 19, 1850, by P.		
Matthewson	5	142/3
GARDINER, W[illia]m M., of Mansfield, m. Phila **PENNINGS**, of		
Ashford, July 4, 1851, by George Soule	5	106

	Vol.	Page
GARDINER, (cont.)		
W[illia]m M., blacksmith, ae 23, b. R. I., res.		
Mansfield, m. Phila **JENNINGS,** ae 28, b. Mansfield,		
July 4, 1851, by Rev. George Soule	5	148-9
GARRETTSON, Nathan H., of Worchester, Mass., m. Jane		
HOWARD, of Eastford, Feb. 18, 1844, by Francis		
Williams, Eastford. Intention published	5	88
GAYLAND, [see also **GAYLORD**], Emily, m. Giddings **KEYES,** b.		
of Ashford, Feb. 25, 1829, by Rev. Philo Judson	5	33
GAYLORD, [see also **GAYLAND,** Caroline, of Ashford, m. Edwin		
EATON, of Chaplin, Jan. 12, 1831, by Rev. Philo		
Judson	5	41
Charles Hyde, s. Horace & Mary A., b. Jan. 26, 1837	6	76
Edwin E., s. Harvee, harness maker, ae 47, & Mary A., ae 41,		
b. June 5, 1849	5	132-3
Horace Amidon, s. Horace & Mary A., b. Aug. 26, 1835	6	76
James Guilford, s. Horace & Mary A., b. Mar. 22, 1829	6	76
John Davis, s. Horace & Mary A., b. Dec. 24, 1839	6	76
Luther, m. Salla **PRESTON,** Sept. 27, 1792	4	288
Parmelia, of Ashford, m. Joseph **CONANT,** of Mansfield,		
[Sept.] 4, [1833], by Rev. Reuben Torrey, Eastford	5	51
Sally, m. Zachariah **BICKNELL,** Jr., b. of Ashford, Jan. 21,		
1823, by Rev. Philo Judson	5	8
Samuel Davis, s. Horace & Mary A., b. Oct. 15, 1833	6	76
William Luther, s. Horace & Mary A., b. Oct. 14, 1831	6	76
----, [d.] Luther & Salla, b. July 7, 1793	4	288
----, [d.] Luther & Salla, b. July 10, 1794	4	288
----, [d.] Luther d, Mar. 26, 1795	4	288
----, [d] Luther & Salla b. July 1, 1795	4	288
----la, d. Luther & Salla, b. Dec. 15, 179[7?]	4	288
----raie, s. Luther & Salla, b. Oct. 20, 1801	4	288
GIBBS, John, S. Jacob & Sarah, b. Jan. 31, 1755	1	88
Martha, m. Dyer **CARPENTER,** Sept. 19, 1811	6	21
GIFFORD, ----, child of Jonas, hatter, ae 38, & Eliza Ann, ae 25, b.		
Mar. 21, 1848	5	126-7
GILBORN, Mary Ann, m. John **WALKER,** Mar. 2, 1769	4	32
GILLET, Hannah, m. Mat[t]hew **MARCY,** May 24, 1779	4	120
GILLMORE, Betsey, of Ashford, m. Gurdon **WELCH,** of		
Windham, June 5, 1823, by Rev. Philo Judson	5	10
GILMAN, James H., m. Maria **TROWBRIDGE,** b. of Ashford,		
[Feb.] 27, [1834], by Rev. Reuben Torrey, Eastford	5	53
GILMER, George, of Ashford, m. Gennet **BROCKER,** of New		
Haven, May 13, 1832, by Rev. David Bennett	5	47
GOODALE, GOODAIL, [see also **GOODELL**], Abigail, m. Asa		
EATON, Nov. 5, 1772	4	87
Albert S., s. Vine & Hannah, b. Mar. 4, 1843	6	98
Charles D., s. Vine & Hannah, b. Apr. 14, 1845	6	98
Prissilah, m. John **BEMIS,** Nov. 25, 1778	4	114
GOODELL, [see also **GOODALE**], Catharine, of Ashford, m.		

	Vol.	Page
GOODELL, (cont.)		
Thomas **MANCHESTER,** of Warwick, R. I. ,		
Apr. 3, 1831, by Amos Lyon, J. P.	5	42
Vine, m. Hannah **GRIGGS,** Apr. 3, 1842, by Rev. Ezekiel		
Skinner	5	80
Virgil, of Ashford, m. Olive **JOHNSON,** of East Haddam, Jan.		
13, 1833, by Amasa Lyon, J. P.	5	50
Virgilius M., m. Clarissa **DEANS,** b. of Ashford, Apr. 11,		
1842, by Rev. C. C. Barnes	5	81
----ne, s. Jesse & Abigail, b. Sept. 28, 1774	4	96
GOODENOUGH, GOODNOUGH, Danford F., m. Susan D.		
GREEN, b. of Ashford, Jan. 18, 1841, by Amos		
Babcock	5	77
Mary, of Mansfield, m. Euphrastus **SQUIER,** of Ashford,		
Dec. 29, 1824, by John Warren, J. P.	5	17
GORTON, Susan, m. Charles **BARROWS,** [Feb.] 1, [1837], by		
Rev. Reuben Torrey, Eastford	5	63
GOULD, Aaron, of Ware, Mass., m. Maria **BUGBEE,** of Ashford,		
Dec. 6, 1840, by Rev. Alvin Bennett	5	76
Clariss[a] J., m. Charles P. **HOWE,** b. of Worcester, Mass.,		
June 8, 1845, by E. Dickinson	5	94
Erasmus, s. Jon[a]th[an] & Patience, b. [ ]	4	286
John, s. Jon[a]th[an] & Patience, b. [ ]	4	286
Jonathan, m. Patiance **DYER,** [ ]	4	286
Mary, m. Amos **CARPENTER,** Apr. 3, 1746	2	56
Patience, m. Zera **PRESTON,** Nov. 24, 1816	4	111
----phena, d. Jon[a]th[an] & Patience, [b.], 1799	4	286
GRANT, Clark, m. Sabrina How **CLARK,** June 15, 1819	6	36
Elisha, d. Feb. 8, 1822	6	36
Hamilton, m. Lucy **WILLIAMS,** Apr. 11, 1802	4	45
Jane E., ae 24, b. Willington, res. Ashford, m. Barnes G.		
DUNHAM, shoemaker, ae 28, of Ashford, Feb. 27,		
1849, by Rev. Washington Munger	5	136-7
John Hamilton, s. Hamilton & Lucy, b. Sept. 2, 1802	4	45
Lurinda, of Ashford, m. Rev. James **PORTER,** of Pomfret,		
Apr. 24, 1826, by Rev. Philo Judson	5	22
Marinda, of Ashford, m. William **ROSS,** of Chaplin, [Apr.] 8,		
[1832], by Anson S. Atwood	5	47
Mary R., of Ashford, m. Charles A. **COTTON,** of Hartford,		
Nov. 5, 1833, by Rev. James Porter	5	52
Minor Clark, s. Clark & Sabrina How, b. Aug. 13, 1820	6	36
Nancy, d. Hamilton & Lucy, b. July 14, 1805	4	45
Nelson, s. Hamilton & Lucy, b. Mar. 22, 1804	4	45
GRAVES, Henry, m. Tryphenia **BABBITT,** of Brookfield, Mass.,		
Sept. 18, 1836, by Alvan Underwood	5	61
GRAY, An[n]e, d. Nath[anie]l & Sarah, b. Feb. 15, 1723/4	A	8
Benjamin, s. Nathaniel & Sarah, b. Nov. 13, 1716	A	4
Joseph, [s. Nath[anie]l], b. [ ] at Ham[p]shire	A	8
Samuel, s. Nath[anie]l & Sarah, b. Nov. 8, 1721	A	8

	Vol.	Page
GRANT, (cont.)		
Sarah, d. Nath[anie]l & Sarah, b. May 29, 1719	A	8
Sarah, [d. Nath[anie]l], b. [ ] at Enfield	A	8
William, s. Nathaniel & Sarah, b. Nov. 3, 1713, in Jamaco	A	4
GREEN, GREENE, Ansel H., d. William & Eliza A., b. Sept. 5,		
1841	6	96
Benajah, m Harriet **FREEMAN**, b. of Ashford, Apr. 12, 1822,		
by Reuben Torrey, Eastford	5	6
Benjamin, m. Emily **MORSE**, b. of Ashford, "last evening",		
Feb. 13, 1843, by F. William. Intention published	5	84
Calvin, s. Charles & Mary, b. May 7, 1758	1	110
Charilly M., of Ashford, m. Merrick R. **HIGGINBOTHAM**,		
of Pomfret, [Nov.] 24,[1831], by Rev. Reuben Torrey,		
Eastford	5	46
Elizabeth, Mrs., of Union, m. Josiah **EATON**, of Ashford, Mar.		
6, [1834], by Job Cushman	5	53
Fanny, d. Eben[eze]r & Mary, b. Apr. 16, 1819	6	103
Fred[e]reck, s. Charles & Mary, b. Feb. 13, 1762	3	105
George W., m. Jane M. Bowen, b. of Ashford, Mar. 26, 1846,		
by Francis Williams	5	96
Gilbert, m. Ann Maria **FRANKLIN**, b. of Ashford, Oct. 10,		
1842, by Francis Williams, Eastford. Intention published	5	82
Jerel B., m. Mary W. **HOVEY**, b. of Hartford, Oct. 9, 1837, by		
Rev. Cha[rle]s Hyde	5	66
Luther, s. Charles & Mary, b. Apr. 25, 1760	1	110
Martha S., m. Samuel D. **BEULEY**, Apr. 6, 1845, by Rev.		
Renssalear O. Putney	5	93
Mary, m. Thomas A. **BRAMAN**, b. of Pomfret, [Dec.] 10,		
[1834], by Rev. R. Torrey, Eastford	5	55
Mary Tabor, m.Thomas McDonough **AUSTIN**, b. of Ashford,		
May 28, 1843, by Rev. Ezekiel Skinner	5	85
Orril, m. John **SMITH**, Jr., b. of Ashford, July 4, 1840, by		
Rev. Alvan Underwood, in Westford Parish	5	74
Pessalla, m. [Benj[ami]n] **CHAF[F]E**, Feb. 26, 1741	1	74
Reuben, of East Windsor, m. Maria **WHITON**, of Ashford,		
Jan. 4, 1837, by Alvin Underwood	5	63
Silence, d. Charles & Mary, b. Feb. 10, 175[ ]	1	93
Susan D., m. Danford F. **GOODNOUGH**, b. of Ashford, Jan.		
18, 1841, by Amos Babcock	5	77
GREENSLITT, GREENSLIT, A[u]gustine, s. John & Silome, b.		
Aug. 11, 1792	4	49
Betsa, d. John & Silome, b. June 16, 1796	4	49
Chester, s. John & Silome, b. July 22, 1794	4	49
George W., of Killingly, m. Matilda **PIERCE**, of Sterling, June		
26, 1843, by Rev. Isaac H. Coe. Intention published	5	85
John, m. Silome **PITTS**, June 22, 1790	4	49
Permela, d. John & Silome, b. Nov. 13, 1790 ; d. Dec. 13,		
1791	4	49
GREGGS, [see under **GRIGGS**]		

	Vol.	Page
GRIGGS, GREGGS, GREEGS,		
Abijah, s. [Nathan] & Anna, b. June 27, 1778	4	90
Ann, m. Joseph **BEDLOW**, b. of Ashford, Apr. 21, 1824, by		
Rev. Philo Judson	5	14
Bets[e]y, d. John & Bets[e]y, b. May 12, 1807	4	108
Bets[e]y, w. John d. May 17, 1807	4	108
Daniel A., of Chaplin, m. Betsey **MOSELEY**, of Ashford,		
[Mar.] 27, [1843], by Rev. Cha[rle]s Hyde	5	84
Dorothy, d. Joseph & Rebeckah, b. May 29, 1782	4	74
Elijah, of Abington, Conn., m. Jedido **CHAPMAN**, of Tolland,		
[Sept.] 8, [1831], by Reuben Torrey, Eastford	5	44
Elisha, s. John & Dorothy, b. Sept. 3, 1739	1	71
Elizabeth, d. Lemuel & Hannah, b. Mar. 27, 1782	4	229
Hannah, d. John & Dorothy, b. June 28, 1741	1	71
Hannah, d. John & Dorothy, b. Mar. last day, 1751	2	77
Hannah, d. John, d. Aug. 25, 1751	2	77
Hannah, m. Vine **GOODELL**, Apr. 3, 1842, by Rev. Ezekiel		
Skinner	5	80
Hendrick, s. Jo[seph] & Rebeckah, b. June 25, 1780	4	74
Ichabod, m. Lydia **WRIGHT**, Sept. 8, 1748	2	77
Ichabod, s. Ichabod & Lydia, b. May, 4, 1753 d. Dec. 25, 1755	2	77
Ira, s. John & Bets[e]y, b. Mar. 7, 1805	4	108
Irene, d. John & Dorothy, b. May 29, 1753	1	71
Jane, m. Jonathan K. **RINGE**, [Jan.] 12, [1826], by Rev.		
Reuben Torrey, Eastford	5	21
Jemima, d. Joseph & Rebeckah, b. Oct. 28, 1777	4	74
John, m. Dorothy **SCARBROW**, Dec. 26, 1738, by Lecester		
Grosvener, J. P.	1	71
John, s. John & Dorothy, b. Mar. 16, 1743 ; d. Nov. 2, 1749	1	71
John, s. Joseph & Rebeckah, b. Oct. 5, 1775	4	74
John, m. Bets[e]y **CHAPMAN**, Oct. 22, 1802	4	108
John, s. John & Bets[e]y, b. July 20, 1803	4	108
John, m. Huldah **CARPENTER**, , Nov. 26, 1807	4	108
John, Jr., m. [Clarissa **NYE**], b. of Ashford, Sept. 9, 1824, by		
Reuben Torrey, Eastford [Clarissa **NYE**, b. Jan. 11,		
1804, Exeter, R. I.] [Addition to orginal manuscript]	5	15
John Phillips, s. Parley & Waitey, b. Jan. 25, 1816	6	14
Joseph, s. John & Dorothy, b. Oct. 12, 1748	1	71
Joseph, s. Ichabod & Lydia, b. Mar. 1, 1751	2	77
Joseph, m. Rebeckah **CHAFFEE**, Nov. 17, 1774	4	74
Joseph, s. Joseph & Rebeckah, b. Dec. 13, 1783	4	74
Joseph, Jr., m. Mary **MASON**, Mar. 24, 1814	6	16
Joseph Mason, s. Joseph, Jr. & Mary, b. Feb. 12, 1820	6	16
Justis, s. Joseph & Rebeckah, b. Aug. 13, 1787	4	74
Justus, of Ashford, m. Mrs. Lucinda **LYON**, of Eastford, Oct.		
3, 1854, by Rev. Charles Chamberlain	5	111
Lemuel, s. Ichabod & Lydia, b. May 25, 1755	2	77
Lemuel, m. Hannah **GROSVENOR**, Mar. 23, 1775	4	229

	Vol.	Page
GRIGGS, GREGGS, GREEGS, (cont.)		
Lois, m. John **ELLIS**, Dec. 9, 1790	4	68
Lona Loiza, d. Parley & Waitey, b. Oct. 19, 1820	6	14
Louisa, of Ashford, m. Daniel L. **PRATT**, of Southbridge, Feb. 10, 1842, by Francis Williams, Pastor, Eastford	5	80
Lucian Davison, s. John & Bets[e]y, b. Sept. 23, 1811	4	108
Lucy, d. Nathan & Anna, b. Aug. 7, 1772	4	90
Lucy, m. Shuba[e]l **SNOW**, 2d, Feb. 3, 1794	4	276
Mary, d. John & Dorothy, b. Feb. 12, 1744/5	1	71
Mary, m. Jonathan **BEMIS**, Jan. 20, 1774	4	74
Mary Hastings, d. Joseph, Jr. & Mary, b. Nov. 18, 1816	6	16
Mary S., of Ashford, m. Abner **UNDERWOOD**, of Woodstock, Apr. 15, 1844, by Rev. L. W. Blood	5	89
Nathan, s. Ichabod & Lydia, b. June 2, 1749	2	77
Nathan, m. Anna **HODGES**, Feb. 6, 1772	4	90
Olive, d. Joseph & Rebeckah, b. Jan. 23, 1793	4	74
Olive, m. David **LATHROP**, Nov. 14, 1811	6	16
Olive Maria, d. Parley & Waitey, b. Apr. 18, 1818	6	14
Parley, s. Joseph & Rebeckah, b. Sept. 16, 1790	4	74
Parley, m. Waitty **PHILLIPS**, Apr. 11, 1815	6	14
Patian[c]e, d. John & Dorithy, b. Dec. 23, 1746	1	71
Permelia, d. Joseph, Jr. & Mary, b. Jan. 2, 1815	6	16
Phebe, d. Nathan & Anna, b. Mar. 26, 1776 ; d. Nov. 22, 1776	4	90
Reuben, s. Nathan & Anna, b. Oct. 4, 1782	4	90
Roxey, d. Lemuel & Hannah, b. Mar. 9, 1784	4	229
Sarah, d. Joseph & Rebeckah, b. Sept. [ ], 1776	4	74
Sarah, m. Amos **ABBOTT**, Apr. 9, 1800	4	39
Sibbell, d. Nathan & Anna, b. Oct. 11, 1784	4	90
Syball, m. Amos **CHAPMAN**, Nov. 25, 1807	6	11
GROSVENOR, Ezra, m. Sarah **CARPENTER**, May 4, 1786	4	246
Ezra, s. Ezra & Sarah, b. Apr. 7, 1787	4	246
Hannah, m. Lemuel **GRIGGS**, Mar. 23, 1775	4	229
Roswell, s. Ezra & Sarah, b. Jan. 26, 1789	4	246
Rufus, s. Ezra & Sarah, b. Nov. 11, 1790	4	246
GROVER, Betsey, m. Rufus **FARNHAM**, Nov. 26, 1801	4	70
GURLEY, W[illia]m Y., m. Mary A. **TIFT**, Apr. 15, 1844, by Rev. Washington Munger	5	89
HADDICK, Martha, m. Asa **CHEDLE**, Nov. 5, 1760	3	109
HADSON, Albert, of Ashford, m. Mary J. **FLINT**, of Hampton, Oct. 23, 1842, by Rev. Cha[rle]s Hyde	5	82
HALE, Daniel, s. John & Mehitable, b. Jan. 10, 1773	4	57
James, s. James & Sarah, b. Feb. 9, 1716	A	7
James, Jr., m. Elezebeth **BICKNELL**, May 17, 1739, by Rev. James Hale	1	77
James, Rev., d. Nov. 22, 1742	1	77
James, s. James & Elezebeth, b. May 7, 1744	1	77
James, s. James & Elisabeth, b. Mar. 20, 1757	4	40
James, s. John & Mehitable, b. Mar. 10, 1774	4	57

HALE, (cont.)	Vol.	Page
Johan[n]ah, d. James Jr. & Elezebeth, b. Aug. 24,1740	1	77
Joanna, m. Ele[a]zar WARNER, Apr. 29, 1762	3	60
John, s. James & Sarah, b. Apr. 19, 1715, at Swanzey "in that part now called Barrington"	A	7
John, s. Rev. James, d. June 17, 1738	1	77
John, s. James & Elezebeth, b. Mar. 27, 1742 ; d. July 6, 1742	1	77
John, s. James & Elez[ebet]h, b. Oct. 12, 1747	1	77
John, m. Mehetable KNOWLTON, Apr. 14, 1772	4	57
Laura West, d. Zachariah & Claris[s]a, b. Aug. 24, 1807	4	95
Mehitable, d. Joh[n] & Mehitable, b. Mar. 20, 1775	4	57
Orrin, s. John & Mehitable, b. July 8, 1791	4	57
Robart, s. James & Elezebath, b. Oct 17, 1749	1	77
Samuel, s. James & Elesabeth, b. Apr. 12, 1754	4	40
Sam[ue]ll, s. John & Mehitable, b. June 10, 1790 ; d. June 20, 1790	4	57
Sarah, d. James & Elez[ebeth], b. Apr. 16, 1743 ; d. June 5, 1743	1	77
Sarah, d. James & Elez[ebet]h, b. Oct. 23, 1745	1	77
Sarah, m. Thomas SCOTT, Feb. 16, 1769	4	27
Zachariah, s. James & Elizabeth, b. Aug. 20, 1751	1	77
Zachariah, s. James & Elisabeth, b. Jan. 15, 1756	4	40
Zachariah, m. Clarissa WEST, [ ]	4	95
HALL, Anna, d. Josiah, Jr. & Rheuby, b. Oct. 7, 1792	4	231
Eleazer, of Norwich, m. Sarah SNOW, of Ashford, [Aug.] 12,[1832], by Rev. R. Torrey, Eastford	5	48
Freeman, s. Josiah, Jr. & Rheuby, b. May 24, 1797	4	231
Isaac, s. Robert & Mary, b. Mar. 16, 1777	4	87
Isaac, s. Isaac & Eda, b. Nov. 4, 1800	4	43
Jesse T., of Stafford, m. Lois M. CHAPMAN, of Ashford, Apr. 3, 1850, by Rev. Ezekiel Skinner	5	105
John, Jr., of Holland, Mass., m. Emeline P. CHAPMAN, of Ashford, Aug. 13, 1848, by Rev. Ezekiel Skinner	5	103
Joseph, m. Mrs. Mary LAMB, b. of Eastford, Nov. 17, 1844, by Francis Williams	5	92
Josiah, m. Hannah WOOD, Mar. 22, 1796	4	49
Mary, d. Robe[r]t & Mary, b. June 12, 1775	4	87
Mary, m. James BOSTON, Sept. 14, 1843, by Nathan B. Lyon, J. P.	5	85
Parker, s. Josiah, Jr. & Rheuby, b. Apr. 19, 1795	4	231
Phyluria, d. Isaac & Eda, b. Feb. 10, 1799	4	43
Robert, m. Mary LEE, Nov. 17, 1774	4	87
Salley, d. Robert & Mary, b. Oct. 12, 1779	4	87
Sophia, d. Josiah, Jr. & Rheuby, b. Mar. 10, 1800	4	231
HAMILTON, George W., of Ashford, m. Harriet S. LEWIS, of Pomfret, Mar. 2, 1845, by Rev. Geo[r]ge Mixter	5	93
HAMMOND, Asa, m. Lois DURGY, Jan. 12, 1758	1	105
Asa, s. Asa & Lois, b. May 27, 1758	1	105
Asa, s. Asa, d. Aug. 4, 1760	3	51

	Vol.	Page
HARBUCK, (cont.)		
Ashford, Sept. 3, 1821, by Rev. Philo Judson	5	3
HARDCASTLE, Mary Alic[e], b. New York City, res. Ashford, d.		
Sept. 17, 1848, ae 11 m.	5	138-9
HARDEY, James, m. Susanna **MANARD,** Jan. 9, 1784	4	233
HARDINGS, Lorenzo, of Medford, Mass., m. Hannah C. **KENT,** of		
Ashford, Dec. 1, 1838, by Rev. Ezekiel Skinner	5	69
HARKING, Mary, of Windham, m. John **JENNINGS,** Sept. 13,		
1821, by Philo Judson	5	4
HARRINGTON, Mary M., m. William D. **MARTIN,** b. of Ashford,		
Feb. 25, 1845, by Rev. Cha[rle]s Hyde	5	93
HARRIS, Abijah, m. Mary **KNOWLTON,** Nov. 29, 1739, by James		
Hale	1	30
Julia, of Ashford, m. Luther **SIMONS,** of Mansfield, Dec. 19,		
1844, by Rev. Geo[rge] Mixter	5	92
Mary, m. Francies **PEIRCE,** Jan, [ ], 1761	1	25
Parker, of Mansfield, m. Anna **BETTIS,** of Ashford, Oct. 8,		
[1826], by Ezekiel Skinner	5	24
Percey, m. Levi **WOODWARD,** Oct. 24, 1799	4	266
Sarah, m. George **WHITMAN,** b. of Mansfield, Mar. 22, 1840,		
by Amos Babcock	5	73
Susanna, m. Solomon **PRESTON,** June 13, 1799	4	54
HART, HARTE, HARD, Benjamin, s. Constant & Sarah, b. Mar. 4,		
1752 ; d. same day	2	30
John, s. Constant & Sarah, b. Apr. 23, 1750	2	30
Josiah, s. Constant & Sarah, b. Aug. 18, 1748	2	72
Sarah, w. Constant, d. Mar, 12, 1752	2	30
HARTSHORN, HARTSON, John L., of Chaplin, m. Mary Jane		
HARTSON, of Ashford, Apr. 25, [1836], by Amos		
Babcock	5	59
Mary Jane, of Ashford, m. John L. **HARTSHORN,** of Chaplin,		
Apr. 25, [1836], by Amos Babcock	5	59
HARVEY, Agnes, twin with Albert, d. Alfred, farmer, ae 41, &		
Dolly, ae 36, b. Aug. 3, 1850	5	146-7
Albert, twin with Agnes, s. Alfred, farmer, ae 41, & Dolly, ae		
36, b. Aug, 3, 1850	5	146-7
Alfred, Jr., d. Aug. 10, 1848, ae 6 (Perhaps "Howey")	5	136-7
Alfred, s. Alfred, farmer, ae 39, & Dolly, ae 34, b. Oct. 20,		
1848	5	132-3
Almira, m. John W. **JUDSON,** Jan. 5, 1808	4	114
Amasa, of Palmer, Mass., m. Almira **MOSELEY,** of Ashford,		
May 27, 1845, by Rev. Cha[rle]s Hyde	5	94
Asahel, of Palmer, m. Mary A. **NETTLETON,** of Stafford,		
Nov, 29, 1849, by Rev. Ezekiel Skinner	5	104
Asahel, factory operative, of Palmer, Mass., m. Mary A.		
NETTLETON, of Stafford, Ct. , Nov. 29, 1849, by		
Ezekiel Skinner	5	142-3
----, twin d. & s. Alfred, farmer, ae 40, & Dolly, ae 35, b. Aug.		
3, 1850	5	140-1

	Vol.	Page
HARWOOD, [see also HAYWARD], Lydia, m. Ezra		
HAYWARD, Dec. 4, 1800	4	30
Martha, m. Ebenezer MASON, Jr. Jan. 12, 1804	4	91
Sarah, m. Allen BOSWORTH, Nov. 18, 1802	4	233
HASKELL, Betsey, m. David KEYES, b. of Ashford, Apr. 22,		
"last" [1821], by Rev. Stephen Haskell. Intention		
published	5	3
HASKINS, Rebackah, m. Edward MARCY, Jan. 22, 1729, by Rev.		
Mr. Wills	1	35
HASTAN, Huldah, d. Philip & Huldah, b. Jan. 12, 1800 ; d. Sept.		
12, 1800	4	118
Huldah, d. Philip, d. Sept. 12, 1800	4	118
Mira, d. Philip & Huldah, b. June 11, 1796	4	118
Patty, d. Philip & Huldah, b. Dec. 16, 1797 ; d. Aug. 26, 1800	4	118
Philip, m. Huldah DIMMICK, Sept. 21, 1794	4	118
Timothy, s. Philip & Huldah, b. Aug. 17, 1801	4	118
HASTINGS, Mary, m. Ebenezer MASON, Jr., June 21, 1774	4	75
HATCH, John B., of Union, m. Prescilla L. CHAPMAN, of		
Ashford, [Sept.] 6, [1835], by Dexter Munger	5	57
HAVENS, Amanda, m. Orrin WILSON, b. of Ashford, Dec. 3,		
1843, by Rev. L. W. Blood	5	86
Louisa, m. John MOORE, Feb. 22, 1829, by Levi Work, J. P.	5	34
HAWES, HAWS, Clara, d. Eli & Susanna, b. Dec. 2, 1786 ; d.		
Sept. 18, 1792	4	11
Emery C., of Springfield, Mass., m. Mary A. DOW, of		
Ashford, May 3, 1847, by Charles Peabody	5	100
Harriet M., of Ashford, m. Marcus NEFF, of Chaplin, Aug. 22,		
1836, by Rev. Rodolphus Lanphear	5	62
Sarah, d. Eli & Susanna, b. Sept. 22, 1781	4	11
HAYNES, Prudence, m. Timothy SUMNER, Oct. 26, 1817	6	88
HAYWARD, HAWARD, [see also HETYARD & HARWOOD,		
Abigail, w. Nathaniel, d. June 28, 1777	3	14
Abijah, s. Stephen & Lucy, b. May 31, 1779	4	93
Amasa, s. John & Ann, b. Oct. 20, 1749	1	55
Amasa, s. Jonathan & Lydia, b. Oct. 16, 1790	4	92
Amos, s. John, Jr. & Rebec[c]ah, b. Oct, 12, 1785	3	69
Amos, m. Mary BURLEY, Nov. 27, 1817	6	30
Amos, s. Amos & Mary, b. June 6, 1822 ; d. July 25, 1831	6	30
Anna, m. Medinah PRESTON, b. of Ashford, Jan. [ ], 1762,		
in Woodstock, by S. Williams	3	76
Anne, d. John & An[n]e, b. Dec. 7, 1740	1	45
Anne, d. Jno, Jr., & Rebeckah, b. Dec. 27, 1779	3	69
Bee, s. Sam[ue]ll, Jr. & Bethiah, b. Nov. 14, 1773 ; d. Sept. 17,		
1775	4	29
Betsey, of Ashford, m. Samuel HOWARD, of Lebanon, Oct.		
30, 1828, by David Bolles, J. P.	5	32
Betty, d. John & Ann, b. Sept. 22, 1753	1	55
Betty, m. Joseph WORK, Jr., July 9, 1771	4	72

	Vol.	Page
HAYWARD, HAWARD,(cont.)		
Betty, d. Stephen & Lucy, b. Mar. 17, 1777	4	93
Buril, [s.] Nath[anie]ll & Abigail, b. June 7, 1767	3	14
Caroline, d. Danforth & Olive, b. Oct. 20, 1814	6	31
Chloe, d. John Jr. & Rachel, b. Apr. 8, 1769	3	69
Danforth, m. Olive CHAPMAN, Sept. 22, 1811	6	31
Danforth, s. Danforth & Olive, b. May 27, 1816	6	31
David, s. John & An[n], b. Apr. 28, 1743	1	45
Dorcas, d. John & Ann, b. Aug. 2, 1735	1	45
Dorcas, m. William WAKEFIELD, Nov. 15, 1751, by Rev.		
Mr. Williams	2	38
Ebenezer, s. Samvel & Sarah, b. Dec. 21, 1751	2	35
Ebenezer, s. Nathaniel & Abigail, b. Nov. 24, 1760	3	14
Edward F., s. Danforth & Olive, b. Jan. 29, 1822	6	31
Edwin, s. Danforth & Olive, b. Apr. 4, 1826	6	31
Elizabath, of Ashford, m. John CHAFFEE, of Woodstock,		
Nov. 4, 1735, by Philip Eastman, J. P.	1	45
Elisabeth, d. Jon[a]th[an] & Lydia, b. Oct. 28, 1785	4	92
Emily, of Ashford, m. Lucian B. FISHER, of Woodstock,		
[Oct.] 28, [1838], by Rev. Reuben Torrey, Eastford	5	69
Ephraim, s. John, Jr. & Rebeckah, b. Oct. 12, 1759	1	107
Ephraim, m. Abigail FARNAM, Feb. 26, 1789 ; d. Aug. 27,		
1831, ae 71	4	260
Ephraim, s. Amos & Mary, b. Sept. 17, 1820	6	30
Ephraim, d. Aug. 27, 1831, ae 71	4	260
Est[h]er, m. Benjamin PALMER, Nov. 11, 1755, by Stephen		
Williams	1	89
Esther, d. John, Jr. & Rebeckah, b. Nov. 19, 1775	3	69
Esther Cornelia, d. Danforth & Olive, b. Sept. 23, 1824	6	31
[E]unis, d. John & Anne, b. Oct. 2, 1745	1	45
[E]unis, d. John, d. Apr. 7, 1754	1	55
[E]unice, d. Samuel & Sarah, b. Aug. 11, 1754	2	35
Eunice, d. John & Ann, b. Sept. 13, 1758	1	102
Ezra, s. John, Jr. & Rebeckah, b. June 19, 1762	3	69
Ezra, s. Nat[haniel] & Abigail, d. July 14, 1777	3	14
Ezra, m. Lydia HARWOOD, Dec. 4, 1800	4	30
Ezra, s. Ezra & Lydia, b. Nov. 29, 1803	4	30
Hannah, d. John & An[n]e, b. Jan. 10, 1736/7	1	45
Hannah, m. Zepheniah DEAN, Oct. 2, 1755, by Mr. Stephen		
Williams	1	94
Hannah, d. John, Jr. & Rebeckah, b. Feb. 17, 1773	3	69
Hannah, [twin with Stephen], d. Jonathan & Lydia, b. Aug. 10,		
1793	4	92
Harmony, m. Aaron TUFTS, Jr. Mar. 13, 1796	4	240
Henery, s. John & Rachal, b. Apr. 24, 1767	3	69
Henery, s. Ezra & Lydia, b. Apr. 2, 1805	4	30
Huldy, d. John & An[n]e, b. Dec. 30, 1747	1	46
Jemimah, d. Sam[ue]ll & Sarah, b. Jan. 31, 1742/3	2	35

	Vol.	Page
HAYWARD, HAWARD, (cont.)		
Jemimah, d. Samvel [& Sarah], d. June 26, 1749	2	35
Jemimah, d. Samvel & Sarah, b. Apr. 29, 1750	2	35
John, m. Ann CARPENTER, Nov. 11, 1734, by Philip		
Eastman, J. P.	1	45
John, s. John, Jr. & Rebeckah, b. Jan. 26, 1765	3	69
John, s. Danforth & Olive, b. June 20, 1818	6	31
Jonathan, d. Nov. 23, 1734	1	45
Jonathan, s. Jon & An[n]e, b. Dec. 24, 1738	1	45
Jonathan, s. John & Ann, b. May 6, 1755 ; d. Apr. 14, 1754		
*Two persons. Error in combining. (Correction to		
original manuscript)	1	55
Jonathan, s. Joseph & Prudence, b. Apr. 4, 1759	2	26
Jonathan, s. Jonathan & Lydia, b. Sept. 1, 1783	4	92
Joseph, m. Prudence DEEN, Sept. 18, 1751	2	26
Joseph, s. Joseph & Prudence, b. Sept. 12, 1752	2	26
Joseph, [s. Danforth & Olive], b. July 17, 1832	6	31
Joseph Lafayette, s. Philip & Betsey, b. Sept, 8, 1824	6	50
Julius, s. Danforth & Olive, b. Jan. 7, 1813	6	31
Kezia, d. Nath[anie]ll & Abigail, b. June 8, 1773 ; d. Sept. 23,		
1775	3	14
Levinah, d. John, Jr. & Rebeckah, b. Aug. 11, 1777	3	69
Lucy Anne, [d. Danforth & Olive], b. Dec. 28, 1829	6	31
Lydia, d. Jonath[an] & Lydia, b. Aug. 26, 1781	4	92
Lydia, d. Ezra & Lydia, b. Mar. 22, 1802	4	30
Manassah, s. John, Jr. & Rebeckah, b. Nov. 25, 1763	3	69
Marcy, d. John & Rebec[c]ah, b. May 31, 1782	3	69
Marvin, s. Amos & Mary, b. Sept. 23, 1825	6	30
Mary, d. Joseph & Prudence, b. May 15, 1754	2	26
Mary, m. Thomas TAFT, b. of Ashford, Sept. 29, 1829, by		
Dexter Bullard	5	36
Mary W., d. Danforth & Olive, b. Dec. 19, 1819	6	31
Matilda, d. Sam[ue]ll, Jr., d. Feb. 24, 1782	4	29
Mehetabel, s. Sam[ue]ll & Sarah, b. Feb. 12, 1743/4	2	35
Nathan, s. Jonathan & Lydia, b. Dec. 9, 1776	4	92
Nath[anie]ll, m. Abigail SNOW, Apr. 13, 1759	3	14
Nath[anie]ll, s. Nath[anie]ll & Abigail, b. July 19, 1770 ; d.		
Jan. 13, 1772	3	14
Nathaniel, m. Prissilla CHUB[B], Nov. 13, 1777	3	14
Palmer, s. Jon[a]th[an] & Lydia, b. July 18, 1796	4	92
Phebe, d. Sam[ue]ll, Jr. & Bethiah, b. Oct. 23, 1772 ; d. Sept.		
8, 1775	4	29
Philip, Esq., m. Mrs. Betsey WOODWARD, May 14, 1823, by		
Rev. Philo Judson	5	9
Philip, m. Betsey WOODWARD, May 14, 1823	6	50
Prissilla, m. Comfort CARPENTER, Nov. 15, 1786	4	251
Rebackah, d. Sam[ue]ll & Sarah, b. Aug. 19, 1745	2	35
Rebeckah, d. John Jr. & Rachel, b. Dec. 25, 1770	3	69

	Vol.	Page
HAYWARD, HAWARD (cont.)		
Reuben, s. Amos & Mary, b. Mar. 3, 1827	6	30
Rosetta, m. Otis **LUMBARD**, b. of Ashford, Sept. 16, 1829, by		
Rev. Philo Judson	5	36
Sam[ue]ll, m. Sarah **WOODCOCK**, June 17, 1741	2	35
Sarah, m. Uriah **CARPINTER**, Nov. 28, 1733, by Philip		
Eastman, J. P.	1	44
Sarah, d. Samvel & Sarah, b. Mar. 5, 1747/8	2	35
Sarah, d. Nath[anie]ll & Abigail, b. Apr. 29, 1764	3	14
Sarah, m. Jacob **PRESTON**, May 31, 1770	4	44
Sarah, d. Nath[anie]ll & [Abigail], d. Sept. 29, 1775	3	14
Stephen, s. John & Ann, b. Feb. 3, 1757	1	95
Stephen, s. Stephen & Lucy, b. Apr. 24, 178[ ]	4	93
Stephen, [twin with Hannah], s. Jonathan & Lydia, b. Aug. 10,		
1793	4	92
Susanna, d. Jonath[an] & Lydia, b. Dec. 11, 1778	4	92
William, s. Joseph & Prudence, b. Apr. 10, 1756* (*Entry		
crossed out)	1	92
William, s. Joseph & Prudence, b. June 10, 1756	2	26
Zephaniah, s. Jonathan & Lydia, b. Oct. 13, 1788	4	92
----, d. Benjamin & Hannah, b. Feb. 19, 1766	4	10
----, [child] of Benjamin & Hannah, b. Mar. 15, 1768	4	10
HEATH, David, s. Ebenezer & Hannah, b. Apr. 9, 1757	1	97
David, s. Ele[a]zer, [ ]	4	3
Ebenezer, s. Eleazer[ ]	4	3
Frank, s. Ira & Hannah, b. Aug. 26, 1826	6	21
HEBBARD, [see under **HIBBARD**]		
HENCHER, HENTCHER, [see under **HINTCHER**]		
HENDEE, HENDY, HINDE, Abel, m. Cynthia **TOPLIFF**, Apr. 4,		
1813	6	32
Abigial, d. Josiah & Bethsheba, b. Aug. 16, 1735	1	21
Abigaill, d. Josiah [& Bethsheba], d. Dec. 3, 1740	1	21
Abigail, d. Josiah & Bethsheba, b. May, 18, 1742 ; d. Dec. 11,		
1744	1	21
Alva, s. Josiah & Tamma, b. May 9, 1781	4	89
Amasa, s. Josiah & Hepzibah, b. Mar. 6, 1797	4	89
An[n]is, d. John & An[n]is, b. Sept. 20, 180[ ]	4	287
Ariel, s. Josiah & Tamma, b. May 18, 1779	4	89
Barshab, w. Josiah, d. Oct. 25, 1759	3	3
Billy, s. John & Annis, b. Jan. 30, 17[ ]	4	287
Caleb, s. Josiah & Bathsheba, b. Nov. 29, 1730	1	21
Caleb, m. Hannah **HOLMES**, Jan. 1, 1751/2	2	34
Caleb, s. Caleb & Hannah, b. Aug. 24, 1756	2	34
Charles, s. John & Annis, b. Mar. 20, 1800	4	287
Charlotte, d. Abel & Cynthia, b. Apr. 6, 1815 ; d. Mar. 29,		
1816	6	32
Cyril, [see under **Syrril**]		
Daniel, s. Josiah & Hepzibah, b. Mar. 6, 1792	4	89

	Vol.	Page
HENDEE, HENDY, HINDE, (cont.)		
Elizabeth, d. Josiah & Bethsheba, b. July 19, 1733	1	21
Esther, d. Caleb & Hannah, b. Sept. 17, 1761	2	34
Hannah, d. Caleb & Hannah, b. Jan. 30, 1759	2	34
Hannah, m. Benj[ami]n OWEN, Oct. 11, 1786	4	249
Henry Holman, s. Abel & Cynthia, b. Apr. 27, 1817	6	32
Ichinil*, s. Caleb & Hannah, b. May 20, 1767, (*Perhaps Syrril?)	2	34
John, s. Josiah & Bethsheba, b. Apr. 27, 1740 ; d. May 9, 1757	1	21
John, s. Caleb & Hannah, b. Mar. 21 1770	4	35
John, m. Lucy MARTIN, Dec. 25, 1790	4	287
John, s. John & Annis, b. Dec. 19, [ ]	4	287
John, m. Annis RUSS, July [ ]	4	287
Josiah, m. Bethsheba LARNED, Jan. 9, 1728/9, by Dan[i]el Baker	1	21
Josiah, s. Josiah & Bethsheba, b. Dec. 13, 1737 ; d. Dec. 5, [1740]	1	21
Josiah, s. Calab & Hannah, b. Jan. 25. 1753	2	34
Josiah, m. Kesiah MASON, Mar. 5, 1760	3	3
Josiah, m. Tamma CLARK, Nov. 16, 1775	4	89
Josiah, s. Josiah & Tamma, b. Aug. 24, 1776	4	89
Josiah, m. Hipzibah BUTLER, Feb. 16, 1791	4	89
Lucius Eaton, s. Abel & Cynthia, b. May 30, 1821	6	32
Lucy, d. John & Annis, b. Dec.[ ]	4	287
Lucy, w. John, d. [ ]	4	287
Luther Topliff, s. Abel & Cynthia, b. Apr. 18, 1819	6	32
Mary, d. Caleb & Hannah, b. Feb. 15, 1755	2	34
Mehetable, d. Caleb & Hannah, b. May, 13, 1764	2	34
Orrin, s. John & Annis, b. July 8, 179[ ]	4	287
Sarah, d. Josiah & Bethsheba, b. June 5, 1731	1	21
Stephen, s. Josiah & Tamma, b. Jan. 13, 1786	4	89
Syrril(?), s. Caleb & Hannah, b. May 20, 1767 (Ichinil?)	2	34
Tammy, w. Josiah, d. Jan. 21, 1789	4	89
William, s. Josiah & Tamma, b. Aug. 16, 1783	4	89
HENFIELD, HENDFIELD, HINDFIELD, Benjamin, m. Bridget LEWIS, Feb. 18, 1778	4	119
Lewis, s. Benj[ami]n & Bridget, b. Feb. 12, 1783	4	119
Lucinda, m. Abner BOUTELL, b. of Ashford, Apr. 24, 1821, by Rev. Isaac Hall	5	3
Polley, d. Benj[ami]n & Bridget, b. Apr. 4, 1785	4	119
William, s. Benjamin & Bridget, b. Dec. 16, 1780	4	119
HEWES, Lyman D., m. Harriet M. CLARK, b. of Ashford, Feb. 13, 1831, by Rev. Philo Judson	5	42
HEWET, Polly, of Eastford, m. Simson LARNED, of Dudley, Mass., Apr. 16, 1846, by Edward F. Brooks	5	97
HIBBARD, HEBBARD, Anna, d. Ele[a]zer & Hannah, b. Apr. 19, 1764	3	51
Anna, m. Benj[ami]n WRIGHT, Mar. 19, 1783	4	234

	Vol.	Page
HIBBARD, HEBBARD (cont.)		
Anna, m. [Mat]thew **BOLL[E]S**, Sept. 15, 1793	4	280
Marvin, of Mansfield, m. Zilpha **ROBBINS**, of Ashford, Aug.		
30, 1826, by Rev. Philo Judson	5	23
Silas, of Coventry, Tolland County, m. Experience		
WOODWARD, of Ashford, June 18, 1823, by Rev.		
Philo Judson	5	10
HICKS, Arba, m. Laura **TROWBRIDGE**, Sept. 30, 1824, by		
Reuben Torrey, Eastford	5	15
HIGGINBOTHAM, Lyman S., m. Almira **SHERMAN**, b. of		
Ashford, Aug. 3, 1840, by Rev. R. W. Allen, Eastford	5	74
Merrick R., of Pomfret, m. Charilly M. **GREEN**, of Ashford.		
[Nov.], 24, [1831], by Rev. Reuben Torrey, Eastford	5	46
Phebe Ann, of Ashford, m. Elisha **MOREY**, of Pomfret, Sept.		
12, 1841, by Rev. Charles C. Barnes	5	78
HIGGINS, HEGGINS, HIGANS, Easter, d. Thomas, & Est[h]er, b.		
Aug. 11, 1754	1	84
Sarah, m. John **SOUTHWORTH**, Jan. 19, 1744/5, at		
Providence, by Rev. John Chackley	2	45
Thomas, s. Thomas & Easter, b. Feb. 21, 1750	1	91
Thomas, m. Easter **DEANS**, Nov. 11, 1753	1	81
HILL, HILLS, HIL, Abigail, m. Peter **EASTMAN**, Oct. 17, 1762	3	17
Bethiah, d. Squire & Dorathy, b. Sept. 25, 1771	4	110
Betsey A., Mrs., of Williamantic, m. Craft **EASTMAN**, of		
Grafton, Mass., Mar. 22, 1851, by Rev. P. Mathewson	5	106
Bets[e]y W., m. Craft **EASTMAN**, shoemaker, of Ashford, her		
2d h., Mar. 2, 1851, by P. Mathewson	5	148-9
David, s. Sylvester & Olive, b. Apr. 17, 1812	4	257
Ebenezer, s. Squire & Dorathy, b. Feb. 10, 1778	4	110
Johanna, [d.], Elisabeth Eastman, b. May 2, 1756	3	105
Johannah, m. Jesse **THOMSON**, [ ]	4	88
Philo, of Marlborough, m. Betsey W. **BUTLER**, of Ashford,		
[May] 9,[1836], by Rev. J. Hall	5	59
Polly, d. Squire & Dorathy, b. Sept. 15, 1773	4	110
Squire, m. Dorathy **WALKER**, Oct. 25, 1770	4	110
Zaccheus, s. Squire & Dorathy, b. Mar. 16, 1776	4	110
HILLIARD, (Correction made on original manuscript & placed in		
correct order) Clarissa, m. Jared **WENTWORTH**, b. of		
Ashford, Oct. 12, [1826]	5	24
HIMES, HYMES, HIAMS, Alva, s. Potter & Rebeckah, b. Dec. 10,		
1797	4	104
James, s. Potter & Rebeckah, b. May 22, 1794	4	104
James, m. C[h]loe **CURTISS**, b. of Ashford, Mar. 31, 1822, by		
Nathan Hayward, J. P.	5	6
James, m. Sally **WALKER**, b. of Westford, Nov. 9, 1851, by		
Rev. Ezekiel Skinner	5	108
Lydia, m. Joseph **SCARBOROUGH**, Jan. 2, 1783	4	278
Mary, m. Stephen **SCARBOROUGH** July 4, 1782	4	32

	Vol.	Page
HIMES, HYMES, HIAMS, (cont.)		
Mary, wid., of Ashford, m. Benoni **WALKER**, of Union, July 24, 1836, by Edward S. Keyes, J. P.	5	61
Miriam had s. Adolphas Owen, b. Jan. 8, 1787	4	233
Potter, m. Polly **SNOW**, b. of Ashford, May 25, 1825, by Nathan Hayward, J. P.	5	19
Sally, m. Simeon **SMITH**, Feb. 23, 1804	4	237
HINDEE, [see under **HENDEE**]		
HINDFIELD, [see under **HENFIELD**]		
HINTCHER, HINCHER, HENCHER, HENTCHER, Barsheba, d. Oliver & Elisabeth, b. Mar. 17, 1763	3	27
Isaac, s. Oliver & Elisabeth, b. Jan. 28, 1759	3	27
John, s. Oliver & Elisabeth, b. Mar. 21, 1770 ; d. Sept. 21, 1775	3	27
Mary, w. Oliver, d. Sept. 4, 1754	1	84
Mary, w. Oliver, d. Sept. 4, 1754	3	27
May, d. Will[ia]m & Persealla, b. Apr. 17, 1740	1	46
Oliver, m. Mary **KENDAL**, Oct. 8, 1752	3	27
Oliver, m. Elisabeth **FLINT**, Apr. 20, 1758	3	27
William, s. Oliver & Mary, b. Mar. 28, 1753	3	27
HIRES Sally, wid., of Brookfield, Mass., m. W[illia]m **JOHNSON**, of Ashford, Sept. 22, 1823, by Michael Richmond, J. P.	5	11
HISCOCK, Clarissaa, of Townsend, Vt., m. Otis **MOORE**, of Ashford, Sept. 24, 1826, by Rev. Amos Babcock, Jr. Intention publilshed	5	23
Luke, m. Hannah **HOLMAN**, b. of Woodstock, June 26, 1845, by Rev. Renssalear O. Putney, at North Ashford	5	94
Zelotes P., of Woodstock, m. Harmony C. **CHAFFEE**, of Ashford, July 15, 1844, by Rev. Cha[rle]s Hyde	5	90
HITCHCOCK, Mary, of Ashford, m. Joseph **DORSET**, of Union, Jan. 14, 1821, by Rev. Isaac Hall	6	26
HOAR, HORE, Mary, m. Jonathan **CHAPMAN**, Jr., Sept. 5, 1771	4	46
Sarah, m. Joseph **WORK**, Mar. 4, 1760	1	107
HODGES, Anna, m. Nathan **GRIGGS**, Feb. 6, 1772	4	90
Elizabeth, m. Philip **EASTMAN**, Jr., [ ]	4	5
Sarah, m. Robert **PARRY**, Sept. 5, 1764	4	26
HODGKINS, Nathan D., of Eastford, m. Alice **ROBBINS**, of Ashford, Jan. 28, 1850, by Rev. Ezekiel Skinner	5	104
Nathaniel, Jr., of Hampton, m. Lucretia **PRESTON**, of Ashford, June 12, 1827, by Rev. Luke Wood	5	27
HOLLOWAY, Weeden, of Ashford, m. Ruth **LAMPHEAR**, of Pomfret, Jan. 30, 1823, by Edward Keyes, J. P.	5	8
HOLMAN, Hannah, m. Luke **HISCOCK**, b. of Woodstock, June 26, 1845, by Rev. Renssalear O. Putney, at North Ashford	5	94
Mary, of Ashford, m. Stephen A. **LAMB**, Jr., of Willington, Oct. 5, [1826], by Ezekiel Skinner	5	24
Mary, of Ashford, m. Alvin W. **BENNETT**, of Wilbraham,		

HOLMAN, (cont.)	Vol.	Page
Mass., Apr. 20, 1842, by Rev. Alvin Bennett	5	81
Roxy, m. John TYLER, Jr., b. of Ashford, Jan. 11, 1838, by Alvan Underwood	5	67
HOLMES, HOLMS, Annah, m. James SNOW, Nov. 13, 1771	4	51
Arhoda, w. Josiah, d. Apr. 2, 1748	2	70
Betsay, d. Josiah & Sarah, b. Mar. 22, 1770	2	69
Betsai, d. Josiah & Sarah, b. Mar. 22, 1770	4	38
Calvin, s. Joseph & Hannah, b. Feb. 25, 1766	3	48
David, s. Josiah & Sarah, b. Jan. 19, 1751/52	2	70
David, Dr., m. Betsey PRESTON, [Feb.] 5, [1837], by Rev. R. Torrey, Eastford	5	64
Edward, s. John, Jr. & Lois, b. Sept. 18, 1762	3	22
Edward, [twin with John], s. Joseph & Hannah, b. Oct. 27, 1770	3	48
Elisabeth, d. Joseph & Han[n]ah, b. Sept, 2, 1761	3	48
Ezra, s. Moses & Keziah, b. July 8, 1756	2	29
Frederick, of Pomfret, m. Abigail SEAMANS, of Ashford, Apr. 19, 1840, by Rev. Amos Snell	5	73
Hannah, m. Caleb HENDEE, Jan. 1, 1751/2	2	34
Hannah, d. John, Jr. & Lowis, b. Nov. 19, 1754	1	86
Hannah, m. Abel SIMMONS, Jr., Nov. 3, 1774	4	121
Hartwell P., of Ashford, m. Julia A WITHEY, of Pomfret, Dec. 5, 1844, by Francis Williams	5	92
Isaac, m. Rachel KEEDY, Nov. 21, 1733, by Capt. Adams Justis	1	3
Isaac, m. Mary SKINNER, Oct. 19, 1761	1	3
Isaac, s. Joseph & Hannah, b. May 21, 1774	3	48
Jeen, d. Samuell & Mary, b. Feb. 28, 1756	1	92
John, s. Josiah & Sarah, b. Mar. 24, 1753	2	70
John, m. Lois TIFFANY, Jan. 30, 1754	1	82
John, [twin with Edward,], s. Joseph & Hannah, b. Oct. 26, 1770	3	48
John, Jr., d. Aug. 21, 1776	3	22
John H., m. Catherine M. VINTON, b. of Willington, June 22, 1851, by Rev. Ezekiel Skinner	5	106
Joseph, m. Hannah COYE, Dec. 3, 1760	3	48
Josiah, s. Josiah & Rhoda, b. Mar. 2, 1748	2	70
Josiah, s. Josiah & Arhoda, b. Mar. 3, 1748 ; d. Nov. 2, 1748	2	70
Josiah, m. Sarah WORK, Apr. 4, 1751, by Rev. Mr. John Bass	2	70
Josiah, s. Josiah & Sarah, b. Aug. 28, 1755 ; d. Sept. 17, 1755	2	70
Josiah, s. Josiah & Sarah, b. Aug. 17, 1758	2	70
Josiah, m. Sarah DUNTEN, Oct. 27, 1757	2	70
Lois, d. John, Jr. & Lois, b. Jan. 25, 1776	3	22
Luther, s. Joseph & Hannah, b. Oct. 9, 1763	3	48
Lyd[i]a, [d. Moses & Keziah], b. Sept, 10, 1759	2	29
Mary, d. Joseph & Hannah, b. Apr. 5, 1768	3	48
Mehetebel, m. Ebenezer MASON, May 11, 1748, by T. Tiffany, J. P.	2	71

	Vol.	Page
HOLMES, HOLMS, (cont.)		
Molly, d. Josiah & Sarah, b. June 22 1762	2	70
Moses, s. Moses & Kezia, b. Mar. 11, 1748/9	2	29
Rachal, d. John, Jr. & Lois, b. Oct. 4, 1756	1	96
Rebeckah, w. Isaac, d. Oct. 15, 1759	1	3
Rhoda, see under Arhoda		
Samuell, m. Mary **EWINS,** Aug. 1, 1754	1	84
Sarah, w. Josiah, d. Aug. 29, 1755	2	70
Sarah, d. Josiah & Sarah, b. July 7, 1760	2	70
Serena, m. John **SMITH,** Dec. 27, 1802	4	21
Stephen, s. Josiah & Sarah, b. Feb. 27, 1767	2	69
Stephen, s. Josiah & Sarah, b. Feb. 27, 1767	4	38
Tabatha, d. John & Lois, b. Jan. 28, 1760	3	22
HOLT, Alfred, s. Abial & Sally, b. Feb. 25, 1806	4	87
Arnold, s. Abial & Sally, b. Sept. 24, 1816	4	87
Clarina, d. Silus & Mary, b. Nov. 6, 1769	4	31
Elisabeth, m. James **HOWS,** June 2, 1774	4	78
Henry, s. Rufus & Betsey, b. June 19, 1817	6	21
Lucenda, d. Silus & Mary, b. July 26, 1773	4	31
Lucy, m. Jedidiah **DANA,** Jr. Nov. 27, 1770	4	249
Lucy, m. Aaron **WALKER,** Jan. 26, 1809	4	47
Polley, d. Uriah & Margaret, b. Mar. 2, 1782	4	75
Roxalana, m. Eben[eze]r **SUMNER,** June 13, 1782	4	232
Sally, d. Uriah & Margaret, b. Sept. 18, 1780	4	75
Sanford, s. Abial & Sally, b. Feb. 5, 1815	4	87
Silas, d. Oct. 22, 1773	4	31
Uriah, m Margaret **MASON,** Nov. 11, 1779	4	75
HORE, [see under **HOAR** and **HOVEY**]		
HORSGOOD, [see also **OSGOOD**], Dercus, m. Benjamin **SNOW,**		
July, 5, 1764, by Elijah Whiton, Esq.	4	20
HORTON, Betsey, d. Moses & Silance, b. Apr. 5, 1785	4	242
Betsey, m. Oliver **BOWEN,** Mar. 7, 1837, by Rev. Reuben Torrey, Eastford	5	64
Chauncey, m. Amanda **CHAFFEE,** b. of Ashford, Sept. 30, 1824, by Rev. W[illia]m Storrs	5	16
Dwight Barnum, s. Alva & Lucia M., b. July 21, 1840	6	96
Lucius, m. Huldreth **THAYER,** Apr. 1, 1832, by Rev. Joseph P. Tyler	5	47
Molley, d. Moses & Silance, b. Mar. 23, 1783	4	242
Moses, m. Silance **WILSON,** Oct 17, 1780	4	242
Moses, s. Moses & Silance, b. July 25, 1794	4	242
Salley, d. Moses & Silance, b. Oct. 20, 1796	4	242
Silence, housekeeper, d. Sept. 18, 1848 ae 85	5	138-9
Simion, s. Moses & Silance, b. Aug. 2, 1792	4	242
Solomon, s. Moses & Silance, b. Oct. 20, 1787	4	242
William. s. Moses & Silance, b. Mar. 23, 1781	4	242
HOUGH, Sarah J., ae 27, of Eastford, m. Dwight R. **ADAMS** instructor, ae 27, of Canterbury, Oct. [ ], 1849, by		

	Vol.	Page
HOUGH, (cont.)		
Charles Peabody	5	142-3
HOVEY, Abigail, m. Rev. William **STORRS**, Dec. 12, 1790	4	268
Mary W., m. Jerel B. **GREEN**, b. of Hartford, Oct. 9, 1837, by		
Rev. Cha[rle]s Hyde	5	66
Sarah, m. [Arau]nah **SNOW**, No[v], [ ]	4	286
HOWARD, Anson Ezra, s. Ezra, Jr. & Betsey, b. June 20, 1842	6	93
Calista, of Ashford, m. John **WHITFORD**, Jr. of Woodstock,		
Mar. 16, 1835, by Rev. Reuben Young	5	55
Danforth Milton, [s. John & Lydia], b. Apr. 12, 1832	6	79
David, Jr., m. Percy **PAIN**, May 14, 1807	6	3
David, farmer, d. May 11, 1848, ae 68	5	128-9
Dorothy Rosetta, [d. John & Lydia], b. Aug. 4, 1827	6	79
Ezra, d. Oct. 30, 1840	6	93
Hannah, m. Charles **SEAMANS**, b. of Ashford, Aug. 24, 1840,		
by Rev. Amos Snell	5	75
Hannah Elizabeth, d. Ezra, Jr., b. July 13, 1840	6	93
Henry, d. July, 28, 1834, ae 29 y.	6	80
Hiram, s. Nathan & Susanna, b. Oct. 5. 1802	4	235
Jane, of Eastford, m. Nathan H. **GARRETTSON**, of		
Worchester, Mass., Feb. 18, 1844, by Francis Williams,		
Eastford Intention published	5	88
John, m. Lydia **HOWARD**, Oct. 2, 1825	6	79
Lucy P., of Ashford, m. Daniel **BARTLETT**, of Woodstock,		
June 27, 1836, by Rev. Leonard Gage	5	60
Lucy Paine, d. David, Jr. & Percy, b. Apr. 10, 1815	6	3
Lydia, m. John **HOWARD**, Oct. 2, 1825	6	79
Martha Louisa, d. David, Jr. & Percy, b. Apr. 18, 1811	6	3
Mary, d. Nathan & Susanna, b. Aug. 31, 1809	4	235
Matilda, m. George B. **SEAMANS**, b. of Ashford, Sept. 25,		
1836, by Leonard Gage	5	62
Nathan, m. Susanna **ONLEY**, Nov. 26, 1801	4	235
Percy, housekeeper, d. Apr. 30, 1848, ae 63	5	128-9
Ranson, m. Melissa **TOWNE**, b. of Belchertown, Mass., [Jan.]		
10, [1838], by Rev. Erastus Benton	5	67
Rosetta, d. Nathan & Susanna, b. Aug. 31, 1806	4	235
Samuel, of Lebanon, m. Betsey **HAYWARD**, of Ashford, Oct.		
30, 1828, by David Bolles, J. P.	5	32
Warner, s. Nathan & Susanna, b. Aug. 8, 1804	4	235
HOWE, HOW, HOWS, [see also **HAWS**], Almira, d. Nehemiah &		
Mary, b. July 26, 1781	4	31
Asenah, d. James & Elizabeth, b. Oct. 4, 1774	4	78
Benjamin, m. Sall **EWING**, Sept. 13, 1766	4	37
Charles, s. Benj[ami]n & Sall, b. Apr. 24, 1769	4	37
Charles P., m. Clariss[a] J. **GOULD**, b. of Worcester, Mass.,		
June 8, 1845, by E. Dickinson	5	94
Daniel, of Mansfield, m. Caroline **JONES**, of R. I. Sept. 23,		
1833, by Ezekiel Skinner	5	52
James, m. Elisabeth **HOLT**, June 2, 1774	4	78

	Vol.	Page
HOWE, HOW, HOWS, (cont.)		
Joshua, s. Eben[eze]r & Pressillah, b. [ ]	4	69
Lydia, m. Alexander **EWING,** Jr., Aug. 5, 1760, by Shubael		
Conant, J. P., of Mansfield	4	18
Patty, m. Benjamin **BUTLER,** Dec. 12, 1793	4	50
Sabrina, d. Nehemiah & Mary, b. July 11, 1775	4	31
Sall, d. Benj[ami]n & Sall, b. Feb. 29, 1767	4	37
Thomas, s. Eben[eze]r & Pressillah, b. Oct. 3, 1773	4	69
William Nelson, of Woodstock, m. Harriet Chapman		
THRESHER, of Ashford, June 27, 1836, by Alvan		
Underwood, of Westford	5	60
HOWEY*, Alfred, Jr., d. Aug. 10, 1848 ae 6 (*Perhaps		
"**HARVEY**")	5	136-7
HOWLET, Parley, of Woodstock, m. Elizabeth **BARTLETT,** of		
Ashford, Mar. 4, 1827, by Edward S. Keyes, J. P.		
Intention published	5	26
Phebe, m. Amos **SNELL,** b. of Ashford, Sept. 9, [1828], by		
Rev. Ezekiel Skinner	5	32
HOXSIE, Joseph T., of Richmond, R. I. m. Almira S. **LYON,** of		
Ashford, [Oct.] 4, [1835], by Rev. Reuben Torrey,		
Intention published Oct. 2, 1835	5	57
HUDSON, Minerva, m. William **LYON,** b. of Ashford, Apr. 16,		
1843, by Rev. Nathan T. Hunt, of Abington, Pomfret,		
Eastford	5	85
HUGHES, HUSE, Adaline Ann, d. Jonathan & Sylvania Ann, b.		
Apr. 15, 1839	6	103
Arial, s. Jonathan & Eunice, b. May 13, 1785	4	94
Asa Andrews, s. Jona[than] & S]ylvania] Ann, b. Mar. 13,		
1845	6	103
Edmund, s. Jonathan & Eunice, b. June 25, 1781	4	94
Elial, s. Orrin & Mehetable, b. July 10, 1804 ; d. Aug. 13,		
1804	6	9
Emeline Josephine, d. Jon[atha]n & S[ylvania] Ann, b. Feb. 10,		
1841	6	103
Eunice, w. Jonathan, d. Apr. 25, 1789	4	94
Jonathan, s. Jonathan & Euniss, b. June 17, 1774	4	94
Jonathan, m. Eunice **FULLER,** Dec. 16, 1790	4	94
Jonathan, s. Orrin & Mehetable, b. Jan. 22, 1812	6	9
Jonathan E., m. Sylvana A. **SQUIER,** b. of Ashford, [July] 2,		
[1837], by Rev. Leonard Gage	5	65
Lyman J. s. Orrin & Mehetable, b. Oct. 16, 1806	6	9
Lyman J., m. Sarah **SMITH,** b. of Ashford, Aug. 24, 1851, by		
Rev. P. Mathewson	5	107
Miranda, d. Jon[a]th[an] & Eunice, b. Oct. 4, 1791	4	94
Orrene, d. Jonathan & Eunice, b. Nov. 14, 1778	4	94
Parley, s. Jonathan & Eunis, b. Apr. 29, 1766(sic) (1776?)	4	94
Rufus, s. Jon[a]th[an] & Eunice, b. Sept. 19, 1793	4	94
Sally, d. Orrin & Mehetable, b. Aug. 10, 1814	6	9

	Vol.	Page
HUGHES, HUSE, (cont.)		
Sinda, d. Jon[a]th[an] & Eunice, b. May 28, 1797	4	94
Sybil, d. Jon[a]th[an] & Eunice, b. May 4, 1795	4	94
HUMPHREY, HUMPHRY, HUMPHERY, Abel, s. Samvel &		
Mary, b. Sept. 12, 1748	1	59
Abagail, d. John & Hannah, b. Mar.7, 1748/9 ; d. same day	1	63
Ann, m. Thad[d[eus **WATKINS,** July 21, 1724	A	8
Arther, d. Jan. 30, 1752, in the 89th y. of his age	1	80
Asa, s. Sam[ue]ll & Mary, b. Sept. 9. 1738	1	59
Benj[ami]n, s. John & Hannah, b. May 5, 1746	1	1
Benjamin, s. John, d. Sept. 23, 1748	1	63
Bettey, d. Eben[eze]r & Lucy, b. Dec. 9, 1778	4	52
David, s. Sam[ue]ll & Mary, b. Mar. 27, 1743	1	59
Dorithy had d. Marriam b. Jan. 7, 1748/9 ; reputed father James		
DANIELSON	1	12
Dorothy, d. John & Hannah, b. June 25, 1730	1	1
Ebenezer, s. Sam[ue]ll & Mary, b. Dec. 27, 1739	1	58
Ebenezer, s. Eben[eze]r & Lucy, b. May 9, 1774	4	52
Elezebeth, d. Sam[ue]ll & Mary, b. May 3, 1741	1	59
Hannah, d. John & Hannah, b. Sept. 11, 1728	1	1
Hannah, m. Jonathan **AVERY,** Jr., Dec. 6, 1749, by Rev. John		
Bass	2	19
John, m. Hannah **RUSSEL[L],** Dec. 4, 1727, by James Hale	1	1
John, s. John d. Sept. 16, 1748	1	63
John, s. Eben[eze]r & Lucy, b. Jan. 1, 1795	4	52
John, s. John & Hanna, [ ]	1	1
Joseph, s. Eb[e]n[eze]r & Lucy, b. Mar. 16, 1782	4	52
Marriam, d. Dorithy Humphrey, b. Jan. 7, 1748/9 ; reputed		
father James **DANIELSON**	1	12
Mary, d. John & Hannah, b. July 5, 1734	1	1
Mary, m. Eben[eze]r **EATON,** May 12, 1753	3	10
Mehetable, m. William **WATKINS,** Mar. 17, 1717/8	A	4
Nathan, s. John & Hannah, b. Oct. 8, 1739 ; d. May 1, 1740	1	1
Nathan, s. Samuel & Mary, b. July 11, 1746	1	59
Nathan, s. Samuel [& Mary], d. July 3, 1748	1	59
Polley, d. Abel & Sarah, b. Jan. 15, 1776	4	103
Rachel, d. John & Hannah, b. Apr. 2, 1732	1	1
Rachel, w. Arther, d. Feb. 9, 1744, in the 78th y. of her age	1	80
Rachall, m. John **PITTS,** Jan. 10, 1754	1	86
Sam[u]el, m. Mary **CARPENTER,** Feb. 9, 1737/8	1	59
Sarah, d. John & Hannah, b. June 17, 1737	1	1
Serviah, see under Zerviah		
Tabitha, m. Edward **TIFFANY,** Jan. 27, 1725/6, by Rev. James		
Hale	A	10
Tabitha, m. Edward **TIFFANY,** Jan. 27, 1725/6, by Rev. James		
Hale	1	14
Serviah, d. John & Hannah, b. Dec. 7, 1743	1	1
HUNT, James, of Hampton, m. Pershsey **SNOW,** of Ashford, Feb.		

	Vol.	Page
HUNT, (cont.)		
7, 1821, by Reuben Torrey	5	2
HUNTINGTON, Alfred, s. Nathan & Elether, b. Aug. 29, 1804	4	104
Amelia, d. Andrew & Zerviah, b. Aug. 16, 1811	4	274
Andrew, m. Zeruiah **SMITH**, Feb. 3, 1790	4	274
Andrew, s. Andrew & Zeruiah, b. Aug. 1, 1795 ; d. Aug. 18, 1800	4	274
Andrew, s. Andrew & Zerviah, b. Dec. 7, 1813 ; d. Jan. 4, 1827	4	274
Anna, d. Andrew & Zeruiah, b. June 4, 1792 ; d. Jan. 11, 1795	4	274
Bettey, d. Nathan & Elither, b. Mar. 24, 1801	4	104
Calvin, [twin with Luther], s. Elisha & Ruth, b. June 14, 1778	4	105
Dan, s. Andrew & Zeruiah, b. Feb. 19, 1806	4	274
Eben[eze]r, name credited in original index to page 1, but information regarding same is missing	4	1
Elethiah, d. May 24, 1833	4	104
Elijah, s. Elijah & Abigail, b. May 21, 1772	4	105
Elisha, m. Ruth **CASE**, June 12, 1777	4	105
Elisha , s. Andrew & Zeruiah, b. May 23, 1793	4	274
Elisha D., m. Lucia M. **DAY**, b. of Eastford, Aug. 11, 1844, by Francis Williams	5	90
Enoch Smith, s. Andrew & Zeruiah, b. Sept. 30, 1804	4	274
Hannah, m. Nathan **LILLEY**, Nov. 25, 1800 ; d. July 25, 18[ ]	4	11
Hannah, m. Samuel **WOODWARD**, b. of Ashford, Dec. 24, 1843, by Rev. L. W. Blood, Eastford	5	87
Harriet, of Eastford, m. Edward E. **DAVIS**, of Newburyport, Mass., June 30, 1846, by Francis Williams	5	97
Harrey, s. Nathan & Elether, b. Oct. 1, 1802	4	104
Horatio, s. Andrew & Zeruiah, b. Nov. 27, 1797 ; d. Aug. 15, 1800	4	274
John, s. Nathan B. & Matilda W., b. Oct. 6, 1834	6	80
Lucy, d. Andrew & Zeruiah, b. Aug. 28, 1800; d. Jan. 12, 1804	4	274
Luther, [twin with Calvin], s. Elisha & Ruth, b. June 14, 1778	4	105
Mariah, d. Nathan B. & Matilda W., b. Sept. 4, 1836	6	80
Matilda, d. Andrew & Zeruiah, b. Dec. 26, 1808	4	274
Matilda, of Ashford, m. Frances P. **CLARK**, of Chaplin, Mar. 22, 1836, by Rev. Alvan Underwood	5	59
Nancy, d. Nathan & Elether, b. Sept. 9, 1808	4	104
Nancy, m. Lemuel **SARKIS**, Aug. 6, 1837, by Rodolphus Lanphear	5	65
Nathan, m. Elither **BUTLER**, May 31, 1798	4	104
Nathan B., m. Matilda **WHITON**, b. of Ashford, May 8, 1833, by Rev. James Porter	5	51
Nathan Belcher, s. Andrew & Jeruiah, b. Feb. 22, 1810	4	274
Prince, s. Jack & Silva, b. Feb. 27, 1795	4	66
Sarah Ann Lillie, d. Alfred & Caroline, b. Dec. 20, 1831	6	78
Sophia, d. Andrew & Zeruiah, b. May 4, 1791	4	274
Sophia, m. Elisha **BYLES**, Jan. 28, 1813	6	4
Susan Elizabeth, d. Alfred & Caroline, b. Mar. 28, 1837	6	78

	Vol.	Page
HUNTINGTON, (cont.)		
Susannah, m. Anderson **DANA**, June 1, 1757	3	5
Theodore G., of N. Hadley, Mass., m. Eliza **SUMNER**, of Ashford, Feb. 17, 1841, by Rev. Nathan S. Hunt, of Abington, Pomfret	5	77
Thomas, s. Nathan & Elither, b. Jan. 17, 1799	4	104
Zeruiah, d. Andrew & Zeruiah, b. Mar. 29, 1803 ; d. May 23, 1804	4	274
HUNTLY, Sally, m. Asa **SMITH**, July 8, 1809	4	67
HURLBURT, Amelia, of Ashford, m. Joseph **WHITFORD**, of Woodstock, Mar. 19, 1822, by Reuben Torrey	5	5
HUTCHINSON, HUTCHERSON, Benjamin, index credits name to page 4, but data regarding same is missing	4	4
Elisha, Rev., m. Jerusha **CADWELL**, July 16, 1778	4	108
Mary, d. Rev. Elisha & Jerusha, b. Mar. 1, 1782	4	108
Samuel, s. Rev. Elisha & Jerusha, b. July 9, 1779	4	108
Susanna, d. Rev. Elisha & Jerusha, b. Mar. 16, 1784	4	108
HYDE, Elizabeth R., of Ashford, m. Isaiah C. **THATCHER**, of Rochester, Mass., Jan. 7, 1845, by Rev. Cha[rle]s Hyde	5	92
IDE, Independent, m. Lydia **LEONARD**, b. of Ashford, Jan. 8, 1833, by Rev. Philo Judson	5	50
John B., farmer, b. Webster, Mass., res. Ashford, d. Jan. [ ], 1851, ae 22	5	150-1
Lavina, of Ashford, m. Corlis **BENNETT**, of Tolland, [Apr.] 9, [1838], by Rev. Cha[rle]s Hyde	5	67
Liberty, farmer, b. Attleborough, Mass., res. Ashford, d. Jan. [ ], 1851, ae 73	5	150-1
Lydia Ann, of Ashford, m. Ebenezer S. **ROSS**, of Mansfield, Mar. 22, 1843, by Rev. Cha[rle]s Hyde	5	84
INGALLS, James W., s. Warren, farmer, ae 68, & Hannah, ae 42, b. Aug. 22, 1850	5	146-7
Warren, of Pomfret, m. Hannah K. **MARCY**, of Ashford, Aug. 26, 1849, by Reuben Marcy, J. P.	5	104
Warren, farmer, ae 67, b. Pomfret, res. Ashford, m. 2d w. Hannah **MARCY**, ae 40, b. Ashford, Aug. [ ], 1849, by Reuben Marcy	5	142-3
INGREHAN, Myre, d. Sarah Badger, b. Feb. 2, 1798	4	88
IRONS, Jacob, s. Amasa, Jr., farmer, ae 23, & Susan, ae 31, b. Oct. 11, 1848	5	134-5
JACKSON, ----, 1st s. Caleb & Mary, b. Sept. 27, 1720 ; d. Sept. 28, 1720	A	6
JAMES, [see also JANES], Abigail, of Ashford, m. David **JONES**, of Chaplin, Oct. 5, 1837, by Amos Babcock	5	66
Almira, Mrs., of Ashford, m. John **ROSS**, of Chaplin, Mar. 23, 1851, by Rev. Ralph V. Lyon	5	108
Arthusa, of Ashford, m. Elisha **LORD**, of Abington, Pomfret, Sept. 14, 1846, by Francis Williams, Intention published Sept. 13, 1846, in Abington Meeting-house	5	98

	Vol.	Page

JAMES, (cont.)

Benj[ami]n, Jr., m. Cynth[i]a **RUSSELL**, Feb. 20, 1794	4	37
Benjamin, of Union, m. Hannah **KIMBALL**, of Ashford, Apr. 8, 1834, by Rev. Stephen Fairbanks	5	53
Benj[ami]n Raynals, s. Benj[ami]n, Jr. & Cynth[i]a, b. Nov. 22, 1796	4	37
Betsey, of Palmer, Mass., m. John W. **CURRIER**, of North Troy, Vt., Apr. 15, 1849, by Rev. Ezekiel Skinner	5	103
Betsey, ae 43, of Palmer, Mass., m. John W. **CURRIER**, mechanic, ae 52, b. Ashford, res. North Troy, Vt., Apr. 15, 1849, by Rev. Ezekiel Skinner	5	136-7
Diana, d. Benj[ami]n, Jr. & Cinth[i]a, b. Oct. 15, 1794 ; d. Mar. 6, 1796	4	37
Ebenezer, m. Eunice **DEAN**, b. of Ashford, July 14, 1836, by Amos Babcock	5	60
Elisabeth, m. Jonathan **CHAFFEE**, Jr., Nov. 4, 1802	4	245
Hannah Diana, d. Benj[ami]n, Jr. & Cynthia, b. June 10, 1801	4	37
Jonathan, s. Amos & Jean, b. Oct. 23, 1768	4	70
Jonathan, s. Benj[ami]n, Jr. & Cynth[i]a, b. Apr. 13, 1799	4	37
Jonathan A., m. Betsey **EASTMAN**, Mar. 23, 1826, by Rev. Amos Babcock, Jr. Intention published	5	22
Josiah R., m. Almira **CAMPBELL**, Union, resident of Westford, Oct. 26, 1836, by Alvan Underwood	5	63
Lucius Lyon, s. James & Cynthia, b. Apr. 2, 1809	4	25
Lucy, of Ashford, m. Warner **MARCY**, of Union, Jan. 6, 1831, by Rev. Ezekiel Skinner	5	41
Maria Thursa, m. Calvin **WHITNEY**, b. of Ashford, May, 29, 1823, by Rev. Reuben Torrey, Eastford	5	22
Miriam, m. Samuel **ROBBINS**, [ ] 9, 1797	4	7
Patience, m. Moses **RATHBUN**, Jan. 21, 1790	4	264
Polly, m. David **CARPENTER**, b. of Ashford, Feb. 23, 1834, by Rev. Ezekiel Skinner	5	53
Rhoda, d. Benjamin, Jr. & Cynthia, b. Mar. 7, 1803	4	37
Rhoda, of Ashofrd, m. David **MARCY**, of Union, Sept. 14, 1826, by Rev. Amos Babcock, Jr. Intention published	5	23
Sabrina, m. Hosea C. **ROBBINS**, b. of Ashford, Nov. 9, 1834, by Amos Babcock	5	55

JANES, , [see also **JAMES & JONES**], Arthusa Delocia, d. Walter

& Cynthia, b. Mar. 16, 1807 (Perhaps "Jam[e]s"?)	4	25
Edwin Edward, s. Walter & Cynthia, b. Feb. 14, 1815 (Perhaps "Jam[e]s"?)	4	25
George Washington, s. Walter & Cynthia, b. Dec. 7, 1816 (Perhaps "Jam[e]s"?)	4	25
Josiah, s. Thomas & Ruth, b. Nov. 11, 1792	4	70
Parthena Polly, d. Walter & Cynthia, b. June 21, 1812 (Perhaps "Jam[e]s"?)	4	25
Timothy, s. Thomas & Ruth, b. Nov, 1, 1795	4	70

Vol. Page

JENNINGS, JENINS, GENEINGS, GENINGS, GENNINGS,
JENENS, JENING, Annah, m. Jonathan CUTLER, Apr. 16, 1733,
    by Rev. James Hale   1   13
  Esther, m. Elijah CHAPMAN, Mar. 25, 1793   4   101
  [E]unes, d. Robert & Sarah, b. July 23, 1755   2   59
  Eunice, m. Joseph PECK, Mar. 14, 1782   4   30
  Hannah, d. Robert & Sarah, b. Mar. 9, 1753   2   59
  Hannah, m. Benjamin CHUBBS, Jan. 28, 1773   4   65
  Joannah, d. Jonathan & Keziah, b. May 4, 1750   1   A
  Johana, d. Jonathan & Keziah, b. Nov. 2, 1743   1   65
  John, m. Mary HARKING, of Windham, Sept. 13, 1821, by
    Philo Judson   5   4
  Jonathan, m. Keziah ROOD, May 10, 1742, by Rev. Mr. Hale   1   65
  Keziah, d. Jonathan & Keziah, b. Mar. 15, 1747/8   1   65
  Leb[b]eus, s. Robert & Sarah, b. Aug. 28, 1750   2   59
  Lede, d. Jonathan, d. Feb. 27, 1742/3   1   65
  Lois, m. [William] WATKINS, Aug. 18, 1788   4   6
  Nathan, of Willington, m. Wid. Anna FITTS, of Ashford, Aug.
    11, 1828, by Rev. Philo Judson   5   31
  Phila, ae 28, b. Mansfield, m. W[illia]m M. GARDINER, her
    3d h., blacksmith, ae 23, b. R. I., res. Mansfield, July 4,
    1851, by Rev. George Soule   5   148-9
  Zefaniah, s. Jonathan & Keziah, [b.] Jan. 26, 1745/6   1   65
JEWIT[T], Phebe, m. Elijah PHILLIPS, Jr., Jan. 23, 1800   4   45
JINKS, Anna, m. Daniel PERKINS, Feb. 13, 1791   4   272
JOHNSON, Abigail, d. Isaac & Mary, b. Sept. 19, 1752   2   79
  Annah, d. Isaac & Mary, b. Aug. 23, 1754   1   85
  Caleb, d. Oct. 23, 1778   2   43
  Cyril, s. Reuben & Anna, b. Oct. 8, 1783   4   64
  Daniel, s. Reuben & Anna, b. July 8, 1778   4   64
  Diah, s. Reuben & Anna, b. Sept. 27, 1775   4   64
  Dyania, d. William & Polley, b. May 25, 1802   4   25
  Dianna, m. Warren WHITNEY, b. of Ashford, Oct. 19, 1824,
    by Amos Babcock, Elder, Intention published   5   15
  Drusiller, d. Caleb & Easther, b. Jan. 29, 1752   2   43
  Edwin, m. Emily COOLEY, b. of Ashford, [Jan.] 1, [1843], by
    Rev. Cha[rle]s Hyde   5   83
  Elisha, of Mansfield, m. Betsey S. SMITH, of Ashford, Nov.
    27, 1826, by Rev. Philo Judson   5   25
  Hannah, m. Neal EASTMAN, Oct. 13, 1759, by Rev. Mr.
    Stephen Williams   1   106
  Hiram, ae 49, b. Vermont, res. Sturbridge, m. 2d w. Persis
    BABBITT, ae 59, b. N. Brookfield, Mass., Sept. 24,
    1848, by Rev. Cha[rle]s S. Adams   5   136-7
  James, of Thompson, m. Mary PARKS, of Ashford, Oct. 7,
    1835, by W[illia]m Livesey, Elder   5   57
  Jemimah, d. Caleb & Est[h]er, b. Sept. 30, 1753   2   43
  Lorana, of Ashford, m. Stephen FORD, of Chaplin, May, 5,

	Vol.	Page
JOHNSON, (cont.)		
1832, by Rev. Philo Judson	5	47
Marverick, m. Jemima **BUTLER,** Oct. 25, 1787	4	259
Mary, m. Benjamin **WALKER,** Jr., Mar. 26, 1758	1	101
Mary, m. William **SNOW,** June 6, 1770	4	39
Merrell E, s. Edwin, bootmaker, ae 27, & Emily ae 27 b. Feb. 5, 1850	5	140-1
Nancy, d. William & Polley, b. July 23, 1798	4	25
Olive, of East Haddam, m. Virgil **GOODELL,** of Ashford, Jan. 13, 1833, by Amasa Lyon, J. P.	5	50
Olover, s. Reuben & Anna, b. Feb. 21, 1781	4	64
Perses, d. Caleb & Esther, b. June 29, 1769	2	43
Relief, m. Jonathan **SNOW,**Jr., Apr. 24, 1794	4	280
Reuben, s. Reuben & Anna, b. Nov. 6, 1771 ; d, Nov. 9, 1775	4	64
Reuben, s. Reuben & [Anna], d. Nov. 9, 1775	4	64
Ruth, d. Caleb & Easter, b. Feb. 18, 1766	2	43
Sarah, m. Nathaniel **BUGBE,** Jan. 22, 1746	2	23
Sarah, m. Nath[anie]ll **EATON,** Jr., Nov. 13, 1755, by James Bicknell, J. P.	1	90
Sarah, m. Amasa **TIFFANY,** Nov. 26, 1789	4	259
Sarah, ae 20, m. Isaac N. **CHILD,** shoemaker, ae 25, b. Woodstock, res. Eastford, Jan. 1, 1848, by Francis Williams	5	128-9
Sibbel, m. Josiah **EATON,** Oct. 24, 1754, by James Bicknell, Esq.	1	87
Sibbel, d. Caleb & Easter, b. Jan. 1, 1756	2	43
Stephen, s. Caleb & Easter, b. Aug. 21, 1764	2	43
Sybil, see under Sibbel		
W[illia]m, of Ashford, m. Wid. Sally **HIRES,** of Brookfield, Mass., Sept. 22, 1823, by Michael Richmond, J. P.	5	11
JONES, [see also **JANES**], Abel, s. Benjamin & Prudence, b. Jan. 26, 1755	1	89
Caroline, of R. I., m. Daniel **HOW,** of Mansfield, Sept. 23, 1833, by Ezekiel Skinner	5	52
David, of Chaplin, m. Abigail **JAMES,** of Ashford, Oct. 5, 1837, by Amos Babcock	5	66
Marsylva, m. Benjamin **EASTMAN,** Nov. 8, 1796	4	18
Mary, m. Billings **BUGBEE,** May 13, 1815	6	37
Susan, m. Parley Veits **SNOW,** Dec. 17, 1812	6	98
JORDAN, Baziah, m. Ezekiel **COLLER,** June 12, 1823, by Ezekiel Skinner	5	10
Jemima, m. Thomas **WHITEHOUSE,** b. of Ashford, Feb. 19, [1826], by Ezekiel Skinner	5	21
JUDSON, Almira Harve, d. John W. & Almira, b. Oct. 25, 1808	4	114
Andrew, Rev., m. Elisabeth **WORK,** Jan.7, 1779	4	112
Andrew, Rev., m. Marah **WORK,** Mar. 13, 1785	4	112
Andrue Thompson, s. Andrew & Elisabeth, b. Nov. 29, 1784	4	112
Andrew W., m. Lucy B. **MATTHEWS,** b. of Eastford, June 16, 1844, by Francis Williams	5	90

	Vol.	Page
JUDSON, (cont.)		
Crissa, of Eastford, m. Rev. Asa **KING,** of		
Canterbury, June 16, 1844, by Francis Williams	5	90
Elisabeth Mary, d. Rev. Andrew & Mary, b. Nov. 24, 1785	4	112
John W., m. Almira **HARVE,** Jan. 5, 1808	4	114
John Work, s. Rev. Andrew & Elisabeth, b. July 8, 1782	4	112
John Work, s. John W. & Almira, b. Dec. 29, 1810 ; d. Apr.		
16, 1811	4	114
Jose, s. Rev. [Andrew] & Elisabeth, b. Feb. 6, 1780	4	112
Silvester Gilbert, s. Rev. Andrew & Mary, b. Feb. 15, 1788	4	112
Zuinglius, s. Rev. Andrew & Mary, b. Jan. 30, 1790	4	112
JUSTIN, Abijah Fuller, s. Amos & Lois, b. Nov. 20, 1813	6	27
Amos, m. Lois **FULLER,** May 25, 1810	6	26
Elisha, s. Amos & Lois, b. Sept. 22, 1811	6	27
Elizabeth Ann, d. Amos & Lois, b. Dec. 9, 1819	6	27
Julia Ann Lois, d. Amos & Lois, b. Dec. 23, 1815	6	27
Laura Ann, d. Amos & Lois, b. June 23, 1817	6	27
Laura Ann, m. Alfred H. **POTTER,** b. of Ashford, Sept. 6,		
1836, by Rev. Stephen Cushing	5	61
KASSON, Asher, s. Samuel & Polley, b. June 18, 1788	4	41
Roswell, s. Samuel & Polley, b. May 21, 1787	4	41
KEEDY, Rachel, m. Isaac **HOLMES,** Nov. 21, 1733, by Capt.		
Adams Justis	1	3
KEEP, Josiah O., of Brookfield, Mass., m. Eliza Ann		
SOUTHWORTH, of Ashford, Sept. 21, 1836, by Rev.		
Stephen Cushing	5	61
KEEZER, John L., of Union, m. Lois S. **CHAPMAN,** of Ashford,		
Oct. 11, 1835, by Rev. Alvan Underwood, Westford	5	57
KEITH, Isaac, of Easton, Mass., m. Abigail **DEAN,** of Ashford,		
Feb. 8, 1829, by Rev. Reuben Torrey, Eastford	5	33
James M., s. Merrill & Mary W., b. May 9, 1836	6	92
John, m. Mrs. Lucinda **BROWN,** b. of Eastford, Mar. 16, 1840,		
by Rev. R. W. Allen, Eastford	5	74
Merrill A., m. Mary W. **OLNEY,** b. of Ashford, Sept. 30,		
1831, by Rev. Benjamin Paine	5	44
Royal, of Douglass, Mass., m. Martha **BUTLER,** of Ashford,		
May 2, 1837, by Rev. J. Hall	5	64
Susan K., d. Merrill & Mary W., b. Oct. 29, 1838	6	92
KENDALL, KENDAL, KENDEL, KENDELL, KINDAL, Abigail,		
d. Isaac & Hannah, [b.] [ ] 3, 1715	A	7
Abigail, d. Joshua & Mary, b. Oct. 9, 1741 ; d. Feb. 19, 1748/9	1	67
Abigail had s. James P[ ]orle, b. Nov. 11, 1773	4	123
Abigail, d. Aug. 25, 1784	4	86
Abijah, s. David & Jane, b. Feb. 26, 1739/40	1	28
Almira, d. Eli & Triphenia, b. Aug. 11, 1792	6	22
Almon, s. Jacob & Prudence, b. Aug. 2, 1764	3	4
Amos, [twin with Mary], s. Isaac & Eleaner, b. Apr. 10, 1724	A	8
Amos, s. Joshua & Mary, b. Oct. 6, 1746	1	67
Amos, s. Isa[a]c, d. sometime in the year 1746 at Cape Briton	1	47

	Vol.	Page
KENDALL, KENDAL, KENDEL, KENDELL, KINDAL, (cont.)		
Amos, m. Servial CHAPMAN, Jan. 29, 1772	4	69
Amos, s. Elias & Lois, b. Dec. 11, 1805	4	69
Amos, m. Lois CLARK, Sept. 25, 1805	4	69
Asa, s. Jacob & Prudance, b. June 10, 1770	3	4
Bets[e]y, d. Isaac & Rachel, b. Sept. 25, 1785 ; d. Dec. 1, 1790	4	239
Betsey, d. Isaac & Rachel, b. Aug. 26, 1794	4	239
Cha[u]ncey, s. Smith & Elisabeth, b. Mar. 31, 1796	4	44
Chester, s. Joseph, Jr. & Molley, b. May 25, 1787	4	250
Daniel, s. David & Mehetable, b. May 29, 1785	4	86
David, s. Isaac & Hannah, b. Aug. 1, 1717	A	7
David, m. Jane ADAMS, Feb. 8, 1738/9, by Rev. Mr. Avery	1	28
David, m. Ha[nnah] KENDAL, Mar. 22, 1764	3	127
David, Jr., m. Mehitable STILES, Feb. 23, 1775	4	86
Da[v]id, d. Dec. 16, 1777	4	86
Ebenezer, s. Joshua & Mary, b. Apr. 24, 1756	1	103
Edmund Augustus, s. Elias & Lois, b. Oct. 14, 1813	4	69
Elener, w. Isaac, d. May 5, 1727	A	5
Ellinah, m. Jacob CHAPMAN, Mar. 17, 1762	3	121
Ele[a]nor, d. Isaac & Eleanor, b. Apr. 5, 1827 ; d. Apr. 2, next following (1727?)	A	2
Eli, s. Isaac, Jr. & Mary, b. Mar. 25, 1767	3	40
Eli, s. Eli & Triphenia, b. July 27, 1794	6	22
Elias, s. Joseph & Mary, b. Sept. 30, 1774	3	103
Elias, m. Lois SMITH, Feb. 10, 1803	4	69
Eliza Hatt, d. Simeon & Anna, b. Aug. 11, 1822 ; d. Apr. 5, 1823	6	42
Ellen, d. David, d. Apr. 16, 1798	4	86
Erastus, s. Elias & Lois, b. Dec. 30, 1815	4	69
Est[h]er, d. Isaac & Mary, b. Mar. 2, 1763	3	40
Esther, d. Isaac, d. May 16, 1786	3	40
Esther, d. Isaac & Rachel, b. July 17, 1790 ; d. Mar. 3, 1793	4	239
Esther, d. Isaac & Rachel, b. Apr. 17, 1798	4	239
Esther, d. Jan. [ ], 1850, ae 50	5	144-5
Eunis, d. Joshua & Mary, b. Feb. 23, 1759	1	103
Eunice, d. David & Mehetable, b. July, 19, 1784	4	86
Eunice, m. Benjamin WHEATON, b. of Ashford, Jan. 28, 1844, by Rev. Esekiel Skinner	5	87
Hannah, d. Isaac & Hannah, b. July 24, 1707 (See also Mary)	A	7
Hannah, w. Isaac, d. Aug. 1, 1717	A	7
Hannah, d. Isaac, Jr. & Mary, b. June 2, 1737; d. Apr. 27, 1740	1	6
Hannah, d. Isaac, Jr. & Mary, b. May 6, 1741	1	6
Ha[nnah], m. David KENDAL, Mar. 22, 1764	3	127
Isaac, s. Isaac & Hannah, b. July 4, 1709	A	7
Isaac, Jr., m. Mary CHAPMAN, Mar. 15, 1731/2 by Mr. James Hale	1	6
Isaac, s. Isaac, Jr. & Mary, b. Oct. 6, 1734	1	6
Isaac, d. May 21, 1748	1	5

	Vol.	Page
KENDALL, KENDAL, KENDEL, KENDELL, KINDAL, (cont.)		
Isaac, Jr., m. Mary RUSSELL, July 3, 1760	3	40
Isaac, s. Isaac, Jr. & Mary, b. May 7, 1761	3	40
Isaac, d. Oct. 15, 1776	3	40
Isaac, m. Rachel MARCY, Dec. 16, 1784	4	239
Isaac, s. Isaac & Rachel, b. Dec. 27, 1787	4	239
Isaac, Jr., m. Nancy SMITH, Mar. 25, 1810	4	273
Isreal(?), s. Isaac, Jr. & Mary, b. Mar. 1, 138/9(sic) (Probably 1738/9)	1	6
Jacob, m. Prudence BEEBE, Jan. 12, 1761	3	4
James, s. Isaac, Jr. & Mary, b. Oct. 6, 1745	1	5
James, s. David, d. Feb. 3, 1768	3	127
James P[ ]orle*, s. Abigàil, b. Nov. 11, 1773 *(Carle?)	4	123
John, s. Isaac, Jr. & Mary, b. July 6, 1743	1	6
John, s. Jsaack, Jr. d. Oct. 27, 1756	1	95
John, s. Elias & Lois, b. Feb. 2, 1808	4	69
Joseph, s. Joshua & Mary, b. Oct. 15, 1738	1	67
Joseph, m. Mary DEARING, Nov. 6, 1760	3	103
Joseph, s. Joseph & Mary, b. Sept. 13, 1762	3	103
Joseph, m. Wid. Hannah SMITH, June 20, 1776	3	103
Joshua, s. Isaac & Hannah, b. Dec. 5, 1712	A	7
Joshua, Capt., d. Feb. 9, 1767	3	103
Justus, s. Smith & Elisabeth, b. Feb.7, 1788 ; d. Apr. 30, 1789	4	44
Louis, d. Joseph & Mary, b. Mar. 19, 1771	3	103
Lois, d. Smith & Elisabeth, b. Jan. 24, 1794	4	44
Louisa, d. Isaac, Jr. & Nancy, b. Apr. 1, 1816	4	273
Lucy Holt, d. David, Jr. & Mehetable, b. Mar. 26, 1779 ; d. July 11, 1786	4	86
Lucy Holt, d. David, d. July 11, 1786	4	86
Luna, d. Jacob & Prudence, b. Sept. 17, 1762	3	4
Lymon, s. Joseph & Hannah, b. May, 6, 1784	3	103
Mary, [twin with Amos], d. Isaac & Eleaner, b. Apr. 10, 1724	A	8
Mary*, m. John DIMOCK, Oct. 10, 1728 (*Overwritten to read "Hannah")	1	A
Mary, d. Isaac, Jr. & Mary, b. Sept. 15, 1732	1	6
Mary, m. John TRISCOT, Nov, 23, 1749, by Rev. Mr. John Bass	2	22
Mary, m. Oliver HINTCHER, Oct. 8, 1752	3	27
Mary, d. Joshua & Mary, b. May 31, 1753	1	67
Mary, d. Isaac, Jr. & Mary, b. Feb. 1, 1765	3	40
Mary, d. Oct. 16, 1768	3	103
Mary, w. Joseph, d. Oct. 20, 1775	3	103
Mary, d. Elias & Lois, b. July 20, 1818	4	69
Mary, m. Sewell S. EMERSON, b. of Ashford (Westford), Jan. 21, 1836, by Rev. Alvan Underwood	5	58
Mary Burgess, d. Isaac & Elenor, d. Apr. 8, 1722	A	7
Mason Sherman, s. Isaac, Jr. & Nancy, b. Feb. 25, 1812	4	273
Midine Preston, s. Joseph, Jr. & Molley, b. Nov. 24, 1788	4	250

	Vol.	Page
KENDALL, KENDAL, KENDEL, KENDELL, KINDAL (cont.)		
Nancy, housekeeper, d. Nov. 24, 1848, ae 62	5	136-7
Nathan, s. Smith & Elisabeth, b. Mar. 13, 1798	4	44
Olive, d. Smith & Elisabeth, b. Nov, 21, 1791	4	44
Oliver, s. Joseph & Mary b. May 5, 1769	3	103
Patiance, m. David EATON, July 20, 1749, by Sqr. Bicknel	1	63
Pearly, s. Joseph & Hannah, b. Apr. 23, 1777	3	103
Phebe, d. Joshua & Mary, b. Sept. 23, 1743	1	67
Phebe, d. Joshua [& Mary], d. Feb. 11, 1748/9	1	67
Phebe, d. Isaac, Jr. & Mary, b. May 6, 1769	3	40
Phebe, m. Peter TUFTS, July 4, 1780	4	240
Phebe, m. Zachariah BICKNELL, Jr., Dec. 13, 1787	4	253
Polly, d. Smith & Elisabeth, b. Feb. 15, 1790	4	44
Rebeckah, d. Isaac & Elenor, b. May 19, 1721	A	7
Rebeckah, m. John TRISKET, Oct. 18, 1743, by Rev. Mr. John Bass	2	31
Rocksa, d. Isaac, Jr. & Mary, b. Sept. 4, 1771	3	40
Roxana, d. Eli & Tryphenia, b. June 24, 1798	6	22
Rufus, s. Isaac & Mary, b. Sept. 21, 1774	3	40
Sabin, s. Smith & Elisabeth, b. June 15, 1786	4	44
Samuel, s. David & Jene, b. Apr. 6, 1751	1	28
Sarah, m. Aaron TUFTS, Dec. 25, 1766	3	24
Sarah, d. David, Jr. & Mehitable, b. Oct. 27, 1776	4	86
Sarah, m. John ALLEN, Jan. 1, 1784	4	240
Simeon Marcy, s. Isaac & Rachel, b. Aug. 18, 1792	4	239
Smith, s. Joseph & Mary, b. Aug. 10, 1765	3	103
Smith, m. Elisabeth SABIN, Feb. 9, 1786	4	44
Thais, d. Jacob & Prudence, b. Aug. 9, 1768	3	4
Theda, d. David & Hanna[h], b. Apr. 17, 1767	3	127
Tryphenia, [twin with Tryphosa], d. Eli & Tryphenia, b. July 17, 1803	6	22
William, s. Isaac & Elenor, b. Apr. 1, 1719	A	7
William, m. Patiance WARD, Jan. 1, 1740/41, by Rev. Mr. James Hale	1	47
William, s. Will[ia]m & Patian[c]e, b. Oct. 27, 1741	1	47
William, d. Apr. 5, 1748	1	47
William EATON, s. Eli & Tryphenia, b. June 11, 1800	6	22
Zeruiah, w. Amos, d. Aug. 11, 1804	4	69
Zerviah, d. Elias & Lois, b. Oct. 11, 1810	4	69
Ziba, s. Jacob & Prudence, b. Mar. 19, 1766	3	4
Zube, d. David & Jane, b. Feb. 2, 1748	1	27
---mes, s. David & Hannah, b. Oct. 11, 1765 (James?)	3	127
-----, s. Mason S., farmer & E[ ], b. May [ ], 1850	5	140-1
KENT, Betsey, of Ashford, m. Bradley BARROWS, of Mansfield, Nov. 12, 1840, by Rev. Ezekiel Skinner	5	75
Hannah C., of Ashford, m. Lorenzo HARDINGS, of Medford, Mass., Dec. 1, 1838, by Rev. Ezekiel Skinner	5	69
KEYES, KEIYES, KEYS, KYE, KYES, Aavis, d. Samson &		

	Vol.	Page
KEYES, KEIYES, KEYS, KYE, KYES, (cont.)		
Abiga[i]l, b. Dec. 30, 1763	3	42
Abigail, d. Samson & Abigail, b. Dec. 20, 1758	1	111
Abigail, w. Samson, d. Aug. 21, 1801	3	42
Amasa, s. Jonas & Esther, b. Mar. 11, 1771	4	46
Amos, s. Ephriam & Sarah, b. Aug. 20, 1761	3	61
Andrew F., s. Joseph F. & Clarissa, b. May 13, 1832	6	86
Anna, d. Samson & Abigail, b. Sept. 1, 1743	1	69
Anna, m. Tho[ma]s KNOWLTON, Apr. 5, 1759	3	32
Anna, d. Edward & Mary, b. Mar. 8, 1798	4	256
Asac, s. Epherim & Sarah, b. June 5, 1742 ; d. Aug. 27, 1742	1	57
Avis, d. Ephraim & Sarah, b. Apr, 2, 1764	3	61
Caroline, m. Fielder S. SNOW, b. of Ashford, "last evening", [Mar. 24, 1836], by Rev. J. Hall	5	59
Charlotte, of Ashford, m. John HARBUCK, of Sharon, N. Y., Sept, 3, 1821, by Rev. Philo Judson	5	3
Clarrasa, d. John & Mary, b. Apr. 30, 1768	4	9
David, s. Solomon & Sarah, b. Apr. 20, 1765	3	65
David, m. Sally SUMNER, Jan. 30, 1793	4	114
David, s. Solomon & Esther, b. Sept. 7, 1798	4	244
David, s. Edward & Sarah, b. Jan. 31, 1808	4	256
David, m. Betsey HASKELL, b. of Ashford, Apr. 22, last [1821], by Rev. Stephen Haskell, Intention published	5	3
David L., s. Joseph F. & Clarissa, b. Mar. 31, 1838	6	86
Delotia, d. David & Sally, b. Aug. 9, 1793	4	114
Destotia, m. Joshua LEWIS, Apr. [ ], 1819 (Delotia?)	6	30
Edward, s. Epherem & Sarah, b. Feb. 7, 1745/6	1	57
Edwar[d], s. Solomon & Sarah, b. June 4, 1759	3	65
Edward, m. Mary WORK, June 16, 1779	4	256
Edward, s. Edward & Mary, b. Jan. 20, 1793	4	256
Edward, m. Sarah WHITMAN, Feb. 15, 1801	4	256
Edward, Esq., d. May 1, 1827	4	256
Edward Sumner, s. Edward Sumner & Hannah, b. Sept. 30, 1815	6	59
Elias, s. Solomon & Sarah, b. Apr. 14, 1757	1	98
Elias, s. Solomon & Sarah, b. Apr. 14, 1757	3	65
Ellias, d. Feb. 22, 1767	3	12
Elias, s. Edward, d. June 23, 1801	4	256
Elisabeth, d. Solomon & Sarah, b. Jan. 22, 1761	3	65
Elisabeth, d. Edward, d. May 13, 1803	4	256
Elizabeth, d. Edward Sumner & Hannah, b. Jan. 31, 1824	6	59
Epherem, [s. Elias & Mary], b. July 4, 1715	2	47
Epherem, m. Sarah WADKIN, June 22, 1737,by Rev. Mr. Hale	1	57
Epharam, s. Epharem & Sarah, b. Jan. 27, 1737/8	1	57
Ephraim, Jr., m. Abigail CHAFFE[E], Dec. 20, 1760	3	12
Esther, d. Edward & Mary, b. Jan. 23, 1791	4	256
Esther, d. Edward Sumner & Hannah, b. Nov. 29, 1819	6	59
Frederick, s. Ephraim & Sarah, b. Sept. 20, 1756	1	57

	Vol.	Page
KEYES, KEIYES, KEYS, KYE, KYES, (cont.)		
Giddings, m. Emily **GAYLAND**, b. of Ashford, Feb. 25, 1829		
by Rev. Philo Judson	5	33
Giddings Whitman, s. Edward & Sarah, [b.] Aug. 31, 1802	4	256
Hannah, d. Ephraim & Sarah, b. Jan. 21, 1754	1	57
Hannah, m. Levi **CARPENTER**, Jan. 13, 17[ ]	4	7
Hannah, w. Edward S., d. July 6, 1828	6	59
Hannah Maria, d. Edward Sumner & Hannah, b. May 27, 1826	6	59
Harriet, d. Sampson, Jr. & Lucy, b. June 18, 1789	4	262
Henery, s. Ephraim & Sarah, b. Dec. 16, 1758	1	107
Herbert Williams, s. Giddings W. & Emily G., b. Nov. 2, 1834	6	80
Huldah, d. Solomon & Esther, b. Dec. 14, 1789	4	244
Isaiah, [twin with Solomon], s. Solomon & Esther, b. July 22, 1793	4	244
James, s. Samson & Abigail, b. May 29, 1752	1	70
James H., s. Edward S. & Nancy, b. Oct. 22, 1830	6	59
Jeremiah, s. Solomon & Esther, b. Apr. 2, 1796	4	244
Jerome, s. Edward Sumner & Hannah, b. Nov. 15, 1817	6	59
John, s. Samson & Abigail, b. Oct, 24, 1745	1	69
John, of Ashford, s. of Samson, m. Mrs. Mary **WALES**, d. of Capt. Elisha **WALES**, of Ashford, Sept. 28, 1767, by Nath[anie]ll Wales, Jr., J. P.	4	9
Jonah, s. Ephraim & Sarah, b. Aug. 30, 1748	1	57
Joseph Flagg, s. Edward & Sarah, b. Nov. 23, 1803	4	256
Julius, of Ashford, m. Abigail H. **BROWN**, of Mansfield, Oct. 5, 1837, by Rev. R. Torrey, Eastford	5	66
Justis, s. Solomon & Sarah, b. Sept. 10, 1767	3	65
Justus, s. Edward & Mary, b. Nov. 9, 1780	4	256
Lucy, m. Abraham **PRESTON**, June 1, 1773	4	116
Lucy, m. Sampson **K[E]YES**, Jr., Nov. 15, 1787	4	262
Mareshal, [s. Ephraim & Abigail], b. Sept. 23, 1764	3	12
Mary, [d. Elias & Mary], b. Jan. 19, 1721/2	2	47
Mary, m. Ebenezer **DIMOCK**, Sept. 27, 1739, by Rev. James Hale	1	15
Mary, w. Elias, d. Nov. 27, 1753, ae 58	2	47
Mary, d. Samson & Abigail, b. Dec. 30, 1756	1	98
Mary, w. Edward, d. Mar. 9, 1798	4	256
Mary, m. Horatio **WOODWARD**, Dec. 31, 1809	6	29
Mary Ann, d. Edward Sumner & Hannah, b. Aug. 5, 1821	6	59
May A., of Ashford, m. Stephen H. **WEBSTER**, of Dudley, Mass., Oct. 5, 1841, by Rev. Charles C. Barnes	5	79
Meriam, d. Ephraim & Sarah, b. Sept. 6,[ ], (Entry crossed out)	1	57
Meriam, d. Ephraim & Sarah, d. Aug. 14, 1753	1	57
Miriam, d. Epheram & Sarah, b. Sept. 2, 1743	1	57
Miriam, d. Ephraim & Abigail, b. Oct. 15, 1762	3	12
Olive, d. Samson & Abigail, b. Sept. 13, 1747	1	69
Olive, d. Samson, d. Oct. 27, 1748	1	70
Olive, d. Samson & Abigail, b. Sept. 18, 1749	1	70

	Vol.	Page
KEYES, KEIYES, KEYS, KYE, KYES, (cont.)		
Olive Loisa, d. Cyrel & Margaret, b. Nov. 21, 1823	6	59
Parcy, d. Solomon & Sarah, b. Jan. 20, 1763	3	65
Parcy, d. Solomon & Esther, b. Aug. 8, 1786	4	244
Penelope, of Ashford, Conn., m. Ira **PECK**, of Marion, Ga., Mar. 7, 1824, by Rev. W[illia]m Storrs	5	12
Persce, s. Solomon & Sarah, b. Jan. 20, 1763	3	65
Polli, d. Solomon & Sarah, b. June 20, 1773	3	65
Polley, d, Edward & Mary, b. Nov. 9, 1788	4	256
Ruth, d. Steven & Abigail, b. Sept. 27, 1742	1	63
Salla, d. Solomon & Sarah, b. Oct. 14, 1769	3	65
Salla, d. Edward & Mary, b. Oct. 10, 1795	4	256
Samson, [s. Elias & Mary], b. Nov, 21, 1719	2	47
Samson, m. Abigail **BROOKS**, Sept. 22,1742,by Rev. Mr. Hale	1	69
Samson, s. Samson & Abigail, b. Oct. 30, 1761	3	42
Sampson, Jr., m. Lucy **K[E]YES**, Nov, 15, 1787	4	262
Samson, d. Mar. 14, 1805	3	42
Sampson, of Ashford, m. Percy **BABCOCK**, of Liberty, N. Y., Jan. 6, 1824, by Rev. Philo Judson	5	12
Sarah, d. Ephraim & Sarah, b. Apr. 27, 1755	1	101
Sarah, m. Nathan **WALES**, Dec. 22, 1771	4	66
Sarah M., d. Joseph F. & Clarissa, b. Sept. 11, 1833	6	86
Solomon, [s. Elias & Mary], b. July 15, 1728	2	47
Solomon, m. Sarah **SUMNER**, May 9, 1754, by Esq. Bicknell	1	83
Solomon, s. Solomon & Sarah, b. Mar. 28, 1755	1	88
Solomon, s. Solomon & Sarah, b. Mar. 28, 1755	3	65
Solomon, [twin with Isaiah], s. Solomon & Esther, b. July 22, 1793	4	244
Stephen, [s. Elias & Mary], b. July 15, 1717	2	47
Stephen, s. Sampson, Jr. & Lucy, b. Oct. 19, 1790	4	262
Steven, m. Abigail **PEABODY**, of Pomfret, Oct. 7, 1741, by Rev. Mr. William, of Pomfret	1	63
William, s. Epherem & Sarah, b. Feb. 12, 1739/40	1	57
William, name credited in original index to page 2 but information regarding same is missing	4	2
Zackariah, [s. Elias & Mary], b. Jan. 5, 1723/4	2	47
Zechariah, s. Sampson & Abigail, b. Oct. 2, 1754	1	87
Zilphah, d. Ephraim, Jr. & Abigail, b. Sept. 25, 1760	3	12
Zilpha, m. Clark **ROB[B]INS**, Nov. 16, 1780	4	115
-------, s. Elias & Mary, b. Jan. 5, 1723/4	A	8
KIDDER, John, m. Elizabeth **NICOLS**, b. of Mansfield, May 7, 1838, by Amos Babcock	5	68
KILBURN, Laura, m. Jacob Nash **TORREY**, Feb. 12, 1815	6	17
KIMBALL, KIMBAL, Almira, d. Stephen & Salla, b. Feb. 21, 1806	4	76
Alvan, m. Matilda **FARNAM**, Apr. 1, 1806	4	122
Alvan, s. Alvan & Matilda, b. Mar. 7, 1807	4	122
Andrew Fuller, s. Asahel & Hannah, b. Dec. 26, 1805	6	10
Asahel, m. Hannah **FULLER**, Apr. 17, 1803	6	10

	Vol.	Page
KIMBALL, KIMBAL, (cont.)		
Betsey, d. Sam[ue]ll & Betsey, b. Feb. 22, 1785 ; d. Nov. 19, 1785	4	243
Eleazer, s. Sam[ue]ll, Jr. & Betsey, b. Dec. 24, 1787	4	243
Hannah, of Ashford, m. Benjamin **JAMES,** of Union, Apr. 8, 1834, by Rev. Stephen Fairbanks	5	53
Harrice, s. Stephen & Salla, b. Jan. 12, 1799	4	76
Harriot, d. Stephen & Salla, b. Mar. 15, 1797	4	76
Lucey, d. Sam[ue]ll, Jr. & Betsey, b. Sept. 22, 1781	4	243
Orra, s. Sam[ue]ll, Jr, & Betsey, b. June 1, 1783	4	243
Polley, d. Stephen & Salla, b. Oct. 9, 1795	4	76
Rachel, d. Samuel & Anna, b. May 10, 1765	3	102
Samuel, Jr., m. Betsey **PEARL,** Mar. 9, 1781	4	243
Stephen Hyde, s. Stephen & Salla, b. June 26, 1804	4	76
KING, Asa, Rev., of Canterbury, m. Crissa **JUDSON,** of Eastford, June 16, 1844, by Francis Williams	5	90
Lydia, m. Benjamin **READ,** Jr., Aug. 26, 1747	3	99
Sybil, m. John **MASON,** Oct. 21, 1778	4	113
KINGSBURY, Ebenezer, m. Sophia C. **BOUTELL,** b. of Ashford, Apr. 7, 1829, by Rev. Philo Judson	5	35
KINGSLEY, Sarah, m. James **OULD,** Mar. 20, 1753	4	16
Sarah, m. James **OULD,** Mar. 21, 1753	1	92
KINNE, Elisabeth, m. Jeremiah **UTLEY,** Jr., Nov. 18, 1756	1	98
KNIGHT, Anthony W., m. Susan L. **SMITH,** b. of Johnston, R. I., Oct. 23, 1845, by Isaac Sherman	5	95
Darius, of Chaplin, m. Sophronia **SIMMONS,** of Ashford, Mar. 16, 1842, by Rev. Cha[rle]s Hyde	5	80
Emma J., d. Albert S., carpenter, & Marcia, b. Nov. 10, 1848	5	134-5
Merrick, Rev., of Chaplin, m. Abigail **WARD,** of Westford, June 10, 1851, by Rev. Charles S. Adams	5	109
Merrick, clergyman, ae 33, b. Northampton, res. Chaplin, m. Abigail **WARD,** Jr,., ae 28, b. Ashford, June[ ], 1851, by Rev. C. S. Adams	5	148-9
KNOWLTON, KNOLTON, Abil, s. Abraham & Molley, b. Apr. 9, 1772	3	119
Abel, m. Birsha **DIMOCK,** Apr. 16, 1795	4	119
Abigail, d. Tho[ma]s & Anna, b. June 20, 1768	3	32
Ab[r]aham, s. Robert & Hannah, b. Apr. 3, 1740	1	19
Abraham, m. Molly **KNOX,** May 26, 1760	3	119
Abraham, s. Abraham & Molley, b. Dec. 17, 1774 ; d. Dec. 13, 1775	3	119
Abraham, s. Abraham & Molley, b.July 11, 1776; d. Sept. 6, 1777	3	119
Acksa, d. W[illia]m & Mehitable, b. Aug. 29, 1772	3	6
Achsah, m. Jonas **HANNAH,** Jan. 16, 1797	4	229
Albert Fay, s. Samuel & Elizabeth F., b. July 4, 1840	6	94
Almira, d. Jonathan & Zerviah, b. Sept. 7, 1811	4	38
Almira, w. John, d. Feb. 17, 1821	6	19
Almira Calysta, d. John & Almira, b. Aug. 8, 1820	6	19

	Vol.	Page
KNOWLTON, KNOLTON, (cont.)		
Amanda, d. Jonathan & Zerviah, b. Aug. 27, 1805	4	38
Amanda, d. Daniel, 2nd & Hannah, b. June 24, 1807	4	67
Amanda, m. Daniel B. **READ**, b. of Ashford, Mar. 27, last,		
[1825], by Ezekiel Skinner	5	18
Amanda, of Ashford, m. Lewis **TOPLIFF**, of Mansfield, Oct.		
15, 1835, by Amos Babcock, Elder, Intention published	5	57
Amasa, s. Abraham & Molly, b. Feb. 26, 1764	3	119
Amos, s. Abraham & Molley, b. Mar. 20, 1783	3	119
Amos, m. Nancy **WEBB**, Sept. 13, 1804	4	28
Anna, d. William & Mehitable, b. Dec. 19, 1758	1	102
Anna, d. Tho[ma]s & Anna, b. June 8, 1771 ; d. June 4, 1772	3	32
Anna, d. Thomas & Anna, b. Mar. 19, 1773	3	32
Anna, m. Josiah **EATON**, Apr. 23, 1780	4	14
Anna, w. Col. Thomas, d. May 22, 1808	3	31
Arnon, s. Stephen & Hannah, b. Jan. 28, 1800	4	259
Arnon, m. Susan **WENTWORTH**, b. of Ashford, Mar, 4,		
[1830], by Rev. Ezekiel Skinner	5	38
Asher, s. Amos & Nancy, b. Jan. 3, 1807	4	28
Asher, m. Elvira K. **KNOWLTON**, b. of Ashford, Mar. 25,		
1840, by Rev. Alvin Bennett	5	73
Bridget, w. Tho[ma]s, d. June 9, 1777	3	44
Calista R., of Ashford, m. Hiram **TUFTS**, of Eastford, Apr. 5,		
1848, by Charles Peabody	5	102
Catherine Spring, m. Frederick **CHAFFEE**, Jr., June 12, 1814	6	9
Charles Clark, s. Jonathan W. & Harriet M., b. Sept. 22, 1844	6	100
Chester, s. Tho[ma]s & Hepsibah, b. Oct. 12, 1787	3	44
Danford, s. Daniel, 2d, & Hannah, b. May 5, 1814	4	67
Dan[i]el, m. Serviah **WADKINS**, Nov. 7, 1745	2	60
Daniel, m. Elisabeth **FARNUM**, Nov. 3, 1763	3	20
Daniel, s. Daniel & Elisabeth, b. Dec. 7, 1765	3	20
Daniel, s. Tho[ma]s & Bridget, b. Feb. 8, 1766	3	44
Daniel, s. Thomas & Bridget, d. Sept. 6, 1777	3	44
Daniel, s. Abraham & Molley, b. Mar. 17, 1781	3	119
Daniel, m. Rebec[c]ah **FENTON**, Apr. 24, 1788	3	20
Daniel, Jr., m. Betsey **BIRCHARD**, Apr. 4, 1793	4	60
Daniel, 2d, m. Hannah **KNOWLTON**, Nov. 24, 1803	4	67
David Palmer, s. Palmer & Harriet, b. Nov. 16, 1833	6	85
Ebenezer, s. Stephen & Hannah, b. Apr. 3, 1810	4	259
Ebenezer, m. Eliza Ann **LYON**, b. of Ashford, Apr. 8, 1838,		
by Rev. Amos Babcock	5	68
Edwin, s. Daniel, 2d & Hannah, b. June 24, 1825	4	67
Elisabeth, d. Daniel & Eles[a]b[e]th, b. Mar. 24, 1768	3	20
Elisabeth, w. Daniel, d. June 1, 1786	3	20
Elisabeth, m. Fredrick **CHAFFE[E]**, Mar. 6, 1788	4	254
Elvira K., m. Asher **KNOWLTON**, b. of Ashford, Mar. 25,		
1840, by Rev. Alvin Bennett	5	73
Elvira Keziah, d. Daniel, 2nd, & Hannah, b. Sept. 14, 1816	4	67

	Vol.	Page
KNOWLTON, KNOLTON (cont.)		
Maria Jarritt, d. Anson & Susan, [b.] Sept. 10, 1838	6	76
Mariam, m. Abner **WOODWARD**, Apr. 15, 1790	4	260
Marius, s. Stephen & Hannah, b. Feb. 4, 1806	4	259
Martha, d. Daniel & Elisabeth, b. Feb. 24, 1777	3	20
Martha, m. Charles Willis **BRANDAN**, June 12, 1796	4	19
Martha, m. Benjamin F. **EASTMAN**, b. of Ashford, May 22, last, [1826], by Ezekiel Skinner	5	23
Marvin, s. Daniel & Rebec[c]ah, b. Sept. 3, 1794	3	20
Marvin, m. Calista **LEONARD**, Apr. 19, 1820	6	43
Mary, m. Abijah **HARRIS**, Nov. 29, 1739, by James Hale	1	30
Mary, m. Ezekiel **TIFFANY**, Mar. 9, 1748/9, by Rev. Mr. John Bass	2	81
Mary, d. Thomas & Bridget, b. Jan. 15, 1758	1	99
Mary, d. Ebenezer & Eliza A., b. May 20, 1845	6	95
Mary Ann, d. Amos & Nancy, b. Feb. 26, 1811	4	28
Mary E., d. Jonathan W. & Harriet M., b. Apr. 23, 1846	6	100
Mehetable, m. John **HALE**, Apr. 14, 1772	4	57
Mehitable, [twin with Ephraim], d. William & Mehitable, b. Apr. 27, 1774	3	6
Meriam, d. Abraham & Molly, b. Dec. 15, 1766	3	119
Merian, of Ashford, m. Miram **CADA**, of Hartford, Nov. 24, 1831, by Rev. David Bennett	5	45
Miner, s. Daniel, 2d & Hannah, b. Sept. 25, 1804	4	67
Miriam, d. Daniel, 2nd, & Hannah, b. Mar. 15, 1809	4	67
Molley, w. Abr[aham], d. July 8, 1819, ae 76	3	119
Nancy Miranda, d. Asha & Elvira, b. Jan. 23, 1841	6	95
Nathan, s. Abraham & Molley, b. Aug. 11, 1778	3	119
Nathaniel, [twin with Manassah], s. Daniel & Elisabeth, b. Dec. 24, 1770	3	20
Nathaniel, s. Daniel, Jr. & Betsey, b. Jan. 7, 1794	4	60
Nathaniel, s. Ebenezer & Eliza A., b. May 19, 1843	6	95
Orson, s. Stephen & Hannah, b. Nov. 10, 1803 ; d. Sept. 4, 1817	4	259
Palmer, s. Jon[a]th[an] & Zerviah, b. Dec. 28, 1807	4	38
Persis, d. Abraham & Molly, b. Apr. 2, 1770 ; d. Dec. 6, 1775	3	119
Polly, d. Thomas & Anna, b. Jan. 11, 1767	3	32
Polly, m. [Ste]phen **FITTS**, [ ]	4	283
Ralph Harrison, s. Anson & Susan, b. June 19, 1835	6	76
Rebecca F., of Ashford, m. Samuel **PAUL**, Jr., of Union, Sept. 16, 1838, by Rev. Geo[rge] Mixter	5	68
Reubecca Fenton, d. Marvin & Calissta, b. Aug. 3, 1821	6	43
Reuben, s. Ezra & Abigail, b. Oct, 1, 1791 ; d. Apr. 15, 1792	4	270
Robart, s. Robart & Hannah, b. May 27, 1735 ; d. Nov. 1, 1739	1	19
Robart, s. Daniel & Serviah, b. Feb. 6, 1747/8	2	60
Robert, d. Dec. 29, 1774	1	19
Rosina C. P. F., ae 20, m. Hiram **TUFTS**, farmer, ae 26, b. Ashford, res. Eastford, Apr. 5, 1848, by Charles Peabody	5	128-9

	Vol.	Page
KNOWLTON, KNOLTON, (cont.)		
Rosina C. P. F., [d. Marvin & Calista], b. Feb. 12, 1828	6	43
Roxse, d. Ezra & Abigail, b. Apr. 4, 1788	4	270
Rufus, s. Ezra & Abigail, b. July 1, 1793	4	270
Salena Newell, d. Marvin & Calista, b. June 30, 1823	6	43
Saley, d. Tho[ma]s & Anna, b. Nov. 23, 1763	3	32
Salley, m. Samuel UTLEY, Dec. 6, 1781	4	228
Salla, d. Ezra & Abigail, b. Dec. 8, 1790	4	270
Sally, d. Amos & Nancy, b. Apr. 23, 1805	4	28
Sally, m. Chauncey **WARREN,** b. of Ashford, Apr. 9, 1823, by Rev. Jonathan Goodwin, at Mr. Amos Knowlton's	5	8
Samson, s. Tho[ma]s & Anna, b. Feb. 8, 1770	3	32
Samson, s. Thomas [& Anna], d. Sept. 10, 1777	3	32
Samuel, s. Stephen & Hannah, b. Nov. 2, 1813	4	259
Samuel, m. Elizabeth F. **WOODWARD,** b. of Ashford, Oct. 14, 1839, by Rev. Alvin Bennett	5	72
Sarah, d. Robert & Hannah, b. Aug. 17, 1731 ; d. Oct. 28, 1739	1	19
Sarah, d. Abraham & Molly, b. Jan. 20, 1765	3	119
Sarah, d. Abraham, d. Oct. 6, 1775	3	119
Silence N., of Ashford, m. Samuel **PAUL,** Jr., of Union, Apr. 17, 1742, by Rev. Cha[rle]s Hyde	5	81
Stephen, s. Abraham & Molley, b. Sept. 7, 1768	3	119
Stephen, s. William & Mehitable, b. Sept. 10, 1768	3	6
Stephen, s. Stephen & Hannah, b. Apr. 17, 1797	4	259
Stephen, farmer, d. Sept. 15, 1849, ae 81	5	144-5
Steven, s. Dan[i]el & Seuviah, b. July 8, 1746	2	60
Thomas, s. Robert & Hannah, b. Apr. 26, 1733	1	19
Thomas, m. Bridget **BOSWORTH,** Dec. 8, 1756	1	95
Tho[ma]s, m. Anna **KEYES,** Apr. 5, 1759	3	32
Tho[ma]s, s. Tho[ma]s & Anna, b. July 13, 1765	3	32
Tho[ma]s, Col., d. Sept. 16, 1776	3	32
Thomas, m. Hepsibah [ ], Sept. 24, 1778	3	44
Thomas, s. Tho[ma]s & Hepsibah, b. June 18, 1781	3	44
William, b. Aug. 9, 1733, at Boxford, Mass. ; d. Jan. 9, 1784	3	6
William, d. Mar. 24, 1753	1	80
William, m. Mehetiable **EATON,** Dec. 15, 1757	1	102
William, s. William & Mehitable, b. Jan. 1, 1767	3	6
Zerviah, housekeeper, b. Willington, res. Ashford, d. May 16, 1848, ae 70	5	128-9
KNOX, Archable, [s. Archable & Margaret], b. Feb. 1, 1763	4	25
Archable, d. Feb. 8, 1763	4	25
Betsey, m. Gurdon **ROBINSON,** Sept. 14, 1817	6	15
Daniel, s. Samvel & Sarah, b. Apr. 6, 1749	2	26
Daniel, d. Oct. 17, 1776	3	33
Geddeth, d. Sam[ue]ll & Sarah, b. Dec. 15, 1755	2	26
Genne, m. John **WARD,** Dec. 7, 1773	4	91
James, [s. Archable & Margaret], b. June 20, 1755	4	25
John, [s. Archable & Margaret], b. Mar. 20, 1757	4	25

KNOX, (cont.)   Vol.   Page
  John, of Ashford, m. Sibel **BURNAP**, of Windham,
    Nov. 30, 1773   4   91
  Luse, d. Samvel & Sarah, b. Apr. 8, 1752   2   26
  Lucy, m. David **ROBBINS**, Jr., Nov. 6, 1771   4   86
  Marcy, [d. Archable & Margaret], b. Dec. 31, 1758   4   25
  Marg[a]ret, w. Archibald, d. June 7, 1767   3   33
  Mather, [s. Archable & Margaret], b. Sept. 20, 1753   4   25
  Molly, m. Abraham **KNOWLTON**, May 26, 1760   3   119
  Samuel, d. Jan. 30, 1789, in the 73rd y. of his age   2   26
  Sarah, w. Sam[ue]ll, d. Feb. 23, 1792, ae 75   2   26
  William, [s. Archable & Margaret], b. Nov. 2, 1761   4   25
KYES, [see under **KEYES**]
LAMB, Mary, Mrs., m. Joseph **HALL**, b. of Eastford, Nov. 17,
    1844, by Francis Williams   5   92
  Ruth, m. David **WHITING**, Apr. 27, 1809   6   21
  Samuel, m. Nancy **CONVERSE**, Dec. 12, 1812   6   3
  Stephen A., Jr., of Willington, m, Mary **HOLMAN**, of
    Ashford, Oct. 5, [1826], by Ezekiel Skinner   5   24
  Stephen Avery, s. Nathan & Abiah, b. Jan. 17, 1776   4   96
  Thomas Knowlton, s. Samuel & Nancy, b. Dec. 1, 1813   6   3
  -----, [d.] Nathan & Abiah, b. Apr. 24, 1781   4   96
  -----, [d.] Nathan & Abiah, b. June 30, 1783   4   96
  -----, [d.] Nathan & Abiah, b. Nov. 15, 1785   4   96
  -----, [child] of Nathan & Abiah, b. Feb. 2, 1788   4   96
  -----, [child of] Nathan & Abiah, b. Apr. 3, 1790   4   96
LAMBARD, [see under **LOMBARD**]
LAMPHEAR, Jared, s. Solomon & Charlotte, b. Dec. 7, 1825   6   44
  Jedidiah, s. Solomon & Charlotte, b. June 24, 1823   6   44
  Maria, d. Solomon & Charlotte, b. Jan. 3, 1817   6   44
  Mary, d. Samuel & Sarah, b. July 20, 1783   4   31
  Mary, d. Jared, farmer, ae 25, & Harriet M., ae 23, b. Mar. 22,
    1851   5   146-7
  Ruth, d. Samuel & Sarah, b. Aug. 19, 1785   4   31
  Ruth, of Pomfret, m. Weeden **HOLLOWAY**, of Ashford, Jan.
    30, 1823, by Edward Keyes, J. P.   5   8
  Samuel, s. Samuel & Sarah, b. July 31, 1787   4   31
LANE, John W., of Worcester, m. Catharine F. **THOMAS**, of
    Ashford June 9, 1845, by Francis Williams. Intention
    published   5   94
LARNED, Bethsheba, m. Josiah **HENDEE**, Jan. 9, 1728/9, by
    Dan[i]el Baker   1   21
  Simson, of Dudley, Mass., m. Polly **HEWET**, of Eastford, Apr.
    16, 1846, by Edward F. Brooks   5   97
LASELL, LAISELL, LARSELL, Isaac, s. Thomas, d. Oct. 30,
    1754   1   90
  James, s. John & Elisabeth, b. Sept. 18, 1772   4   76
  John, m. Elisabeth **DANA**, Apr. 18, 1770   4   76
  Thomas, s. Thomas, d. Nov. 8, 1754   1   90

	Vol.	Page
LASELL, LAISELL, LARSELL, (cont.)		
Thomas, d. Apr. 21, 1765	4	21
Thomas, s. John & Elisabeth, b. Nov. 11, 1770	4	76
lATHAM, Elizabeth, m. Denison **CONVERSE,** Mar. 24, last,		
[1830], by Reuben Torrey, Eastford	5	39
Eugene E., s. Joseph B. & Percy K., b. May 11, 1839	6	65
James E., s. Joseph B. & Percy K., b. Nov. 3, 1842	6	65
Joseph B., m Percy K. **BULLARD,** b. of Ashford, [Jan.] 23,		
[1827], by Rev. Reuben Torrey, Eastford	5	26
Joseph Birding, s. Joseph B. & Percy R., b. Nov. 4, 1828	6	65
Lorenzo Bullard, s. Joseph B. & Percy, b. July 28, 1830	6	65
Monroe F., s. Joseph B. & Percy K., b. Jan. 3, 1844	6	65
Percy K., d. Joseph B. & Percy K., b. Sept. 25, 1834	6	65
William Henry, s. Joseph B. & Percy K., b. Dec. 25, 1836	6	65
LATHROP, LOTHROP, Amasa D., shoemaker, b. Mass., res.		
Ashford, d. May [ ], 1850, ae 23	5	150-1
Caroline, d. Erastus & Sally, b. Nov. 27, 1824	6	66
David, m. Olive **GRIGGS,** Nov. 14, 1811	6	16
Eliza Ann, d. Erastus & Sally, b. Apr. 1, 1820	6	66
Elizebeth, d. Benjamin & Sibble, b. Feb. 11, 1754	1	82
Erastus, m. Sally **BALEY,** Sept. 21, 1807	6	66
Gardner, s. Erastus & Sally, b. Mar. 31, 1808; d. Aug. 18, 1810	6	66
Harriet M., d. Erastus & Sally, b. Mar. 12, 1818	6	66
John W., s. Erastus & Sally, b. Jan. 9, 1816	6	66
Julia B., d. Erastus & Sally, b. Dec. 2, 1812	6	66
Julia B., of Ashford, m. William H. **DIVINE,** of Hartford, Oct.		
29, 1832, by Rev. Philo Judson	5	49
Laura, d. David & Olive, b. Jan. 23, 1815	6	16
Lyman Griggs, s. David & Olive, b. Sept. 1, 1813	6	16
Mary, d. Erastus & Sally, b. Sept. 23, 1822	6	66
Sally, d. Erastus & Sally, b. Dec. 2, 1814	6	66
William, s. Erastus & Sally, b. Feb. 1, 1810	6	66
LAWRANCE, LARANE, Lida, d. Sam[ue]ll & Lida, b. Aug. 9,		
1742	1	A
William, s. Sam[ue]ll & Lydia, b. Feb. 12, 1740/41	1	A
LAWSON, Ebenezer, m. Elisabeth **SESSIONS,** Jan. 6, 1785, by		
John Sessions, J. P.	4	236
Elisabeth, d. Eben[eze]r & Elisabeth, b. Sept. 4, 1790	4	236
Ira, of Union, m. Anny **BARTLETT,** of Ashford, [Jan.] 15,		
[1837], by Rev. Reuben Torrey, Eastford	5	63
Julia Ann, m. Origin **PRESCOTT,** b. of Ashford, Nov. 6,		
1843, by Francis Williams	5	86
Nicholas, s. Eben[eze]r & Elisabeth, b. June 15, 1785	4	236
Rockey, d. Eben[eze]r & Elisabeth, b. Sept. 4, 1792	4	236
Sessions, s. Eben[eze]r & Elisabeth, b. Aug. 4, 1787	4	236
Thomas, s. Eben[eze]r & Elisabeth, b. Jan. 23, 1789	4	236
LAWTON, Betsey, of Chaplin, m. Rowland J. **BOLLES,** of		
Pomfret, Jan. 2, 1853, by Rev. P. Mathewson	5	109
LEACH, LEAH, Asa, of Thompson, m. Sarah **MCINTIRE,** of		

	Vol.	Page
LEACH, LEAH, (cont.)		
Ashford, Apr. 7, 1843, by Rev. Ezekiel Skinner	5	85
Ehezekiah, s. Richard & Amate, b. June 10, 1742	1	74
Marg[a]ret, [w. Richard], d. Jan. [ ], 1738	1	74
Marg[a]ret, d. Richard & Amate, b. Feb. 17, 1739/40	1	74
Prissilla, m. Tho[ma]s CHAPMAN, 3rd, Dec. 18, 1777	4	252
Richard, m. Marg[a]ret KNOWLTON, Mar. 17, 1736	1	74
Richard, m. Amate BUGBE, May 2, 1739	1	74
Sarah, d. Richard & Marg[a]ret, b. Nov. 16, 1736	1	74
LEAR (?), Sarah, m. Samuel **PARRY**, Sept. 25, 1783 (**LOAS**?)	4	42
LEBRET, Elezebeth, m. John **BUGBE[E]**, Nov. 9, 1732	1	26
LEE, Abigail, m. Thomas **BRAGG,** b. of Ashford, Dec. 6, 1768, by Elijah Whiton, J. P.	4	47
Abigail, m. Charles **LORD,** Dec. 19, 1799	4	33
Daniel, s. Henery & Rebeckah, b. June 27, 1770 ; d. Oct. 15, 1775	4	27
Elisha, s. Henery & Rebeckah, b. Oct. 20, 1765	4	27
Hannah, d. John & Abigail, b. June 15, 1749	1	85
John, d. Apr. 5, 1774	3	15
John, s. Henery & Rebeckah, b. Feb. 26, 1773 ; d. Sept. 26, 1775	4	27
Lowes, d. Henery & Rebeckah, b. Feb. 7, 1775	4	27
Mary, d. [John] & Abigail, b. May 14, 1751	1	85
Mary, m. Robert **HALL,** Nov. 17, 1774	4	87
Mary, m. William **PERKINS,** Feb. 12, 1795	4	282
Mary, d. Sept. 30, 1797	3	15
Rebeckah, d. Henery & Rebeckah, b. May 10, 1768 ; d. Sept. 28, 1775	4	27
Rebeckah, d. Henery & Rebeckah, b. Mar. 17, 1777	4	27
LEONARD, LEANARD, LENARD [see also **LARNED**], Abigail, m. James **FULLER,** Dec. 12, 1717 (Perhaps Abigail **YENARD**?)	A	4
Calista, m. Marvin **KNOWLTON** Apr. 19, 1820	6	43
Daniel, of Union, m. Isabel M. **PLACE,** [Oct.] 26,[1825], by Rev. Reuben Torrey, Eastford	5	20
Dexter M., of Mansfield, m. Jerusha **WOODWARD** of Ashford, Oct. 20, 1826, by William Ely, V. D. M., Mansfield	5	24
Lydia, m. Independent **IDE,** b. Ashford, Jan. 8, 1833, by Rev. Philo Judson	5	50
Olive, housekeeper, b. Bolton, res. Ashford, d. June 14, 1849, ae 72	5	138-9
Phebe, m. William **BROWN,** b. of Ashford, Nov. 10, [1824], by Ezekiel Skinner	5	16
Recompense, s. Benj[ami]n & Mary, b. Aug. 31, 1771	4	52
LEOPARD, Betsey, m. Luther **CHAPMAN,** Aug, 8, 1805	4	27
LEWIS, LEWES, [see also **LOAS**], Abby, of Brooklyn, Conn., m. David **FLOYD,** of Long Island, [June] 6, [1825], by		

LEWIS, LEWES, (cont.)	Vol.	Page
Reuben Torrey, Eastford	5	19
Ama, d. Israel & Ama, b. June 1, 1791	4	229
Anne, [d. Edward & Bridget], b. May 6, 1751	1	48
Anne, d. Daniel & Sarah, b. Sept. 6, 1782	4	235
Anson, s. Stephen & Sally, b. Nov. 11, 1811	6	44
Asa, of Hampton, m. Louisa LYON, of Ashford, Oct. 1, 1837, by Rev. Erastus Benton, Eastford	5	65
Bridget, d. Edward & Bridget, b. Dec. 25, 1736	1	48
Bridget, d. Edward, d. June 23, 1753	1	48
Bridget, [d. Edward & Bridget], b. Jan. 24, 1755	1	48
Bridget, m. Benjamin HENFIELD, Feb. 18, 1778	4	119
Cynth[i]a, d. Daniel & Sarah, b. Mar. 10, 1777	4	235
Daniel, s. Edward & Bridget, b. Apr. 5, 1745	1	48
Daniel, m. Sarah LYON, Sept. 2, 1776	4	235
Daniel, s. Daniel & Sarah, b. Feb. 10, 1788	4	235
David Keyes, s. Joshua & Destotia, b. Sept, 3, 1821	6	30
Dorathoy, d. John & Martha, b. Dec. 30, 1739	1	3
Dyer, s. Edward & Bridget, b. Apr. 17, 1741	1	48
Edward, m. Bridget TRISKET, Jan. 7, 1735/6, by Rev. Mr. Eleazer Williams	1	48
Edward, s. Edward & Bridget, b. May 16, 1747 ; d. Feb. 3, 1748/9	1	48
Edward, s. Daniel & Sarah, b. Aug. 27, 1780	4	235
Edwin P., m. Susan A. CHAPMAN, Nov. 5, 1848, by Rev. Charles Peabody	5	103
Emily M., of Ashford, m. David K. OWEN, of Hartford, Oct. 17, 1842, by Francis Williams	5	82
Enuch, [twin with Stephen], s. Israel & Ama, b. Dec. 30, 1785	4	229
Gardiner, s. Gardner & Roxey, b. Oct. 18, 1813	6	21
Gardner, s. Israel & Ama, b. Oct. 22, 1780	4	229
George, s. Stephen & Sally, b. Jan. 17, 1819	6	44
Hannah, d. Edward & Bridget, b. May 13, 1748	1	48
Harriet S., of Pomfret, m. George W. HAMILTON, of Ashford, Mar. 2, 1845, by Rev. Geo[rge] Mixter	5	93
Henry, s. Stephen & Sally, b. June 4, 1816	6	44
Israel, s. Israel & Ama, b. Feb. 19, 1783	4	229
Joseph, s. John & Martha, b. Mar. 8, 1732/3	1	3
Joshua, s. Israel & Ama, b. Dec. 9, 1788	4	229
Joshua, m. Destotia KEYES, Apr. [ ], 1819	6	30
Levina, d. Daniel & Sarah, b. Nov. 23, 1778	4	235
Levina, d. Daniel, d. Oct. 8, 1794	4	235
Martha, w. John, d. Apr. 12, 1740	1	40
Mary, d. John & Martha, b. Apr. 17, 1737	1	3
Mary, d. Gardner & Roxey, b. Nov. 21, 1810	6	21
Perice, d. Daniel & Sarah, b. Dec. 24, 1785	4	235
Philamilea, d. Daniel & Sarah, b. Aug. 29, 1790	4	235
Phila M., housekeeper, b. Middletown, res. Ashford, d. Dec. 31, 1850, ae 60	5	150-1

	Vol.	Page
LEWIS, LEWES, (cont.)		
Richard, s. Edward & Bridget, b. Apr. 29, 1739	1	48
Sarah, d. John & Martha, b. May 11, 1735	1	3
Sarah, w. Daniel, d. Apr. 8, 1813	4	235
Stephen, [twin with Enuch], s. Israel & Ama, b. Dec. 30, 1785	4	229
Sibbil, [d. Edward & Bridget], b. July 29, 1753	1	48
Thomas, s. Edward & Bridget, b. Apr. 18, 1743	1	48
Thomas, m. Mrs. Mary **RUS[S]EL**, b. of Ashford, Nov. 18, 1762, in Woodstock, by Stephen Williams	3	75
Thomas, s. Daniel & Sarah, b. Aug. 9, 1795	4	235
LILLEY, Alma, of Union, m. Abner **SMITH**, of Ashford, Mar. 2, 1842, by Rev. Francis Williams, Eastford	5	80
Hannah, w. Nathan, d. July 25, 18[ ]	4	11
Nathan, m. Hannah **HUNTINGTON**, Nov. 25, 1800	4	11
LINCOLN, LINKHORN, Charlotte Sophia, [d. George & Laura], b. Jan. 23, 1834	6	94
Delia Meredeth, [d. George & Laura], b. Nov. 27, 1831	6	94
Dwight, s. George & Laura, b. May 1, 1827	6	94
Emily, m. Ralph **DURKEE**, Nov. 22, 1847, by Cha[rle]s Peabody	5	102
Emily A., ae 18, of Ashford, m. Ralph **DURKEE**, hatter, ae 21, b. Mansfield, res. Ashford, Nov. 22, 1847, by Charles Peabody	5	128-9
Eveline O., m. Whitman C. **DURKEE**, b. of Ashford, Nov. 23, 1846, by Charles Peabody	5	98
Eveline Orville, d. Samuel & Hannah H., b. Mar. 31, 1826	6	60
George, s. George & Laura, b. June 24, 1825	6	94
Hannah, m. Joseph **RUSSEL[L]**, May 13, 1742, by Rev. Mr. James Hale	1	58
Hannah, housekeeper, b. Norwich, res. Ashford, d. Jan. 1, 1850, ae 49	5	144-5
Julia, m. Cha[u]ncey **NEFF**, of Chaplin, Apr. 1, 1824, by Edward Keyes, J. P.	5	13
Laura Elizabeth, d. George & Laura, b. Sept. 14, 1829	6	94
Lorin, of North Windham, m. Elizabeth S. **PARKER**, of Ashford, Feb. 17, 1845, by Rev. Geo[rge] Mixter	5	93
Sarah A., of Ashford, m. Alonzo **MARTIN**, of Hampton, Mar, 22, 1825, by Rev. Philo Judson	5	18
William, m. Caroline **PALMER**, b. of Ashford, "last evening", [Apr. 1, 1835], by Rev. Job Hall	5	56
William Henry, s. William & Caroline, b. Nov. 20, 1835	6	85
LINDSEY, Silas T., Dr., of Union, m. Salome M. **CHAPMAN**, of Ashford, Nov. 4, 1851, by Rev. Samuel J. Curtis, of Union	5	107
LOAS (?), [see also **LEWIS**], Sarah, m. Samuel **PARRY**, Sept. 25, 1783	4	42
LOMBARD, LUMBARD, LAMBARD, Cynthia, d. July [ ], 1850, ae 5 m.	5	144-5

	Vol.	Page
LOMBARD, LUMBARD, LAMBARD (cont.)		
Danforth Otis, [s. Otis & Rosetta], b. June 3, 1838	6	82
Emerson, of Brimfield, (Mass.), m. Phebe Ann **TUFTS**, of		
Ashford, June 22, 1835, by Rev. R. Torrey, Eastford	5	57
James Henry, [s. Otis & Rosetta], b. Jan. 11, 1843	6	82
Julia M., milliner, b. Middletown, res. Ashford, d. Aug. 25,		
1850, ae 18	5	150-1
Juliaetta Maria, [d. Otis & Rosetta], b. Jan. 2, 1832	6	82
Louisa E., b. Middletown, res. Ashford, d. Aug. 3, 1850, ae 3	5	150-1
Mary Sophia, [d. Otis & Rosetta], b. Apr. 14, 1834	6	82
Otis, m. Rosetta **HAYWARD**, b. of Ashford, Sept. 16, 1829,		
by Rev. Philo Judson	5	36
Rosetta Howard, [d. Otis & Rosetta], b. Sept, 6, 1840	6	82
Sarah, d. July [ ], 1850, ae 5	5	144-5
Susan Sorepta, [d. Otis & Rosetta], b. June 25, 1836	6	82
-----, d. Otis, farmer, & Lydia, b. Mar. [ ], 1850	5	140-1
LOOMIS, LOMIS, LUMMIS, LUMMISS, LUMMUS, Aaron, s.		
Rev. Aaron & Persis, b. Jan. 29, 1828	6	63
Abigail, d. Aug. 15, 1848, ae 57	5	138-9
Benjamin, s. Nath[anie]ll & Sarah, b. Jan. 15, 1773	4	28
Chester, s. John & Clirana, b. July 2, 1797	4	122
Chester, s. W[illia]m & Christian, b. Feb. 8, 1822	6	32
Clarissa, of Ashford, m. Abiel **DURHAM**, of Hampton, Nov.		
22, 1820, by W[illia]m Storrs	5	1
Clarissa, of Ashford, m. Abiel **DURKEE**, of Hampton, Nov.		
22, 1820, by W[illia]m Storrs	6	26
Clyrana, d. John & Cylrana, b. Feb. 19, 1786; d. Mar. 29, 1786	4	122
Clirana, d, John & Clirana, b. Mar. 20, 1790	4	122
Emily, d. John & Freelove, b. Feb. 2, 1807	4	264
Emmeline, d. Isaac & Abigail, b. Sept, 22, 1828	6	67
Henery, s. Nath[anie]ll & Sarah, b. Oct. 26, 1775	4	28
Isaac, s. John & Clirana, b. Dec. 27, 1794	4	122
Isaac, m. Abigail **SAUNDERS**, b. of Ashford, Apr. 24, 1827,		
by Rev. Levi Wood, Westford	5	27
Jedediah, s. Nath[anie]ll & Sarah, b. Feb. 26, 1778	4	28
John, m. Clirana **BURNHAM**, Jan. 18, 1781	4	122
John, s. John & Clirana, b. Jan. 30, 1782	4	122
John, Jr., m. Freelove **SAUNDERS**, Apr. 23, 1806	4	264
John Henry, s. Isaac & Abigail, b. Nov. 4, 1831	6	67
Joseph, s. Nath[anie]ll & Sarah, b. Oct. 29, 1770	4	28
Marg[a]ret, d. Nath[anie]ll, Jr. & Sarah, b. Apr. 1, 1769	4	28
Mary Ann, d. William & Christian, b. Jan. 29, 1820	6	32
Nath[anie]ll, Dea., d. Dec. 8, 1769	4	28
William, s. John & Clyrania, b. Nov. 25, 1787	4	122
William, m. Christian **FITTS**, Sept. 23, 1817	6	32
LORD, Caroline Emma, d. Charles & Abigail, b. Dec. 16, 1803	4	33
Charles, m. Abigail **LEE**, Dec. 19, 1799	4	33
Charles, s. Charles & Abigail, b. Jan. 23, 1801	4	33

LORD, (cont.)	Vol.	Page
Elisha, of Abington, Pomfret, m. Arthusa JAMES,		
of Ashford, Sept. 14, 1846, by Francis Williams.		
Intention published Sept. 13, 1846, in Abington Meeting-		
House	5	98
William, s. Charles & Abigail, b. Sept. 23, 1802	4	33

LUMBARD, [see under **LOMBARD**]

LUMMIS, [see under **LOOMIS**]

LYON, A[a]ron, s. Gould & Elezebeth, b. July 10, 1746	1	60
Abigail, m. Jonathan CHAFFEE, June 1, 1727, by Rev. James		
Hale	A	11
Abigail, d. Seth, d. Aug. 19, 1760	1	11
Abigail had s. John Cheney SUMNER, b. Apr. 14, 17[ ]	3	105
Allis, m. John RUSSEL[L], July 10, 1750	2	48
Almira S., of Ashford, m. Joseph T. HOXSIE, of Richmond,		
R. I., [Oct.} 4, [1835], by Rev. Reuben Torrey.		
Intention published Oct. 2, 1835	5	57
Amasa, s. Ephraim & Esther, b. Nov. 19, 1771	3	67
Amasa, s. Nathan & Patience, b. Jan. 3, 1789	4	258
Amasa, m. Kezekiah* KNOWLTON, Jan. 3, 1805 (*Keziah?)	4	116
Amasa, 2d, m. C[h]loe BUGBEE, b. of Ashford, Mar. 18,		
1842, by Rev. Ezekiel Skinner	5	80
Amasa Knowlton, s. Amasa & Keziah, b. July 4, 1806	4	116
Angenette, d. William & Minerva, [b.] Oct. 4, 1845	6	25
Anna, d. Henry & Anna, b. Sept. 22, 1779	4	247
Betsey, w. William, d. Jan. 23, 1827	6	25
Bet[t]ee, d. Ephraim & Esther, b. June 25, 1776	3	67
Bradford, m. Cordelia F. ANDREW, b. of Ashford, Jan. 31,		
1830, by Rev. Philo Judson	5	38
Charlotte Ann, of Ashford, m. William L. LYON, of Hampton,		
Sept. 15, 1835, by Daniel G. Sprague	5	57
Clara, d. Edmund & Lucinda, b. Dec. 28, 1831	6	24
Deloria, d. Amasa & Keziah, b. Oct. 15, 1811	4	116
Deloria, see also Dototia		
Dolly, m. Champlain WILBOUR, b. of Ashford, May, 18,		
1828, by Daniel G. Sprague, Intention published	5	31
Dototia, m. John W. TROWBRIDGE, b. of Ashford, [Apr.]		
10, [1827], by Rev. Reuben Torrey, Eastford	5	27
Dototia, see also Deloria		
Edmund, s. Nathan & Patience, b. Sept. 21, 1797	4	258
Edmund, m. Lucinda EASTMAN, Dec. 1, 1819	6	24
Edmund Harvey, s. Edmund & Lucinda, b. Dec. 6, 1828	6	24
Edward H., of Eastford, m. Mrs. Amanda E. WITHEY, of		
Ashford, Nov. 18, 1854, by Rev. Charles Chamberlain	5	111
Edward Sebray(?), s. Tomson & Eliza, b. Sept. 2, 1843	6	89
Eleanor Ruth, d. Tomson & Eliza, b. May 21, 1840	6	89
Elijah, s. Nathan & Patience, b. Jan. 13, 1792	4	258
Elijah, s. William & Betsey, b. Sept. 28, 1823	6	25
Eliphelet, s. Gould & Elezebeth, b. Jan. 18, 1739/40	1	60

LYON, (cont.)	Vol.	Page
Eliza Ann, m. Ebenezer **KNOWLTEN**, b. of		
Ashford, Apr. 8, 1838, by Rev. Amos Babcock	5	68
Elezebeth, [d. Gould & Elezebeth], b. Mar. 3, 1733	1	60
Elisabeth, m. Solomon **WELCH**, Apr. 17, 1755	3	13
Elizabeth, d. Henry & Anna, b. Sept. 25, 1767	4	247
Elizabeth, m. Benjamin **FITTS**, Mar. 6, 1836, by Reuben		
Torrey, Eastford	5	58
Ellen M., d. Tomson & Eliza, b. June 18, 1832	6	89
Emeline, of Ashford, m. Samuel D. **MERRICK**, of Willington,		
Mar. 14, last [1839], by Rev. Erastus Benton	5	70
Ephraim, m. Est[h]er **BENNETT**, July 5, 1762	3	67
Ephraim, s. Ephraim & Esther, b. Mar. 15, 1767	3	67
Ephraim, d. May 25, 1798	3	67
Ephraim, m. Lois **BOSWORTH**, of Ashford, June 18, 1832, by		
Amasa Lyon, J. P.	5	48
Esther, m. Nathanael **ABBITT**, Jr., Apr. 16, 1734, by Philip		
Eastman, J. P.	1	29
Esther, [d. Gould & Elezebeth], b. Dec. 19, 1736	1	60
Est[h]er, m. Nathan **WATKINS**, Aug. 20, 1761	3	13
Esther, d. Ephraim & Esther, b. Mar. 1, 1765	3	67
Esther, m. Nathan **BURNAM**, Dec. 13, 1781	4	241
Esther, m. Ezra P. **ARNOLD**, b. of Eastford, Oct. 19, 1846, by		
Francis Williams	5	97
Esther E., d. Tomson & Eliza, b. Sept, 6, 1830	6	89
Evalina, d. James & Polley, b. July 31, 1815	4	115
George, s. William & Betsey, b. Jan. 10, 1822	6	25
Gould, m. Elizabeth **CHAPMAN**, Apr. 12, 1726	A	10
Hennery, [s. Gould & Elezebeth], Apr. 2, 1738	1	60
Henry, s. Henry & Anna, b. Feb. 18, 1769	4	247
James, s. Ephraim & Esther, b. May 11, 1784	3	67
James, m. Polly **TROWBRIDGE**, Jan. 29, 1808	4	115
Jeremiah Everett, s. Henry & Anna, b. Nov. 4, 1776	4	247
Gerusha Sabrina, d. Edmund & Lucinda, b. Jan. 26, 1834	6	24
John, s. Henry & Anna, b. May 1, 1785	4	247
Joseph, d. Nathan & Patience, b. Apr. 26, 1799	4	258
Joseph, s. William & Betsey, b. Feb. 28, 1825	6	25
Julia M., of Eastford, m. Zebulon R. **WILLSON**, of Uxbridge,		
Mass., Sept 7, 1845, by Francis Williams, Eastford	5	95
Lafayette, s. William & Minerva, b. Mar. 4, 1844	6	25
Lois, d. Ephraim & Esther, b. Mar. 18, 1780	3	67
Lois, m. Gurdon **ROBINSON**, Nov. 30, 1808	6	15
Louis, d. James & Polley, b. Dec. 3, 1810	4	115
Lorenzo, m. Maria M. **LYON**, Mar. 6, 1836, by Reuben		
Torrey, Eastford	5	58
Louisa, of Ashford, m. Asa **LEWIS**, of Hampton, Oct. 1, 1837,		
by Rev. Erastus Benton, Eastford	5	65
Lucinda, Mrs., of Eastford, m. Justus **GRIGGS**, of Ashford,		
Oct. 3, 1854, by Rev. Charles Chamberlain	5	111

LYON, (cont.)	Vol.	Page
Lucy, d. Ephraim & Esther, b. Dec. 24, 1773	3	67
Marcus, s. Amasa & Keziah, b. July 1, 1809 ; d. Apr. 29, 1810	4	116
Maria M., m. Lorenzo LYON, Mar. 6, 1836, by Reuben Torrey, Eastford	5	58
Marvin, of Abington, m. Sarah Ann SCRANTON, of Ashford, [Apr.] 6, [1828], by Rev. Reuben Torrey, Eastford	5	31
Mary, d. Seth & Abigaill, b. June 16, 1728	1	11
Mary, d. James & Polley, b. Aug. 16, 1808	4	115
Mary, m. Augustus DODGE, b. of Ashford, [Feb.] 3, [1831], by Rev. Reuben Torrey, of Eastford	5	41
Mary Ann, d. Edmund & Lucinda, b. Apr. 18, 1826	6	24
Mehetable, d. Seth & Abigail, b. Jan. 6, 1726/7	A	10
Mehetebel, m. Joseph CHUBB, Apr. 10, 1749, by Mr. Bass	2	27
Melissa S., d. Tomson & Eliza, b. Mar. 16, 1838	6	89
Nancy, d. Henry & Anna, b. Feb. 9, 1765	4	247
Nathan, s. Ephraim & Est[h]er, b. Apr. 29, 1763	3	67
Nathan, m. Patience BADGER, Apr. 10, 1788	4	258
Nathan Bennet, s. Nathan & Patience, b. Mar. 25, 1790	4	258
Nathan T., s. Tomson & Eliza, b. Jan. 19, 1834	6	89
Noah, s. Gould [& Elezebeth], b. Nov. 1, 1743	1	60
Noah, s. Henry & Anna, b. Dec. 25, 1774	4	247
Phebe, m. Samuel PRESTON, Aug. 27, 1806	6	31
Philander, m. Philena UTLEY, Nov. 28, 1839, by Rev. Ezekiel Skinner	5	72
Phillina, d. Nathan & Patience, b. Nov. 27, 1795	4	258
Parsela, d. Seth & Abigail, b. Mar. 22, 1741	1	11
Prissillah, m. Ebenezer CHENEY, Mar. 2, 1760	3	110
Rebec[c]ah, d. Henry & Anna, b. Dec. 25, 1772	4	247
Rebecca, m. James TROWBRIDGE, Jr., Mar. 30, 1809	6	40
Richard, s. Henry & Anna, b. July 1, 1770 ; d. July 1, 1770	4	247
Richard, s. Henry & Anna, b. July 23, 1771	4	247
Sabrina Sophia, d. Edmund & Lucinda, b. [ ] ; d. Sept. 22, 1823	6	24
Samantha Lucinda, d. Edmund & Lucinda, b. Oct. 20, 1823	6	24
Sarah, d. Gould & Elezebeth, b. [ ] 31, 1731 (sic)	1	60
Sarah, m. Samuel WATKINS, Jan. 20, 1765	4	56
Sarah, m. Daniel LEWIS, Sept. 2, 1776	4	235
Sarah A., of Eastford, m. Newman S. MARCY, of Willington, Oct. 1, 1844, by Francis Williams	5	91
Seth m. Abigail RUSSELL, Mar. 29, 1725/6	A	10
Seth, s. Seth & Abigail, b. July 24, 1734	1	11
Sophronia, d. Amasa & Keziah, b. Jan. 4, 1813	4	116
Susan, factory operative, d. July 17, 1849, ae 27	5	136-7
Thompson, s. Nathan & Patience, b. Dec. 5, 1793	4	258
Thompson, m. Eliza WEEKES, b. of Ashford, Nov. 23, 1828, by Rev. Philo Judson	5	32
Willard, s. James & Polley, b. Sept, 19, 1813	4	115
William, s. Nathan & Patience, b. July 2, 1801	4	258

	Vol.	Page
LYON, (cont.)		
William, m. Betsey **WEEKES,** May 31, 1820	6	25
William, m. Minerva **HUDSON,** b. of Ashford, Apr. 16, 1843,		
by Rev. Nathan T. Hunt of Abington, Pomfret, Eastford	5	85
William L., of Hampton, m. Charlotte Ann **LYON,** of Ashford,		
Sept. 15, 1835, by Daniel G. Sprague	5	57
Winthrop D., m. Maria C. **SEARS,** b. of Ashford, Nov. 29,		
1838, by Rev. Alvan Underwood	5	70
Zerviah, d. Ephraim & Esther, b. Mar. 3, 1769	3	67
----, st. b. s. Warren W., merchant, ae 34, & Marriette, ae 28, b.		
Apr. 30, 1851	5	148-9
MAGOON, Elisebeth, m. Jacob **FULLER,** Apr. 1, 1719, by Rev.		
James Hale	1	11
MAIN, Betsey, d. Tho[ma]s & Lucy, b. Sept. 3, 1780	4	60
Charles, s. Tho[ma]s & Lucy, b. July 14, 1794	4	60
Chester, s. Tho[ma]s & Lucy, b. Nov. 15, 1776	4	60
Eunice, d. Thomas & Lucy, b. Nov. 13, 1788	4	60
Joseph, s. Tho[ma]s & Lucy, b. Aug. 13, 1783	4	60
Lucinda, d. Tho[ma]s & Lucy, b. Nov, 27, 1791	4	60
Lucy, d. Tho[ma]s & Lucy, b. June 18, 1778	4	60
Lydia Pimbleton, d. Tho[ma]s & Lucy, b. Aug. 5, 1799	4	60
Thomas Tyler, s. Tho[ma]s & Lucy, b. Aug. 8, 1774	4	60
William, s. Tho[ma]s & Lucy, b. Mar. 13, 1786	4	60
MAINER, Salla, m. [Lovell **SNOW**], Apr. 7, 17[ ]	4	285
MANARD, Susanna, m. James **HARDEY,** Jan. 9, 1784	4	233
MANCHESTER, Thomas, of Warwick, R. I., m. Catharine		
GOODELL, of Ashford, Apr. 3, 1831, by Amos Lyon,		
J. P.	5	42
MARCH, Betsey, m. Roswel[l] **BROWN,** Nov. 24, 1788	4	256
MARCY, MERCY, Bethyer, d. R[e]uben & Rachel, b. July 29,		
1773	3	35
Betsey, d. Mat[t]hew & Hannah, b. June 24, 1781 ; d. Sept. 24,		
1781	4	120
Betsey, d. Matthew & Hannah, b. Oct. 16, 1783	4	120
Betsa, m. Ebenezer **BYLES,** Mar. 21, 180[ ]	4	281
Claras[s]a, m. Chester **MASON,** Jan. 13, 1814	6	2
David, of Union, m. Rhoda **JAMES,** of Ashford, Sept. 14,		
1826, by Rev. Amos Babcock, Jr. Intention published	5	23
Dorkas, d. Sam[ue]ll & Mary, b. May 24, 1727	A	5
Dorcas, d. Zebadiah & Pressilla, b. Mar. 15, 1768	3	45
Edward, m. Rebackah **HASKINS,** Jan. 22, 1729, by Rev. Mr.		
Wills	1	35
Edward, s. Edward & Rebackah, b. Mar. 3, 1730/31	1	35
Edward, s. R[e]uben & Rachel, b. Apr. 22, 1768	3	35
Edward, Capt., d. Jan. 8, 1774	1	44
Elisabeth, m. Thomas **TIFFANY,** Jr., Apr. 19, 1753, by Mr.		
Stephen Williams	1	88
Emeline C., of Holland, Mass., m. William H. **BUGBEE,** of		
Stafford, Dec. 17, 1849, by Rev. Ezekiel Skinner	5	104

MARCY, MERCY, (cont.),

Emeline C., of Holland, Mass., m. William H. **BUGBEE**, of		
Stafford, Dec. 17, 1849, by Ezekiel Skinner	5	142-3
Hannah, d. Zebadiah & Pressilla, b. July 2, 1766	3	45
Hannah, d. Matthew & Hannah, b. Jan. 17, 1787	4	120
Hannah, ae 40, b. Ashford, m. Warren **INGALLS**, farmer, ae		
67, b. Pomfret, res. Ashford, Aug. [ ], 1849, by Reuben		
Marcy	5	142-3
Hannah H., m, Hiram B. **BURNHAM**, b. of Ashford, [May] 5,		
[1839], by Rev. Erastus Benton	5	70
Hannah K., of Ashford, m. Warren **INGALLS**, of Pomfret,		
Aug, 26, 1849, by Reuben Marcy, J. P.	5	104
Jerusha, d. Edward & Rebeckah, b. Sept. 21, 1739 ; d. July [ ],		
1742	1	35
Jerusha, [d. R[e]uben & Rachal], b. Aug. 17, 1759	3	35
Jerusha, d. R[e]uben & Rachel, b. Aug. 19, 1759* (*Entry		
crossed out)	3	35
Jerusha, d. Ma[t]thew & Hannah, b. Aug. 1, 1782	4	120
John, s. Sam[ue]ll & Mary, b. July 23, 1724	A	10
John S., of Woodstock, m. Delotia **BUGBEE**, of Ashford, Sept.		
1, [1845], by Rev. Renesalaer O. Putney, North Ashford	5	95
John Sulyvan, s. Oren & Polley, b. Mar. 25, 1800	4	278
Joseph W., m. Lois **BUGBEE**, b. of Ashford, Apr. 22, 1832,		
by Rev. Leonard Gage	5	47
Joseph Work, s. Oren & Polley, b. Nov. 20, 1797	4	278
Levina, d. Zebadiah & Prissilla, b. Jan. 27, 1763	3	45
Lydia, d. Reuben & Rachal, b. Aug. 3, 1779	3	35
Lydia, of Ashford, m. Thomas **CUSHMAN**, of Willington,		
Feb. 13, 1828, by Rev. Philo Judson	5	30
Marah, d. Oren & Polley, b. July 17, 1806	4	278
Martha, d. Zebadiah & Prissilla, b. Oct. 29, 1769	3	45
Martha C., of Ashford, m. George W. **DARLIN**, of Dorset, Vt.,		
May 17, 1847, by Charles Peabody	5	100
Mary, m. Thomas **OLNEY**, b. of Ashford, Jan. 10, 1826, by		
Nathan Hayward, J. P.	5	21
Mat[t]hew, s. R[e]uben & Rachal, b. Aug. 27, 1757	3	35
Mat[t]hew, m. Hannah **GILLET**, May 24, 1779	4	120
Matthew, d. Mar. 14, 1802	4	120
Newman S., of Willington, m. Sarah A. **LYON**, of Eastford,		
Oct. 1, 1844, by Francis Williams	5	91
Olive, of Ashford, m. Henry **PARKEE**, of Abington, Jan. 1,		
1826, by Rev. Amos Babcock. Intention published	5	21
Prudy, housekeeper, b. Charlton, Mass., res. Ashford, d. Sept.		
21, 1849, ae 80 (Perhaps Prudy **MOREY**)	5	144-5
Rachal, d. R[e]uben & Rachal, b. Oct. 12, 1761	3	35
Rachel, m. Isaac **KENDAL**, Dec. 16, 1784	4	239
Rebackah, d. Edward & Rebeckah, b. May 24, 1737	1	35
Rebeckah, w. Edward, d. Dec. 14, 1748	1	44

	Vol.	Page

MARCY, MERCY, (cont.)

Rebeckah, d. R[e]uben & Rachal, b. Jan. 3, 1764	3	35
R[e]uben, s. Edward & Rebeckah, b. Nov. 28, 1732	1	35
Reuben, m. Rachel **WATSON**, Nov. 18, 1756	1	95
R[e]ubin s. R[e]uben & Rachel, b. Mar. 23, 1766	3	35
Reuben E., s. Reuben, farmer & Clarissa, b. Dec. 31, 1848	5	132-3
Salla, m. Sam[ue]ll **BICKNELL**, Jr., Nov. 14, 1799	4	252
Sarah, d. Edward, b. June 11, 1744	1	35
Sarah, d. Reuben & Rachel, b. Apr. 23, 1777	3	35
Sarah, of Ashford, m. Lucius C. **UTLEY**, of Hampton, Jan. 7, 1836, by Rev. J. Hall	5	58
Sarah M., m. Cyril W. **SMITH**, b. of Ashford, Jan. 1, 1844, by Rev. L. W. Blood, Eastford	5	87
Simeon, s. Edward & Rebackah, b. Apr. 7, 1735 ; d. July 18, [1742]	1	35
Simeon, s. Edw[ar]d, b. Feb. 5, 1742/3 ; d. Mar. 1, next after	1	35
Simeon, s. R[e]uben & Rachel, b. Aug. 19, 1770	3	35
Thomas, s. Zebadiah & Prissilla, b. Mar. 25, 1770	3	45
Warner, of Union, m. Lucy **JAMES**, of Ashford, Jan. 6, 1831, by Rev. Ezekiel Skinner	5	41
----, s. Edward, b. Sept. 13, 1741, st. b.	1	35
----, s. Edward [& Rebackah], b. Jan. 20, 1747/8 ; d. same day	1	35

MARGAIN, David, of Old Brimfield, Mass., m. Harriet **BROWN**, of Ashford, Nov. 16, 1826, by Rev. Amos Babcock, Jr.

Intention published	5	25

MARTIN, Alonzo, of Hampton, m. Sarah A. **LINCOLN**, of Ashford, Mar. 22, 1825, by Rev. Philo Judson

	5	18
Julina, m. Stephen **WHITAN**, Mar. 27, 1806	6	58
Lucy, m. John **HENDEE**, Dec. 25, 1790 ; d. July [ ]	4	287
W[illia]m C., of Woodstock, m Emily **FISHER**, of Ashford, Mar. 31, 1852, by Rev. Bela Hicks	5	109
William D., m. Mary M. **HARRINGTON**, , b. of Ashford, Feb. 25, 1845, by Rev. Cha[rle]s Hyde	5	93

MASH, Experiance, m. Edward **SUMNER**, Jr., Mar. 21, 1754, by Esq. Whe[e]ler, of Plainfield

	1	83

MASON, MAYSON, Alas, d. John & Dorothy b. Jan. 28, 1743/4

	2	41
Alva, s. Eben[eze]r, Jr. & Mary, b. Aug. 9, 1786	4	75
Asa, s. Ebenezer & Mehetable, b. June 23, 1759	2	71
Billey, s. Eb[e]n[eze]r, Jr. & Mary, b. Feb. 17, 1788	4	75
Chester, s. Eben[eze]r, Jr. & Mary, b. June 10, 1793	4	75
Chester, m. Claras[s]a **MARCY**, Jan. 13, 1814	6	2
Dauid, s. Robert & Hannah, b. Feb. 16, 1742/3	1	34
David, s. Eben[eze]r, Jr. & Mary, b. July 27, 1784	4	75
Desire Patian[c]e, d. Eliphelet & Susan[n]ah, b. Feb. 20, 1745/6	2	40
Dorothy, m. Jonathan **CORTICE**, Nov. 16, 1752	2	41
Ebenezer, m. Mehetebel **HOLM[E]S**, May 11, 1748, by T. Tiffany, J. P.	2	71
Ebenezer, s. Ebenezer & Mehetebel, b. Mar. 27, 1749	2	71

	Vol.	Page
MASON, MAYSON, (cont.)		
Ebenezer, Jr., m. Mary HASTINGS, June 21, 1774	4	75
Ebenezer, s. Eben[eze]r, Jr. & Mary, b. Oct. 2, 1782	4	75
Ebenezer, Jr., m. Martha HARWOOD, Jan. 12, 1804	4	91
Ebenezer King, s. John & Sybil, b. Oct. 28, 1790	4	113
Elijah, s. Eliphelet & Susan[n]ah, b. Feb. 12, 1743/4	2	40
Eliphalet, s. Ebenezer & Mehitable, b. Sept. 17, 1757	2	71
Eliph[a]let, s. Eben[eze]r, Jr. & Mary, b. June 23, 1780	4	75
Elezebeth, d. Robert & Hannah, b. Jan. 19, 1740/41	1	34
Elisabeth, d. Robart, d. Apr. 20, 1749	2	40
Elisabeth, d. Soloman & Sarah, b. Aug. 28, 1754	1	85
Elisabeth, d. Solomon & Sarah, b. May, 9, 1766	3	33
[E]unis, d. John & Dorithy, b. Feb. 10, 1745/6	2	41
Hannah, d. Robert & Hannah, [b.] May 6, 1745	1	34
Hannah, d. Robart, d. May 25, 1747	2	40
Hannah, m. John WRIGHT, June 12, 1756	1	9
Hannah, d. Robert & Hannah, b. Sept, 18, 1722	A	6
Hitty, d. Eben[eze]r, Jr. & Martha, b. Oct. 18, 1804	4	91
Jarvis, s. John & Sybil, b. Aug. 12, 1794	4	113
John, s. John & Dorithy, b. Jan. 30, 1748	2	41
John, m. Sybil KING, Oct. 21, 1778	4	113
John, s. John & Sybil, b. Jan. 18, 1780	4	113
Kesiah, m. Josiah HENDE, Mar. 5, 1760	3	3
Lydia, d. Robert, & Hannah, b. Mar. 11, 1746/7	1	34
Lydia, d. Robart, d. May 13, 1748	2	40
Lydia, d. Joseph & Marthy, b. Aug. 3, 1754	1	85
Margreet, d. Ebenezer & Mehetable, b. Aug. 13, 1754	2	71
Margaret, m. Uriah HOLT, Nov. 11, 1779	4	75
Mary, d. John & Dor[o]thy, b. May 15, 1752 ; d. Sept. 14, 1754	2	41
Mary, m. Joseph GRIGGS, Jr., Mar. 24, 1814	6	16
Mehetable, d. Ebenezer & Mehetable, b. [ ] 30, 1752 ; d. Sept. 11, 1754	2	71
Mehitable, d. Ebe[neze]r, Jr. & Mary, b. Aug. 23, 1776	4	75
Mehetable, d. Eben[eze]r, d. Apr. 1, 1801	4	75
Peggy, d. Eben[eze]r, Jr. & Mary, b. June 7, 1795	4	75
Pelatiah, s. Solomon & Sarah, b. Dec. 2, 1763 ; d. Dec. 13, 1763	3	33
Polly, d. Eb[eneze]r, Jr. & Mary, b. May 26, 1790	4	75
Robert, m. Hannah TRESKET, Aug. 23, 1739	1	34
Robart, d. Feb. 6, 1748/9	2	40
Robert, s. John & Dor[o]thy, b. Nov. 12, 1755	2	41
Rufus, s. Eben[eze]r, Jr. & Mary, b. May 23, 1775 ; d. July 29, 1776	4	75
Rufus, s. Ebe[neze]r, Jr. & Mary, b. May 3, 1778	4	75
Salla, d. John & Sybil, b. Jan. 29, 1788 ; d. Nov. 10, 1789	4	113
Sarah, d. Solomon & Sarah, b. Aug. 7, 1760	3	33
Solomon, s. Robert & Hannah, b. Apr. 25, 1725	A	9

	Vol.	Page

MASON, MAYSON, (cont.)

Solomon, m. Sarah **SMITH**, Nov. 15, 1753	1	81
[So]lomon, s. Solomon & Sarah, b. Jan. 6, 1759	1	108
Stephen, s. John & Dorothy, b. Oct. 5, 1750	2	41
Stephen, s. John & Sybil, b. Oct. 29, 1785 ; d. Dec. 13, 1785	4	113
Susan[n]ah, m. David **PRESTON**, June 22, 1747	2	66
Zebbina, s. John & Sybel, b. Feb. 19, 1782	4	113
------, child of John & Dor[o]thy, b. Sept. 9, 1754 ; d. same day	2	41
MASSBEY, Thirza, of Ashford, m. John **ROUSE**, of Groton, Apr. 1, 1821, by Thomas Dow, J. P.	5	2
MATTERSON, [see under **MATTHEWSON**]		
MATTHEWS, Lucy, b., m. Andrew W. **JUDSON**, b. of Eastford, June 16, 1844, by Francis Williams	5	90
Nathan, of Killingly, m. Sophronia **SNOW**, of Ashford, [Sept.] 12, [1836], by Rev. Reuben Torrey, Eastford	5	62
Pascal H., m. Adeline M. **BASS**, b. of Eastford, June 30, 1844, by Francis Williams, Eastford	5	90
William, m. Cynthia **CHAPMAN** Sept. 17, 1827, by Amasa Lyon, J. P.	5	28
MATTHEWSON, MATHEWSON, MATTHERSON, MARTHERSON, MATHERSON, MATTERSON, Charles, m. Rebec[c]ah **WATKINS**, Jan. 30, 1782	4	122
Harriet, of Ashford, m. Elisha O. **WARREN**, of Stafford, Nov. 29, 1829, by Levi Work, J. P.	5	36
Ira, s. Charles & Rebec[c]ah, b. Feb. 1, 1783	4	122
Nancy, d. Charles & Reb[ec]cah, b. Aug. 15, 1782	4	122
Nathan, s. Lois Peck, b. Apr. 13, 1785	4	103
[**MATTOCKS**], **MATOCKS**, John Willard, s. John & Abigail, b. May 25, 1780	4	90
Joseph, s. John & Abigail, b. Aug. 1, 1783	4	90
MAY, W[illia]m R., of Pomfret, m. Elizabeth H. **CLARK** , of Ashford, Nov. 27, 1846, by Rev. Rensselaer O. Putney	5	99
McGAURY, John, joiner, b. Ireland, res. New Hartford, d. July 18, 1848, ae 55	5	128-9
McINTIRE, Jesse, of Mansfield, m. Caroline **PARKER**, of Ashford, Oct. 23, 1843, by Rev. Cha[rle]s Hyde	5	86
Sarah, of Ashford, m. Asa **LEACH**, of Thompson, Apr. 7, 1843, by Rev. Ezekiel Skinner	5	85
MELVIN, Lidiah, d. Benjamin & Lidiah, b. June 4, 1721	A	6
-----, d. Benjamin & Lidea, b. June 24, 1723	A	8
MERCER, James, of Union, m. Hannah W. **BOSS**, of Ashford, Sept. 15, 1831, by Rev. Stephen Hitchcock	5	44
MERCY, [see under **MARCY**]		
MERRICK, Samuel D., of Willington, m. Emeline **LYON**, of Ashford, May 14, last [1839], by Rev. Erastus Benton	5	70
MESSENGER, MESSINGER, James, s. Rev. James & Elisabeth, b. Mar. 5, 1770	4	39
James, Rev., d. Jan. 6, 1782	4	39

	Vol.	Page
MESSENGER, MESSINGER, (cont.)		
Joel, m. Sarah **STORRS**, Jan. 26, 1790	4	46
Sally, d. Joel & Sarah, b. Feb. 26, 1792	4	46
Storrs, s. Joel & Sarah, b. Oct. 13, 1794	4	46
William, s. Rev. James & Elisabeth, b. June 15, 1776	4	39
[METCALF], METCALFE, MEDCEILFF, MEDCALF,		
B[e]ulah, m. Nathan **BICKNELL**, Nov. 18, 1762	3	108
Margaret E., d. Job, farmer, ae 32, b. July 15, 1849	5	132-3
Mary, d. Jonathan & Beulah, b. Apr. 11, 1761	3	index
MILLER, Betsey, m. Numan **WILLSON**, b. of Ashford, Jan. 1,		
1841, by Rev. R. W. Allen, Eastford	5	77
Catharine E., m. Almeran S. **SHIRTLEFF**, Dec. 19, 1847, by		
Rev. Washington Munger	5	102
Eliza, m. John **BRIERLY**, b. of Southbridge, Mass., Mar, 27,		
1844, by Rev. Stephen Cushing	5	88
George, shoemaker, ae 21, b. Providence, R. I., res. Ashford,		
m. Mary Ann **COOK**, ae 26, b. Killingly, Ct., July 23,		
1848, by Cha[rle]s S. Adams	5	128-9
John R., m. Amy A. **CARD**, b. of Ashford, Nov. 28, 1850, by		
Rev. Lyman Leffingwell	5	106
John R., farmer, ae 22, b. N. Y. State, res. Ashford, m. Amey		
A. **CARD**, ae 19, b. Mass., Nov. [ ], 1850, by Lyman		
Leffington	5	148-9
Maria D., d. Augustus, blacksmith, ae 28, & Martha, ae 25, b.		
May 27, 1849	5	132-3
Mercy, of Ashford, m. Henry **POLLOCK**, of Thompson, Oct.		
12, 1823, by Thomas Dow, J. P.	5	11
William, m. Rhoda **PHILLIPS**, b. of Ashford, Oct. 6, 1822, by		
Philo Judson	5	7
MINER, [see also **MAINER**] Lucretial, m. Shubael **PRESTON**,		
Nov. 9, 1794	4	26
MIXER, MIXTER, Anne, d. John & Abigail, b. Oct. 28, 1715	A	2
Ezra, s. John & Abigail, b. July 15, 1712	A	1
Lovisa, m. Daniel S. **ARNOLD**, b. of Ashford, Apr. 15, 1845,		
by Rev. Geo[rge] Mixter	5	93
Rebeckah, d. John & Abigail, d. Feb. 14, 1717/8	A	3
MOORE, Austin, of Union, m. Sally **MOORE**, of Westford, Nov.		
24, 1825, by Rev. Philo Judson, at Westford	5	20
Cather[i]ne, housekeeper, d. Oct. 18, 1849, ae 50	5	144-5
Emily, m. James **CHAPMAN**, b. of Ashford, Jan. 1, 1829, by		
Rev. Ezekiel Skinner	5	32
Esther Minerva, d. John, 2d, & Esther, b. Sept. 13, 1831	6	84
John, m. Louisa **HAVENS**, Feb. 22, 1829, by Levi Work, J. P.	5	34
Martha Naomi, d. John, 2d, & Esther, b. Apr. 26, 1847	6	84
Otis, of Ashford, m. Clarissa **HISCOCK**, of Townsend, Vt.		
Sept. 24, 1826, by Rev. Amos Babcock, Jr. Intention		
published	5	23
Sally, of Westford, m. Austin **MOORE**, of Union, Nov. 24,		

	Vol.	Page
MOORE, (cont.)		
1825, by Rev. Philo Judson, at Westford	5	20
Susan M. A. M., d. John, 2d, & Esther, b. May 9, 1838	6	84
MOREY, Abigail, m. Hale **WHITING,** Nov. 7, 1793	4	278
Elisha, of Pomfret, m. Phebe Ann **HIGGINBOTHAM,** of Ashford, Sept. 12, 1841, by Rev. Charles C. Barnes	5	78
Lucy, milliner, d. Dec. 31, 1847, ae 44	5	130-1
Prudy, housekeeper, b. Charlton, Mass., res. Ashford, d. Sept. 21, 1849, ae 80	5	144-5
MORGAN, [see under **MARGAIN**]		
MORSE, Albert, of Union, m. Laura **ROBBINS,** of Ashford, Sept. 26, 1847, by Ezekiel Skinner	5	101
Danforth, b. Dec. 27, 1802	6	77
Danforth, of Union, m. Rebeckah **WITHNER,** of Ashford, Apr. 1, 1830, by Edward S. Keyes, J. P.	5	38
Emily, m. Benjamin **GREEN** b. of Ashford, last evenig, Feb. 13, 1843, by F. Williams. Intention published	5	84
Jedediah, b. Sept. 9, 1809	6	77
John S., shoemaker, b. Thompson, res. Ashford, d. Dec. [ ], 1848, ae 51	5	138-9
Loiza, d. Joseph & Olive, b. Apr. 20, 1807 (sic)	4	257
Lucius, of Union, m. Lodhia **SCARBOROUGH,** of Ashford, Nov. 24, 1830, by Rev. Stephen Hitchcock	5	40
Mary, m. Henry H. **ARNOLD,** b. of Ashford, [June] 4, [1837], by Rev. Reuben Torrey, Eastford	5	64
Moses, s. Joseph & Olive, b. Apr. 24, 1807	4	257
Otis, of Union, m. Lydia **WATTNER,** of Oxford, Nov. 25, 1823, by Nathan Hayward, J. P.	5	11
MOSELEY, MOSLEY, Alexander Burnham, s. Tho[ma]s & Salley, b. Mar. 12, 1813	4	29
Almira, d. Nathan & Mary, b. June 20, 1814	6	17
Almira, of Ashford, m. Amasa **HARVEY,** of Palmer, Mass., May 27, 1845, by Rev. Cha[rle]s Hyde	5	94
Betsey, of Ashford, m. Daniel A. **GRIGGS,** of Chaplin, [Mar.] 27, [1843], by Rev. Cha[rle]s Hyde	5	84
Dixsy, d. Nathan & Mary, b. Aug. 14, 1816	6	17
Elisty Sophia, d. Thomas & Salley, b. Nov. 25, 1806	4	29
Elizabeth, d. Nathan & Mary, b. June 27, 1808	6	17
Elizabeth, of Ashford, m. Samuel S. D. **WRIGHT,** of Mansfield, Jan. 14, 1830, by Rev. Philo Judson	5	37
Esther, d. Thomas & Salley, b. Jan. 20, 1809	4	29
Hannah, m. John **CLARK,** Oct. 4, 1816	4	109
John, s. Sam[ue]ll & Lucy, b. Sept. 14, 1769	3	130
July Anna, d. Tho[ma]s & Sally, b. Jan. 2, 1815	4	29
Lewis W., of Hampton, m. Gracey **CROSS,** of Ashford, Dec. 12, 1824, by Jared Andrus, Chaplin	5	16
Mahala, of Ashford, m. Asa B. **EGERTON,** of Mansfield, Nov. 16, 1829, by Amasa Lyon, J. P.	5	36
Mary Ann, d. Nathan & Mary, b. May 16, 1812	6	17

	Vol.	Page
MOSELEY, MOSLEY, (cont.)		
Mary Ann, m. Jabez **BOWEN** b. of Ashford, [Mar.] 17, [1834],		
by Rev. Reuben Torryey, Eastford	5	53
Nathan, s. Nathan & Mary, b. Feb. 27, 1806	6	17
Nathan James, s. Selden & Mariah, b. Aug. 29, 1833	6	89
Selden*, s. Nathan & Mary, b. June 16, 1810 (*correction on		
original manuscript)	6	17
Sarah Smith, d. Thomas & Salley, b. Aug. 12, 1804	4	29
Selden, m. Maria **FITTS**, b. of Ashford, Oct. 11, 1832, by Rev.		
Philo Judson	5	49
Thomas, m. Salley **BUCKLAND**, Sept. 22, 1803	4	29
----ah, d. [Sam[ue]ll & Lucy], b. May 22, 1763	3	130
----ler, s. Sam[ue]ll & Lucy, b. Sept. 9, 1767	3	130
----sa, d. Sam[ue]ll & Lucy, b. [ ]er, 24, 1772	3	130
----ar, s. Sam[ue]ll & Lucy, b. Apr. 13, [ ]	3	130
MOULTON, MOULTEN, Louise M., of Stafford, ae 22, m. Alfred		
A. **WHITE,**, of Monson, Mass., cabinet maker, ae 30, s.		
of Esbon & Patty, Apr. 29, 1846, in North Ashford, by		
Rev. Rennsalear O. Putney, of N. Ashford. Intention		
published 14 d. in Monson	5	97
Mehetebel, m. John **PERRY**, Jr., Oct. 26, 1732, by Rev.		
Richerd Treet	1	43
MOUTTAN*, Sophia, of Ashford, m. Levie **SAVERY**, of Union,		
May 18, 1828, by Nehemiah Bardsley (*MOULTEN?)	5	31
MUMFORD, Betsey, d. Jeremiah & Betsey, b. Sept, 8, 1794	4	241
Electa, d. Jeremiah & Betsey, b. Sept. 7, 1799	4	241
Electa, of Ashford, m. Aaron **DAVIS**, of Dudley, Mass., Oct.		
20, 1824, by Reuben Torrey, Eastford	5	16
Elias, s. Jeremiah & Betsey, b. Apr. 28, 1783	4	241
Ira, s. Jeremiah & Betsey, b. Dec. 8, 1791 ; d. Aug. 2, 1795	4	241
Jeremiah, s. Jeremiah & Betsey, b. July 5, 1797	4	241
Maning, s. Jeremiah & Betsey, b. Aug. 23, 1801	4	241
Marinda, d. Jeremiah & Betsey, b. Nov. 9, 1805	4	241
Miranda, of Ashford, m. Samuel B. **DURFEE**, of Providence,		
R. I., Dec. 27, 1831, by Rev. Benjamin Paine	5	46
Nancy, d. Jeremiah & Betsey, b. Oct. 26, 1787 ; d. Dec. 9,		
1788	4	241
Salla, d. Jeremiah & Betsey, b. June 18, 1785; d. Dec. 12, 1788	4	241
Salla, d. Jeremiah & Betsey, b. Nov. 11, 1789	4	241
MUNGER, Alfred J., s. Washington, minister, & Louisa, b. Nov. 7,		
1848	5	132-3
Mary, d. Dexter, b. Dec. 17, 1834	6	75
MURPHY, James J., pedler, b. Willington, res. Ashford, d. Nov. 22,		
1849, ae 20	5	144-5
Sarah T., of Ashford, m. Nathan **GALLUP**, Jr., of Windham,		
Feb. 17, 1850, by Rev. P. Mathewson, of the Tolland		
Baptist Church	5	104
Sarah T., ae 18, b. Ashford, m. Nathan **GALLUP**, Jr., pedler,		

	Vol.	Page
MURPHY, (cont.)		
ae 21, b. Windham, res. Ashford, Feb. 19, 1850, by P.		
Matthewson	5	142-3
NEFF, Cha[u]ncey, of Chaplin, m. Julia **LINCOLN**, Apr. 1, 1824,		
by Edward Keyes, J. P.	5	13
Marcus, of Chaplin, m. Harriet M. **HAWES**, of Ashford, Aug.		
22, 1836, by Rev. Rodolphus Lanphear	5	62
NESBITT, Agnes, d. Robert & Mary, b. Jan. 6, 1790	4	255
Catharine, d. Robert & Mary, b. Aug. 31, 1788	4	255
NETTLETON, Mary A., of Stafford, m. Asahel **HARVEY**, of		
Palmer, Nov. 29, 1849, by Rev. Ezekiel Skinner	5	104
Mary A., of Stafford, Ct., m. Asahel **HARVEY**, factory		
operative, of Palmer, Mass., Nov, 29, 1849, by Ezekiel		
Skinner	5	142-3
NEWPORT, Erastus, m. Eliza Ann **DAVIS**, b. of Ashford, May 29,		
1831, by Rev. David Bennett	5	43
Hannah, Mrs., m. Samuel **ELDREDGE**, May 17, 1840, by		
Edward S. Keyes, J. P.	5	74
Melissa, m. Henry H. **DAVIS**, b. of Ashford, Apr. 3, [1842],		
by Francis Williams, Eastford	5	80
NEWTON, Calvin, of Norwich, Vt., m. Serepta **WHIPPLE**, of		
Ashford, Oct. 6, 1834, by Rev. Job Hall	5	54
Hiram, of Brookfield, Mass., m. Maria **WHITON**, of Ashford,		
Dec. 29, 1833, by Job Cushman	5	52
NICHOLS, NICKOLS, NICOLDS, NICOLS, Anna, d. Will[ia]m		
& Anna, b. Mar. 13, 1747/8	2	68
Elisabeth, m. John **SNOW**, Nov. 15, 1770	4	82
Elizabeth, m. John **KIDDER** h. of Mansfield, May 7, 1838, by		
Amos Babcock	5	68
Lucinda, d. Jon[a]th[an] & Rebec[c]a, b. Mar. 17, 1794	4	253
Lucy, d. Jonathan & Rebec[c]ah, b. Feb. 11, 1790	4	253
Mary, d. William & Anna, b. Apr. 13, 1752	2	68
Rebec[c]ah, d. Jonathan & Rebac[c]ah, b. Feb. 14, 1788	4	253
Sarah, d. Jon[a]th[an] & Rebec[c]a, b. Mar. 6, 1792	4	253
NICKERSON, William, of Smithfield, R. I., m. Amanda **SQUIER**,		
of Ashford, Aug. 18, 1839, by Amos Babcock	5	71
NORTHUP, Adaline, of Chaplin, m. George **DUNHAM**, of		
Mansfield, Nov. 23, 1845, by Rev. Geo[rge] Mixter	5	95
NOTT, Eliph[a]let, s. Stephen & Debo[r]ah, b. June 25, 1773	3	41
Rhoda, m. Benj[ami]n, **WALKER**, Jr, Mar. 29, 1787	4	261
NOYES, Nathan, of Hartford, m. Elizabeth **SUMNER**, of Ashford,		
May 22, 1826, by Rev. Philo Judson	5	23
OLNEY, ONLEY, Abibatena, m. Elias **CHAPMAN**, Jr. Oct. 19,		
1814	6	35
Mary W., m. Merrill A. **KEITH**, b. of Ashford, Sept. 30, 1831,		
by Rev. Benjamin Paine	5	44
Susanna, m. Nathan **HOWARD**, Nov. 26, 1801	4	235
Thomas, m. Mary **MARCY**, b. of Ashford, Jan. 10, 1826, by		
Nathan Hayward, J. P.	5	21

	Vol.	Page
OLNEY, ONLEY, (cont.)		
William Pitt, m. Matilda **RICHARDS,** b. of Ashford,		
[Nov.] 5, [1838], by Rev. Reuben Torrey, Eastford	5	69
W[illia]m Pitt, m. Lydia **RICHARDS,** b. of Ashford, [Mar.]		
17, [1834], by Rev. R. Torrey, Eastford	5	53
ORCUTT, Gurdin, s. Jacob & Abigail, b. Oct. 5, 1773 (Entry		
crossed out)	4	55
Henry Willard, s. William & Emeline, b. Nov. 4, 1831	6	74
Jacob, m. Abigail **CHAFFE[E],** Jan. 1, 1771	4	55
Jacob, s. Jacob & Abigail, b. Aug. 30, 1771	4	55
Jehu, s. Jacob & Abigail, b. Jan. 31, 1773	4	55
Joseph, s. Joseph & Sarah, b. July 6, 1717, in Swanzey	A	4
OSGOOD, [see also **HORSGOOD**], Jeremiah, s. Daniel & Ruth, b.		
Sept. 1, 1762	3	107
OULD, OULDS, Daniel, s. James & Sarah, b. Apr. 5, 1759	4	16
Ebenezer, s. James & Sarah, b. Sept. 18, 1755	1	92
Ebenezer, s. James & Sarah,* b. Sept. 18, 1755 (*First written		
"Elizabeth")	4	16
Eliger, s. James & Sarah, b. May 12, 1767	4	16
Elizabeth, d. James & Elisabeth, b. July 6, 1752	1	91
Elizabeth, d. James & Elizabeth, b. July 11, 1752	4	16
Elisabeth, w. James, d. Aug. 4, 1753, in the 33rd y. of her age	1	91
Ellidise, d. James & Sarah, b. Mar. 18, 1769	4	16
George, s. James & Elizabeth, b. June 17, 1750	4	16
George, s. James & Elizabeth, b. June 24, 1750	1	91
James, m. Sarah **KINGSLEY,** Mar, 20, 1753	4	16
James, m. Sarah **KINGSLEY,** Mar. 21, 1754	1	92
John, s. James & Sarah, b. May 31, 1757	4	16
Methiah, m. Abraham **FOSTER,** Sept. 21, 1769	4	30
Sarah, d. James & Sarah, b. Apr. 2, 1761	4	16
Timothy, s. James & Sarah, b. Mar. 6, 1763	4	16
Tryphena, d. James & Sarah, b. June 29, 1765	4	16
OWEN, OWENS, Adolphas, s. Miriam Himes, b. Jan. 8, 1787	4	233
Almyra, d. Eben[eze]r & Deborah, b. Aug. 30, 1788	4	59
Amasa, s. Timo[thy] & Keziah, b. Aug. 12, 1766	2	56
Bathsheba, d. Ele[a]zer & Jarusha, b. July 30, 1748	2	28
Benj[ami]n, m. Hannah **HENDEE,** Oct. 11, 1786	4	249
Betsey, d. Eleazer, Jr. & Abigail, b. Nov. 11, 1786	4	238
Betsey, d. Benj[ami]n & Hannah, b. Feb. 1, 1796	4	249
Daniel, m. Abigail **PIERCE,** Apr. 25, 1745	1	84
Daniel, s. Da[nie]ll, b. Mar. 3, 1746 ; d. Nov. 21, 1751	1	84
Daniel, s. Ele[a]zar & Jarusha, b. Jan. 15, 1759	2	28
Daniel, s. Eben[eze]r & Deborah, b. Jan. 16, 1797	4	59
David K., of Hartford, m. Emily M. **LEWIS,** of Ashford, Oct.		
17, 1842, by Francis Williams	5	82
Deborah, d. Eben[eze]r & Deborah, b. Mar. 20, 1794	4	59
Ebenezer, s. Ele[a]zer & Jarusha, b. Feb. 13, 1749/50	2	28
Ebenezer, m. Deborah **FULLER,** June 1, 1772	4	59

	Vol.	Page
OWEN, OWENS, (cont.)		
Ebene[ze]r, [twin with Nathaniel], s.		
Eben[eze]r & Deborah, b. Oct. 26, 1778	4	59
Ele[a]zer, m. Jarusha **RUSS**, Feb. 20, 1744, by Rev. Mr. John		
Bass	2	28
Ele[a]zar, s. Ele[a]zar & Jarusha, b. Apr. 16, 1761	2	29
Elijah, s. Timothy & Keziah, b. Aug. 22, 1768	2	56
Elijah F., of Chaplin, m. Lucinda **BROWN**, of Ashford, Dec.		
17, 1843, by Rev. L. W. Blood	5	86
Ella, d. Eben[eze]r & Deborah, b. Nov. 22, 1790	4	59
Esther, d. Ele[a]zer & Jarusha, b. Feb. 20, 1747	2	28
Esther, d. Ebenezer & Deborah, b. Feb. 11, 1775	4	59
Hannah, m. Abraham **RUSS**, Oct. 25, 1738, by Rev. Mr. James		
Hale	1	66
Hannah, d. Tim[othy] & Keziah, b. Aug. 30, 1765	2	56
Hannah, d. Benj[ami]n & Hannah, b. Aug. 9, 1789	4	249
Hulda, [d. Daniel], b. Apr. 17, 1752	1	84
Hulda, d. Timothy & Keziah, b. Apr. 8, 1763; d. Apr. 18, 1763	2	56
James, [s. Daniel], b. Apr. 2, 1750	1	84
James, s. Eben[eze]r & Deborah, b. Oct. 30, 1772 ; d. Nov. 3,		
1775	4	59
James, s. Eben[eze]r & Deborah, b. Mar. 14, 1777	4	59
Jemima, d. Ele[a]zar & Jerush[a], b. Aug. 16, 1765	2	29
Jarusha, d. Ele[a]zer & Jarusha, b. May 25, 1745	2	28
Keziah, d. Timothy & Keziah, b. Mar. 23, 1761	2	56
Leonard, s. Eleazer, Jr. & Abigail, b. Sept. 6, 1788	4	238
Lucy, d. Eben[eze]r & Deborah, b. July 3, 1786	4	59
Lucy, d. Benj[ami]n & Hannah, b. July 1, 1793	4	249
Lucy, m. Samuel **WHIPPLE**, b. of Ashford, Sept. 22, 1834, by		
Rev. Job Hall	5	54
Lydia, d. Da[nie]l, b. Jan. 6, 1748, O. S.	1	84
Mary, d. Ele[a]zer & Jarusha, b. Feb. 13, 1752	2	28
Miriam, d. Eleazer & Jarusha, b. May 15, 1754	2	28
Miriam, d. Eb[e]n[eze]r & Deborah, b. Aug. 5, 1782	4	59
Nathaniel, [twin with Ebene[ze]r], s. Eben[eze]r & Deborah, b.		
Oct, 26, 1778	4	59
Olenda, d. Benj[ami]n & Hannah, b. Aug. 21, 1791	4	249
Perse, d. Timothy & Keziah, b. May 12, 1771	2	56
Polley, d. Eben[eze]r & Deborah, b. Apr. 26, 1781	4	59
Prissillah, d. Ele[a]zar & Jerusha, b. May 15, 1763	2	29
Rainor, s. Eben[eze]r & Deborah, b. Aug. 27, 1792	4	59
Ralph, s. Eleazer, Jr. & Abigail, b. June 3, 1785	4	238
Ruth, d. Benj[ami]n & Hannah, b. Sept. 19, 1798	4	249
Salley, d. Eb[e]n[eze]r & Deborah, b. Aug. 2, 1784	4	59
Silas, s. Benj[ami]n & Hannah, b. Dec. 4, 1787	4	249
Timothy, s. Ele[a]zer & Jarusha, b. Nov. 10, 1756	2	28
Willard, s. Eleazer, Jr. & Abigail, b. Nov. 2, 1791	4	238
William Fuller, s. Eben[eze]r & Deborah, b. Sept. 15, 1800	4	59
PACKER, [see also **PARKER**], David, rake & plough maker, b.		

	Vol.	Page
PACKER, (cont.)		
Groton, res. Ashford, d. July 1, 1848, ae 76	5	128-9
Pardon, s. Rebeckah, b. Sept. 4, 1797	6	12
Rebeckah had s. Pardon, b. Sept. 4, 1797	6	12
PAINE, PAIN, PAYNE, Catharine R., m.		
Reuben **SPAULDING**, of		
Pomfret, Apr. 13, 1846, by Francis Williams	5	96
Elias, s. Noah & Surviah, b. Jan. 1, 1777	4	53
Hannah, d. Noah & Surviah, b. Oct. 1, 1773	4	53
John [twin with Noah], s. Noah & Surviah, b. Sept. 9, 1778	4	53
John, of Union, m. Harriet **STODDARD**, of Mansfield, Apr.		
17, 1836, by Amos Babcock	5	59
Lucy, d. Noah & Surviah, b. Dec. 19, 1771	4	53
Noah, [twin with John], s. Noah & Surviah, b. Sept. 9, 1778	4	53
Percy, m. David **HOWARD**, Jr., May 14, 1807	6	3
Sarah, d. Noah & Surviah, b. Apr. 5, 1775	4	53
PALMER, Benjamin, m. Est[h]er **HAYWARD**, Nov. 11, 1755, by		
Stephen Williams	1	89
Benj[ami]n, s. Benj[ami]n & Easter, b. Mar. 26, 1759	1	104
Benjamin, s. Benjamin & Martha, b. Jan. 30, 1785	4	20
Caroline, d. Stephen F. & Percy, b. Dec. 28, 1804	4	242
Caroline, m. William **LINCOLN**, b. of Ashford, last evening		
[Apr. 1, 1835], by Rev. Job Hall	5	56
Catharina, d. Benj[ami]n & Martha, b. Sept. 1, 1794	4	20
Chauncey, s. Benj[ami]n & Martha, b. June 19, 1792	4	20
Chauncey, m. Hannah P. **DEAN**, b. of Ashford, Nov. 3, 1836,		
by Rev. Stephen Cushing, Eastford	5	63
Elihu, s. Benj[ami]n & Esther, b. Aug. 14, 1768	3	66
Est[h]er, d. Benj[ami]n & Est[h]er, b. Feb. 16, 1763	3	66
Esther, m. Alfred **WHALEY**, Nov. 9, [1823], by Anson S.		
Atwood	5	11
Esther Hayward, d. Stephen F. & Percy, b. Jan. 29, 1803	4	242
Friend, s. Benj[ami]n & Martha, b. Mar. 14, 1787	4	20
George, s. Benj[ami]n & Martha, b. Aug. 1, 1801	4	20
George, m. Deborah **BICKNELL**, Oct. 9, 1826, by Rev. Philo		
Judson	5	24
Hannah P., ae 35, m. 2d h. Thompson **RICHMOND**, farmer,		
ae 33, b. Ashford, res. Wisconsin, Apr. 28, 1850, by		
Lyman Leffingwell	5	142-3
James, s. Benj[ami]n & Esther, b. May 28, 1777	3	66
James Nelson, s. James & Lora, b. July 19, 1803	4	89
John, s. Benj[ami]n & Est[h]er, b. Mar. 12, 1761	3	66
John, s. Joseph & Sally, b. Apr. 7, 1789 ; d. Aug. 30, 1808	4	106
John Devotian, s. Stephen F. & Percy, b. Jan. 13, 1810	4	242
Joseph, s. Benjamin & Est[h]er, b. Dec. 8, 1756	1	94
Joseph, Dr., m. Salley **WELD**, May 20, 1778	4	106
Joseph, s. Joseph & Salley, b. Oct. 10, 1781	4	106
Joseph, Jr., m. Tabitha **SIMMONS**, Apr. 23, 1823, by Philo		
Judson	5	9
Joseph, Dr., d. Mar. 13, 1825, ae 68	4	106

	Vol.	Page
PALMER, (cont.)		
Laura, d. Benj[ami]n & Martha, b. Oct. 21, 1796	4	20
Laura, m. Horace **SHIPPEE**, b. of Ashford, Nov. 24, 1831, by Rev. Philo Judson	5	45
Loisa Wild, d. Stephen F. & Percy, b. Oct. 9, 1814	4	242
Louisa W., of Ashford, m. Nehemiah T. **ADAMS**, of Hampton, Oct. 19, 1836, by Rev. J. Hall	5	62
Martha Sumner, d. Stephen F. & Percy, b. June 27, 1807	4	242
Mary Weld, d. Joseph & Sally, b. Sept. 21, 1786 ; d. Feb. 1, 1788	4	106
Nathan, s. Benjamin & Esther, b. Nov. 28, 1766	3	66
Percy, w. Stephen F., d. July 16, 1825, ae 44	6	71
Percy S., of Ashford, m. William T. **ALMY**, of Norwich, Jan. 8, 1845, by Rev. Cha[rle]s Hyde	5	93
Percy Simmons, d. Stephen F. & Percy, b. Nov. 4, 1823	4	242
Rachal, d. Benj[ami]n & Est[h]er, b. Mar. 19, 1765	3	66
Rachel, m. Asaph **SMITH**, Jr., June 7, 1783	4	92
Ruth, d. Benj[ami]n & Esther, b. May 17, 1770	3	66
Sarah, d. Joseph & Sally, b. May 14, 1792	4	106
Sarah, d. Mar. 22, 1830, ae 72	4	106
Sarah Ann, d. Stephen F. & Percy b. Aug. 12, 1817	4	242
Sarah W., of Ashford, m. Edwin **ROBINSON**, [of] Mobile, Ala., last evening, [June 23, 1836], by Rev. J. Hall	5	60
Stephen Fielder, s. Joseph & Salley, b. Dec. 21, 1778	4	106
Stephen Fielder, m. Percy **SIMMONS**, Jan. 7, 1802	4	242
Stephen Fielder, s. Stephen F. & Percy, b. Jan. 19, 1821	4	242
Stephen Fielder, s. Stephen F. & Percy, d. May 6, 1825, ae 5 y.	6	71
Tabitha, of Ashford, m. Charles **CLARKE**, of Brooklyn, Sept. 30, 1833, by Rev. James Porter	5	52
Tabitha Simmons, d. Stephen F. & Percy, b. Feb. 19, 1812	4	242
Thomas, s. Joseph & Salley, b. May 4, 1784 ; d. Dec. 30, 1812	4	106
Thomas, s. Benj[ami]n & Martha, b. Feb. 4, 1789	4	20
Titus, s. Benj[ami]n & Martha, b. Aug. 4, 1799	4	20
PAREL, Eunice, m. Tho[ma]s **DAVISON**, Aug. 26, 1779	4	108
PARKEE, Henry, of Abington, m. Olive **MARCY**, of Ashford, Jan. 1, 1826, by Rev. Amos Babcock. Intention published	5	21
PARKER, Alvin, of Windham, Vt., m. Rhoda **BUGBEE**, of Ashford, Oct. 10, 1841, by Rev. Samuel J. Curtis, Union	5	79
Angelina, d. Reuben & Chloe, b. Feb. 26, 1796	4	261
Anna, d. Reuben & Anna, b. July 12, 1791	4	261
Anna, w. Reuben, d. Sept. 8, 1791	4	261
Anna E., m. Thomas J. **TAFT**, b. of Ashford, Feb. 18, 1839, by Rev. Alvin Bennett	5	70
Calvin, s. Reuben & Anna, b. Nov. 29, 1789	4	261
Caroline, d. Pardon & Fanny, b. Jan. 16, 1823	6	72
Caroline, of Ashford, m. Jesse **McINTIRE**, of Mansfield, Oct. 23, 1843, by Rev. Cha[rle]s Hyde	5	86
Charles, of Mansfield, m. Anna **UTLEY**, of Ashford, Jan. 7, last [1827], by Rev. Ezekiel Skinner	5	26

PARKER, (cont.)	Vol.	Page
Charles H., s. Pardon & Fanny, b. July 11, 1830	6	72
Elizabeth S., of Ashford, m. Lorin LINCOLN, of North		
Windhan, Feb. 17, 1845, by Rev. Geo[rge] Mixter	5	93
Elvira, d. Pardon & Fanny, b. July 13, 1828	6	72
Esther M., m. Edwin P. DUDLEY, b. of Ashford, Dec. 23,		
1851, by Rev. P. Mathewson	5	108
Jacob, s. Jacob & Sarah, b. Nov. 17, 1725	A	9
Joanna, m. Josiah CHAFFE, Jr., Mar. 26, 1789	4	257
John, s. Jacob, Jr. & Sarah, b. May 12, 1731	1	8
Lora, d. Reuben & Chloe, b. Nov. 12, 1794	4	261
Lorin, of Mansfield, m. Mary Ann SQUIER, of Ashford, June		
3, 1838, by Amos Babcock	5	68
Mary Ann, m. William F. CHAFFEE, b. of Ashford, May 12,		
1840, by Rev. Alvan Underwood	5	74
Miner, of Mansfield, m. Lucy FAY, of Ashford, Mar. 11, 1821,		
by Rev. Philo Judson	5	2
Origin P., m. Mary H. WILSON, b. of Ashford, June 20, 1836,		
by Rev. Stephen Cushing, Eastford	5	60
Orpha, d. Reuben & Chloe, b. Aug. 10, 1793	4	261
Rebeckah, of Mansfield, m. Roger BARROWS, of Ashford,		
Sept. 24, 1826, by Rev. Philo Judson	5	24
Reuben, m. Anna EATON, Oct. 9, 1788	4	261
Reuben, m. Chloe CANADA, Aug. 5, 1792	4	261
PARKHURST, [see also PARKIS], Polly, housekeeper, b.		
Plainfield, res. Eastford, d. Apr. [ ], 1849, ae 72	5	138-9
Stephen, farmer, b. Plainfield, res. Eastford, d. Aug. 6, 1848, ae		
80	5	130-1
PARKIS, [see also PARKHURST], Mary, m. Rastus SPAULDING,		
b. of Ashford, May 22, 1844, by Francis Williams	5	89
PARKS, Mary, of Ashford, m. James JOHNSON, of Thompson,		
Oct. 7, 1835, by W[illia]m Livesey, Elder	5	57
PARRISH, PARISH, Almira, m. David Dana Nelson WEEKS, b.		
of Ashford, Dec. 23, 1827, by Amasa Lyon, J. P.	5	29
Jared, m. Irene CHAPMAN, b. of Ashford, June 2, 1822, by		
Rev. Philo Judson	5	6
Jerusha, m. Daniel CARY, b. of Ashford, Dec. 5, 1822, by		
Rev. John Paine, of Hampton	5	7
Parker, of Woodstock, m. Lucy FITTS, of Pomfret, Sept. 22,		
1830, by Rev. Reuben Torrey, Eastford	5	40
----rd, s. Eliphaz, d. Feb. 14, 1795	4	282
----rathy (?), w. Eliaphaz, d. Mar. 14, 1795	4	282
----lisha, s. Eliphaz, d. Apr. 5, 1795	4	282
PARRY, [see under PERRY]		
PARSONS, [see under PERSONS]		
PAUL, PAULLE, Ethan, of Union, m. Mary Ann RICHMOND, of		
Ashford, May 18, 1826, by N[i]ch[olas] B. Brardsey,		
Union	5	22
Jeduthan, of Tolland, m. Julia BOSWORTH, of Ashford,		

PAUL, PAULLE, (cont.)	Vol.	Page
Feb. 7, 1831, by Daniel Knowlton, J. P.	5	41
Samuel, Jr., of Union, m. Rebecca F. KNOWLTON, of		
Ashford, Sept. 16, 1838, by Rev. Geo[rge] Mixter	5	68
Samuel, Jr., of Union, m. Silence N. KNOWLTON, of		
Ashford, Apr. 17, 1842, by Rev. Cha[rle]s Hyde	5	81
PEABODY, Abigail, of Pomfret, m. Steven KEYES, Oct. 7, 1841,		
by Rev. Mr. William, of Pomfret	1	63
Abigail, d. Ephraim & Abigail, b. June 10, 1755	1	98
Abigail, d. Ephraim & Abigail, b. June 10, 1755	4	43
Abigail, m. Samuel SUMNER, Apr. 10, 1777	4	106
Hannah, d. Ephraim & Abigail, b. Aug. 31, 1758	4	43
Mary, d. Ephraim & Abigail, b. May 18, 1753	1	82
Mary, d. Ephraim & Abigail, b. May, 18, 1753	4	43
Mary, m. Allen BOSWORTH, Apr. 4, 1782	4	233
PEAK, [see under PECK]		
PEARL, Abigail, [twin with Rufus], d. Rufus & Abigail, b. Nov. 21,		
1817 ; d. June 14, 1837	6	12
Abigail, m. Jared RICHMOND, b. of Ashford, [June] 5,		
[1832], by Rev. Samuel S. Mallory, of Willington	5	48
Anna, d. Nathan & Elesabeth, b. Aug. 1, 1758, n. s.	3	125
Azulah, [d. Nathan & Elesabeth], b. Oct. 10, 1762, n. s.	3	125
Betsey, m. Samuel KIMBAL, Jr., Mar. 9, 1781	4	243
Desire, w. Rufus, d. Sept. 15, 1816	6	12
Elisha, s. Rufus & Abigail, b. Mar. 7, 1819	6	12
Elesabeth, d. Nathan & Elesabeth, b. July 6, 1757, n. s.	3	125
Marcy, m. William BUFFINGTON, Jr., Jan. 1, 181[ ]	4	95
Nathan, [s. Nathan & Elesabeth], b. Mar. 8, 1764, o. s. , d. in		
Nov. same year	3	125
Rufus, m. Abigail BYLES, Oct. 27, 1816	6	12
Rufus, [twin with Abigail], s. Rufus & Abigail, b. Nov. 21,		
1817	6	12
Rufus, d. June 22, 1819, ae 32	6	12
Rufus, of Hartford, m. Abigail S. CHAFFEE, of Ashford, May		
6, 1840, by Rev. Alvan Underwood	5	74
Timothy, s. Nathan & Elizabeth, b. Apr. 20, 1752, o. s.	3	125
PECK, PEAK, PECAK, PICK, Abihu, s. Ebenezer, d. Jan. 31,		
1848/9	2	39
Alason, of Abington, Pomfret, m. Abigail CARPENTER, of		
Ashford, [Apr.] 13, [1829], by Rev. Reuben Torrey,		
Eastford	5	35
Anna, d. John & Jerusha, b. Sept. 10, 1768	3	19
Betsey, m. Jared SNOW, Nov. 27, 1817	6	18
Daniel, s. John & Elisabeth, b. Sept. 18, 1762	3	19
Elisha, s. John & Jerusha, b. Mar. 25, 1777	3	19
Elisha, m. Sarah BADGER, Sept. 23, 1802	4	34
Elisha, of Abington Society, Pomfret, m. Mary WHITMAN, of		
[Westford Society], Oct. 29, 1844, by R. V. Lyon, in		
Westford Society	5	92

PECK, PEAK, PECAK, PICK, (cont.)	Vol.	Page
Elezeb[e]th, m. Thomas **PERRY**, Oct. 9, 1732,		
by John Chandler, Esq.	1	42
Elezebeth, d. Ebenezer & Elezebeth, b. Aug. 13, 1744	2	39
Elezebeth, d. Ebenezer, d. Mar. 3, 1748/9	2	39
Elisabeth, d. John & Elisabeth, b. Apr. 18, 1757	1	97
Elisabeth, w. John, d. June [ ], 1767	3	19
Eunis, d. John & Jerusha *, b. Sept. 25, 1770 (*First written		
"Elizabeth)	3	19
Hannah, d. Joseph & Eunice, b. Mar. 17, 1796	4	30
Ira, of Marion, Ga., m. Penelope **KEYES**, of Ashford, Conn.,		
Mar. 7, 1824, by Rev. W[illia]m Storrs	5	12
Iry, s. Joseph & Eunice, b. Feb. 17, 1788	4	30
Jason, s. Joseph & Eunice, b. Jan. 12, 1791	4	30
John, m. Elisabeth **DENNERSON**, June 18, 1755	1	96
John, s. John & Elisabeth, b. Oct. 7, 1759 ; d. May 18, 1760	3	19
John, s. John & Jerusha, b. May 8, 1767	3	19
John, m. Jerusha **PRESTON**, Aug. 25, 1767	3	19
John, Jr., m. Rebeckah **BADGER**, Nov. 12, 1788	4	230
Joseph, s. John & Elisabeth, b. Aug. 14, 1758	1	101
Joseph, m. Eunice **JEN[N]ING** Mar. 14, 1782	4	30
Lebbeus J., of Canton, m. Emeline **FLINT**, of Ashford, Nov.		
24, 1831, by Rev. Joseph P. Tyler	5	46
Lemuel, s. Joseph & Eunice, b. Sept. 12, 1784	4	30
Levi, s. Joseph & Eunice, b. Aug. 25, 1789 ; d. Jan. 25, 1790	4	30
Lois had s. Nathan Matterson, b. Apr. 13, 1785	4	103
Lorenza, d. Joseph & Eunice, b. May 22, 1794	4	30
Lydia, d. John & Elisabeth, b. Dec. 25, 1766	3	19
Minerva, d. Elijah (sic) & Sarah, b. Apr. 19, 1809 (Probably		
Elisha)	4	34
Molly, d. John & Elisabeth, b. Jan. 29, 1756	1	96
Oliver, s. John & Jerusha*, b. Aug. 7, 1772 (First written		
"Elizabeth")	3	19
Oliver, s. John, Jr. & Rebec[c]ah, b. Sept. 13, 1789	4	230
Polly, d. Elisha & Sarah, b. July 29, 1803	4	34
Rhode, d. John & Elisabeth, b. Feb. 3, 1761	3	19
Rhoda, m. Reuben **CHAPMAN** Nov. 21, 1782	4	242
Roxey, d. Joseph & Eunice, b. June 25, 1786	4	30
Sarah, m. David **CHAPMAN**, Aug. 3, 1793	4	51
Stoddard, s. Joseph & Eunice, b. May 20, 1799	4	30
PELER, David, of Ashford, m. Elizabeth **AVERELL**, of Preston,		
Dec. 7, 1722, by Rev. Salmon Treat, at Preston	A	6
PENNIMAN Elkanan, of Woodstock, m. Hannah **SAMSON**, of		
Ashford, [May] 12, [1831], by Rev. Reuben Torrey,		
Eastford	5	43
PENNINGS, Phila, of Ashford, m. W[illia]m M. **GARDINER**, of		
Mansfield, July 4, 1851, by George Soule	5	106
PERKINS, Abigail, d. Isaac & Tamesin, b. Feb. 5, 1773, in		
Mansfield	4	109

	Vol.	Page
PERKINS, (cont.)		
Andrew, s. W[illia]m, & Mary, b. Mar. 26, 1796	4	282
Benjamin, s. [Isaac] & Tamesin, b. June 24, 1782	4	109
Charles, [twin with ----], s. Will[ia]m & Mary, b. Jan. 17, 1809	4	282
Daniel, m. Anna JINKS, Feb. 13, 1791	4	272
Eleazer, s. [Isaac] & Tamasin, b. June 22, 1784	4	109
Eleazer, s. Isaac & Tamesin, d. Sept. 11, 1790	4	109
Eleazer, s. Will[ia]m & Mary, b. Aug. 13, 1802	4	282
George, s. Will[ia]m & Mary, b. Dec. 24, 1803	4	282
Isaac, m. Tamesin CHAPLIN, July 5, 1770, in Mansfield	4	109
Isaac, s. Isaac & Tamesin, b. Apr. 29, 1780	4	109
Isaac, s. W[illia]m & Mary, b. July 23, 1797	4	282
Jinks, s. Daniel & Anna, b. Feb. 7, 1792	4	272
John, s. Isaac & Tamezin*, b. Sept. 22, 1774 (First written "Tabathy")	4	75
John, s. Isaac & Tamesin, b. Sept. 22, 1774 ; d. July 16, 1776	4	109
John, s. Isaac, d. July 16, 1776	4	75
John, s. Isaac & Tamezin*, b. July 29, 1776 (First written "Tabathy"	4	75
John s. Isaac & Tamesin, b. July 29, 1776	4	109
John, m. Esther COLTON, Feb. 20, 1804	4	43
John, s. William & Mary, b. Feb. 5, 1811	4	282
Laura Colton, d. John & Esther, b. Jan. 2, 1805	4	43
Louisa, d. W[illia]m & Mary, b. Dec. 22, 1804	4	282
Mary, d. I[saac] & Tamesin, b. Mar. 5, 1790	4	109
Mary, d. W[illia]m & Mary, b. Dec. 22, 1800	4	282
Nancy, d. Daniel & Anna, b. Aug. 26, 1794	4	272
Sylvany, d. Daniel & Anna, b. Nov. 18, 1796	4	272
William, d. Isaac & Tamesin, b. Feb. 22, 1771, in Mansfield	4	109
William, m. Mary LEE, Feb. 12, 1795	4	282
William Lee, s. W[illia]m & Mary, b. Jan. 22, 1799	4	282
----misin, d. W[illia]m & Mary, b. Feb. 10, 1807	4	282
----, [twin with Charles], s. W[illia]m & Mary, b. Jan. 17, 1809; d. Jan. 18, 1809	4	282
PERRIN, Sarah, m. Ebenezer SUMNER, May 26, 1788	4	232
PERRY, PARRY, Abigail, d. John, Jr. & Mehetebel, b. Nov. 29, 1736 ; d. Aug. [ ], 1742	1	43
Abagial, d. John, Jr. & Mehetebel, b. May 5, 1745	1	43
Abigail, m. Benjamin CHENEY, May 30, 1765	4	14
Abijah, s. John & Mehitabel, b. May 27, 1749	2	39
Aleser, d. Sam[ue]ll & Elisabeth, b. Feb. 19, 1773	3	124
Alithier, w. Samuel, d. Sept. 8, 1782	4	42
Anne, d. Robert & Sarah, b. Dec. 28, 1764	4	26
Arba, s. Obadiah & Jemmima, b. June 3, 1764	3	57
Arba, s. Obadiah & Jemima, b. Aug. 5, 1770	3	57
Benjamin, s. Sam[ue]ll & Ellithiah, b. Aug. 22, 1764	3	124
Bridget, d. John & Bridget, b. Apr. 18, 1729	1	23
Bridget, m. Benjamin SUMNER, Oct. 31, 1748	2	51
Bridget, d. Sam[ue]ll & Ellatheah, b. Feb. 10, 1769	3	70

	Vol.	Page
PERRY, PARRY, (cont.)		
Clarina, d. Robert & Sarah, b. Mar, 31, 1770	4	26
Cyrus, [s. John & Rachal], b. June 20, 1762	3	124
Dorkis, d. Tho[ma]s & Elezebeth, b. Dec. 22, 1741	1	42
Dyar, s. Obadiah & Jemima, b. Mar. 8, 1775	3	57
Ebenezer, s. John & Mehetebel, b. Mar. 27, 1747	1	43
Ebenezer, s. John & Mehitabel, b. Oct.5, 1751	2	39
Ebenezer, d. Oct. 15, 1782	4	42
Elezebeth, d. Thomas & Elezebeth, b. Aug. 23, 1736	1	42
Elizabeth, d. Nov. 8, 1753	1	42
Elizabeth, d. John & Mahitibel, b. Jan. 18, 1754 ; d. Oct. 11, 1757	2	39
Elisabeth, m. Samuell **ALLEN**, May 30, 1754, by Mr. Stephen Williams, of Woodstock	1	83
Elesabeth, d. John, d. Oct. 12, 1757	1	100
Elisabeth, d. John & Rebeckah, b. Oct. 30, 1757	3	124
Elizabeth, d. Obadiah & Jemima, b. Aug. 3, 1768	3	57
Elisabeth, d. Robert & Elisabeth, b. Sept. 27, 1771	4	26
Epheram, s. Tho[ma]s & Elizebeth, b. Feb. 14, 1739/4	1	42
Easter, m. Nathan[i]el **EATON**, May 31, 1727, by Rev. James Hale	1	10
Hannah, d. Obadiah & Jemima, b. June 3, 1766	3	57
Harmey, d. Obadiah & Jemima, b. May 27, 1785	3	57
James, s. Obadiah & Jemima, b. Apr. 7, 1777	3	57
John, Jr., m. Mehetebel **MOULTEN**, Oct. 26, 1732, by Richerd Treet	1	43
John, s. John, Jr. & Meheteble, b. Sept. 8, 1733	1	43
John, Capt., d. Feb. 3, 1745/6	1	23
John, Jr., m. Rebecca **BADGER** May 2, 1755, by Stephen Williams	1	95
John, 3rd, s. John, Jr. & Rebecca, b. Dec. 18, 175[torn]	1	95
John, s. Sam[ue]ll & Elisabeth, b. Dec. 19, 1770	3	70
Joseph, [twin with Sarah], s. Samuel & Alethier, b. Mar. 15, 1778 ; d. Apr. 25, 1778	4	42
Kezia, d. Obadiah & Jemima, b. Aug. 16, 1779	3	57
Lydia, [m. Thad[deu]s **WADKINS**, Jr.], [ ], 1757	3	131
Mary, d. Tho[ma]s & Elezebeth, b. May 22, 1738	1	42
Mary, m. Ebenezer **BICKNELL**, Dec. 1, 1755, by James Bicknell, J. P.	1	90
Mehetebel, d. John, Jr. & Mehetebel, b. Sept. 12, 1738	1	43
Mehitable, d. Sam[ue]ll & Allethere, b. Aug. 4, 1759	1	106
Mehetable, m. John **SUMNER**, Jan. 5, 1761	3	34
Obadiah, s. John, Jr. & Mehetebel, b. July, 27, 1740	1	43
Obadiah, m. Jemmima **WINTCHESTER**, Mar. 18, 1762	3	57
Pairsia, d. Robert & Sarah, b. Oct. 14, 1768	4	26
Polly, d. Obadiah & Jemima, b. Oct. 15, 1772	3	57
Robert, m. Sarah **HODGES**, Sept. 5, 1764	4	26
Robert, s. Robert & Elisabeth, b. Dec. 18, 1773	4	26

	Vol.	Page
PHINEY, (cont.)		
Thomas Preston, s. Thomas & Anna, b. June 21, 1792	4	272
PICK, [see under **PECK**]		
PIDGE, Anne, d. Jonathan & Sarah, b. May 15, 1756	2	29
Bey[t]y, d. Jonathan & Sarah, b. Apr. 25, 1750	2	29
Henery, b. June 11, 1753	1	81
Jonathan, m. Sarah **BARRY**, Apr. 13, 1749	2	29
PIERCE, PEIRCE, PIRCE, Abigail, m. Daniel **OWEN**, Apr. 25, 1745	1	84
Asa, s. William & Hannah, b. Apr. 18, 1757	1	109
Edward, s. Francis, b. [ ], 29, 1765	2	62
Eli, s. Francies & Mary, b. Apr. 12, 1761	1	25
Elizabeth, m. Jonathan **EASTMAN**, Nov. 23, 1749, by Rev. John Bass	2	19
Francies, m. Mary **HARRIS**, Jan. [ ], 1761	1	25
[Francis], Jr., m. Elisabeth [Smith?], [ ], 14, 1762	3	133
Hannah, d. W[illia]m, b. May 23, 1750 ; d. Nov. 24, 1751	1	83
Hannah, d. William & Hannah, b. Dec. 31, 1752	1	83
Hoopstill, d. Francis & Deb[o]roh, b. Nov. 22, 1749 ; d. Apr. 8,* 1754 (*Perhaps "3")	2	62
Lucy, m. Jesse **WILLSON**, b. of Ashford, Dec. 11, 1825, by Nathan Hayward, J. P.	5	20
Lidia, d. Frances & Debroah, b. Apr. 11, 1733	1	8
Martha, d. Summers, b. Apr. 20, 1755	1	90
Mary, d. Frances & Deb[o]roh, b. June 14, 1737	1	8
Mary, d. Oct. 15, 1741	1	25
Mary, of Ashford, m. Shadrick **THAYER**, of Munson, Mass., Dec. 24, 1827, by Nathan Hayward, J. P.	5	30
Maryone, d. Frances & Deb[o]roh, b. Mar. 10, 1741/2	1	25
Maryoney, d. Frances, d. Dec. 29, 1748	2	62
Matilda, of Sterling, m. George W. **GREENSLIT**, of Killingly, June 26, 1843, by Rev. Isaac H. Coe. Intention published	5	85
Molly, d. Francis, b. Apr. 23, 1767	2	62
Nancy, of Ashford, m. James **DODGE**, of Woodstock, Jan. 3, 1836, by Edward S. Keyes, J. P.	5	58
Nathanael, s. Frances & Deborah, b. Feb. 17, 1734/5	1	25
Nathan[i]el, s. Frances, d. Aug. 19, 1741	1	25
Nathan[i]el, s. Frances & Deb[o]roah, b. Jan. 23, 1743/4	1	25
Nathan[i]el, s. Frances, d. Dec. 28, 1748	2	62
Stephen, s. Frances & Deb[o]roah, b. July 2, 1739	1	8
Stephen, d. Oct. 1, 1741	1	25
Stephen, s. Frances & Deb[o]roah, b. Sept. 17, 1745	1	25
Stephen, s. Frances, d. Dec. 25, 1748	2	62
William, [s. William & Hannah], b. June 28, 1759	1	109
William, s. Francies & Mary, b. Dec. 21, 1762	1	25
----, 1st s. [Francis, Jr. & Elisabeth], b. & d. June [ ], 1763	3	133
----, s. Francis, Jr. & Elisa[beth], b. June 18, 1765	3	133

	Vol.	Page
PIKE, John, m. Betsey **CHAMBERLAIN**, June 28, 1804	4	287
PITTS, PITS, Benjamin, s. John & Rachal, b. Nov. 6, 1754	1	86
Benjamin, m. Freelove **WHIPPLE**, Sept. 19, 1776	4	110
Elisabeth, d. John & Rachal, b. June 28, 1770	3	73
James, s. Benj[ami]n & Freelove, b. Dec. 5, 1780	4	110
Jeremiah, s. John & Susan[n]ah, b. Aug. 12, 1735	1	8
Jeremiah, s. John, Jr. & Rachal, b. Jan. 24, 1758	1	101
Jeremiah, m. Irena **YOUNGLOOVE**, Apr. 17, 1780	4	267
Jeremiah, m. [ ], Apr. 27, 1780	4	106
John, m. Susan[n]ah **PRESTON**, Jan. 23, 1729, by Rev. Mr. Hale	1	8
John, s. John & Susan[n]ah, b. Aug. 25, 1733	1	8
John, m Rachall **HUMPHRY**, Jan. 10, 1754	1	86
John, s. John & Rachall, b. June 24, 1756	1	94
John, s. John, Jr., d. May 4, 1758	1	101
John, d. Jan. 5, 1764	1	8
John, s. John & Rachal, b. Mar. 28, 1768	3	73
Lois, d. John & Rachel, b. Jan. 6, 1760	1	106
Marcy Whipple, d. Benj[ami]n & Freelove, b. Dec. 14, 1783	4	110
Patiance, d. John & Susan[n]ah, [b.] May 6, 1738	1	8
Perley, s. Jeremiah & Irena, b. Sept. 20, 1791	4	267
Persa, d. Jeremiah & Irena, b. Feb. 6, 1787	4	267
Rachel, d. Jeremiah & Irena, b. Feb. 25, 1783	4	267
Rebeckah, d. John & Susan[n]ah, b. May 22, 1740	1	8
Rebecca, m. Joel **CARPENTER**, July 3, 1755, by Stephen Williams	1	89
Salla, d. Jeremiah, b. Feb. 1, 1781	4	106
Salla, d. Jeremiah & Irena, b. Feb. 1, 1781	4	267
Saloma, d. John & Rachal, b. Mar. 24, 1766	3	73
Silome, m. John **GREENSLITT**, June 22, 1790	4	49
Samuel, s. John, Jr. & Rachel, b. Nov. 20, 1762	3	73
Samuel, s. Jeremiah & Irena, b. Mar. 31, 1785	4	267
Sarah, d. John & Susan[n]ah, b. May 23, 1731	1	8
PLACE, Isabel M., m. Daniel **LEONARD**, of Union, [Oct.] 26,[1825], by Rev. Reuben Torrey, Eastford	5	20
Jane E., d. Stephen, farmer, ae 42, & Jane E., ae 26, b. Apr. 11, 1850	5	142-3
Sarah, m. Asaph **SMITH**, Dec. 19, 1749, by James Bicknell, Esq.	2	52
PLATT, Peter, m. Emily L. **BICKNELL**, b. of Ashford, Nov. 13, 1853, by Rev. P. Mathewson	5	110
POLLOCK, Henry, of Thompson, m. Mercy **MILLER**, of Ashford, Oct. 12, 1823, by Thomas Dow, J. P.	5	11
POPE, Thomas, of Farmington, m. Flora **WILLIAMS**, of Tolland, Jan. 12, 1841, by Rev. Cha[rle]s Hyde	5	76
PORTER, Abigail, d. Betholomy & Anne, b. June 20, 1759	2	30
Abigail, m. Asa **RUSS**, Sept. [ ], 1790	4	27
Annah, d. Betholomy & Anne, b. Sept. 19, 1757	2	30

	Vol.	Page
PORTER, (cont.)		
Annah had d. Clarra, b. Apr. 6, 1784	4	71
Bartholomy, m. Anna **BUGBEE**, Oct. 9, 1751	2	30
Clarra, d. Annah, b. Apr. 6, 1784	4	71
James, Rev., of Pomfret, m. Lurinda **GRANT**, of Ashford, Apr. 24, 1826, by Rev. Philo Judson	5	22
Manuel, of Palmer, Mass., m. Mary **BROWN**, of Ashford, d. of Anna, Sept. 10, 1821, by John Warren, J. P.	5	4
POTTER, Abigail, d. Philip & Abigail, b. May 10, 1780	4	275
Alfred H., m. Laura Ann **JUSTIN**, b. of Ashford, Sept. 6, 1836, by Rev. Stephen Cushing	5	61
Almira, d. Philip & Abigail, b. Dec. 29, 1785	4	275
Bartholomew, s. Phillip & Abigail, b. Aug. 23, 1778	4	275
Bartholomew, of Willington, m. Sarah **PRESTON**, of Ashford, Mar. 25, last, [1829], by Rev. Ezekiel Skinner	5	34
David, s. Philip & Abigail, b. Apr. 1, 1784	4	275
Elisabeth, d. Silas & Elisabeth, [b.] Mar. 14, 1788	4	80
Elisabeth, d. Philip & Abigail, b. June 6, 1788	4	275
Elisabeth, m. Daniel **WHITING**, Apr. 14, 1808	4	275
Har[r]iat, d. Silas & Elisabeth, b. Mar. 29, 1801	4	80
Harriet, of Ashford, m. Noah M. **COBURN**, of Union, Oct. 3, 1824, by Nathan Hayward, J. P.	5	15
John, s. Silas & Elisabeth, b. June 19, 1794	4	80
John Foster, s. John & Dorothy, b. Mar, 3, 1822	6	46
Julia, m. Joseph W. **SNELL**, shoemaker, ae 24, b. Ashford, res. Auburn, Mass., Aug. 20, 1849, by Cha[rle]s Peabody	5	142-3
Julia A., of Ashford, m. Joseph W. **SNELL**, of Auburn, Mass., Aug. 13, 1849, by Charles Peabody, Intention published	5	103
Luther Warren, s. John & Dorothy, b. June 27, 1824	6	46
Maria, d. Silas & Elisabeth, b. Apr. 3, 1804	4	80
Mariah, of Ashford, m. Benjamin **CORBIN**, of Union, June 2, 1830, by Rev. Ezekiel Skinner	5	39
Marius Newton, s. John & Dorothy, b. Mar. 9, 1823	6	46
Philip, s. Philip & Abigail, b. Feb. 14, 1782	4	275
Rouse, m. Sally S. **STOWELL**, b. of Ashford, Nov. 29, 1837, by Rev. Rodolphus Lanphear	5	67
Silas, m. Elisabeth **WARREN**, Dec. 6, 1786	4	80
Silas, s. Silas & Elisabeth, b. May 14, 1789	4	80
Susanna, d. Silas & Elisabeth, b. May 17, 1791	4	80
Wil[liam] Ellery, s. Phillip & Abigail, b. Sept. 19, 1791	4	275
POWEL, Irane, m. John **BICKNELL**, Dec. 24, 1751, o.s.	1	82
POWERS, Lydia, d. Cyrus & Rachel*, b. Mar. 10, 1778 *(First written "Lydia")	4	76
PRATT, Asa, m. Betsey **PRESTON** b. of Ashford, [Apr.] 17, [1823], by Reuben Torrey, Eastford	5	9
Daniel L., of Southbridge, m. Louisa **GRIGGS**, of Ashford, Feb. 10, 1842, by Francis Williams, Pastor, of Eastford	5	80
Henry Preston, s. Asa & Bethiah, b. July 24, 1824	6	55
Moses K., d. Jan. 6, 1850, ae 2	5	144-5

	Vol.	Page
PRATT, (cont.)		
Moses Kelley, s. Joseph, farmer, ae 57, & Arsena,		
ae 35, b. Apr. 21, 1848	5	126-7
Sarah Elizabeth, d. Asa & Bethiah, b. Apr. 3, 1826 ; d. Apr.		
17, 1826	6	55
PRESCOTT, Orrigen, s. Clarasa Snow, b. Feb. 26, 1818	4	71
Origin, m. Julia Ann **LAWSON**, b. of Ashford, Nov. 6, 1843,		
by Francis Williams	5	86
PRESTON, Abial, m. Meletiah **SMITH**, July 27, 1756	1	97
Abigail, w. Enos, d. Nov. 8, 1781	4	50
Abigail, d. Zera & Mary Ann, b. Mar. 6, 1784	4	111
Abraham, s. Enos & Abigail, b. Aug. 5, 1771	4	50
Abraham, m Lucy **KEIYES**, June 1, 1773	4	116
Adeline, m. John **ADAMS**, b. of Ashford, Apr. 29, 1824, by		
Rev. W[illia]m Storrs	5	14
Allis, d. Enos & Abigail, b. Oct. 12, 1773	4	50
Alva, s. Enos & Abigail, b. Mar. 9, 1779	4	50
Ambros[e], s. Jacob & Mary, b. Apr. 11, 1774	3	9
Amos, s. John & Mary, b. Oct. 9, 1756	1	97
Amos, s. Benjamin & Barshebe, b. Dec. 29, 1765	4	24
Amos, s. Benjamin, d. July 31, 1776	4	24
Ann, d. Jacob & Sarah, b. Nov. 29, 1770	4	44
Anna, m. Elisha **PHILLIPS**, July 9, 1764	3	52
Anna, m. Thomas **PHINEY**, Nov. 7, 1791	4	272
Anna, d. Zera & Mary Ann, b. Sept. 7, 1792	4	111
Anne, d. John & Ele[a]ner, b. Aug. 7, 1741	1	53
Anne, d. Medina & Annah, b. Oct. 19, 1774	3	76
Anne, d. Shubael & Lucretial, b. Sept. 24, 1798	4	26
Anson, s. Tiras & Easther, b. June 30, 1773 (sic)	4	68
Bathashaba, d. Jan. 22, 1813, ae 83	4	24
Benjamin, m. Barshaba **SNOW**, Nov. 17, 1763	2	55
Benjamin, s. Benjamin & Barshaba, b. June 26, 1773	2	55
Benjamin, s. Benj[ami]n & Barshaba, b. June 26, 1773	4	24
Benjamin, d. Dec. 1, 1798	4	24
Bethier, d. Esek & Sally, b. June 16, 1804	4	279
Betsey, d. Jacob & Sarah, b. Nov. 30, 1780	4	44
Betsey, d. Esek & Sally, b. Dec. 3, 1806	4	279
Betsey, m. Asa **PRATT**, b. of Ashford, [Apr.] 17, [1823], by		
Reuben Torrey, Eastford	5	9
Betsey, m. Zuinglius **BULLARD**, Jr., Nov. 15, 1824, by Amos		
Babcock, Elder. Intention published	5	16
Betsey, m. Dr. David Holmes, [Feb.] 5, [1837], by Rev. R.		
Torrey, Eastford	5	64
Calvin, s. John, Jr. & Sarah, b. Apr. 11, 1765	3	16
Charles, s. Jacob, Jr. & Mary, b. Apr. 3, 1765	3	9
Charles, s. Zera & Hannah, b. May 10, 1796	4	111
C[h]loe, d. Jacob & Mary, b. Mar. 12, 1780	3	9
Chloey, m. James **BOUTWELL**, Nov. 15, 1781	4	119
Chloe, d. Abr[aham] & Lucey, b. July 11, 1785	4	116

	Vol.	Page
PRESTON, (cont.)		
Clarissa, d. Solomon & Susanna, b. Apr. 16, 1800	4	54
Clarissa C., of East Ashford, m. W[illia]m E. CHENEY, of		
Manchester, May 13, 1835, by Rev. R. Torrey, East		
Ashford	5	56
Daniel, s. Daniel & Dinah, b. May 4, 1763	3	12
David, m. Susan[n]ah MASON, June 22, 1747	2	66
David, s. David & Susannah, b. Feb. 25, 1758	2	66
Deziah, d. James H. & Deziah, b. Feb. 23, 1822	6	33
Dinah, d. Daniel & Dinah, b. Sept. 13, 175[ ]	1	99
Dorcas, d. Medine & Annah, b. Sept. 16, 1779	3	76
Earl Clap[p], s. Esek & Salla, b. Nov. 25, 1796	4	279
Ebinezer, s. William & Mary, b. Nov. 6, 1754 ; d. Nov. 13,		
1754	2	66
Eleazer, s. Hovey & Phebe, b. Apr. 27, 1778	4	68
Elisabeth, d. Zera & Hannah, b. Aug. 6, 1803	4	111
Ermina, d. Solomon & Susanna, b. Aug. 16, 1801	4	54
Ermina, of Ashford, m. Eliphalet BROWN, of Windham, Mar.		
27, 1829, by Rev. Luke Wood	5	34
Esek, s. Medina & Annah, b. Mar. 31, 1770	3	76
Esek Judson, s. Esek & Sally, b. May 25, 1802	4	279
Etharlinda, d. Jacob & Sarah, b. Jan. 13, 1784	4	44
Eunis Ford, d. Daniel & Dinah, b. Mar. 12, 1759	1	104
Flannda, of Ashford, m. Orrin WITTER, of Chaplin, Mar. 31,		
1824, by Rev. Philo Judson	5	13
Foster, s. Jacob, Jr. & Mary, b. July 22, 1769	3	9
Fredus, s. Shubael & Lucretial, b. Nov. 15, 1796	4	26
Gilbert Howard, s. Reuben & Lucy, b. Nov. 13, 1820	6	34
Hannah, d. John, Jr. & Sarah, b.[ ], 1771 ; d. Apr. 27, 1773	3	16
Hannah, d. Tiras & Easther, b. Aug. 20, 1775	4	68
Hannah, d. Zera & Mary Ann, b. Nov. 14, 1781	4	111
Hannah, w. Zera. d. Apr. 27, 1814	4	111
Harriet, m. Daniel Brewster DORSETT, [b. of Wastford], Nov.		
16, [1841], by Francis Williams	5	79
Harriet Matilda, d. John A. & Emily, b. May 23, 1849	6	102
Hattie Matilda, d. John A., merchant, ae 25, of Stafford, &		
Emily, ae 27, b. May 23, 1849	5	134-5
Henry, of Fredrickstown, Va., m. Sarah WINCHESTER, of		
Ashford, Jan. 7, 1801	4	69
Hovey, s. John & Mary, b. Nov. 13, 1750	1	86
Hovey, m. Phebe BARNEY, Nov. 23, 1773	4	68
Hovey, s. Hovey & Phebe, b. Dec. 30, 1775	4	68
Hovey, s. Hovey & Phebe, b. Dec. 30, 1775	4	83
Hovey, d. June 5, 1819, ae 69	4	68
Jacob, m. Sarah HAYWARD, May 31, 1770	4	44
Jacob, s. Jacob & Sarah, b. Mar. 27, 1774	4	44
Jerusha, m. John PECK, Aug. 25, 1767	3	19
John, s. David & Susan[n]ah, b. Oct. 25, 1756	2	66

	Vol.	Page
PRESTON, (cont.)		
Olever, s. Benj[ami]n & Barshebe, b. Feb. 13, 1768	4	24
Pamelia, of Ashford, m. Augustus **CORBIN,** of Union, May 7, 1829, by Rev. Ezekiel Skinner	5	35
Peggy Smith, d. Zera & Hannah, b. Apr. 24, 1800	4	111
Persa, d. Tiras & Easther, b. Oct. 5, 1777	4	68
Persis, housekeeper, d. Mar. 22, 1850, ae 76	5	144-5
Phebe, d. David & Susan[n]ah, b. Mar. 9, 1750	2	66
Phebe, d. Hovey & Phebe, b. Aug. 25, 1794	4	68
Philip, s. John, Jr. & Sarah, b. Dec. 5, 1760 ; d. Aug. 18, 1765	3	16
Polley, d. Zeph[aniah] & Mary, b. Oct. 6, 1797	4	65
Reubin, s. Zeph[aniah] & Mary, b. Aug. 26, 1792	4	65
Rhoda, d. Medina & Annah, b. Apr. 7, 1777	3	76
Rhoda, m. Samuel **SIBLEY,** b. of Ashford, Aug. 28, [1839], by Rev. Reuben Torrey, Eastford	5	72
Roswel[l], s. Jacob, Jr. & Mary, b. Sept. 15, 1771	3	9
Ruth, d. William, d. Oct. 23, 1754	2	66
Ruth, [d. W[illia]m & Mary], b. June 5, 1760	1	111
Sally, d. William, Jr. & Deziah (?), b. Mar. 10, 1770	4	41
Sally, d. Jacob & Sarah, b. June 24, 1772	4	44
Salla, m. Luther **GAYLORD,** Sept. 27, 1792	4	288
Sally Clap[p], d. Esek & Sally, b. July 31, 1798	4	279
Salvester, see under Sylvester		
Samantha, d. Nathan, b. Aug. 12, 1819	6	27
Samuel, s. William & Mary, b. July 12, 1752 ; d. Oct. 6, 1754	2	66
Samuel, s. Jacob, Jr. & Mary, b. Feb. 19, 1763	3	9
Samuel, s. Medine & Annah, b. June 14, 1783	3	76
Samuel, m. Phebe **LYON,** Aug. 27, 1806	6	31
Samuel H., m. Harriet E. **WHITNEY,** b. of Ashford, Nov. 23, 1851, by Rev. P. Mathewson	5	107
Samuel Hayward, s. Jacob & Sarah, b. May 2, 1786	4	44
Samuel Howard, s. Samuel & Phebe, b. June 26, 1825	6	31
Sarah, d. Abial & Melatiah, b. [ ]cem[b]er 8, 1759	1	110
Sarah, d. John, Jr. & [Sarah], d. Aug. 13, 1765	3	16
Sarah, d. John, Jr. & Sarah, b. Mar. 21, 1767	3	16
Sarah, d. Jacob & Mary, b. May 18, 1767	3	9
Sarah, of Ashford, m. Bartholomew **POTTER,** of Willington, Mar. 25, last [1829], by Rev. Ezekiel Skinner	5	34
Lucretia, of Ashford, m. Nathaniel **HODGKINS,** Jr., of Hampton, June 12, 1827, by Rev. Luke Wood	5	27
Lucy, d. Abraham & Lucy, b. Dec. 4, 1779	4	116
Margaret S., of Ashford, m. Thomas **FULLER,** of Hampton, Mar. 4, 1827, by Rev. Philo Judson	5	26
Mary, d. William & Mary, b. Oct. 19, 1755	1	90
Mary, m. David **EATON,** Jr., June 29, 1757	1	107
Mary, m. Jonathan **CURTISS,** Jan. 12, 1775	2	41
Mary, d. Jacob & Mary, b. June 23, 1776	3	9
Mary, m. Stephen **CHANDLER,** June[ ], 1784	3	3

PRESTON, (cont.)	Vol.	Page
Mary Ann, w. Zera, d. Feb. 9, 1794	4	111
Mary Ford, d. Hove[y] & Phebe, b. June 27, 1764 (sic)	4	68
Masselvea, d. Jacob & Sarah, b. June 23, 1788	4	44
Medinah, m. Anna HAYWARD, b. of Ashford, Jan. [ ], 1762 in Woodstock, by S. Williams	3	76
Medina Fitch, d. Samuel & Phebe, b. Mar, 2, 1817	6	31
Mehetabel, d. David & Susan[n]ah, b. Apr. 19, 1748	2	66
Minerva, d. Solomon & Susanna, b. Aug. 5, 1807	4	54
Minerva, m. Alfred CHAFFEE, b. of Ashford, May 24, 1837, by Alvan Underwood	5	64
Molly, d. Medinah & Anna, b. Sept. 17, 1762	3	76
Molley, d. John, Jr. & Sarah, b. Mar. 6, 1769	3	16
Nance, d. Abr[aham] & Lucy, b. June 12, 1783	4	116
Nathan, s. Zephaniah & Mary, b. Oct. 25, 1786	4	65
Olever, s. Benj[ami]n & Barshebe, b. Feb. 13, 1768	4	24
Pamelia, of Ashford, m. Augustus CORBIN, of Union, May 7, 1829, by Rev. Ezekiel Skinner	5	35
Peggy Smith, d. Zera & Hannah, b. Apr. 24, 1800	4	111
Persa, d. Tiras & Easther, b. Oct. 5, 1777	4	68
Persis, housekeeper, d. Mar. 22, 1850, ae 76	5	144-5
Phebe, d. David & Susan[n]ah, b. Mar. 9, 1750	2	66
Phebe, d. Hovey & Phebe, b. Aug. 25, 1794	4	68
Philip, s. John, Jr. & Sarah, b. Dec. 5, 1760 ; d. Aug. 18, 1765	3	16
Polley, d. Zeph[aniah] & Mary, b. Oct. 6, 1797	4	65
Reubin, s. Zeph[aniah] & Mary b. Aug. 26, 1792	4	65
Rhoda, d. Medina & Annah, b. Apr. 7, 1777	3	76
Rhoda, m. Samuel SIBLEY, b. of Ashford, Aug. 28, [1839], by Rev. Reuben Torrey, Eastford	5	72
Roswel[l], s. Jacob, Jr. & Mary, b. Sept. 15, 1771	3	9
Ruth, d. William, d. Oct. 23, 1754	2	66
Ruth, [d. W[illia]m & Mary], b. June 5, 1760	1	111
Sally, d. William, Jr. & Deziah (?), b. Mar. 10, 1770	4	41
Sally, d. Jacob & Sarah, b. June 24, 1772	4	44
Salla, m Luther GAYLORD, Sept. 27, 1792	4	288
Sally Clap[p], d. Esek & Sally, b. July 31, 1798	4	279
Salvester, see under Sylvester		
Samantha, d. Nathan, b. Aug. 12, 1819	6	27
Samuel, s. William & Mary, b. July 12, 1752 ; d. Oct. 6, 1754	2	66
Samuel, s. Jacob, Jr. & Mary, b. Feb. 19, 1763	3	9
Samuel, s. Medine & Annah, b. June 14, 1783	3	76
Samuel, m. Phebe LYON, Aug. 27, 1806	6	31
Samuel H., m. Harriet E. WHITNEY, b. of Ashford, Nov. 23, 1851, by Rev. P. Mathewson	5	107
Samuel Hayward, s. Jacob & Sarah, b. May 2, 1786	4	44
Samuel Howard, s. Samuel & Phebe, b. June 26, 1825	6	31
Sarah, d. Abial & Melatiah, b. [ ]cem[b]er 8, 1759	1	110
Sarah, d. John, Jr. & [Sarah], d. Aug. 13, 1765	3	16
Sarah, d. John, Jr. & Sarah, b. Mar. 21, 1767	3	16

	Vol.	Page
PRESTON, (cont.)		
Sarah, d. Jacob & Mary, b. May 18, 1767	3	16
Sarah, of Ashford, m. Bartholomew **POTTER**, of Willington,		
Mar. 25, last [1829], by Rev. Ezekiel Skinner	5	34
Sardis, s. Hovey & Phebe, b. Apr. 5, 1792	4	68
Seldon, s. Nathan, b. Sept. 16, 1817	6	27
Shuba[e]l, s. Jacob & Mary, b. Nov. 20, 1758	3	9
Shuba[e]l, s. Median & Annah, b. May 16, 1772	3	76
Shubael, m. Lucretial **MINER**, Nov. 9, 1794	4	26
Solomon, s. Benj[ami]n & Barshebe, b. Sept. 10, 1770	4	24
Solomon, m. Susanna **HARRIS**, June 13, 1799	4	54
Stephen, s. Medina & Anna, b. Dec. 29, 1767	3	76
Sukey Clap[p], d, Esek & Salla, b. Oct. [ ], 1795; d.		
Mar. 21, [ ]	4	279
Susan E., m. Nelson **SPAULDING**, b. of Ashford, Mar. 9,		
1841, by Rev. Ezekiel Skinner	5	77
Susan[n]ah, m. John **PIT[T]S**, Jan. 23, 1729, by Rev. Mr. Hale	1	8
Susannah (?), d. David & Susannah, b. Jan. 16, 1753* (*Entry		
crossed out)	2	66
Salvester, s. Zera & Mary Ann, b. June 3, 1780	4	111
Tabithy, d. Abr[aham] & Lucy, b. May 17, 1781	4	116
Tabatha, d. Zephaniah & Mary, b. Aug. 12, 1788	4	65
Talithamimia, d. Hovey & Phebe, b. Jan. 10, 1790	4	68
Tathelhamma, m. Alfred **BROWN**, b. of Ashford, Aug. 1,		
1830, by Luke Wood	5	39
Tiras, s. John & Mary, b. Oct. 6, 1752	1	86
Tiras, m. Easter **EATON**, Nov. 2, 1773	4	68
Willard, s. Zera & Mary Ann, b. Oct. 3, 1790 ; d. Nov. 14,		
1790	4	111
William, s. W[illia]m & Mary, b. Mar. 27, 1758	1	111
William, s. Zera & Mary Ann, b. July 6, 1788	4	111
William Earl, s. Earl C. & Harriet, b. June 20, 1822	6	56
Zephaniah, s. Medina & Annah, b. Dec. 24, 1764	3	76
Zephaniah, m. Mary **BISHOP**, May 25, 178[ ]	4	65
Zephaniah, s. Esek & Salla, b. Feb. 14, [ ]	4	279
Zera, m Mary Ann **WALKER**, Oct. 7, 1779	4	111
Zera, m. Hannah **SMITH** Apr. 20, 1794	4	111
Zera, s. Zera & Hannah, b. Dec. 12, 1794	4	111
Zera, m. Patience **GOULD**, Nov. 24, 1816 ; d. July 16, 1821,		
ae 62	4	111
Zera, d. July 16, 1821, ae 62	4	111
-----, [ ] to Benja[min], [ ]	4	289
PRICE, [E]unis, d. William & Mary, b. July 29, 1736	1	30
John, s. William & Mary, b. Mar. 13, 1726	A	5
Leah, w. William, d. Oct. 21, 1719	A	6
Mary, d. William & Mary, b. July 24, 1732	1	30
Samuel, s. William & Mary, b. Sept. 9, 1724	A	8
Sarah, d. William & Mary, b. Aug. 1, 1734	1	30
Susannah, d. Will[ia]m & Mary, b. July 6, 1722	A	5

	Vol.	Page
PRICE, (cont.)		
Susannah, d. Feb. 5, 1724/5	A	9
Susan[n]ah, d. Will[ia]m & Mary, b. Sept. 23, 1729	1	30
William, s. William & Mary, b. May 7, 1720	A	6
William, Sr., d. Mar. 25, 1723	A	9
William, s. William, d. Jan. 9, 1724/5	A	9
Will[ia]m, s. William & Mary, b. May 15, 1739	1	30
PROCTER, Easter, m. Joseph **RUSS**, Jr., Jan. 27, 1731/2, by Rev. James Hale	1	36
PROUD, Daniel Knowlton, s. Daniel Bardin & Amanda, b. Jan. 22, 1826	6	62
Else, m. Elihu **CHAFFEE**, Aug. 31, 1806	6	61
Erasmus, m. Mary N. **WEAVER**, b. of Woodstock, Dec. 25, 1832, by Rev. Elias C. Sweet	5	50
William Palmer, s. Daniel Bardin & Amanda, b. Oct. 23, 1827	6	62
PUTNAM, Ruth, m. Frederick F. **SIBLEY**, b. of Ashford, Nov. 27, 1839, by Rev. Alvan Underwood	5	72
RANDALL, James, of Ashford, m. Caroline **RAWSON**, of Charlton, Mass., Aug. 31, 1845, by Rev. Renssalear O. Putney, North Ashford	5	95
Lidy Ann, m. George W. **SHARP**, June 6, 1831, by Rev. Reuben Torrey, Eastford	5	43
Nancy, d. James, farmer, of Stafford, ae 26, black & Catherine, ae 22, b. Jan. 3, 1849	5	134-5
Reuben, m. Waitey **BROOKS**, b. of Ashford, Jan. 16, 1827, by Rev. Luke Wood'	5	25
RATHBURN, RATHBUN, Benja[min], s. Moses & Patience, b. Dec. 1, 1790	4	264
Content, d. Moses & Patience, b. July 12, 1801	4	264
David, m. Nancy **WALES**, July 9, 1789 (Entry crossed out)	4	264
Hannah, m. [Jo]hn **WESTON**, Apr. 24, 1803	4	10
Lyman, s. Moses & Patience, b. July 16, 1799	4	264
Moses, m. Patience **JAMES**, Jan. 21, 1790	4	264
Polley, d. Moses & Patience, b. July 10, 1797	4	264
Rhoda, d. Moses & Patience, b. July 1, 1792	4	264
Sarah, of Thompson, m. Nathan C. **BARTLETT**, of Ashford, Sept. 13, 1840, by Henry Work, J. P.	5	75
RAWSON, Caroline, of Charlton, Mass., m. James **RANDALL**, of Ashford, Aug. 31, 1845, by Rev. Renssalear O. Putney, North Ashford	5	95
RAZE, RAZEE, Amos, of Bellingham, Mass., m. Hannah **SPINK**, of Ashford, July 1, 1839, by Rev. Rueben Torrey, of Eastford	5	71
Emeline, m. Thomas P. **BABCOCK**, Dec. 23, 1814	6	23
READ, REED, Alce, m. Elihu **CHAFFEE**, Aug. 31, 1806	4	100
Allethere, m. Sam[ue]ll **PARRY**, Nov. 18, 1758	1	106
Augustia Villars, d. Daniel & Augusta, b. Feb. 13, 1799	4	282
Benjamin, m. Mary **WILLSON**, Aug. 19, 1722	A	6
Benjamin, s. Benjamin & Mary, b. May 15, 1723	A	7

	Vol.	Page
READ, REED, (cont.)		
Benjamin, Jr., m. Lydia **KING**, Aug. 26, 1747	3	99
Benj[ami]n, s. Benj[ami]n & Lydia, b. June 6, 1759 ; d. Dec. 6, 1759	3	99
Celinda, see under Syllinda		
Daniel, s. Matthew & Dorothy, b. Jan. 11, 1779	4	36
Daniel, m. Aurgusta **FENTON**, July 5, 1798	4	282
Daniel, m. Mrs. Salome **DUNHAM**, b. of Ashford, Sept. 13, 1848, by Charles Peabody	5	103
Daniel, farmer, ae 70, of Ashford, m. 2d w. Saloma **DUNHAM**, ae 60, Sept. 27, 1848, by Rev. Charles Peabody	5	136-7
Daniel B., m. Amanda **KNOWLTON**, b. of Ashford, Mar. 27, last, [1825], by Ezekiel Skinner	5	18
Daniel Bardine, s. Daniel & Augustia, b. Feb. 6, 1801	4	282
David, s. Mat[t]hew & Dorothy, b. Jan. 29, 1784	4	36
Dorothy, Mrs., of Norwich, m. Rev. Timothy **ALLEN**, of Ashford, Jan. 6, 1761, by Rev. Peter Powers, Newent Norwich	3	20
Eliza, d. Daniel & Augustia, b. July 2, 1807	4	282
Eliza, m. Benjamin R. **SKINNER**, b. of Ashford, June 13, last, [1827], by Rev. Ezekiel Skinner	5	28
Elizebath, m. Benjamin **RUSSEL[L]**, 3rd, Oct. 11, 1750, by Rev. John Bass	2	22
Emeline, d. Matthew & Lydia, b. Feb. 10, 1825	6	22
Filenda, d. Daniel & Augustia, b. Nov. 5, 1802	4	282
Frances, d. Matthew & Lydia, b. Feb. 3, 1819	6	22
Hannah, m. Abel **SIMONS**, Dec. 21, 1747	1	67
Hannah, m. Abel **SEMONS**, Dec. 21. 1747	2	68
Hannah, d. Benjamin & Lydia, b. July 16, 1753	3	99
James, s. Benj[ami]n & Lydia, b. Oct. 10, 1751	3	99
John, s. Benj[ami]n & Lydia, b. Feb. 26, 1750 ; d. Oct. 5, 1755	3	99
Loes, d. Benj[ami]n & Lydia, b. Sept. 23, 1756	3	99
Lydia, d. Benj[ami]n & Lydia, b. Oct. 14, 1762	3	99
Martha Jane, d. Daniel & Augustia, b. Oct. 22, 1818	4	282
Mary, w. Benjamin & d. of Dea Isa[a]c **KENDEL**, d. Mar. 27, 1749	1	47
Mary, d. Benj[ami]n & Lydia, b. Oct. 21, 1760	3	99
Mary, d. Ma[t]thew & Dorothy, b. July 14, 1772	4	36
Mary, d. Mat[t]hew, d. Dec. 22, 1775	4	36
Mary Brown, d. Daniel & Augustia, b. Sept. 25, 1804	4	282
Mat[t]hew, s. Mat[t]hew & Dorothy, b. Nov. 3, 1776	4	36
Mercy, m. Thomas **TIFFANY**, Jr., June 11, 1719, by Dan[ie]ll Smith, Justice	1	2
Olive, d. Mat[t]hew & Dorothy, b. Oct. 8, 1781	4	36
Polly, m. Azel **HANKES**, June 1, 1806	4	93
Reuben, s. Matthew & Dorothy, b. Oct. 3, 1774	4	36
Reuben, s. Mat[t]hew, d. Dec. 25, 1775	4	36

	Vol.	Page
READ, REED. (cont.)		
Syllinda, d. Math[t]hew & Dorothy, b. May 25, 1770	4	36
Syllenda, m. Othnial **WOODWARD**, Jan. 27, 1793	4	53
Thankfull, m. Sam[ue]ll **EASTMAN**, Feb. 25, 1742/3	2	32
Tho[ma]s, s. Benj[ami]n & Lydia, b. July 26, 1748	3	99
William Dwight, s. Daniel & Augustia, b. Dec. 17, 1809	4	282
REYNOLDS, Samuel G., m. Eliza **ANTHONY**, [Feb.] 16, [1824],		
by Reuben Torrey, Eastford	5	12
[RHOADES], RHOODES, ROADES, Amasa, m. Lydia S. **ROSS**,		
Sept. [ ], 1824	6	68
Cordelia Jane, d. Amasa & Lydia, b. [ ] 26, 1827	6	68
Jason W., of Chaplin, m. Nancy **FITTS**, of Ashford, Nov. 25,		
1830, by Rev. Ezekiel Skinner	5	40
Lucius Dwight, s. Amasa & Lydia, b. Dec. 21, 1829	6	68
Polly Malinda, d. Amasa & Lydia, b. Jan. 21, 1825	6	68
RICE, Alice, see under Elles		
Deborah, m. Samuel **BE[C]KNAL**, Nov. 13, 1755	4	107
Deborah, m. Sam[ue]ll **BICKNELL**, Nov. 14, 1755	1	105
Eliphalet, s. John & Mary, b. Oct. 24, 1746	1	7
Elizabeth, d. Samuel & Sarah, b. Apr. 19, 1718	A	3
Elisabeth, d. John, b. Aug. 17, 1752, o.s.	1	7
Elles, d. John, d. Mar. 17, 1726/7	1	7
John, s. Sam[ue]ll & Sarah, b. Mar. 29, 1724	A	8
John, m. Mary **EASTMAN**, Oct. 22, 1724	A	9
John, s. John & Mary, b. Apr. 11, 1738	1	7
Mary, w. John, d. Mar. 9, 1754	1	7
Molle, d. John & Mary, b. Apr. 9, 1749	1	7
Philip, s. John & Mary, b. Dec 16, 1732/3	1	7
Rebeckah, d. Samuel & Sarah, b. July 8, 1730	1	15
Samuel, s. John & Mary, b. Nov. 8, 1730	1	7
Sarah, d. John & Mary, b. Jan. 19, 1727/6	A	10
Sarah, d. John & Mary, b. May 3, 1728	1	7
Sarah, d. Samuel & Sarah, b. June 27, 1728	1	15
Sarah, d. John & Mary, b. Jan. 17, 1734/5	1	7
Sarah, m. Jonathan **DEXTER**, Feb. 5, 1751	4	15
Simeon, s. Samuel & Sarah, b. May 4, 1722	A	5
Susannah, d. John & Mary, b. Mar. 22, 1724	A	9
-----, st. b. s. John, b. Apr. 26, 1745	1	7
RICH, Abigail, d. Jonathan & Sarah, b. Oct. 3, 1719	A	6
Betsey, m. Ezra **SOUTHWORTH**, Apr. 22, 1823	6	46
RICHARDS, Abigail C., m. Augustus A. **SPAULDING**, b. of		
Ashford, Nov. 7, 1843, by Francis Williams, Eastford	5	86
Asa, s. Asa & Drusilla, b. Oct. 10, 1782	4	33
Asa, Jr., m. Mary **ASHCRAFT**, Aug. 19, 1804	4	102
Aurel, [s.] Reuben & Olive, b. Nov. 1, 1805	4	79
Becca, d. Asa & Drusilla, b. Dec. 11, 1789	4	33
Cinthia, d. Asa & Drusilla, b. Aug. 31, 1778	4	33
Eliza, d. Moses & Betsey, b. June 25, 1818	6	37

RICHARDS, (cont.)	Vol.	Page
Eliza, m. James J. **SLADE**, b. of Ashford,		
Nov. 3, 1841, by Rev. Cha[rle]s Hyde	5	79
Fanny, d. Asa & Drusilla, b. July 15, 1787	4	33
Fanny, m. James **EATON**, May 1, [ ]	4	97
Harriet A., d. Aug. 22, 1848, ae 2 1/2 y.	5	136-7
Harriet M., of Ashford, m. Lyman **FITTS**, of Pomfret, June 2,		
1847, by Charles Peabody	5	100
Harriet Mariah, d. Moses & Betsey, b. Oct. 16, 1820	6	37
Josiah, s. Asa & Drusilla, b. June 28, 1792	4	33
Lucius, s. Moses & Betsey, b. Nov. 17, 1812	6	37
Lucius, m. Emeline **SIBLEY**, b. of Ashford, [Nov.] 28, [1839],		
by Rev. Reuben Torrey, Eastford	5	72
Lydia, m. W[illia]m Pitt **OLNEY**, b. of Ashford, [Mar.] 17,		
[1834], by Rev. R. Torrey, Eastford	5	53
Matilda, m. William Pitt **OLNEY**, b. of Ashford, [Nov.] 5,		
[1838], by Rev. Reuben Torrey, Eastford	5	69
Moses, m. Betsey **BICKNELL**, Dec. 12, 1811	6	37
Norman, s. Asa, Jr. & Mary, b. Sept. 7, 1805	4	102
Rebecca, see under Becca		
Reuben, s. Asa & Drusilla, b. Oct. 25, 1776	4	33
Reuben, m. Olive **SUMNER**, Sept. 16, 1802	4	79
Sally, d. Asa & Drusilla, b. June 22, 1780	4	33
Sunmer, s. Reuben & Olive, b. Nov, 8, 1803	4	79
Sumner, m. Abigail **BURNHAN**, Mar. 20, 1827 by Rev.		
Reuben Torry, Eastford	5	27
Truman, s. Asa, Jr. & Mary, b. Nov. 15, 1807	4	102
W[illia]m Henry, b. Middletown, res. Ashford, d. Sept. 22,		
1850, ae 7	5	150-1
RICHMOND, Abigail, d. Jared D., & Abigail, b. Nov. 29, 1838	6	78
Andrew, [s. Charles & Hannah], b. Nov. 15, 1819	6	8
Charles, s. Charles & Hannah, b. Feb. 18, 1816	6	8
Eleazer, s. Michael & Polly, b. July 10, 1825	6	7
Emeline Mary Ann Maria, d. Danforth & Clarissa, b. July 4,		
1827	6	75
Emily, d. Michael & Polly, b. May 13, 1821	6	7
Emily, of Westford, m. Dr. John A. **PRESTON**, of		
Southampton, L. I., Sept, 8, 1847, by Rev. H. N. Wilson,		
of Southampton, L. I.	5	101
Emily, ae 24, of Ashford, m. John Augustus **PRESTON**,		
physician, ae 23, b. Ashford, res. Southampton, L. I.,		
Sept. 8, 1847, by Hugh N. Willson	5	128-9
Eunice, m. Capt. Amos **BUGBEE**, b. of Ashford, Apr. 15,		
1822, by Rev. James Grow, of Pomfret	5	6
Eunice, m. Amos **BUGBEE**, Apr. 15, 1822	6	49
Francis Josias, s. J[ared] D., b. July 21, 1834	6	78
Hannah A., [d. Charles & Hannah], b. Sept. 11, 1817	6	8
James, s. Michael & Polly, b. June 3, 1823	6	7
Jared, m. Abigail **PEARL**, b. of Ashford, [June] 5, {1832}, by		

	Vol.	Page
RICHMOND, (cont.)		
Rev. Samuel S. Mallory of Willington	5	48
Jared Dewing, s. Abner & Eunice, b. Mar. 29, 1804	6	8
John, s. Jared D. & Abigail, b. May 19, 1837	6	78
Julette, d. Michael & Polly, b. Jan. 1, 1820	6	7
Juliaette, of Ashford, m. Edwin S. **CHILDS**, of Woodstock, [Aug. 28, 1843,], by D. Bullard	5	85
Mary, d. Michael & Polly, b. Jan. 1, 1816	6	7
Mary Ann, d. Abner & Eunice, b. Sept. 12, 1806	6	8
Mary Ann, of Ashford, m. Ethan **PAUL**, of Union, May 18, 1826, by N[i]ch. B. Brardsey, Union	5	22
Michael, m. Polly **BYLES**, Mar. 3, 1814	6	7
Phebe, of Ashford, m. George **COLLINS**, of Wilbraham, Mass., Nov. 30, 1820, by Rev. Philo Judson	6	26
Philo, s. Jared D. & Abigail, b. Jan. 16, 1836	6	78
Susan, d. Abner & Eunice, b. Apr. 27, 1811	6	8
Susan, d. Jared D. & Abigail, b. Apr. 6, 1833	6	78
Susa[n] P., of Ashford, m. Amasa **CARPENTER**, of Woodstock, Oct. 7, 1830, by Rev. Samuel Backus	5	40
Thompson, s. Michael & Polly, b. Nov. 29, 1817	6	7
Thompson, farmer, ae 33, b. Ashford, res. Wisconsin, m. 2d w. Hannah P. **PALMER**, ae 35, Apr. 28, 1850, by Lyman Leffingwell	5	142-3
-----, s. Michael & Sally, b. Jan. 12, 1815 ; d. Feb. 3, 1815	6	7
RIDER, Anna, of Ashford, m. Adin **UNDERWOOD**, of Union, Feb. 6, 1843, by J. M. Bidwell	5	84
Hannah, of Ashford, m. Samuel **RIDER**, of Austinburg, Ohio, Sept. 27, 1821, by Rev. William Storrs	5	5
Jerremiah Post, m. Betsey **BROWN**, b. of Ashford, Nov. 30, 1820, by Rev. Isaac Hall	5	1
Jeremiah Post, m. Betsey **BROWN**, b. of Ashford, Nov. 30, 1820, by Rev. Isaac Hall	6	26
Pamelia, m. Ezekiel E. **WYMAN**, b. of Ashford, Feb. 1, 1843, by J. M. Bidwell	5	83
Samuel, of Austinburg, Ohio, m. Hannah **RIDER**, of Ashford, Sept. 27, 1821, by Rev. William Storrs	5	5
RIGBE, Dorothy, m Peltiah **BUGBE[E]**, Nov. 4, 1747, by Rev. Mr. John Bass	2	23
RINGE, Jonathan K., m. Jane **GRIGGS**, [Jan.] 12, [1826], by Rev. Reuben Torrey, Eastford	5	21
Samuel, s. Jonathan K. & Joanna D., b. Nov. 11, 1826	6	64
·Thomas, s. Jonathan & Joanna D., b. Mar. 20, 1828	6	64
RISS, [see under **ROSS**]		
ROATH, Alice R., m. Hosea C. **ROBBINS**, Nov. 21, 1819	6	41
ROBBINS, ROBINS, Abigail, d. Clark & Zilpha, b. July 15, 1792	4	115
Alice, d. Hosea C. & Alice, b. Mar. 1, 1827	6	41
Alice, d. Sept. 13, 1833, ae 33 y.	6	41
Alice, of Ashford, m. Nathan D. **HODGKINS**, of Eastford, Jan. 28, 1850, by Rev. Ezekiel Skinner	5	104

	Vol.	Page
ROBBINS, ROBINS, (cont.)		
Amasa s, Clark & Zilpha, b. Jan. 28, 1786	4	115
Amas, s. Clark, d. Aug. 3, 1807	4	115
Azuba, d. Tho[ma]s & Azuba, b. Feb. 22, 1786	4	224
Benjamin, s. Joseph & Luce, b. June 11, 1764	2	63
Benjamin, m. Lois **CARPENTER**, Oct. 21, 1784	4	237
Benjamin, s. Benj[ami]n & Lois, b. July 13, 1785	4	237
Benj[ami]n, s. Benj[ami]n & Lois, b. May 14, 1790	4	237
Betty, m. Francis **CURTISS**, Nov. 17, 1768	4	33
Carthrine, d. David & Carthrine, b. Jan. 24, 1762	3	54
Clark, s. Joseph & Luce, b. Sept. 10, 1759	2	63
Clark, m. Zilpha **KEYES**, Nov. 16, 1780	4	115
Clark, s. Clark & Zilpha, b. Feb. 28, 1796	4	115
Sinthe, d. Tho[ma]s & Azuba, b. Feb.7, 1793	4	224
Syril, s. Tho[ma]s & Azuba, b. Jan. 26, 1784	4	224
David, Jr., m. Lucy **KNOX**, Nov. 6, 1771	4	86
David, Jr., d. Dec. 4, 1776	4	86
David, s. Clark & Zilpha, b. Feb. 3, 1782	4	115
David, s. Samuel & Miriam, b. Oct. 27, [ ]	4	7
Ebenezer, s. Ebenezer & Zuriah, b. Oct. 23, 1825	6	63
Ebenezer, of Chaplin, m. Betsey **UTLEY**, of Ashford, Dec. 22,		
1833, by Rev.. L. S. Hough, of Chaplin	5	52
Elisha, m. Lucy Ann **BURNHAM**, b. of Ashford, May 1, 1842,		
by Rev. Charles C. Barnes	5	81
Elisha Keyes, s. Hosea C. & Alice, b. July 21, 1820	6	41
Elizabeth, d. Thomas & Azuba, b. Feb.7, 1782	4	224
Elvira, of Ashford, m. Joseph F. **DAWLEY**, manufacturer, b.		
R. I., res. Willington, Mar. 24, 1850, by Washington		
Munger	5	142-3
Ephraim, s. Clark & Zilpha, b. Mar. 21, 1788	4	115
Easter, d. Joseph, b. July 29, 1758 ; d. Aug. 27, 1758	2	63
Esther, d. John & Hannah, b. Sept. 18, 1773	4	45
Esther, w. Ebenezer, d. Feb. 26, 1817	6	63
Esther, d. Ebenezer & Zuriah, b. May 20, 1820	6	63
Esther, m. George **TYLER**, b. of Ashford, Sept. 18, 1839, by		
Rev. Alvan Underwood	5	71
Fanny E., of Ashford, m. William **ROWAND**, of Eastford,		
Dec. 27, 1847, by Rev. Ezekiel Skinner	5	102
Fanny Emeline, d. Hosea C. & Alice, b. Apr. 21, 1829	6	41
Hezekiah, s. Benj[ami]n & Lois, b. Dec. 18, 1786	4	237
Hosea C., m. Alice R. **ROATH**, Nov. 21, 1819	6	41
Hosea C., m. Sabrina **JAMES**, b. of Ashford, Nov. 9, 1834, by		
Amos Babcock	5	55
Hosea Clark, s. Clark & Zilpha, b. Jan. 10, 1798	4	115
Hosea Clark, s. Clark & Zilpha, b. Jan. 10, 1799	4	115
Hosea Dexter, [s. Hosea C. & Alice], b. May 13, 1831	6	41
Huldah, d. John & Hannah, b. Mar. 25, 1772	4	45
Ira, s. Benj[ami]n & Lois, b. Feb. 8, 1794 ; d. Feb. 26, 1794	4	237

	Vol.	Page
ROBBINS, ROBINS, (cont.)		
[Job*], m. Cynth[i]a [ ],Apr. 2, 1767 (*Supplied from the index)	4	6
John, s. Joseph & Luce, b. Apr. 12, 1749	2	63
Joseph, s. Joseph & Luse, b. May 2, 1747 ; d. Apr. 27, 1759	2	63
Joseph, s. Benj[ami]n & Lois, b. Oct. 9, 1788	4	237
Laura, d. Hosea C. & Alice, b. Nov. 11, 1822	6	41
Laura, of Ashford, m. Albert **MORSE**, of Union, Sept. 26, 1847, by Ezekiel Skinner	5	101
Lester, s. Benj[ami]n & Lois, b. June 11, 1793	4	237
Lois, d. Benj[ami]n & Lois, b. Sept. 18, 1792	4	237
Lucinda, d. Tho[ma]s & Azuba, b. Apr. 12, 1795	4	224
Luce, d. Joseph & Luce, b. Aug. 22, 1750	2	63
Lucy, d. Tho[ma]s & Azuba, b. Feb. 23, 1788	4	224
Lucy, d. May [ ], 1850, ae 18	5	144-5
Lydia, d. John & Hannah, b. Sept. 7, 1770	4	45
Marsha, [twin with Marshel], d. Clark, & Zilpha, b. July 29, 1794 ; d. July 6, 1794 (sic)	4	115
Marshel, [twin with Marsha], s. Clark & Zilpha, b. July 29, 1794	4	115
Mary, d. Ebenezer & Esther, b. Feb. 24, 1817	6	63
Mary Jerusha, d. Ebenezer & Zuriah, b. Oct. 26, 1822	6	63
Nathan, s. Joseph, b. Dec. 17, 1753	2	63
Polley, d. Clark & Zilpha, b. May 24, 1790	4	115
[Pr]ysilla, m. David **CHAFFE[E]**, Nov. 6, 1761	3	128
Pursia, d. Clark & Zilpha, b. Jan. 27, 1784	4	115
Rufus, s. Ebenezer & Esther, b. Apr. 25, 1816	6	63
Samuel, s. David, Jr. & Lucy, b. Feb. 25, 1775	4	86
Samuel, m. Miriam **JAMES**, [ ] 9, 1797	4	7
Sarah, d. David, Jr. & Lucy, b. Jan. 20, 1773 ; d. Sept. 27, 1775	4	86
Sarah, m. John Henery **SAGERS**, June 20, 1781	4	231
Sophia, d. Tho[ma]s & Azuba, b. Nov. 22, 1797	4	224
Thomas, s. Joseph & Luce, b. Aug. 29, 1756	2	63
Thomas, m. Azuba **SQUIRE**, May 10, 1781	4	224
Thomas, s. Tho[ma]s & Azuba, b. Nov. 30, 1790	4	224
Thomas S., of Weathersfield, m. Martha C. **SEARS**, of Ashford, Aug. 29, 1832, by Francis Wood, Clerk, Willington	5	48
Timothy, s. Joseph & Luce, b. Mar. 11, 1752 ; d. Apr. 23, 1759	2	63
William, s. Hosea C. & Alice, b. Oct. 31, 1824	6	41
Zilpha, d. Clark & Zilpha, b. Sept. 2, 1802	4	115
Zilpha, of Ashford, m. Marvin **HIBBARD**, of Mansfield, Aug. 30, 1826, by Rev. Philo Judson	5	23
----ail, d. David & Carthrine, [b.] [ ] 14, 1759	1	110
----, [child of Job] & Cynth[i]a, [b.] Jan. 7, 1768	4	6
----, [child of Job] & Synth[i]a, b. Aug. 1, 1771	4	6
----, [child of Job] & Synth[i]a, b. June 25, 1773	4	6
----, [child of Job] & Santh[i]a, b. June 23, 1775	4	6

	Vol.	Page
ROBBINS, ROBINS, (cont.)		
----, [child of Job] & Synth[i]a, b. May 6, 1777	4	6
----, [child of Job] & Synth[i]a, b. May 24, 1779	4	6
ROBINSON, Amasa, m. Marcia **BOUTWELL**, b. of Ashford, last		
evening, [June 1, 1835], by Rev. Job Hall	5	56
Anna, d. Timothy & Anna, b. [ ] 24, 1777	4	98
Edwin, [of] Mobile, Ala., m. Sarah W. **PALMER**, of Ashford,		
last evening, [June 23, 1836], by Rev. J. Hall	5	60
Gurdon, m. Lois **LYON**, Nov. 30, 1808	6	15
Gurdon, m. Betsey **KNOX**, Sept. 14, 1817	6	15
Joshua, s. Gurdon & Lois, b. Feb. 27, 1811	6	15
Levina, m. Samuel **WALKER**, Nov. 25, 1803	4	68
Lois, w. Gurdon, d. Mar. 12 1817	6	15
Lydia, d. Timothy & Anna, b. Oct. 27, [ ]	4	98
Mehetable, m. Stephen **BUTLER**, Mar. 6, 178[ ]	4	15
Nanna, m. Asaph **SMITH**, Jr., Jan. 3, 1797	4	92
Reuben, of Mansfield, m. Anna **CHAFFEE**, of Ashford, Feb.		
13, 1822, by Rev. W[illia]m Storrs	5	5
Thankful, m. Elijah **FARNAM**, Aug. 4, 1793	4	273
[ ]illiam, s. Amasa & Harmony, b. Oct. 15, 1792	4	8
----iah, d. Amasa & Harmony, b. Aug. 25, 1790	4	8
----er, s. Amasa & Harmony, b. Oct. 15, 1796	4	8
----, d.Timothy & Anna, b. Feb. 2, 17[ ]	4	98
ROCKWELL, Maria, m. Horace **STONE**, b. of Sturbridge, Mass.,		
Oct. 25, 1844, by Francis Williams	5	91
ROGERS, Alva, s. Moses & Lois, b. June 18, 1776	4	104
Alva, m. Desire **EATON**, Sept. 8, 1803	4	105
Asa, of Willington, m. Prescilla **WHITON**, of Ashford, May		
21, 1823, by Rev. W[illia]m Storrs	5	10
Ishmael, s. Ichabond & Persala, b. Mar. 9, 1745/6	2	44
Jarvis, s. Alva & Desire, b. Sept. 13, 1805	4	90
Joseph, d. Ichabond, & Persella, b. Aug. 4, 1744	2	44
Leiscter Holt, s. Alva & Desire, b. Jan. 5, 1804	4	90
Lucia, d. Moses & Lois, b. May 28, 1771	4	104
Mary Humphrey, d. Alva & Desire, b. Sept. 10, 1807	4	90
Olive, m. Abel **DOW**, Sept. 28, 1784	4	267
Sarah, d. Ichabond & Persala, b. Feb. 12, 1747/8	2	44
Sarah, m. Stephen **CHANDLER**, July 3, 1790	3	3
----, [child of Jonah] & Deliverance, b. July 18, 1767	4	8
----, [child of Jonah] & Deliverence, b. Dec. 18, 1768	4	8
----, [child of Jonah] & Deliverance, b. Sept. 19, 1770	4	8
---h, [child of Jonah] & Deliverance, b. Sept. 14, 1772	4	8
ROOD, Keziah, m. Jonathan **JENENS**, May 10, 1742, by Rev. Mr.		
Hale	1	65
ROSE, Isreal G., Rev., of Canterbury, m. Percey **CLARK**, of		
Ashford, [Nov.] 22, [1826], by Rev. Reuben Torrey,		
Eastford	5	25
Mary R., m. Gilbert **SPAULDING** b. of Eastford, Nov. 11,		

	Vol.	Page
ROSE, (cont.)		
1844, by Francis Williams, Eastford	5	92
ROSS, [see also **ROUSE** and **RUSS**], Abraham, s. Joseph &		
Presilla, b. May 12, 1713, in Framingham	A	5
Ebenezer S., of Chaplin, m. Elizabeth [ ], of Ashford, Dec.		
1, [1824], by Ezekiel Skinner	5	17
Ebenezer S., of Mansfield, m. Lydia Ann **IDE**, of Ashford,		
Mar. 22, 1843, by Rev. Cha[rle]s Hyde	5	84
Jerusha, d. Joseph & Presilla, b. Mar. 30, 1722	A	7
John, s. Joseph & Pressilla, b. July 19, 1716	A	5
John, of Chaplin, m. Mrs. Almira **JAMES**, of Ashford, Mar.		
23, 1851, by Rev. Ralph V. Lyon	5	108
Joseph, s. Joseph & Presilla, b. Aug. 2, 1710, in Andover	A	5
Lydia S., m. Amasa **RHOODES**, Sept. [ ], 1824	6	68
Presillah, d. Joseph & Presilla, b. Apr. 21, 1720	A	6
William, s. Samuel & Sarah, b. Mar. 26, 1726 (Written		
"RISS")	A	5
William, of Chaplin, m. Marinda **GRANT**, of Ashford, [Apr.]		
8, [1832], by Anson S. Atwood	5	47
ROUSE, [see also **ROSS** and **RUSS**], John, of Groton, m. Thirza		
MASSBEY, of Ashford, Apr. 1, 1821, by Thomas Dow,		
J. P.	5	2
ROWAND, William, of Eastford, m. Fanny E. **ROBBINS**, of		
Ashford, Dec. 27, 1847, by Rev. Ezekiel Skinner	5	102
ROYCE, Abigail, m. Charles **BRANDON**, Apr. 1, 1773	4	90
Emily Josephine, d. Harrison, silk manufacturer, of Manchester		
, ae 31, & Louisa, ae 22, b. June 29, 1848	5	126-7
Louisa Isabel, d. Harrison, shoemaker, ae 33, of Willington,		
& Louisa, ae 23, b. Jan. 26, 1850	5	142-3
RUSS, [see also **ROUSE** and **ROSS**], Abel, s. Timothy & Deborah,		
b. Aug. 8, 1783	4	83
Abigail, d. John & Rebeckah, b. Dec. 27, 1741	1	58
Abraham, m. Hannah **OWEN**, Oct. 25, 1738, by Rev. Mr.		
James Hale	1	66
Abraham, s. Abraham & Hannah, b. Oct. 29, 1741 ; d. Jan. 6,		
1741/2	1	66
Abraham, s. Abraham & Hannah, b. May 29, 1745	1	66
Almira, d. Asa & Abigail, b. Feb. 26, 1792	4	27
Amaziah, s. Asa **RUSS** & Sabra **SNOW**, b. May 19, 1789*		
(*Entry crossed out)	2	74
Amaziah, m. Tryphena **FARNHAM**, Nov. 10, 1811	4	26
Amy, d. Abraham & Hannah, b. June 10, 1749	1	66
Anis, s. John & Rebacah, b. Feb. 24, 1746/7	1	58
Anis, d. John & Rebeckah, b. Feb. 9, 1748/9	1	58
Annis, m. John **HENDEE**, July [ ]	4	287
Asa, s. Azari[a]h & Marcy, b. Aug. 28, 1762	3	70
Asa, m. Abigail **PORTER**, Sept. [ ], 1790	4	27
Asa, d. Mar. 26, 1838	4	27
Azariah, s. Abraham & Hannah, b. June 19, 1739	1	66

RUSS, (cont.)	Vol.	Page
Azariah, m. Marcy **BENJAMIN**, May 21, 1761	3	66
Benjamin, s. Joseph, Jr. & Patian[c]e, b. Apr. 3, 1736	1	49
Benjamin, s. Joseph, Jr., d. Oct. 11, 1736	1	49
Benj[ami]n, s. Joseph & Patian[c]e, b. Oct. 16, 1745	1	50
Benjamin, s. Timothy & Deborah, b. Oct. 8, 1773	4	83
Bethiah, d. Azariah & Mary, b. Aug. 3, 1771	3	70
Bethiah, [twin with Polley], d. Asa & Abigail, b. Aug. 22, 1795 ; d. Jan. 14, 1822	4	27
Bethiah, d. Asa, d. Jan. 14, 1822	4	27
Charity, d. Joseph & Patian[c]e, b. Feb. 13, 1743/4	1	36
Dan, of Chaplin, m. Mary Ann **BROWN**, of Ashford, Nov. 30, 1837, by Amos Babcock	5	66
Daniel, s. Abraham & Hannah, b. Jan. 21, 1756	1	90
Eleazer, s. Azariah & Marcy, b. Feb. 10, 1783	3	70
Elizebath, d. Abraham & Hannah, b. Aug. 19, 1743	1	66
Elezebeth, d. Abraham & Hannah, b. Mar. 29, 1747 ; d. Aug. 19, 1753	1	66
Easther, w. Joseph, Jr., d. Apr. 22, 1734	1	49
Hannah, [twin with Priscel[l]a], d. Abraham & Hannah, b. Feb. 23, 1742/3	1	66
Hannah, d. Abraham, d. May 15, 1756	1	95
Hulda, d. Azariah & Marcy, b. Jan. 16, 1765	3	70
Hulda had s. Silvanus. b. June 5, 1795	4	111
Jarusha, m. Ele[a]zer **OWEN**, Feb. 20, 1774, by Rev. Mr. John Bass	2	28
John, m. Rebeckah **WOOD**, Nov. 3, 1737, by Rev. Mr. Eleazer Williams	1	58
John, s. John & Rebac[c]ah, b. May 21, 1745	1	58
Joseph, Jr., m. Easter **PROCTER**, Jan. 27, 1731/2, by Rev. James Hale	1	36
Joseph, s. Joseph, Jr. & Est[h]er, b. Nov. 17, 1732	1	36
Joseph, Jr., m. Patien[c]e **BALDWEN**, Jan. 22, 1734/5	1	49
Mary, d. John & Reback[ah], [b.] Oct. 22, 1743	1	58
Nancy, d. Asa & Abigail, b. Mar. 9, 1799	4	27
Nancy, m. Elias L. **UPTON**, b. of Ashford, May 12, 1839, by Rev. Alvin Bennett	5	70
Patian[c]e, d. Joseph & Patian[c]e, b. Aug. 13, 1742	1	49
Polley, [twin with Bethiah], d. Asa & Abigail, b. Aug. 22, 1795	4	27
Priscel[l]a, [twin with Hannah], d. Abraham & Hannah, b. Feb. 23, 1742/3	1	66
Reuben, s. Ezraiah & Mary, b. Apr. 27, 1774	3	70
Ruth, d. Azariah & Mary, b. July 6, 1769	3	70
Salla, m. Simeon **BEMISS**, July 26, 1793	4	277
Sarah, d. Azariah & Marcy, b. Mar. 10, 1777	3	70
Simbroniss, s. Azariah & Mary, b. July 6, 1767	3	70
Silvanus, s. Hulda, b. June 5, 1795	4	111
Sibbel, d. Timothy & Deborah, b. [ ] 28, 1774	4	83
Weltha, d. Asa & Abigail, b. June 3, 1794	4	27

	Vol.	Page
RUSSELL, RUSSEL, Abigail, m. Seth **LYON**, Mar. 29, 1725/6	A	10
Abigail, d. John & Allice, b. Sept. 26, 1753	2	48
Abigail, s. Ezekiel & Tabitha, b. May 19, 1755	2	44
Abilene, d. John & Allice, b. Apr. 12, 1764	2	48
Anna, d. Joseph & Hannah, b. June 24, 1758	2	24
Anna, d. Benj[ami]n & Pheba, b. Nov. 25, 1770	3	47
Benjamin, m. Sarah **PARRY**, July 13, 1724	A	8
Benjamin, s. Benj[ami]n, Jr. & Sarah, b. Jan. 26, 1728/9	1	17
Benjamin, 3rd, m. Elizebath **RE[E]D**, Oct. 11, 1750, by Rev.		
John Bass	2	22
Benj[ami]n, s. Joseph & Hannah, b. Nov. 26, 1753	2	24
Benjamin, d. Oct. 5, 1754	1	17
Benjamin, Jr., d. Oct. 7, 1754	1	17
Benjamin, s. Benjamin & Elizabeth, b. July 30, 1755	2	22
Benj[ami]n, 3rd, m. Pheebe **SMITH**, Feb. Last day, 1757	1	98
Synth[i]a, d. John & Allice, b. Jan. 22, 1771	3	46
Synthy, d. John, Jr. & Rebeckah, b. Oct. 5, 1772	4	47
Cynth[i]a, m Benj[ami]n **JAMES**, Jr., Feb. 20, 1794	4	37
David, s. Benj[ami]n & Pheebe, b. June 10, 1758	1	101
Ebenezer, s. John & Allice, b. Feb. 15, 1773	3	46
Eleasar, s. Benj[ami]n & Phebe, b. Nov. 15, 1761	3	47
Elijah, s. Benj[ami]n & Phebe, b. Oct. 5, 1768	3	47
Elisha, s. Joseph & Hannah, b. Sept. 29, 1746	1	58
Elizabeth, d. Benjamin, 3rd & Elizabeth, b. July 28,1751	2	22
Elezabeth, d. Benj[ami]n, 3rd, & [Elizabeth], d. Aug. 27,		
1754, o.s.	2	22
Elisabeth, w. Benj[ami]n, d. Dec. 6, 1756	1	98
Elizabeth, d. John & Allice, b. Jan. 13, 1760	2	48
Ezekiel, s. Benjamin & Sarah, b. Jan. 24, 1724/5 ;		
d. Mar. 3,, following	A	9
Ezekiel, s. Ezekiel & Tabitha, b. June 22, 1751	2	44
Hannah, d. Benj[ami]n, Jr. & Sarah, b. Mar. 24, 1725/26 ; d.		
same day	1	17
Hannah, m. John **HUMPHRY**, Dec. 4, 1727, by James Hale	1	1
Hannah, d. Joseph & Han[n]ah, b. June 8, 1749	2	24
Hannah, d. John, Jr. & Rebeckah, b. June 8, 1768	4	47
Israel, s. John 2d, & Elisabeth, b. June 10, 1791	4	228
John, s. Benjamin, Jr. & Sarah, b. Oct. 11, 1730	1	17
John, s. Joseph & Hannah, b. Oct. 16, 1742	1	58
John, Jr., m. Rebeckah **WILLSON**, May 1, 1766	4	47
John, m. Allis **LYON**, July 10, 1750	2	48
John, s. John & Allice, b. Apr. 3, 1758	2	48
John, Jr., m. Elisabeth [ ], Jan. 23, 1781	4	228
Jonathan, s. John Jr. & Rebeckah, b. May 21, 1770	4	47
Joseph, s. Benjamin & Mary, b. June 5, 1717	A	1
Joseph, m. Hannah **LINKHORN**, May 13, 1742, by Rev. Mr.		
James Hale	1	58
Josiah, s. Joseph & Hannah, b. May 7, 1756	2	24

	Vol.	Page
RUSSELL, RUSSEL, (cont.)		
Justin, s. John, Jr. & Elisabeth, b. Sept. 18, 1787	4	228
Levi, s. John & Allice, b. May 6, 1776	3	46
Levi, s. John, Jr. & Elisabeth, b. Nov. 25, 1782	4	228
Mary, d. Benjamin, Jr. & Sarah, b. July 8, 1733	1	17
Mary, d. Joseph & Hannah, b. Oct. 3, 1744	1	58
Mary, m. Inglesbee **WORK**, Aug. 8, 1750, by Mr. Bass	2	21
Mary, m. Isaac **KENDAL**, Jr., July 3, 1760	3	40
Mary, Mrs., m. Thomas **LEWIS**, b. of Ashford, Nov. 18, 1762, in Woodstock, by Stephen Williams	3	75
Mary had s. Nathan, b. July 30, 1773	2	24
Mehitibal, d. John & Allis, b. Nov. 21, 1751	2	48
Nabby, d. John, 3d*, & Elisabeth, b. July 28, 1789 (*John, Jr.?)	4	228
Nathan, s. Joseph & Hannah, b. Apr. 7, 1751	2	24
Nathan, s. Mary, b. July 30, 1773	2	24
Parley, s. John & Rebeckah, b. Oct. 28, 1777	4	47
Phebe, d. Benj[ami]n & Phebe, b. Dec. 16, 1766	3	47
Phebe, m. John **CLARK**, Nov. 25, 1779	4	109
Polley, d. John, Jr. & Elisabeth, b. Nov. 16, 1784	4	228
Robert, s. Ezekill & Tabitha, b. May 15, 1757	2	44
Sally, d. Benjamin & Phebe, b. Feb. 28, 1774	3	47
Sarah, d. Benjamin, Jr. & Sarah, b. Feb. 26, 1726/7	A	10
Sarah, d. Benjamin, 3rd, & Elizebet[h], b. June 17, 1753 ; d. Oct. 8, 1754	2	22
Sarah, d. John & Allice, b. Jan. 11, 1756	2	48
Sarah, w. Benj[ami]n, Jr., d. Dec. 9, 1786	1	17
Smith, s. James & Lydia, b. Nov. 14, 1786	4	243
Stephen, s. Benj[ami]n & Phebe, b. Jan. 28, 1765	3	47
Tabitha, d. Ezeki[e]l & Tabitha, b. Aug. 19, 1749	2	44
Thomas, s. John & Allice, b. Sept. 24, 1761	2	48
Zurviah, m. Izra **SMITH**, Sept. 27, 1738	1	68
SABIN, SABINE, Benj[ami]n, m. Elisabeth **BURNHAM**, May 10, 1763 ; d. Sept. 12, 1783	4	34
Elisabeth, d. Benj[ami]n & Elisabeth, b. Oct. 19, 1769	4	34
Elisabeth, m. Smith **KENDAL**, Feb. 9, 1786	4	44
J. May, of Woodstock, m. Mrs. Eunice **THOMPSON**, of Eastford, Jan. 5, 1846, by Francis Williams	5	96
SAGERS, John, s. John Henery & Sarah, b. Feb. 1, 1782	4	231
John Henery, m. Sarah **ROB[B]INS**, June 20, 1781	4	231
SALTER, Orrin, s. William & Sarah, b. Mar. 28, 1798	4	244
Polly, d. William & Sarah, b. Dec. 4, 1795	4	19
SAMSON Alphonso Delestrain, s. Charles & Lydia, b. Dec. 10, 1813	6	2
Charles, m. Lydia **BARNES**, Mar. 4, 1813	6	2
Hannah, of Ashford, m. Elkanan **PENNIMAN**, of Woodstock, [May] 12, [1831], by Rev. Reuben Torrey, Eastford	5	43
Lydia, w. Charles, d. Jan. 23, 1814	6	2

	Vol.	Page
SANGER, C[h]loe, d. Jonathan & Lydia, b. Aug. 2, 1748	2	78
[E]unis, d. Nath[anie]ll & Mary, b. Apr. 16, 1745	2	51
Hannah, m. Hezekiah **ELDRIDGE,** Dec. 25, 1786	3	129
Mary, d. Jonathan & Lydia, b. Dec. 15, 1745	2	78
Nathaniel, s. Jonathan & Lydia, b. July 17, 1754	2	78
Zeruiah, d. Jonathan & Lydia, b. Mar. 20, 1744	2	78
Zerviah, m. Jonathan **KNOWLTON,** Apr. 4, 1802	4	38
SARKIS, Lemuel, m. Nancy **HUNTINGTON,** Aug. 6, 1837, by		
Rodolphus Lanphear	5	65
SAUNDERS, Abigail, m. Isaac **LOOMIS** b. of Ashford, Apr. 24,		
1827, by Rev. Levi Wood, Westford	5	27
Asael, s. [E]sek & Abigail, b. May 21, 1781	4	290
Aurilla, of Ashford, m. Clark **WILBUR,** of Brooklyn, Apr. 14,		
1824, by Rev. W[illia]m Storrs	5	14
[D]eborah, d. Esek & [A]bigail, b. Dec. 4, 1779	4	290
Delia, d. Stephen & Sophronia, b. Feb. 3, 1824	6	57
Esek, s. Esek & [Ab]igail, b. Dec. 28, 1784	4	290
Freelove, m. John **LOOMIS,** Jr., Apr. 23, 1806	4	264
Maria, d. [Esek & Abig]ail, b. Feb. 17, 1799	4	290
Orilla, d. Esek, b. July 2, 1797	4	290
Philip, s. [Esek] & Abigail, b. May 15, 1789	4	290
Sally, d. Esek & [Abigail], b. Mar. 28, 1788	4	290
Sophronia, d. Stephen & Sophronia, b. Dec. 10, 1825	6	57
Stephen, m. Sophronia **WHITON,** b. of Ashford, Apr. 10,		
1823, by Rev. W[illia]m Storrs	5	9
Stephen Osborn, s. Stephen & Sophronia, b. June 16, 1829	6	57
-----, d. Esek & Abigail, [b.] Apr. 21, 1783	4	290
---ustus, s. Esek & Abigail, b. [ ] 14, 1786	4	290
----, s. Esek & Abigail, b. [ ], [ ]0, 1793	4	290
----, [d.] Esek & Abigail, b. July [ ]	4	290
----, [child] of [Esek] & Abigail, b. [ ]	4	290
SAVERY, Levie, of Union, m. Sophia **MOULTAN,** of Ashford,		
May 18, 1828, by Nehemiah Bardsley (**MOUTTAN?**)	5	31
SAWTELLE Amaziah, of Hartford, m. Abigail **BOSWORTH,** of		
Ashford, May 6, 1829, by Rev. Philo Judson	5	35
SCARBOROUGH, SCARBROUGH, SCARBROW,		
SCARBROTH, Abigail, d. Stpehen & Marg[a]ret, b. July 29, 1754	2	42
Abigail, d. Sept. 26, 1755	1	90
Abigail, d. Joseph & Lydia, b. June 8, 1788	4	278
Abigail, m. William **ALBRO,** b. of Ashford, [Mar.] 8, 1829, by		
Rev. Reuben Torrey, Eastford	5	33
Chester, s. Stephen & Mary, b. Mar. 29, 1788	4	32
Danforth, s. Stephen & Mary, b. Aug. 24, 1799	4	32
Dorothy, d. John & Dorothy, b. Oct. 25, 1735	1	46
Dorothy, m. John **GREEGS,** Dec. 26, 1738, by Lecester		
Grosvener, J. P.	1	71
Dorothy, m. Ezekiel **BADGER,** Apr. 3, 1755, by Mr. Stephen		
Williams, of Woodstock	1	88

SCARBOROUGH, SCARBROUGH, SCARBROW,	Vol.	Page
SCARBROTHE, (cont.)		
Elias, s. Stephen & Mary, b. Mar. 8, 1786	4	32
Elisha, s. Stephen & Marg[a]ret, b. Apr. 15, 1763	2	42
Elisha, m. Prudence TUCKER, Apr. 21, 1791	4	279
Hannah, d. Stephen & Marg[a]ret, b. Sept. 18, 1744	2	42
Hannah, d. Elisha & Prudence, b. Dec. 7, 1791	4	279
Huldah, m. Horace CONVERSE, b. of Ashford, Sept. 3, [1837], by Rev. Elias Sharpe, at the home of Alfred Brown, Westford Society	5	65
James, s. Joseph & Lydia, b. May 10, 1785	4	278
John, s. Stephen & Marg[a]ret, b. Feb. 12, 1745/6	2	42
John, s. Stephen & Mary, b. July 19, 1792	4	32
John, s. Elisha & Prudence, b. Aug. 19, 1804	4	279
Josep[h], s. Stephen & Marg[ar]it, b. Nov. 26, 1756	2	42
Joseph, m. Lydia HYMES, Jan. 2, 1783	4	278
Joseph, s. Joseph & Lydia, b. Sept. 1, 1794	4	278
Joseph P., of Eastford, m. Esther W. YOUNG, of Ashford, June 16, 1851, by Jared D. Richmond, J. P.	5	106
Joseph P., shoemaker, ae 30, b. Ashford, res. Eastford, m. Esther W. YOUNG, June 16, 1851, by J. D. Richmond	5	148-9
Lodhia, of Ashford, m. Lucius MORSE, of Union, Nov. 24, 1830, by Rev. Stephen Hitchcock	5	40
Lydia, m. Palmer CARPENTER, Jr., Oct. 7, 1839, by Elder Henry Greenslit. Intention published	5	71
Marg[a]rit, d. Stephen & Marg[a]ret, b. June 26, 1759	2	42
Margarit, d. Joseph & Lydia, b. Aug. 17, 1791	4	278
Margaret, m. Magaldus BROWN, Mar. [ ], 1817	6	83
Mary, d. Stephen & Marg[a]ret, b. May 11, 1749	2	42
Mercia, d. Elisha & Prudence, b. Apr. 8, 1796	4	279
Polley, d. Stephen & Mary, b. Aug. 20, 1790	4	32
Roxey, d. Stephen & Mary, b. Apr. 16, 1796	4	32
Sarah, d. John & Dorothy, b. Dec. 25, 1733	1	46
Stephen, m Marg[a]ret STOEL, Feb. 1, 1743/4, by Rev. Mr. John Bass	2	42
Stephen, s. Stephen & Marg[a]rit, b. Oct. 7, 1752	2	42
Stephen, m. Mary HIAMS, July 4, 1782	4	32
Stephen, s. Stephen & Mary, b. Sept. 12, 1794	4	32
Stephen, m. Elizabeth CARPENTER, b. of Ashford, Mar. 8, 1821, by Rev. Stephen Haskell	5	2
Stephen, s. Stephen & Elizabeth, b. Jan. 20, 1822	6	39
Theodore, of Brooklyn, m. Caroline SIMMONS, of Ashford, May 20, 1839, by Rev. Cha[rle]s Hyde	5	71
SCOTT, SCOT, Ellis, m. Daniel SQUIRE, Nov. 13, 1754	1	100
Millisent, m. John SQUIRE, Dec. 19, 1751	1	100
Thomas, m. Sarah HALE, Feb. 16, 1769	4	27
SCRANTON, Desire N., of Ashford, m. George W. CLOUGH, of Warwick, R. I., Oct. 26, 1828, by Amos Babcock, Elder. Intention published	5	32

	Vol.	Page
SESSIONS, Elisabeth, m. Ebenezer **LAWSON**, Jan. 6, 1785, by		
John Sessions, J. P.	4	236
SHARP, George W., m. Lidy Ann **RANDALL**, June 6, 1831, by		
Rev. Reuben Torrey, Eastford	5	43
SHAW, Annah, m. Stephen **SNOW**, Apr. 29, 1756	2	72
SHEPARD, James, d. Mar. 20, 1795	4	82
SHERMAN, Abigail, m. Benjamin **SNOW**, Feb. 27, 1804	4	88
Allton, see under Alton		
Almira, d. Zeph[aniah] & Betsey, b. May 11, 1820	4	272
Almira, m. Lyman S. **HIGGINBOTHAM**, b. of Ashford, Aug.		
3, 1840, by Rev. R. W. Allen, Eastford	5	74
Allton, s. Zeph[aniah] & Betsey, b. Jan. 23, 1813	4	272
Alton, m. Huldah **EDGERTON**, b. of Ashford, Nov. 27, 1834,		
by W[illia]m Livesey, Elder, Eastford	5	55
Daniel, s. Zeph[aniah] & Betsey, b. Dec. 22, 1814	4	272
Daniel, m. Eveline **CHAPMAN**, b. of Ashford, Jan. 13, 1837,		
by Rev. Stephen Cushing	5	65
Eliza, m. Ezra **SOUTHWORTH**, Nov. 28, 1812	6	46
Ellina Ann, d. Allton & Huldah M., b. Mar. 14, 1840	6	99
Isaac, s. Zeph[aniah] & Betsey, b. Sept. 30, 1816	4	272
Isaac, m. Lemira **PRESTON**, b. of Ashford, Oct. 12, 1836, by		
Rev. Stephen Cushing, Eastford	5	62
Isaac, m. Freedy **SIMMONS** b. of Ashford, [Feb.] 4, [1838],		
by Rev. Erastus Benton, Eastford	5	67
James Edward, s. Isaac & Freda, b. Oct. 24, 1839	6	94
John, s. Zeph[aniah] & Betsey, b. Apr. 15, 1818	4	272
John, m. Laura L. **EDGERTON**, b. of Ashford, Feb. 6, 1842,		
by Rev. Charles C. Barnes	5	80
Latan, s. Zeph[aniah] & Betsey, b. Nov. 22, 1808	4	272
Mason S., m. Eveline **WHITMORE**, b. of Ashford, Feb. 27,		
1821, by Philo Judson	5	2
Nancy Maria, d. Zeph[aniah] & Betsey, b. Mar. 9, 1824	4	272
Sarah Matilda, d. Zephaniah & Betsey, b. Jan. 12, 1826	4	272
Zephaniah, m. Betsey **ALLTON**, Nov. 15, 1804	4	272
Zephaniah, s. Zephaniah & Betsey, b. Aug. 21, 1806	4	272
SHIPPEE, SHIPPEY, Henrietta Eliza, d. William G., farmer, ae 30,		
& Wealthey, ae 31, b. Aug. 15, 1847	5	126-7
Horace, m. Laura **PALMER**, b. of Ashford, Nov. 24, 1831, by		
Rev. Philo Judson	5	45
SHIRTLEFF, SHURTLIFF, SHIRTLIF, SHITLEFF, Almeran S.,		
m. Catharine E. **MILLER**, Dec. 19, 1847, by Rev.		
Washington Munger	5	102
Betsey, m. Frederick **CHAFFEE**, Nov. 13, 1814	4	254
Catharine Spring, d. Sylvanus & Elizabeth, b. Sept. 3, 1827	6	60
Daniel, hat braider, ae 25, of Ashford, m. Harriet **FULLER**, ae		
20, b. Providence, R. I., Apr. 27, 1849, by Isaac Sherman	5	136-7
Daniel **KNOWLTON**, s. Sylvanus & Elizabeth, b. Nov. 24,		
1823	6	60

	Vol.	Page
SHIRTLEFF, SHURTLIFF, SHIRTLIF, SHITLEFF, (cont.),		
Elizabeth, m. Stephen **STORY**, b. of Ashford, Apr. 21, 1844,		
by Rev. Geo[rge] Mixter	5	89
Elizabeth K., m. George W. **WESTBRIDGE**, Apr. 11, 1831,		
by Rev. David Bennett	5	42
Elizabeth K., d. Daniel, mechanic, ae 27, & Harriet, ae 23, b.		
Aug. 17, 1850	5	146-7
Elizabeth K., d. Daniel K., straw braider, ae 28, & Harriet,		
ae 23, b. Aug. 17, 1850	5	148-9
Elizabeth Knowlton, d. Sylvanus & Elizabeth, b. Mar. 28, 1815	6	60
Henry Milton, s. Almiran, mechanic, ae 31, & Catharine, ae 19,		
b. Oct. 12, 1850	5	146-7
Lorenzo Wells, s. Sylvanus & Elizabeth, b. Mar. 5, 1817 ; d.		
Jan. 24, 1818	6	60
Martha Almira, d. Sylvanus & Elizabeth, b. July 23, 1825	6	60
Salvia Almarin, s. Sylvanus & Elizabeth, b. Feb. 17, 1819	6	60
Susan Maria, d. Sylvanus & Elizabeth, b. Dec. 28, 1820	6	60
Susan[n]ah, d. Silvinus, b. [ ]	4	3
Silvinus, s. Silvinus. b. [ ]	4	3
Sylvanus, m. Elizabeth **CHAFFEE**, Mar. 4, 1813	6	60
Sylvanus Sumer, s. Sylvanus & Elizabeth, b. Aug. 27, 1813	6	60
SHUMWAY, Albert, s. John P. & Jerusha C., b. Mar. 15, 1843 ; d.		
Oct. 11, 1843, ae 6 m. 26 d.	6	91
Charles L., s. John P. & Jerusha C., b. Dec. 21, 1831	6	91
Dwight, s. John P. & Jerusha C., b. Dec. 2, 1837	6	91
Jerusha C., housewife, b. Mansfield, res. Ashford, d. Apr. 4,		
1849, ae 38	5	136-7
Jerush C., [w. John P.] d. Apr. 4, 1849	6	91
John P., b. June 29, 1808 ; m. Jerusha C. **ATWOOD**, Nov. 11,		
1830	6	91
Millen s. John P. & Jerusha C., b. Sept. 2, 1840	6	91
Orrel A., d. John P. & Jerusha C., b. Nov. 17, 1833	6	91
SIBLEY, Aaron, s. Ezekiel & Hannah, b. June 5, 1779	4	103
Aaron, s. John & Esther, b. Apr. 11, 1799	4	276
Benjamin Franklin, s. Samuel & Sally, b. Apr. 23, 1831	6	71
Charles, s. John & Esther, b. July 4, 1801	4	276
Emeline, m. Lucius **RICHARDS**, b. of Ashford, [Nov.] 28,		
[1839], by Rev. Reuben Torrey, Eastford	5	72
Ezekiel, m. Hannah **CAVARY***, Sept. 24, 1778 (***CARARY**)	4	103
Ezekiel, m. Sarah **YEMMONS**, [ ]	4	103
Frederick F., m. Ruth **PUTNAM**, b. of Ashford, Nov. 27, 1839,		
by Rev. Alvan Underwood	5	72
John, m. Esther **BELLAMAY**, Apr. 4, 1793	4	276
John, s. John & Esther, b. June 6, 1797	4	276
Phebe, m. Daniel **SQUIRE**, Sept. 20, 1768	3	21
Prissilla, m. Ephraim **SQUIRE**, Dec. 31, 1778	4	121
Samuel, m. Rhoda **PRESTON**, b. of Ashford, Aug. 28, [1839]		
by Rev. Reuben Torrey, Eastford	5	72

	Vol.	Page
SIBLEY, (cont.)		
Sarah, w. Ezekiel, d. Apr. 29, 1778	4	103
SIMMONS, SIMONS, SEMONS, [see also **SEAMONS**], Abel m.		
Hannah **REED,** Dec. 21, 1747	1	67
Abel, m. Hannah **READ,** Dec. 21, 1747	2	68
Abel, Jr., m. Hannah **HOLMES,** Nov. 3, 1774	4	121
Abel, s. Abel, Jr. & Hannah, b. Aug. 13, 1787	4	121
Abel Henry, s. Alva & Tryphena, b. Mar. 14, 1824	4	81
Albert, of Mansfield, m. Eunice **CHAFFEE,** of Ashford, Nov. 28, 1831, by Rev. David Bennett	5	45
Alva, s. Abel, Jr. & Hannah, b. June 23, 1778	4	121
Alva, m. Tryphena **BURNHAM,** Dec. 4, 1800	4	81
Benjamin C., m. Mariet **BYLES,** b. of Ashford, Apr. 29, 1824, by Rev. Philo Judson	5	14
Benj[ami]n Clark, s. Abel, Jr. & Hannah, b. May 16, 1790	4	121
Caroline, d. Alva & Tryphena, b. Jan. 27, 1826	4	81
Caroline, of Ashford, m. Theodore **SCARBOROUGH,** of Brooklyn, May 20, 1839, by Rev. Cha[rle]s Hyde	5	71
Chloe, d. Abel & Hannah, b. July 13, 1749	1	67
Edwin S., s. Benj[ami]n C. & Maryette, b. Jan. 19, 1837 ; d. Sept. 27, 1846	6	84
Elizabeth, d. Abel & Hannah, b. Sept. 3, 1759	4	22
Elizabeth, d. Alva & Tryphena, b. Dec. 8, 1809	4	81
Elizabeth, m. Charles **SNELL,** b. of Ashford, Mar. 27, 1831, by Rev. Ezekiel Skinner	5	42
Ellen Percy, d. Benj[ami]n C. & Maryette, b. May 24, 1846	6	84
Emery, of Woodstock, m. Sarah **DUNN,** of Ashford, May 19, 1844, by Erastus Dickinson	5	89
Freda, d. W[illia]m & Chloe, b. Dec. 4, 1812	4	253
Freedy, m. Isaac **SHERMAN,** b. of Ashford, [Feb.] 4, [1838], by Rev. Erastus Benton, Eastford	5	67
Guilson, s. William & Chloe, b. Dec. 9, 1802	4	253
Hannah, d. Abel & Hannah, b. Sept. 6, 1761	4	22
Hannah, w. Abel, d. Dec. 1, 1765	4	22
Hannah, d. Alva & Tryphena, b. Mar. 16, 1814	4	81
Harriet, d. Alva & Tryphena, b. Mar. 8, 1804	4	81
Harriet, m. Ichabod **BARTHBY,** b. of Ashford, Oct. 24, 1827, by Rev. Philo Judson	5	29
Harriet, d. Benj[ami]n C. & Maryette, b. Nov. 4, 1827	6	84
Hezekiah, of Woodstock, m. Patty **CARPENTER,** of Ashford, Jan. 11, 1829, by Levi Works, J. P.	5	33
John, s. Abel, Jr. & Hannah, b. Sept. 16, 1775	4	121
John Holmes, s. Alva & Tryphena, b. Nov. 21, 1811	4	81
Joseph B., m. Lucinda H. **CLARK,** b. of Ashford, Feb. 19, 1829, by Rev. Philo Judson	5	33
Joseph Burnham, s. Alva & Tryphena, b. Oct. 12, 1801	4	81
Laura Ann, d. Benj[ami]n C. & Maryette, b. Sept. 8, 1825	6	84
Leonard, s. Abel, b. Sept. 15, 1787	4	22
Lucinda H., m. George **CADY,** b. of Ashford, Apr. 14, 1841,		

	Vol.	Page
SIMMONS, SIMONS, SEMONS, (cont.)		
by Rev. Cha[rle]s Hyde	5	78
Luther, of Mansfield, m. Julia **HARRIS**, of Ashford, Dec. 19,		
1844, by Rev. Geo[rge] Mixter **(SIMONS)**	5	92
Lyman, s. Abel, b. Aug. 29, 1783	4	22
Mary, d. W[illia]m & Chloe, b. Apr. 10, 1805	4	253
Mary, of Ashford, m. Abram **BRIGGS**, of Cambin, Apr. 1,		
1824, by Edward Keyes, J. P.	5	13
Olive, d. Abel, b. Feb. 9, 1785	4	22
Percy, d. Abel, Jr. & Hannah, b. Dec. 17, 1780	4	121
Percy, m. Stephen Fielder **PALMER**, Jan. 7, 1802	4	242
Percy, d. Alva & Tryphena, b. Nov. 5, 1816	4	81
Pheba, d. Abel & Hannah, b. Sept. 29, 1763	4	22
Polley, d. Abel, b. Apr. 2, 1780	4	22
Rebec[c]a, d. Abel & Hannah, b. June 3, 1751	1	67
Roxie, d. Abel, b. Jan. 1, 1782	4	22
Sarah Byles, d. Benj[ami]n C. & Maryette, b. Dec. 23, 1829	6	84
Sarah M., dressmaker, ae 24, b. R. I., m. Smith W. **EVANS**,		
millwright, ae 27, b. Burrillville, R. I., res. Burrillville, R.		
I., Mar. 10, 1850, by Ezekiel Skinner	5	142-3
Seffrane, d. W[illia]m & Chloe, b. July 25, 1807	4	253
Sophronia, d. Alva & Tryphena, b. Jan. 11, 1806	4	81
Sophronia, of Ashford, m. Darius B. **WILCOX**, of West		
Greenwich, R. I., [Jan.] 20, [1828], by Rev. Reuben		
Torrey	5	30
Sophronia, of Ashford, m. Darius **KNIGHT**, of Chaplin, Mar.		
16, 1842, by Rev. Cha[rle]s Hyde	5	80
Stephen, s. Abel & Hannah, b. Nov. 7, 1765	4	22
Sylvester, name credited in original index to page 2, but		
information regarding same is missing	4	2
Tabitha, d. Abel, Jr. & Hannah, b. Apr. 2, 1783	4	121
Tabitha, m. Joseph **PALMER**, Jr., Apr. 23, 1823, by Philo		
Judson	5	9
William, s. Abel, b. Sept. 13, 1778	4	22
William, m. Chloe **SKINNER**, Nov. 25, 1801	4	253
SIMONS, [see under **SIMMONS**]		
SKINNER, Anna, m. Joseph **ABBOT[T]**, Mar. 6, 1794	4	275
Benjamin R., m. Eliza **READ**, b. of Ashford, June 13, last,		
[1827], by Rev. Ezekiel Skinner	5	28
Chloe, m. William **SIMMONS**, Nov. 25, 1801	4	253
Ele[a]zar, s. Joseph & Elizabeth, b. Nov. 18, 1761	4	31
Huldah, m. Nathan **ABBOT[T]**, Oct. 16, 1808	4	240
Jon[a]than, m. Mary W. **CLARK**, b. of Ashford, Mar. 22,		
1838, by Rev. Erastus Benton, of Eastford	5	68
Joseph, m. Mrs. Elisabeth **BRAYFORD**, b. of Ashford, Dec.		
15, 1762, at Woodstock, by Stephen Williams	3	64
Martha A., of Ashford, m. Richard **BOONE**, of Berlin, N. Y.,		
Feb. 26, 1844, by Rev. Ezekiel Skinner	5	88
Martha A., m. Seldon **CURTIS**, June 5, 1853, by Rev. Ezekiel		

SIMMONS, SIMONS, SEMONS, (cont.)	Vol.	Page
Skinner, Westford	5	110
Mary, m. Isaac HOLMES, Oct. 19, 1761	1	3
SLADE, SLEAD, SLEADE, SLAIDE, SLATE, Elesabeth, m. Elias		
CHAPMAN, Feb. 12, 1778	4	62
James J., m. Eliza RICHARDS, b. of Ashford, Nov. 3, 1841,		
by Rev. Cha[rle]s Hyde	5	79
James Josephus, s. Jonathan & Amey, b. July 5, 1816	4	276
Lauritta, d. Jonathan & Amey, b. Sept. 27, 1813	4	276
Lydia Josephine, d. Thomas S., farmer, ae 47, & Hannah P., ae		
33, b. Mar. 28, 1848	5	126-7
Maria, d. Jonathan & Amey, b. Oct. 20, 1804	4	276
Mariah, m. Stephen CHAPMAN, Jr., b. of Ashford, Sept. 16,		
1824, by John Nichols	5	15
Nelson Wheaton, s. Jonathan & Amey, b. July 7, 1802	4	276
Phebe, m. Jacob CHAPMAN, Jr., Apr. 16, 1805	4	272
Sarah Ann, d. Jonathan & Amey, b. Aug. 8, 1811	4	276
Thompson, s. Jonathan & Amey, b. Oct. 27, 1806	4	276
SLATE, [see under SLADE]		
SLEAD, [see under SLADE]		
SMEED, Adolphus, of Mansfield, m. Almire SQUIERS, of Ashford,		
Oct. 25, 1832, by Rev. Ezekiel Skinner	5	49
SMITH, Aaron, s. Hubbard & Kezia, b. Feb. 26, 1782	4	100
Aavis, see under Avis		
Abagail, d. Nehemiah & Ann, b. Aug. 14, 1751	2	54
Abigail, d. Eben[eze]r & Martha, b. Apr. 28, 1770	4	15
Abigail, d. Simeon & Anna, b. Feb. 2, 1777	4	38
Abijah, Jr., m. Judith WHITON, Aug. 28, 1783	4	235
Abijah, s. Abijah & Judith, b. Sept. 9, 1792	4	235
Abner, of Ashford, m. Alma LILLEY, of Union, Mar. 2, 1842,		
by Rev. Francis Williams, Eastford	5	80
Adalette Orissa, d. Ezra W. & Louisa, b. Mar. 28, 181[ ]	6	21
Albert C., m. Arabella FISHER, b. of Hartford, June 24, 1829,		
by Rev. Philo Judson	5	35
Alva, s. Asaph, Jr. & Rachel, b. Feb. 26, 1795	4	92
Alvergins, s. Isaiah & Susannah, b. Jan. 29, 1756 ; d. Mar.		
16, 1756	1	91
Amos, s. Hezekiah & Meriam, b. Nov. 21, 1758	4	11
Ann, d. Nehemiah & Ann, b. Aug. 21, 1758	2	54
Ann, w. Nehemiah, d. Sept. 9, 1801	2	55
Anna, d. Simeon & Anna, b. Jan. 1, 1774	4	38
Anna, d. Eb[e]n[eze]r & Martha, b. Oct. 11, 1776	4	15
Anna, w. Simeon, d. Apr. 12, 1791	4	38
Anna, d. Simeon & Sally, b. Aug. 20, 1806	4	237
Asa, m. Sally HUNTL[E]Y, July 8, 1809	4	67
Asa Williams, d. Hosea & Lydia, b. May 20, 1818	6	21
Asaph, m. Sarah PLACE, Dec. 19, 1749, by James Bicknell,		
Esq.	2	52
Asaph, Jr., m. Rachel PALMER, June 7, 1783	4	92

SMITH, (cont.)

	Vol.	Page
Asaph, Jr., m. Nanna **ROBINSON**, Jan. 3, 1797	4	92
Asenath, d. Eben[eze]r & Martha, b. Sept. 19, 1789	4	15
Aavis, d. John, Jr. & Meriam, b. Dec. 16, 1769	4	42
Aavis, d. John, Jr. & Meriam, b. Dec. 29, 1773	4	42
Avis, d. Hezekiah & Rebeckah, b. June 3, 1816	6	12
Benjamin, s. Ezra & Judah, b. Oct. 29, 1749	1	68
Benjamin, s. Ezaa, d. Aug. 30, 1754	2	82
Bethyah, d. Nehemiah & Ann, b. Oct. 19, 1749	2	54
Betsey, d. Hezekiah & Rebeckah, b. June 5, 1801	6	12
Betsey S., of Ashford, m. Elisha **JOHNSON**, of Mansfield, Nov. 27, 1826, by Rev. Philo Judson	5	25
B[e]ulah, d. Josiah & Mary, b. Feb. 1, 1768	3	117
Caroline M., d. Abner P., shoemaker, & Alma, b. Apr. 11, 1849	5	132-3
Caroline M., d. July [ ], 1850, ae 1	5	144-5
Chester, s. Olover & Avis, b. June 7, 1792	4	271
Chloe, d. Eben[eze]r & Martha, b. Apr. 19, 1774	4	15
Charasa, d. Pheba **PHILLIPS**, b. Jan. 19, 1768	4	29
Clarary, d. Olover & Avis, b. Aug. 1, 1790	4	271
Craft, s. John, Jr. & Mary, b. Oct. 13, 1795	4	21
Cyril W., m. Sarah M. **MARCY**, b. of Ashford, Jan. 1, 1844, by Rev. L. W. Blood, Eastford	5	87
Daniel, s. Ezra & Judath, b. Mar. 19, 1750/51	2	82
Daniel, s. Ezra, d. Sept, 21, 1754	2	82
Darius, s. Hubbard & Kezia, b. June 18, 1780	4	100
David, m. Mehetebel **CHUBB**, Aug. 28, 1733, by Sqr. Eastman, J. P.	1	36
David, d. Mar. 28, 1776	1	36
David, m. Sarah **CONLY**, Apr. 13, 1809	4	12
Ebenezer, s. Sam[ue]ll & Zephara, b.Aug. 12, 1741	1	55
Ebenezer, s. Asaph & Sarah, b. Mar. 13, 1750	2	52
Ebenezer, s. Ebe[neze]r & Martha, b. Aug. 16, 1772	4	15
Edward, [s. Sam[ue]ll, Jr. & Meheteble], b. May 3, 1762	1	56
Ele[a]ner, [d. John, Jr. & Sarah], b. Aug. 2, 1745	1	69
Eleazer, s. Josiah & Mary, b. Nov. 7, 1762	3	117
Eli, [s. Sam[ue]ll, Jr. & Meheteble], b. Oct. 17, 1759	1	56
Elias, s. Solomon & Rebec[c]a, b. Dec. 6, 1775	4	77
Elisha, s. Simeon & Anna, b. Nov. 20, 1783	4	38
Elisha, s. Eben[eze]r & Martha, b. July 24, 1791	4	15
Elizabeth, d. Ezra & Judath, b. Apr. 6, 1753	2	82
Elizabeth, d. Ezra, d. Sept. 16, 1754	2	82
Elisabeth, d. Ezra & Carthrine, b. Aug. 10, 1756	2	76
Elisabeth, m. [Francis] **PEIRCE**, Jr., [ ] 14, 1762	3	133
Elisabeth, [d. George & Delight], b. July 26, 1763	4	35
Elisabeth, m. Jabez **WEBB**, Apr. 9, 1776	4	269
Elizabeth Orcelia, d. Barak, b. Jan. 13, 1824	6	45
Ephraim, s. Isaiah & Susannah. b. Mar. 4, 1763	4	20
Erastus, see under Urastus		
Esther M., m. Josiah **HAMMOND**, farmer, of Ashford, Dec.		

SMITH, (cont)	Vol.	Page
22, 1850, by P. Mathewson	5	148-9
Eunice, of Woodstock, m. William **HARBINGER**, of		
Providence, R. I., Jan. 11, 1852, by Rev. Ezekiel Skinner	5	109
Ezra, m. Judath **BOSWORTH**, May 23, 1745	1	68
Ezra, m. Carthrine **SPRING**, Nov. 13, 1755	2	76
Ezra, s. Ezra, d. Nov. 19, 1758	2	76
Ezra, s. Simeon & Anne, b. Dec. 20, 1767	4	38
Ezra E., s. Simeon & Sally, b. Nov. 28, 1820	4	237
Ezra, see also Izra		
Ezra W., of Ashford, m. Ama L. **CLARK**, of Chaplin, Feb. 28,		
1843, by F. Williams. Intention published	5	84
George, d. Apr. 27, 1807	4	35
Green *, [triplet with Washington & Trumbull], s. Eben[eze]r		
& Martha, b. Nov. 29, 1781 (*First written "Hancock")	4	15
Gregrorys, s. Josiah & Mary, b. Mar. 31, 1764	3	117
Hannah, d. Nehemiah & An[n]e, b. Apr. 19, 1747	2	54
Hannah, d. Ezra & Judath, b. Feb. 28, 1747/8	1	68
Hannah, d. John, Jr. & Sarah, b. Feb. 28, 1747/8	1	69
Hannah, m. Ebenezer **WALKER**, Jan. 10, 1754	1	82
Hannah, m. William **WALKER**, Sept, 15, 1769	4	41
Hannah, d. Simeon & Anna, b. Apr. 14, 1789	4	38
Hannah, [d. George & Delight], b. Feb. 22, 1771	4	35
Hannah, wid., m. Joseph **KENDELL**, June 20, 1776	3	103
Hannah, d. Solomon & Rebeka, b. Sept. 12, 1777	4	77
Hannah, d. Asaph, Jr. & Rachel, b. Oct. 30, 1785	4	92
Hannah, m. Zera **PRESTON** Apr. 20, 1794	4	111
Hannah, m. Ebenezer **CHAFFEE**, b. of Ashford, Mar. 21,		
1822, by Rev. W[illia]m Storrs	5	5
Harriet, d. Hezekiah & Rebeckah, b. Jan. 19, 1815	6	12
Hephzibath, [d. John, Jr. & Sarah], b. Mar. 1, 1748	1	69
Hiram, of Stafford, m. Mary Ann **WHITEHOUSE**, of Ashford,		
Nov. 26, 1827, by Rev. Luke Wood	5	29
Horatio, see under Oratio		
Hosea, s. John, Jr. & Mary, b. July 10, 1788	4	21
Hosea, m. Lydia **BOUTEVEL**, Jan. 12, 1814	6	21
Hosea, d. Oct. 3, 1844	6	21
Hubbart, [s. John, Jr. & Sarah], b. Nov. 24, 1750	1	69
Hubbard, [m.] Kezia **SNOW** [ ]	4	100
Isaiah, s. Isaiah & Susannah, b. July 7, 1758	1	104
Izra, m. Zurviah **RUSSEL[L]**, Sept. 27, 1738	1	68
Izra, see also Ezra		
James, [s. George & Delight], b. Feb. 2, 1769	4	35
James, m. Deborah **WILLIAMS**, Feb. 23, 1790	4	266
James, index credits name to page 4, but information regarding		
same is missing	4	4
James P., s. Asaph, Jr. & Rachel, b. May 9, 1789	4	92
Jedediah, s. Sam[ue]ll, Jr. & Meheteble, b. Nov. 11, 1754	1	56
Jemime, [d. John, Jr. & Sarah], b. Mar. 30, 1739 ; d. Oct. 19,		

	Vol.	Page
SMITH, (cont.)		
1740	1	69
Jemima, d. Hubbard & Kezia, b. May 7, 177[ ]	4	100
Jerusha, [s. Sam[ue]ll, & Meheteble], b. May 3, 1757	1	56
Jerusha, [d. George & Delight], b. June 20, 1767	4	35
Jerusha, d. Eben[eze]r & Martha, b. Mar. 22, 1787	4	15
Jerusha, m. Shuba[e]l SNOW, Aug. 23, 1787	4	25
Joel, s. James & Deborah, b. Feb. 12, 1791	4	266
John, Jr., m. Sarah YOEMONS, Mar. 1, 1738	1	69
John, [s. John, Jr. & Sarah], b. Oct. 26, 1743	1	69
John, d. Dec. 15, 1752	1	80
John, s. Solomon & Rebakah, b. Apr. 21, 1781	4	77
John, m. Serena HOLMES, Dec. 27, 1802	4	21
John, s. John, d. Jan. 17, 1808, ae 25	4	21
John, Jr., m. Orril GREEN, b. of Ashford, July 4, 1840, by		
Rev. Alvan Underwood, in Westford Parish	5	74
John C., of Ashford, m. Mrs. Polly THRASKER, of Stafford,		
Apr. 13, 1834, by Nathaniel Sheffield, Elder	5	54
John Cot[t]on, s. Asa & Sally, b. [ ] 8, 1809 (sic)	4	67
John Dorrance, s. Hosea & Lydia, b. Feb. 24, 1815	6	21
Joshua, s. Sam[ue]ll & Zephara, b. Apr. 9, 1743	1	55
Joshua, s. Josiah & Mary, b. Dec. 27, 1765	3	117
Josiah, m. Mary STOEL, Dec. 6, 174[ ]	3	117
Josiah, m. Mary WATKINS, Dec. 29, 1761	3	117
Josiah, s. Hubbard & Kezia, b. Dec. 1, 1776	4	100
Judath, w. Ezra, d. July 12, 1754	2	82
Judith, d. Abijah & Judith, b. Sept. 28, 1788	4	235
Lemuell, s. Abijah & Mary, b. May 9, 1751	1	81
Lodeme, d. Isaiah & Susannah, b. Jan. 10, 1755 ; d. Jan. 28,		
1755	1	91
Lois, d. Samuel & Zep[h]ara, b. Aug. 25, 1749 ; d. June 20,		
1750	1	55
Lowes, d. Pelatiah & Mary, b. Aug. 27, 1754	1	92
Lois, m. Elias KENDAL, Feb. 10, 1803	4	69
Lory Elelary, d. David & Sarah, b. Aug. 9, 1810	4	12
Lucius, s. Hezekiah & Rebeckah, b. Apr. 12, 1810	6	12
Lucy, d. Simeon & Lucy, b. July 20, 1794	4	38
Mariam, [d. George & Delight], b. Dec. 25, 1759	4	35
Mariam, see also Meriam		
Martha, d. Eben[eze]r & Martha, b. Aug. 16, 1767	4	15
Martha, d. Abijah, Jr. & Judith, b. Mar. 3, 1784	4	235
Mary, [d. John, Jr. & Sarah], b. July 25, 1740	1	69
Mary, w. Josiah, d. Jan. 10, 1761	3	117
Mary, w. Josiah, d. June 18, 1770	3	117
Mary, d. Eb[e]n[eze]r & Martha, b. Oct. 17, 1784	4	15
Mary, W. John, d. Apr. 6, 1801	4	21
Matilda, m. Elijah WHITON, Nov. 25, 1802	4	87
Matilda, see also Metilda		
Meletiah, m. Abial PRESTON, July 27, 1756	1	97

SMITH, (cont.)   Vol.   Page

Meriam, w. John, d. Oct. 23, 1778   4   42

Meriam, see also Mariam

Metildia, d. Simeon & Anna, b. June 26, 1781   4   38

Metildia, see also Matilda

Molley, d. Simeon & Anne, b. Aug. 12, 1770   4   38

Molley, m. Billarcha **SNOW,** May 17, 1781   4   227

Molley, d. John, Jr. & Mary, b. Sept. 12, 1790   4   21

Nancy, d. John, Jr. & Mary, b. June 5, 1786   4   21

Nancy, m. Isaac **KENDAL,** Jr., Mar. 25, 1810   4   273

Nehemiah, m. Ann **TIFFANY,** Dec. 25, 1745, by Rev. Mr.
Bass   2   54

Nehemiah, d. Dec. 10, 1800   2   55

Nelson, s. Hezekiah & Rebeckah, b. Apr. 11, 1806   6   12

Newton, s. Cyrel W., farmer, of Hartford, & Sarah U., b. Sept.
10, 1848   5   132-3

Oliver, s. Samuel, Jr. & Mehitabel, b. [J]une 7, 1748 ; d. Feb.
18, 1748/9   1   56

Oratio, s. Solomon & Rebekah, b. May 16, 1779   4   77

Otis, s. John, Jr. & Meriam, b. Oct. 31, 1771   4   42

Parker, s. Hezekiah & Rebeckah, b. Feb. 23, 1812   6   12

Pat[t]y, d. John & Mary, b. Mar. 22, 1801   4   21

Patty, m. William **BOUTELL,** b. of Ashford, Apr. 21, 1825,
by Rev. Philo Judson   5   18

Peter, m. Sarah **CONANT,** Sept. 11, 1768   4   16

Phebe, d. David & Mehitebel, b. Nov. 25, 1734   1   36

Pheebe, m. Benj[ami]n **RUSSELL,** 3rd, Feb. last day, 1757   1   98

Polly, d. Abijah & Judith, b. Nov. 28, 1790   4   235

Polley, m. Perkins B. **WOODWARD,** Apr. 4, 1793   4   274

Polley, d. Asaph, Jr. & Rachel, b. June 18, 1793   4   92

Pricil[l]a, d. David & [Mehitebel], b. [Jan. 31, 1735/6] ; d. Jan.
31, 1735/6   1   36

Rachel, w. Asaph, Jr., d. Dec. 26, 1795   4   92

Ransom, [s. Sam[ue]ll, Jr. & Meheteble], b. Sept. 20, 1765   1   56

Rebeckah, d. Hezekiah & Rebeckah, b. Apr. 1, 1814   6   12

Rodney, s. Hezekiah & Rebeckah, b. Nov. 18, 1804   6   12

Rosanna, d. Hubbard & Kezia, b. Oct. 25, 1783   4   100

Ruth, m. Jacob **WILSON,** May 21, 1741   3   100

Ruth, d. Hezekiah & Rebeckah, b. July 24, 1803   6   12

Ruth, housekeeper, d. July [ ], 1850, ae 65   5   144-5

Ruth M., m. Josiah **HAMMOND,** Dec. 22, 1850, by Rev. P.
Mathewson   5   106

Sally, d. Simeon & Sally, b. July 21, 1809   4   237

Samuel, Jr., m. Mehitabel **WADKENS,** Nov. 7, 1745, by Mr.
Bass   1   56

Samuel, s. Samuel, Jr. & Mehitabel, b. Jan. 15, 1749/50   1   56

Sam[ue]ll, d. Mar. 1, 1753   1   80

Sarah, m. Solomon **MASON,** Nov. 15, 1753   1   81

Sary, [d. George & Delight], b. Sept. 22, 1764   4   35

	Vol.	Page
SMITH, (cont.)		
Sarah, m. Lyman J. **HUGHES,** b. of Ashford,		
Aug. 24, 1851, by Rev. P. Mathewson	5	107
Silas, s. John, Jr. & Meriam, b. Jan. 14, 1775	4	42
Silence, d. Pelatiah & Mary, b. Nov. 2, 1755	1	92
Silance, [child of George & Delight], b. Feb. 22, 1773 ; d. Apr.		
7, 1773	4	35
Silvester, s. Hubbard & Kezia, b. Oct. 20, 1778	4	100
Simeon, s. Izara & Surviah, b. Nov. 10, 1741	1	68
Simeon, s. Nehemiah & Anna, b. July 4, 1755	2	54
Simeon, m. Anne **BYLES,** Feb. 18, 1766	4	38
Simeon, s. Simeon & Anna, b. Apr. 12, 1779	4	38
Simeon, Esq., d. Jan. 16, 1799	4	38
Simeon, m. Sally **HIMES,** Feb. 23, 1804	4	237
Simeon, m. Lucy **WALDOW,** [ ]	4	38
Solomon, [s. John, Jr. & Sarah], b. Aug. 21, 1749	1	69
Solomon, m. Rebeckah **CRAIN,** Oct. 28, 1773	4	77
Stephen, [s. Abjiah & Mary], b. Oct. 9, 1752 ; d. Dec. 25, 1753	1	81
Stephen, s. Benjamin & Hannah, b. June 24, 1773	4	11
Stephen, s. Solomon & Rebeckah, b. Sept. 9, 1774	4	77
Steven, s. Abijah, Jr. & Judith, b. June 13, 1785 ; d. May		
16, 1789	4	235
Susan L., m. Anthony W. **KNIGHT,** b. of Johnston, R. I., Oct.		
23, 1845, by Isaac Sherman	5	95
Susy, d. Simeon & Sally, b. Sept. 16, 1804	4	237
Sylvester, see under Silvester		
Thomas, s. Nehemiah & An[n]e, b. May 30, 1748 ; d. June 29,		
1749	2	54
Thomas, s. Nehemiah & Ann, b. May 17, 1753	2	54
Trumbull, [triplet with Washington & Green*], s. Eben[eze]r &		
Martha, b. Nov. 29, 1781 (*First written "Hancock")	4	15
Urastus, s. Solomon & Rebeckah, b. Oct. 8, 1783	4	77
Washington, [triplet with Trumbull & Green*], s. Eben[eze]r &		
Martha, b. Nov. 29, 1781 (*First written "Hancock")	4	15
W[illia]m, of Williamstown, County of Orange, State of Vt., m.		
Mary **WORK,** of Ashford, Conn., [Feb.] 16, 1823], by		
Reuben Torrey, Eastford	5	8
William B., s. Simeon & Sally, b. Sept. 4, 1814	4	237
Zebina, s. Hubbard & Kezia, b. Aug. 15, 1785	4	100
Zerviah, d. Ezra & Judath, b. Mar. 30, 1746	1	68
Zeruiah, d. Ezra, d. June 12, 1748	1	68
Zerviah, d. Simeon & Anna, b. Oct. 15, 1772	4	38
Zeruiah, m. Andrew **HUNTINGTON,** Feb. 3, 1790	4	274
----nl, s. Jabez & Chloe, b. Apr. 19, 1811	4	10
----raniss, s. Jabez & Chloe, b. Sept. 9, 1813	4	10
----uis*, d. Jabez & Chloe, b. June 5, 1815 (*Perhaps "ais")	4	10
----, s. Elias K., farmer, ae 36, & Susan M., ae 33, b. July 23,		
1851	5	146-7

SNELL, Amos, m. Phebe **HOWLET,** b. of Ashford, Sept. 9, [1828],

	Vol.	Page
SNELL. (cont.)		
by Rev. Ezekiel Skinner	5	32
Charles, m. Elizabeth **SIMMONS**, b. of Ashford,		
Mar. 27, 1831, by Rev. Ezekiel Skinner	5	42
Ebenezer, s. W[illia]m & Sarah, b. July 13, 1760	3	7
Eunice, m. Jonathan **FARNHAM**, Mar. 20, 1794	4	246
Joseph W., of Auburn, Mass., m. Julia A. **POTTER**, of		
Ashford, Aug. 13, 1849, by Charles Peabody. Intention		
published	5	103
Joseph W., shoemaker, ae 24, b. Ashford, res. Auburn, Mass.,		
m. Julia **POTTER**, Aug. 20, 1849, by Cha[rle]s Peabody	5	142-3
Lorenzo, s. W[illia]m & Sarah, b. Jan. 20, 1759 ; d. Jan. 30,		
1759	3	7
Sally, m. David **CHISON**, b. of Ashford, Oct. 17, 1831, by		
Rev. Ezekiel Skinner	5	44
W[illia]m, m. Sarah **BARNEY**, Dec. 26, 1758	3	7
SNOW, Abigail, d. Joseph & Sarah, b. Oct. 8, 1736	1	54
Abigail, w. Sam[ue]ll, d. Jan. 12, 1747/8	1	54
Abigail, m. Nath[anie]ll **HAYWARD**, Apr. 13, 1759	3	14
Abigail, m. Charles **WEEKS**, b. of Ashford, Feb. 29, 1824, by		
Rev. Philo Judson	5	12
Alice, see under Elas		
Alva, s. William & Mary, b. Mar. 16, 1781	4	39
Alva, s. Stephen & Polleysena, b. May 29, 1782	4	226
Amasa, s. Stephen & Annah, b. June 19, 1766	2	72
Amaziah, s. Oliver & Ursula, b. Apr. 21, 1764	2	73
Amaziah, s. Sabara, b. May 19, 1789	2	74
Amzaiah, see Amaziah Russ		
Aminda, d. Sam[ue]ll & Molley, b. Apr. 13, 1790	4	61
Amos, s. Joseph, Jr. & Mary, b. Sept. 20, 1765	3	74
Amos, m. Eunice **BURNHAM**, June 27, 1797	4	20
Amos, d. Sept. 13, 1805	4	20
Andrew **BROUGHTON**, s. Clarissa, b. Feb. 11, 1828	4	71
Anna, w. Stephen, d. Nov. 8, 1790, in the 60th y. of her age	2	72
Annis, d. Jonath[an] & Hannah, b. May 1, 1778	4	58
[Ara]una (?), s. Robert & Sarah, b. Feb. 14, 1757	1	95
[Arau]nah, m. Sarah **HOVEY**, No[v]. [ ]	4	286
Ariel, s. Simeon & Lydia, b. Feb. 28, 1788	4	36
Asa, s. Oliver, d. July 4, 1754	2	73
Asa, s. Oliver & Elizabeth, b. Aug. 26, 1754	2	73
Aseph, s. Oliver & Elizabeth, b. Dec. 26, 1752	2	73
Barshaba, m. Benjamin **PRESTON**, Nov. 17, 1763	2	55
Benj[ami]n, m. Keziah **FREEMAN**, Oct. 20, 1737, by Rev.		
Mr. Eleazer Williams	1	65
Benj[ami]n, s. Benj[ami]n & Keziah, b. Aug. 10, 1738, ; d.		
Oct. 30, 1740	1	65
Benj[ami]n, s. Benj[ami]n & Keziah, b. Nov. 20, 1740 ; d. Dec.		
15, "next after"	1	65
Benj[ami]n, s. Joseph & Sarah, b. Jan. 23, 1743/4	1	54

	Vol.	Page
SNOW, (cont.)		
Benjamin, d. Apr. 22, 1752	1	65
Benjamin, m. Dercus **HORSGOOD**, July 5, 1764,		
by Elijah Whiton, Esq.	4	20
Benjamin, s. W[illia]m & Mary, b. Oct. 27, 1778	4	39
Benjamin, m. Abigail **SHERMAN**, Feb. 27, 1804	4	88
Benjamin, s. Benj[ami]n & Abigail, b. Aug. 22, 1808	4	88
Billarcha, m. Molley **SMITH**, May 17, 1781	4	227
Billarcha, see also Billashey & Billy Arkey		
Billashey, Jr., m. Frances D. **TROWBRIDGE**, Dec. 26, 1828,		
by Levi Works, J. P. (Billarkey?)	5	33
Billings, s. Simeon & Lydia, b. Apr. 29, 1790	4	36
Bille, s. Joseph & Sarah, b. Oct. 24, 1759	1	106
Billy, m. Olive **CLARK**, Dec. 11, 1787	4	16
Billy Arkey, s. Samuel, 3rd, & Hannah, b. Sept. 18, 1757	1	100
Billy Arkey, see also Billarcha and Billashey		
Billy Clark, s. Billy & Olive, b. Nov. 13, 1796	4	16
Chloey, d. Joseph, Jr. & Mary, b. Apr. 7, 1780	3	74
Cillista, d. Simeon & Lydia, b. July 22, 1804	4	36
Cillista, see also Elista M.		
Cinthy, see under Cynthia		
Clarine, d. William & Mary, b. Oct. 10, 1772	4	39
Clarina, m. John **BAILEY**, Aug. 30, 1792	4	75
Claras[s]a had d. Lucretia **ASPINWILL**, b. Mar. 30, 1807	4	71
Claras[s]a had s. Orrigen **PRESCOTT**, b. Feb. 26, 1818	4	71
Claras[s]a had s. Timothy Dwight **DIMICK**, b. Feb. 27, 1820	4	71
Clarissa had s. Andrew **BROUGHTON**, b. Feb. 11, 1828	4	71
Clark, s. Billy & Olive, b. July 21, 1789 ; d. Oct. 25, 1790	4	16
Clark, s. Billy, d. Oct. 25, 1790	4	16
Clyna, d. Billarky & Molley, b. Nov. 1, 1788	4	227
Sinthy, d. Salvenus & Rebeckah, b. Aug. 12, 1758	2	47
Cinthy, d. Belarke & Molley, b. July 29, 1786	4	227
Cynthia, m. Wheedon **CLARK**, b. of Ashford, Feb. 3, 1825, by		
Rev. Philo Judson	5	17
Daniel, s. Samuel & Molley, b. Apr. 30, 1779	4	61
David Johnson, s. Benj[ami]n & Abigail, b. Oct. 28, 1809	4	88
Diadamy, d. Oliver & Elizabeth, b. Nov. 13, 1750	2	73
Diademy, d. Oliver, d. July 6, 1754	2	73
Diademy, d. Oliver & Elisabeth, b. June 29, 1756	2	73
Diedamia, d. Silas & Eunice, b. Sept. 16, 1787	4	230
Dudley, s. Jonathan & Hannah, b. Sept. 30, 1784	4	58
Dudley, m. Almira **STOCKBRIDGE**, b. of Ashford, [Mar.] 4,		
[1825], by Allen Barnes, Elder	5	17
Ebenezer, s. Sam[ue]ll, Jr. & Hannah, b. Oct. 26, 1747	1	68
Ebenezer, s. Sam[ue]ll, Jr., d. Sept. 24, 1754	1	88
Eben[eze]r, s. Sam[ue]ll, d. Mar. 22, 1762	1	45
Ebene zer, s. Sam[ue]ll & Hannah, b. June 26, 1762	1	51
Ebenezer, s. Robert & Sarah, b. Apr. 10, 1766 ; d. same day	3	107
Edmund, s. James & Annah, b. Aug. 11, 1773	4	51

SNOW, (cont.)	Vol.	Page
Elas, d. Joseph & Sarah, b. Sept. 23, 1741	1	54
Ele[a]zer, s. Billarcha & Molley, b. May 7, 1782	4	227
Eli, s. Salvenus & Rebeckah, b. Feb. 20, 1773	3	1
Eli, s. Silas & Eunice, b. Apr. 15, 1789	4	230
Elias, s. Sam[ue]ll, Jr. & Molley, b. Jan. 22, 1785	4	61
Eliph[a]let, s. Joseph, Jr. & Mary, b. July 7, 1784	3	74
Elista M., of Ashford, m. Smith BENNETT, of Monroe, Oct. 2, 1831, by Rev. David Bennett	5	45
Elista M., see also Cillista		
Elizabeth, d. Samuel, Jr. & Sarah, b. July 11, 1734 ; d. Apr. 1, 1737, in the 3rd y. of her age	1	32
Elezebeth, d. Sam[ue]ll, Jr. & Sarah, b. Sept. 28, 1739	1	32
Elisabeth, w. Oliver, d. May 14, 1761	2	73
Elisabeth, d. Salvenus & Rebeckah, b. July 7, 1766	3	1
Elizabeth, d. Oliver & Ursula, b. Nov. 6, 1768	2	73
Elisabeth, m. Sam[ue]ll W[H]IPPLE, Jan. 27, 1771	4	60
Emerson, s. Smith & Sarah, b. Aug. 1, 1828	6	54
Erastus, s. James & Annah, b. Apr. 9, 1782	4	51
Easther, d. Samvel, Jr. & Hannah, b. July 24, 1745	1	68
Esther, m. Ephraim SPAULDING, May 20, 1772	4	73
Eunis, d. Jonathan & Hannah, b. Apr. 6, 1776	4	58
Eunice, d. Silas & Eunice, b. Sept. 4, 1784	4	230
Eunice, w. Parley, d. Mar. 13, 1834, ae 67	4	271
Eunice S., of Ashford, m. Reuben M. BARLOW, of Woodstock, Apr. 17, 1844, by R. V. Lyon	5	89
Eunice Sophia, d. Parley V. & Susan, b. Jan. 23, 1826	6	98
Ezra, s. Joseph & Sarah, b. June 19 1755	1	99
Fanny, d. James & Annah, b. Dec. 9, 1791	4	51
Fielder S., m. Caroline KEYES, b. of Ashford, last evening, [Mar. 24, 1836], by Rev. J. Hall	5	59
Frana (?), s. Robert & Sarah, b. Feb. 14, 1757	1	95
Freeman, s. William & Mary, b. Apr. 20, 1771	4	39
Freeman, m. Lois CHAPMAN, May 18, 1797	4	48
Freeman, s. Freeman & Lois, b. Apr. 3, 1798	4	48
Hannah, d. Sam[ue]ll, Jr. & Hannah, b. July 2, 1754	1	87
Hannah[h], d. Robert & Sarah, b. July 15, 1761	3	107
Hannah, d. Robert, d. June 28, 1787	3	107
Hannah, d. Sam[ue]ll, Jr. & Molley, b. Oct. 3, 1787	4	61
Hannah, d. Silas & Eunice, b. Feb. 15, 1793	4	230
Hannah, m. Darbey DADEY, b. of Ashford, Sept. 21, 1851, by Rev. P. Mathewson	5	107
Hannah, d. Sam[ue]ll, Jr. & Sarah, b [ ]	1	32
Harney* M., s. Parley V. & Susan, b. Mar. 20, 1817 (*Harvey?)	6	98
Harriot, d. Simeon & Lydia, b. Apr. 16, 1793	4	36
Harriet M., of Ashford, m. Philander WYLLYS, of Windham, Jan. 1, 1846, by Francis Williams	5	96
Harvey, s. Parley & Eunice, b. July 17, 1799 ; d. Dec. 29, 1803	4	271

SNOW, (cont.)	Vol.	Page
Harvey, see also Harney		
Henry, s. Parley & Eunice, b. Jan. 20, 1794	4	271
Henry C., m. Mrs. Harriet A. STEBBINS, b. of Ashford, Feb. 13, 1834, by Thomas Dow, J. P.	5	53
Henry Veits, s. Parley V. & Susan, b. Feb. 23, 1815, at Becket	6	98
Hollis Anthony, s. Jared W. & Betsey, b. Oct. 21, 1818	6	18
Hulda, m. Timothy DIMMUCK, Dec. 21, 1767	4	54
James, s. Joseph & Sarah, b. June 11, 1749	1	54
James, m. Annah HOLMES, Nov. 13, 1771	4	51
James, s. James & Annah, b. Sept. 27, 1777	4	51
Jared, m. Betsey PECK, Nov. 27, 1817	6	18
Jared Warner, s. Shuba[e]l, 2d, & Lucy, b. Jan. 30, 1797	4	276
Jemima, d. Oliver & Ursula, b. Feb. 1, 1775	2	74
Jesse, s. Benjamin & Darcus, b. Jan. 3, 1765	4	20
Jesse, s. James & Anna, b. Jan. 17, 1780	4	51
Joanna, d. Simeon & Lydia, b. Mar. 30, 1802, ; d. Sept. 16, 1806	4	36
John, s. Stephen & Annah, b. Nov. 16, 1762	2	72
John, m. Elisabeth NICHOLS, Nov. 15, 1770	4	82
John, s. John & Elisabeth, b. Aug. 30, 1774	4	82
Jonathan, s. Joseph & Sarah, b. Aug. 13, 1752	1	54
Jonathan, m. Hannah CHUBB, Mar. 30, 1773	4	58
Jonathan, s. Jonathan & Hannah, b. Jan. 21, 1774	4	58
Jonathan, Jr., m. Relief JOHNSON, Apr. 24, 1794	4	280
Joseph, of Ashford, m. Sarah CORNEL, of Willmantown, May 7, 1735, by Rev. Mr. James [Hale]	1	54
Joseph, s. Joseph & Sarah, b. Nov. 15, 1738	1	54
Joseph, Jr., m. Mary CHANDLER, Nov. 18, 1762	3	74
Joseph, s. Joseph, Jr. & Mary, b. Mar. 31, 1772	3	74
Joseph, d. Feb. 6, 1787	1	54
Joseph, Jr., m. Desire SWIFT, Jan. 1, 1788	3	74
Julia A., d. Parley V. & Susan, b. Sept. 5, 1823	6	98
Julia A., m. Henry N. SQUIER, b. of Ashford, Jan. 3, 1841, by Amos Babcock	5	76
Justus, s. Joseph, Jr. & Mary, b. Nov. 26, 1769	3	74
Kezia, d. Joseph & Sarah, b. May 20, 1746	1	54
Keziah had s. Shuba[e]l b. Sept. 23, 1766	4	23
Kezia, m. Hubbard SMITH, [ ]	4	100
Lemuel, s. Joseph, Jr. & Mary, b. July 22, 1777	3	74
Levi, s. Salvenus & Rebeckah, b. Nov. 5, 1760	3	1
Louis, d. James & Annah, b. Aug. 18, 1775	4	51
Lois, d. Freeman & Lois, b. Nov. 13, 1799	4	48
Louisa, s. [d.] Smith & Sarah, b. Feb. 6, 1826	6	54
[Lovell], m. Salla MAINER, Apr. 7, 17[ ]	4	285
Lowel*, s. Robert & Sarah, b. Sept. 4, 177[ ] (*Perhaps Lovell?)	3	107
Luseena, d. Salvenus & Rebeckah, b. Nov. 15, 1775 ; d. Dec. 7, 1775	3	1

SNOW, (cont.)	Vol.	Page
Lucena, d. Silas & Eunice, b. Mar. 17, 1783	4	230
Lucia, d. Amos & Eunice, b. Nov. 23, 1804	4	20
Lucius, s. Amos & Eunice, b. Aug. 14, 1801 ; d.		
Mar. 22, 1804	4	20
Lucius J., s. Parley V. & Susan, b. Apr. 21, 1820	6	98
Lucretia ASPINWILL, d. Clarasa b. Mar. 30, 1807	4	71
Lucy, d. Samuel & Molley, b. Sept. 14, 1782	4	61
Lucy, d. Sam[ue]ll, d. Dec. 11, 1790	4	61
Lucy B., m. Benjamin B. ANDREWS, b. of Ashford, Mar. 8,		
1830, by Rev. Philo Judson	5	38
Lucy Belinda, d. Shubael & Lucy, b. July 3, 1809	4	276
Lydia, d. Simeon & Lydia, b. June 2, 1799	4	36
Mary, d. Joseph, Jr. & Mary, b. Mar. 18, 1768	3	74
Mary, w. Joseph, Jr., d. Mar. 11, 1787	3	74
Mary, d. Freeman & Lois, b. Nov. 23, 1803	4	48
Mary, m. Calvin CLARK, [June] 12, [1825], by Rev. Reuben		
Torrey, Eastport* (*Eastford?)	5	19
Mary Ann, of Ashford, m. Elisha FENTON, of Chaplin, Nov.		
30, 1851, by Rev. P. Mathewson	5	108
Mary E. T., m. Sylvanus D. WEEKS, Jan. 15, 1843, by F.		
Williams. Intention Published	5	83
Mary Johnson, [twin with Mason Sherman], d. Benj[ami]n &		
Abigail, b. Aug. 27, 1805 ; d. Nov. 11, 1805	4	88
Mary Thirza, d. Jared W. & Betsey, b. Nov. 3, 1821	6	18
Mason Sherman, [twin with Mary Johnson], s. Benj[ami]n &		
Abigail, b. Aug. 27, 1805	4	88
Mehetable, d. Robert & Sarah, b. Apr. 5, 1767	3	107
Mehetable, m. Isaac FARNAM, Oct. 15, 1792	4	84
Meriam, d. Billarcky & Molley, b. Mar. 20, 1793	4	227
Minerva Marion (?), d. Jared W. & Betsey, b. Apr. 13, 1827	6	18
Mynor, s. Joseph & Desire, b. May 24, 1788	3	74
Molly, d. Sam[ue]ll & Hannah, b. Dec. 18, 1759	1	51
Molly, d. Samuel, Jr. & Molly, b. July 25, 1776	4	61
Molley, d. W[illia]m & Mary, b. Apr. 22, 1786	4	39
Mynor, see under Minor		
Myra, d. Billarky & Molley, b. Oct. 31, 1790	4	227
Nabby Maranda, d. Benj[ami]n & Abigail, b. July 12, 1807	4	88
Nathan, s. Oliver & Elisabeth, b. Dec. 10, 1759	2	73
Oliver, m. Elizebeth PHILIPS, Apr. 12, 1748	2	73
Oliver, s. Oliver & Elizebath, b. Mar. 14, 1749	2	73
Oliver, m. Ursula STREETER, July 6, 1763	2	73
Oliver, d. Mar. 18, 1796	2	74
Orrigen PRESCOTT, s. Claras[s]a, b. Feb. 26, 1818	4	71
Parle, s. Oliver & Ursule, b. Nov. 6, 1765	2	72
Parley, farmer, b. Middletown, res. Ashford, d. Apr. 18, 1851		
ae 85	5	150-1
Parley V., farmer, d. Aug. 3, 1850, ae 60	5	150-1
Parley Vaiets, s. Parley & Eunice, b. Feb. 18, 1790, at Bicket,		

	Vol.	Page
SNOW, (cont.)		
in Barkshire County	4	271
Parley Veits, m. Susan **JONES,** Dec. 17, 1812	6	98
Pershey, of Ashford, m. James **HUNT,** of		
Hampton, Feb. 7, 1821, by Reuben Torrey	5	2
Phena, d. Sam[ue]ll & Molly, b. May 12, 1793	4	61
Pleiades, d. Parley & Eunice, [b.] Nov. 6, 1792 ; d. Aug. 6,		
1843	4	271
Pollexena, d. Stephen, dJr. & Pollexena, b. Nov. 8, 1784	4	226
Polly, m. Potter **HIMES,** b. of Ashford, May 25, 1825, by		
Nathan Hayward, J. P.	5	19
Ralph, s. James & Annah, b. Dec. 1, 1784	4	51
Rebeckah, m. Jacob **BOUTLE,** Oct. 11, 1739	1	60
Rebeckah, d. Salvenus & Rebeckah, b. Nov. 12, 1777	3	1
Reuby, d. Shuba[e]ll, 2d, & Lucy, b. June 4, 1794	4	176
Rhoda, d. William & Mary, b. Jan. 28, 1777	4	39
Rhodolphus Frederic, s. Stephen, Jr. & Pollisena, b. June 6,		
1787	4	226
Robert, s. Robert & Sarah, b. June 19, 1763	3	107
Rowsel, s. Samuel & Molley, b. Feb. 22, 1781 (Roswell?)	4	61
Roswell, s. Samuel, d. Sept. 4, 1790	4	61
Roxa, d. Billey & Olive, b. Sept. 3, 1791	4	16
Ruth, m. Samuel **FOSTER,** Dec. 3, 1724	A	10
Ruth, m. Samuel **FOSTER,** Dec. 3, 1724	1	39
Sabra, d. Oliver & Ursula, b. Mar. 5, 1771	2	74
Sabara had s. Amaziah, b. May 19, 1789	2	74
Sabra had s. Amaziah **RUSS,** s. Asa **RUSS,** b. May 19, 1789*		
(* Entry crossed out)	2	74
Salla, d. Eben[eze]r & Abigail, b. Nov. 2, 1788	4	80
Sallenda, d. William & Mary, b. Dec. 2, 1782	4	39
Sallome, d. William & Mary, b. July 14, 1775	4	39
Salome, d. Freeman & Lois, b. Dec. 9, 1801	4	48
Selvenus, s. Samuel, Jr. & Sarah, b. Mar. 17, 1731/2	1	32
Salvanus, m. Rebakah **CORRARY,** Nov. 9, 1752, by James		
Bicknell, J. P.	2	47
Sam[ue]ll, s. Sam[ue]ll & Hannah, b. Sept. 3, 1743	1	68
Samuel, Lieut., d. Dec. 19, 1743, in the 74th y. of his age	1	54
Samvel, d. Nov. 8, 1748	1	68
Samvel, s. Samvel, Jr. & Hannah, b. Feb. 9, 1749/50	1	68
Samuell, d. Dec. 24, 1756, in the 65th y. of his age	1	32
Sam[ue]ll, [twin with Semeon], s. John & Elisabeth, b. Jan. 28,		
1772	4	82
Samuel, Jr., m. Molly **WILLSON,** Nov. 25, 1773	4	61
Samuel, s. Sam[ue]ll, Jr. & Molley, b. Sept. 3, 1774 d. May		
17, 1726	4	61
Samuel, d. Apr. 22, 1791	1	45
Sanford W., s. Parley V. & Susan, b. May 20, 1828	6	98
Sarah, d. Samuel, Jr. & [Sarah], b. Jan. 4, 1724, at Woborn ; d.		
May 17, 1726	1	32

SNOW, (cont.)	Vol.	Page
RSarah, d. Sam[ue]ll & Sarah, b. Apr. 29, 1726	A	10
Sarah, d. Samuel & Sarah, b. Apr. 29, 1726	A	32
Sarah, d. Salvanus & Rebeckah, b. Oct. 25, 1753	1	47
Sarah, d. Robert & Sarah, b. Jan. 6, 1756 ; d. Jan. 26, 1756	2	95
Sarah, d. Joseph & Mary, b. Oct. 11, 1774	1	74
Sarah, w. Sam[ue]ll, d. Nov. 16, 1790, in the 95th y. of her age	3	32
Sarah, w. Joseph, d. Oct. 8, 1797, in the 85th y. of her age	1	45
Sarah, of Ashford, m. Eleazer HALL, of Norwich, [Aug.] 12, [1832], by Rev. R. Torrey, Eastford	1	48
Sarah, d. Robert & Sarah, [b.] Mar. [ ]	5	109
[Sarah], w. Araunah, d. Dec. 1, [ ]	1	286
Sarah Phidelia, d. Jared W. & Betsey, b. Mar. 30, 1835	4	18
Sardine, s. Parley & Eunice, b. July 15, 1796	6	271
Selah, s. Stephen & Annah, b. Sept. 28, 1768	4	72
Shuba[e]l, s. Keziah, b. Sept. 23, 1766	2	23
Shuba[e]ll, s. Robert & Sarah, b. Mar. 29, 1770	4	107
Shuba[e]l, m. Jerusha SMITH, Aug. 23, 1787	3	25
Shuba[e]l, 2d, m. Lucy GRIGGS, Feb. 3, 1794	4	276
Sibbel, see under Sybel	4	
Silas, s. Salvenus & Rebeckah, b. Nov. 5, 1760* (*Entry crossed out)	2	47
Silas, s. Samuel & Hannah, b. Nov. 5, 1760* (*Entry crossed out)	3	1
Silus, [twin with Solomon], s. Oliver & Elisabeth, b. Apr. 18, 1761	2	73
Silas, m. Eunice FARNAM, Dec. 16, 1782	4	230
Silas, s. Silas & Eunice, b. June 26, 1791	4	230
Silve, d. Salvenus & Rebeckah, b. Sept. 24, 1763	3	1
Simeon, s. Joseph, Jr. & Mary, b. Sept. 1, 1763	3	74
Semeon, [twin with Sam[ue]ll, s. John & Elisabeth, b. Jan. 28, 1772	4	82
Simeon, s. Simeon & Lydia, b. Jan. 15, 1796	4	36
Smith, s. Billarky & Molley, b. Aug. 18, 1784	4	227
Solomon, [twin with Silus], s. Oliver & Elisabeth, b. Apr. 18, 1761	2	73
Sophrona, d. Benj[ami]n & Abigail, b. Aug. 31, 1811	4	88
Sophronia, of Ashford, m. Nathan MATTHEWS, of Killingly, [Sept.] 12, [1836], by Rev. Reuben Torrey, Eastford	5	62
Stephen, m. Annah SHAW, Apr. 29, 1756	2	72
Stephen, s. Stephen & Annah, b. Oct. 18, 1757	2	72
Stephen, m. Polleysana BUGBEE, Feb. 10, 1781	4	226
Steven, s. Sam[ue]ll, Jr. & Sarah, b. July 5, 1738 (1730 ?)	1	32
Susan, d. Parley V. & Susan, b. Feb. 18, 1814, at Becket	6	98
Sibbel, d. Salvenus & Rebeckah, b. May 26, 1769	3	1
Sibbell, d. Salvenus, d. July 30, 1773	3	1
Sybel, m. Jacob BOUTELL, Oct. 24, 1827, by Israel P. Fuller, Stafford, Conn.	5	28
Sylvanus, see under Salvanus		

	Vol.	Page
SNOW, (cont.)		
Thankfull, d. Stephen & Annah, b. Nov. 4, 1759	1	105
Thankfull, d. Stephen & Annah, b. Nov. 4, 1759	2	72
Thankfull, m. Samuel **BUGBE[E]**, Nov. 27, 1777	4	118
Timothy, s. Sam[ue]ll, Jr. & Sarah, b. Sept. 20, 1737, ; d. Apr. 9, 1749	1	32
Timothy, s. Samuel, Jr. & Hannah, b. Apr. 13, 1752	1	51
Timothy, s. Sam[ue]ll, Jr., d. Aug. 31, 1754	1	87
Timothy, s. Salvinus & Rebeckah, b. Dec. 8, 1755	1	90
Timothy Dwight **DIMICK**, s. Clarasa, b. Feb. 27, 1820	4	71
Tryphenia, m. Nelson **WORK**, b. of Ashford, Dec. 12, 1824, by Rev. Philo Judson	5	17
Ursula, w. Oliver, d. Apr. 9, 1804	2	74
Willard, s. Jonathan & Hannah, b. Deca. 30, 1782	4	58
Willard, s. Jonathan, d. July 28, 1784	4	58
William, s. Benjamin & Keziah, b. Apr. 26, 1750	1	65
William, m. Mary **JOHNSON**, June 6, 1770	4	39
William, s. Will[ia]m & Mary, b. July 12, 1784	4	39
William, s. Freeman & Lois, b. Dec. 15, 1805	4	48
William, d. July 23, 1815	4	39
Zibe, s. Oliver & Ursule, b. Mar. 26, 1766 ; d. Mar. 29, 1766	2	72
----na, d. Jonathan, Jr. & Releif, b. Sept. 29, 1794	4	280
----lard, s. Jonathan, Jr. & Relief, b. Oct. 2, 1798	4	280
----liae, d. Jon[a]th[an], Jr. & Relief, b. Jan. 11, 1797	4	280
---- Hovey, s. Araunah & Sarah, b. July 25, [ ]	4	286
----, d. Sanford, farmer, ae 21, & Minerva, ae 22, b. May 19, 1849	5	132-3
----, s. Sanford W., farmer, ae 22, & Hannah M., ae 22, b. May 13, 1850	5	140-1
----ell, [child of Lovell] & Salla, b. Jan. 25, 17[ ]	4	285
----, [child] of Lovell & Salla, b. Sept. 16, 17[ ]	4	285
----, [child] of Lovell & Salla, b. Jan. [ ]	4	285
----, d. Araunah & Sarah, b. Ja[n]. [ ]	4	286
----h, d. Araunah & Sarah, b. [ ] ; d. Apr. [ ]	4	286
----ah, d. Araunah & Sarah, b. Ap[r]. [ ]	4	286
----n, s. Araunah & Sarah, b. Jun[e] [ ]	4	286
----, s. Araunah & Sarah, b. Oct. [ ]	4	286
----, d. Araunah & Sarah, b. O[ ]	4	286
----e, d. Araunah & Sarah, b. [ ]	4	286
-----ina, d. Araunah & Sarah, b. [ ]	4	286
SOUTHERBY, Chloe, of Pomfret, m. William M. **COREY**, of Hampton, Dec. 12, 1842, by Rev. F. Williams	5	83
SOUTHWARD, Easter, d. John & Sarah, b. May 3, 1755	2	45
Jemima, d. John & Sarah, b. Apr. 3, 1753	2	45
Thomas, s. John & Sarah, b. Apr. 24, 1751	2	45
SOUTHWARTS, Austin S., of Mansfield, m. Orrel S. **ATWOOD**, of Willington, Feb. 2, 1836, by Amos Babcock	5	58
SOUTHWORTH, Alva, s. John & Levina, b. Jan. 11, 1773	6	19
Anna, d. John & Levina, b. Sept. 26, 1782 ; d. Oct. 30, 1782	6	19

SOUTHWORTH, (cont.)	Vol.	Page
Anna, d. John & Levina, b. Feb. 26, 1784	6	19
Betsey, d. John & Levina, b. Jan. 14, 1787	6	19
Eliza, w. Ezra, d. May 12, 1822	6	46
Eliza Ann, d. Ezra & Eliza, b. Sept. 19, 1813	6	46
Eliza Ann, of Ashford, m. Josiah O. KEEP, of Brookfield, Mass., Sept. 21, 1836, by Rev. Stephen Cushing	5	61
Ezra, m. Eliza SHERMAN, Nov. 28, 1812	6	46
Ezra, m. Betsey RICH, Apr. 22, 1823	6	46
Ezra, d. Dec. 16, 1829	6	46
Harriet, d. Ezra & Eliza, b. Oct. 3, 1814	6	46
Harriet, m. Lorenzo BULLARD, b. of Ashford, Mar. 5, 1835, by W[illia]m Livesey, Elder	5	56
John, m. Sarah HEGGINS, Jan. 19, 1744/5, by Rev. John Chackley, at Providence	2	45
John, s. John & Sarah, b. Jan. 3, 1746/7	2	45
John, m. Levina DANA, Feb. 20, 1770	6	19
John, s. John & Levina, b. Mar. 20, 1775 ; d. Apr. 15, 1777	6	19
Joseph, s. John & Sarah, b. Mar. 12, 1760	2	45
Joseph Ezra, s. Ezra & Betsey, b. Jan. 26, 1828	6	46
Mary, d. John & Sarah, b. Nov. 12, 1745	2	45
Mary, d. Palmer, merchant, ae 33, of N. Y. & Ashford, & Diadamia, ae 30, b. Oct. 14, 1850	5	148-9
Mason S., m. Sophia L. SPINK, b. of Ashford, June 6, 1842, by Rev. Francis Williams. Intention published	5	81
Mason Slade, s. Ezra & Eliza, b. June 16, 1816	6	46
Nancy Holmes, d. Ezra & Betsey, b. July 13, 1824	6	46
Palmer, [twin with Permelia], s. Ezra & Eliza, b. Apr. 14, 1818	6	46
Palmer, m. Diadama ARNOLD, b. of Ashford, Apr. 15, 1845, by Rev. Geo[rge] Mixter	5	93
Permelia, [twin with Palmer], d. Ezra & Eliza, b. Apr. 15, 1818; d. Mar. 11, 1819	6	46
Polly, d. John & Levina, b. Apr. 3, 1780	6	19
Polly, m. Leonard BOSWORTH, Mar. 12, 1809	6	10
Sarah, d. John & Sarah, b. Apr. 3, 1749	2	45
Sarah, d. John & Levina, b. Mar. 1, 1778	6	19
Sarah, m. Royal BURNHAM, [July] 15, [1832], by Reuben Torrey, Eastford	5	48
Sarah Sophia, d. Ezra & Betsey, b. May 13, 1826	6	46
Stephen, s. John & Levina, b. Apr. 10, 1771	6	19
Stephen, s. John & Levina, d. Aug. 30, 1775	6	19
William, s. John & Sarah, b. Feb. 5, 1758	2	45
SPARKS, Amos, s. Isaiah & Philisity, b. Sept. 24, 1792	4	239
Erastus, s. Isaiah & Philisity, b. Sept. 29, 1789	4	239
Isaiah, m. Filisity DAWSET, Dec. 9, 1779	4	239
Isaiah, s. Isaiah & Philisity, b. Dec. 16, 1783 ; d. May 27, 1785	4	239
Isaiah, d. Dec. 7, 1794	4	239
Lawrance, s. Isaiah & Philisity, b. Mar. 18, 1782	4	239
Martin, s. Isaiah & Philisity, b. Aug. 30, 1785	4	239

	Vol.	Page
SPARKS, (cont.)		
Mehetabel, d. Isaiah & Philisity, b. Sept. 14, 1787	4	239
Stephen, s. Isaiah & Philisity, b. Aug. 24, 1780	4	239
SPAULDING, SPALDING, Abigail, d. Josiah & Priscilla, b. Mar. 28, 1778	3	28
Allva, s. Ephraim & Esther, b. May 30, 1773	4	73
Alvah, s. Ephraim, d. Apr. 27, 1796	4	73
Alva, s. Edmund & Mary, b. June 29, 1810	4	103
Andrew, s. Edmund & Mary, b. Dec. 12, 1813	4	103
Augustus A., m. Abigail C. **RICHARDS,** b. of Ashford, Nov. 7, 1843, by Francis Williams, Eastford	5	86
Azuba, of Ashford, Eastford Society, m. William **BARBER,** of Pomfret, Mar. 4, 1823, by Rev. Philo Judson	5	8
Betsa, d. Ephraim & Esther, b. Sept. 2, 1775	4	73
Cena, d. Ephraim & Esther, b. Sept. 29, 1780	4	73
Cynthia, d. Josiah & Priscilla, b. Apr. 2, 1767	3	28
Dua, s. Ephraim & Esther, b. Sept. 26, 1782	4	73
Dua, m. Marcy **WARREN,** Apr. 30, 1807	4	56
Edmund, s. Ephraim & Esther, b. Sept. 27, 1784	4	73
Edmund, m. Mary **CHANDLER,** Sept. 20, 1809	4	103
Elisha, s. Josiah & Prissilla, b. Feb. 28, 1763	3	28
Eliza, m. Nelson **WHITFORD,** [May] 31, [1837], by Rev. R. Torrey, Eastford	5	64
Ephraim, s. Josiah & Priscilla, b. Sept. 30, 1769	3	28
Ephraim, m. Esther **SNOW,** May 20, 1772	4	73
Ephraim, m. Hannah **STOWEL,** Sept. 1, 1808	4	73
[E]rastus, m. Mary **PARKIS,** b. of Ashford, May 22, 1844, by Francis Williams	5	89
Esther, w. Ephraim, d. July 17, 1806, in the 61st y. of her age	4	73
Gilbert, m. Mary R. **ROSE,** b. of Eastford, Nov. 11, 1844, by Francis Williams, Eastford	5	92
John, s. Josiah & Pressella, b. Jan. 10, 1774	3	28
Josiah, s. Josiah & Priscilla, b. Mar. 12, 1765	3	28
Luuis*, s. Edmund & Mary, b. Apr. 10, 1815 (*Perhaps "Luc[i]us"?)	4	103
Mary, of Ashford, m. Thomas W. **DELPHY,** of Exeter, [Dec.] 25, [1827], by Rev. Reuben Torrey, Eastford	5	30
Nelson, m. Susan E. **PRESTON,** b. of Ashford, Mar. 9, 1841, by Rev. Ezekiel Skinner	5	77
Olive, m. Cyrus **BROWN,** Apr.4, 1820, by Edward Keyes, J.P.	6	32
Rastus, see under Erastus		
Reuben, of Pomfret, m. Catharine R. **PAINE,** Apr. 13, 1846, by Francis Williams	5	96
Selendia, d. Josiah & Priscilla, b. Aug. 31, 1771	3	28
Solomon, s. Josiah & Prissilla, b. Feb. 20, 1761	3	28
SPINK, Hannah, of Ashford, m. Amos **RAZEE,** of Bellingham, Mass., July 1, 1839, by Rev. Reuben Torrey, of Eastford	5	71
Rufus Stafford, of Pomfret, m. Susanna **BROWN,** of Ashford, Sept. 24, 1826, by Nathan Hayward, J. P.	5	23

	Vol.	Page
SPINK, (cont.)		
Sophia L., m. Mason S. **SOUTHWORTH**, b. of		
Ashford, June 6, 1842, by Rev. Francis Williams.		
Intention published	5	81
Susan, m. Lyman **COOLY**, b. of Ashford, Apr. 25, 1830, by		
Rev. Philo Judson	5	39
SPOKE, Pierre V. C., m. Alice W. **FREEMAN**, b. of Ashford, Nov.		
13, 1831, by Rev. Ezekiel Skinner	5	45
SPRAGUE, Almira, m. Horace **CONVERSE**, [Sept.] 4, 1834, by		
Reuben Torrey, Eastford	5	54
Sarah, of Ashford, m. Samuel H. **BAXTER**, of Mansfield, Nov.		
8, 1841, by Rev. Charles C. Barnes	5	79
SPRING, Catharine, d. Josiah & Catharine, b. Mar. 3, 1750	1	30
Carthrine, m. Ezra **SMITH**, Nov. 13, 1755	2	76
Carthrine, m. Joseph **FARNUM**, Mar. 15, 1770	4	71
Josiah, s. Josiah & Catharine, b. Oct. 26, 1743 ; d. Oct. 5, 1748	1	30
Josiah, d. June 14, 1755	1	89
Keziah, d. Josiah & Catheran, b. Oct. 21, 1745	1	30
Nathanael, s. Nath[anie]ll & Marther, b. Sept. 16, 1749	2	25
Samuel, s. Josiah & Catherin, b. Sept. 20, 1747	1	30
Sarah, d. Josiah, d. Apr. 26, 1759	1	109
SQUIRE, SQUIER, SQUIR, SUIER, Abner, s. Daniel & Phebe, b.		
May 6, 1769 ; d. Nov. 7, 1775	3	21
Adaline L., d. Henry W., farmer, ae 87, & Julia A. ae 27, b.		
Jan. 6, 1851	5	146-7
Albert C., s. Henry N., farmer, ae 36, & Julia S., ae 26, b.		
Aug. 13, 1848	5	132-3
Alice, see also Ellis		
Alles, d. Philip & Elisabeth, b. Jan. 6, 175/51 * (*Date so		
written in the original)	3	65
Almire, of Ashford, m. Adolphus **SMEED**, of Mansfield, Oct.		
25, 1832, by Rev. Ezekiel Skinner	5	49
Amanda, of Ashford, m. William **NICKERSON**, of Smithfield,		
R. I, Aug. 18, 1839, by Amos Babcock	5	71
Ann, d. Philip & Elezebeth, b. Mar. 24, 1724	1	22
Azuba, m. Thomas **ROBBINS**, May 10, 1781	4	224
Calvin, s. Daniel & Ellis, b. Nov. 9, 1763	3	21
Catharine Maria, d. John W., & Phila, b. Oct. 1, 1816	4	53
Catharine Mariah, of Ashford, m. Renssalear **CANADA**, of		
Chaplin, Aug. 30, 1834, by Amos Babcock, Elder	5	54
Christana, d. John W. & [Phila], b. Mar. 5, 1831	4	53
Clerasa, d. John W. & Phila, b. June 7, 1812	4	53
Daniel, s. Philip & Elizabeth, b. Mar. 16, 1730/31	1	22
Daniel, m. Ellis **SCOT[T]**, Nov. 13, 1754	1	100
Daniel, [twin with Ellis], s. Daniel & Ellis, b. Apr. 5, 1756	1	100
Daniel, m. Phebe **SIBLEY**, Sept. 20, 1768	3	21
Edward Hart, s. John W. & Phila, b. Mar. 2, 1829	4	53
Elijah, [s. John & Millisant], b. July 23, 1852 ; d. Oct. 15,		
1754	1	100

	Vol.	Page
SQUIRE, SQUIER, SQUIR, SUIER, (cont.)		
Elijah, s. Daniel & Ellis, b. May 3, 1760 ; d. Mar. 11, 1761	3	21
Elijah, s. Daniel & Ellis, b. Jan. 31, 1762	3	21
Elizabeth, d. Philip & Elizabeth, b. July 2, 1718	A	5
Elezebeth, d. Philip & Elezebeth, b. July 2, 1718	1	22
Elisabeth, [d. John & Millisant], b. Apr. 7, 1756	1	100
Elisabeth, d. Aug. 15, 1800	1	22
Elizabeth Jane, m. David M. WHITE, b. of Ashford, Jan. 16, 1853, by Rev. Chester Tilden	5	109
Ellener, d. Philip & Elisabeth, b. Nov. 18, 1756	2	65
Ellis, [twin with Daniel], d. Daniel & Ellis, b. Apr. 5, 1756	1	100
Ellis, w. Dan[ie]ll, d. Aug. 26, 1767	3	21
Ellis, see also Alles		
Ephraim, s. Philip & Elizabeth, b. Feb. 9, 1747/8	2	65
Ephraim, m. Prissilla SIBLEY, Dec. 31, 1778	4	121
Ephraim, s. Ephraim & Prissilla, b. Nov. 10, 1784	4	121
Ephraim, s. Ephraim, d. Feb. 26, 1791	4	121
Ephraim, d. Aug. 17, 1841, ae 93, 6 m.	4	121
Ephraim Westley, s. John W. & Phila, b. May 13, 1824	4	53
Esther, d. Daniel & Ellis, b. Mar. 2, 1766	3	21
Ethan, s. Ephraim & Prissilla, b. July 3, 1779	4	121
Euphrastus, of Ashford, m. Mary GOODENOUGH, of Mansfield, Dec. 29, 1824, by John Warren, J. P.	5	17
Ezek[i]el, s. Ezek[i]el & Mary, b. Oct. 19, 1755	1	93
Fanna Sophia, d. John W., b. Sept. 27, 1833	4	53
Hannah, [d. John & Millisant], b. Apr. 7, 1754	1	100
Harri[e]t Capernaun, d. John W. & Phila, b. Dec. 19, 1826	4	53
Henry N., m. Julia A. SNOW, b. of Ashford, Jan. 3, 1841, by Amos Babcock	5	76
James Ralph, s. Nathan & Anna, b. Oct. 11, 1814	6	40
Joab, s. Daniel & Phebe, b. Apr. 20, 1771	3	31
Joab, s. Daniel & Phebe, b. Apr. 20, 1771* (*Entry crossed out)	4	50
Joab, s. Daniel & Phebe, b. May 25, 1775 ; d. Oct. 18, 1775	3	21
Joel, s. Ephraim & Prissilla, b. Sept. 7, 1798	4	121
John, s. Philip & Elezebeth, b. May 24, 1727	1	22
John, m. Millisent SCOT[T], Dec. 19, 1751	1	100
John Wisley, s. Ephraim & Prissilla, b. Jan. 15, 1792	4	121
John Westley, m. Phila CANADA, Jan. 26, 1812	4	53
Josiah, s. Phillip & Elisabeth, b. Mar. 5, 1764	2	65
Leah, d. Thomas & Grace, b. Apr. 2, 1717	A	4
Leah, m. Caleb CHUB[B], June 20, 1743, by Sqr. Grosvener	2	62
Lorenzo Clark, s. Nathan & Anna, b. May 26, 1816	6	40
Louis A., of Ashford, m. Elias L. UPTON, of Tolland, Dec. 12, 1833, by Amos Babcock	5	52
Martha, d. Philip & Elezebeth, b. Mar. 10, 1728/9	1	22
Martha, d. Philip & Elisabeth, b. June 23, 1762	2	65
Mary, d. Philip & Elizabeth, b. Nov. 1, 1716	A	5

	Vol.	Page
SQUIRE, SQUIER, SQUIR, SUIER, (cont.)		
Mary, d. Philip & Elezebeth, b. Nov. 1, 1716	1	22
Mary, d. Philip [& Elezebeth], d. May 15, 1736, ae 19 y, &		
about 7 m.	1	22
Mary, d. Philip & Elisabeth, b. May 2, 1750	2	65
Mary, d. Daniel & Ellis, b. Sept. 26, 1758	1	103
Mary, d. Philip & [Elisabeth], d. Sept. 6, 1762	2	65
Mary Ann, d. John W. & Phila, b. May 17, 1819	4	53
Mary Ann, of Ashford, m. Lorin **PARKER,** of Mansfield,		
June 3, 1838, by Amos Babcock	5	68
Meriam, [d. John & Millisant], b. Dec. 17, 1757	1	100
Molly, d. Philip & Elisabeth, b. May 27, 1773	2	65
Nathan, m. Anna **FITCH,** Jan. 19, 1811	6	40
Nathan, m. Chloe **WHITHOUSE,** Nov. 12, 1854, by Rev. J. B.		
Maryat	5	111
Nathan Henry, s. Nathan & Anna, b. Oct. 26, 1812	6	40
Orrin E., laborer, ae 22, b. Ashford, res. Willington, m.		
Cordelia E. **BARROWS,** ae 17, b. Mansfield, Aug. 5,		
1849, by Washington Munger	5	142-3
Phebe, d. Daniel & Phebe, b. Jan. 21, 1773	3	21
Philenia Ann, d. Nathaniel & Anna, b. Aug. 4, 1824	6	40
Philip, m. Elizabeth **FULLER,,** Oct. 27, 1715, by Ebenezer		
Williams, of Mansfield	A	5
Philip, m. Elezeb[e]th **FULLER,** Oct. 17, 1715, by Ele[a]er		
Willi[a]ms, of Mansfield	1	22
Philip, s. Philip & Elizabeth, b. Sept. 2, 1720	A	5
Philip, s. Philip & Elezebeth, b. Sept. 2, 1720	1	22
Philip, m. Elizeb[e]th **YEMONS,** Aug. 31, 1747, by James		
Bicknell, Esq.	2	65
Philip, s. Philip & Elisabeth, b. Nov. 6, 1758	2	65
Philip, m. Anna **STOWEL,** b. of Ashford, Jan. 25, 1826, by		
Ezekiel Skinner	5	21
Polley, d. Ephraim & Prissilla, b. July 4, 1783	4	121
Prissilla, d. Ephraim & Prissilla, b. Mar. 25, 1789 ; d. Feb. 22,		
1791	4	121
Priscilla, wid. Ephraim d. Aug. 22, 1842	4	121
Rachel, m. Will[ia]m **CHUB[B]**, Nov. 13, 1745, by Rev. Mr.		
Bass	2	53
Ruth, d. Philip & Elizabeth, b. Mar. 26, 1722	A	6
Ruth, d. Philip & Elezebeth, b. Mar. 26, 1722	1	22
Ruth, m. Jacob **BOSWORTH,** Oct. 6, 1743	2	49
Ruth Amelia, d. John W. & Phila, b. Sept. 1, 1821	4	53
Sarah, d. Philip & Elisabeth, b. Jan. 11, 1755	2	65
Sarah, d. Ephraim & Prissilla, b. Feb. 28, 1781	4	121
Stephen, s. Philip & Elisabeth, b. Nov. 7, 1766	2	65
Stephen, s. Philip, d. Oct. 12, 1773	2	64
Stephen, s. Ephraim & Prissilla, b. Nov. 22, 1786	4	121
Stephen, s. Ephraim, d. Feb. 27, 1791	4	121

	Vol.	Page
SQUIRE, SQUIER, SQUIR, SUIER, (cont.)		
Stephen Fielder, s. Nathan & Anna, b. Dec. 3, 1820	6	40
Sylvana A., m. Jonathan E. **HUSE**, b. of Ashford, [July] 2,		
[1837], by Rev. Leonard Gage	5	65
Thomas, m. Grace **DRICE**, Dec. 4, 1716	A	3
Timothy, s. Philip & Elizebath, b. May 20, 1734	1	22
William, s. Philip & Elisabeth, b. Aug. 23, 1760	2	65
----, d. Philip & Elizabeth, b. Mar. 4, 1720	A	8
----, d. John & Millisent, b. Nov. 3, 1759	4	10
----, s. John & Millisent, b. Oct. 13, 1761	4	10
----, s. John & Millisent, b. Nov. 18, 1765	4	10
----on, s. John & Millisent, b. Apr. 20,1766	4	10
----al, d. John & Millisent, b. June 15, 1768	4	10
----id, s. John & Millisent, b. Oct. 29, 1770	4	10
----, d. Bradley, farmer, & Nan, b. July [ ], 1849	5	134-5
STANLEY, Jeremiah, name credited in orginal index to page 1, but		
information regarding same is missing	4	1
STAPLES, Eunice, m. John **CLARK**, Aug. [ ], 1812	4	109
Seth, farmer, b. Uxbridge, Mass., res. Ashford, d. May [ ],1848	5	130-1
STARKWEATHER, Jabez, Jr., of Mansfield, m. Dedama **ARNOld**,		
of, Ashford, Jan. 26, 1830, by Rev. Ezekiel Skinner	5	38
STEBBINS, STIBBENS, STIBBINS, STEBENS, Elisabeth, m.		
Zechariah **BICKNELL**, Apr. 22, 1756	2	57
Elisabeth, d. Thomas & Sarah, b. Apr. 4, 1776	4	55
Elisabeth, m. Jonathan **STOWELL**, Nov. 28, 1800	4	32
Emaly, d. Tho[ma]s, Jr. & Salla, b. Feb. 2, 1806	4	280
Erastus, s. Tho[ma]s & Sarah, b. Feb. 1, 1788	4	55
Giles, s. Tho[ma]s & Sarah, b. Feb. 22, 1786	4	55
Giles, m. Anna **WOOD**, Nov. 4, 1810	6	4
Hannah, d. Tho[ma]s & Sarah, b. May 24, 1780	4	55
Harriet A., Mrs., m. Henry C. **SNOW**, b. of Ashford, Feb. 13,		
1834, by Thomas Dow, J. P.	5	53
Harriet Ann, d. Giles & Anna, b. Aug. 13, 1812	6	4
James, s. Thomas & Sarah, b. Dec. 10, 1782 ; d. Sept. 25, 1785	4	55
Rufus, s. Tho[ma]s & Sarah, b. Oct. 17, 1772	4	55
Sally, d. Thomas & Sarah, b. June 6, 1774	4	55
Sally, d. Thomas, d. May 10, 1795	4	55
Thomas, m. Sarah **TIFFANY**, Jan. 14, 1772	4	55
Thomas, s. Tho[ma]s & Sarah, b. Jan. 12, 1778	4	55
Thomas, Jr., m. Sally **TORREY**, Jan. 22, 1805	4	280
STEDMAN, STEADMAN, Chloe, m. [Samu]el **EATON**, Sept. 23,		
1765, by Elijah Whiton, J. P.	4	12
Elisha, s. Nathan, Jr. & Prudance, b. Sept. 29, 1765	4	14
Nathan, father of Nathan, Jr., d. Apr. 27, 1771	4	14
Polley, d. Nathan & Prudence, b. Dec. 19, 1773	4	14
William, s. Nathan & Prudence, b. July 8, 1771	4	14
Winship, s. Nathan, Jr. & Prudence, b. Sept. 29, 1767	4	14
STERNS, Joseph, d. Aug. 18, 1735, at the home of Nath[anie]ll		

	Vol.	Page
STERNS, (cont.)		
Eaton	1	10
STEVENS, Jenne, of Killingly, m. Richerd **TOPPING** late of		
Killingly, Mar. 19, 1746/7, by Rev. Mr. Bass	2	59
Sally, m. Abijah **BROOKS,** Dec. 19, 1811	6	15
STEVENSON, Ellen W., of Brookfield, Mass., m. Nathan		
WALKER, Apr. 16, 1848, by Rev. Ezekiel Skinner	5	102
STILES, Asel, s. Moses & Phebe, b. May 21, 1739	1	75
John, s. Moses & Phebe, b. Aug. 19, 1740	1	75
Mary, d. Moses & Phebe, b. Oct. 31, 1742	1	75
Mehitable, m. David **KENDALL,** Jr., Feb. 23, 1775	4	86
Moses, m. Phebe **CRAIN,** Jan. 8, 1735, by Rev. Mr. Mosle	1	75
Moses, s. Moses & Phebe, b. Oct. 17, 1735	1	75
Phebe, d. Moses & Phebe, b. Jan. 11, 1737/8	1	75
Samuel, s. Moses & Phebe, b. Feb. 1, 1746/7	1	75
Sarah, d. Moses & Phebe, b. July 24, 1747	1	75
STOCKBRIDGE, Almira, m. Dudley **SNOW,** b. of Ashford, [Mar.]		
4, [1825], by Allen Barnes, Elder	5	17
STODDARD, Harriet, of Mansfield, m. John **PAYNE,** of Union,		
Apr. 17, 1836, by Amos Babcock	5	59
Lyd[i]a, d. Joshua & Sarah, b. Aug. 8, 1757	1	98
STOEL, [see under **STOWELL**]		
STONE, Hopkins, of Cranston, R. I., m. Mary **BOSWORTH,** of		
Ashford, Jan. 2, 1825, by Levi Work, J. P.	5	17
Horace, m. Maria **ROCKWELL,** b. of Sturbridge, Mass., Oct.		
25, 1844, by Francis Williams	5	91
W[illia]m H., of Southbridge, Mass., m. Electa **CURTIS,** of		
Ashford, Oct. 26, 1846, by Rev. R. V. Lyon, Westford		
Society	5	99
STORRS, Aaron Hovey, s. Rev. William & Abigail, b. Jan. 20,		
1806	4	268
Abigail, d. Rev. Will[ia]m & Abigail, [b.] Sept. 15, 1791	4	268
Abigail, housekeeper, b. Mansfield, res. Ashford, d. May 17,		
1850, ae 80	5	144-5
Bezalell, s. Henry [& Polley], b. July 4, 1803	4	4
Crissa, d. Rev. Will[ia]m & Abigail, b. Mar. 15, 1793	4	268
Edwin, of Mansfield, m. Laura **WRIGHT,** of Ashford, Sept.		
26, [1838], by Amos Babcock	5	69
Lucius(?), s. Rev. William & Abigail, b. Feb. 28, 1800	4	268
Melanthan, s. William, Jr. & Harriet Elizabeth, b. Oct. 2, 1823	6	47
Rosetta C., of Ashford, m. Amos **WOOD,** of Worchester,		
Mass., Apr. 11, 1837, by Alvan Underwood	5	64
Rosetta Cecelia, d. Rev. William & Abigail, b. July 23, 1813	4	268
Sarah, m. Joel **MESSINGER,** Jan. 26, 1790	4	46
William, Rev., m. Abigail **HOVEY,** Dec. 12, 1790	4	268
William, s. Rev. William & Abigail, b. Sept. 2, 1796	4	268
William, Jr., m. Hannah E. **WOODWARD,** b. of Ashford, Oct.		
14, 1822, by Rev. W[illia]m Storrs	5	7
William, Rev., d. Nov. 30, 1824	4	268

STORRS, (cont.)

	Vol.	Page
William, s. William, Jr. & Harriet Elizabeth, b. Dec. 28, 1824	6	47
William R., of Willimantic, m. Harriet **WHITON**, of Westford, June 9, 1850, by Rev. Charles S. Adams	5	109
W[illia]m R., depot master, ae 25, b. Ashford, res. Windham, m. Harriet **WHITON**, ae 24, of Ashford, June 14, 1850, by Cha[rle]s S. Adams	5	142-3
----, [child of] Henry & Polley, b. [ ] 1800	4	4
----, Fitch, s. Henry [& Polley b.] [D]ec. 23, 1791	4	4
STORY, Irena, m. Daniel B. **CORRY,** Mar. 31, 1833, by Rev. David Bennett	5	51
Sally, housekeeper, b. Lebanon, res. Ashford, d. Nov. 25, 1849, ae 68	5	144-5
Stephen, m. Elizabeth **SHIRTLEFF,** b. of Ashford, Apr. 21, 1844, by Rev. Geo[rge] Mixter	5	89
William, farmer, d. June 25, 1851, ae 74	5	150-1
STOWELL, STOEL, STOWIEL, Alladuran, [child of] Jonathan, Jr. & Rhoda, b. Feb. 6, 1766	4	42
Amasa, s. Jonathan, Jr. & Rhode, b. Nov. 27, 1762	3	118
Anna, m. Phillip **SQUIER,** b. of Ashford, Jan. 25, 1826, by Ezekiel Skinner	5	21
Archelus, s. Jonathan & Rhode, b. Apr. 7, 1764	3	118
Archalus, m. Olive **BUGBE[E],** Nov. 4, 1791	4	19
Artemisia, d. Seth & Dinah, b. Nov. 7, 1784	4	40
Hannah, m. Ephraim **SPAULDING,** Sept. 1, 1808	4	73
John, [s. Jonathan, Jr. & Rhoda], b. July 18, 1769	4	42
Jonathan, s. Jonathan & Margaret, b. Apr. 19, 1740	1	43
Jonathan, m. Rhode **WILLSON,** Apr. 4, 1762	3	118
Jonathan, m. Elisabeth **STEBBINS,** Nov. 28, 1800 ; d. May 5, 1801	4	32
Marg[a]ret, m. Stephen **SCARB[O]ROUGH,** Feb. 1, 1743/4, by Rev. Mr. John Bass	2	42
Mary, m. Josiah **SMITH,** Dec. 6, 174[ ] ; d. Jan. 10, 1761	3	117
Mary, m. Jobe **TYLER** Apr. 25, 1751, by Rev. Mr. John Bass	1	93
Mary, [d. Jonathan, Jr. & Rhoda], b. Sept. 17, 1768	4	42
Meary, m. Thomas **CHENEY,** Oct. 4, 1792	4	72
Mehitable, m. John **WRIGHT,** Jr. Mar. 14, 1756	1	94
Meriam, d. Jonathan & Marg[ar]et, b. May 29, 1737	1	43
Rylla, d. Amasa & Bathsheb, b. July 15, 17[ ]	4	9
Sally S., m. Rouse **POTTER,** b. of Ashford, Nov. 29, 1837, by Rev. Rodolphus Lanphear	5	67
Sally Stebbins, d. Jonathan & Elisabeth, b. Nov. [ ], 1801	4	32
Sarah, m. Warren **PERRY** b. of Ashford, Sept. 28, 1824, by Edward Keyes, J. P.	5	15
STRANAHAN, Joshua C., of Plainfield, m. Lucy **FARNHAM,** of Ashford, Apr. 20, 1824, by Rev. Luke Wood, Westford	5	31
STREETER, Hiram B., of Southbridge, m. Lucy Ann **TROWBRIDGE,** of Ashford, Nov. 8, 1846, by Rev.		

	Vol.	Page
STREETER, (cont.)		
Edward A. Lyon	5	98
Lucy, m. Albigence **CHAFFEE,** Sept. 15, 1811	6	1
Ursula, m. Oliver **SNOW,** July 6, 1763	2	73
STRICKLAND, Aaron Tuffts, s. Nathan & Deborah, b. Dec. 24,		
1790	4	244
Salla, d. Nathan & Deborah, b. Dec. 19, 1796	4	244
STRONG, Alvin, of Pike Grove, Wis., m. Melissa **TROWBRIDGE,**		
of Ashford, June 10, 1846, by Rev. Edward A. Lyon	5	98
Anna, m. John **WHITMAN,** Apr. 30, 1812	4	236
Marion, m. Horatio **AMIDON,** Oct. 14, 1819	6	56
STUART, Levi, of Hartford, m. Katharine **SUMNER,** of Ashford,		
May 10, 1824, by Rev. Philo Judson	5	14
SUMNER Abigail, w. Samuel, d. Mar. 3, 1778	4	106
Abigail Peabody, d. Sam[ue]ll & Lydia, b. Sept. 13, 1786	4	106
Alce, d. Robert & Jemima, b. Oct. 2, 1787	4	252
Amasa, s. John & Mehetable, b. Oct. 19, 1767	3	34
Azel, s. Sam[ue]ll & Lydia, b. Jan. 19, 1789	4	106
Benjamin, m. Bridget **PARRY,** Oct. 31, 1748	2	51
Benjamin, s. John & Mehetable, b. Aug. 15, 1764	3	34
Benjamin, s. James F. & Adah, b. Feb. 17, 1788	4	77
Betsey, d. John & Mehetable, b. June 8, 1778	3	34
Bets[e]ly, [twin with Polley], d. James F. & Adah, b. June 6,		
1785 ; d. Mar. 22, 1789	4	77
Bridget, d. Edward & Sarah, b. Dec. 26, 1744	1	18
Catharine, d. Sam[ue]ll, 3rd, & Salla, b. May 20, 1804	4	101
Clap, s. Edward & Sarah, b. Sept. 9, 1749	1	18
Clarice, d. Robert & Jemima, b. Jan. 17, 1785	4	252
Daniel, s. Eben[eze]r & Sarah, b. Jan. 15, 1802	4	232
Daniel H., s. Timothy & Prudence, b. Jan. 25, 1822 ; d. Apr.		
13, 1826	6	88
Drusilla, d. James F. & Adah, b. Apr. 13, 1777	4	77
Ebenezer, s. Edward & Sarah, b. Nov. 18, 1737	1	18
Ebenezer, [s. Edward, Jr. & Experience], b. Aug. 5, 1757	1	100
Eben[eze]r, m. Roxalana **HOLT,** June 13, 1782	4	232
Ebenezer, s. Capt. John & Mehitable, b. Apr. 22, 1785	3	34
Ebenezer, m. Sarah **PERRIN,** May 26, 1788	4	232
Ebenezer, s. Eben[eze]r & Sarah, b. Mar. 26, 1793	4	232
Edward, s. Edward & Sarah, b. Nov. 26, 1728	1	18
Edward, Jr., m. Experiance **MASH,** Mar. 21, 1754, by Esq.		
Whe[e]ler, of Plainfield	1	83
Edward, s. Edward, Jr. & Experiance, b. Mar. 5, 1772	3	62
Elizea, d. Sam[ue]ll, 3rd, & Salla, b. Dec. 19, 1801	4	101
Eliza, of Ashford, m. Theodore G. **HUNTINGTON,** of N.		
Hadley, Mass., Feb. 17, 1841, by Rev. Nathan S. Hunt,		
of Abington, Pomfret	5	77
Elizebeth, d. Edward & Sarah, b. Mar. 31, 1731/2	1	18
Elisabeth, [d. Edward, Jr. & Experience], b. Nov. 5, 1755	1	100
Elisabeth, m. Joseph **WOODWARD,** Jr., Jan. 11, 1774	4	67

SUMNER, (cont.)	Vol.	Page
Elizabeth, of Ashford, m. Nathan NOYES, of		
Hartford, May 22, 1826, by Rev. Philo Judson	5	23
Elizabeth, see under Elizabeth BICKNELL	1	80
Ephraim Peabody, s. Samuel & Abigail, b. Mar. 3, 1778	4	106
Experience, d. Edw[ar]d, Jr. & Experience, b. Dec. 17, 1769	3	62
Hannah, d. Edward & Sarah, b. Sept. 20, 1739	1	18
Hannah, m. Christopher WEBBER, Mar. 23, 1762	3	106
Hannah, d. Edward, Jr. & Experience, b. Jan. 9, 1774	3	62
Hannah, m. Ephraim ALLEN, Mar. 6, 180[ ]	4	84
Harmony, d. Clap & K[e]ziah, b. June 10, 1772	4	78
Increase J., of Syracuse, N. Y. m. Susan E. SUMNER, of		
Eastford, June 2, 1847, by Francis Williams	5	100
Irena, m. [E]lijah DEANS, Sept. 27, 1791	4	10
Irane, d. James F. & Adah, b. Apr. 15, 1793	4	77
James Fitch, s. Benjamin & Bridget, b. July 29, 1749	2	51
Jane, d. Capt. John, d. Feb. 19, [ ], ae 12	3	34
Joan, d. John & Mehitable, b. Jan. 14, 1771	3	34
John, s. Edward & Sarah, b. Feb. 14, 1735/6	1	18
John, m. Mehetable PARRY, Jan. 5, 1761	3	34
John, s. John & Mehitable, b. Sept. 11, 1774	3	34
John, s. Eben[eze]r & Sarah, b. Aug. 26, 1799	4	232
John Cheney, s. Abigail LYON, b. Apr. 14, 17[ ]	3	105
John E., s. Timothy & Prudence, b. Dec. 31, 1825	6	88
John Newman, m. Polley ALLEN, June 8, 1797	4	24
Katharine, of Ashford, m. Levi STUART, of Hartford, May 10,		
1824, by Rev. Philo Judson	5	14
Louisa J., d. Timothy & Prudence, b. Nov. 30, 1829	6	88
Lucy, d. Benj[ami]n & Bridget, b. Aug. 25, 1761	2	51
Lucy, d. Benj[ami]n & Bridget, b. Aug. 25, 1761	3	42
Lucy, d. Benj[ami]n & Bridget, b. Oct. 25, 1761	2	51
Lydia, d. Sam[ue]ll & Lydia, b. Feb. 28, 1791	4	106
Lydia, d. Eben[eze]r & Sarah, b. June 18, 1797	4	232
Lydia, m. Isaac WARREN, b. of Eastford, Nov. 15, [1841], by		
Francis Williams	5	79
Marcelia A., d. Timothy & Prudence, b. July 20, 1832	6	88
Maria, of Ashford, m. Seth VINTON, Jr., of Willington, Jan. 6,		
1824, by Nathan Hayward, J. P.	5	11
Mary, d. Edward & Sarah, b. Mar. 17, 1733/4	1	18
Mary, d. Edward [& Sarah], d. Mar. 25, 1740	1	18
Mary, d. Edward & Sarah, b. Aug. 31, 1741	1	18
Mary, d. Edward, Jr. & Experiance, b. June 9, 1759	1	109
Mary, m. Daniel ALLEN, Jr., Feb. 19, 1764	4	33
Mary, d. Eb[eneze]r & Sarah, b. May 18, 1804	4	232
Mehitable, d. John & Mehitable, b. Apr. 29, 1769	3	34
Molly, d. John & Mehitable, b. Dec. 11, 1762	3	34
Myra, d. Eben[eze]r & Roxalana, b. Apr. 17, 1783	4	232
Olive, d. Sam[ue]ll & Lydia, b. Apr. 4, 1783	4	106
Olive, m. Reuben RICHARDS, Sept. 16, 1802	4	79

SUMNER, (cont.)   Vol.   Page

	Vol.	Page
Olive, housekeeper, d. Aug. [ ], 1848, ae 74	5	138-9
Oliver, s. Sam[ue]ll & Lydia, b. Sept. 27, 1784	4	106
Percey, d. John & Mehetable, b. Sept. 28, 1780	3	34
Perrin, s. Eben[eze]r & Sarah, b. May 13, 1791	4	232
Polley, [twin with Betsy], d. James F. & Adah, b. June 6, 1785	4	77
Robert, s. John & Mehetable, b. Sept. 18, 1761	3	34
Robert, m. Jemima [ ], Dec. 22, 1784	4	252
Roxalana, d. Eben[eze]r & Roxalana, b. [ ]	4	232
Roxalana, w. Eben[eze]r, d. [ ]	4	232
Sally, m. David **KEYES**, Jan. 30, 1793	4	114
Samuel, s. Benj[ami]n & Bridget, b. Jan. 5, 1754	2	51
Samuel, s. Edward & Experience, b. Oct. 4, 1764	3	62
Samuel, m. Abigail **PEABODY**, Apr. 10, 1777	4	106
Samuel, m. Lydia **UTLEY** Jan. 3, 1782	4	106
Sarah, d. Edward & Sarah, b. Feb. 25, 1729/30	1	18
Sarah, m. Solomon **KEYES**, May 9, 1754, by Esq. Bicknell	1	83
Sarah, d. Edward, Jr. & Experiance, b. June 5, 1759	3	62
Sarah, d. John & Mehitable, b. Oct. 28, 1772	3	34
Sarah, d. James Fitch & Adah, b. Oct. 29,1774	4	77
Sarah, m. Jason **WOODWARD**, June 20, 1782	4	224
Sarah, d. Eben[eze]r & Sarah, b. Apr. 30, 1795	4	232
Susan E., of Eastford, m. Increase J. **SUMNER**, of Syracuse, N. Y., June 2, 1847, by Francis Williams	5	100
Sibil, d. Beniamin [& Bridget], b. Sept. 10, 1751	2	51
Sibel, d. James F. & Adah, b. May 29, 1782	4	77
Timothy, s. Eben[eze]r & Sarah, b. Oct. 5, 1789	4	232
Timothy, m. Prudence **HAYNES**, Oct. 26, 1817	6	88
Timothy, farmer, b. Ashford, res. Eastford, d. July 7, 1848, ae 59	5	130-
Timothy P., s. Timothy & Prudence, b. Feb. 29, 1820	6	88
Tryphenia, m. Capt. Jason **WOODWARD**, b. of Ashford, Jan. 28, 1821, by Rev. Philo Judson	5	2
William, s. James F. & Adah, b. Aug. 13, 1779	4	77
----, child of Edward, Jr. & Experience, b. Nov. 28, 1754 ; d. same day	1	100
SWAN, Calvin S., of Northfield, Mass., m. Rhoda **BROWN**, of Ashford, Conn., Feb. 12, 1824, by Rev. Ella Dunham	5	12
SWIFT, Charles, of Darby, m. Francis **UTLEY**, of Ashford, May 3, 1836, by Amos Babcock	5	59
Desire, m. Joseph **SNOW**,Jr., Jan. 1, 1788	3	74
John Sanford, s. Sanford, farmer, of Sturbridge, Mass., ae 28, & Lucinda, ae 22, b. Dec. 31, 1847	5	126-7
TAFT, [see also **TIFT** and **TUFFTS**], Eliza J., d. Jathan W., mechanic, ae 33, of Stafford, & Sally, ae 34, b. Nov. 29, 1848	5	134-5
George W., m. Candace **CARPENTER**, b. of Montague, Mass., July 20, 1839, by Rev. Alvan Underwood	5	71
Jotham W., of Grafton, Mass., m. Sally E. **COE**, of Ashford,		

	Vol.	Page
TAFT, (cont.)		
Nov. 7, 1836, by Rev. Alfred Burnham	5	63
Minjamin (?), m. Sarah **TAFT,** b. of Blackstone, Mass., May 1, 1846, by Rev. Edward A. Lyon	5	98
Philena, m. Wells **CHAMBERLAIN,** b. of Ashford, [Feb.] 17, [1840], by Rev. Reuben Torrey, Eastford	5	73
Sarah, m. Minjamin (?) **TAFT,** b. of Blackstone, Mass., May 1, 1846, by Rev. Edward A. Lyon	5	98
Thomas, m. Mary **HAYWARD,** b. of Ashford, Sept. 29, 1829, by Dexter Bullard	5	36
Thomas J., m. Anna E. **PARKER,** b. of Ashford, Feb. 18, 1839, by Rev. Alvin Bennett	5	70
TALBOT, Roxey Ann, m. Henry A. **WILLARD,** b. of Ashford, Oct. 7, 1832, by Rev. Elias C. Sweet	5	49
TANDO, Mary, of Weathersfield, m. Harlow E. **BARROWS,** of Mansfield, Sept. 13, 1834, by Amos Babcock	5	54
TANNER, Elnathan, s. Joseph & Wealthy, b. Mar. 19, 1817	6	13
Rufus Pearl, s. Joseph & Wealthy, b. Nov. 14, 1815	6	13
Stephen, m. Mary **CARTER,** b. of Ashford, Jan. 14, 1827, by Rev. Luke Wood	5	25
TAYLOR, TAYLER, Abigail, m. Elijah **FITCH,** Sept. 24, 1745, by Mr. McKinstry	2	52
Lavinia, m. Sumner **WOODWARD,** b. of Ashford, June 18, 1820, by Philip Hayward, J. P.	5	1
Levina, m. Samuel **WOODARD,** b. of Ashford, June 18, 1820, by Philip Hayward, J. P.	6	24
Mary J., d. Apr. 12, 1850, ae 7	5	144-5
THATCHER, THACHER, Hannah, d. John & Elizabeth, b. Jan. 28, 1724/5	A	9
Hannah, d. Samvel & Hannah, b. July 6, 1751	2	18
Isaiah C., of Rochester, Mass., m. Elizabeth R. **HYDE,** of Ashford, Jan. 7, 1845, by Rev. Cha[rle]s Hyde	5	92
John, s. Samvel & Hannah, b. May 24, 1750	2	18
Joseph, s. Sam[ue]ll & Hannah, b. Sept. 30, 1756	2	18
Peter, s. John & Elizabeth, b. Dec. 12, 1720	A	5
Peter, s. Sam[ue]ll & Hannah, b. Sept. 2, 1758	2	18
Samuel, s. John & Elizabeth, b. May 29, 1723	A	7
Samvel, m. Hannah **DIMMUCK,** Dec. 18, 1749	2	18
Samuell, Jr., [s.] Samuell & Hannah, b. Nov. 24, 1753	2	18
THAYER, Huldreth, m. Lucius **HORTON,** Apr. 1, 1832, by Rev. Joseph P. Tyler	5	47
Ruth, of Amherst, Mass., m. Palmer **DODGE,** of Belchertown, Mass., [Aug.] 13, [1824], by Ezekiel Skinner	5	14
Shadrick, of Munson, Mass., m. Mary **PIERCE,** of Ashford, Dec. 24, 1827, by Nathan Hayward, J. P.	5	30
THOMAS, Catharine F., of Ashford, m. John W. **LANE,** of Worcester, June 9, 1845, by Francis Williams. Intention published	5	94
Charles, of R. I., m. Sarah **WEEKS,** of Ashford, Nov. 26,		

THOMAS, (cont.)	Vol.	Page
1829, by Amasa Lyon, J. P.	5	37
Henry, m. Almira CLARK, b. of Ashford, Mar. 18, 1844, by L. W. Blood	5	88
Hiram, m. Emma F. CHAPMAN, Jan. 23, 1844, by Francis Williams, Eastford	5	87

THOMPSON, TOMSON, THOMSON, TOMSEN, Abel, s. David

& Patience, b. Jan. 25, 1761	3	71
An[n]e, d. John & Elenor, b. Feb. 19, 1723/4	A	9
Benj[ami]n, s. Jesse [& Johannah], b. Apr. 21, 1776	4	88
Brainard, m. Sarah TUFTS, b. of Eastford, Apr. 29, 1845, by Francis Williams	5	94
Demaris, d. Stephen & Eunice, b. Aug. 17, 1798	6	7
Dianna, d. Stephen & Eunice, b. Jan. 7, 1816	6	7
Enos, s. James & Rachel, b. Jan. 2, 1772	4	255
Eunice, Mrs., of Eastford, m. J. May SABINE, of Woodstock, Jan. 5, 1846, by Francis Williams	5	96
James, s. David & Patience, b. Jan. 15, 1765	3	71
Jesse, m. Johannah HILL, [ ]	4	88
John, m. Sarah CHAMBERLIN, Oct. 4, 1770	4	65
Mat[t]hew, s. Mat[t]hew & Mary, b. Nov. 1, 1719	A	6
Patience, d. David & Patience, b. Nov. 9, 1763	3	71
Prudence, d. John & Sarah, b. Sept. 3, 1771	4	65
Roswell, s. James & Rachel, b. Oct. 13, 1775. Recorded Jan. or Feb. 1789	4	255
Sarah, of Ashford, m. Chester W. CARDER, of Killingly, Jan. 11, 1837, by Rev. Reuben Torrey, Eastford	5	63
Uriel, s. John & Sarah, b. June 14, 1773	4	65

THRASKER, Polly, Mrs., of Stafford, m. John C. SMITH, of

Ashford, Apr. 13, 1834, by Nathaniel Sheffield, Elder	5	54

THRESHER, Harriet Chapman, of Ashford, m. William Nelson

HOW, of Woodstock, June, 27, 1836, by Alvan Underwood, of Westford	5	60
THRIFT, Lydia, d. John & Zean, b. Dec. 5, 1778	4	227

THROOP, Mary, m. Thomas CHAPMAN, Jan. 26, 1729, by Rev.

Mr. Solomon Williams	1	52
TIFFANY,TIFFENY, Abigail, d. Thomas & Marcy, b.Aug. 10,1720	A	6
Abiga[i]ll, d. Tho[ma]s, Jr. & Mercy, b. Aug. 10, 1720	1	2
Alicena, d. Simeon & Easther, b. Dec. [ ]	4	99
Amasa, s. Ezekiel & Mary, b. Nov. 6, 1767	2	81
Amasa, m. Sarah JOHNSON, Nov. 26, 1789	4	259
Ann, m. Nehemiah SMITH, Dec. 25, 1745, by Rev. Mr. Bass	2	54
An[n]e, d. Thomas & Mercy, b. July 7, 1723	A	7
Anne, d. Tho[ma]s, Jr. & Mercy, b. July 7, 1723	1	2
Bethyah, d. Thomas & Marcy, b. Nov. 18, 1721	A	5
Bethyah, d. Tho[ma]s, Jr. & Mercy, b. Nov. 18, 1721	1	2
Bethyah, of Lym[e], m. Eleazer TIFFENY, of Ashford, Dec. 23, 1734, by Justice Lord, of Lym[e]	1	44
Bethiah, d. Eleazer & Bethyah, b. Oct. 24, 1735	1	44

TIFFANY, TIFFENY, (cont.)	Vol.	Page
Bethyah, m. David **EATON**, Mar. 11, 1741/2, by Rev. James Hale	1	64
Betsey, d. Simeon & Esther, b. Apr. 23, 1781 ; d. June 3, 1781	4	99
Betsey, d. Sim[eon] & Esther, b.Jan. 18, 17[ ] ; d. May 4,1780	4	99
Clark, s. William & Molley, b. June 20, 1778	4	89
David, s. Edward & Tabitha, b. Mar. 16, 1732 ; d. Sept. 6,1742	1	14
Edward, m. Tabitha **HUMPHREY**, Jan. 27, 1725/6, by Rev. James Hale	A	10
Edward, m. Tabitha **HUMPHRY**, Jan. 27, 1725/6, by Rev. James Hale	1	14
Edward, s. Edward & Tabitha, b. Dec. 16, 1728 ; d. Sept. 19, 1742	1	14
Edward, s. Edward & Tabitha, b. Aug. 25, 1743 ; d. Nov. 27, 1748	1	14
Edward, d. July 29, 1770	1	13
Eleazer, of Ashford, m. Bethyah **TIFFENY**, of Lym[e], Dec. 23, 1734, by Justice Lord, of Lym[e]	1	44
Ezekiel, s. Thomas & Mercy, b. Dec. 30, 1724	A	8
Ezekiel, s. Tho[ma]s, Jr. & Mercy, b. Dec. 30, 1724	1	24
Ezekiel, m. Mary **KNOWLTON**, Mar. 9, 1748/9, by Rev. Mr. John Bass	2	81
Ezekiel, s. Ezekiel & Mary, b. Mar. 12, 1763	2	81
Ezra, s. Ezekiel & Mary, b. June 27, 1765	2	81
Hannah, d. Edward & Tabitha, b. Mar. 28, 1727	A	10
Hannah, d. Edward & Tabitha, b. Mar. 28, 1727	1	14
Hannah, d. Thomas, Jr. & Mar[cy], b. Nov. 11, 1733	1	2
Hannah, w. Thomas, d. Mar. 7, 1733/4	1	2
Hannah, d. Thomas & Mercy, d. Oct. 13, 1742, in the 9th y. of her age	1	51
Hannah, m. Benjamin **CLARK**, Dec. 17, 1747	2	25
Kezia, d. Nath[anie]ll & Keziah, b. June 2, 1727	A	6
Lois, d. Edward & Tabitha, b. Oct. 6, 1734	1	14
Lois, m. John **HOLMES**, Jan. 30, 1754	1	82
Marcy, d. Ezekiel & Mary, b. Dec. 1, 1755	2	81
Mary, d. Thomas & Mercy, b. Nov. 24, 1726	A	10
Mary, d. Tho[ma]s, Jr. & Mercy, b. Nov. 24, 1726	1	2
Mary, d. Tho[ma]s, Jr., d. Feb.10,1741/2, in the 16th of her age	1	51
Mary, d. Edward & Tabatha, b. July 9, 1747	1	14
Molley, w. William, d. July 3, 1778	4	89
Nathan, s. Nathan[i]el & Keziah, b. May 14, 1733	1	29
Nathaniel, m. Keziah **WARD**, Sept. 6, 1726	A	6
Nath[anie]ll, s. Nath[anie]ll & Kezia, b. May 1, 1731	1	29
Percey, d. Simeon & Esther, b. Jan. 7, 1786	4	99
Sarah, d. Tho[ma]s, Jr. & Marcy, b. June 27, 1736	1	51
Sarah, d. Tho[ma]s, d. Oct. 30, 1748, in the 13th y. of her age	1	51
Sarah, d. Ezekiel & Mary, b. Nov. 26, 1749	2	81
Sarah, m. Thomas **STIBBINS**, Jan. 14, 1772	4	55

	Vol.	Page
TIFFANY, TIFFENY, (cont.)		
Selina, d. Tho[ma]s & Elisabeth, b. July 30, 1777	4	110
Semeon, s. Thomas, Jr. & Marcy, b. Aug. 24, 1732	1	2
Simeon, s. Thomas, d. Sept. 21, 1742, in the 11th y. of his age	1	51
Simeon, s. Ezekiel & Mary, b. May 29, 1751	2	81
[Simeon], [m.] Esther **CLARK**, Dec. 28, 1775	4	99
Simeon, s. Simeon & Esther, b. July 26, 178[ ] ; d. Sept. 5, 1782	4	99
Stephen, s. Amasa & Sarah, b. Feb. 21, 1792	4	259
Thomas, Jr., m. Mercy **REED**, June 11, 1719, by Dan[ie]ll Smith, Justice	1	2
Thomas, s. Thomas, Jr. & Marcy, b. Dec. 30, 1728/9	1	2
Thomas, Jr., m. Elisabeth **MARCY**, Apr. 19, 1753, by Mr. Stephen Williams	1	88
Thomas, d. Jan. 29, 1768	1	2
Thomas, m. El[i]sabeth **FOLLET**, Apr. 15, 1777	4	110
Thomas, d. May 31, 1778	4	110
Thomas, s. Amasa & Sarah, b. July 27, 1796	4	259
William, s. Ezekiel & Mary, b. July 30, 1753	2	81
William, m. Molly **CLARK**, Nov. 16, 1775	4	89
William, s. William & Molly, b. Sept. 26, 1776	4	89
----, s. Ezekiel, b. Nov. 5, 1772	2	81
----ty, d. Simeon & Esther, b. Dec. 13, 1776	4	99
TIFT, [see also **TAFT** and **TUFFTS**], Mary A., m. W[illia]m Y. **GURLEY**, Apr. 15, 1844, by Rev. Washington Munger	5	89
TILDEN, Mary, m. Augustus **DODGE**, b. of Ashford, Apr. 5, 1835, by W[illia]m Livesey, Elder	5	56
TOBIE, Clement, of Dover, Mass., m. Dilotia **WILSON**, of Ashford, Jan. 1, 1823, by Reuben Torrey	5	7
TOPLIFF, Cynthia, m. Abel **HENDEE**, Apr. 4, 1813	6	32
Lewis, of Mansfield, m. Amanda **KNOWLTON**, of Ashford, Oct. 15, 1835, by Amos Babcock, Elder. Intention published	5	57
TOPPING, TOPPIN, Richerd, late of Killingly, m. Jenne **STEVENS**, of Killingly, Mar. 19, 1746/7, by Rev. Mr. Bass	2	59
Richard, d. Dec. 31, 1790	3	105
TORREY, TORRY, Ann, d. John & Sarah, b. Jan. 31, 1730	1	34
Anna, d. Rev. Reuben & Ann, b. May 12, 1832	6	55
David, m. Eunice **BICKNAL**, Feb. 12, 1778	4	95
David, m. Lydia **BARROWS**, Dec. 28, 1790	4	95
David, d. May 5, 1833	4	95
David Bicknell, s. David & Eunice, b. Apr. [ ]	4	95
David Kilburn, s. Jacob N. & Laura, b. Sept. 6, 1815	6	17
Eliza E., d. Rev. Reuben & Ann, b. Sept. 23, 1821 ; d. Aug. 27, 1823	6	55
Eunice, d. David & Eunice, b. Aug. 23, [ ]	4	95
Eunice, w. David, d. Mar. 9,[ ]	4	95

	Vol.	Page
TORREY, TORRY, (cont.)		
George Bicknell, s. J[acob] N., b. Mar. 9, 1833, at S. Canton	6	17
Jacob, s. James, d. May 14, 1756	1	97
Jacob Nash, s. David & Eunice, b. Mar. 14, 1[ ]	4	95
Jacob Nash, m. Laura **KILBURN**, Feb. 12, 1815	6	17
Jacob Tudor, s. Jacob N. & Laura, b. Jan. 16, 1831	6	17
James, s. James & Sarah, b. May 27, 1752	1	85
James, d. July, 18, 1756	1	97
James Nash, s. Jacob N. & Laura, b. Dec. 3, 1821	6	17
John Frink, s. Jacob N. & Laura, b. Apr. 14, 1817	6	17
Laura Ann, d. Jacob N. & Laura, b. Apr. 1, 1824	6	17
Lydia, d. David & Lydia, b. Nov. 26, 17[ ]	4	95
Lydia, w. David, d. May 18, 1792	4	95
Maria, d. Rev. Reuben & Ann, b. May 2, 1826	6	55
Martha E., d. Rev. Reuben & Ann, b. June 29, 1824	6	55
Mary Elizabeth, d. Jacob N. & Laura, b. Aug. 26, 1826	6	17
Micaiah, s. James & Sarah, b. July 12, 1755	1	97
Michajah, s. James & Sarah, b. July 12, 1755	1	101
Micajah, s. James, d. Apr. 4, 1756	1	97
Polley, d. David & Eunice, b. Feb. 16, 1[ ]	4	95
Sally, m. Thomas **STEBBINS**, Jr., Jan. 22, 1805	4	280
Sarah, d. David & Eunice, b. May 2, 1779	4	95
Solomon, s. James, d. June [ ]	1	97
Susan, d. Rev. Reuben & Ann, b. Jan. 24, 1823	6	55
Thomas Stebbins, s. Jacob N. & Laura, b. July 27, 1819	6	17
Tudor Jacob, s. Jacob N. & Laura, b. Sept. 28, 1828 , d. June 9, 1831	6	17
Wayland, s. Rev. Reuben & Ann, b. Jan. [ ], 1828	6	55
TOWN, TOWNE, Mary A., of Union, m. Charles M. **ARNOLD**, of Ashford, Mar. 1, 1846, by Rev. Rensselaer O. Putney	5	96
Melissa, m. Ransom **HOWARD**, b. of Belchertown, Mass., [Jan.] 10, [1838], by Rev. Erastus Benton	5	67
TRACY, Edmund, s. Nehemiah & Meriam, b. July 4, 1767	4	29
Irena, d. Nehemiah & Miriam, b. June 27, 1769	4	29
Julia R., of Seconk, Mass., m. Richard A. **BROWN**, of R. I., May 16, 1823, by Philip Hayward, J. P.	5	9
TREADWAY, William **WAISE**, s. Dyer & Jerush[a], b. July 1, 1804	4	28
TRESCOT, [see under **TRISCOT**]		
TRISCOT, TRISKET, TRESKET, TRESCOT, TRISCOTT,		
Abiel, m. David **WRIGHT**, Feb. 17, 1732, by Rev. Eleazer Williams	1	43
An[n]e, [twin with Elener], d. John & Rebeckah, b. June 25, 1748 ; d. Mar. 25, 1748/9	2	31
Bridget, m. Edward **LEWES**, Jan. 7, 1735/6, by Rev. Mr. Eleazer Williams	1	48
Elener, [twin with An[n]e], d. John & Rebeckah, b. June 25, 1748	2	31

	Vol.	Page
TRISCOT, TRISKET, TRESKET, TRESCOT, TRISCOTT,(cont)		
Hannah, m. Robert MASON, Aug. 23, 1739	1	34
Hannah, d. Joseph & Irana, b. June 21, 1781	4	81
Hezekiah, s. Joseph & Irena, b. Dec. 11, 1789	4	81
Irena, d. Joseph & Irena, b. May 9, 1788	4	81
Jerusha, d. Joseph & Irena, b. Apr. 16, 1784	4	81
Jesse, s. Joseph & Irene, b. Nov. 13, 1773	4	81
John, m. Rebeckah KENDAL, Oct. 18, 1743, by Rev. Mr. John Bass	2	31
John, s. John & Rebackah, b. July 14, 1746 ; d. Sept. 6, 1748	2	31
John, m. Mary KENDEL, Nov. 23, 1749, by Rev. Mr. John Bass	2	22
John, s. John & Mary, b. Dec. 4, 1756	2	22
John, d. Aug. 20, 1757	2	22
John, s. Joseph & Irena, b. Sept. 14, 1775	4	81
Joseph, s. John & Mary, b. Sept. 20, 1753	2	22
Joseph, m. Irene FOLLET, Nov. 30, 1773	4	81
Joseph, s. Joseph & Irena, b. Feb. 13, 1779	4	81
Mary, d. Joseph & Irena, b. Mar. 24, 1787	4	81
Nathan, s. Joseph & Irena, b. Sept. 24, 1777	4	81
Rebeckah, w. John, d. June 26, 1749	2	31
Rebeccah, d. John & Mary, b. May 30, 1751	2	22
Sarah, d. John [& Rebeckah], d. Oct. 16, 1748	2	31
Sarah, d. John & Rebacah, b. Nov. 18, 1744	2	31
Susanna, d. Joseph & Irena, b. Jan. 26, 1783	4	81
TROWBRIDGE, Amasa, s. John W. & Delotia, b. Feb. 10, 1831	6	100
Amos, m. Luretta CARPENTER, Feb. 10, 1813	6	20
Arsinoe, d. Elisha & Esther, b. July 23, 1816	4	277
Asaph, s. Elisha & Esther, b. Dec. 3, 1813	4	277
Caroline, m. Hiram TUFTS, b. of Eastford, Apr. 29, 1845, by Francis Williams	5	94
Catherine, d. Ephraim & Hannah, b. Jan. 28, 1830	6	16
Charles, s. Ephraim & Hannah, b. Apr. 20, 1840	6	16
Edward, s. Ephriam & Hannah, b. Mar. 29, 1832	6	16
Elethiah, d. Ephriam & Hannah, b. July 12, 1825	6	16
Elisha, m. Esther WORK, Nov. 14, 1793	4	277
Elisha, s. John W. & Delotia, b. Apr. 25, 1833	6	100
Elisha Ranson, s. Elisha & Esther, b. Jan. 9, 180[ ]	4	277
Eliza, d. Ephraim & Hannah, b. May 30, 1823	6	16
Ephraim, m. Hannah WORK, Apr. 29, 1818	6	16
Esther, d. Elisha & Esther, b. Mar. 7, 1794	4	277
Eveline, C., m. Calvin C. WHE[E]LOCK, of Southbridge, Mass., Feb. 8, 1847, by Rev. Edward A. Lyon, Eastford	5	100
Fanny, m. Augustus BOLLES, Nov. 27, 1798	4	29
Frances, d. Elisha & Esther, b. Sept. 26, 179[ ]	4	277
Frances D., m. Billashey SNOW, Jr., Dec. 26, 1828, by Levi Works, J. P.	5	33
Frederick A., s. Philander & Harriet, b. Jan. 20, 1835	6	100

	Vol.	Page
TROWBRIDGE, (cont.)		
Hannah, d. Ephraim & Hannah, b. Feb. 5, 1819	6	16
Hannah, m. Frances G. **WATKINS,** b. of Eastford, July 14, 1844, by Francis Williams	5	90
Henry, s. Ephraim & Hannah, b. Aug. 14, 1837	6	16
Horace, s. James, Jr. & Rebecca, b. May 28, 1809	6	40
Horace, of North Providence, R. I., m. Lucy **BURNHAM,** of Ashford, last evening, [Aug. 31, 1836], by Rev. J. Hall	5	61
Ingoldsby W., s. Philander & Harriet, b. Mar. 9, 1845	6	100
J. Augustus, s. Ephraim & Hannah, b. Oct. 13, 1834	6	16
James, Jr., m. Rebecca **LYON,** Mar. 30, 1809	6	40
James, Jr., m. Nancy **LYON,** Jan. 6, 1811	6	40
James, Jr., m. Catharine S. **WORK,** Dec. 16, 1846, by Charles Peabody	5	99
John W., m. Dototia **LYON,** b. of Ashford, [Apr.] 10, [1827], by Rev. Reuben Torrey, Eastford	5	27
John Work, s. Elisha & Esther, b. May 2, 180[ ]	4	277
Junius, s. James, Jr. & Nancy, b. June 13, 1817	6	40
Laura, m. Arba **HICKS,** Sept. 30, 1824, by Reuben Torrey, Eastford	5	15
Lucy Ann, of Ashford, m. Hiram B. **STREETER,** of Southbridge, Nov. 8, 1846, by Rev. Edward A. Lyon	5	98
Luretta, w. Amos, d. Aug. 21, 1818	6	20
Malissa, see under Melissa		
Maria, d. Amos & Luretta, b. Dec. 4, 1813	6	20
Maria, m. James H. **GILMAN,** b. of Ashford, [Feb.] 27, [1834], by Rev. Reuben Torrey, Eastford	5	53
Marius, s. Amos & Luretta, b. Nov. 27, 1815	6	20
Mary, d. Eilsha & Esther, b. May 31, 179[ ]	4	277
Mary Ann, d. Ephraim & Hannah, b. Jan. 8, 1821	6	16
Mary Ann, m. Eldridge G. **WATKINS,** b. of Eastford, Aug. 27, 1844, by Francis Williams, Eastford	5	91
Mary Work, m. Lorenzo **BOLLES,** Oct. 13, 1819	6	103
Malissa, d. James, Jr. & Nancy, b. Sept. 10, 1814	6	40
Melissa, of Ashford, m. Alvin **STRONG,** of Pike Grove, Wis., June 10, 1846, by Rev. Edward A. Lyon	5	98
Philander, s. Elisha & Esther, b. Nov. 26, 1807	4	277
Polly, m. James **LYON,** Jan. 29, 1808	4	115
Rebecca, w. James, d. Aug. 27, 1810	6	40
Rebecca, d. James, Jr. & Nancy, b. May 22, 1812 ; d. Nov. 18, 1813	6	40
Sarah D., d. Philander & Harriet, b. May 2, 1840	6	100
Susan, d. Amos & Luretta, b. Oct. 18, 1817	6	20
Thursa, d. James, Jr. & Nancy, b. Jan. 29, 1819	6	40
TRUESDEL, TRUSDAL, Jonathan, s. Tho[ma]s & Judeth, b. Apr. 4, 1741	1	44
Mary, d. Tho[ma]s & Judeth, b. July 8, 1743	1	44
TRUMBULL, Jude, b. Thompson, res. Ashford, d. Sept. 24, 1847,		

TRUMBULL, (cont.)	Vol.	Page
ae 83	5	130-1
TUBBS, Martha, m. Samuel EATON, Dec. 11, 1777	4	12
TUCKER, Prudence, m. Elisha SCARBOROUGH, Apr. 21, 1791	4	279
Zeba, s. Rufus & Abigail, b. Feb. 8, 1780	4	111
TUFTS, TUFFTS, TUFT, [see also TAFT and TIFT], Aaron, m.		
Bridget UTLEY, Dec. 19, 1754	3	24
Aaron, m. Sarah KENDAL, Dec. 25, 1766	3	24
Aaron, s. Aaron & Sarah, b. May 17, 1773	3	24
Aaron, Jr., m. Harmony HAYWARD, Mar. 13, 1796	4	240
Aaron, s. Aaron, Jr. & Harma, b. July 4, 1798 ; d. Mar. 21,		
1804	4	240
Abigail, d. John & Abigail, b. July 3, 1777	4	123
Olice, m. John BA[D]GER, May 12, 1778 (sic)	4	118
Bridget, d. Aaron & Bridgit, b. Apr. 17, 1758	3	24
Bridgit, w. Aaron, d. Aug. 16, 1759	3	24
Chester, s. Peter & Phebe, b. Feb. 8, 1783	4	240
Danforth Hayward, s. Aaron, Jr. & Harmony, b. May 4, 1805	4	240
Hiram, m. Caroline TROWBRIDGE, b. of Eastford, Apr. 29,		
1845, by Francis Williams	5	94
Hiram, of Eastford, m. Calista R. KNOWLTON, of Ashford,		
Apr. 5, 1848, by Charles Peabody	5	102
Hiram, farmer, ae 26, b. Ashford, res. Eastford, m. 2d w.		
Rosina C. P. F. KNOWLTON, ae 20, Apr. 5, 1848, by		
Charles Peabody	5	128-9
Lovia M., m. Cassander BROWN, b. of Ashford, [Jan.] 5,		
[1840], by Rev. Reuben Torrey, Eastford	5	73
Maria, d. Aaron, Jr., d. Mar. 30, 1804	4	240
Peter, s. Aaron & Bridget, b. Mar. 8, 1756	3	24
Peter, d. Oct. 23, 1757 (Date of year is blurred)	1	99
Peter, m. Phebe KENDAL, July 4, 1780	4	240
Peter, s. Peter & Phebe, b. Apr. 10, 1781	4	240
Phebe Ann, of Ashford, m. Emerson LAMBARD, of Brimfield,		
(Mass.), June 22, 1835, by Rev. R. Torrey, Eastford	5	57
Salla, d. Aaron & Sarah, b. Sept. 24, 1767	3	24
Sallay, d. John & Abigail, b. Oct. 23, 1783	4	123
Salla, d. Aaron, Jr. & Harma, b. Nov. 28, 1796	4	240
Samuel, s. Peter & Phebe, b. Aug. 14, 1785	4	240
Sarah, m. Brainard THOMPSON, b. of Eastford, Apr. 29,		
1845, by Francis Williams	5	94
Thomas Knowlton, s. Aaron & Sarah, b. Mar. 12, 1776	3	24
Thomas Knowlton, s. Aaron, Jr. & Harmany, b. Jan. 7, 1807	4	240
TURNER, Harlow P., of Mansfield, m. Marion UTLEY, of Ashford,		
Jan. 7, 1830, by Rev. Ezekiel Skinner	5	37
----, female, b. Springfield, Mass., Ashford, d. June[ ],		
1849, ae 6 m.	5	138-9
TWISS, Louisa S., of Ashford, m. James PHELPS, of Webster,		
Mass., Nov, 8, 1840, by Rev. Charles Hyde	5	75
Relief A., of Ashford, m. William A. DESPEAN, of Grafton,		

	Vol.	Page
TWISS, (cont.)		
Mass., July 17, 1841, by Rev. Ezekiel Skinner	5	78
TYLER, TILER, Betsey, m. Palmer **CONVERSE,** b. of Ashford,		
June 5, 1821, by Rev. Isaac Hall	5	3
Catthrine, d. Job & Martha, b. Feb. 12, 1773	3	8
Cumfo[r]t, s. Job & Martha, b. Feb. 27, 1764	3	8
David, s. Job & Martha, b. Aug. 8, 1761	3	8
Eben[eze]r, s. Job & Martha, b. Dec. 27, 1757	3	8
George, m. Esther **ROBBINS,** b. of Ashford, Sept. 18, 1839,		
by Rev. Alvan Underwood	5	71
Jobe, m. Mary **STOWEL,** Apr. 25, 1751, by Rev. Mr. John		
Bass	1	93
Job, m. Martha **CHAFFE,** Oct. 6, 1767	3	8
Job, s. Job & Martha, b. June 22, 1767	3	8
John, s. Job & Martha, b. Mar. 12, 1770	3	8
John, Jr., m. Roxy **HOLMAN,** b. of Ashford, Jan. 11, 1838, by		
Alvan Underwood	5	67
Sam[ue]ll, s. Job & Martha, b. Apr. 12, 1759	3	8
William, s. Job & Martha, b. Oct. 4, 1775	3	8
----, d. David & Elizabeth, b. Mar. 4, 1724	A	8
UNDERWOOD, Abner, of Woodstock, m. Mary S. **GRIGGS,** of		
Ashford, Apr. 15, 1844, by Rev. L. W. Blood	5	89
Adin, of Union, m. Anna **RIDER,** of Ashford, Feb. 6, 1843, by		
J. M. Bidwell	5	84
Alvin, of Monson, Mass., m. Ann Maria **FLINT,** of Ashford,		
June 29, 1842, by Rev. J. M. Bidwell	5	81
UPTON, Albert Palmer, s. Elias L. & Nancy, b. July 6, 1846	6	101
Arnold Beder, s. Elias L. & Nancy, b. Jan. 18, 1842	6	101
Elias L., of Tolland, m. Louis A. **SQUIER,** of Ashford, Dec.		
12, 1833, by Amos Babcock	5	52
Elias L., m. Nancy **RUSS,** b. of Ashford, May 12, 1839, by		
Rev. Alvin Bennett	5	70
Henry Harrison, s. Elias L. & Nancy, b. Dec. 22, 1839	6	101
USTICK, Hannah, d. Rev. Tho[ma]s & Hannah, b. Dec. 1, 1778	4	105
Jane, [twin with Stephen Clegg], s. Rev. Thomas & Hannah, b.		
Sept. 5, 1773, in New York City	4	105
Sarah, d. Rev. Tho[ma]s & Hannah, b. Jan. 27, 1775, in New		
York City	4	105
Stephen Clegg, [twin with Jane], s. Rev. Thomas & Hannah, b.		
Sept. 5, 1773, in New York City	4	105
Thomas Whitear, s. Rev. Tho[ma]s & Hannah, b. Oct. 19, 1776	4	105
UTLEY, UTLY, Almira, d. Jacob & Sarah, b. Jan. 17, 1800	4	225
Alvah, s. Jonath[an] & Mary, b. Feb. 1, 1777	4	59
Ama, d. John & Ama, b. May 25, 1770	4	67
Anna, d. James & Mary, b. Sept. 7, 1745	1	12
Anna, d. Joel & Abigail, b. Feb. 21, 1776	4	30
Anna, d. Nathan & Sally, b. May 5, 1805	6	29
Anna, of Ashford, m. Charles **PARKER,** of Mansfield, Jan. 7,		
last, [1827], by Rev. Ezekiel Skinner	5	26

	Vol.	Page
UTLEY, UTLY, (cont.)		
Anne, m. Samuel **WAKEFIELD**, Feb. 5, 1761	4	48
Anne, d. Jeremiah & Elesabeth, b. Jan. 10, 1768	3	51
Asa, s. William & Sarah, b. June 12, 1751	2	25
Augustus, s. Jacob & Sarah, b. Mar. 21, 1795	4	225
Betsey, of Ashford, m. Ebenezer **ROBBINS**, of Chaplin, Dec. 22, 1833, by Rev. L. S. Hough, of Chaplin	5	52
Bridget, d. William & Sarah, b. Jan. 2, 1753	2	25
Bridget, m. Aaron **TUFTS**, Dec. 19, 1754	3	24
Charles Cotesworth, s. Nathan & Sally, b. July 24, 1812	6	29
Charlock, d. Jonathan & Mary, b. Nov. 6, 1771	4	59
Chloe, d. Jeremiah & Elesabeth, b. Jan. 9, 1766	3	51
Chrissa, d. Jacob & Sarah, b. Sept. 11, 1790	4	225
Clara, d. Joel & Abigail, b. June 30, 1780	4	30
Clarice, d. Jonath[an] & Mary, b. Aug. 2, 1778	4	59
Daniel, s. Jer[emia]h, Jr. & Elesabeth, b. Sept. 18, 175[ ]	1	99
Daniel, s. Jeremiah, Jr. & Elisabeth, b. Sept. [ ]	1	98
Deabody, s. W[illia]m & Sarah, b. Jan. 31, 1769	2	25
Ede, d. Nathan, d. Feb. 28, 1765	4	36
Edmund, s. Jacob & Sarah, b. Dec. 18, 1804	4	225
Elisha, s. Jeremiah & Elisabeth, b. May 29, 1769	3	51
Eliza, d. Sam[ue]ll & Sarah, b. Oct. 21, 1801	4	233
Elesabeth, d. Jeremiah & Elesabeth, b. Mar. 15, 1764	3	51
Erastus, s. Jacob & Sarah, b. Mar. 26, 1786 ; d. Mar. 31, 1787	4	225
Frances, d. Nathan & Sally, b. Sept. 28, 1817	6	29
Francis, of Ashford, m. Charles **SWIFT**, of Darby, May 3, 1836, by Amos Babcock	5	59
Fre[e]love, d. Jeremiah & Elisabeth, b. May 14, 1771	3	51
Hannah, d. Nathan & Hannah, b. Apr. 23, 1769	4	36
Hastin, s. Harvey, b. Mar. 16, 1804	4	228
Jacob, m. Sarah **CRARY**, Dec. 5, 1781	4	225
Jacob, d. Apr. 8, 1813	4	225
Jacob Barlow, s. Nathan & Sally, b. Aug. 20, 1814	6	29
Jeremiah, Jr., m. Elisabeth **KINNE**, Nov. 18, 1756	1	98
Joel, s. James & Mary, b. Aug. 29, 1743	1	12
Joel, d. May 21, 1782	4	30
John, s. Jonath[an] & Mary, b. July 9, 1780	4	59
John, s. Nathan & Sally, b. Nov. 4, 1808	6	29
John, d. July 4, 1818, ae 80	4	67
Keziah, b. Ashford, m. 3rd h. Reuben W. **BAKER**, laborer, b. Pomfret, res. Ashford, May [ ], 1850, by Cha[rle]s Peabody	5	142-3
Linda, m. Joseph **WILSON**, Apr. 11, 1790	4	34
Linda, m. Joseph **WILLSON**, Apr. 11,, 1790	4	117
Loidice, d. John & Ama, b. Oct. 30, 1765	4	67
Loidice, d. Jacob & Sarah, b. Apr. 2, 1782	4	225
Laodicea, m. David **WRIGHT**, May 11, 1806	4	277
Lucius C., of Hampton, m. Sarah **MARCY**, of Ashford, Jan. 7,		

	Vol.	Page
UTLEY, UTLY, (cont.)		
1836, by Rev. J. Hall	5	58
Lydia, m. Samuel SUMNER, Jan. 3, 1782	4	106
Maria, d. Nathan & Sally, b. Dec. 12, 1806	6	29
Marion, of Ashford, m. Harlow P. TURNER, of Mansfield,		
Jan. 7, 1830, by Rev. Ezekiel Skinner	5	37
Mary, d. Joel & Abigail, b. Nov. 22, 1769	4	30
Mirenda, d. Jacob & Sarah, b. Aug. 27, 1802	4	225
Nancy, d. Jacob & Sarah, b. Feb. 4, 1788	4	225
Nathan, m. Sally CONANT, Dec. 25, 1804	6	29
Oliver, s. William & Sarah, b. May 4, 1765	2	25
Orpah, d. Jacob & Sarah, b. July 21, 1797	4	225
Patience, d. Jonath[an] & Mary, b. Apr. 10, 1775	4	59
Phebe, d. Jeremiah, b. Apr. 12, 1759	1	106
Phebe, d. Jeremiah & Elesabeth, b. Apr. 12, 1759	3	51
Philena, m. Philander LYON, Nov. 28, 1839, by Rev. Ezekiel		
Skinner	5	72
Polley, d. Sam[ue]ll & Salley, b. Feb. 10, 1784	4	228
Polly, d. Jacob & Sarah, b. Mar. 4, 1784	4	225
Rufus, s. Nathan & Hannah, b. Nov. 11, 1767	4	36
Salley, d. Samuel & Salley, b. July 18, 1782	4	228
Samuel, m. Salley KNOWLTON, Dec. 6, 1781	4	228
Samuel, m. Sarah EASTMAN, Jan. 7, 1790	4	233
Samuel, d. Sept. 13, 1801	4	233
Seth, s. Samu[ue]ll & Sarah, b. Aug. 27, 1795	4	233
Sibbel, d. John & Ama, b. Aug. 16, 1772	4	67
Simeon, s. Jeremiah & Elesabeth, b. Mar. 9, 1762	3	51
Stephen, s. Joel & Abigail, b. Nov. 20, 1773	4	30
Stephen, m. Coziah COLLAR, b. of Ashford, Dec. 6, 1830, by		
Rev. Philo Judson	5	41
Stephen, farmer, d. Feb. 15, 1848, ae 75	5	128-9
Sybil, see under Sibbel		
Thomas, s. Joel & Abigail, b. Mar. 21, 1778	4	30
Timothy, s. Sam[ue]ll & Sarah, b. July 10, 1797	4	233
Vilura, d. Nathan & Sally, b. May 16, 1820	6	29
Vine, s. John & Ama, b. Feb. 9, 1768	4	67
Vine, s. Jacob & Sarah, b. Jan. 3, 1793 ; d. Oct. 13, 1795	4	225
Volney C., farmer, of Ashford, d. Apr. 1, 1848, ae 25	5	128-9
William, s. W[illia]m & Sarah, b. Oct. 21, 1754	2	25
----byl, m. [ ], Oct. 20, 1796	4	290
VANRUM, [see also FARNHAM, Ruth, m. Hezikiah CORBAN, b.		
of Ashford, July 27, 1849, by Charles Peabody.		
Intention published	5	103
VINTON, Catherine M., m. John H. HOLMES, b. of Willington,		
June 22, 1851, by Rev. Ezekiel Skinner	5	106
Hosea, of Woodstock, m. Wealthy Matilda AMMIDOW, of		
Ashford, Jan. 28, 1841, by Rev. Alvin Bennett	5	77
Samuel, of Hartford, m. Elizabeth BELDING, of Ashford, Nov.		
10, 1850, by Rev. F. P. Coe	5	105

	Vol.	Page
VINTON, (cont.)		
Seth, Jr., of Willington, m. Maria SUMNER, of		
Ashford, Jan. 6, 1824, by Nathan Hayward, J. P.	5	11
WADKINS, [see under WATKINS]		
WAKEFIELD, WAKFIELD, Abigail, d. Sam[ue]ll & Hannah, b.		
Feb. 27, 1744	2	38
Alice, see under Ellis		
Amasa, [s. Samuel & Anne], b. Apr. 23, 1769	4	48
Anne, [d. Samuel & Anne], b. Jan. 30, 1770	4	48
Dorcas, d. William & Dorcas. b. Jan. 25, 1755	1	86
Elizebeth, d. Sam[ue]ll & Hannah, b. July 2, 1741	2	38
Ellis, d. John & Ellis, b. Feb. 12, 1765	2	38
Eunis, d. William & Dorcas, b. Feb. 25, 1757	2	38
Fanney, [d. Samuel & Anne], b. Feb. 23, 1763	4	48
Joseph, [twin with Samuel, s. Samuel & Anne], b. Apr. 8,		
1767; d. Jan. 4, 1770	4	48
Mary, d. Samuel, Jr. & Elesabeth, b. Nov. 10, 1754	1	86
Nathaniel, [s. Samuel & Anne], b. Mar. 19, 1765	4	48
Oliver, [s. Samuel & Anne], b. Sept. 10, 1761	4	48
Peteshall, s. Sam[ue]ll & Hannah, b. Mar. 6, 1746/7	2	38
Samuel, m. Anne UTLEY, Feb. 5, 1761	4	48
Samuel, [twin with Joseph], s. [Samuel & Anne], b. Apr. 8,		
1767	4	48
Sibel, d. William & Dorcas. b. Apr. 29, 1752	2	38
Walker, s. Sam[ue]ll & Hannah, b. May 26, 1739	2	38
William, m. Dorcas HAYWARD, Nov. 15, 1751, by Rev. Mr.		
Williams	2	38
WALBRIDGE, Leander, m. Emily BAKER, b. of Ashford, Nov.		
20, 1853, by Rev. P. Mathewson	5	110
WALDOW, Lucy, m. Simeon SMITH, [ ]	4	38
WALES, Annah, d. Ebe[neze]r & Annah, b. Nov. 7, 1775	4	84
Chloe, m. Jonathan AVERY, Nov. 29, 1773	4	70
Daraus (?), s. Nathan & Sarah, b. Sept. 2, 1781	4	93
Ebenezer, m. Annah BABCOCK, Dec. 26, 1773	4	84
Eleas[er], s. Nathan & Sarah, b. Sept. 14, 1778	4	93
Elisha, s. Nathan & Sarah, b. Jan. 9, 1773	4	66
Elisha, s. Nathan & Sarah, b. Jan. 9, 1773	4	93
Elisha Smith, m. Mary WATKINS, Mar. 7, 1775	4	84
Ephraim, s. Nathan & Sarah, b. Nov. 22, 1774, at Norwich	4	93
George, s. Nathan & Sarah, b. Feb. 20, 1780	4	93
Hannah, d. Elisha & Mary, b. June 19, 1760	3	36
Lorinda, d. Nathan & Sarah, b. Aug. 19, 1776	4	93
Mary, Mrs., d. of Capt. Elisha WALES, of Ashford, m. John		
KEYES, of Ashford, s. of Samson, Sept. 28, 1767, by		
Nath[anie]ll Wales, Jr., J. P.	4	9
Miriam, d. Elisha Smith & Mary, b. Mar. 28, 1778	4	84
Nathan, m. Sarah KEYES, Dec. 22, 1771	4	66
Sally, d. Elisha Smith & Mary, b. Jan. 16, 1776	4	84
Sally, d. E. Smith & Annah, b. Jan. 16, 1776* (*Entry crossed		

WALES, (cont.)	Vol.	Page
out	4	84
WALKER, Aaron, s. Samuel & Ellice, b. Jan. 20, 1776	4	99
Aaron, m. Lucy **HOLT**, Jan. 26, 1809	4	47
Aaron, d. Nov. 1, 1815	4	47
Abigail, d. Nathaniel & Jemima, b. May 11, 1721	A	5
Abigail, d. John & Mary, b. Aug. 8, 1771	4	32
Abigail, w. Ephraim, d. Oct. 13, 1808	3	104
Abner, s. Samuel & Ellice, b. Apr. 7, 1791	4	99
Abner Chaffee, s. W[illia]m, Jr. & Sylvia, b. Oct. 13, 1819	4	78
Ama, d. Eben[eze]r & Hannah, b. June 25, 1769	3	26
Amasa, s. Ebenezer & Hannah, b. Mar. 21, 1767	3	26
Anna, m. Gordin **BIRCHARD**, Sept. 16, 1798	4	59
Anna, d. Sam[ue]l & Livina, b. June 27, 1813	4	68
Asenath, s. (sic) Samuel, Jr. & Ellice, b. Nov. 9, 1785	4	99
Benjamin, s. Nathaniel & Rebecca, b. Aug. 4, 1709	A	1
Benj[ami]n, [s. Benj[ami]n & Mary], b. Feb. 28, 1728 ; d. the 6th of Mar. following	1	33
Benjamin, s. Benjamin & Mary, b. July 20, 1730	1	33
Benjamin, Jr., m. Mary **JOHNSON**, Mar. 26, 1758	1	101
Benjamin, [J]r., s. Benj[ami]n & Mary, b. Sept. 9, 1760	1	111
Benj[ami]n, Jr., m. Rhoda **NOTT**, Mar. 29, 1787	4	261
Benoni, of Union, m. Wid. Mary **HIMES**, of Ashford, July 24, 1836, by Edward s. Keyes, J. P.	5	61
Bethiah, w. Eben[eze]r, d. Oct. 10, 1771	4	41
Botoo[y], d. Benj[ami]n, Jr. & Rhoda, b. Apr. 29 1790	4	261
Caleb, s. Will[ia]m & Hannah, b. Mar. 16, 1773	4	41
Caleb, s. Caleb & Abigail, b. Jan. 26, 1796 ; d. Jan. 29, 1796	4	40
Caleb, m. Abigail **DIMICK**, Oct. 23, 1796	4	40
Calvin, [twin with Luther], s. Will[ia]m & Hannah, b. Jan. 15, 1775	4	41
Calvin, [twin with Luther, s. Will[ia]m & Hannah], d. Feb. 19, 1775	4	41
Debbe, d. Benj[ami]n, Jr. & Rhoda, b. Jan. 24, 1788	4	261
Dorathy, m. Squire **HILL**, Oct. 25, 1770	4	110
Ebenezer, s. Benjamin & Mary, b. July 23, 1731	1	33
Ebenezer, m. Hannah **SMITH**, Jan. 10, 1754	1	82
Ebenezer, s. Obediah & Mary, b. June 12, 175[ ]	1	81
Ebenezer, s. Ebenezer & Hannah, b. Dec. 21, 1760	3	26
Eben[eze]r, d. July 5, 1799	4	41
Edward, s. Nathaniel & Jemima, b. Sept. 23, 1725	A	9
Edward, d. Jan. 13, 1731/2, ae 41 y. & about 6 wks.	1	3
Elisa, d. Samuel & Ellice, b. Dec. 11, 1794	4	99
Eliza, d. Caleb & Abigail, b. Nov. 23, 1799	4	40
Elezebeth, [twin with Mary], d. Benj[ami]n & Mary, b. May 14, [1726] ; d. [May] 15, 1726	1	33
Elizebeth, d. Benj[ami]n & Mary, b. July 11, 1729	1	33
Elisabeth, d. Will[ia]m & Hannah, b. Jan. 11, 1771	4	41
Elisabeth, d. Sam[ue]ll & Thiah, b. Nov. 8, 1785	4	49

	Vol.	Page
WALKER, (cont.)		
Elisabeth, m. Experiance J. **AMIDON,** Jan. 5, 1807	4	60
Ephraim, s. Benjamin & Mary, b. Feb. 15, 1734/5	1	33
Ephriam, s. James & Sarah, b. Oct. 21, 1793	4	266
Ephriam, d. Mar. 21, 1811	3	104
Esther, d. Benj[ami]n, Jr., b. Aug. 9, 1770	3	132
Eveline, d. Palmer & Mary, b. Nov. 16, 1835	6	73
Francis, s. W[illia]m & Sylvia, b. Mar. 1, 1817	4	78
Hannah, [twin with Susan[n]ah], d. Nathaniel & Jemimah, b. Mar. 24, 1728	1	3
Hannah, d. Benjamin & Mary, b. May 9, 1737 ; d. July 9, 1737	1	33
Hannah, d. Ebenezer & Hannah, b. Aug. 11, 1756	1	93
Hannah, d. Benjamin, Jr. & Mary, b. Feb. 7, 1759	1	103
Hannah, d. Sam[ue]l & Ellice, b. June 4, 1779	4	99
Harmany, d. Sam[ue]l & Livina, b. Sept. 3, 1809	4	68
Harvey, s. Timothy & Joanna, b. Feb. 2, 1818 (sic) (1808?)	4	105
Hezekiah, d. (sic) Nathaniel & Jemima, b. July 8, 1723	A	7
Huldah Ainsworth, d. Palmer & Mary, b. Sept. 13, 1839	6	73
Israel, s. Nathaniel & Jemima, b. Mar. 18, 1719	A	5
Jacob. s. Stephen & Hannah, b. Nov. 4, 1775	4	80
James, s. Eb[nezer] & Hannah, b. July 9, 1762	3	26
James, s. Stephen & Hannah, b. Sept. 18, 1778	4	80
James, m. Sarah **FLINT,** June 14, 1787	4	266
James Harvey, s. James & Sarah, b. Mar. 30, 1790	4	266
Jemimah, d. Obadiah & Mary, b. Jan. 29, 1743/4	2	50
John, s. Benj[ami]n & Mary, b. Nov. 10, 1743	1	34
John, m. Mary Ann **GILBORN,** Mar. 2, 1769	4	32
John, s. John & Mary, b. June 19, 1774	4	32
John, d. Nov. 11, 1776	4	32
John, s. Sarah, of Union b. Oct. 22, 1847	5	126-7
John Milton, s. Timothy & Joanna, b. May 2, 1804	4	105
John Palmer, s. Palmer & Mary, b. Jan. 24, 1832	6	73
Jonathan Case, s. Samuel & Ellice, b. Jan. 5, 1799	4	99
Joseph, s. Benjamin & Mary, b. Mar. 24, 1746 ; d. Mar. 18, 1769	1	38
Joseph, s. John & Mary Ann, b. Oct. 2, 1769	4	32
Joseph, s. Parley & Rebeckah, b. Mar. 10, 1803	4	81
Joseph, [s. Palmer & Mary], b. May 31, 1833	6	73
Judah, d. Will[ia]m & Hannah, b. May 17, 1769	4	41
Judith, m. Abner **CHAFFEE,** Dec. 9, 1790	4	21
Keziah Abiga[i]l, d. Obadiah & Mary, b. June 22, 1746	2	50
Lemuel, s. W[illia]m & Sylvia, b. Aug. 12, 1812	4	78
Levi, s. Timothy & Joanna, b. Mar. [ ], 1810	4	105
Levine, w. Samuel, d. Sept. 28, 1815	4	68
Life, [twin with Linbe(?)], child of Sam[ue]ll, Jr. & Ellice, b. July 1, 17[ ]	4	99
Liman, s. Timothy & Joanna, b. Nov. 5, 1805	4	105
Linbe(?), [twin with Life(?), child of Sam[ue]ll, Jr. & Ellice		

WALKER, (cont.)	Vol.	Page
b. July 1, 17[ ]	4	99
Lucius, s. Sam[ue]ll & Livina, b. May 10, 1806	4	68
Lucy Main, d. Aaron & Lucy, b. Nov. 11, 1813	4	47
Luther, [twin with Calvin], s. Will[ia]m & Hannah, b. Jan. 15, 1775 ; d. Feb. 18, 1775	4	41
Lydia, d. Sam[ue]ll & Livina, b. Sept. 30, 1804	4	68
Maria Trumbull, d. Aaron & Lucy, b. July 11, 1810	4	47
Mary, [twin with Elezebeth], d. Benj[ami]n & Mary, b. May 14, [1726] ; d. [May] 15, 1726	1	33
Mary, d. Benjamin & Mary, b. Sept. 1, 1732	1	33
Mary, m. James AVERIL, Mar. 3, 1757	1	103
Mary Ann, d. Ebenezer & Hannah, b. Aug. 20, 1757	1	101
Mary Ann, m. Zera PRESTON Oct. 7, 1779	4	111
Milo, s. Timothy & Joanna, b. Oct. 25, 1821	4	105
Minerva, s. Timothy & Joanna, b. July 21, 1813	4	105
Minerva, of Ashford, m. Willard FULLER, of Willington, May 19, 1831, by Rev. Luke Wood	5	43
Nathan, s. Peter & Sarah, b. Dec. 28, 1795	4	266
Nathan, m. Ellen W. STEVENSON, of Brookfield, Mass., Apr. 16, 1848, by Rev. Ezekiel Skinner	5	102
Nathaniel, s. Nathaniel & Rebecca, b. Sept. 23, 1707	A	1
Nathan[i]el, s. Obadiah & Mary, b. July 6, 1748	2	50
Obadiah, s. Nathaniel & Jemima, b. Feb. 3, 1715	A	1
Peter, m. Hannah FULLER, Mar. 17, 1748	2	76
Peter, s. Peter & Hannah, b. Oct. 2, 1748 ; d. same day	2	76
Peter, s. Samuel & Ellice, b. Aug. 22, 1783	4	99
Peter, m. Sarah CARPENTER, Nov. 13, 1783	4	266
Phebe, d. Samuel & Ellice, b. July 22, 1793 ; d. Dec. 24, 1793	4	99
Philo, s. John M. & Caroline, b. July 2, 1833	6	91
Rebeckah, d. Nathaniel & Jemima, b. Mar. 7, 1717	A	3
Rebeckah, d. John & Mary, b. June 22, 1776	4	32
Ruth, d. Benjamin & Mary, b. May 15, 1738	1	34
Ruth, d. James & Sarah, b. Dec. 15, 1791	4	266
Sally, m. James HIMES, b. of Westford, Nov. 9, 1851, by Rev. Ezekiel Skinner	5	108
Sam[ue]ll, [s. Benjamin & Mary], b. May 1, 1742	1	33
Sam[ue]ll, s. Benjamin & Mary, b. May 1, 1742	1	34
Samuell, m. Thiah CRARY, Nov. 15, 1769	4	49
Samuel, Jr., m. Ellese CASE, Dec. 14, 1775	4	99
Samuel, s. Sam[ue]ll & Thiah, b. Nov. 8 , 1776	4	49
Samuel, s. Sam[ue]ll, Jr. & Ellice, b. May 24, 1781	4	99
Samuel, d. June 1, 1791	4	49
Samuel, m. Levina ROBINSON, Nov. 25, 1803	4	68
Sarah, d. Eben[eze]r & Hannah, b. Oct. 22, 1763	3	26
Sarah A., m. Joseph C. BURNHAM, b. of Ashford, Nov. 26, 1846, by Rev. Edward A. Lyon, Eastford	5	99
Seth, of Brookfield, Mass., m. Lucretia WHITON, of Ashford, Nov. 5, 1837, by Alvan Underwood	5	66

WALKER, (cont.)	Vol.	Page
Stephen, m, Hannah **WILLSON**, Nov. 24, 1774	4	80
Stephen, s. Stephen & Hannah, b. May 15, 1780	4	80
Susan, d. Palmer & Mary, b. Sept. 10, 1837	6	73
Susan[n]ah, [twin with Hannah], d. Nathaniel & Jemimah, b. Mar. 24, 1728	1	3
Sylvia Healey, d. W[illia]m, Jr. & Sylvia, b. Dec. 23, 1814	4	78
Timothy, s. Caleb & Abigail, b. May 18, 1797 ; d. July 24, 1800	4	40
Timothy, s. Sam[ue]ll & Thiah, b. May 27, 1781	4	49
Timothy, m. Joanna **WHITON**, Jan. 24, 1804	4	105
Timothy, s. Timothy & Joanna, b. Dec. 2, 1819	4	105
Truman, s. Sam[ue]ll & Livina, b. Nov. 18, 1807	4	68
Vina Emala, d. Sam[ue]ll & Livina, b. July 31, 1811	4	68
Welthey, d. Peter & Sarah, b. Sept. 16, 1789	4	266
William, m. Hannah **SMITH**, Sept. 15, 1769	4	41
William, s. William & Hannah, b. July 22, 1781	4	41
William, Jr., m. Sylvia **CORBIN**, May 28, 1806	4	78
William Corbin, s. W[illia]m, Jr. & Sylvia, b. Sept. 11, 1810	4	78
----, d. Benj[ami]n, Jr. & Mary, b. Aug. 14, 1763	3	132
WARD, Abigail, d. Ichabod & Abigail, b. Oct. 29, 1822	6	53
Abigail, of Westford, m. Rev. Merrick **KNIGHT**, of Chaplin, June 10, 1851, by Rev. Charles S. Adams	5	109
Abigail, Jr., ae 28, b. Ashford, m. Merrick **KNIGHT**, clergyman, ae 33, b. Northampton, res. Chaplin, June[ ], 1851, by Rev. C. S. Adams	5	148-9
Amos, s. Jacob & Hannah, b. Mar. 16, 1734/5	1	40
Ebenezer, s. William & Rachel, b. Apr. 11, 1719	A	7
Elisabeth, d. Joel & Elisabeth, b. Dec. 7, 1773	4	73
Elisabeth, d. Joel & Elisabeth, b. Dec. 7, 1773	4	82
Elizabeth, d. Ichabod & Abigail, b. Feb. 21, 1815	6	53
Hannah, d. Jacob & Hannah, b. Apr. 24, 1729	1	40
Hannah, d. Joel & Elisabeth, b. May 23, 1775	4	82
Ichabod, s. Joel & Elizabeth, b. Nov. 21, 1786	4	82
Jacob, s. Jacob & Hannah, b. Sept. 22, 1727	1	40
James, s. Jacob & Hannah, b. Feb. 16, 1732/3	1	40
Jesse, s. William & Rachel, b. Aug. 11, 1729	1	28
Joel, m. Elisabeth **WOODWARD**, Jan. 13, 1773	4	73
John, s. William & Rachel, b. Nov. 9, 1716	A	7
John, m. Genne **KNOX**, Dec. 7, 1773	4	91
John, d. Oct. 20, 1776	4	91
Keziah, m. Nathaniel **TIFFANY**, Sept. 6, 1726	A	6
Lusenda, d. John & Genne, b. Feb. 19, 1774	4	91
Mary, d. Jacob & Hannah, b. Sept. 16, 1737	1	40
Moses, s. William & Rachel, b. Sept. 7, 1722	A	7
Obadiah, s. William & Rachel, b. Feb. 9, 1724/5	A	9
Patiance, m. William **KENDALL**, Jan. 1, 1740/1, by Rev. Mr. James Hale	1	47
Pat[t]y, d. Joel & Elizabeth, b. July 3, 1779	4	82

WARD, (cont.)	Vol.	Page
Patty, m. Samuel **WORK**, Jan. 9, 1800	4	77
Persis, d. John & Genne, b. May 31, 1776	4	91
Peter, s. Jacob & Hannah, b. Dec. 22, 1730	1	40
Phebe, d. Joel & Elizabeth, b. Oct. 22, 1782	4	82
Uriah, s. Will[ia]m & Rachel, b. Feb. 2, 1715	A	7
William, s. William & Rachel, b. Aug, 9, 1721 ; d. Oct. 9, 1721	A	7
WARNER, Abigail, d. Ele[a]zar & Joanna, b. Dec. 27, 1765	3	60
Abigail, d. Eleazer & Joanna, b. Sept. 5, 1787	3	60
Delight, d. Eleazer & Joanna, b. Mar. 24, 1789	3	60
Ele]a]zar, m. Joanna **HALE**, Apr. 29, 1762	3	60
Ele[a]zar, s. Ele[a]zar & Joanna, b. Sept. 27, 1767	3	60
Eliph[a]let, s. Ele[a]zar & Joanna, b. Apr. 29, 1771	3	60
Elisha, s. Thomas & Elisabeth, b. May 30, 1756	1	93
Elisabeth, d. Ele[a]zar & Joannah, b. Feb. 19, 1763	3	60
James, s. Ele[a]zar & Joanna, b. Nov. 5, 1773	3	60
Joanna, d. Ele[a]zar & Joanna, b. Sept. [ ], 1772	3	60
Joanna, d. Eleazer & Joanna, [b.] July 30, 1784	3	60
Samuel, s. Ele[a]zer & Joanna, b. Jan. 26, 1769	3	60
Thomas, s. Thomas & Elisabeth, b. Jan. 16, 1753	1	89
Thomas, s. Ele[a]zar & Joan[n]ah, b. Feb. 28, 1764	3	60
WARREN, Calvin, s. John & Elisabeth, b. Feb. 2, 1770	4	91
Chauncey, m. Sally **KNOWLTON**, b. of Ashford, Apr. 9, 1823, by Rev. Jonathan Goodwin, at Mr. Amos Knowlton's	5	8
Elisha O., of Stafford, m. Harriet **MATHEWSON**, of Ashford, Nov. 29, 1829, by Levi Work, J. P.	5	36
Elisabeth, m. Silas **POTTER**, Dec. 6, 1786	4	80
Hannah, d. John, Jr. & Hannah, b. Nov. 29, 1798	4	86
Isaac, m. Lydia **SUMNER**, b. of Eastford, Nov. 15, [1841], by Francis Williams	5	79
John, s. John & Elisabeth, b. Nov. 21, 1776	4	91
John, Jr., m. Hannah **FULLER**, Dec. 29, 1797	4	86
Lucinda, d. John, Jr. & Hannah, b. Aug. 22, 1804	4	86
Lucinda, m. Levi **WORK**, June 26, 1808	4	287
Lucinda, of Ashford, m. Thomas **CHANDLAR**, of Pomfret, Dec. 12, last, [1826], by Rev. Ezekiel Skinner	5	25
Luther, s. John & Elisabeth, b. May 21, 1773	4	91
[Lu]ther, m. Pamela **WOODWARD**, [cr. 29, 1803	4	98
Luther, m. Mrs. Olive **DURKEE**, Sept. 30, 1847, by Charles Peabody	5	101
Luther, farmer, ae 75, of Ashford, m. 2d w. Olive **DURKEE**, ae 51, b. Mansfield, res. Ashford, Sept. 30, 1847, by Charles Peabody	5	128-9
Lydia, m. Elias **DIMMICK**, Jan. 26, 1785	4	257
Marcy, m. Dua **SPALDING**, Apr. 30, 1807	4	56
Prescott, s. Luther, 2d. farmer, & Harriet, b.Aug. 20,. 1848	5	132-3
Roxey Lendy, d. John & Elisabeth, b. Nov. 17, 1775	4	91

WARREN, (cont.)	Vol.	Page
Sibbil, d. John & Elisabeth, b. May 9, 1776	4	91
Susan M., D. Thomas & Lydia, b. Mar. 23, 1834	6	102
Sybil, see under Sibbil		
Thomas, s. Luther & [Pam]ela, b. Feb. 12, 1805	4	98
Thomas, m. Lydia WENTWORTH, Mar. 27, 1833, by Rev.		
David Bennett	5	51
WATERS, [see also WATHNER and WATROUS], Edward B., of		
Providence, R. I. m. Mary CHESTER, of Ashford, Oct.		
6, 1847, by Charles Peabody	5	101
Sarah, d. Isreal & Sarah, b. July 7, 1780	4	117
WATHNER, WATTNER, [see also WITHNER], Harvey, of		
Union, m. Julia Ann WHITE, of Ashford, May 16, 1833,		
by Rev. James Porter	5	51
Lydia, of Oxford, m. Otis MORSE, of Union, Nov. 25, 1823,		
by Nathan Hayward, J. P.	5	11
Palmer, m. Mary YOUNG, b. of Ashford, Apr. 19, 1831, by		
Edward S. Keyes, J. P.	5	42
WATKINS, WADKINS, WADKENS, Abigail, d. Sam[ue]l &		
Sarah, b. Apr. 6, 1774	4	56
Adolphus, s. Jedidiah & Nabby, b. Jan. 26, 1783	4	281
Advina, [d. Samuel & Sarah], b. Feb. 9, 1765	4	56
Alexander, [twin with Sarah, s. Amasa] & Anna, b. Aug. 2,		
1756	3	105
Allen, s. Nathan & Est[h]er, b. Feb. 5, 1771	3	13
Amasa, [s. Will[ia]m & Mehetebell], b. Apr. 30, 1730	1	56
Amasa, m. Anna WORK, Sept. 12, 175[ ]	3	105
Amasa, s. Amasa & Anna, b. May 17, 1765	3	105
Amasa, [twin with a dau.], s. William & Lois, b. Mar. 12, 1797	4	6
Ann, m. Obadiah BROWN, May 9, 1744, by Rev. Mr. John		
Bass	2	46
Anna, d. William & Mehetable, b. Jan. 29, 1721	A	11
Anna, m. Amos BADCOCK, Oct. 25, 1737	1	73
Anna, m. Jonathan AVEREL Dec. 4, 1783	4	283
An[n]e, d. Thad[d]eas & An[n]e, b. May 25, 1728	1	12
Anne, d. Amasa & Anna, b. Dec. 17, 1760	3	105
Arte, s. Jedidiah & Nabby, b. Apr. 6, 1789	4	281
Benjamin, s. Edward & Mary, b. May 12, 1751	2	21
Betsey W., d. Fielder & Mariah, b. Dec. 7, 1837	6	74
Betty, d. Amasa & Anna, b. Apr. 27, 1769	3	105
Bodwell, s. [Samuel & Sarah], b. Dec. 3, 1761	4	56
Cassinai, s. Jedidiah & Nabby, b. Jan. 24, 1787	4	281
Charles, s. Alpheus & Allice, b. Feb. 28, 179[ ]	4	287
Chloe, d. Nathan & Est[h]er, b. June 29, 1762	3	13
Edward, s. William & Mehetable, b. Apr. 3, 1723	A	11
Edward, m. Mary WATKINS, June 29, 1749, by Rev. Mr.		
John Bass	2	21
Edward, s. Nathan & Est[h]er, b. June 11, 1764	3	13
Eldridge G., m. Mary Ann TROWBRIDGE, b. of Eastford,		

	Vol.	Page
WATKINS, WADKINS, WADKENS, (cont.)		
Aug. 27, 1844, by Francis William, Eastford	5	91
Elijah, s. Phineas & Mary, b. Dec. 8, 1754	1	87
Elijah, s. Phineas & Mary, b. Dec. 8, 1764	2	40
[E]unis, [d. Will[ia]m & Mehetebell], b. Apr. 13, 1737	1	56
Fielder, s. Jedidiah, b. Mar. 16, 1800	4	267
Fielder, m. Mariah **WENTWORTH,** b. of Ashford, Mar. 25,		
[1829], by Rev. Ezekiel Skinner	5	34
Frances G., m. Hannah **TROWBRIDGE,** b. of Eastford, July		
14, 1844, by Francis Williams	5	90
Grant, s. Jedidiah & Nabby, b. May 29, 1791	4	281
Hannah, d. Will[ia]m & Mehetebel, b. Jan. 27, 1741/2	1	56
Hannah, d. John & Hannah, b. Aug. 11, 1753	1	87
Hiram, s. Jedidiah, b. June 22, 1802	4	267
James, s. John & Hannah, b. Oct. 26, 1755	1	91
James, s. Nathan & Est[h]er, b. Aug. 18, 1766	3	13
Jedediah, s. Will[ia]m & Meheteble, b. Oct. 5, 1739	1	56
Jedediah, s. Amasa & Anna, b. July 29, 1767	3	105
John, s. Thad[d]eus & An[n]e, b. Mar. 2, 1724/5	A	9
John, m. Hannah **FLETCHER,** Oct. 26, 1749	1	87
John, s. John & Hannah, b. Mar. 1, 1750	1	87
John, s. Amasa & Anna, b. Mar. 28, 1754	3	105
John, [s. Samuel & Sarah], b. Mar. 28, 1767	4	56
John, s. Amasa, d. Feb. 10, 1775	3	105
John, o. Jedidiah & Nabby, b. Jan. 22, 1785	4	281
Lyman Bruce, s. Fielder & Maria, [b.] June 23, 1830	6	74
Mariam, [d. Will[ia]m & Mehetebell], b. Feb. 18, 1735	1	56
Mary, m. Edward **WATKINS,** June 29, 1749, by Rev. Mr.		
John Bass	2	21
Mary, m. Josiah **SMITH,** Dec. 29, 1761	3	117
Mary, m. Elisha **SMITH,** Mar. 7, 1775	4	84
Mehetable, d. William & Mehetable, b. June 3, 1728	A	11
Mehitabel, m. Samuel **SMITH,** Jr., Nov. 7, 1745, by Mr. Bass	1	56
Mehetable, d. Amas[a] & Anna, b. Oct. 18, 1758	3	105
Nabby, d. Jedidiah & Nabby, b. July 30, 1793	4	281
Nathan, [s. Will[ia]m & Mehetebell], b. June 29 1732	1	56
Nathan, s. John & Hannah, b. Sept. 19, 1751	1	87
Nathan, m. Est[h]er **LYON,** Aug. 20, 1761	3	13
Nehemiah, m. Bethyah **BUGBEE,** May 25, 1726	A	10
Onor, [child of Samuel & Sarah], b. Nov. 17, 1771	4	56
Phinehas, s. Ne[he]miah & Bethiah, b. June 21, 1728	1	8
Phineas, m. Mary **FULLER,** Oct. 24, 1752, by Tho[ma]s		
Tiffany, Esq. Mr. Mil[l]s paid * for him & c (*Uncertain)	2	40
Polly, d. Amasa & Anna, b. Nov. 13, 1773	3	105
Rachel, d. Thad[d]eus & An[n]e, [b.] Sept. 1, 1726	A	11
Rebec[c]a, d. Amasa & Anna, b. Feb. 16, 1763	3	105
Rebec[c]ah, m. Charles **MATTHERSON,** Jan. 30, 1782	4	122
Rhode, d. Nathan & Est[h]er, b. Feb. 1, 1769	3	13

	Vol.	Page
WATKINS, WADKINS, WADKENS, (cont.)		
Samuel, m. Sarah **LYON**, Jan. 20, 1765	4	56
Samuel, d. June 8, 1776	4	56
Sarah, d. William & Mehetable, b. Aug. 9, 1718	A	11
Sarah, m. Epherem **KYE**, June 22, 1737, by Rev. Mr. Hale	1	57
Sarah, [twin with Alexander, d. Amasa] & Anna, b. Aug. 2, 1756	3	105
Sarah, [d. Samuel & Sarah], b. July 19, 1770	4	56
Seuviah, d. Will[ia]m & Mehetebell, b. Apr. 28, 1728	1	56
Serviah, m. Dan[i]el **KNOWLTON**, Nov. 7, 1745	2	60
Thad[d]eus, m. Ann **HUMPHREY**, July 21, 1724	A	8
Thad[d]eaus, s. Thad[d]eas & An[n]e, b. Nov. 19, 1729	1	12
Thad[d]eas, s. Edward & Mary, b. Nov. 19, 1749	2	21
[Thaddeus], m. Lydia [**PERRY***], [ ], 1757 (*Illegible. Perhaps Torry)	3	131
Theda, d. Alpheus & Allice, b. Mar. 2, 1795	4	287
Vine, s. Amasa & Anna, b. May 7, 1771	3	105
William, m. Mehetable **HUMPHREY**, Mar. 17, 1717/8	A	4
William, s. Amasa & Anna, b. Feb. 14, 175[ ]	3	105
William, s. Nathan & Est[h]er, b. July 28, 1773	3	13
[William], m. Lois **JENNENS**, Aug. 18, 1788	4	6
Zerviah, see under Seuviah and Serviah		
----, child [of Nehemiah & Bethyah], b. Feb. 25, [1727]	A	10
---ard, s. Thad[deu]s & Lydia, b. Aug. 5, 1757	3	131
----, d. Thad[deu]s, Jr. [& Lydia], b. Dec. 9, 1757	3	131
----s, d. thad[deu]s, Jr. & [Ly]dia, b. Feb. 7, 1760	3	131
----nnah, d. Thad[deu]s & [Ly]dia, b. May 31, 1762	3	131
----, [child] of William & Lois, b. Jan. 6, 1789	4	6
----, s. William & Lois, b. Mar. 27, 1791	4	6
----, [child] of William & Lois, b. Oct. 10, 1793	4	6
----, [twin with Amasa], d. William & Lois, b. Mar. 12, 1797	4	6
WATROUS, WATEROUS, WARTEROUS, WARTERS,		
Elizabeth, d. William & Mary, b. Mar. 1, 1784	4	13
Elisabeth, m. Jonathan **WEEKS**, May 30, 1797	4	13
Sarah, d. William & Mary, b. Jan. 5, 1775	4	13
Washington, s. William & Mary, b. Dec. 2, 1780	4	13
William Chedle, s. William & Mary, b. Mar. 8, 1777	4	13
William, of Pomfret, County of Windsor, State of Vt., m. Experience **CASE**, of Ashford, Sept. 21, 1823, by Thomas Dow, J. P.	5	11
WATSON, Joanna, d. Azbura **WINCHESTER**, b. Oct. 11, 1819	6	103
Molley, m. David **BROWN**, Nov. 23, 1777	4	117
Rachel, m. Reuben **MERCY**, Nov. 18, 1756	1	85
WEAVER, Mary N., m. Erasmus **PROUD**, b. of Woodstock, Dec. 25, 1832, by Rev. Elias C. Sweet	5	50
WEBB, Anna, d. Jabez & Elisabeth, b. Feb. 20, 1786	4	269
Bets[e]y, d. Jabez & Elisabeth, b. June 27, 1778	4	269

	Vol.	Page
WEBB, (cont.)		
Betsey, m. Jedediah **WENTWORTH,** May 9, 1799	4	24
Ezra, s. Jabez & Elisabeth, b. Nov. 30, 1794	4	269
Jabez, m. Elisabeth **SMITH,** Apr. 9, 1776	4	269
Jabez, s. Jabez & Elisabeth, b. Mar. 15, 1777	4	269
James, s. Jabez & Elisabeth, b. Oct. 26, 1780 ; d. Apr. 28, 1782	4	269
James, s. Jabez & Elisabeth, b. Dec. 10, 1782	4	269
Nancy, m. Amos **KNOWLTON,** Sept. 13, 1804	4	28
Polley, d. Jabez & Elisabeth, [b.] Aug. 15, 1792	4	269
WEBBER, Christopher, m. Hannah **SUMNER,** Mar. 23, 1762	3	106
Herman, s. Christopher & Hannah, b. May 11, 1763	3	106
Justice, s. Christopher & Hannah, b. Nov. 10, 1764	3	106
Mary, d. Christopher & Hannah, b. Nov. 14, 1766	3	106
WEBSTER, Areta, d. Platiah & Ruth, b. Apr. 4, 1759	1	104
Chester, m. Hannah **DOUGLASS,** b. of Ashford Woods, [Nov.] 28, [1839], by Rev. Reuben Torrey, Eastford	5	72
Stephen H., of Dudley, Mass., m. May A. **KEYES,** of Ashford, Oct. 5, 1841, by Rev. Charles C. Barnes	5	79
WEDGE, James N., s. Moses & Mary, b. Jan. 20, 1821	6	38
Moses, m. Mary Ann **DRAPER,** Apr. 4, 1819	6	38
Sarah, of Ashford, m. William **CROUCH,** of Brimfield, Mass., Apr. 2, 1838, by Rev. Reuben Torrey, Eastford	5	67
WEEKS, WEEKES, Abigail, d. Charles & Abigail, b. Apr. 7, 1826	6	68
Amos, Jr., m. Lucretia **BADGER,** Oct. 29, 1837, by Amasa Lyon, J. P.	5	66
Amos K., s. Charles & Abigail, b. July 23, 1824	6	68
Benjamin Dwight, s. Charles & Abigail, b. Feb. 12, 1829	6	68
Betsey, m. William **LYON,** May 31, 1820	6	25
Charles, m. Abigail **SNOW,** b. of Ashford, Feb. 29, 1824, by Rev. Philo Judson	5	12
Charles, m. Mary Ann **SEGICK,** b. of Eastford, Aug. 18, 1844, by Francis Williams	5	91
David Dana Nelson, m. Almira **PARRISH,** b. of Ashford, Dec. 23, 1827, by Amasa Lyon, J. P.	5	29
Eliza, m. Thompson **LYON,** b. of Ashford, Nov. 23, 1828, by Rev. Philo Judson	5	32
Elizabeth, Mrs., of Windham, m. Capt. Amos **CHAFFEE,** of Ashford, Oct. 27, 1844, by Jared D. Richmond, J. P.	5	91
Frank, m. Lucetta P. **BADGER,** b. of Ashford, Dec. 11, 1842, by Rev. F. Williams	5	83
Henry Lee, s. Amos & Lucretia Ann, b. Sept. 18, 1843	6	99
Jonathan, m. Elisabeth **WATROUS,** May 30, 1797	4	13
Jonathan, Jr., m. Philinda **CHAPMAN,** Feb. 24, 1828, by Amasa Lyon, J. P.	5	30
Jonathan, of Ashford, m. Mary **BATES,** of West Greenwich, R. I., [June] 27, [1836], by Rev. Reuben Torrey, of Eastford	5	60
Merriett, d. Charles & Abigail, b. May 27, 1827	6	68
Sarah, of Ashford, m. Charles **THOMAS,** of R. I., Nov. 26, 1829, by Amasa Lyon, J. P.	5	37

	Vol.	Page
WEEKS, WEEKES, (cont.)		
Sylvanus D., m. Mary E. T. **SNOW**, Jan. 15, 1843, by F.		
Williams. Intention published	5	83
WELCH, WELTCH, Basina, d. Solomon & Elisabeth, b. Dec. 6,		
1778	3	13
Daniel, s. Solomon & Elisabeth, b. Sept. 20, 1755	3	13
Elanah, d. John & [Elanah], b. [ ]	4	3
Elenah, w. John, d. [ ]	4	3
Elisabeth, [d. Solomon & Elisabeth], b. Nov. 24, 1757	3	13
Gurdon, of Windham, m. Betsey **GILLMORE**, of Ashford,		
June 5, 1823, by Rev. Philo Judson	5	10
Hannah, m. Josiah **BUGBEE**, Jr., June 14, 1770	4	44
John, [m.] Elanah **CUMMINGS**, [ ]	4	3
Solomon, m. Elisabeth **LYON**, Apr. 17, 1755	3	13
Solomon, [s. Solomon & Elisabeth], b. June 16, 1760	3	13
Thirza, m. James **BUGBEE**, [ ]	6	39
WELD, Salley, m. Dr. Joseph **PALMER**, May 20, 1778	4	106
WELLS, Aaron T., of Middletown, m. Maraett **HAMMOND**, of		
Ashford, Sept. 21, 1829, by Rev. Philo Judson	5	36
James, s. Harrison & Ma[r]y E., b. June 3, 1850	5	142-3
WENTWORTH, Betsey, d. Jedidiah & Betsey, b. Apr. 2, 1800	4	24
Content Ann, of Dear Island, Me., m. Capt. Aaron **AUSTIN**, of		
Suffield, Conn., Nov. 28, 1822, by Edward Keyes, J. P.	5	7
Elizabeth, d. Jed[edia]h & Betsey, b. Jan. 14, 1805	4	24
Jered, s. Jedediah & Betsey, b. Mar. 16, 1803	4	24
Jared, m. Clarissa **HILLIARD**, b. of Ashford, Oct. 12, [1826]	5	24
Jedidiah, m. Betsey **WEBB**, May 9, 1799	4	24
Lydia, m. Thomas **WARREN**, Mar. 27, 1833, by Rev. David		
Bennett	5	51
Mariah, d. Jed[edia]h & Betsey, b. June 9, 1810	4	24
Mariah, m. Fielder **WATKINS**, b. of Ashford, Mar. 25, [1829],		
by Rev. Ezekiel Skinner	5	34
Sally, d. Jedediah & Betsey, b. Oct. 11, 1801	4	24
Susan, d. Jed[edia]h & Betsey, b. Dec. 30, 1807	4	24
Susan, m. Amon **KNOWLTON**, b. of Ashford, Mar. 4, [1830],		
by Rev. Ezekiel Skinner	5	38
WEST, Clarissa, m. Zachariah **HALE**, [ ]	4	95
WESTBRIDGE, George W., m. Elizabeth K. **SHIRTLEFF**, Apr.		
11, 1831, by Rev. David Bennett	5	42
WESTON, [H]arriat Byran, d. John & Hannah, b. Apr. 16, 1804	4	10
[Jo]hn, m. Hannah **RATHBUN**, Apr. 24, 1803	4	10
WHALEY Alfred, m. Esther **PALMER**, Nov. 9, [1823], by Anson		
S. Atwood	5	11
Caroline S., of Ashford, m. William S. **BABCOCK**, of Toledo,		
O., Oct. 24, 1842, by Rev. Cha[rle]s Hyde	5	82
Caroline Sophronia, d. Alfred & Esther, b. Nov. 27, 1824	6	47
Esther H., m. Harden H. **CHESTER**, b. of Ashford, Mar. 30,		
1841, by Rev. Cha[rle]s Hyde	5	78
Stephen Fielder Palmer, s. Alfred & Esther, b. June 1, 1827	6	47

WHITE, (cont.)	Vol.	Page
Ashford. Intention published 14 d. in Monson	5	97
Andrew C., d. Sept. 7, 1847, ae 6	5	130-1
Chloe, housekeeper, b. Uxbridge, Mass., res. Ashford, d. Jan.		
[ ], 1849, ae 80	5	138-9
Cornelia, d. Moses & Betsey, b. Dec. 14, 1833	6	28
David M., m. Elizabeth Jane SQUIER, b. of Ashford, Jan. 16,		
1853, by Rev. Chester Tilden	5	109
Eliza, ae 17, of Ashford, m. W[illia]m WHITE, shoemaker,		
ae 25, b. Douglass, res. Webster, Oct. 24, 1847, by Rev.		
Mr. Bancroft	5	128-9
Eliza B., of Ashford, m. W[illia]m B. WHITE, of Webster,		
Mass., Oct. 24, 1847, by Rev. D. Bancroft, of Willington	5	101
Julia Ann, of Ashford, m. Harvey WATHNER, of Union, May		
16, 1833, by Rev. James Porter	5	51
Keith W., of Uxbridge, Mass., m. Caroline FARNHAM, of		
Ashford, Dec. 7, 1829, by Rev. Luke Wood	5	37
Laura, d. Moses & Betsey, b. July 23, 1818	6	28
Laura, m. Stephen WHITON, b. of Ashford, Oct. 29, 1839, by		
Ebenezer Chaffee, J. P.	5	72
Lovina, of [Ashford], m. Daniel CLARK, of Ellington, Feb.		
12, [ ], by S. M. Wheelock, at Westford	5	50
Maria, d. Moses & Betsey, b. Dec. 3, 1821	6	28
Merrit Paul, s. Moses & Betsey, b. Mar. 4, 1831	6	28
Moses Wood, s. Moses & Betsey, b. June 15, 1828	6	28
Nab[b]y, d. Ezra & Chloe, b. Feb. 5, 1806	4	35
Nehemiah, d. Oct. 3, 1754	1	94
Nehemiah, s. Nehemiah, b. Apr. 30, 1755	1	94
Phebe, d. Keith W. & Caroline, b. Feb. 1, 1831	6	86
Sarah, m. John W. BAKER, b. of Ashford, Sept. 15, 1850, by		
Rev. John M. Hunt	5	105
Sarah, d. James & Mary, b. Jan. [ ]	A	
Sarah H., ae 19, b. Canterbury, m. John W. BAKER, farmer,		
ae 22, of Ashford, Sept. 15, 1850, by Rev. John M. Hunt	5	148-9
Sibbell, d. Nehemiah & Ruth, b. Mar. 17, 1753	1	81
W[illia]m, shoemaker, ae 25, b. Douglass, res. Webster, m.		
Eliza WHITE, ae 17, of Ashford, Oct. 24, 1847, by Rev.		
Mr. Bancroft	5	128-9
W[illia]m B., of Webster, Mass., m. Eliza B. WHITE, of		
Ashford, Oct. 24, 1847, by Rev. D. Bancroft, of		
Willilngton	5	101
WHITEHOUSE, Chester, farmer, d. Apr. [ ], 1848	5	130-1
Chloe, m. Nathan SQUIER, Nov. 12, 1854, by Rev. J. B.		
Maryat	5	111
Mary Ann, of Ashford, m. Hiram SMITH, of Stafford, Nov.		
26, 1827, by Rev. Luke Wood	5	29
Sarah A., of Ashford, m. Albert WILLIAMS, of Willington,		
Nov. 25, last, [1827], by Rev. Ezekiel Skinner	5	29
Thomas, m. Jemima JORDAN, b. of Ashford, Feb. 19, [1826],		

	Vol.	Page
WHITEHOUSE, (cont.)		
by Ezekiel Skinner	5	21
WHITFORD, Calista J., d. John, farmer, ae 38, & Calista, ae 35, b.		
July 1, 1849	5	134-5
John, Jr., of Woodstock, m. Calista **HOWARD**, of Ashford,		
Mar. 16, 1835, by Rev. Reuben Young	5	55
John, cooper, b. Dudley, Mass., res. Ashford, d. Jan. 23,		
1848, ae 72	5	130-1
Joseph, of Woodstock, m. Amelia **HURLBURT**, of Ashford,		
Mar. 19, 1822, by Reuben Torrey	5	5
Nelson, m. Eliza **SPAULDING**, [May] 31, [1837], by Rev. R.		
Torrey, Eastford	5	64
WHITING, Abigail Potter, d. Daniel & Elizabeth, b. Jan. 22, 1820	4	275
Churchill Leach, s. David & Ruth, b. Mar. 26, 1815	6	21
Danford, s. Daniel & Elisabeth, b. Mar. 21, 1813	4	275
Daniel, m. Elisabeth **POTTER**, Apr. 14, 1808	4	275
Daniel, s. Daniel & Elisabeth, b. June 2, 1811	4	275
David, m. Ruth **LAMB**, Apr. 27, 1809	6	21
David Levi, s. Daniel & Elisabeth, b. July 29, 1825	4	275
David Whitfield, s. David & Ruth, b. May 9, 1811	6	21
Edward, s. Calvin & Maria Theresa, b. Apr. 21, 1825 ; d. Oct.		
8, 1827, ae 1 y. 5 m. 18d. (See also **WHITNEY**)	6	54
Eleaner, m. Benj[ami]n **CHAPMAN**, Jr., Mar. 28, 1805	4	77
Elisabeth, d. Daniel & Elisabeth, b. Feb. 21, 1809	4	275
Ellen, [d.] Calvin & Maria Theresa, b. July 31, 1827	6	54
Hale, m. Abigail **MOREY**, Nov. 7, 1793	4	278
Maria Theresa, d. Calvin & Maria Theresa, b. June 23, 1823	6	54
Nathan, s. David & Ruth, b. May 14, 1813	6	21
Nathaniel, s. Hale & Abigail, b. Aug. 13, 1795	4	278
Polly, d. David & Ruth, b. Dec. 7, 1809	6	21
WHITMAN, Abigail, w. John, [d.] Dec. 18, 1810	4	236
Abigail, d. John & Anna, b. July 11, 1815	4	236
Anna, w. John, d. Dec. 18, 1832	4	236
Francis, s. John & Abigail, b. Mar. 9, 1801	4	236
George, m. Sarah **HARRIS**, b. of Mansfield, Mar. 22, 1840, by		
Amos Babcock	5	73
Hannah, d. John & Anna, b. Apr. 12, 1818	4	236
Henry, of Willington, m. Annah **WHEATON**, of Ashford,		
Sept. 28, 1830, by Rev. Ezekiel Skinner, Eastford	5	40
John, s. John & Abigail, b. Feb. 25, 1808	4	236
John, m. Anna **STRONG**, Apr. 30, 1812	4	236
Mary, of [Westford Society], m. Elisha **PECK**, of Abington		
Society, Pomfret, Oct. 29, 1844, by R. V. Lyon, in		
Westford Society	5	92
Philip, s. John & Abigail, b. Aug. 7, 1803	4	236
Sanford, s. John & Anna, b. Feb. 22, 1813	4	236
Sarah, m. Edward K[E]YES, Feb. 15, 1801	4	256
Susan, of Ashford, m. Benjamin L. **BAKER**, of Woodstock,		
Sept. 30, 1838, by Elias C. Scott	5	69

	Vol.	Page
WHITMARSH, Mary, of Ashford, m. Joseph **DORSET**, of Union, Jan. 14, 1821, by Elder Isaac Hall	5	1
WHITMORE, Eveline, m. Mason S. **SHERMAN**, b. of Ashford, Feb. 27, 1821, by Philo Judson	5	2
Francis, m. Betsey **WHITAM**, b. of Ashford, Oct. 24, 1825, by Nich[olas] B. Brardsey	5	20
Harvey, s. Francis & Betsey, b. Dec. 11, 1827	6	58
John, of Ashford, m. Adaline **FERGUSON**, of Hartford, Sept. 18, 1853, by Rev. Ezekiel Skinner	5	110
Joseph, s. Francis & Betsey, b. May 4, 1826	6	58
Laura, of Ashford, m. Charles **BOWEN**, of Pomfret, July 11, 1841, by Rev. Charles C. Barnes	5	78
WHITNEY, Calvin, m. Maria Thursa **JAMES**, b. of Ashford, May 29, 1822, by Rev. Reuben Torrey, Eastford, (See under **WHITING** for record of children)	5	22
Emily, d. Samuel, Jr. & Lucinda, b. Nov. 24, 1819	6	35
Esther, d. Peter & Marcy*, b. Nov. 1, 1778 (*Perhaps **MAREY**)	4	100
Fielder Spaulding, s. Samuel, Jr. & Lucinda, b. Mar. 1, 1817	6	35
Harriet E., m. Samuel H. **PRESTON**, b. of Ashford, Nov, 23, 1851, by Rev. P. Mathewson	5	107
Juneck Williams, s. Samuel, Jr. & Lucinda, b. Apr. 2, 1826	6	35
Mary Ann, d. Samuel, Jr. & Lucinda, b. May 26, 1823	6	35
Sally, of Ashford, m. George **ARNOLD**, of Woodstock, July 11, 1822, by Rev. Isaac Hall	5	6
Samuel, Jr., m. Lucinda **CHAPMAN**, Jan. 21, 1816	6	35
Samuel, farmer, b. Killingly, res. Ashford, d. Jan. 7, 1850, ae 93	5	144-5
Warren, m. Dianna **JOHNSON**, b. of Ashford, Oct. 19, 1824, by Amos Babcock, Elder. Intention published	5	15
---dia, d. Peter & Marcy*, b. Feb. 10, 1781 (*Perhaps Marey)	4	100
WHITON, WHITAN, WHITEN, Abigail, m. Hezekiah **ELDRIDG[E]**, [ ], 16, 1766	3	129
Abigail, s. Boaz & Tryphena, b. Sept. 30, 1788	4	254
Abner, s. Joseph & Joanna, b. Aug. 17, 1788	4	52
Abner, m. Amy **CHAFFEE**, Oct. [ ], 1814	6	43
Abraham, s. Elijah, d. Oct. 5, 1754	1	85
Alice, see under Eles		
Amie, d. Elijah & Hannah, b. Aug. 16, 1773	3	29
Anna, d. Wilson & Mary, b. Mar. 1, 1802	4	250
Ashabel, s. Stephen & Julina, b. July 10, 1813 ; d. Mar. 25, 1814	6	58
Ashabel, s. Stephen & Julina, b. May 11, 1815	6	58
Ash[a]bel, m. Jerusha W. **WHITON**, b. of Ashford, May 4, 1841, by Rev. Alvan Underwood	5	78
Augustus, s. Elijah & Matilda, b. Aug. 25, 1807	4	87
Betsey, d. Joseph, Jr. & Betsey, b. May 15, 1803	4	64
Boz, [twin with Ruth], s. Elijah & Hannah, b. Dec. 24, 1762	3	29

	Vol.	Page

WHITON, WHITAN, WHITEN, (cont.)

	Vol.	Page
Joanna, m. Timothy WALKER, Jan. 24, 1804	4	105
Joanna, d. Joseph, Jr. & Betsey, b. Apr. 2, 1808	4	64
Joanna, m. Aaron FLINT, Nov. 25, 1830, by Rev. Luke Wood	5	41
John, s. Wilson & Mary, b. Oct. 16, 1803	4	250
Joseph, Jr., m. Joanna CHAFFE, Oct. 4, 1770	4	52
Joseph, s. Joseph & Joannah, b. Sept. 24, 1776	4	52
Joseph, d. May 8, 1777	1	27
Judah, [twin with Martha], d. Elijah & Hannah, b. July 8, 1759	1	105
Judith, m. Abijah SMITH, Jr., Aug, 28, 1783	4	235
Judeth Amelia, d. Abner & Amy, b. June 19, 1822	6	43
Julia S., d. Stephen, farmer, ae 39, & Abigail b., ae 32, b. Apr. 7, 1849	5	134-5
Lucinda Ann, d. Chauncey & Lucinda, b. July 29, 1836	6	85
Lucretia, d. Joseph, Jr. & Betsey, b. Aug. 20, 1804	4	64
Lucretia, of Ashford, m. Seth WALKER, of Brookfield, Mass., Nov. 5, 1837, by Alvan Underwood	5	66
Lucy, d. Joseph, Jr. & Betsey, b. Aug. 6, 1806	4	64
Marah, d. James & Mehitable, b. Feb. 11, 1765	3	23
Maria, d. Elijah & Matilda, b. Mar. 13, 1812	4	87
Maria, of Ashford, m. Hiram NEWTON, of Brookfield, Mass., Dec. 29, 1833, by Job Cushman	5	52
Maria, of Ashford, m. Reuben GREEN, of East Windsor, Jan. 4, 1837, by Alvin Underwood	5	63
Martha, [twin with Judah], d. Elijah & Hannah, b. July 8, 1759	1	105
Martha, d. Joseph & Joannah, b. Jan. 25, 1774	4	52
Martha, d. Elijah, d. Jan. 17, 1775	3	29
Mary, d. Stephen & Julina, b. Feb.10, 1807	6	58
Mary, w. Wilson, d. Aug. 22, 1809	4	250
Mary, m. Sylvester G. FARNHAM, b. of Ashford, Mar. 1, 1827, by Rev. Levi Wood	5	26
Mary Matilda, d. Horace & Mary Ann, b. July 18, 1839	6	101
Matilda, d. Boaz & Tryphena, b. Apr. 19, 1800	4	254
Matilda, d. Elijah & Matilda, b. Feb. 15, 1810	4	87
Matilda, m. Nathan B. HUNTINGTON, b. of Ashford, May 8, 1833, by Rev. James Porter	5	51
Mehetable, d. James & Mehitable, b. May 4, 1769	3	23
Mehitabail, d. Wilson & Mary, b. Nov. 11, 1792	4	250
Mercy, d. James & Mehetable, b. Apr. 8, 1767	3	23
Otis, s. Joseph, Jr. & Betsey, b. Jan. 10, 1810	4	64
Persis, d. Wilson & Mary, b. May 26, 1786	4	250
Philena, d. Wilson & Mary, b. Apr. 12, 1797	4	250
Persilla, w. Elijah, d. July 19, 1756	1	94
Pressillah, d. Joseph, Jr. & Joannah, b. Dec. 4, 1771	4	52
Pris[s]il[l]a, m. Nicholas DUDLEY, Nov. 12, 1778	4	231
Prescilla, of Ashford, m. Asa ROYCE*, of Willington, May 21, 1823, by Rev. W[illia]m Storrs *(correction to original copy)	5	10

WILLARD, (cont.)	Vol.	Page
Oct. 7, 1832, by Rev. Elias C. Sweet	5	49
WILLIAMS, Albert, of Willington, m. Sarah S. **WHITEHOUSE**, of		
Ashford, Nov. 25, last, [1827], by Rev. Ezekiel Skinner	5	29
Charles, s. John & Anna, b. Aug. 20, 1772	4	9
Synthya, d. John & Anna, b. Nov. 30, 1768	4	9
Cynthia, m. Ezra **BOUTWELL**, Mar. 25, 1790	4	265
Deborah, m. James **SMITH**, Feb. 23, 1790	4	266
Flora, of Tolland, m. Thomas **POPE**, of Farmington, Jan. 12,		
1841, by Rev. Cha[rle]s Hyde	5	76
Frances, d. John & Anna, b. Sept. 22, 1770	4	9
Isaac, s. John & Anna, b. Dec. 22, 1766	4	9
Lucy, m. Hamilton **GRANT**, Apr. 11, 1802	4	45
Phila Ann, d. Simeon & Sarah, b. Mar. 16, 1811	4	22
Phila Ann, of Ashford, m. George **BUCK**, of Killingly, June 5,		
1831, by Rev. Reuben Torrey, of Eastford	5	43
Susan, m. Horace **FARNHAM**, b. of Westford, Nov. 24, 1844,		
by R. V. Lyon, in Westford Society	5	92
William C., of Roxbury, Litchfield County, m. Justin W.		
COOK, of Ashford, June 9, 1827, by Rev. Philo Judson	5	28
WILSON, WILLSON, Abigail, d. Joseph & Abigail, [b.] Mar. 28,		
1716	1	28
Abigail, [d. Joseph & Abigail], b. Mar. 28, 1736	1	107
Benjamin, d. July 11, 1750	1	26
Selinda, d. Elias & Zuriah, b. Dec. 19, 1789	4	108
Charles, s. Jacob, Jr. & Hannah, b. Feb. 7, 1785	4	83
Dilotia, of Ashford, m. Clement **TOBIE**, of Dover, Mass., Jan.		
1, 1823, by Reuben Torrey	5	7
Elias, s. Isaac, b. May 28, 1769	4	37
Elias, m. Zaruiah **BEMIS**, Oct. 1, 1789	4	108
Elisabeth, [d. Joseph & Abigail], b. Feb. 10, 1745	1	107
Elisabeth, d. Jan. 11, 1766	1	26
Emma Jane, d. Nelson, farmer, ae 36, & Emily, ae 38, b. Nov.		
22, 1847	5	126-7
Esther, d. Joseph & Abigail, [b.] Apr. 6, 1718	1	28
Esther, [d. Joseph & Abigail], b. Apr. 10, 1738	1	107
Frances, s. Joseph & Abigail, b. June 16, 1740	1	28
Frances, [s. Joseph & Abigail], b. June 14, 1740	1	107
Hannah, d. Jacob & Ruth, b. Apr. 4, 1745	3	100
Hannah, m. Stephen **WALKER**, Nov. 24, 1774	4	80
Hannah, d. Jacob, Jr. & Hannah, b. Mar. 31, 1781	4	83
Jacob, s. Joseph & Mary, b. July 10, 1718	A	4
Jacob, m. Ruth **SMITH**, May 21, 1741	3	100
Jacob, s. Jacob, d, Jan. 16, 1748	3	100
Jacob, s. Jacob & Ruth, b. Apr. 5, 1752	3	100
Jacob, s. Jacob, Jr. & Hannah, b. June 6, 1789	4	83
Jacob, d. Dec. 27, 1807	3	100
James, [s. Joseph & Abigail], b. Sept, 11, 1752	1	108
James, s. Jacob, Jr. & Hannah, b. Dec. 22, 1782	4	83

	Vol.	Page
WILSON, WILLSON, (cont,)		
Jesse, m. Lucy **PIERCE**, b. of Ashford, Dec. 11, 1825, by Nathan Hayward, J. P.	5	20
John, [s.Joseph & Abigail], b. Mar. 12, 1747	1	107
Joseph, m. Abigail **BUGBE[E]**, Feb. 28, 1714/15, by Rev. James Hale	1	28
Joseph, s. Joseph & Mary, b. June 25, 1716	A	2
Joseph, d. Dec. 4, 1756	1	108
Joseph, s. Jacob & Ruth, b. Sept. 11, 1764	3	100
Joseph, m. Linda **UTLEY**, Apr. 11, 1790	4	117
Joseph, m. Linda **UTLEY**, Apr. 11, 1790	4	34
Lorry, d. Joseph & Mary, b. July 3, 1801	4	34
Losha, d. Joseph & Mary, b. Jan. 5, 1803	4	34
Maria, d. Joseph & Maria, b. May 23, 1791	4	34
Marvin, s. Joseph & Maria, b. Mar. 14, 1794	4	34
Mary, m. Benjamin **READ**, Aug. 19, 1722	A	6
Mary, [d. Joseph & Abigail], b. Aug. 14, 1742	1	107
Mary, d. Elias & Zariah, b. July 31, 1793	4	108
Mary E., d. Eben, merchant, ae 29, & Sarah, ae 20, b. July 18, 1849	5	134-5
Mary Elizabeth, d. Numan & Betsey, b. Aug. 31, 1841	6	96
Mary H., m. Origin P. **PARKER**, b. of Ashford, June 20, 1836, by Rev. Stephen Cushing, Eastford	5	60
Molly, d. Jacob & Ruth, b. Mar. [ ], 1756	3	100
Molly, m. Samuel **SNOW**, Jr., Nov. 25, 1773	4	61
Numan, m. Betsey **MILLER**, b. of Ashford, Jan. 1, 1841, by Rev. R. W. Allen, Eastford	5	77
Orrin, m. Amanda **HAVENS**, b. of Ashford, Dec. 3, 1843, by Rev. L. W. Blood	5	86
Palmer, s. Jacob, Jr. & Hannah, b. Aug. 15, 1791	4	83
Parker, s. Jacob & Ruth, b. Nov. 22, 1743	3	100
Parker, s. Joseph & Maria, b. Mar. 15, 1796	4	34
Rebeckah, m. John **RUSSELL**, Jr., May 1, 1766	4	47
Rhoda, d. Jacob & Ruth, b. Feb. 12, 1742	3	100
Rhode, m. Jonathan **STOEL**, Apr. 4, 1762	3	118
Roswell, s. Jacob, Jr. & Hannah, b. June 20, 1795	4	83
Ruby, d. Joseph & Maria, b. Sept. 14, 1792	4	43
Ruth, d. Jacob & Ruth, b. Aug. 26, 1750	3	100
Sam[ue]ll, s. Jacob & Ruth, b. May 16, 1754	3	100
Samuel, s. Jacob, Jr. & Hannah, b. May 27, 1787	4	83
Sarah, m. James **COMINS**, of Willington, Mar. 18, 1746/7	2	61
Sarah, [d. Joseph & Abigail], b. Mar. 26, 1750	1	107
Sarah, [d. Joseph & Abigail], d. July 19, 1759	1	108
Seldin, [s.] Joseph & Maria, b. Dec. 22, 1797	4	34
Serviah, [d. Joseph & Abigail], b. Apr. 13, 1755	1	108
Silence, d. Jacob & Ruth, b. June 18, 1762	3	100
Silance, m. Moses **HORTON**, Oct. 17, 1780	4	242
Sophronia, m. William **FARNHAM**, Sept. 5, 1847, by Charles Peabody	5	101

	Vol.	Page
WILSON, WILLSON, (cont.)		
Sophronia, white, ae 28, m. William **FARNHAM**, shoemaker, mulatto, ae 24, of Ashford, Sept. 5, 1847, by Charles Peabody	5	128-9
Sophronia M., d. Thomas, farmer, ae 34, & M., ae 30, b. Feb. 15, 1849	5	132-3
Susan Jane, d. Thomas W., farmer, ae 34, & Susan, ae 30, b. Oct. 8, 1850	5	146-7
Zebulon R., of Uxbridge, Mass., m. Julia M. **LYON**, of Eastford, Sept. 7, 1845, by Francis Williams, Eastford	5	95
Zerviah, see under Serviah		
Zulvah (?), d. Isaac, b. Feb. 24, 1767	4	37
WINCHESTER, WINTCHESTER, Albia, [d. Amariah & Abigail], b. Dec. 27, 1771	4	48
Amariah, s. Amariah & Hannah, b. Aug. 28, 1746	1	27
Amariah, d. Oct. 10, 1766	1	27
Azbura, had d. Joanna **WATSON**, b. Oct. 11, 1819	6	103
Jemmima, m. Obadiah **PARRY**, Mar. 18, 1762	3	57
Joanna **WATSON**, d. Azbura, b. Oct. 11, 1819	6	103
John, s. Amariah & Abigail, b. Sept. 9, 1766	4	48
Sarah, [d. Amariah & Abigail], b. Nov. 5, 1768	4	48
Sarah, of Ashford, m. Henry **PRESTON**, of Fredrickstown, Va., Jan. 7, 1801	4	69
Sarah, name credited in original index to page 1, but information regarding same is missing	4	1
WING, Almira, d. Sylvanus & Anna, b. July 21, 1801	4	83
Desire, d. Thomas, b. [ ]	4	3
Eliza, d. Sylvanus & Anna, b. Sept. 12, 1802	4	83
John, s. Thomas & Judah *, b. [ ] (*changed to "Phebe")	4	3
Phebe, d. Tho[ma]s, [&] [ ]h, [ ]	4	3
Phebe, d. Tho[ma]s & Judah*, [ ] (*Changed to "Phebe")	4	3
Sabrina, d. Sylbanus & Anna, b. Sept. 16, 1799	4	83
Sunner, see under Turner		
Turner, s. Thomas, b. [ ] (Perhaps "Sunner")	4	3
WINTER, Elisabeth, m. Amos **WOODWARD**, Apr. 13, 1776	4	225
WITHEY, Amanda E., Mrs., of Ashford, m. Edward H. **LYON**, of Eastford, Nov. 18, 1854, by Rev. Charles Chamberlain	5	111
Julia A., of Pomfret, m. Hartwell P. **HOLMES**, of Ashford, Dec. 5, 1844, by Francis Williams	5	92
WITHNER, [see also **WATHNER**], Rebeckah, of Ashford, m. Danforth **MORSE**, of Union, Apr. 1, 1830, by Edward S. Keyes, J. P.	5	38
WITTER, Orrin, of Chaplin, m. Flannda **PRESTON**, of Ashford, Mar. 31, 1824, by Rev. Philo Judson	5	13
WOOD, Amos, of Worcester, Mass., m. Rosetta C. **STORRS**, of Ashford, Apr. 11, 1837, by Alvan Underwood	5	64
Anna, m. Giles **STEBBINS**, Nov. 4, 1810	6	4
Cynthia, m. Levi **WOODWARD**, June 7, 1814	4	266
Deborah, [d. Benjamin & Precilla], b. Dec. 19, 1746	2	20

	Vol.	Page
WOOD, (cont.)		
Experiance, [d. Benjamin & Precilla], b. Apr. 30, 1745	2	20
Hannah, m. Josiah **HALL,** Mar. 22, 1796	4	49
James, [s. Benjamin & Precilla], b. Aug. 17, 1748 ; d. Oct. 21, 1748	2	20
Joseph, [s. Benjamin & Precilla], b. Aug. 15, 1743	2	20
Noah, [s. Benjamin & Precilla], b. Dec. 3, 1749	2	20
Rebeckah, m. John **RUSS,** Nov. 3, 1737, by Rev. Mr. Eleazer Williams	1	58
Sarah, [d. Benjamin & Precilla], b. May 2, 1752	2	20
Stephen, m. Ditta **CHAPMAN,** b. of Ashford, Apr. 11, 1824, by Edward Keyes, J. P.	5	13
Zalman G., of Mendon, Mass., m. Emily **WHEATON,** of Pomfret, Mar. 20, 1844, by Rev. Cha[rle]s Hyde	5	88
WOODBURY, Levi, see under Levi Woodbury **CORBIN**	5	126-7
WOODCOCK, WOODCOK, Abigail, w. Samuel, d. July 16, 1754	1	84
Ann, m. Joshua **EATON,** Dec. 14, 1737, by Rev. Mr. Hale	1	70
Anne, w. Sam[ue]ll, d. Jan. [ ], 1739/40	1	23
Easther, m. Jonathan **BAKER,** June 17, 1740	2	33
Mary, m. Benjamin **CHUB[B],** Nov. 15, 1748, by Mr. John Bass	2	75
Samuel, s. Samuel & Anne, b. May 2, 1739 ; d. May 7, 1740	1	23
Sarah, m. Sam[ue]ll **HAYWARD,** June 17, 1741	2	35
WOODWARD, WOODARD, Abner, m. Mariam **KNOWLTON,** Apr. 15, 1790	4	260
Abner Tarbell, s. Charles & Polly, b. July 1, 1821	6	11
Amos, m. Elisabeth **WINTER,** Apr. 13, 1776	4	225
Anna, d. Perkins B. & Polley, b. Jan. 8, 1794	4	274
Ashbel, of Franklin, m. Emeline **BICKNELL,** of Ashford, May 31, 1832, by Rev. Philo Judson	5	48
Benjamin, s. John & Hannah, b. Mar. 14, 1796	4	17
Betsey, d. Amos & Elisabeth, b. Apr. 11, 1780	4	225
Betsey, d. John & Hannah, b. Oct. 23, 1800 ; d. Feb. 23, 1802	4	17
Betsey, Mrs., m. Philip **HAYWARD,** Esq., May 14, 1823, by Rev. Philo Judson	5	9
Betsey, m. Philip **HAYWARD,** May 14, 1823	6	50
Charles Henry, s. Charles & Polly, b. May 16, 1815	6	11
Charlotte, d. Charles & Polly, b. Oct. 25, 1808	6	11
Cristina, d. Perkins B. & Polly, b. Aug. 10, 1810	4	274
Cynthia Ann Chapin, d. Levi & Cynthia, b. Oct. 30, 1817	4	266
Ebenezer Collins, s. Charles & Polly, b. Dec. 6, 1812	6	11
Edward Benoni, s. Samuel & Levina, b. Aug. 1, 1821	6	24
Edward Keyes, s. Horatio & Mary, b. Jan. 6, 1814	6	29
Elisa, d. Perkins B. & Polley, b. Mar. 22, 1801	4	274
Eliza Jane, d. Otis & Eliza, b. Mar. 15, 1836	6	88
Elisabeth, m. Joel **WARD,** Jan. 13, 1773	4	73
Elisabeth, d. Joseph, Jr. & Elisabeth, b. Nov. 25, 1774	4	67
Elisabeth, d. Perkins B. & Polley, b. July 19, 1799 ; d. Aug.		

WOODWARD, WOODARD, (cont.)	Vol.	Page
18, 1800	4	274
Elisabeth, d. Levi & Percey, b. July 25, 1800	4	266
Elizabeth, m. Asa FARNHAM, b. of Ashford, (Westford Society), May 1, 1825, by Levi Smith, at Westford Society)	5	18
Elizabeth, d. Otis, farmer, ae 41, & Eliza, ae 35, b. Apr. 22, 1848	5	126-7
Elizabeth F., m. Samuel KNOWLTON, b. of Ashford, Oct. 14, 1839, by Rev. Alvin Bennett	5	72
Elizabeth Perkins, d. Abner & Eunice, b. Feb. 26, 1812 ; d. Aug. 4, 1814	4	260
Ellen, d. Otis, farmer, ae 42, & Eliza, ae 39, b. June 4, 1850	5	140-1
Emily Fay, d. Levi & Percy, b. July 26, 1805	4	266
Experience, of Ashford, m. Silas HIBBARD, of Coventry, Tolland County, June 18, 1823, by Rev. Philo Judson	5	10
Ezra Smith, s. Perkins B. & Polley, b. Nov. 4, 1805	4	274
George, s. Jason & Sarah, b. Mar. 7, 1795	4	224
George, s. Horatio & Mary, b. May 28, 1816	6	29
Hannah, d. John & Hannah, b. Mar. 17, 1794	4	17
Hannah E., m. William STORRS, Jr., b. of Ashford, Oct. 14, 1822, by Rev. W[illia]m Storrs	5	7
Harriet Sophia, d. Charles & Polly, b. Feb. 16, 1819	6	11
Henry, s. Horatio & Mary, b. May 21, 1820	6	29
Horatio, s. Jason & Sarah, b. June 29, 1785	4	224
Horatio, m. Mary KEYES, Dec. 31, 1809	6	29
Horatio, s. Horatio & Mary, b. July 4, 1818	6	29
Irenea, d. Amos & Elisabeth, b. Feb. 7, 1779	4	225
Janes, s. Horatio & Mary, b. Nov. 23, 1810	6	29
Jason, m. Sarah SUMNER, June 20, 1782	4	224
Jason, s. Jason & Sarah, b. Apr. 21, 1789	4	224
Jason, Capt., m. Tryphenia SUMNER, b. of Ashford, Jan. 28, 1821, by Rev. Philo Judson	5	2
Jelina, of Ashford, m. Francis P. CLARK, of Chaplin, Mar. 11, 1830, by William Ely	5	38
Jerusha, of Ashford, m. Dexter M. LEONARD, of Mansfield, Oct. 20, 1826, by William Ely, V. D. M., Mansfield	5	24
John, m. Hannah BICKNELL, Apr. 24, 1783	4	17
John, s. John & Hannah, b. Mary 29, 1798	4	17
John Brightman, s. Jason, b. Nov. 22, 1833	6	82
Joseph, Jr., m. Elisabeth SUMNER, Jan. 11, 1774	4	67
Levi, s. Joseph & Elisabeth, b. Aug. 19, 1773	4	43
Levi, m. Percey HARRIS, Oct. 24, 1799	4	266
Levi, m. Cynthia WOOD, June 7, 1814	4	266
Levi Dexter, s. Levi, b. Aug. 4, 1824 ; d. Apr. 26, 1825	4	266
Loiza, d. Charles & Polly, b. May 11, 1817 ; d. June 2, 1817	6	11
Lucius, s. John & Hannah, b. Sept. 3, 1803	4	17
Lydia, d. John & Hannah, b. June 16, 1787	4	17
Marcus, s. Othniel & Syllinda, b. Sept. 10, 1804	4	53

	Vol.	Page
WOODWARD, WOODARD, (cont.)		
Martha, m. Amos **BUGBEE**, Mar. 21, 1782	4	226
Mary Adaline, d. Charles & Polly, b. Feb. 18, 1811	6	11
Mary Ann, d. Horatio & Mary, b. Mar. 29, 1812	6	29
Mary Freeman, d. Otis & Eliza, b. Jan. 8, 1838	6	88
Mary Marilla, d. Othniel & Sylenda, b. Jan. 12, 1813	4	53
Orenda, d. John & Hannah, b. July 18, 1785	4	17
Othnial, m. Syllenda **READ**, Jan. 27, 1793	4	53
Pamela, d. Jason & Sarah, b. Sept. 10, 1783	4	224
Pamela, m. [Lu]ther **WARREN**, [ ]cr. 29, 1803	4	98
Percy, w. Levi, d. June 10, 1812	4	266
Perkins B., m. Polley **SMITH**, Apr. 4, 1793	4	274
Perkins Bushnell, s. Joseph & Elisabeth, b. Aug. 17, 1770	4	43
Perkins Bushnell, s. Perkins B. & Polley, b. Sept. 11, 1803	4	274
Phila, d. Jason & Sarah, b. Jan. 8, 1791 ; d. Sept. 14, 1810	4	224
Phila, d. Jason, d. Sept. 14, 1810	4	224
Philitus, s. Levi & Percey, b. June 6, 1803	4	266
Phinehas, s. Perkins B. & Polley, b. Aug. 6, 1797 ; d. Aug. 16, 1800	4	274
Polley, d. Amos & Elisabeth, b. Jan. 1, 1777	4	225
Polly, d. Perkins B. & Polly, b. Aug. 20, 1795 ; d. Aug. 18, 1800	4	274
Polly, d. Perkins B. & Polley, b. Dec. 8, 1807	4	274
Royal, s. Abner & Eunice, b. Nov. 13, 1815	4	260
Salla, d. Jason & Sarah, b. July 7, 1787	4	224
Samuel, s. Jason & Sarah, b. Mar. 12, 1793	4	224
Samuel, m. Levina **TAYLOR**, b. of Ashford, June 18, 1820, by Philip Hayward, J. P.	6	24
Samuel, m. Hannah **HUNTINGTON**, b. of Ashford, Dec. 24, 1843, by Rev. L. W. Blood, Eastford	5	87
Sarah Heart, d. Horatio & Mary, b. May 23, 1822 ; d. Nov. 7, 1823	6	29
Sumner, m. Lavinia **TAYLER**, b. of Ashford, June 18, 1820, by Philip Hayward, J. P.	5	1
Thyne, d. Joseph, Jr. & Elisabeth, b. July 17, 1781	4	67
Timothy, s. John & Hannah, b. Mar. 31, 1790	4	17
William, s. Joseph, Jr. & Elisabeth, b. Aug. 12, 1777 ; d. Aug. 26, 1780	4	67
William, s. John & Hannah, b. Jan. 5, 1792	4	17
WORK, WORKS, Alanson, s. Alex[ande]r & Dorathy, b. Aug. 30,[]	4	9
Elexander, s. Joseph & Joanna, b. Dec. 4, 1746	1	37
Allexander, s. Ingolsbe & Mary, b. Mar. 8, 1763	2	21
Andrew, s. Joseph & Sarah, b. Dec. 22, 1766	3	31
Anna, m. Amasa **WATKINS**, Sept. 12, 175[ ]	3	105
An[n]e, d. Joseph & Elezi[be]th, b. Jan. 22, 1731/2	1	37
Anne, d. Ingoldsbe & Mary, b. Feb. 5, 1771	2	20
Ariel, s. Ingoldsbe & Mary, b. Sept. 29, 1767 ; d. Nov. 29, 1788	2	21

	Vol.	Page

WORK, WORKS, (cont.)

	Vol.	Page
Ariel, s. Alex[ande]r & Dorathy, b. June 4, 179[ ]	4	9
Asa Bolles, s. Henry, Jr. & Maria, b. Dec. 20, 1825	6	34
Asa Smith, s. Alex[ande]r & Dorathy, b. Feb. 9, 179[ ]	4	9
Benjamin, s. Inglesbee & Mary, b. Nov. 26, 1754	2	21
Benjamin, s. Ingolsbe, d. May 27, 1777	2	20
Catherine, m. Erastas **BICKNELL,** b. of Ashford, June 3, 1835, by Rev. R. Torrey, Eastford	5	56
Catharine S., m. James **TROWBRIDGE,** Jr., Dec. 16, 1846, by Charles Peabody	5	99
Elias, [twin with Lyman], s. Alex[ande]r & Dorothy, b. Mar. 15, [ ]	4	9
Elijah, s. Joseph & Sarah, b. May 14, 1773	3	31
Eliza, m. Zachariah **BICKNELL,** Jr., b. of Ashford, Jan. 7, 1841, by Rev. Charles Hyde	5	76
Elezebeth, d. Joseph & Elezebeth, b. May 18, 1737	1	37
Elezebeth, w. Joseph, d. Sept. 25, 1743	1	37
Elisabeth, d. Inglesbee & Mary, b. Feb. 1, 1757 ("**BORK**")	2	21
Elesabeth, m. Calvin **EATON,** Dec. 8, 1757	1	99
Elisabeth, d. Henery & Carthrine, b. Feb. 22, 1767	3	126
Elisabeth, m. Rev. Andrew **JUDSON,** Jan. 7, 1779	4	112
Elisabeth had d. Elisabeth **DOW,** b. Jan. 4, 1792	4	58
Esther, d. Ingoldsbe & Esther, b. June 11, 1772	2	20
Esther, m. Elisha **TROWBRIDGE,** Nov. 14, 1793	4	277
Esther, of Ashford, m. Zenus D. **WIGHT,** of Woodstock, [Feb.] 19, [1833], by Rev. Reuben Torrey, Eastford	5	50
Godfrey, s. Samuel & Patty, b. Apr. 27, 1806	4	77
Hannah, d. Joseph, Jr. & Betty, b. July 23, 1774	4	72
Hannah, m. Ephraim **TROWBRIDGE,** Apr. 29, 1818	6	16
Henery, s. Joseph & Elezebeth, b. June 31, 1739	1	37
Henery, [s. Ingolsbee & Mary], b. Jan. 22, 1751 (sic)("**BORK**")	2	21
Henery, m. [Carthrine] [ ]ng, May 7, 1762	3	126
Henry, Jr., m. Maria **BOLLES,** Apr. 23, 1817	6	34
Ingalsbe, s. Joseph & Elizabeth, b. Feb. 17, 1726/7	A	10
Inglesbee, m. Mary **RUSSEL[L],** Aug. 8, 1750, by Mr. Bass	2	21
[In]goldesby, s. Henery & Carthrine, b. Feb. 8, 1765	3	126
Ingoldsbe, m. Esther **BUGBEE,** July 11, 1771	2	20
[In]goldsby, s. Levi & Lucinda, b. Oct. 28, 1812	4	287
Ingoldsby, d. Mar. 22, 1813	2	20
James, s. Joseph & Sarah, b. Aug. 13, 1776	3	31
James Henry, s. Henry, Jr. & Maria, b. Jan. 22, 1818	6	34
Joanna, d. Mar. 9, 1795, in the 89th y. of her age	4	74
John, s. Joseph & Sarah, b. Oct. 24, 1760	3	31
John, s. Ingoldsby & Esther, b. Nov. 17, 1775	2	20
Joseph, s. Joseph & Elizabeth, b. May 12, 1734	1	37
Joseph, d. Feb. 26, 1760	1	38
Joseph, d. Feb. 26, 1760	1	37
Joseph, m. Sarah **HORE,** Mar. 4, 1760	1	107

	Vol.	Page
WORK, WORKS,(cont.)		
Joseph, s. Joseph & Sarah, b. Sept. 15, 1769	3	31
Joseph, Jr., m. Betty **HAYWARD**, July 9, 1771	4	72
Levi, s. Inglosbe & Esther, [b.] Apr. 25, 1778	2	20
Levi, m. Lucinda **WARRIN**, June 26, 1808	4	287
Levi Tilar, s. Sam[ue]l & Patty, b. Aug. 17, 1802	4	77
Lucian, s. Levi & Lu[c]inda, b. Apr. 12, 1809	4	287
Luce, d. Ingolsbee & Mary, b. Sept. 14, 1765	2	21
Lyman, [twin with Elias], s. Alex[ande]r & Dorothy, b. Mar. 15, [ ]	4	9
Marah, m. Rev. Andrew **JUDSON**, Mar. 13, 1785	4	112
Martha, d. Joseph & Elezebeth, b. June 30, 1741	1	37
Martha, d. Joseph & Sarah, b. Nov. 25, 1764	3	31
Mary, d. Henery & Carthrine, b. Mar. 7, 17[ ]	3	126
Mary, d. Ingolsbee & Mary, b. Jan. 1, 1759 (Written "**BORK**")	2	21
Mary, w. Ingoldsbe, d. Mar. 25, 1771	2	20
Mary, m. Edward **K[E]YES**, June 16, 1779	4	256
Mary, of Ashford, Conn., m. W[illia]m **SMITH**, of Williamstown, County of Orange, State of Vt., [Feb.] 16, [1823], by Reuben Torrey, Eastford	5	8
Molley, d. Joseph, Jr. & Bettey, b. Jan. 28, 1777	4	72
Nelson, m. Tryphenia **SNOW**, b. of Ashford, Dec. 12, 1824, by Rev. Philo Judson	5	17
Percy, d. Joseph, Jr. & Betty, b. Oct. 13, 1772	4	72
Phebe, d. Joseph & Sarah, b. Sept. 21, 1762	3	31
Rebackah, d. Joseph & Elezebeth, b. Sept. 3, 1743	1	37
Samuel, s. Ingolsbe & Esther, b. Nov. 12, 1773	2	20
Samuel, m. Patty **WARD**, Jan. 9, 1800	4	77
Sarah, d. Joseph & Elezebeth, b. Feb. 6, 1729/30	1	37
Sarah, d. Inglesbee & Mary, b. Feb. 25, 1750/51	2	21
Sarah, m. Josiah **HOLMES**, Apr. 4, 1751, by Rev. Mr. John Bass	2	70
Sidney, of Stafford, m. Cindarilla **ATWOOD**, of Ashford, [Nov.] 2, [1834], by Rev. Dexter Munger	5	55
Stephen, s. Joseph & Sarah, b. [ ], st. b.	3	31
Thomas, s. Joseph & Joanna, b. Apr. 28, 1749 ; d. Aug. 9, 1749	1	37
Tomson Judson, s. Sam[ue]l & Patty, b. Aug. 21, 1804	4	77
Ward Augustus, s. Sam[ue]l & Patty, b. Sept. 12, 1800	4	77
WRIGHT, RIGHT, Abiel, d. David & Abiel, b. Feb. 15, 1732/3	1	43
Abial, m. John **BROOKS**, Feb. 15, 1748/9, by Rev. John Bass	2	79
Abigail, d. Eben[eze]r & Mol[l]ey, b. Mar. 28, 1786	4	238
Abigail, d. Benj[ami]n & Anna, [b.] Jan. 4, 1793	4	234
Amasa, [twin with Asa], s. John, Jr. & Mehetable, b. Oct. 13, 1766	3	63
Asa, [twin with Amasa], s. John, Jr. & Mehetable, b. Oct. 13, 1766	3	63

	Vol.	Page
WRIGHT, RIGHT (cont.)		
Benjamin, s. John & Hannah, b. Mar. 19, 1761	3	41
Benj[ami]n, m. Anna **HIBBARD**, Mar. 19, 1783	4	234
Benj[ami]n, s. Benj[ami]n & Anna, b. Feb. 14, 1784	4	234
Caroline, d. David & Laodicea, b. Dec. 1, 1806	4	277
Clark, s. David & Laodicea, b. Aug. 9, 1813	4	277
Cluia, d. John & Hannah, b. June 5, 1763* (*Entry Crossed out)	3	41
Cluia, d. John, Jr. & Mehetable, b. June 5, 1763	3	63
Cybil, see under Sybil		
Daniel, m. Sally **AMIDON**, b. of Ashford, Nov. 8, 1821, by Rev. W[illia]m Storrs	5	5
David, m. Abiel **TRISKET**, Feb. 17, 1732, by Rev. Eleazer Williams	1	43
David, d. Jan. 21, 1736/7	1	43
David, s. John, Jr. & Mehitable, b. July 18, 1759	1	106
David, s. Benj[ami]n & Anna, b. Apr. 30, 1795	4	234
David, m. Laodicea **UTLEY**, May 11, 1806	4	277
David, s. David & Laodicea, b. June 11, 1808	4	277
David, m. Salla **AMIDON**, Nov. 8, 1821	4	277
Dimmis, m. Francis **DAVIS**, b. of Ashford, [Dec.] 26,[1835], by Rev. R. Torrey, Eastford	5	58
Ebenezer, s. John, d. Apr. 8, 1731	1	9
Ebenezer, s. David & Abiel, b. Aug. 22, 1734	1	43
Ebenezer, m. Mol[l]ey **ABBOTT**, Nov. 21, 1784	4	238
Elijah, s. John, Jr. & Mehitable, b. Jan. 22, 1765	3	63
Easther, d. John, Jr. & Judeth, b. Dec. 10, 1739	1	9
Feebe, see under Phebe		
Giles, s. David & Laodicea, b. Mar. 11, 1810	4	277
Hannah, d. Oliver & Rebeckah, b. Sept. 17, 1773	4	11
Hannah, d. Sept. 17, 1782	3	41
John, s. John, Jr. & Judeth, b. Feb. 18, 1732/3	1	9
John, d. Dec. 12, 1755	1	9
John, Jr., m. Mehitable **STOEL**, Mar. 14, 1756	1	94
John, m. Hannah **MASON**, June 12, 1756	1	9
John, Dea., d. Sept. 20, 1774	3	41
Joseph, s. John & Hannah, b. Oct. 6, 1757	1	9
Judah, w. John, Jr., d. July 31, 1753	1	9
Judah, d. John, Jr. & Mehetable, b. July 5, 1761	3	63
Judath, d. John & Judath, b. Feb. 10, 1726/7	A	10
Judeth, d. John, Jr., d. Feb. 7, 1732/3	1	9
Laodice, w. David, d. June 27, 1821	4	277
Laodicea, d. David & Laodice, b. Feb. 26, 1821	4	277
Laura, d. David & Laodicea, b. Aug. 13, 1815	4	277
Laura, of Ashford, m. Edwin **STORRS**, of Mansfield, Sept. 26, [1838], by Amos Babcock	5	69
Leander, [twin with Ledoit], s. David & Laodicea, b. June 14, 1819	4	277

	Vol.	Page
WRIGHT, RIGHT, (cont.)		
Ledoit, [twin with Leander], s. David & Laodicea, b. June 14, 1819	4	277
Louisa, d. David & Salla, b. Aug. 30, 1822	4	277
Lidia, m. Edward BUGBE[E], May 22, 1739	1	47
Lydia, m. Ichabod GRIGGS, Sept. 8, 1748	2	77
Mary, d. John, Jr. & Judeth, b. Sept. 29, 1730	1	9
Mary, m. John ABBOTT, Nov. 21, 1750, by James Bicknell, Esq.	1	17
Mary, d. John, Jr. & Mehitable, b. Apr. 9, 1756	1	94
Mary, d. Eben[eze]r & Mol[l]ey, b. Mar. 24, 1789	4	238
Mason, s. Benj[ami]n & Anna, b. Nov. 15, 1791 ; d. Mar. 5, 1792	4	234
Molley, d. Oliver & Rebeckah, b. May 18, 1769	4	11
Mol[l]ey, w. Eben[eze]r, d. Nov. 16, 1790	4	238
Nathan, s. John, Jr. & Judeth, b. May 22, 1735	1	9
Feebe, d. John, Jr. & Mehitable, b. Oct. 29, 1757 (Phebe)	1	100
Philo, s. David & Laodicea, b. Feb. 16, 1812	4	277
Philo, s. David, d. Mar. 9, 1825	6	51
Philo, s. David & Sally, b. Mar. 2, 1828	6	51
Polley Maria, d. David & Salla, b. June 6, 1824	4	277
Samuel S. D., of Mansfield, m. Elizabeth MOSELEY, of Ashford, Jan. 14, 1830, by Rev. Philo Judson	5	37
Sophronia, d. David & Laodic[e]a, b. June 13, 1817	4	277
Sophronia, of Ashford, m. John ATWOOD, of Mansfield, Mar. 6, 1844, by Rev. Ezekiel Skinner	5	88
Spafford, of Mansfield, m. Julia A. PHELPS, of Chaplin, Feb. 20, 1831, by Rev. Ezekiel Skinner	5	42
Cybil, d. Benj[ami]n & Anna, b. Sept. 7, 1787 (Sybil)	4	234
----, s. Leander, farmer, ae 31, & Sarah H., ae 23, b. July 11, 1851	5	146-7
WYLLYS, Ephraim, of Manchester, m. Susanna CHAFFEE, 2d, of Ashford, [Mar.] 12. [1840], by Daniel Knowlton, J. P.	5	73
Philander, of Windham, m. Harriet M. SNOW, of Ashford, Jan. 1, 1846, by Francis Williams	5	96
WYMAN, Ezekiel E., m. Pamelia RIDER, b. of Ashford, Feb. 1, 1843, by J. M. Bidwell	5	83
YEMMONS, YEMONS, [see also YOEMANS], Elizeb[e]th, m. Philip SQUIER, Aug. 31, 1747, by James Bicknell, Esq.	2	65
Sarah, m. Ezekiel SIBLEY [ ] ; d. Apr. 29, 1778	4	103
[YEOMANS], YOEMONS, [see also YEMMONS], Sarah, m. John SMITH, Jr., Mar. 1, 1738	1	69
YEWARD, Abigail, m. James FULLER, Dec. 12, 1717 (Lenard?)	A	4
YOUNG, Ashley, s. Thomas, Jr. & Polley, b. Sept. 8, 1810	4	58
Calotus (?), s. Thomas, Jr. & Polley, b. Oct. 12, 1807	4	58
Claras[s]a, [twin with Richmond], d. Tho[ma]s, Jr. & Polley, b. Nov. 18, 1824	4	58
David, s. Tho[ma]s & Mable, b. Apr. 6, 1782	4	50
Esther W., of Ashford, m. Joseph P. SCARBOROUGH, of		

	Vol.	Page

YOUNG, (cont.)

	Vol.	Page
Eastford, June 16, 1851, by Jared D. Richmond, J. P.	5	106
Esther W., m. Joseph P. **SCARBOROUGH**, shoemaker, ae 30, b. Ashford, res. Eastford, June 16, 1851, by J. D. Richmond	5	148-9
Forest E., s. Samuel, mechanic, ae 28, of Stafford, & Sarah, ae 19, b. Feb. 18, 1849	5	134-5
Freelove, s. Tho[ma]s, Jr. & Polley, b. Feb. 11, 1813	4	58
Freelove, d. Tho[ma]s, Jr., d. Feb. 3, 1815	4	458
Freelove, d. Tho[ma]s, Jr. & Polley, b. Aug. 27, 1821	4	58
Hannah, d. Tho[ma]s & Mable, b. May 25, 1785	4	50
Harriet, d. Tho[ma]s & Mary Haskings, b. Oct. 11, 1813	4	50
James, s. Tho[ma]s & Mary Haskings, b. May 29, 1818 ; d. June 14, 1818	4	50
James M., s. John A., shoemaker, b. Jan. 7, 1850	5	142-3
Jerome, s. Tho[ma]s, Jr. & Polley, b. July 9, 1817	4	58
Job, s. Thomas & Mary, b. May 15, 1797	4	50
Job, s. Tho[ma]s & Mary Haskings, b. Mar. 12, 1816	4	50
John, s. Tho[ma]s & Mable, b. May 29, 1790	4	50
Justis, s. Tho[ma]s & Mary Haskings, b. July 22, 1811	4	50
Justis, s. Tho[ma]s & Mary, b. July 22, 1811	4	50
Lorenzo, s. Tho[ma]s, Jr. & Polley, b. July 5, 1819	4	58
Mable, d. Tho[ma]s & Mable, b. May 31, 1787	4	50
Mable, w. Thomas, d. Oct. 31, 1795	4	50
Mark, s. Tho[ma]s & Mable, b. Apr. 30, 1792	4	50
Mary, m. Palmer **WATHNER**, b. of Ashford, Apr. 19, 1831, by Edward S. Keyes, J. P.	5	42
Noah, s. Tho[ma]s & Mable, b. Apr. 3, 1794	4	50
Polley, d. Tho[ma]s, Jr. & Polley, b. May 12, 1812	4	58
Ranslier, s. Thomas, Jr. & Polley, b. Apr. 7, 1806	4	58
Richmond, [twin with Claras[s]a], s. Tho[ma]s, Jr. & Polley, b. Nov. 18, 1824	4	58
Samuel, of Stafford, m. Sarah **CHAPMAN**, of Ashford, Dec. 19, 1847, by Rev. Ezekiel Skinner	5	102
Samuel, farmer, ae 27, of Stafford, m. 2d w. Sarah **CHAPMAN**, ae 18, of Ashford, Dec. 13, 1847, by Ezekiel Skinner	5	128-9
Tenta, of Ashford, m. Joseph **CONVERSE**, of Stafford, May 18, 1834, by Amasa Lyon, J. P.	5	54
Thomas, s. Thomas & Mable, b. July 14, 1780	4	50
Thomas, m. Mary **FLINT**, Mar. 2, 1796	4	50
Thomas, Jr., m. Polley **PHILLIPS**, Mar. 27, 1805	4	58
Thomas, d. Oct. 21, 1818	4	50
Tho[ma]s Sailes, s. Tho[ma]s, Jr. & Polley, b. June 17, 1815	4	58
----, d. John A., shoemaker, ae 43, & Angeline, b. May 12, 1851	5	148-9
YOUNGLOOVE, Irena, m. Jeremiah **PITTS**, Apr. 17, 1780	4	267
NO SURNAME, Anna, m. Increase **CHEDAIL**, July 22, 1759	1	109

	Vol.	Page
NO SURNAME, (cont.)		
[Carthrine], m. Henery **WORKS**, May 7, 1762	3	126
Cynth[i]a, m. [Job*] **ROBBINS**, Apr. 2, 1767 (*Supplied from		
index)	4	6
Elisabeth, m. John **RUSSELL**, Jr., Jan. 23, 1781	4	228
Elizabeth, of Ashford, m. Ebenezer S. **ROSS**,of Chaplin, Dec.		
1, [1824], by Ezekiel Skinner	5	17
Experience, m. Elip[h]alet **CASE**, Nov. 26, 1778	3	4
Hannah, d. Eben[eze]r & Hannah, b. Oct. 23, 1760	1	111
Hannah, [d. Timothy & Hannah], b. May [ ]	1	109
Hepsibah, m. Thomas **KNOWLTON** Sept. 24, 1778	3	44
Jemima, m. Robert **SUMNER**, Dec. 22, 1784	4	252
Mary, d. Edward, Jr. & Experience, b. June 9, 1759	1	109
Molley, d. Timothy & Hannah, b. [ ] 26, 1759	1	109
Simeon, s. Boston & Barbe, negroes, b. May 27, 1769	4	66
Suton, s. Jack & Silva, negroes, b. Dec. 17, 1798	4	66

AVON VITAL RECORDS
1830 -1851

	Vol.	Page
BARBER, (cont.)		
Stephen Hubbell	LR2	377
Micah, farmer, ae 75, m. 2nd w. Mary **EMBRE**, ae 66, b.		
Canton, res. Avon, Sept. 17, 1850, by Joel Grant	LR4	385
Michael, m. Mrs. Mary **EMBREE**, b. of [Avon], Sept. 17, 1851*,		
by Rev. Joel Grant, of Cong. Ch. West Avon. Recorded		
May 25, 1851 *(1850?)	LR4	21
BARNES, BARNS, Ella, d. John S., farmer, ae 24, & Abigail, ae 21,		
b. Oct. 12, [1851]	LR4	386
John S., machinist, ae 23, b. Northampton, res. Hartford, m.		
Abiga[i]l R. **WOODRUFF**, ae 30, Jan. 6, 1850, by Rev.		
Mr. Surls	LR4	373
Terry, of South Hampton, Mass., m. Prudence **PRATT**, of		
Saybrook, Ct., July 30, 1837, by Rev. F. H. Case, of East		
Ch.	LR1	572
BARTLETT, Delia J., of [Avon], m. Orestes H. **HAWLEY**, of		
Augusta, Ill., "last evening", by John Bartlett. Dated Apr.		
7, 1840	LR2	375
Mary, of Avon, m. Bela C. **KELLOGG**, [Oct.] 15, [1839], by		
John Bartlett	LR2	375
BEACH, John C., m. Amelia **GATES**, Apr. 30, 1850, by Rev. Stephen		
Hubbel[l], of Cong. Ch.	LR2	384
BEEMAN, BEMAN, Job. m. Chloe A. **MILLER**, Jan. 15, 1851, by		
Rev. Stephen Hubbell	LR4	21
Job, farmer ae 24 of Suffield, m. Chloe **MILLER**, ae 17, b.		
Avon, Jan. 15, [1851], by Stephen Hubbell	LR4	384
BISHOP, Dan F., m. Esther A. **HART**, Mar. 21, 1852, by Rev.		
Stephen Hubbell, of Cong. Ch.	LR4	20
Dan F., m. Esther A. **HART**, Mar. 21, 1852, by Stephen Hubbell	LR4	?
Helen E., m. Robert F. **WOODFORD**, Apr. 2, 1846, by Rev.		
Stephen Hubbell	LR2	381
Joseph, m. Zerviah R. **WOODFORD**, b. of Avon, July 14, 1836,		
by Rev. William Bentl[e]y	LR1	571
Julia A. m. Charles P. **STOW**, Oct. 26, 1843, by Rev. Stephen		
Hubbell, of Cong. Ch.	LR2	379
Lucius S., m. Sarah A. **WOODFORD**, Dec. 30, 1849, by		
Rev. Stephen Hubbel[l], of Cong. Ch.	LR2	384
Mary E., m. Francis **FROST**, May 5, 1852, by Rev. Stephen		
Hubbell, of Cong. Ch.	LR4	22
Maryett, of North Haven, m. Lucius **SPERRY**, of {Avon], "last		
evening", by John Bartlett. Dated Aug. 15, 1845	LR2	380
Sarah M., ae 23, b. Avon, res. Bristol, m. Dan A. **MILLER**,		
mfg., ae 24, b. Avon, res. Bristol, Nov. 25, [1847], by Rev.		
Stephen Hubbell	LR4	316
Sarah M., m. Dan A. Miller, Nov. 25, 1847, by Rev. Stephen		
Hubbell, of Cong. Ch.	LR2	382
Stella, ae 23, m. Harvey **WOODFORD**, farmer, ae 21, of Avon,		
Apr. 16, [1851], by S. Hubbell	LR4	384
Stella M., m. Ha[r]vey **WOODFORD**, Apr. 16, 1851, by Rev.		

	Vol.	Page
BISHOP, (cont.)		
Stephen Hubbell	LR4	?
Stella M., ae 21, of Avon, m. Harvey **WOODFORD**, ae 23, Apr. 16, 1851, by S. Hubbell	LR4	386
Thomas F., farmer, d. July [ ], 1851, ae 88	LR4	384
BLACKWELL, Angeline A., m. James **THOMPSON**, May 10, 1852, by Rev. Stephen Hubbell, of Cong. Ch.	LR4	?
BOOTH, Charlotte A., d. Johnson H., farmer, ae 40 & Charlotte, ae 30, b. Dec. 7, 1847	LR4	316
Johnson H., of Avon, m. Charlotte **CARRIER**, of Marlborough, [Apr. 18, 1887], by Rev. F. H. Case of East Church	LR1	572
Lydia, ae 19, of Avon, m. Francis **STEWARD**, farmer, ae 28, of Farmington, Nov. 15, [1847], by Rev. Stephen Hubbell	LR4	316
Lydia A., m. Josiah S. **BUTLER**, July 6, 1851, by Rev. Stephen Hubbell	LR4	21
Lydia Ann, m. Francis **STEWART**, Nov. 15, 1847, by Rev. Stephen Hubbell	LR2	382
Lydia S., ae 23, b. Avon, res. Avon, m. 2nd h. Josiah S. **BUTLER**, farmer, ae 34, b. Wethersfield, res. Wethersfield, July 6, 1851, by Stephen Hubbell	LR4	384
Mary E., of Avon, m. John L. **FENN**, of Burlington, May 6, 1846, by Rev. T. H. Clark	LR2	381
BOYD, Albert, b. Simsbury, res. Avon, d. Mar.[ ], 1849, ae 3	LR4	350
BRACE, Caroline M., of New Hartford, m. William H. **FOX**, of Hartford, Aug. 24, 1840, by Francis H. Case	LR2	375
BRADFORD, ----, m. [ ] **PANFIELD**, Apr. 18, 1852, by Rev. Joel Grant, of Cong. Ch. West Avon	LR4	20
BRAINARD, Orrin, [of] Lenox, N. Y., m. Elmena **WOODRUFF**, of [Avon], Mar. 9, 1834,by Rev. H. Bushnell, of West Church	LR1	568
BRAW, Rebecca, of Avon, m. Edward **BROCKWAY**, of Simsbury, May 5, 1836, by Rev. Francis H. Case, of East Ch.	LR1	570
BREWER, Eliab, m. Julia A. **SOPER**, Sept. 21, 1843, by Rev. Stephen Hubbell, of Cong. Ch.	LR2	379
BROCKLESBY, Susan, m. Dr. Alfred **KELLOGG**, b. Avon, Apr. 18, 1838, by Rev. F. H. Case, of East Church	LR2	373
BROCKWAY, Edward, of Simsbury, m. Rebecca **BRAW**, of Avon, May 5, 1836, by Rev. Francis H. Case of East Ch.	LR1	570
Joseph B., of Avon, m. Catharine A. Miller, of Granby, Sept. 28, 1834, by Rev. Francis H. Case, of 2nd Church	LR1	569
BRONSON, Newbury, of Winchester, m. Lucy **TILLOTSON**, of Avon, May 8, 1831, by Rev. Francis H. Case of East Ch.	LR1	564
BROOKS, Amy Ursula, of [Avon], m. Nelson **HART**, of Berlin, "yesterday" by John Bartlett. Dated Nov. 4, 1841	LR2	376
BROWN, Isaas H., Dr., m. Mary A. **WOODFORD**, b. of Avon, July 29, 1834, by Rev. Francis H. Case, of 2nd Church	LR1	569
BULKLEY, Charles, m. Helen **WOODRUFF**, b. of [Avon], Mar. 5, [1837], by John Bartlett	LR1	571
Harriet M., m. James **BULLARD**, Jan. 1, 1849, by Rev. Stephen Hubbel[l], of Cong. Ch. in East Avon	LR2	383

BULKLEY, (cont.)   Vol.   Page
  Harriet M., b. Hartford, m. as 2nd w. James **BULLARD**, farmer,
    b. Sheffield, Mass., res. Lee, Mass., Jan. 1, 1849, by Rev.
    Stephen Hubbell   LR4   350
BULLARD, James, farmer, b. Sheffield, Ma.., res. Lee, Mass., m. 2nd
    w. Harriet M. **BUCKLEY**, b. Hartford, Jan. 1, 1849, by
    Rev. Stephen Hubbell   LR4   350
  James, m. Harriet M. **BULKLEY**, Jan. 1, 1849, by Rev. Stephen
    Hubbel[l], of Cong. Ch. in East Avon   LR2   383
BURDWIN, Jesse, of N. Y., m. Charlotte **HADSELL**, of West Avon,
    [Dec. 25, 1851], by Charles B. McLean   LR4   20
  Jesse, of N. Y., m. Charlotte **HADSELL**, of West Avon, [Dec.
    25, 1851], by Charles B. McClean   LR4   ?
BURR, Chester H., of Bloomfield, m. Angeline D. **WILSON**, Nov. 12,
    1835, by Rev. Francis H. Case, of East Ch.   LR1   570
BURRILL, Jane A., of Hartford, m. Jerome B. **NICHOLS**, of
    Westville, "last evening", by John Bartlett. Dated Sept. 21,
    1846   LR2   381
BURT, Nahum, of South Hampton, Mass., m. Anna K. **MILLER**, of
    Avon, Mar. 21, 1837, by Rev. Francis H. Case, of East Ch.   LR1   571
BUTLER, Emeline A., of Burlington, m. Noah **HART**, of [Avon],
    Dec. 7, 1851, by Rev. Joel Grant, of Cong. Ch. West Avon   LR4   ?
  Josiah S., m. Lydia A. **BOOTH**, July 6, 1851, by Rev. Stephen
    Hubbell   LR4   ?
  Josiah S., farmer, ae 34, b. Wethersfield, res. Wethersfield, m.
    2nd w. Lydia S. **BOOTH**, ae 23, b. Avon, res. Avon, July
    6, 1851, by Stephen Hubbell   LR4   384
BYINGTON, Rowena, m. William F. **CURTIS**, b. of Bristol, [June]
    19, [1842], by John Bartlett   LR2   377
CADWELL, Ami, of Bloomfield, m. Fanny **COOK**, of Simsbury,
    Sept. 17, 1837, at Avon, b. Erastus Clapp. O. D. M. LR1   572
CARMAN, George, of Hartford, m. Nancy Ette **WOODFORD**, of
    Avon, [June 6, 1849], by Rev. N. Whiting. of Bapt. Ch.
    Bloomfield   LR2   383
  George C., harness-maker, ae 36, of Hartford, m. Nancy E.
    WOODFORD, milliner, ae 26, of Avon, June 6, 1849, by
    Rev. Niles Whiting   LR4   349
CARPENTER, Ann, of Avon, m. John **WYMAN**, of Union, Dec. 3,
    1832, by Geo[rge] Norton, J. P.   LR1   567
CARRIER, Burton, s. David, farmer, ae 36 & Lucy, ae 34, b. Sept.
    11, [1850]   LR4   384
  Charlotte, of Marlborough, m. Johnson H. **BOOTH**, of Avon,
    [Apr. 18, 1837], by Rev. F. H. Case of East Church   LR1   572
  David, m. Lucy C. **WOODFORD**, Nov. 29, 1849, by Rev.
    Stephen Hubbell, of Cong. Ch.   LR2   384
  David, farmer, ae 34, b. Marlborough, res. Avon, m. Lucy C.
    WOODFORD, ae 28, of Avon, Nov. 29, 1849, by Rev.
    Stephen Hubbell   LR4   371
  William B., of Glastenbury, m. Lucy Ann **MARSHALL**, of

	Vol.	Page

CARRIER, (cont.)
Avon, May 4, 1831, by Frances H. Case, Pastor of East
Church   LR1   564

CARTER, Evita, m. Emma **TAYLOR,** b. of Berkhampsted, Oct. 20,
1831, by Rev. Francis H. Case, of East Cong. Ch.   LR1   565

CASE, Emerson J., s. Jay, farmer, ae 38 & Mary, ae 34, b. Oct. 10*,
[1849], *(First written "Apr. 20")   LR4   372

Lucy R., d. Nathan L., farmer, ae 40 & Abiga[i]l, ae 36, b. Aug.
19, 1849   LR4   371

Luke, of Canton, m. Mrs. Abi S. **THOM[P]SON,** of [Avon], July
18, 1849, by Rev. Joel Grant, of West Avon, Cong. Ch.   LR2   384

Luke, farmer, b. Canton, m. Abi **THOMPSON,** b. New Britain,
res. Canton, July 18, 1849, by Rev. Joel Grant   LR4   349

Lyman, m. Huldah **WATERS,** of Hartford, Nov. 3, 1839, by Rev.
F. H. Case, of East Ch.   LR2   375

Nathan, m. Etna **GILLET,** b. of Avon, Jan. 31, 1833, by Rev.
Francis H. Case, of East Church   LR1   567

Nathan L., m. Abigail W. **HURLBUT,** b. of Avon, May 3, 1836,
by Rev. Francis H. Case, of East Ch.   LR1   570

CHAPMAN, Mary T., of Avon, Ct., m. George W. **HAWLEY,** of
Augusta, Ill., Aug. 31, 1835, by Rev. Francis H. Case. of
2nd Ch.   LR1   570

Robert, of Newington, m. Abigail **WOODRUFF,** of Avon, "last
evening", by John Bartlett. Dated Sept. 24, 1840   LR2   376

[CHAPPELL], CHAPEL, CHAPELL, Charles Z., twin with Stephen
Z., s. Simon D., farmer, ae 33, & Purlina G., ae 30, b. Feb.
7, 1848   LR4   316

Simon D., of New London, m. Purlina G. **HART,** of [Avon],
"last evening", by Joh Bartlett. Dated Jan. 8, 1838   LR2   373

Stephen Z., twin with Charles Z., s. Simon D., farmer ae 33 &
Purlina G., ae 30, b. Feb. 7, 1848   LR4   316

CHIDSEY, Abraham, Dea., of [Avon], m. Mrs. Nancy **BALDWIN,** of
Southbury, Mar. 10, 1833, by Rev. Harvey Bushnell, of
West Church   LR1   567

Alonzo, d. May 4, 1849,. ae 13   LR4   350

Andrew, m. Julia Ett **ALFORD,** Apr. 30, 1846, by Rev. Stephen
Hubbell, of Cong. Ch.   LR2   381

Ann M., of [Avon], m. Roswell **MOORE,** of New Hartford, Nov.
18, 1832, by Rev. Harvey Bushnell, of West Church   LR1   567

Evelina A., of Avon, m. John H. **STEEL,** of West Hartford, Nov.
28, 1833, by Rev. Francis H. Case, of East Ch.   LR1   568

Frank Erwin, [illeg.], s. Julia Elvira, unm., ae 20, b. July 19, 1848   LR4   315

George, m. Maria M. **WOODFORD,** b. of Avon, Mar. 28, 1838,
by Rev. Francis H. Case, of East Ch.   LR2   373

Jeptha C., wheelwright, ae 39 & Lucy A. **CHIDSEY,** ae 38, had
twins, b. Apr. 29, 1848   LR4   314

Jeptha C., mechanic, ae 41 & w. Lucy Ann, ae 40, had s. b. May
24, [1850]   LR4   372

Marion, d. Mar. 25, 1850, ae 16   LR4   373

	Vol.	Page
CHIDSEY, (cont.)		
Martha, m. Amos **WHEELER,** Nov. 28, 1844, by		
Rev. Stephen Hubbell, of East Cong. Ch.	LR2	380
Mary A., m. Ozem **SPERRY,** b. of [Avon], Apr. 30, 1832, by		
Rev. Harvey Bushnell, of West Church	LR1	566
Nancy, ae 23, b. Avon, m. Seth M. **MOSES,** ae 24, of Simsbury,		
Apr. 15, 1851, by S. Hubbell	LR4	386
Nancy M., m. Seth F. **MOSES,** Apr. 15, 1851, by Rev. Stephen		
Hubbell, of Cong. Ch.	LR4	?
Naomi, of [Avon], m. Adna **CRAMPTON,** of Farmington, Nov.		
24, 1831, by Rev. Harvey Bushnell, of West Church	LR1	565
Sarah Ette, m. Deforest **WOLCOTT,** b. of [Avon, Sept.] 19,		
[1841], by John Bartlett	LR2	376
Susan S., m. Tullius C. **HAYDEN,** Feb. 22, 1843, by Rev.		
Stephen Hubbell, of Cong. Ch.	LR2	378
Ursula, m. Ozem **SPERRY,** b. of Avon, Aug. 16, 183[5], by		
Correl Higley, J. P.	LR1	569
Zaccheas, farmer, d. Jan. [, 1850], ae 65	LR4	371
CHURCH, James B., m. Elizabeth T. **GOODRICH,** of Avon, May		
18, 1837, by Rev. William Bentley	LR1	572
CLARK, David, m. Emily **FULLER,** b. of [Avon], "last Evening), by		
John Bartlett. Dated Sept. 11, 1840	LR2	376
David, had st. b. , d. July 13, 1849	LR4	350
Eliza, m. Solomon P. **WILCOX,** b. of [Avon], "last evening", by		
John Bartlett. Dated July 16, 1838	LR2	373
Julia, m. Eldad **WOODRUFF,** b. of Avon, [Sept. 4, 1839], by		
Cornelius B. Everest, Bloomfield	LR2	375
Milla, b. Columbia, Ct., d. Oct. 30, 1850, ae 70	LR4	385
William M., of Farmington, m. Adelia D. **FRENCH,** of [Avon],		
"last evening", by John Bartlett. Dated Jan. 18, 1843	LR2	378
CLYDE, Samuel, of Rome, N. Y., m. Julia **WILCOX,** of Avon, [Sept.		
4, 1831], by George Norton, J. P.	LR1	565
COLLEY, Mary, wid. of Israel, see under Mary **MONTGOMERY**	LR2	382
COLTON, Charlotte A., m. Levi H. **HAMBLIN,** b. of Springfield,		
Mass., Nov. 18, 1840, in Avon, by Rev. W. C. Hoyt, of		
Bloomfield	LR2	376
Eunice L., of Avon, Ct., m. Joel S. **SHUMWAY,** of Montague,		
Mass., "last evening", by John Bartlett. Dated Dec. 5, 1842	LR2	378
COOK, Amelia M., of Simsbury, m. Morgan **STRATTON,** Dec. 31,		
1838, by Rev. Francis H. Case, of East Ch.	LR2	374
Fanny, of Simsbury, m. Ami **CADWELL,** of Bloomfield, Sept.		
17, 1837, at Avon, by Erastus Clapp. O. D. M.	LR1	572
Katharine D., of [Avon], m. Austin B. **MOSIER,** of New		
Brittain, Aug. 19, 1832, by Rev. Harvey Bushnell	LR1	566
COOPER, Helen, housekeeper, b. Barkhampsted, res. Avon, d. Mar.		
25, 1849, ae 18	LR4	350
James, had infant s., d. Mar. 6, 1849, ae 8 w.	LR4	350
John, cotton worker, ae 22 at Avon & w. Helen, ae 18, had d. b.		
Feb. 1, 1849	LR4	350

	Vol.	Page
CORNWALL, Moses, of Granville, Mass., m. Eliza **HUMPHREY**, of [Avon], Nov. 25, 1830, by Rev. Harvy Bushnell, of West Church	LR1	564
COWLES, Chauncey M., of Avon, m. Huldah A. **DAILEY**, of Bristol, [Apr.]20, [1836], by John Bartlett	LR1	570
Elya, housewife, d. June 10, [1850], ae 72	LR4	372
Henrietta C., housewife, d. Feb. 23, 1851, ae 16	LR4	385
Henry C., d. Feb. 6, [1850], ae 1 1/2	LR4	372
William, of [Avon], m. Eunice **HADSELL**, of Burlington, May 25, 1851, by Rev. Joel Grant, Cong. Ch. West Avon	LR4	?
William, mason, ae 71, b. Farmington, res. Avon, m. 2nd w. Eunice **HADSELL**, ae 65, b. Cheshire, res. Burlington, May 25, 1851, by J. Grant	LR4	385
CRAMPTON, Adna, of Farmington, m. Naomi **CHIDSEY**, of [Avon], Nov. 24, 1831, by Rev. Harvey Bushnell, of West Church	LR1	565
CROSS, Elisha, of Tolland, m. Sylvia **SPER[R]Y**, of Avon, Feb. 22, 1834, by Allen Pinney, J. P.	LR1	568
CURTIS, Ebenezer G., m. Mary A. **NORTON**, Oct. 11, 1846, by Rev. Stephen Hubbill, of Cong. Ch.	LR2	381
William A., of Meriden, m. Adeline **HIGLEY**, of Canton, Aug. 22, [1847], by Charles W. Potter	LR2	382
William F., m. Rowenna **BYINGTON**, b. of Bristol, [June] 19, [1842], by John Bartlett	LR2	377
DAILEY, **DAILY**, Huldah, housewife, b. Farmington, res. Avon, d. Jan. 1, [1849], ae 73	LR4	351
Huldah A., of Bristol, m. Chauncey M. **COWLES**, of Avon, [Apr.], 20, [1836], by John Bartlett	LR1	570
DAY, Carlos C., m. Lavilla **WOODRUFF**, b. of [Avon], Sept. 22, 1833, by Rev. Harv[e]y Bushnell, of 1st Church	LR1	567
Thomas Stanley, d. Oct. 12, 1837. Marcus Day, Executor	LR2	376
William D., s. Carloss C., farmer, ae 40 & Lavilla, ae 38, b. Aug. 19, 1851	LR4	384
William P., of Westfield, Mass., m. Catherine E. **GILLETT**, of Avon, Dec. 17, 1833, b Rev. Francis H. Case, of East Church	LR1	568
DEMING, Elmina, ae 39, of Avon, m. Ozem **SPERRY**, butcher, ae 40, of Avon, June 13, 1848, by Rev. Grant	LR4	316
Franklin, m. Emelilne **WOODFORD**, b. of [Avon], July 3, 1832, by Rev. Harvey Bushnell, of West Church	LR1	566
DERRIN, **DERREN**, A. G., farmer & w. Jane had s., b. Feb. 25, [1850]	LR4	371
Ammi G., m. Sarah Jane **WOODFORD**, b. of [Avon], "last evening", by John Bartlett. Dated Dec. 4, 1845	LR2	380
Ammi G., farmer, ae 38, & Sarah P., ae 26, had child, b. Mar. 29, 1848	LR4	315
Ammi G., farmer, ae 40, & w. Jane, ae 29, had d. b. Mar. 21, 1851	LR4	385
DICKINSON, Elizabeth, m. Gideon **GOODRICH**, b. of Avon, Dec.		

	Vol.	Page
DICKINSON, (cont.)		
16, 1832, by Rev. Francis H. Case, of East Church	LR1	567
DOWD, DOUD, Highland, farmer, ae 29, b. Haydensville, Mass., m.		
2nd w. Eunice **FAIRFIELD**, ae 27, June 29,[1850], by Seth		
Higby	LR4	384
Hig[h]land, of Monterey, Mass., Eunice P. **PENFIELD**, of Avon,		
June 29, 1851, by Rev. Seth Higby	LR4	?
Plily S., of Tyringham, Mass., m. Zerah **SPERRY**, of Simsbury,		
Ct., Jan. 1, 1837, by Rev. Francis H. Case, of 2nd Ch.	LR1	571
DRAKE, Asa, m. Mary Ann **RICE**, b. of Barkhempsted, July 27,		
1832, by Rev. Harvey Bushnell, of West Church	LR1	566
DUDLEY, Everet[t], of Bloomfield, m. Achsah **WOODRUFF**, of		
[Avon], Sept. 6, 1838, by John Bartlett	LR2	373
EMBREE, EMBRE, Mary, Mrs., m. Michael **BARBER**, b. of [Avon],		
Sept. 17, 1851* by Rev. Joel Grant, of Cong. Ch. West		
Avon. Recorded May 25, 1851 *(1850?)	LR4	?
Mary, ae 66, b. Canton, res. Avon, m. 2nd h. Micah **BARBER**,		
farmer, ae 75, Sept. 17, 1850, by Joel Grant	LR4	385
ERWIN, Frank, see Frank Erwin **CHIDSEY**	LR4	315
FAIRFIELD, Eunice, ae 27, m. 2nd h. Highland **DOWD**, farmer, ae		
29, b. Haydensville, Mass., June 29, [1850], by Seth Higby	LR4	384
FENN, John L., of Burlington, m. Mary E. **BOOTH**, of Avon, May 6,		
1846, by Rev. T. H. Clark	LR2	381
FILLEY, Betsey, m. William **JACKMAN**, Apr. 24, 1837, by Correl		
Higley, J. P.	LR1	572
FOOT, Henry, of Canton, m. Lemira **WOODRUFF**, of [Avon], "last		
evening", by John Bartlett. Dated Sept. 27, 1838	LR2	374
FORBES, Minerva, of Canton, m. Solomon N. **WADSWORTH**, of		
[Avon], Feb. 2, 1832, by Rev. Harvey Bushnell, of West		
Church	LR1	565
FORD, Cha[u]ncey D., m. Edna A. **NORTH**, Sept. 26, 1852, by Rev.		
Stephen Hubbell, of Cong. Ch.	LR4	22
FOX, William H., of Hartford, m. Caroline M. **BRACE**, of New		
Hartford, Aug. 24, 1840, by Francis H. Case	LR2	375
FRENCH, Aaron D., m. Mary J. **THOM[P]SON**, b. of [Avon], "last		
evening', by John Bartlett. Dated Jan. 12, 1842	LR2	376
Adelia D., of [Avon], m. William M. **CLARK**, of Farmington,		
"last evening", by John Bartlett. Dated Jan. 18, 1843	LR2	378
Avis, of Avon, m. Erastus **HART**, of Burlington, Mar. 28, 1832,		
by Rev. Harvey Bushnell, of West Church	LR1	565
Emma J., d. Aaron D., house carpenter, of West Avon & Mary J.,		
b. Jan. 5, 1849	LR4	349
Jane K., of [Avon], m. Oliver B. **FRENCH**, of Coventry, Oct. 30,		
1833, by Rev. Harv[e]y Bushnell, of 1st Church	LR1	568
Juliaett, m. Ephraim **WOODFORD**, b. of [Avon, Mar.] 13,		
[1843], by John Bartlett	LR2	378
Oliver B., of Coventry, m. Jane K. **FRENCH**, of [Avon], Oct. 30,		
1833, by Harv[e]y Bushnell, Pastor of 1st Church	LR1	568
FRISBIE, Anna, of Middletown, m. Ebenezer **MILLER**, Jr., of Avon,		

FRISBIE, (cont.)

Aug. 10, 1835, by Rev. Francis H. Case, of 2nd Cong. Ch.   LR1   569

Diana, farmers, d. , d. Dec. 7, 1848, ae 24   LR4   350

FROST, Francis, m. Mary E. **BISHOP,** May 5, 1852, by Rev. Stephen
Hubbell, of Cong. Ch.   LR4   22

Jesse D., of Waterbury, m. Almira Jane **HOWLEY,** of Avon,
[July] 9, [1846], by John Bartlett   LR2   381

FULLER, Emily, m. David **CLARK,** b. of [Avon], "last evening", by
John Bartlett. Dated Sept. 11, 1840   LR2   376

Juliette, of [Avon], m. Charles J. **MOSES,** of N. Y. City, Mar.
14, 1852, by Joel Grant   LR4   22

Julius, m. Almira **WOODRUFF,** June 2, 1836, by Correl Higley,
J. P.   LR1   571

Sarah, of Avon, m. Dan H. **GOODWIN,** of Unionville, June 20,
1843, by John Bartlett   LR2   379

GABRIEL, Harriet M., m. Joseph B. **NORTH,** Jan. 24, 1850, by Rev.
Stephen Hubbell, of Cong. Ch.   LR2   384

Harriet M., ae 20, m. Joseph B. **NORTH,** farmer, ae 25, of Avon,
Jan. 24, [1850], by Stephen Hubbell   LR4   373

GAINES, GAINS, George, farmer, ae 27, & Julia, ae 24, had child b.
Apr. 29, 1848   LR4   314

Julia, housekeeper, b. N. Y., res. Avon, d. Sept. 4, 1848, ae 25   LR4   350

GATES, Amelia, m. John C. **BEACH,** Apr. 30, 1850, by Rev. Stephen
Hubble[l], of Cong. Ch.   LR2   384

Sylvester, of East Haddam, m. Sarah **GLEASON,** Jan. 15, 1839,
by Rev. F. H. Case, of East Ch.   LR2   374

GILLETT, GILLET, GILLETTE, Catherine E., of Avon, m. William
P. **DAY,** of Westfield, Mass., Dec. 17, 1833, by Rev.
Francis H. Case, of East Ch.   LR1   568

Etna, m. Nathan **CASE,** b. of Avon, Jan. 31, 1833, by Rev.
Francis H. Case, of East Church   LR1   567

Henry C., m. Lucy L. **HAMLIN,** May 17, 1848, by Rev. Stephen
Hubbell, of Cong. Ch.   LR2   382

Henry C., farmer, m. Lucy L. **HAMLIN,** b. of Avon, May 17,
1848, by Rev. Stephen Hubbell   LR4   314

Rosaline, d. Henry, saw mill tender, ae 24, & Lucy, ae 27, b.
Nov. 18, 1850   LR4   385

William H., s. Henry, saw mill tender, ae 22, of Avon & Lucy, ae
20, b. Mar. 25, 1849   LR4   350

GLEASON, Samuell S., of Ohio, m. Naomi **WOODFORD,** of
[Avon], Sept. 13, 1832, by Rev. Harvey Bushnell, of West
Church   LR1   566

Sarah, m. Sylvester **GATES,** of East Haddam, Jan. 15, 1839, by
Rev. F. H. Case, of East Ch.   LR2   374

GOODRICH, Elizabeth T., of Avon, m. James B. **CHURCH,** May
18, 1837, by Rev. William Bently   LR1   572

Ellen, m. Elisaph **HULL,** June 25, 1848, by Rev. Joel Grant, of
Cong. Ch. of West Avon   LR2   382

	Vol.	Page

GOODRICH, (cont.)

Ellen, milliner, ae 20, b. Avon, m. Elisaph **HULL**, farmer, ae 33,
    b. Oxford, N. Y., June 25, 1848, by Rev. Joel Grant — LR4 — 315

Gideon, m. Elizabeth **DICKINSON**, b. of Avon, Dec. 16, 1832,
    by Rev. Francis H. Case, of East Church — LR1 — 567

Juliann H., m. William W. **WOODFORD**, May 18, 1842, by
    Rev. Stephen Hubbell — LR2 — 377

Maria, m. Isaac **BALDWIN**, b. of Avon, Aug. 1, 1830, by Rev.
    Harvy Bushnell, of the West Church — LR1 — 564

Prudence M., d. Mar. 27, [1849], ae 14 1/2 y. — LR4 — 351

Sarah E., of Avon, m. Cicero **GRISWOLD**, of Bloomfield, Nov.
    15, 1837, by W[illia]m Bentley — LR1 — 572

GOODWIN, Dan H., of Unionville, m. Sarah **FULLER**, of Avon,
    June 20, 1843, by John Bartlett — LR2 — 379

GRANT, John Cowles, s. Rev. Joel, ae 32 & Abigail F., ae 28, b. Apr.
    21, 1848 — LR4 — 315

Mary, d. Joel, minister, ae 35 & Abigail F., ae 31, b. June 18,
    1851 — LR4 — 384

GRAVES, Lucy, of Williamstown, Vt., m. Harlowe **AUSTIN**, of New
    Hartford, Ct., [Mar.] 25, [1837], by Rev. Francis H. Case,
    of East Ch. — LR1 — 571

GRAY, GREY, Charles, m. Maria E. **WHEELER**, Dec. 17, 1848, by
    Rev. Stephen Hubbel[l], of Cong. Ch. — LR2 — 383

Charles, colored, m. Maria E. **WHEELER**, colored, Dec. [ ],
    1848, by Rev. Stephen Hubbell — LR4 — 350

GREEN, Julia, of Wales, Mass., m. Rans[s]alee r **YOUNG**, of South
    Canton, Dec. 15, 1831, by George Norton, J. P. — LR1 — 565

GRISWOLD, Cicero, of Bloomfield, m Sarah E. **GOODRICH**, of
    Avon, Nov. 15, 1837, by W[illia]m Bentley — LR1 — 572

Nathan S., m. Clarinda F. **WOODFORD**, Dec. 25, 1845, by Rev.
    Stephen Hubbell — LR2 — 381

Norman, m. Jane **PRESCOTT**, Dec. 7, 1841, by Rev. Stephen
    Hubbell — LR2 — 377

HACK, Mary Ann, of Granby, m. Levi **RICE**, of Barkhampsted, Nov.
    16, 1842, by John Bartlett — LR2 — 378

HADSELL, Charlotte, of West Avon, m. Jesse **BURDWIN**, of N. Y.,
    [Dec. 25, 1851], by Charles B. McLean — LR4 — ?

Charlotte, of West Avon, m. Jesse **BURDWIN**, of N. Y. , [Dec.
    25, 1851], by Charles B. McLean — LR4 — ?

Eunice, of Burlington, m. William **COWLES**, of [Avon], May
    25, 1851, by Rev. Joel Grant, of Cong. Ch. West Avon — LR4 — ?

Eunice, ae 65, b. Cheshire, res. Burlington, m. 6th h. William
    COWLES, mason, ae 71, b. Farmington, res. Avon, May
    25, 1851, by J. Grant. — LR4 — 385

HAGAN, Mary, of Brookfield, Mass., m. Ebenezar **PARDEE**, of
    Avon, [Sept. 18, 1849], by Barais Sperry, J. P. — LR2 — 384

HAMBLIN, HAMLIN, Levi H., m Charlotte A. **COLTON**, b. of
    Springfield, Mass., Nov. 18, 1840, in Avon, by Rev. W. C.

	Vol.	Page
HAMBLIN, HAMLIN, (cont.)		
Hoyt, of Bloomfield	LR2	376
Lucy L., m. Henry C. JILLET, May 17, 1848, by Rev. Stephen Hubbell, of Cong. Ch.	LR2	382
Lucy L., m. Henry C. GILLETTE, farmer, b. of Avon, May 17, 1848, by Rev. Stephen Hubbell	LR4	314
Maria L., b. Litchfield, m. Robert A. HAWLEY, farmer, ae 30, b. New Haven, res. Avon, May 6, 1849, by Rev. Stephen Hubbell	LR4	349
Maria L., m. Rober A. HAWLEY, May 7, 1849, by Rev. Stephen Hubbel[l], of Cong. Ch.	LR2	383
HART, Amos G., m. Sarah MILLER, Oct. 19, 1851, by Rev. Stephen Hubbell, of Cong. Ch.	LR4	21
Austin A., m. Catharine HART, Nov. 20, 1844, by Rev. Stephen Hubbell, of East Cong. Ch.	LR2	380
Beulah, m. Martin HART, Jan. 4, 1841, by Marcus Day Esq.	LR2	376
Catharine, m. Austin A. HART, Nov. 20, 1844 by Rev. Stephen Hubbell, of East Cong. Ch.	LR2	380
Electa C., of Avon, m. John WOODRUFF, of Unionville, [Sept.] 25, [1842], by John Bartlett	LR2	378
Elvira, m. Erastus WOODRUFF, Jr., b. of [Avon], Apr. 7, [1846], by Alfred Kellogg, J. P.	LR2	381
Emily D., m. Joshua S. HEATH, [May] 16, [1843], by Rev. E. Hart	LR2	378
Erastus, of Burlington, m. Avis FRENCH, of Avon, Mar. 28, 1832, by Rev. Harvey Bushnell, of West Church	LR1	565
Esther A., m. Dan F. BISHOP, Mar. 21, 1852, by Rev. Stephen Hubbell, of Cong. Ch.	LR4	20
Esther A., m. Dan F. BISHOP, Mar. 21, 1852, by Rev. Stepehn Hubbell	LR4	22
Gideon W., of Avon, m. Ann RICE, of Barkhamsted, Nov. 27, 1834, by Rev. F. H. Case, of 2nd Church	LR1	569
Harvey, m. Harriet WOODFORD, b. of [Avon], Sept. 22, 1833, by Harv[e]y Bushnell, of 1st Church.	LR1	567
Jeptha, farmer, d. July 18, [1850], ae 65	LR4	372
Lent, d. Apr. 12, 1837. Marcus Day executor	LR2	376
Linus O., farmer & w. Marian, had d., b. July 26, [1850]	LR4	371
Lucy A., of Avon, m. Ira A. PORTER, of Bristol, June 6, 1852, by Rev. Joel Grant, of Cong. Ch. West Avon	LR4	20
Martha S., d. Gideon W., farmer & Mary S., b. Aug. 25, 1850	LR4	384
Martin, m. Beulah HART, Jan. 4, 1841, by Marcus Day, Esq.	LR2	376
Minerva C., of [Avon], m. Lee L. ROGERS, of New Haven, Feb. 2, 1834, by Rev. Harvey Bushnell, of East Church	LR1	568
Nelson, of Berlin, m. Amy Ursula BROOKS, of [Avon], "yesterday", by John Bartlett. Dated Nov. 4, 1841	LR2	376
Noah, of [Avon], m. Emeline A. BUTLER, of Burlington, Dec. 7, 1851, by Rev. Joel Grant, Cong. Ch. West Avon	LR4	2?
Olive D., m. Horace WOODRUFF, b. of [Avon], "last evening", by John Bartlett. Dated Jan. 30, 1840	LR2	375

Vol.   Page

HART, (cont.)

Purlina G., of [Avon], m. Simon D. **CHAPELL,** of New London,
"last evening", by John Bartlett. Dated Jan. 8, 1838   LR2   373

Susan F., of Avon, m. Newton **ROOT,** of Marlborough, Mar. 25,
1837, by Correl Higley, J. P.   LR1   572

HAWLEY, Almira Jane, of Avon, m. Jesse D. **FROST,** of Waterbury,
[July] 9, [1846], by John Bartlett   LR2   381

Betsey, m. John **WOODFORD,** b. of Avon, [Mar. 14, 1849], by
Jarius C. Leach   LR2   383

Cordelia, m. Franklin **WOODFORD,** b. of [Avon], "last Wed.
evening", by John Bartlett. Dated Sept. 16, 1842   LR2   377

Edwin D., farmer, d. Jan. 31, [1849], ae 23   LR4   351

Eveilin, m. Catharine **WOODRUFF,** b. of [Avon], "last evening",
by John Bartlett. Dated July 31, 1837   LR1   572

George W., of Augusta, Ill., m. Mary T. **CHAPMAN,** of Avon,
Ct., Aug. 31, 1835, by Rev. Francis H. Case, of 2nd Ch.   LR1   570

Harriet A., m. William C. **WOODRUFF,** of [Avon, Oct.] 9,
[1839], by John Bartlett   LR2   375

Jane, of [Avon], m. Franklin A. **TRYON,** of Farmington, "last
Evening", by John Bartlett. Dated May 7, 1847   LR2   382

Lot, grocer, b. Avon, res. Avon, d. Dec. 31, [1848], ae 73   LR4   351

Margaretta, d. Robert A., farmer & Maria J., b. Mar. 2, 1850   LR4   371

Maria N., housewife, b. Farmington, res. Avon, d. July 30,
[1849], ae 45   LR4   351

Naioma, housewife, d. Jan. 25, [1850], ae 63   LR4   372

Orestes H., of Augusta, Ill., m. Delia J. **BARTLETT,** of [Avon],
"last evening", by John Bartlett. Dated Apr. 7, 1840   LR2   375

Robert A., farmer, ae 30, b. New Haven, res. Avon, m. Maria L.
HAMBLIN, b. Litchfield, May 6, 1849, by Rev. Stephen
Hubbell   LR4   349

Robert A., m. Maria L. **HAMLIN,** May 7, 1849, by Rev. Stephen
Hubbel[l], of Cong. Ch.   LR2   383

Sarah, m. Lucius **LUSH,** b. of [Avon, Aug.] 20, [1837], by John
Bartlett   LR1   572

Sylvester, m. Maria N. **HUMPHREY,** b. of [Avon, Mar.] 9,
[1843], by Rev. Richard Woodruff   LR2   378

Sylvester, mechanic, ae 55, b. Farmington, res. Avon, m. 3rd w.
Thankfull M. **SWETT,** ae 49, b. Wethersfield, res. Wells
River, Vt., Jan. 8, 1851, by Mr. McLean   LR4   385

HAYDEN, Tullius C., m Susan S. **CHIDSEY,** Feb. 22, 1843, by Rev.
Stephen Hubbell, of Cong. Ch.   LR2   378

HEATH, Joshua S., m. Emily D. **HART,** [May] 16, [1843], by Rev.
E. Hart   LR2   378

HESS, W[illia]m H., of Naugatuck, m. Catharine S. **WOODRUFF,** of
[Avon], May 6, 1849, by Rev. Joel Grant, of 1st Cong. Ch.   LR2   383

William H., farmer, m. Catharine S. **WOODRUFF,** b. West
Avon, res. Avon, May 6, 1849, by Rev. Joel Grant   LR4   349

HIGLEY, Adeline, of Canton, m. William A. **CURTIS,** of Meriden,

HIGLEY, (cont.)	Vol.	Page
Aug. 22, [1847], by Charles W. Potter	LR2	382
Amelia C., of Avon, m. Allen E. **PHELPS**, of Simsbury, Ct., Aug. 21, 1845, by Geo[rge] B. Atwell	LR2	380
Lyman O., of Simsbury, m. Sarah A. **WOODFORD**, of Avon, [Nov.] 16, [1837], by [Rev. William Bentley]	LR1	572
HILL, Joseph, of New Hartford, m. Ann D. **WOODFORD**, of Avon, [June], 1, [1842], by George B. Atwell	LR2	377
HILTON, James, teamster, ae 30, & Phebe, ae 25, had child b. July 5, 1848	LR4	314
James A., d. Mar. 19, 1850, ae 1	LR4	373
HOLMES, Alanson, of Bridgeport, Ct., m. Ellen E. **SPERRY**, of [Avon], July 28, 1850, by Rev. Joel Grant, of Cong. Ch. West Avon	LR4	21
HUBBELL, Eliza E., housewife, d. Mar. [, 1849], ae 43	LR4	351
HUGHS, Everlen, of Canton, m. Louisa **ROBINS**, of [Avon], May 1, 1831, by Rev. Harvy Bushnell, of West Church	LR1	564
HULL, Elisaph, m. Ellen **GOODRICH**, June 25, 1848, by Rev. Joel Grant, of Cong. Ch. of West Avon	LR2	382
Elisaph, farmer, ae 33, b. Oxford, N. Y., m. Ellen **GOODRICH**, milliner, ae 20, b. Avon, June 25, 1848, by Rev. Joel Grant	LR4	315
HUMPHREY, Eliza, of [Avon], m. Moses **CORNWALL**, of Granville, Mass., Nov. 25, 1830, by Rev. Harvy Bushnell, of West Ch.	LR1	564
Goodwin S., of Bloomfield, m. Charlotte L. **PARDEE**, of Avon, Sept. 18, 1850, by Rev. N. Whiting, of Bapt. Ch., Bloomfield	LR4	21
Maria N., m. Sylvester **HAWLEY**, b. of [Avon, Mar.] 9, [1843], by Rev. Richard Woodruff	LR1	378
HURD, Jane, ae 16, m. Royal **WOODRUFF**, house joiner, ae 24, b. of Avon, Feb. 18, [1849], by Rev. Mr. Viets	LR4	351
HURLBUT, Abigail W., m. Nathan L. **CASE**, b. of Avon, May 3, 1836, by Rev. Francis H. Case, of East Ch.	LR1	570
JACKMAN, William, m. Betsey **FILLEY**, Apr. 24, 1837, by Correl Higley, J. P.	LR1	572
JILLET, [see under GILLETT		
JOHNSON, Daniel B., of East Windsor, m. Harriet N. **WOODRUFF**, of Avon, Apr. 24, 1839, by John Bartlett	LR2	374
KELLOGG, Alfred, Dr., m. Susan **BROCKLESBY**, b. of Avon, Apr. 18, 1838, by Rev. F. H. Case, of East Church	LR2	373
Amelia C., of Avon, m. James **KILBOURN**, of Litchfield, Dec. 12, 1838, by Rev. F. H. Case, of East Ch.	LR2	374
Bela C., m. Mary **BARTLETT**, of Avon, [Oct.] 15, [1839], by John Bartlett	LR2	375
Bela C., harness maker, ae 39, & w. Mary, ae 37, had d., b. July 28, 1851	LR4	386
Jane B., d. Bela C., harness maker, ae 39 & Mary B., ae 32, b. Sept. 21, [1849]	LR4	372
Mary E., m. Edgar M. **WOODFORD**, b. of [Avon], Sept. 7,		

	Vol.	Page
KELLOGG, (cont.)		
1843, by John Bartlett	LR2	379
KELSEY, Enoch, of Wethersfield, m. Caroline M. **WOODRUFF,** of		
[Avon], [Sept.] 18, [1842], by John Bartlett	LR2	377
KILBOURN, Henry, of Wethersfield, m. Caroline G.		
WADSWORTH, of [Avon], Feb. 22, 1836, by John Bartlett	LR1	570
James, of Litchfield, m. Amelia C. **KELLOGG,** of Avon, Dec.		
12, 1838, by Rev. F. H. Case, of East Ch.	LR2	374
Sukey, housewife, b. Farmington, res. Avon, d. July 1, [1849],		
ae 71	LR4	351
KIMBALL, Charles H., m. Henrietta **MILLER,** Nov. 17, 1852, by		
Rev. Stephen Hubbell	LR4	22
Edwin R., m. Harriet F. **THOM[P]SON,** Sept. 18, 1844, by Rev.		
Stephen Hubbell, of East Cong. Ch.	LR2	379
John P., m. Elizabeth C. **WHEELER,** b. of Avon, Oct. 17, 1839,		
by Rev. F. H. Case, of East Ch.	LR2	375
LAMBERT, -----, b. New Hartford, res. Avon, d. Aug. [, 1850], ae 1		
(Male)	LR4	373
LAMPSON, Julius, m. Oliva A. **LAMPSON,** Mar. 13, 1842, by Rev.		
Stephen Hubbell	LR2	377
Oliva A., m. Julius **LAMPSON,** Mar. 13, 1842, by Rev. Stephen		
Hubbell	LR2	377
LEWIS, Washington D., of Farmington, m. Salome E. **ROOD,** of		
[Avon, Oct. 8, 1845], by John Bartlett	LR2	380
LUSH, Lucius, m. Sarah **HAWLEY,** b. of [Avon, Aug.] 20, [1837], by		
John bartlett	LR1	572
Lucius, farmer, ae 37 & Sarah, ae 32, had d., b. July 30, 1849	LR4	351
MCKEE, Moses, of Avon, m. Evelina **ANDRUS,** of Farmington,		
[Nov.] 8, [1842], by John Bartlett	LR2	378
MARSHALL, Lucy Ann, of Avon, m. William B. **CARRIER,** of		
Glastenbury, May 4, 1831, by Rev. Frances H. Case, of East		
Ch.	LR1	564
Rahumah, d. Jan. 19, 1849, ae 82	LR4	349
MILLER, Anna K., of Avon, m. Nahum **BURT,** of South Hampton,		
Mass., Mar. 21, 1837, by Rev. Francis H. Case, of East Ch.	LR1	571
Caroline D., m. Justus M. **ALLING,** Mar. 16, 1842, by Rev.		
Stephen Hubbell	LR2	377
Catharine A., of Granby, m. Joseph B. **BROCKWAY,** of Avon,		
Sept. 28, 1834, by Rev. Francis H. Case, of 2nd Church	LR1	569
Chloe, ae 17, b. Avon, m. Job **BEEMAN,** ae 24, of Suffield, Jan.		
15, [1851], by Stephen Hubbell	LR4	384
Chloe A., m. Job **BEMAN** Jan. 15, 1851, by Rev. Stephen		
Hubbell	LR4	21
Dan A., m. Sarah M. **BISHOP,** Nov. 25, 1847, by Rev. Stephen		
Hubbell of Cong. Ch.	LR2	382
Dan A., mfg., ae 24, b. Avon, res. Bristol, m. Sarah M. **BISHOP,**		
ae 23, b. Avon, res. Bristol, Nov. 25, [1847], by Rev.	LR4	
Stephen Hubbell		316
Ebenezer, Jr., of Avon, m. Anna **FRISBIE,** of Middletown, Aug.		

MILLER, (cont.)

    10, 1835, by Rev. Francis H. Case, of 2nd Cong. Ch.   LR1   569

    Ebenezer, farmer, d. Jan. [ ], 1851, ae 83   LR4   384

    Edward, farmer, ae 47, & Lavinia, ae 39, had child, b. Mar. 19,
    1848   LR4   315

    Edward, farmer, ae 49 & w. Lavina, ae 41, had d., b. June 22,
    1850   LR4   371

    Emily E., m. George **MILLS,** Aug. 31, 1843, by Rev. Stephen
    Hubbell, of Cong. Ch.   LR2   379

    Henrietta, m. Charles H. **KIMBALL,** Nov. 17, 1852, by Rev.
    Stephen Hubbell   LR4   22

    Sarah, m. Amos G. **HART,** Oct. 19, 1851, by Rev. Stephen
    Hubbell, of Cong. Ch.   LR4   21

    Sarah L., m. Dwight E. **MORRON,** May 4, 1852, by Rev.
    Stephen Hubbell   LR4   22

MILLS, George, m. Emily E. **MILLER,** Aug. 31, 1843, by Rev.
    Stephen Hubbell, of Cong. Ch.   LR2   379

    Job, of Franklin, Del. Co., N. Y. m. Eliza **ROBBINS,** of [Avon],
    "last evening", by John Bartlett. Dated Mar. 1, 1842   LR2   377

MONTGOMERY, Mary, wid. of Moody **MONTGOMERY** &
    formerly wid. of Israel **COLLEY,** d. at the house of
    [William Kimball] in the town of Avon on Apr. 13, 1844.
    William Kimball executor of the will of Mary Montgomery.   LR2   382

MOORE, Roswell, of New Hartford, m. Ann M. **CHIDSEY,** of
    [Avon], Nov. 18, 1832, by Rev. Harvey Bushnell, of West
    Church   LR1   567

MORRON, Dwight E., m. Sarah L. **MILLER,** May 4, 1852, by Rev.
    Stephen Hubbell   LR4   22

MORSE, Laura, housekeeper, b. in Farmington, res. Avon, d. Mar. 1,
    1848   LR4   314

MOSES, Charles J., of N. Y. City, m. Juliette **FULLER,** of [Avon],
    Mar. 14, 1852, by Joel Grant   LR4   22

    Seth F., m. Nancy M. **CHIDSEY,** Apr. 15, 1851, by Rev.
    Stephen Hubbell, of Cong. Ch.   LR4   21

    Seth M., ae 24, of Simsbury, m. Nancy **CHIDSEY,** ae 23, b.
    Avon, Apr. 15, 1851, by S. Hubbell   LR4   386

MOSIER, Austin B., of New Brittain, m. Katherine D. **COOK,** of
    [Avon], Aug. 19, 1832, by Rev. Harvey Bushnell   LR1   566

NEIRING, Dolly, housewife, d. Dec. 14, [1849], ae 59   LR4   372

NICHOLS, Jerome B., of Westville, m. Jane A. **BURRILL,** of
    Hartford, "last evening", by John Bartlett. Dated Sept. 21,
    1846   LR2   381

    Jerome B., of Westville, m. Jane A. **BURRILL,** of
    Hartford, "last evening", by John Bartlett. Dated Sept. 21,
    1846   LR2   381

NORTH, Anna Roselle, d. Joseph, farmer, ae 26, & Harriet, ae 21, b.
    Nov. 1, [1850]   LR4   384

    Edna A., m. Cha[u]ncey D. **FORD,** Sept. 26, 1852, by Rev.

	Vol.	Page
NORTH, (cont.)		
Stephen Hubbell, of Cong. Ch.	LR4	22
Harriet F., m. Horace I. **BARBER**, Aug. 16, 1846, by Rev.		
Stephen Hubbell, of Cong. Ch.	LR2	381
Joseph, blacksmith, b. in Farmington, res. Avon, d. Oct. 7, 1847,		
ae 64	LR4	315
Joseph B., m. Harriet M. **GABRIEL**, Jan. 24, 1850, by Rev.		
Stephen Hubbell, of Cong. Ch.	LR2	384
Joseph B., farmer, ae 25, of Avon, m. Harriet M. **GABRIEL**, ae		
20, Jan. 24, [1850], by Stephen Hubbell	LR4	373
Sally M., of [Avon], m. Rowland **WETHERBY**, of Canton, Nov.		
25, 1830, by Rev. Harvy Bushnell, of West Church	LR1	564
NORTON, Elizabeth, m. Chandler **WOODFORD**, b. of Avon, Jan.		
19, 1835, by Amasa Woodford, J. P.	LR1	569
Mary A., m. Ebenezer G. **CURTIS**, Oct. 11, 1846, by Rev.		
Stephen Hubbill, of Cong. Ch.	LR2	381
Seth P., m. Elizabeth **WILCOX**, Jan. 1, 1851, by Rev. Stephen		
Hubbell, of Cong. Ch.	LR4	20
Seth P., m. Elizabeth **WILCOX**, Jan. 1, 1851, by Rev. Stephen		
Hubbell, of Cong. Ch.	LR4	21
Seth P., ae 26, b. Avon, m. 2nd w. Elizabeth **WILCOX**, ae 23, b.		
Simsbury, res. Collinsville, Jan. 1, 1851, by S. Hubbell	LR4	386
PAIN, Nancy A., of Avon, m. Charles **TOMPKINS**, of Southington,		
Mar. 28, 1836, by Correl Higley, J. P.	LR1	570
PARDEE, Charlotte L., of Avon, m. Goodwin S. **HUMPHREY**, of		
Bloomfield, Sept. 18, 1850, by Rev. N. Whiting, of Bapt.		
Ch.,Bloomfield	LR4	21
Charlotte Maria, d. Ebenezer, laborer, ae 23, & Mary, ae 21, b.		
Apr. 15, [1851]	LR4	384
Ebenezar, of Avon, m. Mary **HAGAN**, of Brookfield, Mass.,		
[Sept. 18, 1849], by Barais Sperry, J. P.	LR2	384
Walter, s. Ebenezer, ostler, ae 23 & Mary A., ae 22, b. Nov. 1,		
[1849]	LR4	372
PARK [ ], F. Aurelius, of Collinsville, m. Nancy E. **WOODRUFF**, of		
[Avon], [May 8, 1849], by Rev. Joel Grant, of 1st Cong.		
Ch.	LR2	383
PARKER, Luther A., grocer, ae 26, b, Windsor, Vt., res. Collinsville,		
m. Nancy E. **WOODRUFF**, ae 20, b. West Avon, May 8,		
1849, by Rev. Joel Grant	LR4	349
PECK, Clarence E., s. Major L. & Cordelia A., b. Jan. 21, 1851	LR4	385
D. L., male, d. Mar. 4, [1850], ae 3	LR4	372
George, of Bethlehem, m. Emily **ANDRUS**, of Farmington, July		
20, 1831, by Rev. Harvy Bushnell, of West Church	LR1	564
PENFIELD, Eunice P., of Avon, m. Hig[h]land **DOUD**, of Monterey,		
Mass., June 29, 1851, by Rev. Seth Higby	LR4	21
----, m. [ ] **BRADFORD**, Apr. 18, 1852, by Rev. Joel Grant, of		
Cong. Ch. West Avon	LR4	20
PHELPS, Allen E., of Simsbury, Ct., m. Amelia C. **HIGLEY**, of		
Avon, Aug. 21, 1845, by Geo[rge] B. Atwell	LR2	380

PHELPS, (cont.)

   Eleanor S., m. Oliver W. **WOODFORD**, b. of Avon, Apr. 27,

    1835, by Rev. Francis H. Case, of 2nd Church   LR1   569

   Emerson A., m. Caroline F. **WOODFORD**, Nov. 19, 1844, by

    Rev. Stephen Hubbell, of East Cong. Ch.   LR2   380

   Zophor, of Granby, m. Maria A. **SOPER**, of Hartford, June 4,

    1832, by Rev. Francis H. Case, of 2nd Cong. Church   LR1   566

PHILIPS, W[illia]m C., merchant, ae 30, b. in Winchester, m. Harriet

   J. **ROOD**, dressmaker, ae 22, b. in Sheffield, Mass., Oct.

   18, 1847, by Rev. Mr. Holley   LR4   315

   W[illia]m S., of Winsted, m. Harriet J. **ROOD**, of [Avon], Oct. 1,

   1847, by Rev. P. T. Holly, of Cong. Ch., in Sandisfield,

   Mass.   LR2   382

PIERCE, PEARCE, Daniel L., farmer, ae 26 of Canaan, Ct., m. Ann

   E. **ROOD**, ae 18, b. Sheffield, Mass., June 5, [1850], by

   Stephen Hubbell   LR4   373

   David L., m. Anne Eliza **REOUD**(?), June 12, 1850, by Rev.

   Stephen Hubbell   LR2   384

PORTER, Ira A., of Bristol, m. Lucy A. **HART**, of Avon, June 6,

   1852, by Rev. Joel Grant, of Cong. Ch. West Avon   LR4   20

   Major H., of Unionville, m. Mary A. **THOMPSON**, of Avon,

   May 3, 1852, by Rev. Joel Grant, of Cong. Ch. West Avon   LR4   20

POTTER, Emeline, of Candoe, N. Y., m. Henry E. **TUCKER**, of

   [Avon, Nov. 29, 1836], by John Bartlett   LR1   571

PRATT, Prudence, of Saybrook, Ct., m. Terry **BARNES**, of South

   Hampton, Mass., July 30, 1837, by Rev. F. H. Case, of East

   Ch.   LR1   572

PRESCOTT, Benjamin, of New Haven, m. Jane **WOODFORD**, of

   Avon, Oct. 19, 1831, by Rev. Francis H. Case, of East

   Cong. Ch.   LR1   565

   Jane, m. Norman **GRISWOLD**, Dec. 7, 1841, by Rev. Stephen

   Hubbell   LR2   377

REXFORD, John, of Barkhampsted, m. Henrietta Maria **ALLEN**, of

   Hamden, Nov. 15, [1837], by John Bartlett   LR2   373

RICE, Ann, of Barkhamsted, m. Gideon W. **HART**, of Avon, Nov. 27,

   1834, by Rev. F. H. Case, of 2nd Church   LR1   569

   Levi, of Barkhampsted, m. Mary Ann **HACK**, of Granby, Nov.

   16, 1842, by John Bartlett   LR2   378

   Mary Ann, m. Asa **DRAKE**, b. of Barkhempsted, July 27, 1832,

   by Rev. Harvey Bushnell, of West Church   LR1   566

RICHARDSON, Alice J., d. John, farmer, ae 62, & Emily, ae 43, b.

   Nov. 7, 1848   LR4   351

ROBBINS, ROBINS, Eliza, of [Avon], m. Job **MILLS**, of Franklin,

   Del. Co, N. Y, "last evening", by John Bartlett. Dated Mar.

   1, 1842   LR2   377

   Louisa, of [Avon], m. Everlen **HUGHS**, of Canton, May 1, 1831,

   by Rev. Harvy Bushnell, of West Church   LR1   564

ROGERS, Lee L., of New Haven, m. Minerva C. **HART**, of [Avon],

	Vol.	Page

ROGERS, (cont.)

Feb. 2, 1834, by Rev. Harvey Bushnell, of East Church — LR1 568

ROOD, REOUD, Ann E., ae 18, b. Sheffield, Mass., m. Daniel L.
PIERCE, farmer, ae 26, of Canaan, Ct., June 5, [1850], by
Stephen Hubbell — LR4 373

Anne Eliza, m. David L. **PEARCE,** June 12, 1850, by Rev.
Stephen Hubbell — LR2 384

David A., m. Maria **WOODFORD,** b. of Avon, "last evening" by
John Bartlett. Dated Mar. 24, 1843 — LR2 378

Harriet J., of [Avon], m. W[illia]m S. **PHILIPS,** of Winsted, Oct.
1, 1847, by Rev. P. T. Holly, of Cong. Ch., in Sandisfields,
Mass. — LR2 382

Harriet J., dressmaker, ae 22, b. in Sheffield, Mass., m.
W[illia]m C. **PHILIPS,** merchant, ae 30, b. in Winchester,
Oct. 18, 1847, by Rev. Mr. Holley — LR4 315

Joel E., m. Dorinda H. **WOODFORD,** [Sept. 4, 1844], by Rev.
Niles Whiting, of Bap. Ch. — LR2 379

Salome E., of [Avon] m. Washington D. **LEWIS,** of Farmington,
[Oct. 8, 1845], by John Bartlett — LR2 380

ROOT, Newton, of Marlborough, m. Susan F. **HART,** of Avon, Mar.
25, 1837, by Correl Higley, J. P. — LR1 572

SHUMWAY, Joel S., of Montague, Mass., m. Eunice L. **COLTON,** of
Avon, Ct., "last evening", by John Bartlett. Dated Dec. 5,
1842 — LR2 378

SMITH, Delmore C., b. Hartford, res. Avon, d. Nov. 24, [1848],
ae 2 3/4 y. — LR4 351

George W., of Haverhill, N. H., m. Helen M. **SMITH,** of [Avon],
"last evening", by John Bartlett. Dated Apr. 1, 1844 — LR2 379

Helen M., of [Avon], m. George W. **SMITH,** of Haverhill, N. H.,
"last evening", by John Bartlett. Dated Apr. 1, 1844 — LR2 379

Helen M., d. George, day laborer & Helen M., ae 24, b. Sept. 3,
1848 — LR4 351

Helen M., housewife, d. Dec. 14, [1848], ae 24 — LR4 351

Mary, m. Isaac **WOODFORD,** b. of [Avon], "last evening", by
John Bartlett. Dated Jan. 2, 1845 — LR2 380

Mary, d. Patrick, day laborer, ae 26, & Mary, ae 30, b. Jan. 24,
[1850] — LR4 372

----, laborer, had d., b. Mar. 17, 1851 — LR4 386

SOPER, Julia A., m. Eliab **BREWER,** Sept. 21, 1843, by Rev.
Stephen Hubbell, of Cong. Ch. — LR2 379

Maria A., of Hartford, m. Zophor **PHELPS,** of Granby, June 4,
1832, by Rev. Francis H. Case, of 2nd Cong. Church — LR1 566

SPAULDING, Joseph R., taverner, ae 31, & Jane B., ae 28, had child
b. May 26, 1848 — LR4 314

SPERRY, SPERY, Edwin G., m. Mary E. **WOODFORD,** June 8,
1843, by Rev. Stephen Hubbell, of Cong. Ch. — LR2 378

Ellen E., of [Avon], m. Alanson **HOLMES,** of Bridgeport, Ct.,
July 28, 1850, by Rev. Joel Grant, of Cong. Ch. West

	Vol.	Page
SPERRY, SPERY, (cont.)		
Avon	LR4	21
Emily, d. Zerah, farmer, ae 36 & Catharine, ae 23, b. Oct. 1, 1849	LR4	371
Filena, d. June 29, [1850], ae 65	LR4	371
Lucius, of [Avon], m. Maryett **BISHOP,** of North Haven, "last evening", by John Bartlett. Dated Aug. 15, 1845	LR2	380
Martha, d. Ozem, peddler, ae 42 & Elmina, ae 41, b. Mar. 3, [1851]	LR4	386
Ozem, m. Mary A. **CHIDSEY,** b. of [Avon], Apr. 30, 1832, by Rev. Harvey Bushnell, of West Church	LR1	566
Ozem, m. Ursula **CHIDSEY,** b. of Avon, Aug. 16, 183[5], by Correl Higley, J. P.	LR1	569
Ozem, butcher, ae 40, of Avon, m. Elmina **DEMING,** ae 39, of Avon, June 13, 1848, by Rev. Grant	LR4	316
Sylvia, of Avon, m. Elisha **CROSS,** of Tolland, Feb. 22, 1834, by Allen Pinney, J. P.	LR1	568
Zerah, of Simsbury, Ct., m. Plily S. **DOUD,** of Tyringham, Mass., Jan. 1, 1837, by Rev. Francis H. Case, of 2nd Church	LR1	571
STEDMAN, Jane, of New Hartford, m. Newton **WOODFORD,** of Avon, July 10, 1839, by Cornelius B. Everest, of Bloomfield	LR2	374
STEELE, STEEL, John H., of West Hartford, m. Evelina A. **CHIDSEY,** of Avon, Nov. 28, 1833, by Rev. Francis H. Case, of East Ch.	LR1	568
Martin, s. Martin, mechanic, ae 33 & Susan, ae 30, b. Oct. 30, [1849]	LR4	372
Martin, d. Jan. 1, 1850, ae 1	LR4	373
STEWART, STEWARD, Francis, m. Lydia Ann **BOOTH,** Nov. 15, 1847, by Rev. Stephen Hubbell	LR2	382
Francis, farmer, of Farmington, ae 28, m. Lydia **BOOTH,** of Avon, ae 19, Nov. 15, [1847], by Rev. Stephen Hubbell	LR4	316
Robert N., s. Francis, farmer, ae 28, of Farmington & Lydia A., ae 19, b. Dec. 7, 1847	LR4	316
STOCKBRIDGE, Randolph, m. Jane F. **BARBER,** May 26, 1842, by Rev. Stephen Hubbell	LR2	377
STODDARD, Frederick, s. Horace W., carriage maker, ae 35, & Lucelia, ae 17, b. Feb. 22, 1850	LR4	385
Helen Mary, d. David, wheelwright, ae 26, & Clarissa, ae 23, b. Oct. 8, 1847	LR4	315
Mary Ann, d. Jan. [ ], [1850], ae 38	LR4	371
STOW, Charles P., m. Julia A. **BISHOP,** Oct. 26, 1843, by Rev. Stephen Hubbell, of Cong. Ch.	LR2	379
STRATTON, Morgan, m. Amelia M. **COOK,** of Simsbury, Dec. 31, 1838, by Rev. Francis H. Case, of East Ch.	LR2	374
SULLIVAN, James. s. James, farmer, ae 45 & Catharine, ae 35, b. May 10*, 1850, *(Perhaps "May 18")	LR4	372
Patrick, laborer, had ch. b. July 10, 1849	LR4	350
SWEET, Philip, of Farmington, m. Almira **WOODFORD,** of Avon,		

	Vol.	Page

SWEET, (cont.)

Nov. 7, 1830, by Rev. Harvy Bushnell, of West Church — LR1 564

Thankfull M., ae 49, b. Wethersfield, res. Wells River, Vt. m.,
2nd h. Sylvester HAWLEY, mechanic, ae 55, b.
Farmington, res. Avon, Jan. 8, 1851, by Mr. McLean — LR4 385

TAYLOR, Emma, m. Evits CARTER, b. of Berkhampsted, Oct. 20,
1831, by Rev. Francis H. Case, of East Cong. Ch. — LR1 565

TERRY, Oliver C., m. Ruby L. WOODRUFF, Apr. 3, 1851, by Rev.
Seth Higby — LR4 21

Orwin, laborer, b. Granby, res. Avon, d. Feb. [ ], 1851, ae 39 — LR4 384

THOMPSON, THOMSON, Abi, b. New Britain, res. Canton, m. 2nd
h. Luke CASE, farmer, b. Canton, July 18, 1849, by Rev.
Joel Grant — LR4 349

Abi S., Mrs., of [Avon], m. Luke CASE, of Canton, July 18,
1849, by Rev. Joel Grant, of West Avon Cong. Ch. — LR2 384

Amon, farmer, ae 24, of Avon, m. Jane WOODRUFF, ae 21, b.
Avon, res. Simsbury, May 15, 1851, by J. Burt — LR4 385

Clifford Stanley, s. Stanley, farmer & Julia A., b. Feb. 19, [1850] — LR4 371

Harriet F., m. Edwin R. KIMBALL, Sept. 18, 1844, by Rev.
Stephen Hubbell, of East Cong. Ch. — LR2 379

Harriet N., of [Avon], m. Alonzo WOODFORD, of Burlington,
Sept. 23, [1838], by John Bartlett — LR2 374

Huldah E., m. Hiram WOODRUFF, b. of [Avon], Oct. 16, 1845,
by John Bartlett — LR2 380

James, m. Angeline A. BLACKWELL, May 10, 1852, by Rev.
Stephen Hubbell, of Cong. Ch. — LR4 22

Jane N., m. Guy T. WOODFORD, b. of Avon, Apr. 18, 1839, by
Rev. F. H. Case, of East Ch. — LR2 374

Justus F., farmer, of West Avon & Charlotte E., had d. b. Nov.
16, 1848 — LR4 349

Levi, farmer, d. Feb. 11, 1850, ae 71 — LR4 371

Levi E., m. Nancy WHEELER, June 20, 1832, by Allen McLean — LR1 566

Lorenzo, carpenter, d. May [, 1850], ae 25 — LR4 371

Mary A., of Avon, m. Major H. PORTER, of Unionville, May 3,
1852, by Rev. Joel Grant, of Cong. Ch. West Avon — LR4 20

Mary J., m. Aaron D. FRENCH, b. of [Avon], "last evening", by
John Bartlett. Dated Jan. 12, 1842 — LR2 376

Rockwell, merchant, ae 25, b. Avon, res. New River, La., m.
Sophia TILLOTSON, ae 20, Nov. [ ], 1850, by M. Sexton — LR4 385

Rockwell M., m Sophia TILLOTSON, of West Avon, Oct. 29,
1850, by Rev. J. A. Saxton, of Pres. Ch. Witnesses: Justice
F. Thomson, Charlotte E. Thomson & Betsey Ann Tillotson — LR4 21

Sarah C., m. Thomas H. WELLS, Sept. 1, 1845, by Rev. Stephen
Hubbell, of Cong. Ch. — LR2 380

Stanley T., m. Julia A. TILLOTSON, b. of [Avon], "last
evening", by John Bartlett. Dated Oct. 24, 1845 — LR2 380

TILLOTSON, Julia A., m. Stanley T. THOM[P]SON, b. of [Avon],
"last evening,} by John Bartlett. Dated Oct. 24, 1845 — LR2 380

	Vol.	Page
TILLOTSON, (cont.)		
Lucy, of Avon, m Newbury **BRONSON**, of		
Winchester, May 8, 1831, by Rev. Francis H. Case	LR1	564
Rhoda, housewife, b. Canton, res. Avon, d. Jan. 23, 1851, ae 78	LR4	385
Sophia, of West Avon, m. Rockwell M. **THOM[P]SON**, Oct. 29, 1850, by Rev. J. A. Saxton, of Pres. Ch. Witnesses: Justice F. Thomson, Charlotte E. Thomson & Betsey Ann Tillotson	LR4	21
Sophia, ae 20, m. Rockwell **THOMPSON**, merchant, ae 25, b. Avon, res. New River, La., Nov. [ ], 1850, by M. Sexton	LR4	385
Winthrop R., s. Romanta, farmer, ae 45 & Almira, ae 24, b. Oct. 19, 1848	LR4	351
TOMPKINS, Charles, of Southington, m. Nancy A. **PAIN**, of Avon, Mar. 28, 1836, by Correl Higley, J. P.	LR1	570
TRYON, Franklin A., of Farmington, m. Jane **HAWLEY**, of [Avon], "last evening", by John Bartlett. Dated May 7, 1847	LR2	382
TUCKER, Henry E., of [Avon], m. Emeline **POTTER**, of Candoe, N. Y., [Nov. 29, 1836], by John Bartlett	LR1	571
TYRELL, Catherine B., of Monterey, Mass., m. Martin **WOODRUFF**, of Farmington, May 20, 1849, by Rev. Miles N. Almsted	LR2	383
Catharine, ae 20, b. Monterey, Mass., res. Avon, m. Martin **WOODRUFF**, house joiner, ae 26, of Avon, May [, 1849], by Rev. Mr. Viets	LR4	351
WADSWORTH, Caroline G., of [Avon], m. Henry **KILBOURN**, of Wethersfield, Feb. 22, 1836, by John Bartlett	LR1	570
Catharine E., m. Elisha A. **WOODRUFF**, b. of Avon, [Dec. 17, 1846], by Rev. Charles B. McLean	LR2	382
Solomon N., of [Avon], m. Minerva **FORBES**, of Canton, Feb. 2, 1832, by Rev. Harvey Bushnell, of West Church	LR1	565
WALDBRIDGE, Wing, cotton worker, ae 33, of Avon & w. [ ], ae 31, had d. b. July 14, 1849	LR4	350
WALKER, Robert W., s. Daniel, farmer, ae 39, & Chriscinia, ae 32, b. Nov. 23, 1849	LR4	371
WASHBURN, Erastus W., m. Julia **WOODFORD**, Sept. 14, 1836, by John Bartlett	LR1	571
WATERS, Henry, m. Mary **WILCOX**, b. of Goshen, Ct., Oct. 12, 1835, by Rev. Francis H. Case, of 2nd Ch.	LR1	570
Huldah, of Hartford, m. Lyman **CASE**, Nov. 3, 1839, by Rev. F. H. Case, of East Ch.	LR2	375
WEBSTER, , Chloe T., m. Orris O. **WOODFORD**, b. of Avon, Apr. 19, 1838, by Rev. F. H. Case, of East Church	LR2	373
Eliza P., seamstress, b. in Windsor, res. Avon, d. Mar. 20, 1848, ae 39	LR4	315
Harriet A., m. Chester R. **WOODFORD**, b. of [Avon, Aug.] 18, [1840], by James H. Francis	LR2	376
WELLS, Thomas H., m. Sarah C. **THOM[P]SON**, Sept. 1, 1845, by Rev. Stephen Hubbell, of Cong. Ch.	LR2	380
WETHERBY, Delmore, s. Roland & Sally, b. May 8, 1851	LR4	385

	Vol.	Page

WETHERBY, (cont.)

Rowland, of Canton, m. Sally M. **NORTH,** of [Avon], Nov. 25,
1830, by Rev. Harvy Bushnell, of West Church   LR1   564

WETHERELL, Eva, d. John, carpenter, ae 28, & Matilda, ae 29, b.
Feb. 2, [1850]   LR4   372

WHEELER, Abby Luthera, d. Luther, farmer, ae 39 & Abby, ae 42, b.
Aug. 3, 1850   LR4   386

Amos, m. Martha **CHIDSEY,** Nov. 28, 1844, by Rev. Stepehn
Hubbell, of East Cong. Ch.   LR2   380

Elizabeth C., m. John P. **KIMBALL,** b. of Avon, Oct. 17, 1839,
by Rev. F. H. Case, of East Ch.   LR2   375

Emma Mary, d. Amos, merchant, ae 29 & Martha, ae 27, b. Dec.
11, 1850   LR4   385

Luther, farmer, ae 37 & Abiga[i]l, had ch. b. Jan. 25, 1849   LR4   350

Luther, had infant d. d. [, 1849], ae 8 w.   LR4   350

Maria E., m. Charles **GRAY,** Dec. 17, 1848, by Rev. Stephen
Hubbel[l], of Cong. Ch.   LR2   383

Maria E., colored, m. Charles **GREY,** colored, Deac. [ ], 1848,
by Rev. Stephen Hubbell   LR4   350

Nancy, m. Levi E. **THOM[P]SON,** June 20, 1832, by Allen
McLean   LR1   566

Perley A., s. Amos, merchant, ae 27, of Avon & Martha, b. Jan.
5, 1849   LR4   350

WHITNEY, John G., of Willimantic, m. Ann E. **WOODRUFF,** of
[Avon, May], 3, [1846], by John Bartlett   LR2   381

WILCOX, Amon B., farmer, d. Jan. [ ], 1851, ae 20   LR4   384

Elizabeth, m. Seth P. **NORTON,** Jan. 1, 1851, by Rev. Stephen
Hubbell, of Cong. Ch.   LR4   ?

Elizabeth, m. Seth P. **NORTON,** Jan. 1, 1851, by Rev. Stephen
Hubbell, of Cong. Ch.   LR4   21

Elizabeth, ae 23, b. Simsbury, res. Collinsville, m. as 2nd w.
Seth P. **NORTON,** ae 26, b. Avon, Jan. 1, 1851, by S.
Hubbell   LR4   386

Julia, of Avon, m. Samuel **CLYDE,** of Rome, N. Y., [Sept. 4,
1831], by George Norton, J. P.   LR1   565

Mary, m. Henry **WATERS,** b. of Goshen, Ct., Oct. 12, 1835, by
Rev. Francis H. Case, of 2nd Ch.   LR1   570

Solomon P., m. Eliza **CLARK,** b. of [Avon], "last evening", by
John Bartlett. Dated July 16, 1838   LR2   373

WILLIAMS, Daniel W., teamster, ae 35 & w. Lydia, ae 32, had d., b.
Apr. 18, 1850   LR4   371

WILSON, Angeline D., m. Chester H. **BURR,** of Bloomfield, Nov. 12,
1835, by Rev. Francis H. Case, of East Ch.   LR1   570

WOLCOTT, Deforest, m. Sarah Ette **CHIDSEY,** b. of [Avon, Sept.]
19, [1841], by John Bartlett   LR2   376

Deforest, farmer, ae 38 & w. Sarah E., ae 27, had s. b. May 30,
1849   LR4   351

Harrison, s. Oliver, shoemaker, ae 49 & Lucy, ae 25, b. May 30,

	Vol.	Page
WOLCOTT, (cont.)		
1849	LR4	351
Melvenia V., d. Oliver & Lucy A., b. Dec. 21, 1850	LR4	385
WOODFORD, Almira, of Avon, m. Philip **SWEET,** of Farmington,		
Nov. 7, 1830, by Rev. Harvy Bushnell, of West Church	LR1	564
Alonzo, of Burlington, m. Harriet N. **THOMPSON,** of [Avon],		
Sept. 23, [1838], by John Bartlett	LR2	374
Alonzo & Harriet, had ch. b. Feb. 6, 1848	LR4	316
Amasa, Esq., m. Fanny **WOODFORD,** b. of Avon, Nov. 22,		
1837, by Rev. F. H. Case, of East Ch.	LR2	373
Ann D., of Avon, m Joseph **HILL,** of New Hartford, [June] 1,		
[1842], by George B. Atwell	LR2	377
Arson, of Burlington, m. Cornelia **WOODRUFF,** of [Avon],		
"last week on Wednesday evening", by John Bartlett. Dated		
May 8, 1839	LR2	374
C. R., farmer, ae 36 & w. Harriet A., ae 34, had s. b. Jan. 10,		
[1851]	LR4	384
Caroline F., m. Emerson A. **PHELPS,** Nov. 19, 1844, by Rev.		
Stephen Hubbell, of East Cong. Ch.	LR2	380
Chandler, m. Elizabeth **NORTON,** b. of Avon, Jan. 19, 1835, by		
Amasa Woodford, J. P.	LR1	569
Chester R., m. Harriet A. **WEBSTER,** b. of [Avon, Aug.] 18,		
[1840], by James H. Francis	LR2	376
Clarinda F., m. Nathan S. **GRISWOLD,** Dec. 25, 1845, by Rev.		
Stephen Hubbell	LR2	381
Corydon*, of Burlington, Conn., m. Sylvia **WOODRUFF,** of		
Avon, May 7, 1834, by Rev. Francis H. Case, of 2nd		
Church *(Perhaps "Corydon **WOODRUFF**)	LR1	568
Dennis, s. Evelin, farmer, ae 48 & Emma, ae 42, b. Sept. 21,		
[1849] (First written "Feb. 9)	LR4	372
Dennis, d. Sept. 21, 1850, ae 1	LR4	373
Dorinda H., m. Joel E. **ROOD,** [Sept. 4, 1844], by Rev. Niles		
Whiting, of Bap. Ch.	LR2	379
Edgar M., m. Mary E. **KELLOGG,** b. of [Avon], Sept. 7, 1843,		
by John Bartlett	LR2	379
Edgar M., farmer, of West Avon & Mary E., had s. b. Sept. 27,		
1848	LR4	349
Edgar M., farmer, ae 26 & w. Mary E., ae 28, had d. b. May 18,		
1851	LR4	385
Edward, farmer, ae 43 & Charlotte, ae 39, had d., b. Apr. 3, 1849	LR4	351
Elizabeth, of Avon, m. Abel L. **BARBER,** of Simsbury, Sept. 11,		
1833, by Rev. Francis H. Case, of East Church	LR1	567
Ellen Eliz[a]beth, d. W[illia]m W. **WOODFORD,** farmer, ae 34,		
& Julia Ann H., ae 32, b. Feb. 18, 1848	LR4	315
Emeline, m. Franklin **DEMING,** b. of [Avon], July 3, 1832, by		
Rev. Harvey Bushnell, of West Church	LR1	566
Ephraim, m. Juliaett **FRENCH,** b. of [Avon, Mar.] 13, [1843], by		
John Bartlett	LR2	378
Esther, m. Henry M. **WOODFORD,** Nov. 30, 1843, by Rev.		

	Vol.	Page
WOODFORD, (cont.)		
Stephen Hubbell, of Cong. Ch.	LR2	379
Fanny, m. Amasa **WOODFORD**, Esq., b. of Avon, Nov. 22, 1837, by Rev. F. H. Case, of East Ch.	LR2	373
Fidelia A., m. Amariah **AVERY**, b. of Avon, Sept. 6, 1831, by Rev. Francis H. Case, of East Church	LR1	565
Franklin, m. Cordelia **HAWLEY**, b. of [Avon], "last Wednesday evening", b. John Bartlett. Dated Sept. 16, 1842	LR2	377
Franklin, farmer, of West Avon & Cordelia had s. b. May 28, 1849	LR4	349
Frederick G., s. Chester R., farmer, of Avon & Harriet A., b. Nov. 29, 1848	LR4	349
Guy T., m. Jane N. **THOM[P]SON**, b. of Avon, Apr. 18, 1839, by Rev. F. H. Case, of East Ch.	LR2	374
Harriet, m. Harvey **HART**, b. of [Avon], Sept. 22, 1833, by Harv[e]y Bushnell, of 1st Church	LR1	567
Ha[r]vey, m. Stella M. **BISHOP**, Apr. 16, 1851, by Rev. Stephen Hubbell	LR4	21
Harvey, farmer, ae 21, of Avon, m. Stella **BISHOP**, ae 23, Apr. 16, [1851], by S. Hubbell	LR4	384
Harvey, ae 23, m. Stella M. **BISHOP**, ae 21, of Avon, Apr. 16, 1851, by S. Hubbell	LR4	386
Henry M., m. Esther **WOODFORD**, Nov. 30, 1843, by Rev. Stephen Hubbell, of Cong. Ch.	LR2	379
Henry M., peddler, ae 31 & Esther, ae 26, had child, b. May 27, 1848	LR4	314
Isaac, m. Mary **SMITH**, b. of [Avon], "last evening", by John Bartlett. Dated Jan. 2, 1845	LR2	380
Jane, of Avon, m. Benjamin **PRESCOTT**, of New Haven, Oct. 19, 1831, by Rev. Francis H. Case, of East Cong. Ch.	LR1	565
John, m. Betsey **HAWLEY**, b. of Avon [Mar. 14, 1849], by Jarius C. Leach	LR2	383
Julia, m. Erastus W. **WASHBURN**, Sept. 14, 1836, by John Bartlett	LR1	571
Lucia J., m. Virgil L. **WOODFORD**, [Sept. 4, 1844], by Rev. Niles Whiting, of Bap. Ch.	LR2	379
Lucy C., m. David **CARRIER**, Nov. 29, 1849, by Rev. Stephen Hubbell, of Cong. Ch.	LR2	384
Lucy C., ae 28, of Avon, m. David **CARRIER**, farmer, ae 34, b. Marlborough, res. Avon, Nov. 29, 1849, by Rev. Stephen Hubbell	LR4	371
Maria, m. David A. **ROOD**, b. of [Avon], "last evening", by John Bartlett. Dated Mar. 24, 1843	LR2	378
Mariah F., d. Ephraim, farmer, of West Avon & Juliette, b. Sept. 8, 1848	LR4	349
Maria M., m. George **CHIDSEY**, b. of Avon, Mar. 28, 1838, by Rev. Francis H. Case, of East Ch.	LR2	373
Mary A., m. Dr. Isaac H. **BROWN**, b. of Avon, July 29, 1834, by Rev. Francis H. Case, of 2nd Church	LR1	569

	Vol.	Page
WOODFORD, (cont.)		
Mary E., m. Edwin G. **SPERRY**, June 8, 1843, by Rev. Stephen Hubbell, of Cong. Ch.	LR2	378
Nancy E., milliner, ae 26, of Avon, m. George C. **CARMAN**, harness-maker, ae 36, of Hartford, June 6, 1849, by Rev. Niles Whiting	LR4	349
Nancy Ette, of Avon, m. George **CARMAN**, of Hartford, [June 6,1849], by Rev. N. Whiting. of Bapt. Ch. Bloomfield	LR2	383
Naomi, of [Avon], m. Samuell S. **GLEASON**, of Ohio, Sept. 13, 1832, by Rev. Harvey Bushnell, of West Church	LR1	566
Newton, of Avon, m. Jane **STEDMAN**, of New Hartford, July 10, 1839, by Cornelius B. **EVEREST**, of Bloomfield	LR2	374
Oliver W., m. Eleanor S. **PHELPS**, b. of Avon, Apr. 27, 1835, by Rev. Francis H. Case, of 2nd Church	LR1	569
Orris O., m. Chloe T. **WEBSTER**, b. of Avon, Apr.19, 1838, by Rev. F. H. Case, of East Church	LR2	373
Robert F., m. Helen E. **BISHOP**, Apr. 2, 1846, by Rev. Stephen Hubbell	LR2	381
Sarah A., of Avon, m. Lyman O. **HIGLEY**, of Simsbury, [Nov.] 16,[1837], by [Rev. William Bentley]	LR1	572
Sarah A., m. Lucius S. **BISHOP**, Dec. 30, 1849, by Rev. Stephen Hubbel[l], of Cong. Ch.	LR2	384
Sarah Jane, m. Ammi G. **DERREN**, b. of [Avon], "last evening", by John Bartlett. Dated Dec. 4, 1845	LR2	380
Virgil L., m. Lucia J. **WOODFORD**, [Sept. 4, 1844], by Rev. Niles Whiting, of Bap. Church	LR2	379
William W., m. Juliann H. **GOODRICH**, May 18, 1842, by Rev. Stephen Hubbell	LR2	377
Zerviah R., m. Joseph **BISHOP**, b. of Avon, July 14, 1836, by Rev. William Bentl[e]y	LR1	571
WOODRUFF, Abigail, of Avon, m. Robert **CHAPMAN**,of Newington, "last evening", by John Bartlett. Dated Sept. 24, 1840	LR2	376
Abiga[i]l R., ae 30, m. John S. **BARNS**, machinist, ae 23, b. Northampton, res. Hartford, Jan. 6, 1850, by Rev. Mr. Surls	LR4	373
Achsah, of [Avon], m. Everet[t] **DUDLEY**, of Bloomfield, Sept. 6, 1838, by John Bartlett	LR2	373
Ada, d. Royal, joiner & Jane, b. Dec. 1, [1849]	LR4	372
Almira, m. Julius **FULLER**, June 2, 1836, by Correl Higley, J. P.	LR1	571
Ann E., of [Avon], m. John G. **WHITNEY**, of Williamantic, [May] 3, [1846], by John Bartlett	LR2	381
Caroline M., of [Avon], m. Enoch **KELSEY**, of Wethersfield, [Sept.] 18, [1842], by John Bartlett	LR2	377
Catharine, m. Eveilin **HAWLEY**, b. of [Avon], "last evening", by John Bartlett. Dated July 31, 1837	LR1	572
Catharine S., b. West Avon, res. Avon, m. William H. **HESS**, farmer, May 6, 1849, by Rev. Joel Grant	LR4	349
Catharine S., of [Avon] m. W[illia]m H. **HESS**, of Naugatuck, May 6, 1849, by Rev. Joel Grant, of 1st. Cong. Ch.	LR2	383

WOODRUFF, (cont.)	Vol.	Page

Cornelia, of [Avon], m. Arson **WOODFORD**, "last week on
Wednesday evening", by John Bartlett. Dated May 8, 1839   LR2   374

Darius, of St. Joseph, Florida, m. Esther **WOODRUFF**, of Avon,
[Oct.] 7, [1839], by John Bartlett   LR2   375

Eldad, m. Julia **CLARK**, b. of Avon, [Sept. 4, 1839], by
Cornelius B. Everest, Bloomfield   LR2   375

Elisha A., m. Catharine E. **WADSWORTH**, b. of Avon, [Dec.
17, 1846], by Rev. Charles B. McLean   LR2   382

Elmena, of [Avon] m. Orrin **BRAINARD**, [of] Lenox, N. Y.,
Mar. 9, 1834,. by Rev. H. Bushnell, of West Church   LR1   568

Erastus, Jr., m. Elvira **HART**, b. of [Avon], Apr. 7, [1846], by
Alfred Kellogg   LR2   381

Esther, of Avon, m. Darius **WOODRUFF**, of St. Joseph, Florida,
[Oct] 7, [1839], by John Bartlett   LR2   375

Harriet N., of Avon, m. Daniel B. **JOHNSON**, of East Windsor,
Apr. 24, 1839, by John Bartlett   LR2   374

Helen, m. Charles **BULKLEY**, b. of [Avon], Mar. 5, [1837], by
John Bartlett   LR1   571

Hiram, m. Huldah E. **THOM[P]SON**, b. of [Avon], Oct. 16,
1845, by John Bartlett   LR2   380

Horace, m. Olive D. **HART**, b. of [Avon,], "last evening", by
John Bartlett. Dated Jan. 30, 1840   LR2   375

Jane, ae 21, b. Avon, res. Simsbury, m. Amon **THOMPSON**,
farmer, ae 24, of Avon, May 15, 1851, by J. Burt   LR4   385

John, of Unionville, m. Electa C. **HART**, of Avon, [Sept.] 25,
[1842], by John Bartlett   LR2   378

Lavilla, m. Carlos C. **DAY**, b. of [Avon], Sept. 22, 1833, by Rev.
Harv[e]ly Bushnell, of 1st Church   LR1   567

Lemira, of [Avon], m. Henry **FOOT**, of Canton, "last evening",
by John Bartlett. Dated Sept. 27, 1838   LR2   374

Lucy E., d. Mrs. Harriet A., farmer, b. Nov. 10, 1849   LR4   371

Lucy Margaret, d. W[illia]m C., grocer, ae 35, of Hartford &
Harriet, ae 33, b. Jan. 1, 1848   LR4   315

Martin, of Farmington, m. Catherine B. **TYRELL**, of Monterey,
Mass., May 20, 1849, by Rev. Miles N. Almsted   LR2   383

Martin, house joiner, ae 26, of Avon, m. Catharine **TYRELL**, ae
20, b. Monterey, Mass., res. Avon, May [, 1849], by Rev.
Mr. Viets   LR4   351

Micah, farmer, d. Aug. 31, 1848, ae 70   LR4   349

Nancy E., ae 20, b. West Avon, m. Luther A. **PARKER**, grocer,
ae 26, b. Windsor, Vt., res. Collinsville, May 8, 1849, by
Rev. Joel Grant   LR4   349

Nancy E., of [Avon], m. F. Aurelius **PARK[ ]**, of Collinsville,
[May 8, 1849], by Rev. Joel Grant, of 1st. Cong. Ch.   LR2   383

Royal, house joiner, ae 24, m. Jane **HURD**, ae 16, b. of Avon,
Feb. 18, [1849], by Rev. Mr. Viets   LR4   351

Ruby L., m. Oliver C. **TERRY**, Apr. 3, 1851, by Rev. Seth Higby   LR4   21

	Vol.	Page

WOODRUFF, (cont.)

Sylvia, of Avon, m. Corydon **WOODFORD***,
    of Burlington, Conn., May 7, 1834, by Rev. Francis H.
    Case, of 2nd Church *(Perhaps "**WOODRUFF**")   LR1   568

Thomas D., d. Mar. 10, [1850], ae 9   LR4   372

William C., m. Harriet A. **HAWLEY**, of [Avon, Oct.] 9, [1839],
    by John Bartlett   LR2   375

WYMAN, John, of Union, m. Ann **CARPENTER**, of Avon, Dec. 3,
    1832, by Geo[rge] Norton, J. P.   LR1   567

YOUNG, Rans[s]aleer, of South Canton, m. Julia **GREEN**, of Wales,
    Mass., Dec. 15, 1831, by George Norton, J. P.   LR1   565

NO SURNAME, Mary, stranger. b. Ireland, d. [ ], 1851, ae 40   LR4   386

----, female infant, d. Apr. 1, 1851, ae 1 m.   LR4   386

----, female infant, d. Oct. 1, 1851, ae 6 m.   LR4   386

www.ingramcontent.com/pod-product-compliance
Lightning Source LLC
Chambersburg PA
CBHW071840270326
41929CB00013B/2054